IN THE OFFICE

FEATURED CONTRIBUTOR

TECHNOLOGY AND TODAY'S PARALEGAL

DEVELOPING PARALEGAL SKILLS

ETHICS WATCH

Introduction to Law

Custom 3rd Edition

Roger LeRoy Miller | Mary Meinzinger

CENGAGE
Learning·

Australia • Brazil • Japan • Korea • Mexico • Singapore • Spain • United Kingdom • United States

Introduction to Law: Custom 3rd Edition

Paralegal Today: The Legal Team at Work, Seventh Edition
Miller | Meinzinger

© 2017, 2014, 2010, 2007, 2004, 2000, 1995 Cengage Learning. All rights reserved.

Library of Congress Control Number: 2015939942

For product information and technology assistance, contact us at
Cengage Learning Customer & Sales Support, 1-800-354-9706

For permission to use material from this text or product,
submit all requests online at **cengage.com/permissions**
Further permissions questions can be emailed to
permissionrequest@cengage.com

This book contains select works from existing Cengage Learning resources and was produced by Cengage Learning Custom Solutions for collegiate use. As such, those adopting and/or contributing to this work are responsible for editorial content accuracy, continuity and completeness.

Compilation © 2016 Cengage Learning

ISBN: 978-1-337-04420-2

Cengage Learning
20 Channel Center Street
Boston, MA 02210
USA

Cengage Learning is a leading provider of customized learning solutions with office locations around the globe, including Singapore, the United Kingdom, Australia, Mexico, Brazil, and Japan. Locate your local office at:
www.international.cengage.com/region.

Cengage Learning products are represented in Canada by Nelson Education, Ltd.

For your lifelong learning solutions, visit **www.cengage.com/custom.**

Visit our corporate website at **www.cengage.com.**

Brief Contents

APPENDICES

The Paralegal Profession

CHAPTER 1

Today's Professional Paralegal

CHAPTER OUTLINE

CHAPTER OBJECTIVES

After completing this chapter, you will know:

- What a paralegal is.

- The major tasks paralegals perform.

- The names of professional associations of paralegals.

- The education and training available to paralegals.

- Whether paralegals must be certified or licensed.

- Key skills and attributes of the professional paralegal.

Introduction

The career of a paralegal can be exciting, challenging, and rewarding. Law firms have been giving greater responsibilities to paralegals. The opportunities for paralegals to work outside of law firms (such as in corporations or government agencies) are also expanding. As the profession has grown, the average paralegal salary has increased. According to a recent survey, experienced paralegals earned average compensation of $73,400.[1]

How do you know if you want to become part of this dynamic profession? The first step in finding out is to become familiar with what a paralegal is, the kinds of work paralegals do, and what education and skills are needed. These topics are covered in this chapter. In Chapter 2, you will learn about where paralegals work, how much they earn, and how they got their jobs. As you read through this book, remember that this is only an introduction to the profession and the starting point of your education. You should supplement what you learn in the classroom by networking with paralegals in professional environments. In today's competitive job market, whom you know can sometimes be as important as what you know in getting the job you desire.

What Is a Paralegal?

In this book, we use the terms *paralegal* and *legal assistant*, as is often done in the legal community, but the term paralegal is dominant. Some people or groups may prefer one label to the other, but that does not mean that the labels describe different jobs. Indeed, some persons who are trained professional paralegals may be called something else entirely at their workplace, such as *legal technician* or *legal research specialist*.

Definition of Paralegal

After years of disagreement, two of the major organizations involved reached a consensus on the definition of paralegal. The American Bar Association (ABA), which is a national association for attorneys, and the National Association of Legal Assistants (NALA), which is the largest national organization of paralegals, agree to the following definition:

> A legal assistant, or paralegal, is a person qualified by education, training, or work experience who is employed or retained by a lawyer, law office, corporation, governmental agency or other entity and who performs specifically delegated substantive legal work, for which a lawyer is responsible.[2]

The National Federation of Paralegal Associations (NFPA), another large paralegal association, prefers the term *paralegal*.[3] Members of NFPA were concerned that many attorneys refer to their secretaries as legal assistants and so wanted to distinguish the role of paralegals as professionals. The NFPA gives the following definition for *paralegal*:

> A Paralegal is a person, qualified through education, training or work experience to perform substantive legal work that requires knowledge of legal concepts and is customarily, but not exclusively, performed by a lawyer. This person may be retained or employed by a lawyer, law office, governmental agency or other entity or may be authorized by administrative, statutory or court authority to perform this work. Substantive shall mean work requiring recognition, evaluation, organization, analysis, and communication of relevant facts and legal concepts.[4]

Another major organization, the American Association for Paralegal Education (AAfPE), provides the following definition:

> Paralegals perform substantive and procedural legal work as authorized by law, which work, in the absence of the paralegal, would be performed by an attorney.

American Bar Association (ABA)
A voluntary national association of attorneys. The ABA plays an active role in developing educational and ethical standards for attorneys and in pursuing improvements in the administration of justice.

National Association of Legal Assistants (NALA)
One of the two largest national paralegal associations in the United States; formed in 1975. NALA is actively involved in paralegal professional development.

paralegal or legal assistant
A person qualified by education, training, or work experience who is employed or retained by a lawyer, law office, corporation, governmental agency, or other entity and who performs specifically delegated substantive legal work, for which a lawyer is responsible.

National Federation of Paralegal Associations (NFPA)
One of the two largest national paralegal associations in the United States; formed in 1974. NFPA is actively involved in paralegal professional development.

American Association for Paralegal Education (AAfPE)
A national organization of paralegal educators; the AAfPE was established in 1981 to promote high standards for paralegal education.

Paralegals have knowledge of the law gained through education, or education and work experience, which qualifies them to perform legal work. Paralegals adhere to recognized ethical standards and rules of professional responsibility.[5]

Expanding Roles

Regardless of which term is used, paralegals or legal assistants today perform many functions that traditionally were performed by attorneys. That is why the United States Department of Labor predicts growth in the paralegal profession will continue to be above average. Paralegals perform substantive legal work that they are trained to perform through education, experience, or (usually) both.

What Do Paralegals Do?

Paralegals assist attorneys in many ways. The following is a sampling of some of the tasks that legal assistants typically perform in a law office. Keep in mind that today's paralegals work in many nontraditional settings, including corporations, government agencies, courts, insurance companies, real estate firms, and almost any other entity that uses legal services. Throughout this book, you will read about the specific tasks that paralegals perform in different settings.

A Sampling of Paralegal Tasks

Typically, legal assistants perform the following duties:

- *Conduct client interviews and maintain contact with clients*—provided that the client is aware of the status and function of the paralegal, who does not give legal advice (see the *Ethics Watch* feature on the facing page).

- *Locate and interview witnesses*—to gather relevant facts and information about a lawsuit, for example.

- *Conduct legal investigations*—to obtain, organize, and evaluate information from sources such as police reports, medical records, photographs, court documents, experts' reports, technical manuals, and product specifications.

- *Calendar and track important deadlines*—such as the date by which a certain document must be filed with the court or the date by which the attorney must respond to a settlement offer.

- *Organize and maintain client files*—to keep the documents in each client's file accessible.

- *Conduct legal research*—to identify, analyze, and summarize the appropriate laws, court decisions, or regulations that apply to a client's case.

- *Draft legal documents*—such as legal correspondence, interoffice memoranda, contracts, wills, mortgages, and documents to be filed with the court.

- *File legal documents with courts*—such as complaints, answers, and motions.

- *Summarize witness testimony*—such as when depositions (sworn testimony) are taken of individuals out of court or when the parties have given written statements.

- *Coordinate litigation proceedings*—communicate with opposing counsel, court personnel, and other government officials; prepare necessary documents for trial; and schedule witnesses.

- *Attend legal proceedings*—such as trials, depositions, executions of wills, and court or administrative hearings.

- *Use computers and technology*—to perform many of the above tasks and help expand the social media presence of a firm.

No matter what task is being performed, paralegals have an obligation to meet high ethical standards. You will see the *Ethics Watch* feature in every chapter in the textbook and ethical obligations will be reviewed in detail in Chapter 4.

Paralegals' Duties Vary

The specific tasks that paralegals perform vary depending on the size of the office, the kind of law that the firm practices, and the expertise the paralegal has. If you work in a one-attorney office, for example, you will also perform certain secretarial functions. Tasks include conducting legal research and investigating the facts, copying documents, keying data into the computer, and answering the phone as needed.

If you work in a larger law firm, you usually have more support staff (secretaries, file clerks, and others) to whom you can delegate tasks. Your work may also be more specialized, so you work only on cases in certain areas of law. If you work in a law firm's real estate department, for example, you may deal only with legal matters relating to that area.

Although paralegal duties vary, the tasks that paralegals report spending the most time performing are drafting legal documents, handling client relations, and conducting legal research.

ETHICS WATCH

PARALEGAL EXPERTISE AND LEGAL ADVICE

Paralegals often gain a great deal of knowledge in specific areas of law. If you specialize in environmental law, for example, you will become knowledgeable about environmental claims. In working with a client on a matter involving an environmental agency, you might be tempted to advise the client on which type of action would be most favorable to him or her. Never do so. Only attorneys may give legal advice, and paralegals who give legal advice risk penalties for the unauthorized practice of law. Whatever legal advice is given to the client must come directly from the attorney.

If you speak to a client, the advice must reflect exactly (or nearly exactly) what the attorney said with no modification and must be communicated to the client as directed by the attorney. After consulting with your supervising attorney, for example, you can say to the client that the attorney "advises that you do all that you can to settle the claim as soon as possible."

The rule prohibiting the unauthorized practice of law is stated in Section 1.8 of the NFPA *Model Code of Ethics and Professional Responsibility:* "A paralegal shall comply with the applicable legal authority governing the unauthorized practice of law in the jurisdiction in which the paralegal practices." It is also required by the NALA *Code of Ethics and Professional Responsibility* Canon 4: "A paralegal must use discretion and professional judgment commensurate with knowledge and experience but must not render independent legal judgment in place of an attorney."

FEATURED CONTRIBUTOR

START TODAY

William McSorley

BIOGRAPHICAL NOTE

Bill received his undergraduate degree in journalism from the University of South Carolina, followed by his law degree in 1983. He served as editor-in-chief of *The Paralegal Survival Guide: Facts and Forms,* a publication by the South Carolina Bar Continuing Legal Education Division.

Bill spends the great majority of his time serving as a faculty member and paralegal program director at Midlands Tech in Columbia, SC, where he has taught paralegal students for more than 25 years and has served as director since 2002. He is a member of the American Bar Association, South Carolina Bar Association, and Richland County Bar Association. He also served as a member of the American Bar Association Approval Commission and continues to provide support to the commission as a specially designated site team chair.

Bill is currently on a task force with paralegals, paralegal educators, and members of the South Carolina Bar and Judiciary, studying the potential for paralegal certification in South Carolina.

For those seeking a new career in the legal field, the challenges are many. We are often frozen by uncertainty, and as a result, fail to move forward. So start moving. Start today!

Map out a strategy for yourself. Everyone has his or her own timetable and it's always subject to change, but let's put something down as an initial blueprint. Here is just a sample of a strategy for a full-time student in a two-year paralegal program.

> "Map out a strategy for yourself."

BEFORE YOU BEGIN: Educate yourself on this career path and do a self-assessment. What are the key skills and qualities needed in this profession? Where are the jobs? Ask yourself, "What are my strengths and weaknesses?" How can I improve on my weaknesses and align my skills with those needed for the profession? If you are not good at doing a self-assessment, ask somebody who will give you an honest answer.

Paralegals and Technology

Many paralegals have become the technology experts at law firms. Because lawyers are busy with the practice of law, paralegals are often in the best position to know the firm's working needs. Increasingly, legal assistants take a leading role in reviewing and recommending specialized legal software programs and online databases.

Needless to say, computer skills, technical knowledge, and, increasingly, the ability to use social media productively, are highly valued. Paralegals use software packages for internal case management to organize client files, manage calendars, share research, record reference materials, and track the hours to be billed to clients. Attorneys and paralegals use time and billing software to manage expenses, generate bills, calculate accounts receivable, and produce financial reports. Legal databases available on the Internet allow paralegals to perform sophisticated legal research at their desks. When cases that involve many documents must be prepared for trial, litigation support software can help retrieve, categorize, and index the various materials for presentation. These technologies are discussed in appropriate chapters throughout this book.

What do employers want in a new hire? They want somebody with strong communication skills, a working understanding of the law, a sense of integrity and professionalism, some technological skills, and a positive attitude. Is this you today? Can this be you by the time you graduate? How do you develop these skills?

SEMESTER ONE: Get good grades, get to know your program director and instructors, start making a list of contacts, and get working on a quality résumé. Full-time and adjunct faculty members often are the best place to start networking. They have strong ties to the legal community, appreciate students who do quality work, and are the source of many job placements. Think about developing a draft of a résumé and continue to add to this as you go along. Have it in just an outline form for now.

> " ... getting some experience is key ..."

SEMESTER TWO: Join a local paralegal organization. Try to attend their regular meetings and make some contacts in this organization. The local paralegal organizations can be the best way to find out about job opportunities, learn about the profession, and expand your personal and professional network. I am always impressed by the kindness our local association shows toward student members. Working paralegals remember what it was like to be a student, and they are extremely supportive.

SEMESTER THREE: Work on securing an internship or doing volunteer work at a law office or other legal environment. If your school has a mandatory internship, now is the time to do it. Work on producing a professional résumé. It may be the only opportunity to separate you from a large stack of "applicants" seeking a job, so make yourself stand out from the crowd. My personal preference (though many disagree) is to include references as part of your résumé. In many areas, the legal and business communities are closely knit and having a "known reference"

who can vouch for your good character could be what gets you the interview.

Check out your college's career services resources and discuss your résumé, interviewing skills, and placement opportunities with them. Reach out to your contacts for assistance in securing a position somewhere. Even if your school doesn't require an internship, getting some experience is key, even if you have to volunteer. One of my favorite stories involves a student who finished his volunteer internship, did good work, and asked if he could continue to volunteer since he was learning so much. They couldn't say "no" to free, quality help, so they let him stay on and after a couple of months they created a full-time job for him.

SEMESTER FOUR: Make the final push to get that job you've worked so hard to obtain! At this point, you have a good-looking résumé, you have done a few mock (or real) interviews, and you have worked your network to help identify some potential job opportunities.

Recognizing the importance of strong interpersonal skills, you are getting better every day at being polite and friendly, using proper grammar, and learning to hold your tongue rather than saying something you'll regret later!

You have also developed your technology and research skills and are comfortable with the Microsoft Office Suite or comparable products. You are familiar with the basics of calendaring, billing, and database management. Even if these skills aren't taught in your program, there's nothing stopping you from looking at all the free resources online. If a job comes down to you and another applicant, you want to make sure the "technology advantage" is on your side.

Your graduation may seem ages from now, but I promise it will be here before you know it. So make a plan, try to stick to it, and start today!

Paralegal Education

The first paralegals were legal secretaries who learned through on-the-job training how to perform more complex legal tasks given to them by attorneys. No formal paralegal education programs existed until the late 1960s. Once attorneys realized that using paralegals was cost-effective and benefited both the client and the firm (as you will read in Chapter 3), paralegal education programs began to expand.

According to the ABA's Standing Committee on Paralegals, there are now about a thousand paralegal training programs operating in the United States. A great deal of variety exists in the quality of the education provided. Of course, your formal education is only part of becoming a successful legal professional as the *Featured Contributor* discusses above.

Educational Options

The role of formal paralegal education has become increasingly important in the growth and development of the paralegal profession. Many colleges offer programs. Generally, paralegal education programs fall into one of five categories:

- Two-year community college programs, leading to an associate of arts degree or a paralegal certificate. Programs often require the completion of about 60 semester hours and include some general education requirements.

- Four-year bachelor's degree programs with a major or minor in paralegal studies. A bachelor's degree in paralegal studies usually requires about 120 semester hours, with 50 to 60 of these hours spent on general education courses. A person may be able to select a minor field that enhances desirability in the job market. Conversely, a student who majors in another field—for example, nursing—and obtains a minor in paralegal studies will be very marketable to employers.

- Certificate programs offered by private institutions, usually three to eighteen months in length. Typically, these programs require a high school diploma or the equivalent for admission.

- Postgraduate certificate programs, usually three to twelve months in length, resulting in the award of a paralegal certificate. These programs require applicants to have already earned a bachelor's degree in order to be admitted; some also require applicants to have achieved a certain grade-point average.

- Master's degree programs are offered by several universities, including an increasing number of online programs. These prepare students to work as paralegals, paralegal supervisors, or law office administrators. Some programs offer specific concentrations—for example, dispute resolution or intellectual property.

Because those seeking to become paralegals have diverse educational backgrounds, capabilities, and work experience, no one program is best for everyone. Deciding which program is most appropriate depends on personal needs and preferences.

Paralegal Curriculum—Substantive and Procedural Law

A paralegal's education includes the study of both substantive law and procedural law. Substantive law includes laws that define, describe, regulate, and create legal rights and obligations. For example, a law prohibiting employment discrimination on the basis of age falls into the category of substantive law. Procedural law establishes the methods of enforcing the rights established by substantive law. Questions about what documents need to be filed to begin a lawsuit, when the documents should be filed, which court will hear the case, and which witnesses will be called are all procedural law questions. You will review aspects of both areas in this course and explore in more detail in later courses.

substantive law
Law that defines the rights and duties of individuals with respect to each other's conduct and property.

procedural law
Rules that define the manner in which the rights and duties of individuals are enforced.

The Role of the AAfPE and ABA in Paralegal Education

The American Association for Paralegal Education (AAfPE) was formed to promote high standards for paralegal education. The AAfPE and the ABA are the two major organizations responsible for developing standards and curriculum for paralegal education programs across the nation. California was the first state to require a paralegal to meet certain minimum educational requirements. Although most states do not have such requirements, many employers either require or prefer job candidates with a certain level of education. Some employers select only graduates from established programs. A list of schools offering paralegal programs is available at the AAfPE website, **www.aafpe.org**, in the "Need Help Finding a School?" menu.

In 1974, the ABA established educational standards for paralegal training programs. The ABA guidelines have been revised over time to keep pace with changes in the profession. Paralegal schools are not required to be approved by the ABA. Rather, ABA approval is a voluntary process that gives extra credibility to the schools that successfully apply for it. Programs that meet the ABA's quality standards and that are approved by the ABA are referred to as ABA-approved programs. Of the paralegal education programs in existence, about 260 have ABA approval.

ABA-approved program
A legal or paralegal educational program that satisfies the standards for paralegal training set forth by the American Bar Association.

Certification

Certification refers to formal recognition by a professional group or state agency that a person has met the standards of ability specified by the organization. Generally, this means passing an examination and meeting certain requirements with respect to education and/or experience. The term *certification*, as used here, does not refer to receiving a paralegal certificate. You may obtain a paralegal certificate after completing school, but you will not be considered a *certified paralegal* unless you complete the NALA, NFPA, NALS, AAPI, or state certification process. These certification programs are discussed next. No state requires paralegals to be certified. Although most employers do not require certification, earning a certificate from a professional society or the state can make one more competitive in the labor market and lead to a higher salary (see Chapter 2).

NALA and NFPA Certification

Paralegals who meet the background qualifications set by NALA are eligible to take a two-day, comprehensive examination to become a Certified Legal Assistant (CLA) or, for those who prefer to use the term paralegal, a Certified Paralegal (CP). NALA also sponsors the Advanced Paralegal Certification (APC) program (before 2006, this was called the Certified Legal Assistant Specialty, or CLAS). The APC program provides a series of online courses composed of text lessons, slides, exercises, and interactive tests. NALA offers APC certification to those who are already CLAs or CPs and want to show special competence in a particular field of law. Appendix F provides more detailed information on NALA certification and requirements.

Paralegals who have at least two years of work experience and who have met specific educational requirements can take the Paralegal Advanced Competency Exam (PACE) through NFPA. The PACE is broken down into two tests, one covering general issues and ethics and one on specialty areas. Those who pass the examination use the designation Registered Paralegal (RP). Further information on the PACE program is provided in Appendix G of this book.

Certification by Other Paralegal Organizations

NALS ("the association for legal professionals") offers three certifications:

- Paralegals who have completed an accredited curriculum course or who have one year of work experience may take the basic certification exam (ALS) for legal professionals.
- Paralegals who have three years of work experience or who have earned a prior certification may take the advanced certification exam (PLS) for legal professionals.
- Paralegals who have five years of work experience may take an examination to obtain Professional Paralegal (PP) certification, which was developed by paralegals.

The American Alliance of Paralegals, Inc. (AAPI), also provides a Paralegal Certification Program for paralegals who have at least five years of work experience and have met specific educational requirements.

State Certification

Some states, including California, Florida, Louisiana, North Carolina, and Ohio have implemented voluntary, state certification programs. Details for state programs can be found online. Some state bar associations have information on certification as well. Other states are considering implementing such programs. Generally, paralegal organizations (such as NALA) are in favor of *voluntary* certification and oppose *mandatory* (legally required) certification or state licensing (as you will read in Chapter 4).

certification
Formal recognition by a private group or a state agency that a person has satisfied the group's standards of ability, knowledge, and competence; ordinarily accomplished through the taking of an examination.

Certified Legal Assistant (CLA) or Certified Paralegal (CP)
A legal assistant whose legal competency has been certified by the National Association of Legal Assistants following an examination that tests the legal assistant's knowledge and skills.

Advanced Paralegal Certification (APC)
A credential awarded by the National Association of Legal Assistants to a Certified Paralegal (CP) or Certified Legal Assistant (CLA) whose competency in a legal specialty has been certified based on an examination of the paralegal's knowledge and skills in the specialty area.

Registered Paralegal (RP)
A paralegal whose competency has been certified by the National Federation of Paralegal Associations after successful completion of the Paralegal Advanced Competency Exam (PACE).

Continuing Legal Education

continuing legal education (CLE)
programs
Courses through which attorneys
and other legal professionals extend
their education beyond school.

Paralegals, like attorneys, often enhance their education by attending continuing legal education (CLE) programs. CLE courses, which are offered by state bar associations, commercial providers, law schools, and paralegal associations, are usually seminars and workshops that focus on specific topics or areas of law. Such programs are a good way to learn more about a specialized area of law or keep up to date on the latest developments in software and technology. Many employers encourage their paralegals to take CLE courses and may pay some or all of the costs involved.

Some paralegal organizations, such as NALA and NFPA, require their members to complete a certain number of CLE hours per year as a condition of membership or certification status. NFPA requires certified paralegals to complete 12 hours of CLE every two years. California requires a minimum number of CLE hours from all persons who work as paralegals. Paralegals in California are required to complete four CLE hours in legal ethics every three years and four CLE hours in substantive law every two years.[6]

Paralegal Skills and Attributes

As noted earlier, paralegals now perform many tasks that lawyers customarily performed. Thus, the demands on paralegals to be professional and efficient have increased. To be successful, a paralegal must not only possess specific legal knowledge, but should also exhibit certain aptitudes and personality traits. For example, paralegals need to be able to think logically and to analyze complex issues of law and conflicting descriptions of fact. Some general characteristics that paralegals should have are discussed next.

Analytical Skills

Paralegals are often responsible for gathering and analyzing certain information. A corporate paralegal, for example, may be required to analyze new government regulations to see how they affect the corporation. A paralegal working for the Environmental Protection Agency may be responsible for collecting and studying data on toxic waste disposal and drafting a memo on the matter.

Legal professionals need to be able to break down theories and fact patterns into smaller, more easily understandable components. That is how lawyers formulate arguments and judges decide cases. The process of legal analysis is critical to a paralegal's duties, especially when engaged in factual investigation, trial preparation, and legal research and writing. Analytical reasoning will be discussed in greater depth in Chapters 7 and 9 of this book. For now, it is important that you focus on developing a step-by-step approach to tackling each new subject or task that you encounter. Making analytical thinking a habit will improve your proficiency as a legal assistant.

Communication Skills

Good interpersonal skills are critical to people working in the legal area. The legal profession is a "communications profession" because effective legal representation depends to a great extent on how well a legal professional communicates with clients, witnesses, judges, juries, opposing attorneys, and others. Poor communication can damage a case, destroy a client relationship, and harm one's reputation. Good communication helps to wins cases, clients, and sometimes promotions.

Communication skills involve more than speaking and listening; they also include reading and writing. We look briefly at each of these here. Although we focus on communication skills in the law office setting, these skills are essential to success in any work environment.

Excellent reading skills are a plus in any profession, but they are especially important in the legal arena. As a paralegal, you must not only be able to read well, but also be able to interpret what you are reading, whether it be a statute, a court's decision, or a contract's provision. What other important skills should every paralegal acquire?

© wavebreakmedia/www.Shutterstock.com.

Interpersonal Skills

Good listening skills are an important part of paralegal work. Instructions must be followed carefully. To understand instructions, you must listen to them carefully. Asking follow-up questions helps to clarify anything that you do not understand. In addition, repeating the instructions not only ensures that you understand them but also gives the attorney a chance to add anything that may have been forgotten. Listening skills are particularly important when interviewing clients and other parties relevant to a legal matter. In Chapter 11, you will read in detail about listening skills and techniques that will help you conduct effective interviews. If you can relate well to the person whom you are interviewing, your chances of obtaining useful information are increased (see the *Developing Paralegal Skills* feature on page 13 for more on interviews).

Similarly, there will also be times when you will have to deal with people in your office who are under a great deal of stress. You may have to deal with people you consider to be "difficult." The more effectively you can respond to these people in ways that promote positive working relationships, the more productive you will be as a member of a legal team.

Speaking Skills

Paralegals must be able to speak well. In addition to using correct grammar, legal assistants need to be precise and clear in communicating ideas or facts to others. For example, when you discuss facts learned in an investigation with your supervising attorney, your oral report must explain exactly what you found, or it could mislead the attorney. A miscommunication in this context could have serious consequences if it leads the attorney to take an action that harms the client's interests.

Oral communication also has a nonverbal dimension—that is, we communicate our thoughts and feelings through gestures, facial expressions, and other "body language." For example, if your body language suggests you are uncomfortable with a client, the client will be less responsive to your questions.

DEVELOPING PARALEGAL SKILLS

PROOFREADING LEGAL DOCUMENTS

Geena Northrop, a paralegal, works for a solo practitioner (a one-attorney law firm). Among her duties, she handles some legal writing for the attorney. Geena knows that when creating a legal document, writing the document is only half the job. The rest is proofreading—and not just once. One proofreading is simply not enough to catch every error. Geena has adopted the motto of one of the instructors in her paralegal program: "Proof, proof, and proof again!"

Today, she has set aside time to proofread carefully a last will and testament that her supervising attorney and she created for a client. Geena prints out a copy of the document for proofreading purposes, because she has learned that it is difficult to proofread a document only on a computer screen. Moreover, style and formatting problems are often not as evident on a screen as they are on hard copy.

Her first step in proofreading the document is to make sure that the document reflects all of the relevant information from her notes. Geena reviews her notes point by point from the client interview and from her discussion with the attorney about the will. She compares the notes to the document.

All looks well in this respect, so she proceeds to her second step in proofreading: checking style and format. Are all of the headings in the correct size and font? Is the spacing between headings consistent? Are

all paragraphs properly indented? She finds a couple problems and marks her hard copy to make the appropriate changes. She then reads the document word for word to ensure that there are no grammatical problems, spelling errors, or typos. Finally, she revises the document on her computer, prints it out, and takes it to the attorney for review.

CHECKLIST FOR PROOFREADING LEGAL DOCUMENTS

- When you create a legal document, do not assume that one proofreading is sufficient to catch all problems or errors that the document may contain.

- Print out the document and go through the contents line by line to make sure that it includes all required or relevant information. Many documents contain "boilerplate" that must be checked to be sure earlier entries for other clients are not retained.

- Read through the document again to make sure that the style and formatting elements are consistent throughout.

- Reading a document out loud can be an effective way to catch errors.

- Finally, read through the document word for word to ensure that it is free of grammatical errors, misspelled words, and typos.

Reading Skills

Reading skills involve more than just being able to understand the meaning of written letters and words. Reading skills also involve understanding the *meaning* of a sentence, paragraph, section, or page. As a legal professional, you need to be able to read and comprehend many different types of written materials, including statutes and court decisions. You need to be familiar with legal terminology and concepts so that you know the meaning of these legal writings. You also need to develop the ability to read documents carefully so that you do not miss important distinctions, such as the difference in meaning that can result from the use of *and* instead of *or*. The importance of proofreading as a reading skill is highlighted in the *Developing Paralegal Skills* feature above.

Writing Skills

Good writing skills are crucial to success. Paralegals draft letters, memoranda, and a variety of legal documents. Letters to clients, witnesses, court clerks, and others must

DEVELOPING PARALEGAL SKILLS

INTERVIEWING A CLIENT

Brenda Lundquist is a paralegal in a small firm. She has many responsibilities, including interviewing prospective divorce clients. Using a standard set of forms, Brenda meets with a prospective client and obtains information about the reasons for the divorce, finances and assets, and desired custody arrangements. This information is needed to assist the supervising attorney in determining whether to take the case. The information will also help Brenda in preparing the documents to be filed with the court should the attorney decide to represent the client. Brenda enjoys the work because she likes helping people, and often people who are getting divorced need both emotional and legal support.

CHECKLIST FOR CLIENT INTERVIEWS

- Plan the interview in advance.
- Print out forms and checklists to use during the interview.
- Introduce yourself as a paralegal or legal assistant.
- Explain the purpose of the interview to the client.
- Communicate your questions precisely.
- Listen carefully and be supportive, as necessary.
- Summarize the client's major concerns.
- Give the client a "time line" for what will happen in the legal proceedings.

be clear, well organized, and must follow the rules of grammar and punctuation. Legal documents must also be free of errors. Lawyers are generally attentive to details and they expect legal assistants to be equally so. Remember, you represent your supervising attorney when you write. You will learn more about writing skills in Chapter 9.

Computer Skills

In all professional workplaces, computer skills are now essential. At a minimum, you will be expected to have experience with document creation and to have data-entry skills. Paralegals well versed in the technology now widely used will have an edge in the job market. Paralegal specialists who know how to use sophisticated software, such as database-management systems, and how to adapt new technology, such as social media tools, to the workplace so as to improve efficiency and communication, hold some of the best-paying positions.

We cannot stress enough that to become a successful paralegal, the best thing you can do during your training is to become as knowledgeable as possible about online communications. Throughout this book, you will read about how technology applies to all areas of legal practice. You will also learn how you can use technology to perform various paralegal tasks and to keep up to date on the law. (See this chapter's *Technology and Today's Paralegal* feature on the following page for some online resources for paralegals.)

Organizational Skills

Being well organized is a plus. Law offices are busy places. There are phone calls to be answered and returned, witnesses to get to court and on the witness stand on time, documents to be filed, and checklists and procedures to be followed. If you are able to organize files, create procedures and checklists, and keep things running smoothly, you will be providing a valued service to the legal team and to clients. Importantly, you must organize your time, as discussed in the *In the Office* feature on page 15.

If organization comes naturally to you, you are ahead of the game. If not, now is the time to learn and practice organizational skills. You will find plenty of opportunities to do this as a paralegal student—by organizing your notebooks, devising an efficient tracking system for homework assignments, and creating a study or work schedule and following it. Other suggestions for organizing your time and work, both as a student and as a paralegal on the job, are included in the **Skill Prep: A Paralegal Skills Module** before Chapter 1.

The Ability to Keep Information Confidential

Paralegals are required to have the ability to keep client information confidential. The ability to keep confidences is not just a desirable attribute in a paralegal, but a mandatory one.

TECHNOLOGY AND TODAY'S PARALEGAL

ONLINE RESOURCES FOR PARALEGALS

There are many career resources available online. To keep your skills up to date and to stay on top of developments in the law, you should regularly check such resources.

PARALEGAL ASSOCIATIONS

Many paralegals belong to the National Association of Legal Assistants (NALA) or to the National Federation of Paralegal Associations (NFPA). Both organizations offer excellent gateways for paralegal resources. NALA's website (**www.nala.org**) displays information on many professional certification and continuing education programs. It also provides links to state and local affiliated organizations. The NFPA website (**www.paralegals.org**) offers a continuing education calendar, a gateway to legal research sites, and a variety of career advice. *Paralegal Today,* a magazine for paralegals, also has a website (**www.paralegaltoday.com**) that features salary data, job listings, continuing education information, and downloadable forms.

AMERICAN BAR ASSOCIATION

The ABA is not just for lawyers. The Standing Committee on Paralegals provides career information, continuing education, directories, a gateway to blogs by paralegals, and information on paralegal education standards. Its website notes many meetings for legal professionals that cover many areas of interest.

BRYAN GARNER'S LEGAL WRITING SITE

America's most celebrated legal writing guru, Southern Methodist University law professor Bryan Garner, is best known for his books, which include *The Redbook: A Manual on Legal Style* and *Legal Writing in Plain English*. He is the current editor of the famous *Black's Law Dictionary*. Garner's website, **www.lawprose.org**, offers a bibliography of articles on legal writing, the schedule of legal writing seminars, and a way to subscribe to his "Usage Tips of the Day."

THE PARALEGAL GATEWAY

The Paralegal Gateway (**www.paralegalgateway.com**) focuses on job advice, examples of successful résumés and interviews, and networking tools such as LinkedIn. It also offers links to continuing education resources.

LEGAL NEWS

There is a wide range of online newsletters and websites on specific areas of law produced by law firms. The LawProf blog network (**www.lawprofessorblogs.com**) provides many subject-specific blogs (known as *blawgs*) by law professors that offer commentary on new cases, statutes, and news from trustworthy sources.

IN THE OFFICE

USE TIME WISELY

Paralegals often work on many cases at the same time. To be responsive to job requirements and to meet the needs of clients, set aside time each day to review the demands on your time. Think about what must be done that day as well as what must be completed by certain dates to meet deadlines. Make a list of what you need to accomplish. The list might be built into your calendaring software. Each morning, reevaluate what you got done the day before. If work was not completed, think about why. When working on multiple cases, it is critical to understand what must be accomplished on each case so that one deadline does not "sneak up" on you while you are paying attention to another. Consider adopting a time-management system. There are computer programs and apps to help you stay organized. Find one that works for you.

As you will read in Chapter 4, attorneys are ethically and legally obligated to keep all information relating to the representation of a client strictly confidential unless the client consents to the disclosure of the information. The attorney may disclose this information only to people who are also working on behalf of the client and who therefore need to know it. Paralegals share in this duty. If a paralegal reveals confidential client information to anyone outside the group working on the client's case, the lawyer (and the paralegal) may face consequences if the client suffers harm as a result. The law firm could be sued and the paralegal dismissed. Even if the client is not harmed, lack of confidence can be the end of a career.

Keeping client information confidential means that you, as a paralegal, cannot divulge such information even to your spouse, family members, or closest friends. You should not talk about a client's case in hallways, elevators, or any areas in which others may overhear your conversation. You must be careful when handling client documents that you do not expose them to outsiders. Keeping work-related information confidential is an essential part of being a responsible and reliable paralegal.

Professionalism

Paralegals should behave professionally at all times. That means be responsible and reliable to earn the respect and trust of the attorneys and clients with whom you work. It also means you put aside any personal bias or emotion that interferes with your representation of a client or assessment of a case. Paralegals must be honest and assertive in letting others know what things paralegals can and cannot do (for example, they cannot give legal advice). This is particularly important because not everyone is sure what paralegals do.

As a paralegal, you will find that you are judged not only by your actions and words but also by your appearance, attitude, and other factors. When deadlines approach and the pace of office work becomes somewhat frantic, it can be difficult to meet the challenge of acting professionally. When the pressure is on, it is important to remain calm and focus on completing your task quickly and accurately to ensure quality work. If a client's call or another attorney interrupts you, be aware that the way you react is likely to affect whether others view you as professional. Be courteous and respectful during such interruptions. The paralegal must be detail oriented and accurate, even when working under pressure.

The Future of the Profession

The paralegal profession is a dynamic and expanding field within the legal arena. Paralegals continue to assume a growing range of duties in the nation's legal offices and perform many of the same tasks as lawyers. According to the U.S. Department of Labor, the employment of paralegals should grow "faster than average" and "formally trained paralegals with strong computer and database management skills should have the best employment opportunities."[7] Growth is occurring because law firms and other employers with legal staffs are hiring more paralegals to lower the cost—and increase the availability and efficiency—of legal services.

Those entering the profession today will find a broader range of career options than ever before. In addition, you have the opportunity to help chart the course the profession takes in the future. The paralegal profession has become a popular career choice for many, so the job market is competitive, but formally trained and skilled paralegals have excellent employment potential.

KEY TERMS AND CONCEPTS

ABA-approved program   8

Advanced Paralegal Certification (APC)   9

American Association for Paralegal Education (AAfPE)   3

American Bar Association (ABA)   3

certification   9

Certified Legal Assistant (CLA)   9

Certified Paralegal (CP)   10

continuing legal education (CLE) programs   10

legal assistant   3

National Association of Legal Assistants (NALA)   3

National Federation of Paralegal Associations (NFPA)   3

paralegal   3

procedural law   8

Registered Paralegal (RP)   9

substantive law   8

Chapter Summary / Today's Professional Paralegal

WHAT IS A PARALEGAL?

The terms *paralegal* and *legal assistant* mean the same to some people. The terms *legal technician* or *legal research specialist* may be used in some workplaces. Paralegals perform many of the tasks traditionally handled by attorneys. A paralegal is qualified by education, training, or work experience to be employed by a law office, corporation, governmental agency, or other entity. A paralegal performs delegated substantive legal work, for which a lawyer is responsible.

WHAT DO PARALEGALS DO?

1. *Typical tasks*—Legal assistants may perform the following duties: interviewing and maintaining contact with clients and witnesses, locating and interviewing witnesses, conducting legal investigations, calendaring and tracking deadlines, organizing and maintaining client files, conducting legal research, drafting legal documents, filing legal documents with courts, summarizing witness testimony, coordinating litigation proceedings, attending legal proceedings, and using technology.

2. *Duties often vary*—Paralegals perform different functions depending on where they work and on their abilities and experience. Duties vary according to the size of a law firm and the kind of law practiced by the firm. Paralegals commonly spend significant time performing document management, client relations, and research.

3. *Paralegals and technology*—Technology is the number-one area of expanding paralegal responsibility. Paralegals skilled in using technologies to assist them in performing their duties will excel in the profession.

PARALEGAL EDUCATION

Paralegal education programs have become increasingly important in the growth and development of the profession.

1. *Educational options*—Colleges offer a variety of programs to train paralegals, ranging in length from three months to four years.

2. *Curriculum*—Paralegal education includes coverage of substantive law and of procedural law, as paralegals are involved in most aspects of the legal process.

3. *ABA and AAfPE paralegal education*—The ABA sets voluntary educational standards for paralegal training programs. ABA-approved programs have volunteered to meet the ABA's standards. AAfPE promotes high standards in paralegal education.

4. *Certification*—Certification refers to recognition by a professional group or state agency that a person has met standards of proficiency specified by the group. Generally, this means passing an examination and meeting certain requirements with respect to education and/or experience. Paralegals may be certified by NALA, NFPA, or a state agency. No state requires paralegal certification.

5. *Continuing legal education (CLE)*—Continuing legal education courses are offered by state bar associations and paralegal associations. These programs provide a way to learn more about a specialized area of law or keep up to date on developments in law and technology.

PARALEGAL SKILLS AND ATTRIBUTES

Because paralegals perform many of the tasks that lawyers used to perform, the demands on paralegals to be professional and efficient have increased.

1. *Analytical skills*—These include gathering and analyzing information relevant to legal matters.

2. *Communication skills*—The ability to communicate effectively with clients, witnesses, and others in the legal process is essential. Understanding a legal matter and communicating about it involves reading, speaking, listening, and writing.

3. *Computer skills*—Most legal research is done online, and computers are used to produce most legal documents, familiarity with the tools available makes a paralegal more successful and competitive.

4. *Organizational skills*—Paralegals keep track of numerous legal documents and other matters related to cases and the functioning of a law office, so being well organized is a requirement of the profession.

5. *Keeping confidence*—As paralegals have knowledge of confidential legal matters and help represent clients, protecting information from exposure to others is a major requirement of the job.

6. *Professionalism*—In legal work, responsibility and trust are key. Legal professionals are judged on the basis of actions, words, and attitude.

FUTURE OF THE PROFESSION

The role of paralegals in law continues to grow as the providers of legal services have learned the effectiveness of qualified non-attorney professionals.

QUESTIONS FOR REVIEW

1. What is a paralegal? Is there any difference between a paralegal and a legal assistant?

2. What types of educational programs and training are available to paralegals? Must a person meet specific educational requirements to work as a paralegal?

3. What role does the American Bar Association play in paralegal education?

4. What does *certification* mean?

5. List and describe the skills that are useful in paralegal practice. Do you have these skills?

ETHICS QUESTION

Richard attends a six-month paralegal course and earns a certificate. In the West Coast city where he lives, certified paralegals—those with a CP or a CLA designation—are in great demand in the job market. Richard responds to a newspaper advertisement for a certified paralegal, indicating that he is one. Has Richard done anything unethical? What is the difference between a certificate and certification?

PRACTICE QUESTIONS AND ASSIGNMENTS

1. Using the material found in the chapter, identify which of the following employees are paralegals:

   a. Graciela works in the file room of a major law firm checking out and returning files as they are needed by attorneys.

   b. Maria does all of the typing, filing, and answering phones for two attorneys in a small law office.

   c. Tameko drafts legal documents, meets with clients, and assists her supervising attorney with trials.

   d. Majora, who has an MBA, supervises the day-to-day operations of a 250-attorney law firm.

2. Using the material in the chapter, identify which of the following laws are substantive laws and which are procedural laws:

   a. A law requiring a person to be 16 years old to obtain a driver's license.

   b. A court rule requiring that an answer to a complaint be filed within 21 days of receipt of service of process.

   c. A law requiring a manufacturer of an automobile to replace the vehicle or refund the purchase price if it cannot be repaired.

   d. A law requiring civil lawsuits exceeding $25,000 to be filed with the circuit court.

3. Which national paralegal organizations offer paralegal certification exams and what are the certifications called? Do states offer certifications for paralegals? Is a state certification a license to practice law? Explain your answer.

4. Tom and Sandy are having coffee after their paralegal class. The instructor discussed the debate within the profession about whether to use the term *paralegal* or *legal assistant*. Tom says he agrees with NFPA that the term *paralegal* is preferable because no one will confuse paralegals with legal secretaries. Sandy, who has worked as a legal secretary, is offended by Tom's remarks. What label do you prefer—*legal assistant* or *paralegal*—and why? Is it an important issue?

GROUP PROJECT

This project asks the group to review information on the websites of NALA (www.nala.org) and NFPA (www.para-legals.org) about the organizations' certification programs. The members of the group will do the following tasks to complete the project:

- Student one will determine and summarize the requirements of the NALA certification exams.

- Student two will determine and summarize the requirements of the NFPA certification exams.

- Student three will compile the results in a chart or graph in PowerPoint or Excel.

- Student four will present the results to the class.

INTERNET PROJECTS

1. Browse through the materials on the websites of the National Association of Legal Assistants, or NALA (at **www.nala.org**), and the National Federation of Paralegal Associations, or NFPA (at **www.paralegals.org**). Answer the questions below:

   a. Is there an affiliate of the National Association of Legal Assistants or the National Federation of Paralegal Associations in your city? Where is the nearest affiliate of either of these organizations located?

   b. Are there any regional or local paralegal associations in your area? If so, what are their names, street and e-mail addresses, and phone numbers?

   c. If you located a paralegal organization, does it accept student members, and are there networking opportunities for students?

   d. What other member benefits are offered by these organizations?

2. Review the AAfPE website at **www.aafpe.org**, and the American Bar Association website for paralegals at **www.americanbar.org/groups/paralegals.html**. Answer the following questions:

   a. What role does each of these organizations play in paralegal education?

   b. Click on the link to education on the AAfPE website and to the general approval process information (under Resources) on the ABA website. Review the information on paralegal education and print the first page located for each site. List the benefits of a paralegal education program, or having the approval, of each organization. Can you think of any reasons why a paralegal program would not belong to, or seek approval of either organization?

END NOTES

1. **www.salary.com**. That is the median salary for Paralegal IV. Paralegal managers earn more ($90,900 median) and entry-level paralegals earn less (Paralegal I salary median was $48,850).

2. Source: **www.nala.org**. This information is subject to updates and edits at any time.

3. The members of NFPA voted to remove the term *legal assistant* from their definition of *paralegal* in 2002. The American Association for Paralegal Education took a similar position that year.

4. Reprinted by permission of the National Federation of Paralegal Associations, Inc. (NFPA®) **www.paralegals.org**.

5. Reprinted by permission of the American Association for Paralegal Education.

6. California Business and Professions Code, Sections 6450–6456. Enacted in 2000. California Advanced Specialist (CAS) certification is also available as a specialty exam through NALA to paralegals who possess CLA or CP certification. For more information on this state-specific NALA certification, see Appendix F.

7. See **www.bls.gov/ooh**. (In the search box, type *paralegals*)

CHAPTER 2

Career Opportunities

CHAPTER OUTLINE

CHAPTER OBJECTIVES

After completing this chapter, you will know:

- What types of firms and organizations hire paralegals.

- Some areas of law in which paralegals specialize.

- How much paralegals can expect to earn.

- How to search for an employer.

- How to present yourself to prospective employers.

- How to prepare a career plan and pursue it.

- How to use social media to promote your career.

INTRODUCTION

Paralegals enjoy a wide range of employment opportunities in both the private and the public sectors. They are in demand at law firms because they help provide competent legal services at a lower cost to clients. Most legal assistants work in law offices. However, almost any business that uses legal services, including large corporations, insurance companies, banks, and real estate agencies, employ paralegals. In addition, the government has positions for paralegals at many agencies. Paralegals work in many court systems, county offices, and legal-services clinics across the nation.

This chapter provides you with a starting point for planning your career. In the pages that follow, you will read about where paralegals work and what compensation paralegals receive. You will also learn about the steps you will need to follow to plan your career, locate potential employers, present yourself in social media, and find a job.

Where Paralegals Work

Paralegal employers fall into a number of categories. This section describes the general characteristics of each of the major types of working environments. Regardless of where you work, on-the-job stress is a potential problem, as discussed in the *In the Office* feature on page 23.

Law Firms

When paralegals first began to establish themselves in the legal community in the 1960s, they worked almost exclusively in law firms. Today, law firms continue to hire more paralegals than do any other organizations. Two-thirds of all paralegals work in law firms, but as was just noted, there are opportunities in other organizations. Law firms vary in size from the one-attorney office to the huge "megafirm" with hundreds of attorneys. As you can see in Exhibit 2.1 below, most paralegals work in settings that employ fewer than twenty-five attorneys.

Working for a Small Firm

Many paralegals begin their careers working for small law practices with just one or a few attorneys. To some extent, this is because small law firms (those with twenty-five or fewer attorneys) outnumber large ones. It may also be due to geographic location. For example, a paralegal who lives in a small community may find that the only option is a small legal practice.

FIRM SIZE MATTERS. Working for a small firm offers many advantages to the beginning paralegal. If the firm is a general law practice, you have the opportunity to gain experience in many different aspects of the practice of law. You will learn whether you enjoy working in one area (such as family law) more than another (such as criminal defense work) in the event that you later decide to specialize. Some paralegals also prefer

Number of Attorneys	Percentage of Paralegals	Average Salary
1	14%	$40,796
2–5	29%	$44,261
6–10	18%	$55,530
11–25	17%	$55,098
26–50	13%	$54,635
51–100	6%	$71,837
Over 100	3%	$63,268

EXHIBIT 2.1

Paralegal Employment and Salary by Size of Firm or Legal Department

The data in this exhibit come from survey data reported in *Paralegal Today*.

Paralegals who work for large firms often need to research statutes, court cases, or regulations in the firm's law library. Notebook computers, tablet devices, and smartphones facilitate the ease with which paralegals can do research and communicate with attorneys, clients, and other. What are the pros and cons of working for a large law firm?

the more personal and less formal environment that usually exists in a small law office, as well as the variety of tasks and greater flexibility common in this setting.

Small size may also have disadvantages, however. Paralegals who work for small firms may have less support staff to assist them. This means that if you work in a small law office, your job may involve a substantial amount of secretarial or clerical work.

THINK ABOUT COMPENSATION DIFFERENTIALS. Compensation is another topic of potential concern. Small firms pay, on average, lower salaries than do larger firms, as shown in Exhibit 2.1 on page 21. Generally, the larger the firm, the higher paralegal salaries will be. Small firms also may provide fewer employee benefits, such as pension plans and health benefits. At the same time, however, a small firm may be in a convenient location, may not require an expensive wardrobe, and may provide free parking.

Working for a Large Firm

In contrast to the (typically) more casual environment of the small law office, larger law firms usually are more formal. In a larger firm, your responsibilities will probably be limited to specific, well-defined tasks. For example, you may work for a department that handles (or for an attorney who handles) only certain types of cases, such as real estate transactions. Office procedures and employment policies will also be more clearly defined and may be set forth in a written employment manual.

The advantages of the large firm often include greater opportunities for promotions and career advancement, higher salaries and better benefits packages, more support staff for paralegals, and more sophisticated technology that affords greater access to research resources.

You may see certain characteristics of large law firms as either advantages or disadvantages, depending on your personality and preferences. For example, if you favor the more specialized duties and formal working environment of a large law firm, then you will view these characteristics as advantages. If you prefer to handle a greater variety of tasks and enjoy the more personal atmosphere of the small law office, then you might think the specialization and formality of a large law firm are disadvantages.

Corporations and Other Business Organizations

As already mentioned, many paralegals work outside of law firms. Almost any business that uses legal services may hire paralegals. An increasing number of paralegals work for

IN THE OFFICE

STRESS PROBLEMS

Stress can cause health problems. It is also related to making mistakes at work. When that happens, even more stress is generated. Errors increase when we rush to meet deadlines and have our minds on many things at once.

How can you reduce stress that may result in sloppy work and missed deadlines?

1. Be candid about your workload when a supervisor adds new work.
2. Prioritize your tasks. Determine, perhaps by consulting with your supervising attorney, which projects take priority.
3. Consider asking your supervisor to assign another person in the office to help you.
4. Keep in mind that being aware of stress is a key step in learning to deal with it in an effective way.

Being organized and clear about responsibilities will increase your productivity, concentration, and performance. It will also reduce the likelihood of stress building up in the office.

---

corporate legal departments. In recent years, companies have been bringing more legal work "in house" rather than paying outside law firms for work, so this is a growth area for paralegal employment. Most large companies hire a large staff of in-house attorneys to handle corporate legal affairs. Paralegals who are employed by corporations usually work under the supervision of in-house attorneys.

Paralegals in a corporate setting perform a variety of functions, such as organizing meetings and maintaining necessary records, drafting employee contracts and benefit plans, and preparing financial and other reports for the corporation. Paralegals often help monitor government regulations to be sure the company operates within the law. When the firm is involved in a lawsuit, paralegals may be assigned duties related to that lawsuit. (For more information on the duties of corporate paralegals, see Chapter 18.)

About one-fifth of all paralegals work in corporate environments. Paralegals who are employed by corporations frequently receive higher salaries than those working for law firms. In addition, paralegals who are employed by corporations may work more regular hours. Unlike paralegals in law firms, corporate paralegals typically have not been required to generate a specific number of "billable hours" per year (hours billed to clients for paralegal services performed, to be discussed in Chapter 3).

Government

Paralegals employed by government agencies work in a variety of settings and often specialize in one aspect of the law. Agencies also usually provide excellent benefits and stable work environments, as budgets do not depend on client billing.

Administrative Agencies

Paralegals who work for federal or state government agencies may conduct legal research and analysis, investigate welfare eligibility or disability claims, examine documents (such as loan applications), and many other tasks. At the federal level, the U.S. Department of Justice employs the largest number of paralegals, followed by the Social Security Administration and the Department of the Treasury.

Paralegals who work for government agencies normally work regular hours and tend to work fewer total hours per year (have more vacation time) than paralegals in private law firms. Like paralegals in corporations, they may not have to worry about billable hours, although other measures of productivity are likely to be used. Additionally, paralegals who work for the government usually enjoy comprehensive employment benefits.

Legislative Offices

Legislators in the U.S. Congress and in some state legislatures typically have staff members to help them with their duties. Duties often include legal research and writing, and paralegals sometimes perform such services. For example, a senator who plans to propose an amendment to a certain law may ask a staff paralegal to research the legislative history of that law (to discern the legislature's intention when passing the law—see Chapters 5 and 7) and write up a summary of that history.

Law Enforcement Offices and Courts

Many paralegals work for government law enforcement offices and institutions. As you will read in Chapter 13, which discusses criminal law and procedures, a public prosecutor prosecutes a person accused of a crime. Public prosecutors (such as district attorneys, state attorneys general, and U.S. attorneys) are paid by the government. Accused persons may be defended by private attorneys or, if they cannot afford to hire a lawyer, by *public defenders*—attorneys paid for by the state to ensure that criminal defendants are not deprived of their constitutional right to be represented by counsel. Both public prosecutors and public defenders rely on paralegals for assistance.

Paralegals also find work in other government settings, such as federal or state court administrative offices. Court administrative work ranges from recording and filing court documents (such as the documents filed during a lawsuit—see Chapter 10) to working for a small claims court (a court that handles claims below a specified amount—see Chapter 6). Paralegals also work for bankruptcy courts (see page 29 and Chapter 19 for a discussion of bankruptcy law and practice).

Legal Aid Offices

Legal aid offices provide legal services to those who find it difficult to pay for legal representation. Most legal aid is government funded, although some support comes from private foundations.

Many paralegals who work in this capacity find their jobs rewarding, even though they usually receive lower salaries than they would in other settings. In part, this is because of the nature of the work—helping people in need. Additionally, paralegals in legal aid offices generally assume a wider array of responsibilities than they would in a traditional law office. For example, some federal and state administrative agencies, including the Social Security Administration, allow paralegals to represent clients in agency hearings and judicial proceedings. As you will read in Chapter 4, paralegals normally are not allowed to represent clients—only attorneys can do so. Exceptions to this rule exist when a court or agency permits nonlawyers to represent others in court or in administrative agency hearings.

Freelance Paralegals

freelance paralegal
A paralegal who operates his or her own business and provides services to attorneys on a contract basis. A freelance paralegal works under the supervision of an attorney, who assumes responsibility for the paralegal's work product.

Some experienced paralegals operate as freelancers. Freelance paralegals (also called *independent contractors* or *contract paralegals*) own their own business and perform specific legal work for attorneys on a contract basis. Attorneys who need temporary legal assistance may contract with freelance paralegals to work on particular projects. In addition, attorneys who need legal assistance but cannot afford to hire full-time paralegals might hire freelancers to work on a part-time basis.

Freelancing has advantages and disadvantages. Because freelancers are their own bosses, they can set their own schedules. Thus, they enjoy a greater degree of work flexibility. In addition, depending on the nature of their projects, they may work at home or in attorneys' offices. With flexibility, however, comes added responsibility. A freelance paralegal's income depends on the ability to promote and maintain business. If there are no clients for a month, there is no income. Also, freelancers do not enjoy benefits such as employer-provided medical insurance.

Freelance paralegals work under attorney supervision. Freelancers are not to be confused with legal technicians—often called independent paralegals—who do *not* work under the supervision of an attorney and who provide (sell) legal services directly to the public. These services include helping members of the public obtain and fill out forms for certain legal transactions, such as bankruptcy filings and divorce petitions. As we will see in Chapter 4, legal technicians run the risk of violating state statutes prohibiting the unauthorized practice of law.

legal technician or **independent paralegal**
A paralegal who offers services directly to the public without attorney supervision. Independent paralegals assist consumers by supplying them with forms and procedural knowledge relating to simple or routine legal procedures.

Paralegal Specialties

While many paralegals perform a wide range of legal services, some find it satisfying to specialize in one area. Areas of law in which paralegals report that they work at least some of the time are litigation (52 percent), corporate law (9 percent), contract law (13 percent), and real estate law (11 percent). Other specialties exist, and some are listed in Exhibit 2.2 below. Here, we discuss a few of the areas in which paralegals may specialize, but increasingly, in all practice settings, being able to use technology efficiently is a great asset, as discussed in the *Technology and Today's Paralegal* feature on page 27.

Litigation

Working a lawsuit through the court system is called litigation. Paralegals who specialize in assisting attorneys in this process are called litigation paralegals. Litigation paralegals work in general law practices, small litigation firms, litigation departments of larger law firms, and corporate legal departments. Litigation paralegals often specialize in a certain type of litigation, such as personal-injury litigation (discussed shortly) or product liability cases (which involve injuries caused by defective products).

Litigation paralegal work varies with the substantive law area being litigated. It also varies according to whether it is done on behalf of plaintiffs (those who bring lawsuits) or defendants (those against whom lawsuits are brought). Some litigation paralegals investigate cases, review documents containing evidence, interview clients and witnesses, draft documents to file with the courts, and prepare for hearings and trials. You

litigation
The process of working a lawsuit through the court system.

litigation paralegal
A paralegal who specializes in assisting attorneys in the litigation process.

plaintiff
A party who initiates a lawsuit.

defendant
A party against whom a lawsuit is brought.

Area of Legal Specialty	Average Compensation
Administrative	$39,250
Bankruptcy	$45,380
Contracts	$48,100
Corporate	$61,413
Criminal	$42,820
Employment	$47,289
Environmental	$57,633
Family	$39,078
Insurance	$55,371
Intellectual property	$67,300
Litigation	$53,615
Medical malpractice	$53,191
Personal injury (plaintiff)	$47,680
Probate (wills and estates)	$39,750
Real estate	$45,614
Workers' compensation	$36,200

EXHIBIT 2.2

Average Compensation by Specialty

The authors compiled this exhibit using data from *Paralegal Today*.

will read about litigation procedures and the important role played by paralegals in this process in Chapters 10 through 12.

Corporate Law

corporate law
Law that governs the formation, financing, merger and acquisition, and termination of corporations, as well as the rights and duties of those who own and run the corporation.

Corporate law consists of the laws that govern the formation, financing, structure, and termination of corporations, as well as the rights and duties of those who own and run corporations. Chapter 18 reviews the meaning of these functions and the tasks that corporate paralegals may perform.

Paralegals who specialize in corporate law may work in the legal department of a corporation, or for a law firm that specializes in corporate law. Corporate paralegals often perform such tasks as prepare and file documents with a state agency to set up business entities, maintain corporate records, organize and schedule shareholders' meetings in accordance with state law. As you see on the previous page in Exhibit 2.2, paralegals who work in corporate law generally receive higher salaries than paralegals in some other settings. In addition, corporate paralegals who narrow their expertise to areas such as mergers are among the highest-paid paralegals.

Contract Law

contract
An agreement (based on a promise or an exchange of promises) that can be enforced in court.

Contract law work is common for many lawyers. As you will read in Chapter 15, a contract is an agreement (based on a promise or an exchange of promises) that can be enforced in court. Paralegals who specialize in contracts may work for a corporation's legal department, for a law firm, or for a government agency.

Paralegal work in contract law may involve preparing contracts and forms, and reviewing contracts to determine whether a party to a contract has complied with its terms. In a lawsuit for breach of contract, for example, a paralegal might be asked to look closely at the terms and do some factual investigation to find out whether the contract has been breached (broken). Contract specialists also may conduct research in the law governing contracts, before a contract is formed or during litigation concerning the contract. Because contracts are so common in our legal environment, many paralegals—not just contract specialists—are involved with work relating to contracts.

Real Estate Law

real estate
Land and things permanently attached to the land, such as houses, buildings, and trees.

At law, real estate, or *real property*, consists of land and things attached to the land, such as houses, buildings, and trees. Because of the value of real estate (for most people, a home is the most expensive purchase they will ever make) and the complexities of the transaction, attorneys frequently assist parties that buy or sell real property to make sure that nothing important is overlooked.

Paralegals who specialize in real estate may find employment in a number of environments, including small law firms that specialize in real estate transactions, real estate departments in large law firms, or other business firms that frequently buy or sell real property, banks (which finance real estate purchases), title companies, and real estate agencies. As we discuss in Chapter 16, paralegals working in real estate law often draft contracts for the sale of real estate, draft mortgage agreements, draft and record deeds, and schedule closings on the sale of property.

Personal-Injury Law

tort
A civil wrong not arising from a breach of contract; a violation of a legal duty that causes harm to another.

Much litigation involves claims brought by persons who have been injured in automobile accidents or other incidents as a result of the negligence of others. *Negligence* is a tort, or civil wrong, that occurs when carelessness causes harm to another. Someone who has been injured as a result of another's negligence is entitled under tort law to attempt to obtain compensation from the wrongdoer. (Tort law, including negligence, is discussed in Chapter 14.)

TECHNOLOGY AND TODAY'S PARALEGAL

MORE CAREER OPPORTUNITIES FOR TECH-SAVVY PARALEGALS

Paralegals possessing superior technological skills are in demand. Knowing the basics—document creation, spreadsheets, database management, and online legal research—is essential. Also knowing how to utilize social media such as LinkedIn, Facebook, and Google+ is becoming increasing important. Finally, the use of smartphones and tablets has become part of the life of many paralegals. Here we review some skills that paralegals should master to secure their future in the job market.

MASTER DOCUMENT-CREATION SKILLS

Good document-creation skills are an asset. The faster you can accurately type text or key in data on a computer, the more work you can complete in a shorter time—and, consequently, the more valuable you are to an employer. This is true whether you are creating documents, scheduling court dates, managing calendars, or performing legal research. Make sure your touch-typing skills (typing without looking at the keys) are superior. Practice entering numbers as well as letters so that you can accurately key in court dates and deadlines in calendaring programs and figures in billing programs. Inexpensive or free typing programs are available on the Internet.

BE PROFICIENT WITH OFFICE SOFTWARE

Most law firms use a variety of software applications, including billing programs, e-mail, calendaring, and legal research applications. To be competitive, paralegals should be skilled at using these programs. For example, paralegals are often responsible for keeping track of the deadlines for filing court documents, along with court filing fees and requirements. Local court rules specify the filing dates and fees for different kinds of cases, but these rules change regularly. Missed deadlines are a leading cause of malpractice (professional negligence) lawsuits filed by clients against attorneys.

Calendaring software helps ensure that attorneys do not miss important dates and calculates required fees based on the local court rules. Such software could suit the needs of a small law firm that handles only local cases, but it might not be adequate if the firm handles cases in numerous counties or states. The firm may use an online calendaring service instead. A paralegal who knows about such applications could suggest that the firm use these and other services that enhance productivity.

Look for calendaring apps for smartphones and for iPads and other tablets. Some apps can be integrated and synced with software that you may have in your office, but you must keep the confidentiality of the firm in mind.

TAKE ON NEW CHALLENGES

Evolving technologies provide avenues for paralegals to advance their positions and become indispensable to their firms. For example, many courts now require documents to be filed electronically. Paralegals are often responsible for making sure that these documents are in the proper format and that they include hyperlinks to relevant resources.

Courts also allow electronic discovery—that is, prior to a trial, a party can obtain evidence in electronic form from the opposing party's e-mails, computers, smartphones, and other equipment. Some law firms also take video depositions (testimony from witnesses) when witnesses are unable to appear in person. Paralegals with skill in locating and obtaining electronic evidence or with the ability to film and produce videos are likely to be in demand.

TECHNOLOGY TIP

Along with technological advances come certain legal questions that are considered by the courts. For example, how long does electronic evidence need to be retained on an online or offline computer system? Who should be required to pay for the discovery of electronic evidence? A paralegal who understands the various legal issues surrounding the use of new technologies and who knows how the courts in the area are resolving these disputes will likely become a key member of the legal team.

Paralegals who specialize in personal-injury litigation often work for law firms that concentrate in this field. Legal assistants working in this capacity obtain and review medical and employment records to calculate the client's lost income. These items are needed to determine the plaintiff's damages in a personal-injury lawsuit. Personal-injury paralegals are also hired by insurance companies to investigate claims. Defendants in personal-injury cases are typically covered by insurance, and a defendant's insurance company has a duty to defend an insured customer who is sued.

Insurance Law

insurance
A contract by which an insurance company (the insurer) promises to pay a sum of money or give something of value to another (either the insured or the beneficiary) to compensate for a specified loss.

Insurance is a contract by which an insurance company (the insurer) promises to pay a sum or give something of value to another (either the insured or the beneficiary of the insurance policy) to compensate for a specified loss. Insurance may provide compensation for the injury or death of the insured or another, for damage to the insured's property, or for other losses, such as those resulting from lawsuits. Paralegals who specialize in insurance law may work for law firms that defend insurance companies in litigation brought against the companies. They may also work directly for insurance companies or for companies that buy large amounts of insurance or are self-insured, such as hospitals.

Paralegals may review insurance regulations and monitor an insurance firm's compliance with the regulations. They may also be asked to review insurance contracts, undertake factual and legal investigations relating to insurance claims, or provide litigation assistance in lawsuits involving the insurance company. Paralegals often help in litigation involving insurance. For example, a paralegal may be asked to provide investigative or litigation assistance for a client who is bringing a lawsuit or defending against a personal-injury, malpractice, or other litigation in which insurance is a factor.

Employment and Labor Law

workers' compensation statutes
State laws establishing an administrative procedure for compensating workers for injuries that arise in the course of their employment.

As will be discussed in Chapter 18, laws governing employment relationships are referred to collectively as *employment and labor law*. This body of law includes laws governing health and safety in the workplace, labor unions and union–management relations, employment discrimination, sexual harassment, wrongful termination, employee benefit plans, retirement and disability income, employee privacy rights, minimum wage, and overtime wages.

estate planning
Making arrangements, during a person's lifetime, for the transfer of that person's property to others on the person's death. Estate planning often involves executing a will or establishing a trust fund to provide for others, such as a spouse or children, on a person's death.

Some paralegals specialize in just one aspect of employment law, such as workers' compensation. Under workers' compensation statutes, employees who are injured on the job are compensated from state funds or insurance funds. Paralegals assist persons injured on the job in obtaining compensation from the state workers' compensation program. As mentioned earlier, some state workers' compensation boards allow paralegals to represent clients during agency hearings, which are conducted to settle disputes, or during negotiations with the agencies.

will
A document directing how and to whom the maker's property and obligations are to be transferred on his or her death.

Frequently, working in employment law involves interacting with administrative agencies, such as the Occupational Safety and Health Administration and the Equal Employment Opportunity Commission. Each agency has its own rules and legal procedures. Paralegals who work in employment or labor law must be familiar with the relevant federal and state agencies, as well as with their specific roles in resolving disputes. We cover employment law in Chapter 18 and administrative agencies in Chapter 5.

probate
The process of "proving" the validity of a will and ensuring that the instructions in a valid will are carried out.

Estate Planning and Probate Administration

probate court
A court that probates wills; usually a county court.

Estate planning and probate administration have to do with the transfer of an owner's property, or *estate*, on the owner's death. Through estate planning, the owner decides, before death, how his or her property will be transferred to others. The owner may make a will to designate the persons to whom property is to be transferred. If someone contests the validity of the will, it must be probated (proved) in a probate court. Depending on the size and complexity of the estate, it may take months or longer for the probate court to approve the property distribution and for the property to be transferred to the rightful heirs.

Because the probate process is time consuming and expensive, many people engage in estate planning to try to avoid probate. For example, a person may establish a trust agreement, a legal arrangement in which the ownership of property is transferred to a third person (the *trustee*) to be used for the benefit of another (the beneficiary). Paralegals often are responsible for interviewing clients to obtain information necessary to draft wills and trust agreements, for gathering information on debts and assets, and for locating heirs if necessary (see Chapter 17). A paralegal who is sensitive and caring toward clients, yet professional in explaining and working out procedures, is well suited for this specialty.

trust
An arrangement in which title to property is held by one person (a trustee) for the benefit of another (a beneficiary).

Bankruptcy Law

Bankruptcy law allows debtors to obtain relief from their debts. Bankruptcy law is federal law, and bankruptcy proceedings take place in federal courts (see the discussion of the federal court system in Chapter 6). The goals of bankruptcy law are (1) to protect a debtor by giving him or her a fresh start and (2) to ensure that creditors who are competing for a debtor's assets are treated fairly. The bankruptcy process may provide several types of relief for individuals or business firms. Both large and small firms practice bankruptcy law and hire paralegals who specialize in this area.

Bankruptcy law, to be discussed in Chapter 19, imposes strict requirements, which means that paralegals working in this field may have detailed responsibilities. The paralegal might be responsible for interviewing debtors to obtain information about their income, assets, and debts. This often involves verifying the accuracy of information provided by debtors and ensuring that debtors have completed required credit counseling. The paralegal may also review the validity of creditors' claims and prepare documents that must be submitted to the bankruptcy court.

bankruptcy law
The body of federal law that governs bankruptcy proceedings. The twin goals of bankruptcy law are (1) to protect a debtor by giving him or her a fresh start and (2) to ensure that creditors competing for a debtor's assets are treated fairly.

Intellectual Property Law

Intellectual property consists of the products of individuals' minds—products that result from creative processes. Those who create intellectual property acquire certain rights over the use of that property. Literary works, such as books, and artistic works, such as songs, are protected by *copyright law*. *Trademark law* protects firms' distinctive marks or logos. Inventions are protected by *patent law*. Firms may also have *trade secrets*, such as the formula to make Coca-Cola. The owner of intellectual property rights may sell the rights to another, may collect royalties on the use of the property (such as a popular song) by others, and may prevent unauthorized publishers from reproducing the property without permission. Chapter 15 provides detail about laws governing intellectual property.

intellectual property
Property that results from intellectual, creative processes. Copyrights, patents, and trademarks are examples of intellectual property.

Some law firms (or departments of large law firms) specialize in intellectual property law. Other firms provide a variety of legal services, of which intellectual property law is a part. In addition, corporate legal departments may be responsible for registering copyrights, patents, or trademarks with the federal government.

Paralegals may specialize in intellectual property research regarding existing patents and trademarks. They also assist in compiling patent applications in accordance with detailed regulations, draft documents necessary to apply for trademark and copyright protection, and assist in litigating disputes. Because of the expertise required, paralegal intellectual property specialists are paid more than average (see Exhibit 2.2 on page 25). This is an especially good practice area for paralegals with a science background. In fact, anyone, including a paralegal, with three years of undergraduate science courses can apply to the U.S. Patent and Trademark Office to become a registered patent agent and thus be qualified to prepare patent applications.

Environmental Law

environmental law
All state and federal laws or regulations enacted or issued to protect the environment and preserve environmental resources.

Environmental laws help to protect the environment. These involve the regulation of air and water pollution, protection of property from abuse, natural resource management, endangered species protection, proper hazardous waste disposal, the clean-up of hazardous waste sites, pesticide control, and nuclear power regulation.

Employers of paralegal specialists in environmental law include administrative agencies (such as the federal Environmental Protection Agency (EPA), state natural resource departments, and local zoning boards), environmental law departments of large law firms, law firms that specialize in environmental law, and corporations. For example, a company may employ a paralegal as an environmental coordinator to help maintain compliance with regulations, oversee company environmental programs, and obtain permits for certain kinds of land use. Paralegals working in law firms that handle environmental matters often perform tasks similar to those described previously for litigation and personal-injury paralegals.

Family Law

family law
Law relating to family matters, such as marriage, divorce, child support, and child custody.

Family law, as the term implies, deals with family matters, such as marriage, divorce, alimony, child support, and child custody. We will discuss it in detail in Chapter 17. Family law is governed by state statutes, so if you specialize in this type of law, you will become familiar with your state's particular requirements.

As a family law specialist, you might work for a small law practice, for a family law department in a large law firm, or with a state or local agency, such as a community services agency that assists persons who need help with family-related legal problems. You might research and draft documents that are filed with the court in divorce and adoption proceedings. You might also perform investigations into assets and the grounds for divorce. Paralegals in this area often have extensive contact with clients and need to be skilled at extracting information from sometimes emotionally distraught persons. Those with a background or interest in social work or counseling are particularly well suited to this specialty.

Criminal Law

civil law
Law dealing with the definition and enforcement of private rights, as opposed to criminal matters.

criminal law
Law that governs and defines those actions that are crimes and that subjects persons convicted of crimes to punishment imposed by the government (a fine or jail time).

Law is sometimes classified into the two categories of civil law and criminal law. Civil law is concerned with the duties that exist between persons or between citizens and their governments, excluding criminal matters. Contract law (Chapter 15), for example, is part of civil law. When the EPA demands a company pay a fine for failure to comply with some aspect of environmental regulation, that is an area of civil law.

Criminal law, in contrast, is concerned with wrongs committed against the public. Criminal acts are prohibited by federal or state statutes (criminal law and procedures will be discussed in Chapter 13). In a criminal case, the government seeks to impose a penalty (which could include jail time) on a person who is alleged to have committed a crime. In contrtast, in a civil case, one party tries to make the other party comply with a duty or pay for the damage caused by a failure to comply with a legal obligation.

Paralegals who specialize in criminal law may work for public prosecutors, public defenders (which is discussed in the *Developing Paralegal Skills* feature on the facing page), or criminal defense attorneys. A legal assistant working for the prosecutor's office, for example, might draft search or arrest warrants. A paralegal working for the defense attorney (public or private) might obtain police reports, conduct research, and draft documents to be filed with the court, such as a document arguing that the police violated the defendant's constitutional rights. Although criminal law and civil law are quite different, the trial process is comparable, and paralegals perform similar types of tasks (investigation, summarizing witness testimony, and so forth) in preparation for litigation.

DEVELOPING PARALEGAL SKILLS

WORKING FOR A PUBLIC DEFENDER

Michele Sanchez works as a paralegal for the public defender's office in her county. Today, she has been assigned to go to the county jail to meet with a new client, Geraldine Silverton. Silverton had been arrested for child abuse after her child's school notified the police. According to school officials, the child had bruises all over his body. The child also told his teacher that his mother frequently "beat him up" for no reason at all.

The client, Silverton, is upset and tells Michele that "no way in the world would she harm her boy." Silverton claims that her son was hurt when he fell off the trampoline in their backyard and that he's just "making up" the abuse story to get attention.

Silverton demands to be released from jail immediately. Michele makes a note of Silverton's concerns and then explains the scheduling for the bail hearings.

TIPS FOR MEETING WITH A NEW CLIENT

- Review the police report before meeting with the client.
- During the interview with the client, ask the client for his or her side of the story.
- Listen carefully and supportively to the client, and communicate with empathy.
- Do not appear to judge the client.

Additional Specialty Areas

The listing of specialty areas is not exhaustive. Opportunities for paralegals exist in many other capacities. As the U.S. population ages, for example, more attorneys are focusing on serving the needs of older clients. Elder law is the term used to describe this broad specialty. Paralegals who work in this practice area may be asked to assist in a variety of tasks, including those relating to estate planning (discussed earlier), age-discrimination claims, financial arrangements for long-term care, Medicare and Medicaid, abuse suffered by elderly persons, and the visitation rights of grandparents.

Nurses have found profitable and challenging work as paralegals. A paralegal who is also a trained nurse is able to evaluate legal claims involving injuries, such as those involved in personal-injury, medical-malpractice, or product-liability lawsuits. A specialty area among nurses—and within the legal profession—is that of the legal nurse consultant (LNC). LNCs usually work independently (offering their services on a contract basis) and are typically well paid for contract services. Some LNCs work for law firms, insurance companies, government offices, and risk management departments of companies as salaried employees. The American Association of Legal Nurse Consultants offers a certification program in which nurses who meet the eligibility criteria (including educational credentials and sufficient experience as a legal nurse) and pass an examination can become certified as LNCs.

elder law
A relatively new legal specialty that involves serving the needs of older clients, such as estate planning and making arrangements for long-term care.

legal nurse consultant (LNC)
A nurse who consults with legal professionals and others about medical aspects of legal claims or issues. Legal nurse consultants normally must have at least a bachelor's degree in nursing and significant nursing experience.

Paralegal Compensation

What do paralegals earn? This is an important question for anyone contemplating a career as a paralegal. You can obtain some idea of what paralegals make, on average, from paralegal compensation surveys. Following a discussion of these surveys, we look at some other components of paralegal compensation, including job benefits and compensation for overtime work.

EXHIBIT 2.3

Average Paralegal
Compensation by Experience

Data from 2015 from salary.com. See that website for
definitions of the different paralegal positions and for
job openings.

Position Classification	Average Compensation + Bonus
Paralegal I	$49,034 + $1,800
Paralegal II	$57,339 + $2,200
Paralegal III	$66,192 + $2,600
Paralegal IV	$73,673 + $5,500
Paralegal Supervisor	$71,623 + $8,000
Paralegal Manager	$91,269 + $7,000

Compensation Surveys

Paralegal income is affected by a number of factors. We have already covered the effects of the size of the firm or legal department (see Exhibit 2.1 on page 21) and the specialty area in which the paralegal practices (see Exhibit 2.2 on page 25). Another income-determining factor is the paralegal's years of experience. Typically, as shown in Exhibit 2.3 above, more experienced paralegals enjoy higher rates of compensation. This is particularly noticeable when a paralegal has worked for the same employer for a long period of time.

Another major factor that affects paralegal compensation is geographical location. Exhibit 2.3, like earlier exhibits, illustrates *national* averages. Exhibit 2.4 below, by contrast, shows *regional* averages. As you can see, paralegals working in San Francisco enjoy higher levels of compensation than paralegals in many other cities. Remember, though, that these figures represent averages and can therefore be deceptive. For example, a paralegal working in a suburb of Chicago may not earn as much as a paralegal who works in downtown Chicago.

Keep in mind, too, that salary statistics do not tell the whole story. Although paralegals earn more in California than in Nebraska, the cost of living is higher in California than in Nebraska. This means that your real income—the amount you can purchase with your income—may, in fact, be the same in both states despite the differences in salary. If you are comparing job offers in different cities, be sure to consider the cost of living as well as the pay being offered. Salary statistics also do not reveal another important component of compensation—job benefits.

Job Benefits

Part of your total compensation package as an employee will consist of job benefits. These benefits may include paid holidays, sick leave, group insurance coverage (life, disability, medical, dental), pension plans, and possibly others. Benefits packages vary from firm to firm. Most employers require employees to contribute part of the cost of insurance and retirement benefits. When evaluating any job offer, you need to consider the benefits that you will receive and what these benefits are worth to you. You will read more about the importance of job benefits later in this chapter in the context of evaluating a job offer.

EXHIBIT 2.4

Average Paralegal Salary
in Law Firms by Region

Authors compiled data from *Paralegal Today.*

Area	Median Salary
Midwest	$51,198
Northeast	$61,363
South	$57,643
West	$66,013

Salaries versus Hourly Wages

Most paralegals are salaried employees. That is, they receive a specified annual salary. Others are paid an hourly wage rate for every hour worked. Paralegals are frequently asked to work overtime, and how they are compensated for overtime work usually depends on the employment status. Some firms compensate salaried paralegals for overtime work through year-end bonuses, which are payments made to employees in recognition of their devotion to the firm and the high quality of their work. Paralegals often receive annual bonuses ranging from around $2,000 to around $5,000, depending on years of experience and so forth. Some firms allow salaried employees to take compensatory time off work (for example, an hour off for every extra hour worked). Employees who are paid an hourly wage rate are normally paid overtime wages. In such cases, there may be no bonus or only a small one.

bonus
An end-of-the-year payment to a salaried employee in appreciation for that employee's overtime work, diligence, or dedication to the firm.

Planning Your Career

Career planning involves three key steps. The first step is defining your long-term goals. The second involves coming up with short-term goals and adjusting them to meet the realities of the job market. We look at these two steps in this section. (For some tips on how to succeed in your career, see this chapter's *Featured Contributor* feature beginning on page 34.) Later in this chapter, we discuss the third step: reevaluating your career after you have had some on-the-job experience as a paralegal.

Defining Your Long-Term Goals

You want to define, as clearly as possible, your career goals. This requires personal reflection and self-assessment. What are you looking for in a career? Why do you want to become a paralegal? Is income the most important factor? Is job satisfaction (doing the kind of work you like) the most important factor? Is the environment in which you work the most important factor? Asking yourself these and other broad questions about your personal preferences and values will help you define more clearly your overall professional goals.

Your Goals May Change

Do not be surprised to find that your long-term goals change over time. As you gain experience as a paralegal and your life circumstances alter, you may decide that your long-term goals are no longer appropriate. For example, the level of career involvement that suits you as a single person may not be appropriate should you have children. Similarly, later in life, when your children leave home, you may have different goals with respect to work.

Explore New Challenges

At the outset of your career, you cannot know what opportunities might arise. Throughout your career as a paralegal, you will probably meet paralegals who have made career changes. Many paralegals, for example, decided on the field after several years of working in another profession, such as nursing, law enforcement, business administration, or accounting. Changes within the profession, your own experiences, and new opportunities affect the career choices before you. The realities you face during your career are likely to play a significant role in modifying your long-term goals.

Short-Term Goals and Job Realities

Long-term goals are just that—goals that we hope to achieve over many years or even a lifetime. Short-term goals are the steps we take to realize our long-term goals. As an entry-level paralegal, one short-term goal is to find a job.

FEATURED CONTRIBUTOR

"TIPS TO JUMPSTART YOUR PARALEGAL CAREER"

Antoinette France-Harris, J.D.

BIOGRAPHICAL NOTE

Antoinette France-Harris is a graduate of Harvard University (B.A. *cum laude*, 1992), Columbia University School of Social Work (M.S.W. 1994), and University of Pennsylvania Law School (J.D. 1997). From 1997 to 2002, she was a corporate and estate planning attorney in New York. In 2003, Mrs. Harris became a solo practitioner in Georgia, specializing in real estate, corporate, and estate planning matters. She also works on a *pro bono* basis to assist not-for-profit organizations to incorporate and obtain tax-exempt status. Mrs. Harris began her paralegal teaching career in 2010, when she accepted a full-time position as an instructor with Atlanta Technical College. She taught paralegal students for four years and became program chair. Since fall 2014, Mrs. Harris has been a member of the full-time faculty at Clayton State University.

This is a great time to become a paralegal! With the downturn in the economy, legal employers are turning increasingly to paralegals to meet growing client needs in a cost-effective manner. Opportunities exist in various legal specialties, including bankruptcy and environmental law, which have been deemed recently as hot areas of the law.

So, how does one get started? This article is designed to provide some useful strategies to launch a career in paralegalism. The list is by no means exhaustive, but it will give the reader a starting point on this exciting journey.

TIP 1: FORMAL EDUCATION

Generally, people become paralegals either through on-the-job training or formal education. Many paralegal jobs require an

> **" ... the legal field is constantly evolving"**

associate's degree. For broader appeal, job seekers might pursue a bachelor's degree. Others who already have a bachelor's in a different field might consider a post-baccalaureate certificate in paralegalism instead. Even paralegals who received on-the-job training report that obtaining a degree has opened doors to promotions and salary increases and makes it easier to transition from one employer to the next.

TIP 2: NEVER STOP LEARNING— CONTINUING LEGAL EDUCATION

In this perpetually changing and increasingly technological legal industry, it is important to continuously enhance your education and skills to keep pace. An easy way to do so is by attending timely classes, seminars, and workshops, which will equip you to optimize your usefulness to employers.

Ideally, you will find a job that provides you with a salary consistent with your training and abilities, a level of responsibility that is comfortable (or challenging) for you, and good job benefits. The realities of the job market are not always what we wish them to be, however. You might not find the "right" employer or the "perfect" job when you first start. You may be lucky from the outset, but it may take several attempts before you find the employer and the job that best suit your needs, skills, and talents.

Remember that even if you do not find the perfect job right away, you gain valuable skills and experience in *any* job environment—skills and experience that can help you achieve long-term goals in the future. In fact, you might want to "try on" jobs at

TIP 3: GET CERTIFIED

While they are not required to do so in many states, some paralegals are taking certification exams to distinguish themselves from other job seekers. The National Association of Legal Assistants (NALA) offers the entry-level Certified Legal Assistant/Certified Paralegal (CLA/CP) exam. The National Federation of Paralegal Associations (NFPA) offers the Paralegal Advanced Certification Exam (PACE) and the National Association of Legal Professionals (NALS) offers the Professional Paralegal (PP) exam, both of which require paralegal experience.

TIP 4: IMPROVE YOUR PARALEGAL RÉSUMÉ

Create a résumé that is tailored particularly for employment in this field. The paralegal résumé must highlight skills that every good paralegal should possess. Even if you have not worked as a paralegal, it is critical to accentuate any position that involved research and writing, organizational and communication skills, scheduling appointments or maintaining calendars, and multitasking. Your résumé should be a continual work in progress where trainings, achievements, associations, and the like are added regularly.

> " Your résumé should be a continual work in progress ... "

TIP 5: NETWORK/FIND A MENTOR

It is essential for anyone seeking paralegal employment to meet people in the legal field. Most local bar associations have paralegal sections where you can attend events and network with experienced paralegals and attorneys. These individuals can provide unique insight and act as invaluable sources of information related to employment and advancement opportunities.

TIP 6: BECOME A VOLUNTEER

One of the biggest complaints from job seekers is that most employers are seeking only candidates with legal experience.

Once you have decided to become a paralegal, consider visiting a local law firm and offering your services voluntarily to gain experience. Who can resist free labor? The firm may not have an immediate paralegal opening, but if you make yourself invaluable, a job offer may come eventually. Be sure to add the volunteer experience to your résumé!

TIP 7: TAKE OTHER JOBS IN THE LEGAL ENVIRONMENT

Although you may not have paralegal experience, you undoubtedly have other work experience that a law firm or department may value and for which there is an opening. Once you have an "in" with the firm and the employer becomes more familiar with you, your skills, and your work ethic, eventually you may be considered for a paralegal position.

TIP 8: KEEP ABREAST OF HOT AREAS OF THE LAW

As mentioned previously, the legal field is constantly evolving. Like any other business, it operates on the principles of supply and demand. Conduct thorough research in advance of your job search and consider choosing or changing your area of specialization based on where there is a projected need in the market.

In sum, launching a career as a paralegal will require extreme diligence, dedication, and determination. Setting and achieving short- and long-term goals and deadlines related to the job search will provide a sense of accomplishment throughout the process. To launch a career as a paralegal, you must be bold and willing to step outside of your comfort zone. In the end, your determination will yield great rewards.

different-sized firms and in different specialty areas to see how they "fit" with your particular needs.

Locating Potential Employers

Looking for a job is time consuming and requires attention to detail, persistence, and creativity. Your paralegal education is preparing you, among other things, to do investigative research. The investigative skills that you will use on the job as a paralegal are the ones that you should apply when looking for a job.

Where do you begin your investigation? How can you find out what paralegal jobs are available in your area or elsewhere? How do you know which law firms practice the type of law that interests you? The following suggestions will help you answer these questions.

Networking

Career opportunities often go unpublished. Many firms post notices within their own organizations before publishing online. This opens doors to their own employees before the general public. It also spares employers from having to wade through many applications for a vacant position. If you have connections within an organization, you may be told that a position is opening up before other candidates are aware that an opportunity exists.

More paralegals find employment through networking than through any other means. For paralegals, networking is the process of making personal connections with other paralegals, paralegal instructors, attorneys, and others who are involved in (or who know someone who is involved in) the paralegal or legal profession. Online networking, such as that provided by LinkedIn, is becoming popular as well. Professional organizations and internships offer important networking opportunities.

Join a Professional Association

Students can form a network of paralegal connections through affiliation with professional associations and student clubs. You have already learned about NALA and NFPA, the two largest national associations for legal assistants. Other organizations of paralegals exist across the country. Some such organizations are listed in Appendix E at the end of this book. See if your local paralegal association allows students to be members. If it does, attend meetings and get to know other paralegals who may know of job opportunities in your area. Persons involved with other groups—such as the International Paralegal Management Association, or IPMA (an association of individuals who manage legal assistants), and the state bar association (a state-level association of attorneys)—can also provide valuable inside knowledge of potential job openings.

Network during Internships

Many paralegal education programs include an internship in which students are placed temporarily in a law firm or other work setting. The people you meet in these settings often turn out to be beneficial to you in finding future employment. An intern who has performed well may be offered a full-time position after graduation. Even if you are not interested in working for the firm with which you do your internship, be careful not to "burn your bridges." The legal community is relatively small, and lawyers are more inclined to hire paralegals about whom their colleagues have made positive remarks. Many online social networks, such as Facebook and Google+, are used by professionals to provide and obtain work-related information.

Volunteer

You can develop your skills and expand your professional network by volunteering with a local legal aid group or other organization that provides legal advice and assistance. Many attorneys volunteer for such work, so you may make a valuable connection while you help. You will also gain worthwhile experience and demonstrate to potential employers that you are willing and able to cooperate with other professionals in aiding others.

Finding Available Jobs

Your next effort should be to locate sources that list paralegal job openings. Trade journals and similar publications, such as your local or state bar association's journal, newsletter, or website, may list openings for legal professionals. Increasingly, employers

---

networking
Making personal connections and cultivating relationships with people in a certain field, profession, or area of interest.

state bar association
An association of attorneys within a state. In most states, an attorney must be a member of the state bar association to practice law in the state.

trade journal
A newsletter, magazine, or other periodical that provides a certain trade or profession with information (products, trends, or developments) relating to that trade or profession.

advertise job openings in online publications and turn to online databases to find prospective employees.

Identifying Possible Employers

You should identify firms and organizations for which you might like to work and submit an employment application to them. In a well-organized job search, locate and contact organizations that offer the benefits, salary, opportunities for advancement, work environment, and legal specialty of your choice. Even though these employers may not have vacancies in your field at the moment, you want your job application to be available when an opening occurs. Most firms, if they are interested in your qualifications, will keep your application on file for six months or so and may contact you if a position becomes available. As the *Ethics Watch* feature below discusses, be truthful about your background.

It is a good idea to begin compiling employer information for your job search while you are still completing your studies. Many of the resources you will need are available at the college you attend or through your paralegal program.

Legal Directories

Legal directories provide lists of attorneys, their locations, and their areas of practice. The *Martindale-Hubbell Law Directory*, which you can find online, lists the names, addresses, phone numbers, areas of legal practice, and other data for many lawyers and law firms. It is an excellent resource for paralegals interested in working for law firms or corporate legal departments. *West's Legal Directory* is another valuable source

ETHICS WATCH

THE IMPORTANCE OF INTEGRITY

When looking for a job, be honest with others about your skills and experience. Even though you may want to impress a prospective employer, never give in to the temptation to exaggerate your qualifications. For example, suppose that you are working for a law firm during your internship and would really like to be hired by the firm in the future as a paralegal. In conversations with people in the firm, don't try to impress them by making misleading statements about your qualifications or skills. For instance, suppose you tell your supervisor that your GPA was 3.8 when in fact it was 3.4. This "little white lie" may come back to haunt you in the future. If the firm offers you a permanent job, it will likely check your credentials, including your college or professional school transcripts. Any misrepresentation, no matter how minor it may seem, could doom your chances of being hired. Professional responsibility requires, among other things, that you be honest and pay close attention to detail—not only on the job but also when you are looking for a job.

This scenario is consistent with the NFPA *Model Code of Ethics and Professional Responsibility*, Section 1.3, "A paralegal shall maintain a high standard of professional conduct" and "A paralegal shall avoid impropriety and the appearance of impropriety and shall not engage in any conduct that would adversely affect his/her fitness to practice."

of information (see **lawyers.findlaw.com**). It contains a listing of U.S. attorneys and law firms, state and federal attorneys and offices, and corporate legal departments and general counsel.

Job-Placement Services

Make full use of your school's placement service. Many colleges with paralegal programs provide job-placement services, and ABA-approved schools are required to provide ongoing placement services. Placement offices have personnel trained to assist you in finding a job, as well as in preparing job-search tools, such as your résumé and a list of potential employers. Some schools also offer practice interviews.

A growing trend is to use legal staffing or placement companies (also known as *recruiters*) to locate employment. Usually, the employer pays the fees for the placement company's services, and the company recruits candidates for the paralegal position and arranges interviews. Placement services can be located through paralegal program directors, local paralegal associations, and state bar associations, as well as on the web.

Legal staffing companies place paralegal employees in both temporary (called "contract") and full-time (called "direct-hire") positions. Temporary contract employees are often used when a regular employee needs to take leave or when a special project requires additional paralegals, such as in large-scale litigation cases. Contract jobs can last from a few days to over a year. Long-term contract opportunities can provide valuable work experience in a particular specialty. Direct-hire positions typically provide long-term employment with salary and benefits, which are not provided in most temporary employment contracts.

Marketing Your Skills

Once you locate potential employers, the next step is to market your skills and yourself effectively. Marketing your skills involves three stages: the application process, interviewing for jobs, and following up on job interviews.

Keep in mind that each personal contact you make, whether it results in employment or not, has potential for your future. A firm may not hire you today because it has no openings, but it may hire you a year from now. Therefore, keep track of the contacts you make during your search, be patient, and be professional.

The Application Process

When looking for paralegal employment, you need to assemble and present professional application materials. The basic materials you should create are a résumé, a cover letter, a list of professional references, and a portfolio. The following discussion explains each of these and gives some practical tips on how to create them.

The Résumé

For most job applications, you must submit a personal résumé that summarizes your employment and educational background. Your résumé is an advertisement, and you should invest the time to make it effective. Because human resource representatives in law firms, corporations, and government agencies may receive many résumés for each position they advertise, your résumé should create the best possible impression to gain a competitive edge over other job seekers.

Either generate your résumé yourself or work with a professional résumé-preparation service. Some school placement offices provide assistance. Format each page so that the reader is able to scan it quickly and catch the highlights. You might vary the type size, but never use a type size or style that is difficult to read.

What to Include in Your Résumé

Your name, address, telephone number, e-mail address, and website address, if you have one, belong in the heading of your résumé. The body of the résumé should be simple, brief, and clear. As a general rule, it should contain only information relevant to the job that you are seeking. A one-page résumé is usually sufficient, unless two pages are required to list relevant educational background and work experience. Exhibit 2.5 below shows a sample résumé of a person with paralegal experience, and Exhibit 2.6 on the following page shows one of a person without such experience. Do not put your name and address in the upper left-hand corner, as that area is often stapled.

PROVIDE DETAILS. Divide your résumé into logical sections with headings as shown in the exhibits. Whenever you list dates, such as educational and employment dates, list them chronologically in reverse order. That is, list your most recent educational or work history first. When discussing your education, list the names and locations of the

EXHIBIT 2.5

A Sample Résumé of a Person with Paralegal Experience

ELENA LOPEZ

1131 North Shore Drive
Nita City, NI 48804
Telephone: (616) 555-0102 • E-mail: elopez@nitanet.net

EMPLOYMENT OBJECTIVE

A position as a paralegal in a private law firm that specializes in personal-injury practice.

EDUCATION

2012   Professional Training
Midwestern Professional School for Paralegals, Green Bay, WI
Focus: Litigation Procedures, Legal Investigation, Torts, Arbitration and
Mediation, Case Preparation, and Trial. GPA 3.8.

2009   Bachelor of Arts degree
University of Wisconsin, Madison, WI 53706. Political Science major. GPA 3.1.

PARALEGAL EXPERIENCE

- Caldwell Legal Clinic, Nita City, NI
  Paralegal: June 2012 to the present.
  Responsibilities: Legal research and document review; drafting discovery
  documents, including interrogatories, deposition summaries, and requests for
  admissions; and trial preparation in personal-injury cases.

- Legal Aid Society, Green Bay, WI
  Paralegal: June 2009 to May 2012.
  Responsibilities: Part-time assistance to legal aid attorneys in their
  representation of indigent clients in matters such as divorce, abuse, child
  custody, paternity, and landlord-tenant disputes.

- University of Wisconsin, Madison, WI
  Research Assistant: Political Science Department, January 2007 to May 2009.
  Responsibilities: Research on the effectiveness of federal welfare programs in
  reducing poverty in the United States.

AFFILIATIONS

Paralegal Association of Wisconsin
National Association of Legal Assistants

colleges you have attended and the degrees you have received. You may want to indicate your major and minor concentrations such as "Major: Paralegal Studies" or "Minor: Political Science." When listing work experience, specify your responsibilities in each position. Also include any relevant volunteer work that you have done. Substantive volunteer work is a major asset.

Scholarships or honors should also be indicated. If you have a high grade-point average (GPA), then include the GPA in your résumé. Under the heading "Selected Accomplishments," you might indicate your ability to speak more than one language, or note that you possess another special skill, such as expertise in online research.

NO WORK EXPERIENCE?　What if you are an entry-level paralegal and have no work experience to highlight? What can you include on your résumé to fill out the page? If you are facing this situation, add more information on your educational background

---

EXHIBIT 2.6

A Sample Résumé of a Person without Paralegal Experience

MARCUS BOHMAN

335 W. Alder Street
Gresham, CA 90650
Home Phone: (562) 555-6868 • Mobile: (562) 555-2468 • E-mail: mboh44@gresham.net

---

OBJECTIVE

To obtain a paralegal position in a firm that specializes in real estate transactions.

QUALIFICATIONS

I am a self-motivated, certified paralegal (CLA 2013) with knowledge and background in real estate and a strong academic record (3.7 GPA). In addition to the education listed below, I have completed several courses on real estate financing and possess excellent accounting skills.

EDUCATION

2016	*Bachelor of Arts Degree—ABA-Approved Program* University of La Verne, Legal Studies Program, La Verne, CA Major: Paralegal Studies; Minor: Business Management Emphasis on Real Property and Land-Use Planning, Legal Research and Writing.

EMPLOYMENT

2015–2016	*Intern, Hansen, Henault, Richmond & Shaw* Researched and drafted numerous real estate documents, including land sale contracts, commercial leases, and deeds. Scheduled meetings with clients. Participated in client interviews and several real estate closings. Filed documents with county.
2010–2015	*Office Assistant, Eastside Commercial Property* Maintained files and handled telephone inquiries at commercial real estate company. Coordinated land surveys and obtained property descriptions.
2009–2010	*Clerk, LandPro Title Company* Coordinated title searches and acted as a liaison among banks, mortgage companies, and the title company.
2007–2010	*Clerk, San Jose County Recorder's Office* Handled inquiries from the public and provided instruction to those seeking to look up records via microfiche.

and experience. You can list specific courses that you took, student affiliations, or particular skills—such as computer competency in certain programs—that you acquired during your paralegal training.

Do Not Include Personal Data

Avoid including personal data (such as age, marital status, number of children, gender, or hobbies) in your résumé. Employers are prohibited by law from discriminating against employees or job candidates on the basis of race, color, gender, national origin, religion, age, or disability. You can help them fulfill this legal obligation by not including in your résumé any information that could serve as a basis for discrimination. For the same reason, you would be wise not to include a photograph of yourself with your résumé. It is to your advantage to list volunteer activities, but not hobbies or favorite activities.

Proofread Your Results

Carefully proofread your résumé. Use the spelling checker and grammar checker on your computer, but do not totally rely on them. Have a friend or instructor review your résumé for punctuation, grammar, spelling, content, and visual appearance. If you find an error, you need to fix it. A mistake on your résumé tells the potential employer that you are a careless worker, a message that could ruin your chances of landing a job.

The Cover Letter

To encourage a recruiter to review your résumé, you need to capture her attention with a cover letter that accompanies the résumé. Because the cover letter is usually your first contact with an employer, it should be written carefully. It should be brief, perhaps only two or three paragraphs in length. Exhibit 2.7 on the following page shows a sample cover letter. When possible, you should learn the name of the person in charge of hiring (by phone or e-mail, if necessary) and direct your letter to that person. If you do not know that person's name, use a generic title, such as "Human Resources Manager" or "Paralegal Manager."

CONTENT IS KEY. Your cover letter should point out a few things about yourself and your qualifications for the position that might persuade a recruiter to examine your résumé. As a recently graduated paralegal, for example, you might draw attention to your academic standing at school, your eagerness to specialize in the same area of law as the employer (perhaps listing some courses relating to that specialty), and your willingness to relocate to the employer's city. Your job is to convince the recruiter that you are a close match to the mental picture that he or she has of the perfect candidate for the job. Make sure that the reader knows when and where you can be reached. Often this is best indicated in the closing paragraph of the letter, as shown in Exhibit 2.7 on the following page.

As with your résumé, read through your letter several times and have someone else read it also to make sure that it is free from mistakes and easily understood. You should use the same type of paper for your cover letter as you use for your résumé.

HARD COPY IS BEST. What about e-mailing your cover letter and résumé to prospective employers? This is a difficult question. On the one hand, e-mail is much faster than regular mail. On the other hand, an e-mail résumé does not look as nice. While some firms are accustomed to receiving applications by e-mail, others are not, and attorneys generally prefer traditional résumés. If the job you are applying for was advertised online or if the employer provided an e-mail address for interested job candidates to use, then e-mail is probably appropriate. Generally, though, job candidates who submit applications by e-mail should also send, by regular mail, printed copies of their letters and résumés.

EXHIBIT 2.7
A Sample Cover Letter

ELENA LOPEZ

1131 North Shore Drive
Nita City, NI 48804
Telephone: (616) 555-0102 • E-mail: elopez@nitanet.net

August 22, 2016

Allen P. Gilmore, Esq.
Jeffers, Gilmore & Dunn
553 Fifth Avenue, Suite 101
Nita City, NI 48801

Dear Mr. Gilmore:

I am responding to your advertisement in the *Vegas Law Journal* for a paralegal to assist you in personal-injury litigation. I am confident that I possess the skills and qualifications that you seek.

As you can see from the enclosed résumé, I received my paralegal certificate from Midwestern Professional School for Paralegals after obtaining a Bachelor of Arts degree from the University of Wisconsin. My paralegal courses included litigation procedures, legal research, legal investigation, and legal writing, and I graduated with a G.P.A. of 3.8.

After completing school, I obtained a position with a legal aid office, where I worked for several years and honed my legal research and writing skills. My current position with Caldwell Legal Clinic has provided me with valuable experience in preparing personal-injury cases for trial. I enjoy this area of law and hope to specialize in personal-injury litigation.

I am excited about the possibility of meeting with you to learn more about the position that you have available. A list of professional references is provided in my résumé, and a brief writing sample is attached for your perusal.

Please contact me to schedule an interview. You can contact me by phone after 3:00 p.m., Monday through Friday. I look forward to hearing from you.

Sincerely yours,

Elena Lopez
Elena Lopez

Enclosures

List of Professional References

If a firm is interested in your application, you will probably be asked for a list of references—people the firm can contact to obtain information about you and your abilities. An instructor who has worked closely with you, an internship supervisor who has knowledge of your work, or a past employer who has observed your problem-solving ability would make excellent references. You should have at least three professionally relevant references, but more than five references are rarely necessary. Avoid using the names of family members, friends, or others who are clearly biased in your favor.

List your references on a separate sheet of paper, making sure to include your name, address, and telephone number at the top of the page, in the same format as on your résumé. For each person on the list, include current institutional affiliation or business firm, address, telephone number, fax number, and e-mail address. Make it easy for prospective employers to contact and communicate with your references.

PERMISSION IS REQUIRED.   When creating your list of references, always remember the following rule: never list a person's name as a reference unless you have that person's permission to do so. After all, it will not help you win the position you seek if one of your references is surprised by a call.

Obtaining permission from legal professionals to use them as references also gives you an opportunity to discuss your plans and goals with them, and they may be able to advise you and assist you in your networking. Additionally, it gives you a chance to discuss with them the kinds of experience and skills in which a prospective employer may be interested.

BUILD YOUR CONTACTS.   Start building your list of possible references early in your studies. Dressing professionally in class, volunteering, arriving on time for class, being prepared, and turning in professional work for assignments are all ways to make a good impression on a professor. Keep in touch with those you want to use as references later. The more they know about you, the more effective they will be as a reference.

Your Professional Portfolio

When a potential employer asks you for an interview, have your professional portfolio ready to give to the interviewer. The professional portfolio should contain another copy of your résumé, a list of references, letters of recommendation written by previous employers or instructors, samples of legal documents that you have composed, college or university transcripts, and any other relevant professional information, such as proof of professional certification or achievement. This collection of documents should be well organized and professionally presented. Depending on the size of your portfolio, a cover sheet, a table of contents, and a folder or commercial binder may be appropriate.

SHOW WHAT YOU CAN DO.   The interviewer may be interested in your research and writing skills. Therefore, your professional portfolio should contain several samples of legal writing. If you are looking for your first legal position, go through your paralegal drafting assignments and pull out those that reflect your best work and that relate to the job skills you wish to demonstrate. Working with an instructor or other mentor, revise and improve those samples for inclusion in the portfolio. You might also use documents that you drafted while an intern or when working as a paralegal. These documents make excellent writing samples because they involve real-life circumstances. Be careful, however, and always remember, on any sample document, to completely black out (or "white out") any identifying reference to a client unless you have the client's permission to disclose his or her identity or if the information is not confidential.

Always include a résumé, as well as a list of references, in your professional portfolio, even though you already sent your résumé to the prospective employer with your cover letter. Interviewers may not have the résumé at hand at the time of the interview, and providing a second copy with your professional portfolio is a thoughtful gesture on your part.

FOCUS ON YOUR KEY ATTRIBUTE.   Some interviewers may examine your professional portfolio carefully. Others may keep it to examine later, after the interview. Still others may not be interested in it at all. If there is a particular item in your portfolio that you would like the interviewer to see, make sure you point it out before leaving the interview.

Digital Marketing

An important part of marketing yourself is ensuring that you have a presence online that helps potential employers evaluate your skills. We discuss the effective use of social media for career enhancement in the next section. Here we just note that your entire online presence needs to show that you are a professional who is able to handle the demands of a career that involves confidential information. Employers are likely to drop candidates from the pool of applicants when their social media presence reveals unprofessional photographs or focuses on parties.

As a paralegal, you will have access to personal information about your firm's clients, which can include valuable business information. Law firms and other employers want to be sure that they can rely on their staff to be professional. Your digital image must convey that you are competent, current and organized.

The Interview

After an employer has reviewed your cover letter and résumé, the employer may contact you to schedule an interview. Interviews with potential employers may be the most challenging (and stressful) part of your search for employment.

Every interview will be different. Some will go well, but you will lose out to another candidate. Nonetheless, you have made a good contact, and you may be able to use this interviewer as a resource for information about other jobs. Remember what went right about the interview, and try to build on those positive aspects at the next one. While some interviews may go poorly despite your best efforts, lessons can still be learned from disappointing experiences.

Some interviewers are more skilled at interviewing than others. Some have a talent for getting applicants to open up, while others are confrontational and put a job candidate on the defensive. Still others may be unprepared. They may not have had time to compare applicants' qualifications with the job requirements, for example. Some employers now use a problem-focused interview technique to see how you would respond to a work situation.

As the person being interviewed, you have no control over who will interview you or what the style may be. You do, however, have control over your preparations for the interview. The following discussion will help you with these preparations.

Before the Interview

You can do many things prior to the interview to improve your chances of getting the job. First, do your "homework." Learn as much about the employer as possible. Check with your instructors or other legal professionals to find out if they are familiar with the firm or the interviewer. To see what you can learn about the firm and its members, check the employer's website and consult relevant directories, such as legal and company directories, as well as business publications. Then you can ask questions that indicate knowledge of the organization. Thorough preparation is appreciated and is a sign of professional diligence.

When you are called for an interview, learn the full name of the interviewer so that you will be able to address him or her by name during the interview and properly address a follow-up letter. During the interview, always use Mr. or Ms. in addressing the interviewer unless directed by the interviewer to be less formal.

THINK ABOUT WHAT MAY BE ASKED.   Anticipate and prepare answers for the questions you might be asked during the interview. You will benefit from rehearsing with a friend or with someone from your school's job placement center. For example, if you did not graduate from high school with your class but later received a general equivalency diploma (GED), you might be asked why you dropped out of school. If you have already prepared an answer for this question, it may save you the stress and embarrassment of having to decide, on the spot, how to reduce a complicated story to a brief sentence or two.

You should also prepare yourself to be interviewed by a "team" of legal professionals, such as an attorney, a paralegal, and perhaps others from the firm. Some prospective employers invite others who will be working with a new paralegal to participate in the interviewing process.

Promptness is extremely important. Plan to arrive for the interview at least ten minutes early, and allow plenty of extra time to get there. If the firm is located in an area that is unfamiliar to you, make sure that you know how to get there, how long it will take, and, if you are driving, whether parking is available nearby.

LOOK PROFESSIONAL.   Personal appearance is important. Wear a relatively conservative suit or dress to the interview, and limit your use of jewelry and other accents, such as cologne or perfume. You can find further tips on how to prepare for a job interview by checking online career sites or by looking at books dealing with careers and job hunting.

At the Interview

During the interview, pay attention and listen closely. Interviewers ask questions to decide whether a candidate will fit comfortably into the firm, whether the candidate is organized and competent and will satisfactorily perform the job, and whether the candidate is reliable and will work hard to master the tasks presented. Your answers should be directly related to the questions. If you are unsure of what the interviewer means by a certain question, ask for clarification.

Interviewers use certain question formats to elicit certain types of responses. Four typical formats for questions are the following:

- *Closed-ended questions*—to elicit simple "Yes" or "No" answers.

- *Open-ended questions*—to invite you to discuss, in some detail, a specific topic or experience.

- *Hypothetical questions*—to learn how you might respond to situations that could arise during the course of your employment.

- *Pressure questions*—to see how you deal with uncomfortable situations or unpleasant discussions.

You will learn more about question formats in Chapter 11, where we discuss some techniques that paralegals use when interviewing clients.

SOME TOPICS ARE NOT APPROPRIATE.   Certain questions are illegal or objectionable. These include questions about your marital status, family, religion, race, color, national origin, age, health or disability, or arrest record. You do not have to answer such questions unless you choose to do so. Exhibit 2.8 below shows some examples of

EXHIBIT 2.8

Objectionable or Illegal Questions and Possible Responses

Q. Are you married?

A. If you are concerned that my social life will interfere with work, I can assure you that I keep the two very separate.

Q. Do you have any children yet?

A. That question leads me to believe that you would be concerned about my ability to prioritize my job and other responsibilities. Is that something that you are worried about?

Q. Are you or your husband a member of the Republican Party?

A. That is a private matter. Please realize that my family and political life will not interfere with my ability to do excellent work for your firm.

Q. You're quite a bit more mature than other applicants. Will you be thinking of retiring in the next ten years?

A. I don't understand how my age relates to my ability to perform this job.

how you might respond to these types of questions. Note that because of record-keeping requirements imposed by the federal Equal Employment Opportunity Commission, an employer is likely to ask you to fill out a form that details your race, age, and other personal facts. This information is needed for the record but is not to be discussed in the interview process.

BE READY TO RESPOND. As odd as it may seem, one of the most difficult moments is when the interviewer turns the inquiry around by asking, "Now then, do you have any questions?" Be prepared for this. Before the interview, take time to list your concerns. Bring the list to the interview with you. Questioning the interviewer gives you an opportunity to learn more about the firm and how it uses paralegal services. Questioning the interviewer also reveals how you might interview a client on behalf of the firm. Exhibit 2.9 below lists some sample questions that you might ask the interviewer. You should not raise the issue of salary at the first interview unless you are offered the job. It is also not wise to ask early in the process about vacation time. The employer wants someone eager to work, not to take time off.

After the Interview

You should not expect to be hired as the result of one interview, although occasionally this does happen. Often, two or more interviews take place before you are offered a job. After leaving the interview, jot down a few notes to provide a refresher for your memory should you be called back for another interview. You will impress the interviewer if you are able to "pick up where you left off" from a discussion initiated several weeks earlier. Also, note the names and positions of the people you met during the interview process.

The Follow-Up/Thank-You Letter

A day or two after the interview, but not longer than a week later, you should send a follow-up letter or e-mail to the interviewer. In this brief communication, you can mention again your availability and interest in the position, thank the interviewer for taking the time to interview you, and perhaps refer to a discussion that took place during the interview.

EXHIBIT 2.9

Questioning the Interviewer

Questions that you might want to ask the interviewer include the following:

- What method does the firm use to assign duties to paralegals?
- How do paralegals function within the organization?
- What clerical support is available for paralegals?
- Does the job involve travel? How will travel expenses be covered?
- What technology is used by the firm?
- Does the firm support paralegal continuing education and training programs?
- Will client **contact** be direct or indirect?
- Does the firm have an in-house library and access to computerized research services that paralegals can use?
- Will the paralegal be assigned work in a given specialty, such as real estate or family law?
- When does the job begin?
- What method is used to review and evaluate paralegal performance?
- How are paralegals supervised, and by whom?
- Are paralegals classified as exempt employees by this firm?
- Is there a written job description or employee policy manual for the job that I may review?

You may have left the interview with the impression that the meeting went poorly. But the interviewer may have a different sense of what happened. Interviewers have different styles, and what you interpreted to be a bad interview may just have been a reflection of that interviewer's style. You simply have no way of being certain, so follow through and make yourself available for the job or at least for another meeting. For an example of a follow-up letter, see Exhibit 2.10 below.

Job-Hunting Files

In addition to keeping your professional portfolio materials up to date, you need to construct a filing system to stay on top of your job-search activities. Create a separate file for each potential employer, and keep copies of your letters, including e-mail messages, to that employer in your file, along with any responses. You might also want to keep lists or notes for addresses, telephone numbers, e-mail addresses, dates of contacts, advantages and disadvantages of employment with the various firms that you have contacted or by which you have been interviewed, topics discussed at interviews, and the like. Then, when you are called for an initial or repeat interview, you will have information on the firm at your fingertips. Always keep in mind that when looking for paralegal employment, your "job" is finding work as a paralegal—and it pays to be efficient.

Your files will also provide you with an excellent resource for networking even after you have a permanent position. The files may also provide useful information for a career change in the future.

Salary Negotiations

Sometimes a firm states a salary or a salary range in its advertisement for a paralegal. During a first interview, a prospective employer may offer that information as well. In

---

EXHIBIT 2.10
A Sample Follow-Up Letter

Elena Lopez
1131 North Shore Drive
Nita City, NI 48804
Telephone: (616) 555-0102 • E-mail: elopez@nitanet.net

September 3, 2016

Allen P. Gilmore, Esq.
Jeffers, Gilmore & Dunn
553 Fifth Avenue, Suite 101
Nita City, NI 48801

Dear Mr. Gilmore:

Thank you for taking time out of your busy schedule to meet with me last Thursday about your firm's paralegal position. I very much enjoyed our discussion, as well as the opportunity to meet some of your firm's employees.

I am extremely interested in the possibility of becoming a member of your legal team and look forward to the prospect of meeting with you again in the near future.

Sincerely yours,

Elena Lopez

Elena Lopez

other situations, an applicant does not know what the salary for a certain position will be until he or she is offered the job.

When you are offered a job, be prepared for the prospective employer to indicate a salary figure and ask if that figure is acceptable to you. If it is acceptable, then you have no problem. If you think it is too low, then the situation becomes more delicate. When you have no other job offer and really need a job, you may not want to foreclose this job opportunity by saying that the salary is too low. You might instead tell the prospective employer that the job interests you and that you will consider the offer seriously. Also, remember that salary is just one factor in deciding what a job is worth to you. In addition to salary, you need to consider job benefits and other factors, including those listed in Exhibit 2.11 below

GATHER INFORMATION BEFOREHAND.   Some prospective employers do not suggest a salary or a salary range but rather ask the job applicant what kind of salary he or she had in mind. You can prepare for this question by researching paralegal salaries in the area. You can find information on salaries by checking local, state, and national paralegal compensation surveys. Check first with your local paralegal association to see

EXHIBIT 2.11
Salary Negotiations: What Is This Job Worth to You?

BENEFITS

What benefits are included? • Will the benefits package include medical insurance? • Life insurance? • Disability insurance? • Dental insurance? • What portion, if any, of the insurance premium will be deducted from your wages? • Is there an employee pension plan? • How many paid vacation days will you have? • Will the firm cover your paralegal association fees? • Will the firm assist you with tuition and other costs associated with continuing paralegal education? • Will the firm assist with day-care arrangements and/or costs? • Does the firm help with parking expenses (important in major cities)?

CAREER OPPORTUNITIES

Does the position offer you opportunities for advancement? You may be willing to accept a lower salary now if you know that it will increase as you move up the career ladder.

COMPENSATION

Will you receive an annual salary or be paid by the hour? • If you will receive an annual salary, will you receive annual bonuses? • How are bonuses determined? • Is the salary negotiable? (In some large firms and in government agencies, it may not be.)

COMPETITION

How stiff is the competition for this job? If you really want the job and are competing with numerous other candidates for the position, you might want to accept a lower salary just to land the job.

JOB DESCRIPTION

What are the paralegal's duties within the organization? Do you have sufficient training and experience to handle these duties? • Are you underqualified or overqualified for the job? • Will your skills as a paralegal be utilized effectively? • How much overtime work will likely be required? • How stressful will the job be?

JOB FLEXIBILITY

How flexible are the working hours? • If you work eight hours of overtime one week, can you take a (paid) day off the following week? • Can you take time off during periods when the workload is less?

LOCATION

Do you want to live in this community? • What is the cost of living in this area? Remember, a $50,000 salary in New York City, where housing and taxes are very expensive, may not give you as much real income as a $38,000 salary in a smaller community in the Midwest.

PERMANENCE

Is the job a permanent or a temporary position? Usually, hourly rates are higher for temporary assistance than for permanent employees.

TRAVEL

Will you be required to travel? • If so, how often or extensively? • How will travel expenses be handled? Will you pay them and then be reimbursed by the employer?

if it has collected data on local paralegal salaries. You might also find helpful information in your school's placement office.

Suppose that you have found in your research that paralegals in the community usually start at $39,000 but that many with your education and training start at $46,000. If you ask for $48,000, then you may be unrealistically expensive—and the job offer may be lost. If you ask for $46,000, then you are still "in the ballpark"—and you may win the job.

RESPOND CAREFULLY. Negotiating salaries can be difficult. On the one hand, you want to obtain a good salary and do not want to underprice your services. On the other hand, overpricing your services may extinguish an employment opportunity or eliminate the possibility of working for an otherwise suitable employer. Your best option might be to state a salary range that is acceptable to you. That way, you are not pinned down to a specific figure. Note, though, that if you indicate an acceptable salary range, you invite an offer of the lowest salary—so the low end of the salary range should be the threshold amount that you will accept.

Career Development

Once you have gained several years' experience working as a paralegal, you can undertake the third step in career planning: reevaluating your career goals and reassessing your abilities based on your accumulated experience. Paralegals who want to advance in their careers normally have three options: (1) You can be promoted within an organization, which may include transferring to another department or branch office of the firm. In a small firm there may be no chance for upward movement, but if the position is satisfying and you receive salary increases, then that may not be an issue for you. (2) Even if you are happy at a firm, change, such as retirement of your supervising attorney, can force you to move to another firm, so you want to be sure you are always attractive to another employer. (3) After you have started working you may consider going back to school for additional education. If you are interested in a particular specialty area, course work in that area may help you become more valuable to your current employer or land a job that can advance your career. Alternatively, you might decide to work toward an advanced degree, such as a master's in business administration (MBA), to create new opportunities. Some paralegals opt to go to law school and become attorneys. Whatever your decision, remember that the structure of law practice will continue to evolve, so expanded skills will be valuable.

Using Social Media Effectively

Social media can be a key factor in determining your success in your paralegal career. Yet many professionals don't use it effectively. Your online reputation, often called your digital shadow, will affect how employers, clients, opposing counsel, and others see you. You should assume that all your postings to Facebook, Twitter, Google+, LinkedIn, and other social media can be seen by everyone with whom you interact. As many people have learned, even Snapchat photos, which senders thought disappeared, can be online forever. Make sure that nothing you post diminishes your reputation.

Digital Shadow

You influence how people perceive your digital shadow. Think of it as online reputation management. Your reputation is not something that just happens to you or that you have no influence over. If you invest effort in creating an online reputation, you will see positive results. If you do not pay attention to what exists online and are careless in what you post, people will form their perception based on their searches.

You can invest in your digital shadow in these important ways:

1. Perhaps most important is what you do not do. Do not engage in heated arguments, post unprofessional photos, reveal personal information, suggest you do not work hard, or say negative things about any employer. A lawyer at a New York firm accidentally sent an e-mail to his firm's entire practice group bragging about his two-hour sushi lunch and lack of productivity. Remember: Professionalism is a 24/7 commitment, not something that only occurs during working hours.

2. Post only about important professional events and accomplishments. When you do, accurately present the information without exaggeration. Your goal is to persuade people you are worth working with, recruiting to a new job, or networking with—not to massage your ego.

3. Keep your profiles on career sites such as LinkedIn and social sites such as Facebook consistent and up-to-date. While we often think of Facebook sites as personal—only for friends and family—they can be seen by anyone. Search firms can reveal posted information we thought was private or deleted long ago. If you presume that everything you send can be seen by anyone and can affect your employment future, you will exercise caution. Post only professional photos for your profile pictures on career-related sites such as LinkedIn. (It is often worth investing in a professional photo in business attire for such sites.)

4. Monitor your online presence using tools such as Socialmention.com. What you mean for others to think and know about you may not be the image being perceived by others.

5. Create online content that will give a positive impression of you. Write professionally and clearly, post regularly, and share useful information. Think of how a stranger will view your information, not how those who know you well will view it.

6. Use resources that professional networking sites make available. Many offer online training on how to effectively use their features. Invest time in learning how to get the most out of your digital shadow.

7. Invest 15 minutes per week in managing your digital shadow. Review suggested connections on LinkedIn or other such sites; endorse your connections for their skills (which will often lead them to endorse you); and keep your profiles up to date.

Manage How Others See You

By being proactive and managing your digital shadow, you can enhance your future career prospects and help ensure that those you deal with both online and offline have a positive impression of your professionalism, your abilities, and your work ethic. Remember, employers often look at Facebook and other social media seeking "digital dirt" before hiring someone to get ideas about a person. You control much about how others see you, so spend time cleaning up your profile before applying for jobs.

Social Media Skills Increase Your Value to Employers

Many law firms are just beginning to explore how to use social media in the practice of law. Industry leaders are focusing on increasing productivity within the firm through internal social networks and marketing their services through external social media activities such as Twitter and Facebook.

To succeed in your career, if you are knowledgeable about the latest social media tools, you can assist in your firm's efforts and, thereby, make yourself a more valued employee. While many attorneys are capable of writing useful content for a website or other media site for the firm, they may not have the time, interest, or ability to post effectively, so that is a role you can play. Smaller firms are unlikely to have a media specialist on the payroll, so social media–savvy paralegals can play a leadership role in this area. If your firm does not have a social media policy, volunteer to draft one.

Watching for Opportunities

Use Twitter and other social media to follow employers you might be interested in working for in the future. Many employers now use advertising links on Twitter to find candidates, so following your targeted employers can be helpful in learning about opportunities. Once you've got an interview, you can use your knowledge of the firm gleaned from watching its Twitter feed to ask questions that show you have real interest in the firm. Effective use of Twitter and other social media can help you promote yourself and maximize your chances of landing a good job, keeping a job, and moving to a better job. Promote yourself to help maximize your chances of landing a good job, keeping a job, and moving to a better job.

KEY TERMS AND CONCEPTS

bankruptcy law 29	freelance paralegal 24	probate court 28
bonus 33	independent paralegal 25	real estate 26
civil law 30	insurance 28	state bar association 36
contract 26	intellectual property 29	tort 26
corporate law 26	legal nurse consultant (LNC) 31	trade journal 36
criminal law 30	legal technician 25	trust 29
defendant 25	litigation 25	will 28
elder law 31	litigation paralegal 25	workers' compensation statutes 28
environmental law 30	networking 36	
estate planning 28	plaintiff 25	
family law 30	probate 28	

Chapter Summary / Career Opportunities

WHERE PARALEGALS WORK

1. *Law firms*—More than two-thirds of paralegals work in law firms—most of them in firms employing fewer than twenty attorneys. A small firm allows a legal assistant to gain experience in a number of areas of law and to work in a less formal environment. Paralegals in small firms often earn less than those in large firms, however, and often must perform secretarial duties. Paralegals working for large firms tend to specialize in a few areas of law, enjoy better employee benefits, and have more support staff.

2. *Corporations and other businesses*—About one-fifth of legal assistants work in corporations. Corporate legal departments may have hundreds of attorneys

and paralegals on staff. Paralegals working for corporations work regular hours, do not have to be concerned with billable hours (discussed in Chapter 3), and generally receive above-average salaries. They may specialize in certain aspects of corporate law. In addition, paralegals work in many other public and private institutions, such as insurance companies, banks, real estate companies, title insurance companies, legal-software companies, and law schools.

3. *Government*—Paralegals work in many government administrative agencies, such as the Social Security Administration. Other employment opportunities exist with legislative offices, public prosecutors'

offices, public defenders' offices, and federal and state courts.

4. *Legal aid offices*—Some paralegals find it rewarding to work in legal aid offices, which provide legal services to those who find it difficult to pay for legal representation. These offices are largely funded by the government, but some support comes from private foundations.

5. *Freelance paralegals*—Some experienced paralegals own their businesses and work for attorneys on a contract basis. This work can have more flexible working hours and often can be done from a home office. The success (and income) of a paralegal in this area depends on the person's skill, business sense, and motivation.

PARALEGAL SPECIALTIES

Many paralegals specialize in one or two areas of law. The five areas in which the largest numbers of paralegals currently specialize are litigation, corporate law, contract law, real estate law, and personal-injury law. Other areas in which a legal assistant can specialize include insurance law, employment and labor law, estate planning and probate administration, bankruptcy law, intellectual property law, environmental law, family law, criminal law, elder law, and legal nurse consulting.

PARALEGAL COMPENSATION

Salaries and wage rates for paralegal employees vary. Factors affecting compensation include location, firm size, years of experience, and type of employer (law firm, corporation, or government agency). When evaluating a job, paralegals should consider not only salary or wages but also job benefits, such as insurance coverage, sick/vacation/holiday leave, and pension plans.

PLANNING YOUR CAREER

Career planning involves three steps: defining your long-term career goals, devising short-term goals and adjusting those goals to fit job realities, and reevaluating your career and career goals after you have had some on-the-job experience.

LOCATING POTENTIAL EMPLOYERS

When looking for employment, paralegals should apply the investigative skills that they learned in their paralegal training.

1. *Networking*—Many jobs come through networking with other professionals. You can begin networking while you are a student. If your local paralegal association allows students to become members, join the association. Knowing others in the legal community is a great asset when looking for a job.

2. *Finding available jobs*—You can locate potential employers by reviewing published and posted information about law firms and other possible employers. Advertisements can be found in trade journals, in newspapers, on the Internet, and at your school's placement office. Check legal directories for lists of law offices.

3. *Job-placement services*—

   a. **SCHOOL PLACEMENT SERVICES**—Paralegals should stay in contact with their school's placement office, which is often staffed with personnel trained to assist paralegals with job hunting.

   b. **LEGAL STAFFING OR PRIVATE PLACEMENT COMPANIES**—Paralegals may locate employment through private placement companies. Usually, the employer pays the placement company's fees, and the company recruits candidates for the position and schedules interviews. Placements may be for temporary or long-term positions. Paralegals can find out about job-placement companies through school program directors, local paralegal associations, state bar associations, or the Web.

MARKETING YOUR SKILLS

1. *The application process*—Prepare a professional résumé to outline your educational and work background. Do not include personal details. The cover letter that accompanies your résumé represents you, so draft it carefully. You should also have available a professional portfolio and a list of persons who have agreed to be professional references.

2. *The interview*—Do background research on a firm prior to your interview. Think through the answers you will give to likely questions, and be prepared to ask questions that indicate your interest and knowledge. After an interview, make notes of relevant issues so you can discuss them if called back.

3. *The follow-up/thank-you letter*—After an interview, send a personalized thank-you letter or e-mail expressing continued interest.

4. *Job-hunting files*—Keep your records organized as you look for work by creating a filing system for all your job-search activities.

5. *Salary negotiations*—Some employers will ask you to specify an acceptable salary. Be prepared to give a salary or a salary range, depending on the job requirements. Research information about the salaries paralegals earn in your area.

USING SOCIAL MEDIA EFFECTIVELY

Most people now use social media routinely. It can help you in your job search as employers often look at social media sites for evidence of personal behavior and professionalism. Manage your digital shadow by keeping in mind that your reputation is always on the line. Paralegals may increase their value to a firm by being able to contribute to the social media presence of the firm. Knowledge of effective use of social media tools can help your career in many ways.

■ QUESTIONS FOR REVIEW

1. List and describe the five types of organizations that hire paralegals. Where do most paralegals work?

2. List and briefly describe each of the paralegal specialties discussed in this chapter. Which specialty area or areas interest you the most? Why?

3. How can paralegals locate potential employers? How does networking help paralegals find jobs?

■ ETHICS QUESTION

Sheila, a paralegal with 20 years of bankruptcy law experience, sets up a practice to provide bankruptcy forms and advice directly to the public. She advises a client to file for bankruptcy under Chapter 7, but due to the means test, he should have filed Chapter 13. The wrong advice causes the client distress and added expense. What type of paralegal is Sheila working as? Is it permissible for a paralegal to provide legal services without attorney supervision? Should it be?

■ PRACTICE QUESTIONS AND ASSIGNMENTS

1. Where do most paralegals work? What are some advantages and disadvantages of working for a small law firm? For a large law firm? Which would you prefer to do? Why?

2. Using the material in the chapter, identify which kind of employer the paralegals in the following scenarios work for:

a. Isabella works on a team of one attorney, three paralegals, and two secretaries. They defend product liability cases brought against their employer, a medical-device manufacturer.

b. Ramon works as a case manager for a U.S. district court judge.

c. Miranda works for a county legal aid office that provides low-cost legal services to elderly people in a large city.

d. Anthony works for all of the attorneys in his firm. He has gained a variety of experience as he does all of the clerical work as well as the paralegal work on the various cases his firm handles. He enjoys the casual environment of the office.

e. Felicia's practice is limited to discovery work in the commercial litigation department. The office environment is formal, but she is paid a high salary, along with good benefits, and has opportunities for promotion.

f. Michael provides paralegal services to attorneys in his local community on a contract basis. Most of his work involves support on litigation matters from discovery through trials.

3. What is the difference between a freelance paralegal and a legal technician (also called an independent paralegal)? How would working as a freelance paralegal compare to working for a law firm, or other paralegal employer? How would working as a freelance paralegal compare to working as a legal technician?

4. Using the material in the chapter, identify each of the following types of questions (close-ended, open-ended, hypothetical, pressure) that an interviewer might ask during an interview:

a. Are you available to travel on weekends?

b. Please explain your work history.

c. What would you do in the following situation? Attorney Jones is in trial and at 4 P.M., the judge assigns attorney Jones to research the rules of evidence and bring her findings to him in the morning when the trial resumes. At 5 P.M., attorney Jones asks you to stay and help her do the research, indicating that it will "be a late night."

d. Thinking that you look like a polite person who is not assertive enough to work in a law firm, a human resources manager grabs your paperwork from you and says, "I'll complete that for you. You need to go to the lobby and wait for attorney Smith to interview you." There is clearly plenty of time for you to complete the paperwork.

5. Using the material in the chapter, determine which of the following are illegal questions that an interviewer might ask during a job interview:

a. Are you married?

b. How many children do you have?

c. How do you think that your prior work experience as a social worker will help you in this job as a family law paralegal?

d. You're quite a bit more mature than other applicants. Will you be thinking of retiring in the next ten years?

6. Draft a résumé for yourself using the samples in this chapter for guidance. Think of your strong suits that should be highlighted. Also, write a cover letter that introduces you in a favorable manner.

GROUP PROJECT

The group selects a legal specialty discussed in this chapter. Students one and two find an article about the area from a paralegal publication or website. They each write a one-page summary of the article, including the pros and cons of working in this specialty. Student three interviews a paralegal who works in this practice area, and likewise discusses the pros and cons of the specialty during the interview. Student four summarizes the results of both the research and the interview and presents the results to the class.

INTERNET PROJECTS

1. Go to the American Bar Association's Web pages for paralegals at **www.americanbar.org/groups/paralegals/resources/career_information.html** and review the career and salary information for paralegals.

a. Are jobs posted on the site? If so, click on a job that interests you and make a list of the job duties included in the post. Print and attach a copy of the job posting to your answer.

b. What information is provided (or linked) regarding the growth of the paralegal profession and job opportunities? Is any salary information provided?

c. Search for entry-level paralegal salaries in your area. What are the results? How do they compare to the results for the questions above? Explain differences in the results of your searches.

2. Do an Internet search to see if you can determine which social media site may be most relevant for your career.

a. Provide links to three websites and write two to three paragraphs discussing which results are the best and why. Include your opinion of which site you would choose to promote your career as a paralegal.

b. Using the material in the chapter on using social media, write two to three more paragraphs discussing what you think are the top three ways to manage your digital shadow.

CHAPTER 3

The Inner Workings of the Law Office

CHAPTER OBJECTIVES

After completing this chapter, you will know:

- How law firms are organized and managed.

- Some typical policies and procedures governing paralegal employment.

- The importance of an efficient filing system in legal practice and some typical filing procedures.

- How clients are billed for legal services.

- How law office culture and politics affect the paralegal's working environment.

Introduction

The different environments in which paralegals work makes it impossible to predict exactly how the firm where you will work will be run. Typically, the way in which that firm operates will relate, at least in part, to the firm's form of business organization. Because most paralegals work for private law firms, this chapter focuses on the organization, management, and procedures characteristic of these firms.

First, we look at how the size and structure of a law firm affect the paralegal's working environment. The working environment in a firm owned and operated by one attorney is significantly different from that in a large law firm with two hundred attorneys. Different still is the working climate of a large corporate enterprise or a government agency.

We then look at other aspects of the working environment of paralegals. Most law firms have specific policies and procedures relating to employment conditions, filing systems, billing and timekeeping practices, and financial procedures. Increasingly, firms make use of social media tools. We conclude the chapter with a brief discussion of law office culture and politics.

The Organizational Structure of Law Firms

Law firms range in size from one-attorney firms to megafirms with hundreds of attorneys. Regardless of size, law firms typically organize as sole proprietorships, partnerships, limited liability partnerships, professional corporations, or professional limited liability companies. Because the way in which a business is organized affects the office environment, we next look briefly at each of the major organizational forms of law firms. Organizational forms of businesses in general will be discussed in greater detail in Chapter 18.

Sole Proprietorships

sole proprietorship
The simplest form of business organization, in which the owner is the business. Anyone who does business without creating a formal business entity has a sole proprietorship.

The sole proprietorship is the simplest business form and is often used by attorneys when they first set up legal practices. In a sole proprietorship, one individual—the sole proprietor—owns the business. The sole proprietor is entitled to any profits made by the firm but is also personally liable for all of the firm's debts or obligations. Personal liability means that the owner's personal assets (such as savings and other property) may have to be sacrificed to pay business obligations if the business fails. Because of the personal financial risk faced by a sole proprietor, most sole practitioners are organized as a Professional Corporation (P.C.) or another form, as discussed below.

personal liability
An individual's personal responsibility for debts or obligations. The owners of sole proprietorships and partnerships are personally liable for the debts and obligations incurred by their businesses. If their firms go bankrupt or cannot meet debts, the owners will be personally responsible for the debts.

Solo Practitioner

An attorney who practices law as a sole proprietor is often called a *sole (solo) practitioner*. To save on office overhead expenses, a sole practitioner may share an office with other attorneys. A paralegal may split time among sole practitioners who share office space.

Wide Experience

Working for a sole practitioner with a general practice is a good way for a paralegal to learn law office procedures because the paralegal will perform a wide variety of tasks. Many sole practitioners hire one person to act as secretary, paralegal, administrator, and manager. Paralegals holding such positions would probably handle many tasks: receiving and date-stamping the mail, printing out e-mails, organizing and maintaining the filing system, interviewing clients and witnesses, bookkeeping (receiving payments from clients, preparing and sending bills to clients, and the like), conducting investigations and legal research, drafting legal documents, assisting the attorney in trial preparation and perhaps in the courtroom, and other jobs, including office administration.

Working for a sole practitioner is a good way to find out which area of law you most enjoy because you will learn about procedures relating to many areas. If you work for a sole practitioner who specializes in one area of law, you will have an opportunity to develop expertise in that area. In sum, working in a small law firm gives you an overview of law office procedures and legal practice that will help you throughout your career.

Partnerships

Many law firms with multiple attorneys are organized as partnerships. In a partnership, two or more people do business jointly as partners. A partnership may consist of two or hundreds of attorneys. In a partnership, each partner owns a share of the business and shares in the firm's profits or losses.

In smaller partnerships, the partners may participate equally in managing the partnership. The partners meet to make decisions about clients, policies, procedures, and other matters important to the firm. In larger partnerships, managerial decisions are usually made by a committee of partners, one of whom may be designated as the managing partner.

Partnerships (and professional corporations, which are discussed below) frequently employ attorneys who are not partners and do not share in the profits. Typically, these attorneys are called associate attorneys. They are usually less experienced and may be invited to become partners after working for the firm for several years. Sometimes, firms hire staff attorneys, who will not become partners. Staff attorneys differ from *contract attorneys*, who provide services on a project basis. Many firms also hire law clerks—law students who work for the firm during the summer or part-time during the school year to gain practical legal experience. Law clerks who meet with the approval of the members of the firm may be offered positions as associates when they graduate and pass the bar exam.

Liability of Partners

Like sole proprietors, attorneys in a partnership are personally liable for the debts and obligations of the law firm if it fails. In addition, a partner can be held personally responsible for the misconduct or debts of another partner. For example, suppose a client sues a partner in the firm for malpractice and wins a large judgment. The firm carries malpractice insurance, but it is insufficient to pay the obligation. The court will order the attorney who committed the wrongful act to pay the balance due. Once the responsible attorney's personal assets are exhausted, the assets of the other (innocent) partners can be used to pay the judgment. This unlimited personal liability of partners is a disadvantage for law firms organized as partnerships.

Limited Liability Partnership (LLP)

A form of partnership called the limited liability partnership (LLP) has become increasingly popular. The LLP normally allows professionals to avoid personal liability for the malpractice of other partners. Although LLP statutes vary from state to state, generally state law limits the liability of partners in some way. For example, Delaware law protects each innocent partner from the "debts and obligations of the partnership arising from negligence, wrongful acts, or misconduct." You will read more about LLPs in Chapter 18.

Professional Corporations

A professional corporation (P.C. or PC) is a corporation formed by licensed professionals, such as lawyers or physicians. Like other corporations, it is owned by shareholders, so called because they have purchased the corporation's stock, or shares, and thus own a share of the business. The shareholders share in the profits and losses of the firm in proportion to how many shares they own. Their personal liability, unlike that of partners, may or may not be limited to the amount of their investments, depending on the circumstances and on state law. Limited personal liability is one of the key advantages of this corporate form of business.

---

partnership
An association of two or more persons to carry on, as co-owners, a business for profit.

partner
A person who operates a business jointly with one or more other persons. Each partner is a co-owner of the business firm.

managing partner
The partner in a law firm who makes decisions relating to the firm's policies and procedures and who generally oversees the business operations of the firm.

associate attorney
An attorney working for a law firm who is not a partner and does not have an ownership interest in the firm. Associates are usually less experienced attorneys and may be invited to become partners after working for the firm for several years.

staff attorney
An attorney hired by a law firm as an employee. A staff attorney has no ownership rights in the firm and will not be invited to become a partner in the firm.

law clerk
A law student working as an apprentice with a law firm to gain practical experience.

limited liability partnership (LLP)
A business organizational form designed for professionals who normally do business as partners in a partnership. The LLP limits the personal liability of partners.

professional corporation (P.C.)
A corporation formed by licensed professionals, such as lawyers or physicians. The liability of shareholders is often limited to the amount of their investments.

shareholder
One who purchases corporate stock, or shares, and who thus becomes an owner of the corporation.

professional limited liability company (PLLC)
An organizational form law firms may use in most states to help limit personal liability by separating individuals and the legal entity, the firm.

Most states allow attorneys to form a professional limited liability company (PLLC). The law firm must receive permission from the state bar association. The bar association will likely require that a licensed attorney or group of attorneys operate and own the PLLC. As with other organizational forms, the originating paperwork of the firm is on public file with the secretary of state in each state.

In many respects, the PC or PLLC is run like a partnership, and the distinction among these forms of business organization is often more a legal formality than an operational reality. Because of this, attorneys who organize their business as a PC or PLLC are nonetheless sometimes referred to as partners. For simplicity, in this chapter we will refer to anyone who has ownership rights in a law firm as a partner.

Law Office Management and Personnel

When you take a job as a paralegal, you will learn the relative status of the office personnel. Particularly, you want to know who has authority over you and to whom you are accountable. You also want to know who is accountable to you—whether you have an assistant or a secretary (or share an assistant or a secretary with another paralegal), for example. In a small firm, you will have no problem learning this information. If you work for a larger law firm, the lines of authority may be more difficult to perceive. Your supervisor will probably instruct you on the relative status of the firm's personnel. If you are not sure about who has authority over whom and what tasks are performed by different employees, ask your supervisor.

Professionalism and Courtesy

Regardless of formal lines of authority, it is important to be courteous and professional with everyone. You may outrank a partner's secretary on paper, but if the partner and secretary have a long history of working together, the partner is likely to pay close attention to the secretary's views.

The lines of authority and accountability vary from firm to firm, depending on the firm's size and management preferences. A sample organizational chart for a relatively small law partnership is shown in Exhibit 3.1 below. The partners at the top of the chart are the decision makers in the firm. Next in authority are the associate attorneys. Paralegals are supervised by both the attorneys (in regard to legal work) and the office manager (in regard to office procedural and paralegal-staffing matters). In larger firms,

EXHIBIT 3.1

A Sample Organizational Chart for a Law Partnership

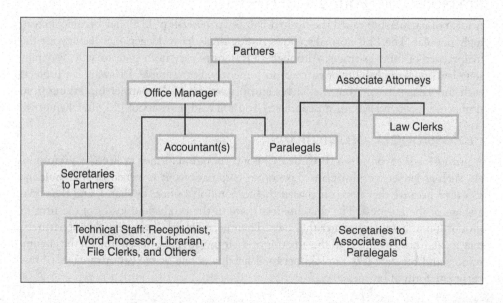

there may be a paralegal manager who coordinates paralegal staffing and programs relating to paralegal educational and professional development.

Besides attorneys and paralegals, law firm employees include administrative personnel. In large firms, the partners may hire a legal administrator to run the business end of the firm. The legal administrator might delegate some authority to an office manager and other supervisory employees.

Variety of Support Staff

In medium-size firms, such as those represented in Exhibit 3.1, an office manager handles the administrative aspects of the firm. The legal administrator or office manager typically is in charge of docketing (calendaring) legal work undertaken by the attorneys; establishing and overseeing filing procedures; implementing new technology, such as new docketing software; ordering and monitoring supplies; and generally making sure that the office runs smoothly and that office procedures are established and followed. In a small firm, the office manager might handle client-billing procedures. The firm represented in Exhibit 3.1 has an accountant to perform this function.

The support personnel in a large law office may include secretaries, receptionists, bookkeepers, file clerks, messengers, and others. Depending on their functions and specific jobs, support personnel may fall under the supervision of any number of other personnel in the firm. In a small firm, just one person—the legal secretary, for example—may perform all of the above-mentioned functions. No matter the size of the office, the need for accuracy and organization is great, as described in the *In the Office* feature below.

Employment Policies

Employees of a law firm, which include all personnel other than the partners or those who work for the firm on a contract basis, are subject to the firm's employment policies. A firm's policies governing employment may be published in an employment manual in larger firms. In smaller firms, these policies are often unwritten. In either case, when you take a job as a paralegal, or perhaps before you accept a position, you will want to become familiar with the firm's conditions of employment.

There will be a policy, for example, on when you may take vacation time and how much you are entitled to take during the first year, second year, and so on. Other policies will govern which holidays are observed by the firm, how much sick leave you

paralegal manager
An employee in a law firm who is responsible for overseeing the paralegal staff and paralegal professional development.

legal administrator
An administrative employee of a law firm who manages day-to-day operations. In smaller law firms, legal administrators are usually called office managers.

office manager
An administrative employee who manages the day-to-day operations of a firm. In larger law firms, office managers are usually called legal administrators.

support personnel
Employees who provide clerical, secretarial, or other support to the legal, paralegal, and administrative staff of a law firm.

employment manual
A firm's handbook or written statement that specifies the policies and procedures that govern the firm's employees and employer-employee relationships.

IN THE OFFICE

KEEP YOUR PRIORITIES CLEAR AND IN ORDER

Staff members in a law office are frequently under pressure to meet deadlines. A paralegal can get caught between attorneys with competing demands or even between the demands of cases being handled by one supervising attorney who is under pressure. Do not let conflicts for your time build up and put you in the middle. Discuss which tasks should be accomplished first. Identify conflicts between you and your supervisor about the best use of your limited time. Other people may forget, or may not know about, work you have to accomplish and may unintentionally be unreasonable in their expectations. Clear communications about what is needed, when work is due, and what gets priority will help you to avoid appearing unresponsive.

can take, when you are expected to arrive at work, and what serves as grounds for the employer to terminate your employment.

Employment policies vary from firm to firm. A leading concern of paralegals (and employees generally) is how much they will be paid, how they will be paid (whether they receive salaries or hourly wages), and what job benefits they will receive. These issues were discussed in Chapter 2, so we will not examine them here. Rather, we look at some other areas of concern to paralegals, including performance evaluations and termination procedures.

Performance Evaluations

Many law firms conduct periodic evaluations to give feedback on performance and to determine if employees will receive raises. Usually, performance is evaluated annually, but some firms conduct evaluations every six months, and some conduct them more often for new employees.

Know What Is Expected of You

Because paralegal responsibilities vary from firm to firm, no one evaluation checklist applies to every paralegal. Some of the factors that may be considered during a performance evaluation are indicated in Exhibit 3.2 below. Note, though, that performance evaluations may be much longer and more detailed than the list in the exhibit. For example, items in that list may have several subheadings. Normally, under each item is a series of options—ranging from "excellent" to "unsatisfactory" or something similar—for the supervisor or attorney to check. Often, written explanations for the rankings are given, especially to explain areas of weak performance.

When you begin work as a paralegal, you should learn at the outset exactly what your duties will be and what performance is expected of you. This way, you will be able to prepare for your first evaluation from the moment you begin working. You will not have to wait months before you learn that you were supposed to be doing something different.

Be Ready

Prepare for evaluations and conduct yourself professionally at all times. Be your own advocate but stay positive. Keep track of your accomplishments, such as the number of billable hours per week or month that you normally generate, so that you can point them out to your supervisor. If you were part of a team that worked many extra hours to win a big case for the firm, mention it during the evaluation. Make your supervisor aware of ways

EXHIBIT 3.2

Factors That May Be Considered in a Performance Evaluation

1. **RESPONSIBILITY**
   Making sure that all tasks are performed on time and following up on all pending matters.

2. **EFFICIENCY**
   Obtaining good results in the least amount of time possible.

3. **PRODUCTIVITY**
   Producing a sufficient quantity of work in a given time period.

4. **COMPETENCE**
   Knowledge level and skills.

5. **INITIATIVE**
   Applying intelligence and creativity to tasks and making appropriate recommendations.

6. **COOPERATION**
   Getting along well with others on the legal team.

7. **PERSONAL FACTORS**
   Appearance, grooming habits, friendliness, and poise.

8. **DEPENDABILITY**
   Arriving at work consistently on time and being available when needed.

in which you save the firm money or contribute to the firm's success. If you master a new software program or pass the CLA (or CP) or PACE exam, tell your supervisor.

Get the Most from Your Performance Evaluation

Both paralegals and their employers can benefit from the discussions that take place during a performance evaluation. In the busy workplace, you may not have much time to talk with your supervisor about issues that do not relate to immediate work needs. Even if you do find a moment, you may feel awkward bringing up the topic of your performance or discussing a workplace problem. Performance evaluations are designed to allow both sides to exchange views on such matters.

During reviews, you will learn how the firm rates your performance. You can gain valuable feedback from your supervisor, learn more about your strengths and weaknesses, and identify the areas in which you need to improve your skills. Do not react negatively to criticisms of your work or conduct. Even during a performance review you are being evaluated. Keeping a positive outlook and showing that you appreciate constructive criticism will impress your supervisor. Discuss how you can make improvements that will enhance your value to the firm.

You can also use the evaluation to give your supervisor feedback on the workplace. This is especially useful if you believe you are capable of handling more complex tasks than you are being assigned. Attorneys sometimes underutilize paralegals because they do not know their capabilities. If you suggest ways in which your knowledge could be put to better use, you may earn more challenging and rewarding responsibilities. Also, if you and your supervising attorney never seem to have the time to meet face-to-face for an evaluation, consider writing up your own evaluation and presenting it to him or her for review.

Employment Termination

Policy manuals almost always deal with the subject of employment termination. A policy handbook will likely specify what kind of conduct can serve as a basis for firing employees. For example, the manual might specify that if an employee is absent more than twelve days a year for two consecutive years, the employer has grounds to terminate the employment relationship. The manual will also probably describe termination procedures.

For instance, the firm might require that it be notified one month in advance if an employee decides to leave the firm; if the employee fails to give such notice, he or she may lose accumulated vacation time or other benefits on termination. Leaving without notice will also make it harder to get a positive recommendation from the firm when you seek another position. Do not burn your bridges with an employer.

In the event that you believe you have been subject to discriminatory treatment in employment and were improperly dismissed, there may be a cause of action (see Chapter 18) that likely requires consulting an attorney who specializes in employment law.

Filing Procedures

Every law firm has some kind of established filing procedures for office work. Efficient procedures are vital because the paperwork generated is substantial. Legal documents must be safeguarded yet be readily retrievable when needed. The need to protect client information is stressed in the *Developing Paralegal Skills* feature on the following page. If a client file is misplaced or lost, the client may suffer costly harm.

Additionally, documents must be filed in such a way as to protect client confidentiality. The duty of confidentiality is discussed in Chapter 4, but is mentioned here because of the extent to which it frames all legal work and procedures. This is particularly true of filing procedures. All information received from or about clients, including files and documents, is considered confidential. A breach of confidentiality by a

DEVELOPING PARALEGAL SKILLS

CONFIDENTIALITY AND CLIENT INFORMATION

One of the most important professional obligations of a paralegal is to treat all of your clients' information as confidential. The obligation to treat information as confidential has been long recognized by the common law, and some jurisdictions even provide criminal sanctions for professionals who violate this duty.

As a general rule, never share *any* information about your clients—even the fact that they are clients—with anyone outside your firm. Don't share "war stories" from work with friends or relatives if doing so could reveal information about the client. Never leave *any* information about your clients where others might see it.

To protect client confidentiality, you should:

- Keep all identifiable information about clients off the cover of files.
- Never leave a file unattended for even a short time in a publicly accessible location such as a library table or courtroom.
- Make sure all client files are removed from internal workspaces where outsiders might be present, such as conference rooms.

- Do not allow outsiders access to computer systems or networks.
- Use only secure networks or encrypted communications systems for transmission of confidential information. Most wireless networks in airports or Internet cafés are *not* secure.
- Password protect all electronic devices on which confidential matters are stored, such as smartphones that receive e-mails.
- Secure your computer when you leave your desk.

The obligation to maintain confidentiality continues even after a file is closed. Your firm should have document-retention policies that detail how long closed files are kept and how they are to be destroyed. Be sure to follow your firm's policies carefully. An excellent guide to such policies is available at **www.americanbar.org**. In the "search" box, type Lee Nemchek and it will take you to articles on this important topic.

---

paralegal or other employee can cause the law firm to incur liability as well as damage to its reputation.

If you work for a small firm, filing procedures may be informal and you may need to assume the responsibility for organizing and developing an efficient and secure filing system. Larger firms normally have specific procedures concerning the creation, maintenance, use, and storage of office files. If you take a job with a large firm, a supervisor will probably train you in office procedures, including filing. Although the trend today, particularly in larger firms, is increasingly computerized filing systems, many firms create "hard copies" to ensure that files are not lost if computer systems crash.

Generally, law offices maintain several types of files. Typically, a law firm's filing system will include client files, work product files and reference materials, and forms files.

Client Files

To illustrate client-filing procedures, we present below the phases in the "life cycle" of a hypothetical client's file. The name of the client is Katherine Baranski. She has just retained (hired) one of your firm's attorneys to represent her in a lawsuit that she wants to bring against Tony Peretto. Because Baranski is initiating the lawsuit, she is referred to as the *plaintiff*. Peretto, because he has to defend against Baranski's claims, is the *defendant*. The name of the case is *Baranski v. Peretto*. Assume that you will be working on the case and that your supervising attorney, who has agreed to represent

Baranski, has just asked you to open a new case file. Assume that you have already verified, through a "conflicts check" (to be discussed in Chapter 4), that no conflict of interest exists.

Opening a New Client File

The first step that you (or a secretary, at your request) will take in opening a new file is to assign the case a file number. For reasons of efficiency and confidentiality, many firms identify their client files by numbers or some kind of numerical and/or alphabetical sequence instead of the clients' names. That is, the *Baranski v. Peretto* case file might be identified by the letters BAPE—the first two letters of the plaintiff's name followed by the first two letters of the defendant's name.

Most law firms use computerized databases to record and track case titles and files. Firms use file labels containing bar codes that contain attorney codes, subject-matter codes, the client's name and file number, and so forth. The databases are also used for contract and billing information.

Typically, law firms maintain a master client list on which clients' names are entered alphabetically and cross-referenced to the clients' case numbers. If file numbers consist of numerical sequences, there is also a master list on which the file numbers are listed in numerical order and cross-referenced to the clients' names.

Adding Subfiles

As work on the *Baranski* case progresses and more documents are generated or received, the file will expand. To ensure that documents will be easy to locate, you create subfiles. One subfile might be created for client documents (such as a contract, will, stock certificate, or photograph) that the firm needs for reference or for evidence at trial. As correspondence relating to the *Baranski* case is generated, you probably add a correspondence subfile. You will also want a subfile for your or the attorney's notes on the case, including research results.

As we will explore in Chapters 10 through 12, litigation involves several stages. As the *Baranski* litigation progresses through these stages, subfiles for documents relating to each stage will be added to the *Baranski* file. Many firms find it useful to color-code or add tabs to subfiles so that they can be readily identified. Often, in large files, an index of each subfile's contents is created and attached to the inside cover of the subfile.

Documents are typically filed within each subfile in reverse chronological order, with the most recently dated document on the top. Usually, to safeguard the documents, they are punched at the top with a two-hole puncher so they can be secured within the file with a clip. Note, though, that an original client document should not be punched or altered in any way. It should always be left loose within the file (or paper-clipped to a copy of the document that *is* punched and secured in the file). For example, if you were holding in the file a property deed belonging to a client, you would not want to alter that document in any way.

File Use and Storage

Often, files are stored in a file room or specific area. Most firms have a procedure for employees to follow when removing files from the storage area. The office staff may be required to replace a removed file with an "out card" indicating the date, the name of the file, and the name or initials of the person who removed it.

Note that documents should not be removed from a client file or subfile. Rather, the entire file or subfile should be removed for use. This ensures that important documents will not be separated from the file and possibly mislaid, misfiled, or lost. Many paralegals make copies of documents in the file for their use. For example, if you are working on the *Baranski* case and need to review certain documents in the file, you might remove them from the file temporarily, copy them, and immediately return the original documents and the file to storage.

Increasingly, firms scan documents into computer files, but certain original paper documents must be retained for clients and to satisfy state law. To improve security of documents stored on computers and at on-offsite locations, a secure password policy is important. Complex passwords that are changed monthly are critical to help reduce hacker access to files. Large firms often have IT specialists, but in smaller firms, you can take a leadership role in helping to develop computer-security policies.

Files and the Cloud

An important information technology trend is "cloud-based computing." That means files and programs are stored online and so are accessible from any computer, smartphone, or tablet connected to the Internet. Law firms are cautious about giving up physical control of confidential information, because they worry about protecting clients' rights to the attorney-client privilege. Be sure to clear any use of cloud storage on your personal devices such as smartphones, tablets, and laptops with your firm. Do not put business information in your iCloud-connected Apple device or on a cloud storage site such as Dropbox without discussing it with your firm.

Even the fact that your firm is representing a client may be something the client wants kept confidential. Storing something as simple as contact information in a mobile phone cloud "app" could result in revealing the fact of a relationship with the law firm. Be particularly cautious about leaving your portable devices logged on to cloud apps while using public wireless networks or in public places where electronic eavesdropping may occur. In general, be cautious about using personal equipment such as smartphones to conduct firm business. Be sure to know if your firm or supervising attorney has a policy about such equipment use.

Closing a File

Assume that the *Baranski* case has been settled out of court and that no further legal work on Baranski's behalf needs to be done. For a time, her file will be retained in the inactive files, but when it is fairly certain that no one will need to refer to it very often, if ever, it will be closed. Closed files are often stored in a separate area of the building or even off-site. Traditionally, many larger law firms stored the contents of old files on microfilm. Today, firms can use scanning technology to scan file contents for storage on hard drives at the firm and on secure off-site servers.

Procedures for closing files vary from firm to firm. Typically, when a case is closed, original documents provided by the client (for example, a deed to property) are returned to the client. Other materials, such as extra copies of documents or cover letters, are destroyed.

Destroying Old Files

Law firms do not have to retain client files forever, and at some point, the *Baranski* case file will be destroyed. Old files are normally destroyed by shredding so that confidentiality is ensured. Because shredded files can be pieced back together, and old computer and copier machine hard drives can be accessed, many firms hire companies that have equipment guaranteed to destroy such materials so recovery is impossible. The National Association for Information Destruction (NAID) certifies firms that will properly destroy files and hard drives. Law firms use great care when destroying client files because a court or government agency may impose a heavy fine on a law firm that destroys a file that should have been retained for a longer time. How long a particular file must be retained depends on many factors, including the nature of the client's legal matters and governing statutes, such as the statute of limitations.

Statutes of limitations limit the time period during which specific types of legal actions may be brought to court. Statutes of limitations for legal-malpractice actions vary from state to state—from six months to ten years after the attorney's last contact with the client. When the statute of limitations in your state expires is an important

statute of limitations
A statute setting the maximum time period within which certain actions can be brought to court or rights enforced. After the period of time has run, no legal action can be brought.

factor in determining how long to retain a client file, because an attorney or law firm will need the information contained in the client's file to defend against a malpractice action. If the file has been destroyed, the firm will not be able to produce any documents or other evidence to refute the plaintiff's claim.

Retention Policy

Your firm will have a document retention policy, and you should become familiar with it. These are policies on retaining documents related to particular matters. Importantly, these policies include the retention of e-mails. Learn how your firm archives e-mails and what your responsibilities are with respect to maintaining those archives. In many cases, e-mails sent through firm computer systems (including smartphones provided by your firm) may be archived even if you delete them.

E-Mail Policy

Not only must you be careful to comply with firm policies on retaining e-mails, but any inappropriate use of a work-related e-mail account or device may leave evidence on servers or in archives. The law is clear that employers have the right to restrict use of company property, such as computers and smartphones given to employees, and can search e-mail files and other transmissions from company property. Guidelines for e-mail professionalism are discussed in the *Technology and Today's Paralegal* feature on page 79.

Work Product Files and Reference Materials

Many law firms keep copies of research projects, legal memoranda, and various case-related documents prepared by the firm's attorneys and paralegals so these documents can be referred to in future projects. In this way, legal personnel do not have to start all over again when working on a claim similar to one dealt with in the past.

Traditionally, hard copies of work product files, or legal-information files, were filed in the firm's law library with other reference materials and publications. Today, work product documents and research materials are often generated on computers and stored on hard drives or other data-storage devices. Often, in large firms, these materials are kept in a central data bank that is accessible by firm personnel. As the *Ethics Watch* feature on the following page reminds us, backing up files is also critical in law firms.

Forms Files

Every law firm keeps on hand various forms that it commonly uses. These forms are usually stored in a forms file. A forms file might include forms for retainer agreements (to be discussed shortly), for filing lawsuits in specific courts, for bankruptcy petitions, for real estate matters, and for many other types of legal matters. Often, to save time, copies of documents relating to specific types of cases are kept for future reference. Then, when the attorney or paralegal works on a similar case, those documents can serve as models, or guides. As noted, these forms may also be kept in a work product file.

Forms files are almost always computerized. Computerized forms have simplified legal practice by allowing legal personnel to generate customized documents within minutes. Forms for many standard legal transactions are available from legal-software companies as discussed in Chapter 8.

forms file
A reference file containing copies of the firm's commonly used legal documents and informational forms. The documents in the forms file serve as models for drafting new documents.

Law Firms and Financial Procedures

In the business of law, the products are legal services that are sold to clients. A major concern of any law firm is to have a clear policy on fee arrangements and efficient procedures to ensure that each client is billed appropriately for the time and costs associated with serving that client. Efficient billing procedures require that attorneys and paralegals keep accurate records of the time they spend working on a given client's case or other legal matter.

ETHICS WATCH

BACK UP YOUR WORK

In using computers on a routine basis we easily forget—while the computer system is working—that a power failure or other problem can occur at any time. Should this happen, current work that has not been saved to a hard drive can be lost. Protect yourself and your firm by having backup copies of all your work, and also have a contingency plan, such as a second computer available to use. File backup can be done both in the office on external hard drives as well as off-site through a service that automatically keeps your files secure in case a catastrophe, such as a fire, destroys the office. There are many automatic backup systems such as Time Machine for Apple products and many devices and services for PCs.

Backing up your work frequently is particularly important and can "save the day" if the computer system crashes or fails. If you routinely back up documents, you may save yourself valuable time that could be required to recreate a document or file. You will also save yourself and the firm from the problem of deciding who will pay—the client or the law firm—for the extra time spent recreating work. Moreover, with backups available, your employer will never be without a crucial document when it's needed. If your office computer system is connected to a server system, you will have online backup on a set time basis.

This practice is consistent with the NFPA *Model Code of Ethics and Professional Responsibility*, which we will discuss in Chapter 4. Section 1.3 of the code states: "A paralegal shall maintain a high standard of professional conduct." Section 1.5 states: "A paralegal shall preserve all confidential information provided by the client or acquired from other sources before, during, and after the course of the professional relationship." Be sure to learn and follow your firm's backup policy.

Tiers of Firms

Law firms differ in their fee structures. Exhibit 3.3 on the facing page shows the general levels of attorney billing rates for partner services. At the top are the elite law firms in the biggest cities like New York and London. These firms primarily focus on complicated business transactions, international deals, and tax matters. The next tier consists of firms that dominate regional markets, such as in Cleveland, Ohio, or San Diego, California. These firms often work with large companies but are more likely to specialize, such as in insurance defense. Just below these firms are the boutique firms handling specialized areas like patents or immigration for high-end clients. Below that come smaller firms with smaller clients.

At the bottom are the legal process outsourcers. This level includes firms that specialize in routine matters requiring the least legal training. These firms often use professionals in India, where wages are much lower, to conduct document review or analyze thousands of e-mails as part of discovery.

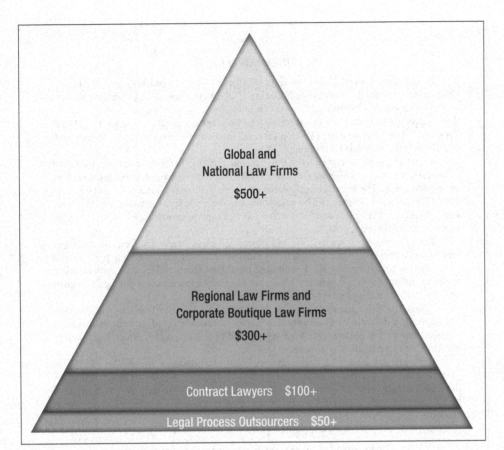

EXHIBIT 3.3
General Structure of Law Firms
and Providers of Legal Services
and Typical Hourly Billing Rate
for Attorney Services

Fee Arrangements

A major ethical concern of the legal profession has to do with the reasonableness of attorneys' fees and the ways in which clients are billed for legal services. State ethics codes governing attorneys require legal fees to be reasonable. The American Bar Association's *Model Rules of Professional Conduct* (to be discussed in Chapter 4) holds that the fees charged by lawyers must be reasonable. The rule then lists the factors that should be considered in determining the reasonableness of a fee. The factors include the time and labor required to perform the legal work, the fee customarily charged in the locality for similar legal services, and the experience and ability of the lawyer performing the services.

Normally, fee arrangements are discussed and agreed on at the outset of any attorney-client relationship. Most law firms require each client to agree, in a signed writing called a retainer agreement, to whatever fee arrangements have been made. Some states require that fee arrangements be stated in writing. The agreement specifies that the client is retaining (hiring) the attorney and/or firm to represent the client in a legal matter and that the client agrees to the fee arrangements set forth in the agreement. Exhibit 3.4 on the following page shows a sample retainer agreement.

Basically, there are three types of fee arrangements: fixed fees, hourly fees, and contingency fees. We examine here each of these types of fees, as well as some alternative fee arrangements. In addition, some legal claims entitle the winning plaintiff to have the defendant pay a reasonable attorney's fee to the plaintiff's lawyer. For example, many states provide for a losing defendant in a contracts case to pay the plaintiff's attorney's fees and costs. To collect requires that the lawyer be able to document his or her time and expenses.

Fixed Fees

The client may agree to pay a fixed fee for a specified legal service. Certain procedures, such as incorporation and simple divorce filings, are often handled on a fixed-fee basis

retainer agreement
A signed document stating that the attorney or the law firm has been hired by the client to provide certain legal services and that the client agrees to pay for those services.

fixed fee
A fee paid to the attorney by his or her client for having provided a specified legal service, such as the creation of a simple will.

EXHIBIT 3.4

A Sample Retainer Agreement

RETAINER AGREEMENT

I, Katherine Baranski, agree to employ Allen P. Gilmore and his law firm, Jeffers, Gilmore & Dunn, as my attorneys to prosecute all claims for damages against Tony Peretto and all other persons or entities that may be liable on account of an automobile accident that caused me to sustain serious injuries. The accident occurred on August 4, 2016, at 7:45 A.M., when Tony Peretto ran a stop sign on Thirty-eighth Street at Mattis Avenue and, as a result, his car collided with mine.

I agree to pay my lawyers a fee that will be one-third (33 percent) of any sum recovered in this case, regardless of whether the sum is received through settlement, lawsuit, arbitration, or any other way. The fee will be calculated on the sum recovered, after costs and expenses have been deducted. The fee will be paid when any money is actually received in this case. I agree that Allen P. Gilmore and his law firm have an express attorney's lien on any recovery to ensure that their fee is paid.

I agree to pay all necessary costs and expenses, such as court filing fees, court reporter fees, expert witness fees and expenses, travel expenses, long-distance telephone and facsimile costs, and photocopying charges. I understand that these costs and expenses will be billed to me by my attorney on a monthly basis and that I am responsible for paying these costs and expenses, even if no recovery is received.

I agree that this agreement does not cover matters other than those described above. This agreement does not cover an appeal from any judgment entered, any efforts necessary to collect money due because of a judgment entered by a court, or any efforts necessary to obtain other benefits, such as insurance.

I agree to pay a carrying charge amounting to the greater of five dollars ($5.00) or four percent (4%) per month on the average daily balance of bills on my account that are thirty (30) days overdue. If my account is outstanding by more than sixty (60) days, all work by the attorney shall cease until the account is paid in full or a monthly payment plan is agreed on.

This contract is governed by the law of the state of Nita.

I AGREE TO THE TERMS AND CONDITIONS STATED ABOVE:

Date: ___2 / 4 / 2017___　　　*Katherine Baranski*

Katherine Baranski

I agree to represent Katherine Baranski in the matter described above. I will receive no fee unless a recovery is obtained. If a recovery is obtained, I will receive a fee as described above.

I agree to notify Katherine Baranski of all developments in this matter promptly, and I will make no settlement of this matter without her consent.

I AGREE TO THE TERMS AND CONDITIONS STATED ABOVE:

Date: ___2 / 4 / 2017___　　　*Allen P. Gilmore*

Allen P. Gilmore
Jeffers, Gilmore & Dunn
553 Fifth Avenue
Suite 101
Nita City, NI 48801

because the attorney can reasonably estimate how much time will be involved in completing the work. Charging fixed fees is increasingly popular with clients who like knowing how much a matter will cost in advance.

Hourly Fees

With the exception of litigation work done on a contingency-fee basis (discussed below), most law firms charge clients hourly rates for legal services. Hourly rates vary widely from firm to firm. Some litigation firms charge high rates ($700 an hour or more) for services of senior partners because of their reputation for high-quality work that results in favorable settlements or court judgments for their clients. In contrast, an attorney just starting up a practice as a sole practitioner will have to charge a lower, more competitive rate (perhaps $100 per hour) to attract clients.

Law firms also bill clients for hourly rates for paralegal services. Because the hourly rate for paralegals is lower than that for attorneys, clients benefit from attorneys' use of paralegal services. Generally, the billing rate for paralegal services depends on the size and location of the firm. According to a compensation survey conducted by *Paralegal Today* billing rates for paralegals begin at about $60 per hour and may exceed $155 per hour. About 40 percent of all billing for paralegal services ranged between $96 and $135 per hour.

Note that although your services might be billed to the client at a certain hourly rate—say, $100—the firm will not actually pay you $100 an hour in wages. The billable rate for paralegal services, as for attorney services, takes into account the firm's expenses for overhead (rent, utilities, employee benefits, supplies, and other expenses).

Contingency Fees

A common practice among litigation attorneys, especially those representing plaintiffs in certain types of cases (such as personal-injury or negligence cases) is to charge the client on a contingency-fee basis. A contingency fee is contingent (dependent) on the outcome of the case. If the plaintiff wins the lawsuit and recovers damages or settles out of court, the attorney is entitled to a percentage of the amount recovered (refer to Exhibit 3.4 on the previous page for an example of a contingency-fee retainer agreement). If the plaintiff loses the lawsuit, the attorney gets nothing for the work and time invested in the case—although the client normally reimburses the attorney for the costs and expenses involved in preparing for trial (costs and expenses are discussed below, in regard to billing procedures).

contingency fee
A legal fee that consists of a specified percentage (such as 30 percent) of the amount the plaintiff recovers in a civil lawsuit. The fee is paid only if the plaintiff wins the lawsuit (recovers damages).

FIXED PERCENTAGE. Often, an attorney's contingency fee is one-fourth to one-third of the amount recovered. The agreement may provide for modification of the amount depending on how and when the dispute is settled. For example, an agreement that provides for a contingency fee of 33 percent of the amount recovered for a plaintiff may state that the amount will be reduced to a lower percentage if the case is settled out of court.

LIMITS ON FEES. The law restricts the use of contingency-fee agreements to certain types of cases. An attorney can request a contingency fee only in civil matters, not in criminal cases. In a civil case, the plaintiff is often seeking monetary damages from the defendant to compensate the plaintiff for injuries suffered. In criminal cases, as you will read in Chapter 13, the government is seeking to punish the defendant for a wrongful act committed against society as a whole. If the defendant is found not guilty of the charges, he will not receive monetary damages that the attorney could share.

Attorneys are also typically prohibited by state law from entering into contingency-fee agreements in divorce cases and probate cases (see Chapter 17) and in workers' compensation cases (see Chapter 18). States usually prohibit contingency fees in these cases because lawmakers have determined that allowing attorneys to share in the proceeds recovered would be contrary to public policy.

Client Trust Accounts

Law firms often require new clients to pay a retainer—an initial advance payment to the firm to cover part of the fee and costs that will be incurred on the client's behalf (such as travel expenses, fax charges, and the like). Some businesses keep an attorney on retainer by paying the attorney a fixed amount every month or year. The attorney handles all normal legal business that arises during that time. Retainer arrangements allow businesses to make legal costs more predictable over time.

retainer
An advance payment made by a client to a law firm to cover part of the legal fees and/or costs that will be incurred on that client's behalf.

trust account
A bank account in which one party (the trustee, such as an attorney) holds funds belonging to another person (such as a client); a bank account into which funds advanced to a law firm by a client are deposited. Also called an *escrow account*.

Funds received as retainers, as well as any funds received on behalf of a client (such as a payment to a client to settle a lawsuit), are placed in a special bank account. This account is usually referred to as a client trust account (or escrow account). The *Developing Paralegal Skills* feature below reviews trust account procedure. It is extremely important that the funds held in a trust account be used *only* for expenses relating to the costs of serving that client's needs. Software programs designed for law offices simplify holding multiple accounts.

In many states, certain trust accounts come under the requirements of Interest on Lawyers' Trust Accounts (IOLTA) programs. All states have IOLTA programs, and most states' lawyers are required to participate. Client funds are deposited in an IOLTA account when the amount is small or is to be held for a short time. In either case, the interest that could be earned for the client is less than the cost of maintaining a separate client account. The funds are instead placed in a single, pooled, interest-bearing trust account. Banks forward the interest earned on the account to the state IOLTA program, which uses the money to fund charitable causes, mostly to support legal assistance for the poor.

Misuse of client funds constitutes a major breach of the firm's duty to its client. An attorney's personal use of the funds, for example, can lead to disciplinary action and possible disbarment, as well as criminal penalties. *Commingling* (mixing together) a client's funds with the firm's funds also constitutes abuse and is one of the most common ways in which attorneys breach their professional obligations. If you handle a client's trust account, you should be especially careful to document your receipt of and use of the funds to protect yourself and your firm against the serious problems that may arise if there are any problems with the account.

Billing and Timekeeping Procedures

As a general rule, a law firm bills its clients monthly. Each client's bill reflects the amount of time spent on the client's matter by the attorney or other legal personnel. Client billing serves an obvious financial function (collecting payment for services

DEVELOPING PARALEGAL SKILLS

CREATING A TRUST ACCOUNT

Louise Larson has been hired to work for Don Jones. Don is just starting his own solo practice of law after years of working with a medium-sized law firm in which he had nothing to do with the firm's financial management. Louise's first assignment is to establish a client trust accounting system.

Don and Louise review the ethical rules regarding client property and funds. These rules require that client funds not be commingled with the lawyer's funds. "It's too easy to 'borrow' from a client's funds when they are in the lawyer's own bank account," explains Don. "Therefore," Don continues, "the first thing we need to do is open a checking account for client trust funds." Don and Louise then discuss what needs to be done

in order to open the trust account and what other bookkeeping procedures will be involved in creating a client trust accounting system.

CHECKLIST FOR CREATING A CLIENT TRUST ACCOUNT

- Obtain and prepare the necessary forms from the bank in which the account will be maintained.
- Devise a bookkeeping method for tracking all fees and expenses for a particular case and/or client.
- Retain all deposit slips and canceled checks.
- Keep a record of payments made to clients.
- Decide who will have access to the account.

A paralegal keeps track of the time she spent in the law office library. Later, she will enter the information into her firm's computerized billing program. Why is accuracy in time tracking so important for both the paralegal and the law firm?

rendered). It also serves a communicative function (keeping the client informed of the work being done on a case), as discussed later in this chapter.

Client bills are usually prepared by a legal secretary or a bookkeeper or, in larger firms, by someone in the accounting department. The bills are based on the fee arrangements made with the client and the time slips collected from the firm's attorneys and paralegals. The time slips (discussed below) indicate how many hours are to be charged to each client and at what hourly rate.

Billable Hours

The *legal fees* billed to clients are based on the number of billable hours generated for work requiring legal expertise. Billable hours are the hours or fractions of hours that attorneys and paralegals spend in client-related work that can be billed directly to clients. The *costs* billed to clients include expenses incurred by the firm (such as court fees, travel expenses, express-delivery charges, and copying costs) on the client's behalf. If an attorney is retained on a contingency-fee basis, the client is not billed monthly for legal fees. The client is normally billed monthly for any costs incurred on the client's behalf.

billable hours
Hours or fractions of hours that attorneys and paralegals spend in work that requires legal expertise and that can be billed directly to clients.

Billing Programs

Typically, a preliminary draft of the client's bill is given to the attorney responsible for the client's account. After the attorney reviews and possibly modifies the bill, it is sent to the client. Exhibit 3.5 on the following page illustrates a sample client bill. Most law firms have computerized billing procedures and use time-and-billing software designed specifically for law offices. Time-and-billing software is based on traditional timekeeping and billing procedures. Familiarity with essential features of such programs, combined with knowledge of the basic principles and procedures involved in client billing, will help you understand whatever type of time-and-billing software your employer may use.

Documenting Time and Expenses

Accurate timekeeping by attorneys and paralegals is crucial because clients cannot be billed for time spent on their behalf unless that time is documented. Traditionally, time slips have been used to document time spent by attorneys and paralegals working for a

time slip
A record documenting, for billing purposes, the hours (or fractions of hours) that an attorney or a paralegal worked for each client, the date on which the work was done, and the type of work done.

EXHIBIT 3.5

A Sample Client Bill

Jeffers, Gilmore & Dunn
553 Fifth Avenue
Suite 101
Nita City, NI 48801

BILLING DATE: February 28, 2017

Thomas Jones, M.D.
508 Oak Avenue
Nita City, NI 48801

RE: Medical-Malpractice Action Brought against Dr. Jones,
     File No. 15789

DATE	SERVICES RENDERED	PROVIDED BY	HOURS SPENT	TOTAL
1/30/17	Initial client consultation	APG (attorney)	1.00	$200.00
1/30/17	Client interview	EML (paralegal)	1.00	74.00
1/30/17	Document preparation	EML (paralegal)	1.00	74.00
2/5/17	Interview: Susanne Mathews (nurse)	EML (paralegal)	1.50	<u>111.00</u>
	TOTAL FOR LEGAL SERVICES			**$459.00**

DATE	EXPENSES			
2/5/17	Hospital charges for a copy of the medical documents			<u>$75.00</u>
	TOTAL FOR EXPENSES			<u>$75.00</u>
	TOTAL BILL TO CLIENT			<u>$534.00</u>

---

client. Today, time slips are incorporated into timekeeping software programs. We look here at *Timeslips*, a commonly used time-and-billing software program created by Sage Software.

In the slip entry form shown in Exhibit 3.6 on the facing page, the user enters his or her name, the task being billed for, the client for whom the work is being performed, the case referenced, and a description of the task. The user then either enters the time spent on the task or turns on an automated stopwatch timer—shown in Exhibit 3.7 on page 74—to track the time spent on the task. Tasks can also be recorded as recurring, and rates can be adjusted according to any special agreements. Notice that in Exhibit 3.6 the time is noted to the minute. While we refer to "hourly billing," the time recorded in client bills should also be expressed in parts of hours, not rounded to whole hours.

Costs incurred on behalf of clients have traditionally been entered on expense slips. Expenses are now usually entered into the billing program on a form similar to the *Time-slips* entry form shown in Exhibit 3.6. The form records a line-by-line description of each expense, along with the quantity and price of each item purchased on behalf of the client.

Billable versus Nonbillable Hours

The time recorded in timekeeping software is charged either to a client (billable hours) or to the firm (nonbillable hours). As mentioned, billable time generally includes the

expense slip

A slip of paper on which any expense, or cost, that is incurred on behalf of a client (such as the payment of court fees or long-distance telephone charges) is recorded.

hours that attorneys and paralegals spend in client-related work that requires legal expertise. For example, the time you spend researching or investigating a client's claim is billable time. So is the time spent conferring with or about a client, drafting documents on behalf of a client, interviewing clients or witnesses, and traveling on a client's behalf, such as going to and from the courthouse to file documents.

Time spent on other tasks, such as administrative work, staff meetings, or performance reviews, is nonbillable time. For example, suppose that you spend thirty minutes photocopying forms for the forms file or a procedures manual for the office. That thirty minutes is not billable time. In *Timeslips*, the user designates whether the task being recorded is billable, as you can see in the "Billing status" box in Exhibit 3.6 above.

Generally, law firms have a legitimate reason for wanting to maximize their billable hours: the financial well-being of a law firm depends to a great extent on how many billable hours are generated by its employees. Nonbillable time ultimately cuts into the firm's revenue used to pay salaries, rent, and other operating expenses. Therefore, the more billable hours generated by the firm's legal professionals, the more successful it will be.

The Pressure to Generate Billable Hours

Attorneys and paralegals face pressure to produce billable hours for the firm. As a paralegal, you may be subject to this pressure and must learn how to handle it. Depending on the firm, a paralegal may be expected to generate between 800 and 2,000 billable hours per year. For example, suppose that your employer expects you to produce 1,800 billable hours per year. Discounting vacation time and holidays (assuming a two-week vacation and ten paid holidays), this equates to 37.5 hours per week. If you work 40 hours a week, you will have only 2.5 hours a week for such nonbillable activities as

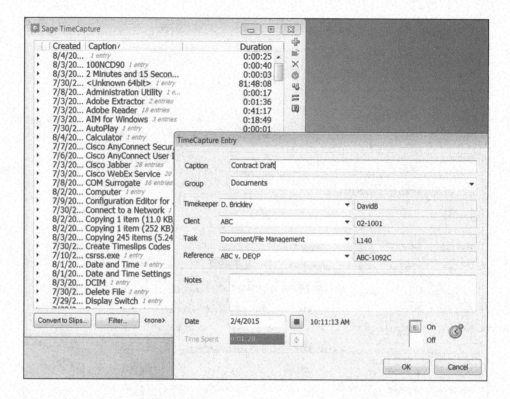

interoffice meetings, performance reviews, coffee breaks, reorganizing your work area, and chatting with others in the office.

Ethics and Client Billing Practices

Because attorneys have a duty to charge their clients "reasonable" fees, legal professionals must be careful in their billing practices. They must not "pad" their clients' bills by including more billable hours than actually worked on behalf of those clients. They also must avoid double billing—billing more than one client for the same time.

Double Billing

double billing

Billing more than one client for the same billable time period.

Sometimes, situations arise in which it is difficult to determine which client should be billed for a particular segment of time. For example, suppose that you are asked to travel to another city to interview a witness in a case for Client A. You spend three hours traveling in an airplane to get to that city. On the plane, you spend two hours summarizing a document relating to a case for Client B. Who should pay for those two hours, Client A, Client B, or both? In this situation, you could argue—as many attorneys do in similar circumstances—that you generated five billable hours, three on Client A's work, since travel time was required for Client A, and two on Client B's case. This is an example of how double billing can occur.

Double billing also occurs when a firm bills a new client for work that was done for a previous client. For example, suppose that an attorney is working on a case for Client B that is very similar to a case handled by the firm a year ago for Client A. The firm charged Client A $2,000 for the legal services. Because much of the research, writing, and other work done on Client A's case can transfer over to Client B's case, the firm is able to complete the work for Client B in half the time.

In this situation, would it be fair to bill Client B $2,000 also? After all, $1,000 of that amount represents hours spent on Client A's case (and for which Client A has already been billed). At the same time, would it be fair to Client A to bill Client B less for essentially the same services? Would it be fair not to allow the firm to profit from cost efficiencies generated by overlapping work? Could the firm split the savings created by the overlapping research ($1,000) with Client B by billing Client B $1,500 instead of $2,000?

The American Bar Association's Response to Double Billing

The American Bar Association (ABA) addressed double billing in a formal ethical opinion. The ABA states that attorneys are prohibited from charging more than one client for the same hours of work. Additionally, the ABA rejected the notion that the firm, and not the client, should benefit from cost efficiencies created by the firm's work for previous clients. "The lawyer who has agreed to bill solely on the basis of time spent is obliged to pass the benefit of these economies on to the client."

Although ABA opinions are not legally binding on attorneys unless they are adopted by the states as law, they carry significant weight in the legal community. Courts, for example, have tended to follow the ABA's position in resolving fee disputes. Typically, a court will not award attorneys' fees that it finds to be "excessive, redundant, or otherwise unnecessary." States will sanction or even disbar an attorney for double billing a client.

Communications and Social Media Tools

Excellent communication skills are a must for law firms to develop and retain clients, to function efficiently as a firm, and to help you develop as a paralegal. (See this chapter's *Featured Contributor* feature on pages 76 and 77 for tips on effective communication.)

Traditional Communications

Sending monthly bills to clients helps keep attorney-client communication channels open, but billing may be inadequate to keep clients informed. The American Bar Association states that a part of professional conduct required of attorneys is to keep their clients reasonably informed about the status of legal matters. This means the attorney, perhaps with the assistance of a paralegal, provides the client with adequate information so they understand the elements of legal matters being handled by the firm. The clients should also know about any legal proceedings that could come about as a result of a particular matter. Attorneys must also respond to inquiries from clients.

As a paralegal, you need to be aware that keeping clients reasonably informed about the progress being made on their cases goes beyond courtesy—it is a legal duty of attorneys. The meaning of "reasonably informed" varies depending on the client and on the nature of the work being done by the attorney. In some cases, a phone call every week or two will suffice to keep the client informed. In other cases, the attorney may ask the paralegal to draft a letter to a client explaining the status of the client's legal matter. Some firms have regular monthly mailings to update clients on the status of their cases. Generally, you should discuss with your supervising attorney how each client should be kept informed of the status of that client's case. (See the *Technology and Today's Paralegal* feature on page 79.)

Copies of all letters and e-mails to a client should, of course, be placed in the client's file. The file should also contain a written record of each phone call made to or received from a client. That way, there is a "paper trail" in the event it is ever necessary to provide evidence of communication with the client. Indeed, this should be done for all phone calls relating to a client's matter. You will learn about the various forms of letters that attorneys send to clients in Chapter 9. Increasingly, attorneys and paralegals communicate with clients via e-mail. Because every paralegal will receive and reply to numerous e-mails, e-mail format and organization is an issue in how a firm functions and is regarded by clients.

Communication by Social Media

The practice of law is an inherently cooperative environment. As a paralegal, you will be part of a team with your supervising attorney, other professionals, and clients. Social media tools help in facilitating collaboration. One of the most important uses of social

FEATURED CONTRIBUTOR

TEN TIPS FOR EFFECTIVE COMMUNICATION

Wendy B. Edson

BIOGRAPHICAL NOTE

Wendy B. Edson received her master's degree in library science (M.L.S.) from the University of Rhode Island and served as law librarian at a Buffalo, New York, law firm. Later, she joined the Paralegal Studies faculty at Hilbert College, in Hamburg, New York, and helped to develop an ABA-approved bachelor's degree program.

As chairperson of the paralegal program, Ms. Edson teaches paralegalism and legal ethics, legal research and writing, and the program's capstone seminar. She developed and now coordinates the internship program. Ms. Edson has lectured to legal professionals on legal research, teaching skills, internships, legal ethics, and curriculum development at the annual conference of the American Association for Paralegal Education and other organizations.

Words! They are the building blocks of human communication. Whether words are exchanged face to face—or by e-mail, phone, fax, or letter—communication is a two-way street. But how do we become skilled at maneuvering the two-way traffic of interpersonal communication? As in driving, we need to follow the "rules of the road." The rules of the road in regard to communication traffic are embodied in the following ten tips.

1. **Establish Communication Equality.** Communication equality does not require that individuals hold equal status in an office or organization, but requires that each party believe in *equal rights* to speak and listen. Observe someone whom you consider to be a good communicator. You will note that he or she demonstrates equality by actively listening and responding appropriately to whoever is speaking. Workplace problems often reflect communication ailments rooted in inequality. A firm belief in communication equality, despite job titles, will help to create a cooperative, productive working environment.

2. **Plan for Time and Space.** Effective communication requires time. Imagine your reaction to a request to work overtime if your supervising attorney took thirty seconds to order you to do the work versus taking two minutes to explain the reason for the request and listening to your response. In the first situation, the attorney saved one and a half minutes but scored "zero" in terms of communication skills. In today's rushed world, it is easy to overlook the

importance of communication skills in morale building and creating a cooperative, efficient workforce.

Effective communicators are aware of how the physical environment in which a conversation takes place can affect the communication process. Communication is always enhanced when the parties have reasonable privacy and are not continually interrupted. Another important factor is physical comfort.

Choosing an inappropriate time and place for communication denies the importance of the matters being discussed and may send the wrong message.

3. **Set the Agenda.** Skilled communicators prepare an *agenda*—whether written or mental—of matters to be discussed in order of their priority. Frequently, both parties bring their respective agendas to a discussion, which means that priorities may need to be negotiated. A subordinate who brings up the topic of desired vacation time when the supervisor is preoccupied with a major project clearly demonstrates that his or her priorities are different from those of the supervisor.

Successful communication requires that the parties first negotiate a *common agenda*—that is, determine jointly the agenda for a particular discussion or meeting and what topics should take priority. Then, the topics can be dealt with one by one, in terms of their relative importance, to the satisfaction of both parties. *Agenda aware-*

ness prevents parties from jumping from topic to topic without successfully resolving anything.

4. **Fine-Tune Your Speaking Skills.** Observe an individual whom you consider to be a good speaker, whether before a group of persons or on a one-on-one basis. What skills does that individual demonstrate? Effective speakers work hard to express thoughts clearly; sometimes, they refer to notes or lists to refresh their memories. Skilled speakers also try to communicate accurately and to talk about matters that they know will interest their listeners. They cultivate *communication empathy*—the sincere effort to put themselves in their listeners' shoes. As you speak to others, pause occasionally and ask yourself: "Would I enjoy listening to what I am saying and how I am saying it?"

5. **Cultivate Listening Skills.** Listening is not just refraining from speaking while another person is talking but is an *active process*—the other half of the communication partnership. An active listener does not interrupt the speaker. If you sense that the speaker is engaging in a monologue, you can use responsive behavior—including body language, attentiveness, and appropriate remarks—to steer the conversation back to a dialogue without cutting off the speaker.

An active listener realizes that listening is an investment in effective communication. By truly responding to what is being said, rather than regarding listening time as insignificant or as a time to plan his or her own remarks, the skilled listener establishes a bond of trust with the speaker. Active listeners avoid preconceived ideas about topics being discussed and assume that they do not know all the answers.

6. **Watch for Body Language.** Body language is nonverbal communication that reflects our emotional state. Physical positions, such as leaning forward or away from the speaker while listening, can reinforce or negate our spoken responses. Body attitudes, whether relaxed (comfortable posture, leaning forward, uncrossed arms and legs, relaxed neck and shoulders) or tense (stiff posture, backing away, crossed arms and legs, rigid neck and shoulders), vividly illustrate our responses before we utter a word. Eye contact is one of the most important tools in the body language tool kit for communication. Interviewers, social workers, and police officers have

learned that steady and responsive eye contact conveys sincerity and credibility.

7. **Put Note Taking in Perspective.** Overinvolvement in note taking detracts from the communication process because opportunities to listen actively, speak responsively, and be sensitive to body language are reduced. The speaker may ramble while the listener records the ramblings in extensive notes.

When it is necessary to take notes, it is helpful to establish some rapport with the speaker or listener before launching the note-taking process. Alternatively, follow-up notes can be a workable solution to the problem. The note taker can devote the interview time to communication and, after the interview, record his or her general impressions of the interview and identify specific issues that need to be discussed further.

> " Eye contact is one of the most important tools in the body language tool kit for communication."

8. **Recognize the Role of Criticism.** *Constructive criticism* focuses on specific actions or behaviors rather than personalities. It is objective rather than subjective. Criticism that is stated calmly and objectively ("We need to rewrite the section on holographic wills") is much more palatable for the person being criticized than is criticism in the form of a personal attack ("You did a terrible job"). By placing emphasis on actions instead of personalities, the parties can more easily work toward a satisfactory solution. If both the critic and the person being criticized can remain calm and can separate actions from personalities, then criticism will usually produce the desired result and *mutual* satisfaction.

9. **Aim for Satisfactory Closure.** Closure means "wrapping up" the communication. Successful communicators know that handling closure properly can leave a participant with a good feeling even if the solution was not exactly what he or she initially desired. Summarizing the discussion and checking for agreement or a need for further discussion will encourage all participants to follow the tenth tip.

10. **Commit to Communicate.** Excellent speakers and listeners have positive, self-confident attitudes that problems can be solved if the "rules of the road" are followed. Skilled communicators cultivate open minds, self-knowledge, and the ability to tolerate differences and empathize with others. They are committed to exercising their rights and responsibilities as speakers and listeners in the communication process.

media is for internal communication among employees. Some of the most constructive ways social media are being used in the legal environment include:

wiki
A Web page that can be added to and modified by anyone or by authorized users who share the site. The most famous example is Wikipedia.

- Private client spaces created to keep clients up to date on case developments.

- Internal wikis where knowledge can be shared.

- Collaborative spaces, secure behind firewalls, where a legal team can share documents.

- Internal community calendars to keep the legal team posted on where team members are and what they are doing, as well as progress on specific tasks.

- Firm-specific Twitter-like services for secure communication among members of the legal team.

- Firm Twitter feeds and other external social media that build the firm's digital shadow and help attract clients.

As a paralegal, you may be called on to play important roles in developing or implementing a social media strategy. This can be an assignment where you can demonstrate your value to the firm.

Some firms have adopted social media strategies to bring in cases and build connections with clients. Showing familiarity with the latest developments in the law is a way that firms can demonstrate knowledge of various areas of the law. Law firm social-media contributors find that the discipline of regular blogging or posting on sites such as Twitter keep their writing skills sharp and their knowledge up to date. Having a strategy is an important part of making a social media effort successful. The Buffalo, New York, law firm of Lippes Mathias Wexler Friedman, for example, has three attorneys blogging on different topics and regularly linking to each other.

Clear Policies

Establishing clear policies governing how the firm and its employees will use the Internet and social media tools is an important element of a media strategy, just as with traditional communications. Any policy should be straightforward and concise, and should include "dos" as well as "don'ts" to encourage appropriate use of the tools. The policy should include specific instructions and examples so that those unfamiliar with social media can understand what is permitted or not. Remember that client confidentiality is critically important in law firms, so any communications policy must address that issue.

Social media policies must comply with the law. The General Counsel of the National Labor Relations Board (NLRB), the federal agency that oversees labor relations in private firms, issued a report addressing some of the restrictions imposed by law on social media policies. The report cautioned employers not to restrict employees from discussing wages or working conditions online, just as they cannot restrict such discussions offline. However, employee comments that are not related to group efforts to address working conditions or wages may be restricted. Employers may restrict employees from pressuring others to "friend" or "like" them, since such behavior can sometimes stray into illegal discriminatory harassment.

Based on a review of lawsuits over social media policies, the book *Navigating Social Media Risks: Safeguarding Your Business* suggests that the key factors determining whether or not a policy is legal are:

- WHEN the social media post was done: during working hours or outside of work.

- WHAT the post discussed: was it an effort to address working conditions or was it about something unrelated? Was it an attempt to organize the employees or mere griping?

- WHO had access to the post? Co-workers or the public? Did co-workers respond (suggesting group action)?

TECHNOLOGY AND TODAY'S PARALEGAL

PROPER AND EFFECTIVE E-MAIL COMMUNICATIONS

E-mail is a standard communication tool for law firms. E-mail is so popular because it is a quick, easy-to-use, and inexpensive way to communicate. In large law firms and corporate enterprises, as well as in government agencies, e-mail messages have largely replaced the printed interoffice memos of the past as well as many letters.

APPLY PROFESSIONAL STANDARDS TO E-MAIL COMMUNICATIONS

Because e-mail is transmitted instantly, it may be difficult to remember that it is also a *written communication*. When we use e-mail we tend to adopt a casual, conversational tone and ignore traditional rules of writing, such as sentence structure, spelling, and capitalization. E-mail is still mail, however, and it should reflect the same professional tone and quality that you use in the firm's paper correspondence. When you send a message to someone (especially a client), you need to use clear and effective language.

There are several things you can do to ensure that your e-mail messages are professional and error free. First, use a spell checker. Typos, misspellings, punctuation errors, and grammatical problems detract from the message and can easily be avoided. Make sure that you also proofread your e-mail carefully because programs will not catch all errors. It helps to print out the draft of an e-mail, let it sit for a while, and review it later when you can see it from a fresh perspective.

Make sure that you use the same form as you would in an ordinary letter (see Chapter 9), with perhaps a few variations—adding your e-mail address below your name in the closing and the word *confidential* at the top (when appropriate), for example. Many law firms have standard signature blocks that note that e-mails are confidential. Do not use quotes or pictures in your signature block. Those belong in your personal e-mail, not in work e-mails.

TIPS FOR FORMATTING E-MAIL MESSAGES

Because e-mail often looks different on the recipient's computer screen than it does on your screen, keep the format simple. Use double spacing between paragraphs rather than indenting with tabs, and do not underline or boldface text (these features often do not transmit clearly from one e-mail system to another). If the message concerns a legal matter and is being sent to a client's workplace or a shared e-mail address, be careful about how you identify the subject of the e-mail. For example, you could write "Documents ready for signature" rather than "Bankruptcy petition complete."

Send attachments in PDF rather than in Word files or similar document-creation programs. That avoids problems in opening documents if recipients do not have the same program, and it prevents differences in platforms from altering the format. Sending PDFs also prevents a recipient from changing the content of a document.

TECHNOLOGY TIP

Always print out a copy of your e-mail and retain it in the client's file so that a record exists. Be sure that any e-mail you send discloses your status as a paralegal (to avoid claims about the unauthorized practice of law). Ask recipients to verify that important messages have been received (such as when you are notifying a person of a court date). E-mail systems often have a function that allows senders to request a "return receipt" to confirm that the message you sent was received. You should respond to incoming e-mail promptly so that the sender knows that you have received the e-mail. Finally, make sure that you know the policies of your firm regarding confidential e-mail. Used carefully, e-mail is an efficient way to fulfill your duties and communicate with clients.

Law Office Culture and Politics

As a paralegal, you will find that each law firm you work for is unique. Even though two firms may be the same size and have similar organizational structures, they will have different cultures, or "personalities." The culture of a given legal workplace is ultimately determined by how the firm's owners (the partners, for example) define the goals of the firm.

Formality versus Reality

Each firm has an internal political structure that may have little to do with the lines of authority and accountability spelled out in the firm's employment manual or other policy statement. An up-and-coming young partner in the firm may, in reality, have more authority than one of the firm's senior partners near retirement. There may be rivalry among associate attorneys for promotion to partnership status, and you can be caught in the middle. In such cases, you may find yourself tempted to take sides, which could jeopardize your own future with the firm.

Unfortunately, paralegals have little way of knowing about the culture and politics of a given firm until they have worked for the firm awhile. Of course, if you know someone who works for the firm, you might gain some advance knowledge about its environment. Otherwise, when you start work, you will need to learn about interoffice politics. Listen carefully whenever a co-worker discusses the firm's staff, and ask questions to elicit information from co-workers about office politics and unwritten policies. This way, you can both prepare yourself to deal with these issues and protect your own interests. After you've worked for the firm for a time, you will be in a position to judge whether the company you have chosen is really the right firm for you.

Issues in Office Culture

Some of the things you should think about when investigating a law firm's culture include:

- Turnover—because it is costly to train new employees, no firm wants to constantly replace staff. If a firm has high turnover, that will tell you that many employees may be unsatisfied with the environment. Ask how long the average employee has been at the firm to get a sense of turnover.

- Competitive compensation—are employees paid based on seniority or are there rewards for exceptional performance?

- Creative benefits—does the firm offer more than the usual package of medical and retirement benefits? Is telecommuting or flextime possible? Are there provisions for emergency backup childcare?

- Does the firm provide candid assessments of performance?

- How does the firm mentor new employees? Will you be assigned a mentor, or will you have to figure out on the job who can guide you?

- What is the firm's philosophy of management and its goals?

- What is the firm vision and brand?

- What does it take to be successful at the firm?

You can ask about these issues in a job interview. You can also learn about many of them by looking at the firm's website, Twitter feed, or other online presence, before your interview. Interviewers are often impressed by job applicants who have taken the time to research the firm before an interview, so be sure to learn as much as you can about the firm beforehand. Your career services office may be able to help with this, and legal directories are often good sources of information on law firms. Note also that firm culture does not remain constant. It changes over time as new employees are hired, older employees retire or move to new opportunities, and clients with different needs appear.

KEY TERMS AND CONCEPTS

Chapter Summary / The Inner Workings of the Law Office

THE ORGANIZATIONAL STRUCTURE OF LAW FIRMS

Law firms can be organized in the following ways:

1. *Sole proprietorship*—In a sole proprietorship, one attorney owns the business and is entitled to all the firm's profits. That individual also bears the burden of any losses and is personally liable for the firm's debts.

2. *Partnership*—In a partnership, two or more lawyers jointly own the firm and share in the firm's profits and losses. Attorneys who are employed by the firm but who are not partners (such as associates and staff attorneys) do not share in the profits and losses of the firm.

Generally, partners are subject to personal liability for all of the firm's debts or other obligations. In many states, firms can organize as *limited liability partnerships,* in which partners are not held personally liable for the malpractice of other partners in the firm.

3. *Professional corporation*—In a professional corporation (P.C.), two or more individuals jointly own the business as shareholders. The owner-shareholders of the corporation share the firm's profits and losses (as partners do) but are not personally liable for the firm's debts or obligations beyond the amount they invested in the P.C.

LAW OFFICE MANAGEMENT AND PERSONNEL

Each law firm has a unique system of management and lines of authority. Generally, the owners of the firm (partners, for example) oversee and manage all other employees. Law firm personnel include associate attorneys; law clerks; paralegals; administrative personnel, who are supervised by the legal administrator or the office manager; and support personnel, including receptionists, secretaries, file clerks, and others.

EMPLOYMENT POLICIES

Employment policies relate to compensation and employee benefits, performance evaluations, employment termination, and other rules of the workplace, such as office hours. Frequently (particularly in larger firms), the policies of the firm are spelled out in an employment manual or other writing. Paralegals must be sure to know their specific responsibilities. Most large firms have policies and procedures that apply to evaluation, promotion, and termination at the firm.

FILING PROCEDURES

Every law firm follows certain filing procedures. In larger firms, these procedures may be written down. In smaller firms, procedures may be more casual and based on habit or tradition.

1. *Client files*—Confidentiality is a major concern and a fundamental policy of every law firm. A breach of confidentiality by anyone in the law office can subject the firm to extensive legal liability. The requirement of confidentiality shapes, to a significant extent, filing procedures. A typical law firm has client files, work product files and reference materials, forms files, and personnel files.

   Proper file maintenance is crucial to a smoothly functioning firm. An efficient filing system helps to ensure that important documents will not be misplaced and will be available when needed. Filing procedures must also maximize client confidentiality and the safekeeping of documents.

2. *Work product files*—Law firms often keep copies of all research materials, support materials related to cases, and legal memoranda. Maintenance of backup files is a requirement.

3. *Form files*—Firms often use standard form files that may have been prepared internally or have been professionally prepared by a service.

LAW FIRMS AND FINANCIAL PROCEDURES

A major concern of any law firm is to have a clear policy on fee arrangements and efficient billing procedures so that each client is billed appropriately.

1. *Tiers of firms*—Top-level firms, which are generally full-service firms in major cities, generally have the highest billing rates, followed by major regional firms. Boutique firms and others fill the needs of different groups of clients.

2. *Fee arrangements*—Types of fee arrangements include fixed fees, hourly fees, and contingency fees. Clients who pay hourly fees are billed monthly for the time spent by attorneys and other legal personnel on the clients' cases or projects, as well as all costs incurred on behalf of the clients.

3. *Client trust accounts*—Law firms are required to place all funds received from a client into a special account called a client trust account. This is to ensure that the client's money remains separate from the firm's money. It is important that the funds held in the trust account be used only for expenses relating to the costs of serving that client's needs.

4. *Billing and timekeeping*—Firms require attorneys and paralegals to document how they use their time. Because the firm's income depends on the number of billable hours produced by employees, firms usually require attorneys and paralegals to generate a certain number of billable hours per year. Double billing presents a major ethical problem for law firms.

COMMUNICATIONS

Attorneys have a duty to keep their clients informed. Paralegals should be aware that this is a legal duty and that they play a significant role in meeting this duty. Sending billing statements to clients is one way to communicate; phone calls, letters, and e-mail messages are other ways to keep clients informed. Firms use a mix of traditional communications and new forms of social media to keep in touch with clients and to help generate new business. Firms need clear policies about communications within the firm and about how the firm presents itself to the outside world.

LAW OFFICE CULTURE AND POLITICS

Each office has its own culture, or personality, which is largely shaped by the attitudes of the firm's owners and the qualities they look for when hiring employees. Each firm also has a political infrastructure that is not apparent to outsiders. Office culture and politics make a great difference in terms of job satisfaction and comfort. Wise paralegals learn as soon as possible from co-workers or others about these aspects of the law office.

QUESTIONS FOR REVIEW

1. List and define the basic organizational structures of law firms discussed in the chapter. What is personal liability?

2. What is the difference between an associate and a partner? Are there attorneys in other roles in law firms? If so, what are their roles? Who supervises the work performed by paralegals?

3. What kinds of files do law firms maintain? What general procedures are typically followed in regard to client files?

4. List and define the different ways law firms bill their clients. What ethical obligations do attorneys have with respect to legal fees?

5. How do lawyers and legal assistants keep track of their time? What is the difference between billable and non-billable hours? What is a client trust account?

ETHICS QUESTIONS

1. Sam Martin, an attorney, receives a settlement check for a client's case. It is made out jointly to Sam and his client. Sam endorses the check and instructs his paralegal to deposit it into his law firm's bank account, instead of the client's trust account, because he wants to take out his fee before he gives the client his portion of the money. Can Sam do this? Why or why not? What should Sam's paralegal do?

2. James Johnson is a sole practitioner. His office is about an hour's drive from the federal district court at which he files many lawsuits. He used to talk on his cell phone to clients as he travelled the two hours to and from the courthouse. He would bill the client on whose behalf he was going to the courthouse for two hours and the clients with whom he talked on the phone for increments of the same two hours. When the American Bar Association issued its rule prohibiting double billing, he was concerned that the rule would drive him out of business due to the drop in income. Is what Johnson is doing ethical? Why or why not?

PRACTICE QUESTIONS AND ASSIGNMENTS

1. Using the material presented in the chapter on the organizational structures of law firms, identify the kind of law practices involved:

   a. Rosa Suefentes practices immigration law. She owns her legal practice, the building, and the office furniture. She leases some office equipment. Rosa employs one secretary and one paralegal.

   b. Mosabi Hamdei owns a general practice law firm with Hassam El-Khouri. They own equal interests in the firm, participate in the firm's management, and share in its profits and losses. Hamdei & El-Khouri also have three associates, six secretaries, and three paralegals who work for the firm.

   c. Ajay Singh, Arun Patel, and Chandra Jindal need to limit their personal liability resulting from a potential legal malpractice claim against their partnership, not all of which will be covered by insurance. They file paperwork with the state to convert to an entity that, in most states, protects innocent partners from debts and obligations arising from negligence, which is the basis for a legal malpractice claim.

2. Using the material in the chapter, identify the following law office personnel:

   a. LaToya works as a paralegal in a large law firm. After twelve years with the firm, she was promoted and now oversees paralegal staffing, assignments, and professional development.

   b. Ani was hired by the partners of a large law firm to manage the day-to-day operations of the firm.

   c. Alicia is an attorney who works as an employee of Marsh & Martin, a law firm with 250 attorneys. She is not on the partnership track.

   d. Jamal is a file clerk for Wright & Goodman.

   e. Michael is a lawyer. He owns O'Dowd & O'Dowd LLP with his sister, Jane.

   f. Kathy is an attorney working on a document-review project in a mass tort litigation case for the BigLaw law firm. Her job will end when the project is completed.

3. Using the material in the chapter on fee arrangements, identify the type of billing that is being used in each of the following examples:

a. The client is billed $200 per hour for a partner's time, $150 per hour for an associate attorney's time, and $125 per hour for a paralegal's time.

b. The attorney's fee is one-third of the amount that the attorney recovers for the client, either through a pretrial settlement or through a trial.

c. The attorney charges $250 to change the name of a client's business firm.

4. A law firm hired to represent a client in a paternity action withdrew from representation of the client while the case was pending, citing irreconcilable differences. In the retainer agreement the client had agreed to pay hourly fees of $475 for the senior attorney, $425 for the junior attorney, $275 for any other attorney in the firm, and $150 for paralegal and law-clerk time. At the time the attorneys withdrew from representation, the client's total bill was $39,561, which she refused to pay. The law firm sued to recover its fee.

a. What argument might the client make to get the fees reduced? Would it make a difference if the typical fee for a paternity case is usually less than $10,000?

b. What argument would the law firm make to support its lawsuit for collecting its fee?

5. A lawyer representing indigent defendants as a court-appointed attorney billed the county courts for more than 24 hours a day on three different days and more than 20 hours a day five other times. On other occasions, she billed between 14 and 19 hours a day. The attorney did not keep detailed records of the hours that she worked, so she often guessed at how much time she had spent on a case. Using the material in the chapter on ethics and client billing practices, explain what this attorney did wrong.

6. Jose Hernandez hires Maria Alvarez, an attorney with the law firm of Alvarez, Banderos & Sedillo, located at 1000 Canyon Road, Phoenix, Arizona, to represent him in a divorce. He agrees to pay attorney Alvarez at a rate of $350 per hour and to pay a paralegal $150 per hour. He also agrees to pay all costs and expenses, such as filing fees, expert-witness fees, court-reporter fees, and other fees incurred in the course of her representation. Using Exhibit 3.4, *A Sample Retainer Agreement*, on page 68, draft a retainer agreement between Jose Hernandez and Maria Alvarez.

GROUP PROJECT

In this project the group will research the use of social media by law firms and present its findings to class. Student one will research for what purpose law firms use social media and what the pros and cons of using social media are. Student two will research statistics on how many law firms use social media. Student three will research statistics on which social media sites law firms use and what the trends are among law firms for using various sites. Student four will summarize and compile the results of the research and will present the group's findings to the class.

INTERNET PROJECTS

1. Go to the American Bar Association Legal Technology Resource Center website at **www.americanbar.org/ groups/departments_offices/legal_technology_ resources.html**. Locate cloud-computing ethics opinions. Is there one from your state? If so, review it and write a one-paragraph summary of it in your own words. If not, do the same for an ethics opinion from another state that addresses storing client files in the cloud. Why is storing client information in the cloud a concern for law firms?

2. Find legal forms on the Internet by going to the following website: **www.legaldocs.com**. List the eight types of forms that are available. Which documents are offered at no charge? Choose five of the forms that are for sale and record their price. What do you see as the advantages and disadvantages of making legal documents available in this way?

3. Research time-and-billing software on the Internet by going to the following website: **www.sagetimeslips. com**. Click on *Overview* to read about the latest version of *Timeslips*. Click on *Features*. Is *Timeslips* limited to one type of billing arrangement or is it flexible? Can it create reports? What else can it do? Select "Free Trial" from the Products and Services menu if you want to try out the program for yourself.

CHAPTER 4

Ethics and Professional Responsibility

CHAPTER OBJECTIVES

After completing this chapter, you will know:

• Why and how legal professionals are regulated.

• Some important ethical rules governing the
conduct of attorneys.

• How the rules governing attorneys affect paralegal
practice.

• The kinds of activities that paralegals are and are
not legally permitted to perform.

• Some of the pros and cons of regulation, including
the debate over paralegal licensing.

Introduction

Paralegals preparing for a career in today's legal arena have a variety of career options. Regardless of which career path you follow, you should have a firm grasp of your state's ethical rules governing the legal profession. When you work under the supervision of an attorney, you and the attorney are team members. You work together on behalf of clients and share in the ethical and legal responsibilities arising as a result of the attorney-client relationship.

In preparing to be a paralegal, you must know what these responsibilities are, why they exist, and how they affect you. The first part of this chapter is devoted to the regulation of attorneys because the ethical duties imposed on attorneys affect paralegals as well. If a paralegal violates a rule governing attorneys, that may result in serious consequences for the client, for the attorney, and for the paralegal. Attorneys are subject to direct regulation by the state.

Paralegals are subject to less regulation, although states may impose more rules if believed desirable. Paralegals are regulated indirectly both by attorney ethical codes and by state laws that prohibit nonlawyers from practicing law. As the paralegal profession develops, professional paralegal organizations, the American Bar Association, and state bar associations continue to issue guidelines that serve to impact paralegals.

The Regulation of Attorneys

Regulate can be defined as "to control or direct in agreement with a rule." To a significant extent, attorneys play critical roles in establishing most of the rules that govern their profession. One of the hallmarks of a profession is the establishment of minimum standards and levels of competence for its members. The accounting profession, for example, has established such standards, as have physicians, engineers, and members of other professions.

Attorneys are also regulated by the state, because the rules of behavior established by the legal profession are adopted and enforced by state authorities. First, by establishing educational and licensing requirements, state authorities ensure that anyone practicing law should be competent. Second, by defining specific ethical requirements for attorneys, the states protect the public against unethical attorney behavior that may affect clients' welfare. Because the rules limiting who can practice law are mostly written and enforced by lawyers, they also serve to assist lawyers by limiting competition from other groups, such as paralegals. We will discuss these requirements and rules shortly. Before we do, however, let's look at how these rules are created and enforced.

Who Are the Regulators?

Key participants that determine what rules govern attorneys and the practice of law, as well as how these rules should be enforced, are bar associations, state supreme courts, state legislatures, and, in some cases, the United States Supreme Court. Procedures for regulating attorneys vary, of course, from state to state. We next look at some of the key regulators.

Bar Associations

Lawyers determine the requirements for entering the legal profession and the rules of conduct practicing attorneys will follow. Traditionally, lawyers have joined together in professional groups (bar associations) at the local, state, and national levels to discuss issues affecting the legal profession and to decide on standards of professional conduct.

In all states, to be admitted to practice, a prospective attorney must pass the state bar examination. Although membership in local and national bar associations is voluntary, membership in the state bar association (called a "unified bar") is mandatory in many states. Many lawyers are also members of the American Bar Association (ABA), the voluntary national bar association discussed in Chapter 1. As you will see, the ABA plays a key role by proposing model (uniform) codes, or rules of conduct, for adoption by the states.

State Supreme Courts

Typically, the state's highest court, often called the state supreme court, is the ultimate regulatory authority in a state. That court decides what conditions (such as licensing requirements, discussed below) must be met before an attorney can practice law within the state and when that privilege will be suspended or revoked. In most states, the state supreme court works with the state bar association. For example, the association may recommend rules and requirements to the court. If the court agrees, it can order the rules to become state law. Under the authority of the courts, state bar associations often handle regulatory functions, including disciplinary proceedings against attorneys who are accused of failing to comply with professional requirements.

State Legislatures

State legislatures regulate the legal profession by passing laws affecting attorneys—such as statutes prohibiting the unauthorized practice of law and statutes concerning ethical conduct of licensed attorneys.

The United States Supreme Court

Occasionally, the United States Supreme Court decides issues relating to attorney conduct. At one time state ethical codes, or rules governing attorney conduct, prohibited lawyers from advertising their services to the public. Restrictions on advertising were determined by the United States Supreme Court to be an unconstitutional limitation on attorneys' rights to free speech. Although there are still restrictions on what attorneys can say in advertisements, lawyer ads on television, billboards, radio, and the Internet are common.

Licensing Requirements

The licensing of attorneys, which gives them the right to practice law, is accomplished at the state level. Each state has different requirements that individuals must meet before they are allowed to practice law and give legal advice.

Basic Requirements

Generally, however, there are three basic requirements:

1. In most states, prospective attorneys must have a bachelor's degree from a university or college and must have graduated from an accredited law school (in many states, the school must be accredited by the ABA), which requires an additional three years of study.

2. A prospective attorney must pass a state bar examination—a rigorous examination that tests the candidate's knowledge of the law. The examination covers both state law (law applicable to the particular state in which the attorney is taking the exam and wishes to practice) and multistate law (law applicable in most states, including federal law). In addition, most states require prospective lawyers to pass the Multistate Professional Responsibility Exam on ethics rules.

3. The candidate must pass an extensive personal background investigation to verify that he or she is a responsible individual and qualifies to engage in an ethical profession. An illegal act committed by the candidate in the past might disqualify the person from being permitted to practice law. Only when these requirements have been met can a person be admitted to the state bar and

licensing
A government's official act of granting permission to an individual, such as an attorney, to do something that would be illegal in the absence of such permission.

practice law in the state. In addition, each federal court requires admission to practice before an attorney can appear in a case filed there. This generally requires a sponsor and an application, but no test.

Licensing and UPL

unauthorized practice of law (UPL)
The performance of actions defined by a legal authority, such as a state legislature, as constituting the "practice of law" without authorization to do so.

Licensing requirements for attorneys are part of a long history of restrictions on entry into the legal profession. Beginning in the 1850s, restrictions on who could (or could not) practice law were put in place by state statutes prohibiting the unauthorized practice of law (UPL). Court decisions relating to unauthorized legal practice also date to this period. By the 1930s, almost all states had legislation prohibiting anyone but licensed attorneys from practicing law. Many of the regulatory issues facing the legal profession—and particularly paralegals—are directly related to these UPL statutes.

Ethical Codes and Rules

The legal profession is also regulated through ethical codes and rules adopted by each state—in most states, by the state supreme court. These codes of professional conduct evolved over time. A major step toward ethical regulation was taken in 1908, when the ABA approved the *Canons of Ethics*, which consisted of ethical principles. The states adopted these canons as law. (Canons are generally accepted principles.)

Today's state ethical codes are based, for the most part, on later revisions of the ABA canons: the *Model Code of Professional Responsibility* (published in 1969) and the *Model Rules of Professional Conduct* (first published in 1983 to replace the *Model Code* and revised many times since then). Although most states have adopted laws based on the *Model Rules*, the *Model Code* is still in effect in some states. New York still uses the *Model Code*, for example, while California and Maine have developed their own rules. You should become familiar with rules that are in effect in your state.

The Model Code of Professional Responsibility

The ABA *Model Code of Professional Responsibility*, often referred to simply as the *Model Code*, consists of nine canons. In the *Model Code*, each canon is followed by sections entitled "Ethical Considerations" (ECs) and "Disciplinary Rules" (DRs). The ethical considerations are "aspirational" in character—that is, they suggest ideal conduct, not necessarily behavior that is required by law. For example, Canon 6 ("A lawyer should represent a client competently") is followed by EC 6-1, which states (in part) that a lawyer "should strive to become and remain proficient in his practice." In contrast, disciplinary rules are mandatory in character—an attorney may be subject to disciplinary action for breaking a rule. DR 6-101 (which follows Canon 6) states that a lawyer "shall not . . . neglect a legal matter entrusted to him."

The Model Rules of Professional Conduct

The 1983 revision of the ABA *Model Code*—referred to as the *Model Rules of Professional Conduct* or, more simply, as the *Model Rules*—represented a major revision of the code. The *Model Rules* replaced the canons, ethical considerations, and disciplinary rules of the *Model Code* with a set of rules organized under eight general headings. Each rule is followed by comments shedding light on the rule's application and how the rule compares with the *Model Code*'s treatment of the same issue.

Because the 1983 *Model Rules* serve as models for the ethical codes of most states, we use the 1983 rules as the basis for our discussion. It is important to note, however, that the ABA's ethics commission periodically updates and revises the *Model Rules* as necessary in light of the realities of modern law practice. The ABA's ethics commission has revised the *Model Rules* to address new ethical concerns raised by technological developments (such as client confidentiality using e-mail). To view the ABA *Model Rules of Professional Conduct*, go to the American Bar Association's website.

Sanctions for Violations

Attorneys who violate the rules governing professional conduct are subject to disciplinary proceedings brought by the state bar association, state supreme court, or state legislature—depending on the state's regulatory scheme. In most states, unethical attorney actions are reported by clients, legal professionals, or others to the ethics committee of the state bar association, which is obligated to investigate each complaint. For serious violations, the state bar association or the court initiates disciplinary proceedings against the attorney.

Formal Sanctions

Sanctions imposed for violations range from a reprimand (a formal "scolding" of the attorney—the mildest sanction but one that can seriously damage an attorney's reputation and practice), to suspension (a more serious sanction in which the attorney is prohibited from practicing law in the state for a given period of time, such as one month or one year), to disbarment (revocation of the attorney's license to practice law in the state—the most serious sanction).

Civil Liability

In addition to these sanctions, attorneys may be subject to civil liability for negligence. As will be discussed in Chapter 14, *negligence* (called malpractice when committed by a professional, such as an attorney) is a tort (a wrongful act) that is committed when an individual fails to perform a legally recognized duty. Tort law allows one who is injured by another's wrongful or careless act to bring a civil lawsuit against the wrongdoer for damages (compensation in the form of money). A client may bring a lawsuit against an attorney if the client has suffered harm because of the attorney's failure to perform a legal duty.

If a paralegal's breach of a professional duty causes a client to suffer substantial harm, the client may sue not only the attorney but also the paralegal. Although law firms' liability insurance policies typically cover paralegals as well as attorneys, these policies do not cover paralegals working on a contract (freelance) basis. Just one lawsuit could ruin a freelance paralegal financially—as well as destroy that paralegal's reputation in the legal community. Hence, obtaining liability insurance is important for freelance paralegals as well as for independent paralegals.

Attorneys and paralegals are also subject to potential criminal liability under federal and state criminal statutes prohibiting fraud, theft, and other crimes.

Attorney Ethics and Paralegal Practice

Because the *Model Rules of Professional Conduct* guide most state codes, the rules discussed in this section are drawn from the *Model Rules*. Keep in mind, though, that your own state's code of conduct is the governing authority on attorney conduct in your state.

As a paralegal, one of your foremost professional responsibilities is to carefully follow the rules in your state's ethical code. You will want to obtain a copy of your state's ethical code and be familiar with its contents. A good practice is to keep the code in your office. It is also helpful to develop a relationship with a trusted mentor at your firm for advice on such issues.

Professional duties—and the possibility of violating them—are involved in almost every task you will perform as a paralegal. Even if you memorize every rule governing the legal profession, you can still violate a rule unintentionally (few people breach professional duties intentionally). To minimize the chances that you violate a rule, you need to know not only what the rules are but also how they apply to the day-to-day realities of your job. In general, avoiding financial dealings and social relationships with clients helps you avoid violating ethical obligations.

reprimand
A disciplinary sanction in which an attorney is rebuked for misbehavior. Although a reprimand is the mildest sanction for attorney misconduct, it is serious and may significantly damage the attorney's reputation in the legal community.

suspension
A serious disciplinary sanction in which an attorney who has violated an ethical rule or a law is prohibited from practicing law in the state for a specified or an indefinite period of time.

disbarment
A severe disciplinary sanction in which an attorney's license to practice law in the state is revoked because of unethical or illegal conduct.

malpractice
Professional misconduct or negligence—the failure to exercise due care—on the part of a professional, such as an attorney or a physician.

damages
Money awarded as a remedy for a civil wrong, such as a breach of contract or a tort (wrongful act).

A paralegal discusses a potential conflict of interest with her supervising attorney. Attorneys and paralegals must be careful to avoid violating the ethical rules of the legal profession, because violations of the rules can have serious professional and financial consequences. What are some ways that you can avoid violating your state's code of ethical conduct?

© Lisa S./www.Shutterstock.com.

The rules relating to competence, confidentiality, and conflict of interest deserve special attention here because they pose particularly difficult ethical problems for paralegals. Other important rules that affect paralegal performance—including the duty to charge reasonable fees, the duty to protect clients' property, and the duty to keep the client reasonably informed—will be discussed elsewhere in this text as they relate to special topics.

The Duty of Competence

Rule 1.1 of the *Model Rules* concerns a fundamental obligation of attorneys—the duty of competence. The Bar Association focuses on the requirement that attorneys provide able representation to their clients. Competency requires knowledge of the law, careful research to ensure being up-to-date, and proper preparation for representation. Most legal representation occurs out of court but requires the same knowledgeable approach. A **breach** (failing to perform) of this duty may subject attorneys to one or more of the sanctions discussed earlier. As a paralegal, you share in this duty when you work on an attorney's behalf.

How the Duty of Competence Can Be Breached

Most breaches of the duty of competence are not intentional. Often, breaches of the duty of competence have to do with inadequate research, missed deadlines, and errors in legal documents filed with the court.

breach
To violate a legal duty by an act or a failure to act.

INADEQUATE RESEARCH. Paralegals do both legal and factual research for attorneys. Depending on the situation, an attorney's first step after meeting with a new client is often to have a paralegal research the facts involved, such as who did what to whom, when, where, and how. If the paralegal fails to discover a relevant fact and the attorney then relies on the paralegal's research in advising the client, the result could be a breach of the duty of competence.

Similarly, a paralegal conducting legal research might breach the duty of competence by failing to find or report a court decision that controls the outcome of a client's case. For example, suppose that a paralegal performs initial research into the law surrounding a particular dispute and reports the findings to the attorney. Then, while the paralegal is working on unrelated cases over the next few months, a state appeals court rules on a case with issues very similar to those involved in the client's dispute. If the paralegal or the attorney does not go back and confirm that the initial research results are still accurate, a ruling that would influence the client's case could be overlooked. This would breach the attorney's duty of competence to the client.

Although attorneys are ultimately responsible for competent representation, paralegals play an important role in providing accurate information to their attorneys. If you are ever unsure of the accuracy of your research results, make sure to let the attorney know of your doubts. Also, keep good notes recording each step you took in conducting research so that you know what still needs to be done. These measures help prevent accidental breaches of the duty of competence.

MISSED DEADLINES. Paralegals often work on several cases at once. Keeping track of every deadline in every case can be challenging. Organization is the key to making sure that all deadlines are met. All dates relating to actions and events for every case or client should be entered on a calendar. Firms typically use computerized calendaring and "tickler" (reminder) systems.

Besides making sure that all deadlines are entered into the appropriate systems, you should also have your own personal calendar for tracking dates that are relevant to the cases on which you are working—and then make sure that you consistently use it. Also, check frequently with your attorney about deadlines.

ERRORS IN DOCUMENTS. Breaches of the duty of competence can involve errors in documents. Incorrect information might be included (or crucial information omitted) in a legal document to be filed with the court. If the attorney fails to notice the error before signing the document, and the document is delivered to the court, a breach of the duty of competence has occurred. Depending on its effect, this breach may expose the attorney to liability for negligence. To prevent these kinds of violations, be especially careful in drafting and proofreading documents.

Generally, if you are ever unsure about what to include in a document, when it must be completed or filed with the court, how extensively you should research a legal issue, or any other aspect of an assignment, ask your supervising attorney for clarification. Make sure that your work is adequately overseen by an attorney to reduce the chances that it contains costly errors. Whether communicating by e-mail or in person, clear communication is critical, as the *In the Office* feature on the following page addresses.

Attorney's Duty to Supervise

Rule 5.3 of the *Model Rules* defines the responsibilities of attorneys to nonlawyer assistants. Attorneys must supervise their assistants to ensure that they behave in accord with the standards of the profession. The rule also specifies the circumstances under which a lawyer is held responsible for conduct by a nonlawyer that violates an attorney's duty. The lawyer is responsible, for example, if she orders improper conduct or ratifies (approves of) it. Lawyers who have managerial authority in a law firm or have supervisory authority over a nonlawyer can also be held responsible for the nonlawyer's unethical conduct if they knew about it and failed to take action to prevent it.

This rule applies not only to lawyers who work in private law firms but also to lawyers in corporate legal departments, government agencies, and elsewhere. In addition, in the statements outlining attorneys' responsibilities toward nonlawyer employees in this area, the ABA commission changed the word *should* to *must*. Attorneys *must* both instruct and supervise nonlawyer employees concerning appropriate ethical conduct as they can be held personally responsible for the ethical violations of their subordinates.

Inadequate Supervision

Because attorneys are legally responsible for their assistants' work, it may seem logical to assume that attorneys will take time to direct that work carefully. In fact, paralegals may find it difficult to ensure that their work is adequately supervised. Most attorneys and paralegals are very busy. Making sure that all paralegals' tasks are properly overseen can be time consuming. At the same time, attorneys—especially if they know their paralegals are competent—often do not take the time to read every document the paralegals draft. Nonetheless, as a paralegal, you have a duty to assist your supervising attorney in fulfilling his or her ethical obligations, including the obligation to supervise your work.

If you ever believe that your attorney is not adequately supervising your work, there are several things you can do:

- Improve communications with the attorney—generally, the more you initiate communication with your supervising attorney, the more likely the attorney will take an active role in directing your activities.

- Ask the attorney for feedback on your work. Sometimes, it helps to place reminders on your calendar to discuss particular issues or questions with the attorney. When the opportunity to talk arises, these issues or questions will be fresh in your mind.

- Attach a note to a document that you have prepared for the attorney, requesting him or her to review the document (or revised sections of the document) carefully before signing it.

Ensuring proper supervision to protect yourself is highlighted in the *Developing Paralegal Skills* feature on the facing page.

IN THE OFFICE

AM I CLEAR?

E-mail is a common form of communication, but it causes problems when not used properly. E-mails are the equivalent of letters or memos. When we write a letter or a memo, we usually read it more than once and think carefully about what we're saying. Too many times, we treat e-mails as if they were oral communications—that is, we write in a chatty and imprecise manner. Before sending any e-mail to a client, print it, read it, be sure it is addressed to the right party, and edit it. Remember that the matter you're discussing is important to the client. Your communication should be professional and clear. You should always follow office e-mail procedures carefully.

If your firm uses social media, you should also use discretion when you create such communications. You are often judged on how carefully you communicate. Keep in mind that social media posts have turned up in lawsuits over office behavior. For example, posts on Facebook or Twitter have crossed the line into sexual harassment. Keep your posts professional, as they represent both you and the firm.

Confidentiality of Information

Rule 1.6 of the *Model Rules* concerns attorney-client confidentiality. This rule is one of the oldest and most important rules of the legal profession. It would be difficult for a lawyer to properly represent a client without such a rule. A client must be able to confide in the attorney so that the attorney can best represent the client's interest. Because confidentiality is one of the easiest rules to violate, a thorough understanding of the rule is essential.

The general rule of confidentiality is that all information relating to representation of a client must be kept confidential. There are exceptions to the rule, which we discuss shortly.

The rule simply states that a lawyer may not reveal "information relating to representation of a client."

EXAMPLE 4.1 You know that a client is the president of a local company. Do you have to keep that information confidential? Suppose you tell a friend, "Mr. X is the president of XYZ Corporation." The fact that X is president is widely known. But in saying that, people are likely to presume that X is a client of your firm. Mr. X may not want it known that he is talking to a lawyer. People who learn that Mr. X has been at the law firm may think "something is up," which is likely true. Confidence has been breached.

Consider another example. Suppose that one evening you told your spouse that you had met Mr. X that day. Your spouse might reasonably assume that your firm was handling some legal matter involving Mr. X and might repeat that to other people.

DEVELOPING PARALEGAL SKILLS

ADEQUATE SUPERVISION

Michael's supervising attorney, Muriel, asks him to prepare two complaints (documents filed with the court to initiate a lawsuit) and gives him specific information needed for the two different cases. Muriel is scheduled to attend a deposition (a pretrial procedure in which testimony is given under oath) in another matter this afternoon and asked Michael to finish the complaints and file them with the court today. Muriel tells Michael to use a complaint from a previous client's case as a model for creating the new complaints, replacing that client's information as necessary.

Michael finishes the work at 3:00 P.M. while Muriel is attending the deposition in the conference room. Michael needs to file the complaints at the courthouse by 5:00 P.M., but, knowing the adequate supervision rule, does not want to file the documents before Muriel has reviewed them. He decides that he must interrupt the deposition so that Muriel can look over the complaints before they

are filed with the court. He flags a few passages that he is unsure about and proceeds into the conference room. Muriel asks the opposing counsel to take a short break so she can step out of the room to review the documents.

TIPS FOR OBTAINING ADEQUATE SUPERVISION

- Always ask your supervising attorney to review your work.
- Use notes or ticklers as reminders to ask for a review.
- Make the review as convenient as possible for your supervising attorney and mark anything that needs particular attention.
- Discuss any ethical concerns with the attorney.
- Be persistent.
- Complete your work in a timely fashion so the attorney can review it.

Because it may be difficult to decide what information is or is not confidential, a good rule of thumb is to regard all information about a client or a client's case as confidential.

Exceptions to the Confidentiality Rule

Rule 1.6, Confidentiality of Information, provides for certain exceptions to the confidentiality rule, each of which we look at here.

CLIENT GIVES INFORMED CONSENT TO THE DISCLOSURE.
The rule indicates that an attorney can reveal confidential information if the client gives informed consent to the disclosure. The attorney must fully explain the risks and alternatives involved in the disclosure for consent to be informed.

> **EXAMPLE 4.2** Suppose an attorney is drawing up a will for a client. The client is leaving certain property to her son and not leaving a share of that property to her daughter. The daughter calls and wants to know how her mother's will reads. The attorney cannot divulge this confidential information because the client has not consented.

In this instance the attorney may explain to the client that if her daughter does not learn about the provisions of the will until after her mother's death, it is more likely that she will contest it in court. After the attorney and client discuss the alternatives, the client can give informed consent to the attorney to disclose information to her daughter.

IMPLIEDLY AUTHORIZED DISCLOSURES.
The ABA rules allow attorneys to make disclosures of information that are presumed necessary to represent clients. This exception is clearly necessary. Legal representation of clients necessarily involves attorneys' assistants who must have access to the confidential information to do their jobs. If a paralegal is working on the client's case he must know what the client told the attorney about the legal matter and must have access to information in the client's file concerning the case.

DISCLOSURES TO PREVENT HARM.
The *Model Rules* recognize that there are certain circumstances in which an attorney should be allowed to disclose confidential information when it is necessary to prevent harm to persons or property. Rule 1.6 specifically lists four exceptions to the confidentiality rule for this purpose:

1. An attorney is allowed to reveal a client's information to prevent possible death or substantial bodily harm.

   > **EXAMPLE 4.3** A client confides to his attorney that he assaulted and nearly killed several people recently. The attorney is not allowed to disclose this information. If that client tells the attorney that he is going to attack a specific person in the future, however, the attorney can disclose this information to prevent likely bodily harm to the person.

   This is addressed further in the *Developing Paralegal Skills* feature on the facing page.

2. In certain situations, an attorney can disclose confidential information to prevent a client from committing a crime or fraud. The crime or fraud must be reasonably certain to result in significant injury to the financial interests or property of another. Also, the client must have used or be using the attorney's services to perpetrate the crime or fraud. If both these conditions are present, then the attorney can disclose information to the extent necessary to enable the affected person to contact the appropriate authorities.

3. If a client used the attorney to help commit a crime or fraud, and the crime or fraud will likely cause injury to the financial interests or property of another, the attorney can disclose confidential information to the extent necessary to prevent or reduce that injury.

DEVELOPING PARALEGAL SKILLS

WHAT IF YOU LEARN YOUR CLIENT IS PLANNING TO COMMIT A CRIME?

Communications between a client and his or her attorney, including those with the attorney's paralegal, are usually covered by the attorney-client privilege. Privileged statements may not be disclosed without the client's consent. When the client makes statements that suggest he or she is going to commit a crime, however, the privilege does not apply.

For example, in one criminal case, the defendant told his lawyer that he was going to attempt to bribe one or more witnesses against him and that if he was unable to do so, he would "whack" the witnesses.[a] Later the defendant also threatened the lawyer. The lawyer reported these threats to the district attorney and withdrew as the

defendant's counsel. The defendant's new lawyer tried to have the first lawyer's testimony about the threats excluded, but failed. Because the defendant had threatened a criminal act (assaulting the witnesses and lawyer) that could involve bodily harm or death, the California appeals court held that privilege did not apply.

State rules on privilege differ, and you should make sure that you understand the range of crimes covered by your state's laws. All states exempt threats of death or serious injury, and such statements should be reported immediately. In addition, some states require reporting of certain criminal acts.

a. *People v. Dang*, 93 Cal.App.4th 1293, 113 Cal.Rptr.2d 763 (2001).

---

4. An attorney can also disclose confidential information to establish a defense to a criminal charge in a controversy between the attorney and the client based on conduct involving the client. Similarly, the attorney may respond to allegations in proceedings regarding the attorney's representation of the client.

DISCLOSURES TO ENSURE COMPLIANCE WITH *MODEL RULES*. If a lawyer is unsure what is required to comply with the *Model Rules of Professional Conduct* in a particular situation, the lawyer can seek legal advice from another lawyer without violating confidentiality.

EXAMPLE 4.4 An attorney who is representing a corporation becomes suspicious that the corporation is engaged in fraud. The attorney is not sure what her professional responsibilities are in that particular situation, so she can seek confidential legal advice to assist her in complying with the *Model Rules*.

DEFENDING AGAINST A CLIENT'S LEGAL ACTION. An attorney may also disclose confidential information if the information is necessary to establish a defense in an action brought by a client against the attorney.

EXAMPLE 4.5 A client sues his attorney for malpractice due to litigation that did not go well. The lawyer might need to reveal confidential information to prove that he was not negligent.

Note, though, that the attorney is permitted to disclose confidential information only to the extent that it is essential to defend the lawsuit.

DISCLOSURES TO COMPLY WITH COURT ORDER OR OTHER LAW. An attorney may also reveal information relating to the representation of a client if ordered to do so by a court or other governmental entity.

EXAMPLE 4.6 An attorney representing a client in a divorce case knows the client is hiding valuable assets from his wife. In that situation, a court could require the attorney to reveal confidential information from the client related to the hidden assets. The attorney should first attempt to persuade the client to disclose the assets. The attorney can reveal as much information as is reasonable to satisfy the needs of the court or other governmental entity.

Violations of the Confidentiality Rule

Naturally, paralegals are tempted to discuss work with family members, co-workers, and friends. As a paralegal, a great temptation you will face is the desire to discuss an interesting case with someone you know.

You can deal with this temptation in two ways: you can decide never to discuss anything concerning legal matters at work, or you can limit your discussion to issues and comments that will not reveal the identity of clients. The latter approach is more realistic for most people, but it requires great care. Something you say may reveal a client's identity, even though you are not aware of it. (See the *Ethics Watch* feature on the facing page.) Developing a reputation for being discreet will enhance your career by encouraging attorneys and clients to confide in you.

CONVERSATIONS OVERHEARD BY OTHERS.　Violations of the confidentiality rule can happen by oversight.

EXAMPLE 4.7 Suppose that you and a secretary in your office are working on the same case and continue, as you walk to the elevator, a conversation about the case. In the hall or on the elevator, your conversation could be overheard, and the confidential information revealed could have an adverse effect on your client's interests.

It is important to avoid the possibility of accidentally revealing confidential information. Therefore, never discuss confidential information when you are in common areas.

ELECTRONIC COMMUNICATIONS AND CONFIDENTIALITY.　**W**henever you talk to or about a client on the telephone, make sure that your conversation will not be overheard by a third party. You may be sitting in your private office, but if your door is open, someone may overhear the conversation. Even employees of the firm should not hear information about cases they are not working on.

Paralegals should take special care when using cell phones. Although conversations on cell phones are difficult to intercept, there is still a security risk. No doubt you have overheard other people talking on their phones as if other people could not hear. Some violations of confidentiality are low-tech, such as talking on the phone in the open, while others are more sophisticated. The *Featured Contributor* on pages 98 and 99 provides more details about electronic security issues.

OTHER WAYS OF VIOLATING THE CONFIDENTIALITY RULE.　There are many other ways in which you can reveal confidential information without intending to do so. A file or document sitting on your desk, if observed by a third party, may reveal the identity of a client or enough information to suggest the client's identity. A computer screen, if visible to those passing by your desk, could convey information to someone not authorized to know that information. You might be speaking to an expert witness about rescheduling a meeting and accidentally let something about the case slip out.

Alternatively, you might be friendly with a paralegal at an opposing attorney's office because the two attorneys have worked on many cases together. You are on the phone trying to work out a date for an important meeting. This paralegal suggests a date, and you tell her that the attorney for whom you work is scheduled to be in court on a specific client's case that day. If you name the client, or indicate that the attorney will be

third party
A person or entity not directly involved in an agreement (such as a contract), legal proceeding (such as a lawsuit), or relationship (such as an attorney-client relationship).

ETHICS WATCH

SOCIAL EVENTS AND CONFIDENTIALITY

You are at a party with some other paralegals. You tell a paralegal whom you know well of some startling news—that a client of your firm, a prominent city official, is being investigated for drug dealing. Although your friend promises to keep this information strictly confidential, she nonetheless tells her husband, who tells a coworker, who tells a friend, and so on. Soon, the news is in the open and the resulting media coverage harms the official's reputation in the community.

Revealing the juicy gossip breached your obligation to the client. If it can be proved that the harm is the result of your breach of the duty of confidentiality, the official could sue you and the attorney and the firm for whom you work for damages.

In this situation, you would have violated the NFPA *Model Code of Ethics and Professional Responsibility*, Section 1.5(f), which states: "A paralegal shall not engage in any indiscreet communications concerning clients." This behavior would also have violated the ABA *Model Guidelines for the Utilization of Paralegal Services*, Guideline 6: "Attorneys may utilize paralegals, but the attorneys must take proper steps to be sure that client confidentiality is protected." Finally, you would have violated the NALA *Code of Ethics and Professional Responsibility*, Canon 7: "A paralegal must protect the confidences of a client."

arguing a particular type of motion in the case, you may breach the duty of confidentiality. As the *Technology and Today's Paralegal* feature on page 100 emphasizes, there are many aspects to confidentiality.

Confidentiality and the Attorney-Client Privilege

All information relating to a client's representation is considered confidential information. Some confidential information also qualifies as privileged information, or information subject to the attorney-client privilege.

The attorney-client privilege can be vitally important during litigation. As you will read in Chapter 10, prior to a trial each attorney is permitted to obtain information relating to the case from the opposing attorney and other persons, such as witnesses. This means that attorneys must exchange certain information about their clients. An attorney need not provide privileged information, however—unless the client consents to the disclosure or a court orders it. Similarly, if an attorney is called to the witness stand during a trial, the attorney may not disclose privileged information unless the court orders it.

What Kind of Information Is Privileged?

State statutes and court cases define what constitutes privileged information. Generally, any communications concerning a client's legal rights or problems fall under the attorney-client privilege.

attorney-client privilege
A rule of evidence requiring that confidential communications between a client and his or her attorney (relating to their professional relationship) be kept confidential, unless the client consents to disclosure.

FEATURED CONTRIBUTOR

SECURING CLIENT INFORMATION IN THE DIGITAL AGE

Anita Whitby

BIOGRAPHICAL NOTE

Anita Whitby is a business law attorney and Park University faculty member. She has extensive experience as a course developer and teacher of legal studies and business law courses. Ms. Whitby is also a textbook reviewer for Cengage Learning and serves on the advisory board for the series known as *Annual Editions: Business Ethics*. Her current research interests include data privacy ethics, intellectual property, and immersive online learning.

The Digital Age has ushered in an array of electronic devices and technology to help streamline law offices. However, the use of such electronic devices and technology presents serious ethical issues. The following best practices will help paralegals avoid common pitfalls associated with the use of popular devices and technology.

> " ... the use of ... electronic devices ... presents serious ethical issues."

E-MAIL ENCRYPTION

When the topic of e-mail security comes up, we often think about it in terms of hackers attacking a computer network. However, it is the act of sending unsecured e-mail communication that is the main source of client data breaches. Communicating with clients via e-mail may seem harmless, but it must be done with extra precaution. Whether you are using a laptop or smartphone, be sure to use encryption software for client communication. Encryption ensures that client informa-

tion is protected. Because the communication cannot be "unlocked" without a "key," misdirected communication is not in danger of being disclosed to a third party.

CLIENT WORKPLACE E-MAIL & CONFIDENTIALITY

What if a client prefers to communicate via e-mail? The American Bar Association recently issued an ethics opinion regarding the attorney's duty to caution clients about communicating sensitive information via workplace e-mail. A prime example is the client who communicates with the law firm through a workplace computer. In this situation, the client does not have an expectation of privacy because the employer's e-mail system is being used. A paralegal should notify the supervising attorney when there is a potential issue about the manner in which a client is communicating sensitive information to the firm.

EXAMPLE 4.8 Suppose that an attorney's client is a criminal defendant. The client tells the attorney that she was near the crime site at the time of the crime, but to her knowledge, no one saw her. This is privileged information that the attorney may disclose only with the client's consent or on a court's order to do so.

work product
An attorney's mental impressions, conclusions, and legal theories regarding a case being prepared on behalf of a client. Work product normally is regarded as privileged information.

WORK PRODUCT. Certain materials relating to an attorney's preparation of a client's case for trial are protected as privileged information under the work product doctrine. Usually, information concerning an attorney's legal strategy for conducting a case is classified as work product and, as such, may be subject to the attorney-client privilege. Legal strategy includes the legal theories that the attorney plans to use in support of the client's claim and how the attorney interprets the evidence relating to the claim.

E-MAIL "RECALL"

Security breaches can result from something as simple as sending an e-mail to the wrong recipient. The e-mail "recall" feature can be used, but the "recall" feature does not work for e-mails that have already been opened. In addition, the recall feature does not always function properly due to firewalls and other network settings. Therefore, a paralegal must be diligent in verifying the correct recipients before e-mail communications are sent. You can opt to use e-mail software that delays outgoing communication for a short period of time before it is sent. That allows extra time to address issues that may arise.

METADATA

Because documents contain metadata, a paralegal must be certain that sensitive information has been properly redacted. Saving a document in PDF format does not "scrub" it of revisions that may have been made. Also, if you use an older version of Adobe software, you may mistakenly believe that it is sufficient to use the markup feature to "strike out" sensitive data. That works when the document is in print form. However, the underlying data still exists in electronic versions of the document and can be readily accessed. Therefore, be sure that electronic documents have been "scrubbed" of metadata. Newer versions of Adobe software allow users to highlight the material and then apply redactions to the document. You can be certain that a document is free of metadata by simply scanning a hard copy of the document and then using that "clean" version of the electronic document for dissemination.

WI-FI HOTSPOTS & WIRELESS PHONES

An often overlooked security danger involves the use of wireless devices to transmit e-mails, texts, and other communication via public Wi-Fi. These networks are unsecured. They should not be used to communicate confidential information. Use a secure mobile hotspot instead. It allows multiple Wi-Fi devices to connect to a secured mobile broadband network.

Wireless phone communication is also of concern because, like public Wi-Fi, it is not always secure. Third parties can use scanners to intercept cell phone calls. Many clients are unaware of the risks or have to be reminded of the potential for an unintended disclosure of their confidential information.

ENCRYPTION, BIOMETRIC TECHNOLOGY & REMOTE WIPES

Smartphones and laptops contain a treasure trove of information, so they must be ecrypted and password protected. Many users employ biometric technology (fingerprint authentication) as an added layer of security. Although biometric technology isn't 100 percent foolproof, many still consider it to be a viable option. With the adoption of "bring your own device" (BYOD) policies, law firms also secure data by programming security software to overwrite files remotely. This is especially helpful for lost or stolen devices because the "remote wipe" erases sensitive data completely.

> ... many clients are unaware of the risks ..."

SOCIAL MEDIA

Social media applications are an ever-increasing source of data breaches because of how quickly malware and viruses can spread through social networks. Avoid clicking on links from dubious sources and never download a third-party application without verifying its source. Use a passphrase instead of a simple password for social media accounts. Create a unique, 15-character passphrase that includes uppercase and lowercase letters, along with symbols and numbers. Update your passphrase often. Last, but not least, avoid the temptation to share work details online.

Certain evidence gathered by the attorney to support the client's claim, however, such as financial statements relating to the client's business firm, would probably not be classified as work product.

CAUTION ADVISED. Because it is often difficult to tell what types of information (including work product) qualify as privileged, paralegals should consult with their supervising attorneys whenever issues arise that may require that such a distinction be made. It is important to note that like any other confidential information relating to a client's case, privileged information is subject to the exceptions to the confidentiality rule discussed above. You should be alert for accidental disclosures by opposing counsel or paralegals. If you think someone on the other side of a case has disclosed confidential information to you, immediately tell your supervising attorney.

TECHNOLOGY AND TODAY'S PARALEGAL

ELECTRONIC COMMUNICATIONS AND CONFIDENTIALITY

Almost everyone has had the experience of sending an e-mail to the wrong recipient or accidentally using "reply to all" instead of "reply" and so broadcasting a personal message to a group. Similarly, law firm employees have sent inappropriate e-mails to partners and clients.

Careless communications can be more than simply embarrassing when they occur in a legal environment: confidential information could be disclosed and privilege lost. Such an incident can damage the sender's employment prospects, the interests of the client, and the reputation of the firm. This is a problem that goes beyond the workplace. Personal Web pages or social networking messages with inappropriate content may be seen by employers, opponents, or clients.

There are four major issues for paralegals to consider when using electronic communications or social media at work and at home:

1. Is a work-related communication truly confidential, or could an opposing party discover it during litigation?
2. Is a communication an appropriate use of the employer's property?
3. What sort of personal information is appropriate to share with the world through Facebook, Twitter, and other services?
4. Is the use of the social media forum consistent with the firm's policies?

CONFIDENTIALITY

Just labeling an e-mail or text message "confidential" does not mean that it will be treated as confidential. Simply adding nonprivileged material to a privileged communication will not protect the nonprivileged portion. Your firm should have a policy about when it is appropriate to send confidential information electronically and when it is not. Seek guidance from your supervising attorney if you have any doubt about the appropriateness of transmitting confidential information. Be particularly careful with your phone, tablet, laptop, or home computer if you are accessing work-related materials on these devices. Leaving a phone in a coffee shop or a computer logged in at home when company is visiting could expose confidential materials to outsiders and cost your client a legal privilege.

PERSONAL USE OF BUSINESS SYSTEMS

Many employers, including law firms, provide employees with communication devices and services, such as smartphones and laptops. Firms often allow some personal use of these devices but retain the right to monitor and audit the content of the e-mails, messages, and Web traffic on them. Be sure to check your employer's policies on appropriate use of such devices before making personal use, such as for e-mail and text messages, of firm-provided hardware or services. If you have a profile on LinkedIn or another service, be sure to ask if you may list the firm as your employer.

There are limits on employers' abilities to monitor personal communications, however. The United States Supreme Court held that a pager text-messaging service could provide an employer with the content of employees' text messages, but emphasized the extent of the measures the employer took to ensure that it did not violate the employees' privacy in reviewing personal use of the employer-provided electronic device.[a] Think carefully about how you are using employer-provided communications devices and systems. Make sure your use is within your employer's policies.

TECHNOLOGY TIP ABOUT ONLINE PERSONAL INFORMATION

Remember, when you post the details of your latest date or pictures of your vacation online, your employer or clients may stumble across those postings simply by Googling your name. Even if you change a Facebook page later, caching by search engines means that an embarrassing picture or post could linger in cyberspace for years. The bottom line: don't post pictures or text online that you would feel uncomfortable showing to your boss. Assume employers and prospective employers will search your name online.

---

a. *City of Ontario, Calif. v. Quon*, 130 S.Ct. 2619 (2010).

When the Attorney-Client Privilege Arises

The attorney-client privilege comes into existence the moment a client communicates with an attorney concerning a legal matter. People sometimes mistakenly assume that there is no duty to keep client information confidential unless an attorney agrees to represent a client and the client signs an agreement. This is not so. The privilege—and thus the duty of confidentiality—arises even if the lawyer decides not to represent the client and even when the client is not charged any fee. Thus, mentioning to a friend that a party called your firm to discuss legal representation, and the firm declined to take the case, could violate the privilege.

Duration of the Privilege

The client is the holder, or "owner," of the privilege. Only the client can waive (set aside) the privilege. Unless waived by the client, the privilege lasts indefinitely. In other words, the privilege continues even though the attorney has completed the client's legal matter and is no longer working on the case.

Privileged information is confidential. If such information is disclosed to others, it is no longer confidential and can no longer be considered privileged. This is another reason why it is so important to guard against accidental violations of the confidentiality rule: if the rule is violated, information that otherwise might have been protected by the attorney-client privilege can be used against the client's interests.

EXAMPLE 4.9 By accident, a paralegal sends, by e-mail, a confidential document to opposing counsel instead of to the client. The document, because it contained the attorney's analysis of confidential client information, might be classified as privileged information under the work product doctrine. The disclosure of the information to the opposing counsel destroyed its confidential character.

Conflict of Interest

A conflict of interest arises when representing one client injures the interests of another client. Model Rules 1.7, 1.8, 1.9, 1.10, and 1.11 pertain to conflict-of-interest situations. The general rule is that an attorney should not represent a client if doing so would be adverse to another client. There should be no representation if there is a significant risk that the attorney's ability to consider, recommend, or carry out an appropriate course of action for the client would be materially (significantly) limited as a result of the attorney's other responsibilities or interests. A classic example of a conflict of interest is when an attorney represents two adverse parties in a legal proceeding. Clearly, in such a situation, the attorney's loyalties must be divided.

conflict of interest
A situation in which two or more duties or interests come into conflict, as when an attorney attempts to represent opposing parties in a legal dispute.

Simultaneous Representation

If an attorney reasonably believes that representing two parties in a legal proceeding will not adversely affect either party's interest, then the attorney is permitted to do so—but only if both parties give informed consent. Normally, attorneys avoid this kind of situation because what might start out as an uncontested proceeding could evolve into a legal battle.

EXAMPLE 4.10 A couple seeking a divorce have agreed how to handle the matter and hire one attorney to represent them both. It is not uncommon for such matters to end up in a nasty dispute. The attorney then faces a conflict of interest: assisting one party could injure the interests of the other.

Because of the potential for a conflict of interest in divorce proceedings, some courts do not permit attorneys to represent both spouses.

Similar conflicts arise when an attorney is asked to handle a family matter and the family members eventually disagree on what the outcome should be. Suppose two adult children request the family lawyer to handle the procedures required to settle their deceased parent's estate. The will favors one child, and the other child decides to challenge the will's validity. The attorney cannot represent both sides without a conflict of interest.

Attorneys representing corporate clients may face conflicts of interest when corporate personnel become divided on an issue.

EXAMPLE 4.11 Finn, an attorney, represents ABC Corporation. Finn typically deals with the corporation's president, Johnson, when giving legal advice. At times, however, Finn deals with other personnel, including Harrison, the corporation's chief accountant. Harrison and Johnson disagree on some issues, and Johnson fires Harrison. Harrison wants attorney Finn to represent him in a lawsuit against the corporation for wrongful termination of his employment. Finn would have a conflict of interest. He could not represent Harrison, but he can continue to represent Johnson and ABC.

Former Clients

The ABA rules express caution when a lawyer may be in a position to represent a new client in a matter that would conflict with the interests of a former client. In such instances, at a minimum, the attorney must notify the former client of the matter and may need to obtain written consent. The rule regarding former clients is closely related to the rule on preserving the confidentiality of a client. The rationale behind the rule is that an attorney, in representing a client, is entrusted with certain information that may be unknown to others. That information should not be used against the client—even after the representation has ended.

JOB CHANGES AND FORMER CLIENTS. The rule concerning former clients does not prohibit an individual attorney or paralegal from working at a firm or agency that represents interests contrary to those of a former client. If that were the situation, many legal professionals would find it hard to change jobs. The rules depend on the specific circumstances. In some situations, when a conflict of interest results from a job change, the new employer can avoid violating the rules governing conflict of interest through the use of screening procedures. That is, the new employer can erect an ethical wall around the new employee so that the new employee remains ignorant about the case that would give rise to the conflict of interest.

WALLING-OFF PROCEDURES. Law offices usually have procedures for "walling off" an attorney or a paralegal from a case when a conflict of interest exists. The firm may announce in a memo to all employees that a certain attorney or paralegal should not have access to specific files and set out procedures to be followed to ensure that access to those files is restricted. Computer documents relating to the case may be protected by passwords or in some other way. Commonly, any hard-copy files relating to the case are flagged with a sticker to indicate that access to the files is restricted.

Firms normally take great care to establish and uphold such restrictions because if confidential information is used in a way harmful to a former client, the former client may sue the firm for damages. In defending against such a suit, the firm must show that it took reasonable precautions to protect that client's interests. The *Developing Paralegal Skills* feature on the facing page summarizes how steps are taken to build an ethical wall.

Other Conflict-of-Interest Situations

Other situations may give rise to conflicts of interest. Gifts from clients may create conflicts of interest, because they tend to bias the judgment of the attorney or paralegal. Certain gifts are specifically prohibited. For example, the *Model Rules* prohibit an attorney from preparing documents (such as wills) for a client if the client gives the attorney or a member of the attorney's family a gift in the will. Note that as a paralegal, you may

ethical wall
A term that refers to the procedures used to create a screen around an attorney, a paralegal, or another member of a law firm to shield him or her from information about a case in which there is a conflict of interest.

DEVELOPING PARALEGAL SKILLS

BUILDING AN ETHICAL WALL

Lana Smith, a paralegal, has been asked by her supervising attorney to set up an ethical wall because a new attorney, Chandra Piper, has been hired from the law firm of Nunn & Bush. While employed by Nunn & Bush, Piper represented the defendant, Seski Manufacturing, in the ongoing case in which Seski is being sued by Joseph Tymes. Smith's firm—and Piper's new employer—represents plaintiff Tymes in that case. Consequently, Piper's work for Nunn & Bush creates a conflict of interest, which Piper has acknowledged in a document signed under oath. Smith makes a list of the walling-off procedures to use to ensure that the firm does not violate the rules on conflict of interest.

CHECKLIST FOR BUILDING AN ETHICAL WALL

- Prepare a memo to the office manager regarding the conflict and the need for special arrangements to ensure that Piper will have no involvement in the Tymes case.
- Prepare a memo to the team representing Tymes to inform them of the conflict of interest and the special procedures to be followed.
- Prepare a memo to the firm giving the case name, the nature of the conflict, the parties involved, and instructions to maintain a blanket of silence with respect to Chandra Piper.
- Arrange for Piper's office to be on a different floor from the team (if possible) to demonstrate, if necessary, that the firm took steps to separate Piper and the team and to prevent them from having access to one another's files.
- Arrange with the office manager for computer passwords to be issued to the team members so that access to computer files on the Tymes case is available only to team members.
- Place "ACCESS RESTRICTED" stickers on the files for the Tymes case.
- Develop a security procedure for signing out and tracking the case files in the Tymes case to prevent inadvertent disclosure of the files to Piper or her staff members.

be offered gifts from appreciative clients at holidays. Generally, such gifts pose no ethical problems. If a client offers you a gift that has substantial value, however, you should discuss the issue with your supervising attorney.

Attorneys also need to be careful about taking on a client whose case may create an "issue conflict." Generally, an attorney cannot represent a client on a substantive legal issue if the client's position is contrary to that of another client being represented by the lawyer—or the lawyer's firm.

Occasionally, conflicts of interest may arise when two family members who are both attorneys or paralegals are involved in the representation of adverse parties in a legal proceeding. Because there is a risk that the family relationship will interfere with professional judgment, generally an attorney should not represent a client if an opposing party to the dispute is being represented by a member of the attorney's family (a spouse, parent, child, or sibling). If you, as a paralegal, are married to or living with another paralegal or an attorney, you should inform your firm of this fact if you ever suspect that a conflict of interest might result from your relationship. Similarly, if you discover that you may have a financial interest in the outcome of a lawsuit that your firm is handling (such as owning stock in a company involved in a lawsuit in which a party is represented by the firm), you should notify the attorney of the potential conflict.

Conflicts Checks

conflicts check
A procedure for determining whether
an agreement to represent a potential client will result in a conflict of
interest.

Whenever a potential client consults with an attorney, the attorney will want to make sure that no potential conflict of interest exists before deciding whether to represent the client. Running a conflicts check is a standard procedure in every law office and one frequently undertaken by paralegals. Before you can run a conflicts check, you need to know the name of the prospective client, the other party or parties that may be involved in the client's legal matter, and the legal issue involved.

Normally, every law firm has some established procedure for conflicts checks, and in larger firms there is usually a computerized database containing the names of former clients and the other information you will need in checking for conflicts of interest.

The Indirect Regulation of Paralegals

Paralegals are regulated *indirectly* in several ways. Clearly, the ethical codes for attorneys just discussed indirectly regulate the conduct of paralegals. Additionally, paralegal conduct is evaluated on the basis of standards and guidelines created by paralegal professional groups that create best practices but do not have the force of law, as well as guidelines for the utilization of paralegals developed by the American Bar Association and various states.

Paralegal Ethical Codes

Paralegals are increasingly self-regulated. Recall from Chapter 1 that the two major national paralegal associations—the National Federation of Paralegal Associations (NFPA) and the National Association of Legal Assistants (NALA)—were formed to define and represent paralegal professional interests on a national level. Both associations adopted codes of ethics defining the ethical responsibilities of paralegals.

NFPA's Code of Ethics

The NFPA's first code of ethics was called the *Affirmation of Responsibility*. The code has been revised several times and, in 1993, was renamed the *Model Code of Ethics and Professional Responsibility*. In 1997, NFPA revised the code, particularly its format, and took the step of appending to its code a list of enforcement guidelines setting forth recommendations on how to discipline paralegals who violate ethical standards promulgated by the code. The full title of NFPA's current code is the *Model Code of Ethics and Professional Responsibility and Guidelines for Enforcement*.

Exhibit 4.1 on the facing page presents the rules from Section 1 of the code, entitled "NFPA Model Disciplinary Rules and Ethical Considerations." For reasons of space, only the rules are included in the exhibit, not the ethical considerations that follow each rule. The ethical considerations are important to paralegals, however, because they explain what conduct the rule prohibits. The full text of NFPA's code (including the rules, ethical considerations, and guidelines for enforcement) is presented in Appendix C of this book.

NALA's Code of Ethics

In 1975, NALA issued its *Code of Ethics and Professional Responsibility*, which, like NFPA's code, has since undergone several revisions. Exhibit 4.2 on page 106 presents NALA's code in its entirety. Note that NALA's code, like the *Model Code of Professional Responsibility* discussed earlier in this chapter, presents ethical precepts as a series of "canons."

Compliance with Paralegal Codes of Ethics

Paralegal codes of ethics express the ethical responsibilities of paralegals generally, and they particularly apply to members of paralegal organizations that adopted the codes.

§1. NFPA MODEL DISCIPLINARY RULES AND ETHICAL CONSIDERATIONS

1.1 A paralegal shall achieve and maintain a high level of competence.

1.2 A paralegal shall maintain a high level of personal and professional integrity.

1.3 A paralegal shall maintain a high standard of professional conduct.

1.4 A paralegal shall serve the public interest by contributing to the improvement of the legal system and the delivery of quality legal services, including *pro bono publico* services.

1.5 A paralegal shall preserve all confidential information provided by the client or acquired from other sources before, during, and after the course of the professional relationship.

1.6 A paralegal shall avoid conflicts of interest and shall disclose any possible conflict to the employer or client, as well as to the prospective employers or clients.

1.7 A paralegal's title shall be fully disclosed.

1.8 A paralegal shall not engage in the unauthorized practice of law.

EXHIBIT 4.1

Rules from Section 1 of NFPA's *Model Code of Ethics and Professional Responsibility and Guidelines for Enforcement*

Only the disciplinary rules are shown in this exhibit. The ethical considerations, which are important to a paralegal's understanding of these rules, can be read in Appendix C of this book.

Reprinted by permission of the National Federation of Paralegal Associations, Inc. (NFPA ©) www.paralegals.org.

Any paralegal who is a member of an organization that has adopted one of these codes is expected to comply with the code's requirements. Compliance with these codes is not legally mandatory. In other words, if a paralegal does not abide by a particular ethical standard of a paralegal association's code of ethics, the association cannot initiate state-sanctioned disciplinary proceedings against the paralegal. The association can, however, expel the paralegal from the association, which may have significant implications for the paralegal's career.

Guidelines for the Utilization of Paralegals

As noted earlier, attorneys are regulated by the state to protect the public from the harms that could result from incompetent legal advice and representation. While licensing requirements may help to protect the public, they also give lawyers something of a monopoly over the delivery of legal services. The increased use of paralegals stems, in part, from the legal profession's need to reduce the cost of legal services. The use of paralegals to do substantive legal work benefits clients because the hourly rate for paralegals is lower than that for attorneys.

For this reason, bar associations (and courts, when approving fees) encourage attorneys to delegate work to paralegals to lower the costs of legal services—and thus provide the public with greater access to legal services.

NALA, the ABA, and many states have adopted guidelines for the utilization of paralegal services. These were created in response to questions concerning the role and function of paralegals within the legal arena that had arisen in earlier years, including the following: What are paralegals? What kinds of tasks do they perform? What are their professional responsibilities? How can attorneys best utilize paralegal services? What responsibilities should attorneys assume with respect to their assistants' work?

NALA's *Model Standards and Guidelines*

NALA's *Model Standards and Guidelines for the Utilization of Paralegals* provides guidance on several important issues. The document lists the minimum qualifications that legal assistants should have and then, in a series of guidelines, indicates what paralegals may and may not do. We will examine these guidelines in more detail shortly. (See Appendix B for the complete text of the annotated version of NALA's *Model Standards and Guidelines*.)

EXHIBIT 4.2

NALA's Code of Ethics and Professional Responsibility

Preamble: A paralegal must adhere strictly to the accepted standards of legal ethics and to the general principles of proper conduct. The performance of the duties of the paralegal shall be governed by specific canons as defined herein so justice will be served and goals of the profession attained.

The canons of ethics set forth hereafter are adopted by the National Association of Legal Assistants, Inc., as a general guide intended to aid paralegals and attorneys. The enumeration of these rules does not mean there are not others of equal importance although not specifically mentioned. Court rules, agency rules and statutes must be taken into consideration when interpreting the canons.

Definition: Legal assistants, also known as paralegals, are a distinguishable group of persons who assist attorneys in the delivery of legal services. Through formal education, training and experience, legal assistants have knowledge and expertise regarding the legal system and substantive and procedural law which qualify them to do work of a legal nature under the supervision of an attorney.

CANON 1.

A paralegal must not perform any of the duties that attorneys only may perform nor take any actions that attorneys may not take.

CANON 2.

A paralegal may perform any task which is properly delegated and supervised by an attorney, as long as the attorney is ultimately responsible to the client, maintains a direct relationship with the client, and assumes professional responsibility for the work product.

CANON 3.

A paralegal must not:

(a) engage in, encourage, or contribute to any act which could constitute the unauthorized practice of law; and

(b) establish attorney-client relationships, set fees, give legal opinions or advice or represent a client before a court or agency unless so authorized by that court or agency; and

(c) engage in conduct or take any action which would assist or involve the attorney in a violation of professional ethics or give the appearance of professional impropriety.

CANON 4.

A paralegal must use discretion and professional judgment commensurate with knowledge and experience but must not render independent legal judgment in place of an attorney. The services of an attorney are essential in the public interest whenever such legal judgment is required.

CANON 5.

A paralegal must disclose his or her status as a legal assistant at the outset of any professional relationship with a client, attorney, a court or administrative agency or personnel thereof, or a member of the general public. A paralegal must act prudently in determining the extent to which a client may be assisted without the presence of an attorney.

CANON 6.

A paralegal must strive to maintain integrity and a high degree of competency through education and training with respect to professional responsibility, local rules and practice, and through continuing education in substantive areas of law to better assist the legal profession in fulfilling its duty to provide legal service.

CANON 7.

A paralegal must protect the confidences of a client and must not violate any rule or statute now in effect or hereafter enacted controlling the doctrine of privileged communications between a client and an attorney.

CANON 8.

A paralegal must disclose to his or her employer or prospective employer any pre-existing clients or personal relationships that may conflict with the interests of the employer or prospective employer and/or their clients.

CANON 9.

A paralegal must do all other things incidental, necessary, or expedient for the attainment of the ethics and responsibilities as defined by statute or rule of court.

CANON 10.

A paralegal's conduct is guided by bar associations' codes of professional responsibility and rules of professional conduct.

The ABA's *Model Guidelines*

In 1991, the ABA adopted its *Model Guidelines for the Utilization of Legal Assistant Services*. The ABA Standing Committee on Paralegals revised these guidelines in 2003 and 2012 by basing them on the ABA's *Model Rules of Professional Conduct*. The document consists of ten guidelines, each followed by a lengthy comment on the origin, scope, and application of the guideline. The guidelines indicate, among other things, the types of tasks that a lawyer may not delegate to a paralegal and, generally, the responsibilities of attorneys with respect to paralegal performance and compensation. For further detail on the revised guidelines, now entitled *Model Guidelines for the Utilization of Paralegal Services*, go to the American Bar Association website and search for "paralegal."

State Guidelines

Most states have adopted some form of guidelines concerning the use of legal assistants by attorneys, the respective responsibilities of attorneys and legal assistants in performing legal work, the tasks paralegals may perform, and other ethically challenging areas. Although the guidelines of some states reflect the influence of NALA's standards and guidelines, they focus largely on state statutory definitions of the practice of law, state codes of ethics regulating the responsibilities of attorneys, and state court decisions. As a paralegal, make sure that you become familiar with your state's guidelines.

The Increasing Scope of Paralegal Responsibilities

The ethical standards and guidelines just discussed, as well as court decisions concerning paralegals, all support the goal of increasing the use of paralegals in the delivery of legal services. Today, paralegals can perform almost any legal task as long as the work is supervised by an attorney and does not constitute the unauthorized practice of law.

Wide Range of Responsibilities

Paralegals working for attorneys may interview clients and witnesses, investigate legal claims, draft legal documents for attorneys' signatures, attend will executions (in some states), appear at real estate closings (in some states), and undertake other types of legal work, as long as the work is supervised by attorneys. When state or federal law allows it, paralegals can also represent clients before government agencies. Paralegals may perform freelance services for attorneys and, depending on state law and the type of service, perform limited independent services for the public.

Legal assistants may also give information to clients on many matters relating to a case or other legal concern. When arranging for client interviews, they let clients know what kind of information is needed and what documents to bring to the office. They inform clients about legal procedures and what clients should expect to experience during the progress of a legal proceeding. As a paralegal, you will be permitted to give clients all kinds of information. Nonetheless, you must make sure that you know where to draw the line between giving permissible advice and giving "legal advice" that only licensed attorneys may give.

Follow ABA Guidelines

The tasks that paralegals are legally permitted to undertake are described throughout this book. As stated in the ABA's guidelines, paralegals may not perform tasks that only attorneys can legally perform. If they do so, they risk liability for the unauthorized practice of law.

The Unauthorized Practice of Law

State statutes prohibit the unauthorized practice of law (UPL). Although the statutes vary, they all aim to prevent nonlawyers from providing legal counsel. These statutes apply to all persons—including paralegals, real estate agents, bankers, insurance agents, and accountants—who might provide services that are typically provided by licensed attorneys.

EXAMPLE 4.12 An insurance agent, talking to a client, offers advice about a possible personal-injury claim. The agent might be liable for UPL.

UPL statutes are not always clear about what constitutes the practice of law. Consequently, courts decide whether a person has engaged in UPL on a case-by-case basis. This may make it difficult to know exactly what activities constitute UPL. To avoid violating UPL laws, a person must be aware of the state courts' decisions on UPL. As we will see below, some states are addressing this problem.

Paralegals, of course, can also refer to the general guidelines for their profession provided by NALA. Guideline 2 in NALA's *Model Standards and Guidelines* prohibits a paralegal from engaging in any of the following activities:

- Establishing attorney-client relationships.
- Setting legal fees.
- Giving legal opinions or advice.
- Representing a client before a court, unless authorized to do so by the court.
- Engaging in, encouraging, or contributing to any act that could constitute the unauthorized practice of law.

State UPL Statutes

Because of the difficulty in predicting with certainty whether a court would consider a particular action to be UPL, some states have made efforts to clarify what is meant by the "practice of law." About half of the states have a formal definition of what constitutes the practice of law, either by statute or by court ruling. For example, the Texas UPL statute provides, in part:

> the "practice of law" means the preparation of a pleading or other document incident to an action or special proceeding or the management of the action or proceeding on behalf of a client before a judge in court as well as a service rendered out of court, including the giving of advice or the rendering of any service requiring the use of legal skill or knowledge, such as preparing a will, contract, or other instrument, the legal effect of which under the facts and conclusions involved must be carefully determined.[1]

The Texas statute also states that this definition is not exclusive and that the state courts have the authority to determine that other activities, which are not listed, also constitute UPL. Other states' definitions focus on various factors, such as appearing in court or drafting legal papers, pleadings, or other documents in connection with a pending or prospective court proceeding. The enforcement of UPL statutes also varies widely among the states. In some states, the attorney general prosecutes violators; in others, a local or state prosecutor enforces UPL statutes, or the state bar association may be in charge of enforcement.

In the following pages, we discuss some of the activities that are considered to constitute UPL in most states. But it must be emphasized that a paralegal should know the details of the UPL statute in the state in which she or he works. Avoiding UPL problems is also discussed in the *Developing Paralegal Skills* feature on the facing page.

The Prohibition against Fee Splitting

An important ethical rule related to the unauthorized practice of law is Rule 5.4 of the *Model Rules of Professional Conduct*. For an attorney or a law firm to split legal fees with a nonlawyer is prohibited. For this reason, paralegals cannot be partners in a law partnership (because the partners share the firm's income), nor can they have a fee-sharing arrangement with attorneys.

DEVELOPING PARALEGAL SKILLS

THE DANGERS OF THE UNAUTHORIZED PRACTICE OF LAW

Every state restricts the "practice of law" to licensed attorneys. State bar associations take this restriction seriously, and they aggressively enforce UPL rules against anyone the bar suspects is infringing on attorneys' control of the practice of law.

Unfortunately, the definition of the "practice of law" is unclear, making it a trap for the unwary. The ABA defines it as "the rendition of services for others that call for the professional judgment of a lawyer." In essence, "practicing" law includes giving legal advice, preparing legal documents, and representing a client in court.

Of course, paralegals routinely do the first two of these. Each is perfectly legal as long as these activities are done under the supervision of a licensed attorney. For example, you will often have to relay legal advice from the attorney to the client. To protect yourself, you must make clear that the advice comes from the lawyer, not you. You can avoid unauthorized practice problems by:

- Being clear that everyone understands you are a paralegal in all communications and meetings by:
  1. Including your title when signing letters, e-mails, and other documents and on your business cards.
  2. Introducing yourself with your title in meetings.

3. Disclosing your status when communicating with a court.

- Ensuring that activities that might be construed to be the "practice of law" are supervised by a licensed attorney by:
  1. Making sure that an attorney reviews and signs off on all legal documents you prepare.
  2. Explicitly stating that the attorney is the source of any legal advice when relaying advice to a client by stating, "I asked Attorney Smith about that and she said . . . ."

- Informing yourself about your state's unauthorized practice rules by:
  1. Researching court decisions, regulations, and state bar opinions on the topic.
  2. Contacting your state paralegal associations and state bar for information and publications on the topic.

Taking care to follow such guidelines will protect the law firm you work for and will protect you, your career, and your firm's clients. Be particularly careful when offering opinions about legal issues on social media sites so that you do not stray into offering legal advice.

One of the reasons for this rule is that it protects the attorney's independent judgment concerning legal matters.

EXAMPLE 4.13 An attorney shares office space with two CPAs (accountants) and the three of them work for some of the same clients. The three form a partnership. Is there a problem? Yes, in this situation, a conflict might arise between the interests of the partnership and the attorney's duty to exercise independent professional judgment about a client's case.

The rule against fee splitting also protects against the possibility that nonlawyers would indirectly, through attorneys, be able to engage in the practice of law.

Giving Legal Opinions and Advice

Giving legal advice goes to the essence of legal practice. After all, a person would not seek out a legal expert if he or she did not want legal advice on some matter. Although a paralegal can communicate an attorney's legal advice to a client, a paralegal cannot independently give legal advice.

The Need for Caution

You need to be careful to avoid giving legal advice even when discussing matters with friends and relatives. Although other nonlawyers often give advice affecting others' legal rights or obligations, paralegals should not do so. For example, when a person gets a speeding ticket, a friend or relative who is a nonlawyer might suggest that the person should argue the case before a judge and explain his side of the story. When a paralegal gives such advice, however, she may be accused of engaging in the unauthorized practice of law. Legal assistants are prohibited from giving even simple, common-sense advice because of the greater weight the recipient might give to the advice of someone who has legal training.

Similarly, you need to be cautious in the workplace. Although you may develop expertise in a certain area of law, you must refrain from advising clients with respect to their legal obligations or rights.

EXAMPLE 4.14 Suppose you are a bankruptcy specialist and know that a client who wants to file for bankruptcy has two options to pursue under bankruptcy law. Should you tell the client about these options and their consequences? No. Advising someone of legal options is dangerously close to advising a person of his legal rights and may therefore constitute the unauthorized practice of law. Even though you may tell the client that he needs to check with an attorney, this does not alter the fact that you are giving advice on which the client might rely.

Be on the Safe Side

What constitutes the giving of legal advice can be difficult to pin down. Paralegals are permitted to advise clients on certain matters, so drawing the line between permissible and impermissible advice may be difficult. To be on the safe side—and avoid potential liability for the unauthorized practice of law—never advise anyone regarding any matter if the advice may alter that person's legal position or legal rights.

Whenever you are pressured to render legal advice—as you surely will be at one time or another by your firm's clients or friends—say that you cannot give legal advice because it is against the law to do so. Paralegals usually find that a frank and honest approach provides the best solution to the problem.

Representing Clients in Court

The rule that only attorneys can represent others in legal matters has a long history. There are two limited exceptions to this rule. First, in 1975 the United States Supreme Court held that people have a constitutional right to represent themselves in court.[2] Second, paralegals are allowed to represent clients before some federal and state government agencies, such as the federal Social Security Administration. Hence, as a paralegal you should know that you are not allowed to appear in court on behalf of your supervising attorney—although local courts in some states have made exceptions to this rule for limited purposes.

Disclosure of Paralegal Status

Because of the close working relationship between an attorney and a paralegal, a client may have difficulty perceiving that the paralegal is not an attorney.

EXAMPLE 4.15 A client calls an attorney's office and is transferred to the attorney's paralegal. The paralegal talks with the client about a legal matter and advises the client that the attorney will be in touch. The client may assume that the paralegal is an attorney and may make inferences based on the paralegal's comments that result in actions with harmful consequences—in which event the paralegal might be charged with the unauthorized practice of law.

To avoid problems, make sure that clients or potential clients know that you are a paralegal and, as such, are not permitted to give legal advice.

Similarly, in correspondence with clients or others, you should indicate your nonattorney status by adding "Paralegal" or "Legal Assistant" after your name. If you have printed business cards, or if your name is included in the firm's letterhead or other literature, also make sure that your status is clearly indicated.

Guideline 1 of NALA's *Model Standards and Guidelines* emphasizes the importance of disclosing paralegal status by stating that all legal assistants have an ethical responsibility to "disclose their status as legal assistants at the outset of any professional relationship with a client, other attorneys, a court or administrative agency or personnel thereof, or members of the general public." Disciplinary Rule 1.7 of NFPA's *Model Code of Ethics and Professional Responsibility* also stresses the importance of disclosing paralegal status. Guideline 4 of the ABA's *Model Guidelines* places on attorneys the responsibility for disclosing the nonattorney status of paralegals.

Attorneys are responsible for the work product of their offices, including the work done by paralegals. Hence, attorneys are required to ensure that clients and other relevant parties, including other attorneys and the courts, know when work has been performed by a paralegal.

Paralegals Freelancing for Attorneys

Some paralegals work on a freelance basis, as discussed in Chapter 2. In a decision in 1992, the New Jersey Supreme Court held that freelance paralegals could be as adequately supervised by the attorneys for whom they worked as are paralegals working inside attorneys' offices. Since that decision, courts in other states, and ethical opinions issued by various state bar associations, have held that freelance paralegals who are adequately supervised by attorneys are not engaging in the unauthorized practice of law.

Legal Technicians (Independent Paralegals) and UPL

As mentioned in Chapter 2, legal technicians (also called independent paralegals) provide "self-help" legal services directly to the public. The courts have had to wrestle with questions such as the following: If an independent paralegal advises a client on what forms are necessary to obtain a simple, uncontested divorce, how to file those forms with the court, how to schedule a court hearing, and the like, do those activities constitute the practice of law?

Generally, the mere dissemination of legal information does not constitute the unauthorized practice of law. There is a fine line, however, between disseminating legal information (by providing legal forms to a customer, for example) and giving legal advice (which may consist of merely selecting the forms that best suit the customer's needs), and the courts do not always agree on just where this line should be drawn.

An Ongoing Problem

Legal technicians continue to face UPL allegations brought against them primarily by UPL committees and state bar associations. In one case, an Oregon appellate court upheld the conviction of Robin Smith for engaging in UPL. The bar association complained that Smith provided consumers with various legal forms, advised them on which forms to use, and assisted them in completing the documents. The court reasoned that by drafting and selecting documents and giving advice with regard to their legal effect, Smith was practicing law.[3]

Some legal technicians faced UPL charges in California when the legislature authorized nonlawyers to provide certain types of legal services directly to the public. Under that law, a person who qualifies and registers with the county as a "legal document assistant" (LDA) may assist clients in filling out legal forms but cannot advise clients which forms to use.[4] After the LDA law passed, the case was settled.

The Controversy over Legal Software

Even publishers of self-help law books and computer software programs have come under attack for the unauthorized practice of law. For example, a Texas Court held that the legal software program *Quicken Family Lawyer* violated Texas's UPL statute.[5] The program provided a hundred different legal forms (including contracts, real estate leases, and wills), along with instructions on how to fill out these forms.

The Texas legislature then amended the UPL statute to reverse the court's ruling. The new law explicitly authorizes the sale of legal self-help software, books, forms, and similar products to the public.[6] Note, however, that the Texas law authorizes these products to be used only for "self-help." The law does not permit persons who are not licensed to practice law to use these programs to give legal advice to others.

Do Paralegals Who Operate as Legal Technicians Engage in UPL?

Debate continues as to whether it is legal, in some situations, for legal technicians to operate without a lawyer's supervision. Generally, unless a state statute or rule specifically allows paralegals to assist the public directly without the supervision of an attorney, paralegals would be wise not to engage in such practices. Most state courts are much more likely to find that a paralegal is engaging in UPL than that a publisher of legal software is doing so. The consequences of violating state UPL statutes can be serious. Any paralegal who contemplates working as a legal technician (independent paralegal) must thoroughly investigate the relevant state laws and court decisions on UPL before offering any services directly to the public and must abide by the letter of the law.

Should Paralegals Be Licensed?

A major issue facing legal professionals is whether paralegals should be subject to direct regulation by the state through licensing requirements. Unlike certification, which was discussed in Chapter 1, licensing involves direct and mandatory regulation, by the state, of an occupational or professional group. When licensing requirements are established for a professional group, such as for attorneys, a member of the group must have a license to practice his or her profession.

Movements toward regulation of paralegals have been motivated in large part by the activities of legal technicians or independent paralegals—those who provide legal services directly to the public without attorney supervision. Many legal technicians call themselves paralegals even though they may have little legal training or experience. At the same time, those who cannot afford to hire an attorney can benefit from the self-help services provided by legal technicians who have training and experience.

General Licensing

general licensing
Licensing in which all individuals within a specific profession or group (such as paralegals) must meet licensing requirements imposed by the state in order to legally practice their profession.

Some states have considered implementing a general licensing program that would require all paralegals to meet certain educational requirements and other specified criteria before being allowed to practice.

For example, the New Jersey Supreme Court Committee on Paralegal Education and Regulation recommended that paralegals be licensed. The committee's report proposed that paralegals be subject to state licensure based on educational requirements and knowledge of the ethical rules governing the legal profession. The New Jersey Supreme Court, however, declined to follow the committee's recommendations. The court concluded that direct oversight of paralegals is best accomplished through attorney supervision rather than through a state-mandated licensing system.

Paralegal Registration

Florida requires registration of paralegals who wish to become a Florida Registered Paralegal (FRP). Initially, experienced paralegals were allowed to register without meeting an educational requirement. Since 2011, however, applicants who wish to be registered must provide proof of educational qualification and must meet certain personal requirements, such as not to have engaged in the unauthorized practice of law. All FRPs are listed on the Florida Bar website.

Paralegals must meet the continuing education (CE) requirement of 30 hours every three-year reporting cycle. At least five of the hours must be in ethics or professionalism. Failure to complete the CE requirement means loss of FRP status. CE courses specifically authorized are provided by the NALA, the NFPA, and the Florida Bar. Other states are considering a similar procedure.

Education and Certification

The law in California defines a paralegal or legal assistant as someone who works under the supervision of an attorney, meets certain educational criteria, and completes required continuing education requirements. Paralegals do not have to register, but an independent paralegal not working under the supervision of an attorney cannot be called a paralegal in California. Independent paralegals can register with the state as a "legal document assistant" (LDA). They prepare documents at the direction of their clients and assist clients in a wide range of areas, from family law to incorporation of businesses. They cannot provide legal advice.

The Louisiana Certified Paralegal Program illustrates another approach. Paralegals who successfully complete the NALA's Certified Legal Assistant (CLA) exam and the Louisiana Certified Paralegal (LCP) exam are certified as a Louisiana Certified Paralegal. The CLA exam tests knowledge of the American legal and judicial systems and four areas of substantive law. The LCP exam focuses on the Louisiana legal and judicial system, ethics, civil procedure, and four areas of substantive Louisiana law.

Direct Regulation—The Pros and Cons

A significant part of the debate over direct regulation has to do with the issue of who should do the regulating. Certainly, state bar associations and government authorities would have a major say in the matter. Yet paralegal organizations and educators, such as NALA, NFPA, and the American Association for Paralegal Education (AAfPE), also want to play a leading role in developing the education requirements, ethical standards, and disciplinary procedures required by a licensing program should one be implemented. One problem is that NFPA, NALA, and the AAfPE have expressed differing views on these matters.

NFPA's Position

NFPA endorses the regulation of the paralegal profession on a state-by-state basis. NFPA asserts that wide-scale regulation of paralegals would improve consumers' access to quality legal services by lowering costs. NFPA favors establishing minimum education requirements to protect the public.

NFPA proposes a two-tiered system of licensing: general licensing and specialty licensing. General licensing by a state board or agency would require all paralegals within the state to satisfy education, experience, and continuing education requirements; it would also subject practicing paralegals to disciplinary procedures by the licensing body. (As mentioned, NFPA has already developed a set of model enforcement guidelines—see Appendix C.) Specialty licensing would require paralegals who wish to practice in a specialized area to demonstrate, by an examination (see the discussion of the PACE examination in Chapter 1 and Appendix G), their proficiency in that area.

NALA's Position

NALA supports voluntary certification (self-regulation) but opposes licensing for paralegals. State licensing would only serve to control entry into the profession and would not improve the quality of the services that paralegals provide.

According to NALA, there is no need to regulate paralegals. Most paralegals work under the supervision of attorneys, who are regulated by state ethical codes. NALA believes that regulation would increase the cost of paralegals to employers. This increase would be passed on to consumers, resulting in higher-cost legal services. NALA therefore considers licensing an unnecessary burden to employers, paralegals, and the public.

AAfPE's Position

The American Association for Paralegal Education (AAfPE) does not take a position on paralegal licensing. AAfPE recommends that states adopt AAfPE's minimum educational standards in any regulatory plan they enact. It contends that paralegals (through associations such as NALA and NFPA) and paralegal educators should present a united front in influencing licensing proposals. Otherwise, by default, the decision will be made by others and will not be subject to their influence.

Other Considerations

While the positions taken by NFPA, NALA, and AAfPE outline the main contours of the debate over regulation, other groups emphasize some different considerations. For example, one of the concerns of lawyers is that if legal technicians are licensed—through limited licensing programs—to deliver low-cost services directly to the public, the business (and profits) of law firms would suffer. Many lawyers are also concerned that if paralegals are subject to mandatory licensing requirements, law firms will not be able to hire and train persons of their choice to work as paralegals.

The Ethical Paralegal

As a professional paralegal, you will have an opportunity to voice your opinion on whether paralegals should be regulated by state governments and, if so, what qualifications should be required. The most important point to remember as you embark on a paralegal career is that you need to think and act in an ethical, professionally responsible manner. Although this takes time and practice, in the legal arena there is little room for learning ethics by "trial and error." Therefore, you need to be especially attentive to the ethical rules governing attorneys and paralegal practice discussed in this chapter. Ethical behavior is required by law, but it is also mandatory if you want other professionals to place their trust and confidence in you.

The *Ethics Watch* features throughout this book offer insights into some ethical problems that arise in various areas of paralegal performance. Understanding how violations can occur will help you anticipate and guard against them as you begin your career. On the job, you can protect the ethics of legal practice by asking questions whenever you are in doubt and by making sure that your work is adequately supervised.

KEY TERMS AND CONCEPTS

Chapter Summary / Ethics and Professional Responsibility

THE REGULATION OF ATTORNEYS

Attorneys are regulated by licensing requirements and by the ethics rules of their state. The purpose of regulation is to protect the public against incompetent legal professionals and unethical attorney behavior.

1. *Who are the regulators?*—Lawyers establish the majority of rules governing their profession through state bar associations and the American Bar Association (ABA), which has established model rules and guidelines relating to professional conduct. Other key participants in the regulation of attorneys are state supreme courts, state legislatures, and (occasionally) the United States Supreme Court.

2. *Licensing requirements*—Licensed attorneys generally must be graduates of a law school and have passed a state bar examination and an extensive personal background check.

3. *Ethical codes and rules*—Most states have adopted a version of either the 1969 *Model Code of Professional Responsibility* or the 1983 revision of the *Model Code*, called the *Model Rules of Professional Conduct*, published by the ABA. The *Model Rules, which* have been adopted in most states, are often amended by the ABA to keep up-to-date with the realities of modern law practice.

4. *Sanctions for violations*—The *Model Code* and *Model Rules* spell out the ethical and professional duties governing attorneys and the practice of law. Attorneys who violate these duties may be subject to reprimand, suspension, or disbarment. Additionally, attorneys (and paralegals) face potential liability for malpractice or for violations of criminal statutes.

ATTORNEY ETHICS AND PARALEGAL PRACTICE

Some of the ethical rules governing attorney behavior pose difficult problems for paralegals, so paralegals should consult their state's ethical code to learn the specific rules for which they will be accountable. The following rules apply in most states.

1. *Duty of competence*—This duty is violated whenever a client suffers harm as a result of the attorney's (or paralegal's) incompetent action or inaction.

   a. Breaching the duty of competence may lead to a lawsuit against the attorney (and perhaps against the paralegal) for negligence. This may arise from faulty research, missed deadlines, or mistakes in documents.

   b. Attorneys must adequately supervise a paralegal's work to ensure that this duty is not breached.

2. *Confidentiality of information*—All information relating to a client's representation must be kept in confidence and not revealed to third parties who are not authorized to know the information.

   a. Paralegals should be careful on and off the job not to discuss client information with third parties. Breaches of confidentiality can include unauthorized persons overhearing telephone conversations or personal comments, or e-mails being sent to parties not intended to see them.

   b. Client confidences can be revealed only in certain circumstances, such as when a client gives informed consent to the disclosure, when disclosure is necessary to represent a client or to prevent harm to persons or property, or when a court orders an attorney to reveal the information.

3. *Confidentiality and the attorney-client privilege*—Some client information is regarded as privileged information under the rules of evidence and receives even greater protection by attorneys and paralegals subject to rules of confidentiality.

4. *Conflict of interest*—This occurs when representing a client injures the interests of another client.

   a. An attorney may represent both sides in a legal proceeding only if the attorney believes that neither party's rights will be injured and only if both clients are aware of the conflict and have given informed consent to the representation. Paralegals also fall under this rule.

   b. When a firm is handling a case and one of the firm's attorneys or paralegals cannot work on the case because of a conflict of interest, that attorney or paralegal must be "walled off" from the case—that is, prevented from having access to files or other information relating to the case.

   c. Normally, whenever a prospective client consults with an attorney, a conflicts check is done to ensure that if the attorney or firm accepts the case, no conflict of interest will arise.

THE INDIRECT REGULATION OF PARALEGALS

Paralegals are regulated indirectly by attorney ethical rules, by ethical codes created by NFPA and NALA, and by guidelines on the utilization of paralegals, which define the status and function of paralegals and the scope of their authorized activities. The ABA and some states have adopted guidelines on the utilization of paralegals. These codes and guidelines provide paralegals, attorneys, and the courts with guidance on the paralegal's role in the practice of law. The general rule is that paralegals can perform almost any legal task that attorneys can (other than represent a client in court) as long as they work under an attorney's supervision.

THE UNAUTHORIZED PRACTICE OF LAW

State laws prohibit nonlawyers from engaging in the unauthorized practice of law (UPL). Violations of these laws can have serious consequences.

1. *State UPL statutes*—Determining what constitutes UPL is complicated by the fact that many state laws give vague or broad definitions. One may look to court decisions in this area of law for guidance.

2. *The prohibition against fee splitting*—Paralegals working for attorneys and legal technicians (independent paralegals) need to be careful not to engage in activities that the state will consider UPL, such as a fee-sharing arrangement with an attorney.

3. *Prohibited acts*—Paralegals should always make clear their professional status so clients are not confused. While paralegals work under the supervision of an attorney, one can be an independent or freelance paralegal and need not be a full-time employee of an attorney. The consensus is that paralegals should not engage in the following acts:

   a. Establish an attorney-client relationship.

   b. Set legal fees.

   c. Give legal advice or opinions.

   d. Represent a client in court (unless authorized to do so by the court).

   e. Encourage or contribute to any act that could constitute UPL.

SHOULD PARALEGALS BE LICENSED?

An issue for legal professionals is whether paralegals should be directly regulated by the state through licensing requirements.

1. *General licensing*—General licensing would establish minimum standards that every paralegal would have to meet in order to practice as a paralegal in the state.

2. *Registration*—Some states, such as Florida, encourage registration of paralegals. While not mandated, it does provide more visibility and professional recognition. Other states, such as California, have education requirements that must be met before one can claim to be a paralegal.

3. *Direct regulation*—The pros and cons of direct regulation through licensing are being debated vigorously by the leading paralegal and paralegal education associations, state bar associations, state courts, state legislatures, and public-interest groups.

▰ QUESTIONS FOR REVIEW

1. Why is the legal profession regulated? Who are the regulators? How is regulation accomplished?

2. How is the paralegal profession regulated by attorney ethical codes? How is it regulated by paralegal codes of ethics?

3. What does the duty of competence involve? How can violations of the duty of competence be avoided?

4. What is the duty of confidentiality? What is the attorney-client privilege? What is the relationship between the duty of confidentiality and the attorney-client privilege? What are some potential consequences of violating the confidentiality rule?

5. How is the practice of law defined? The unauthorized practice of law (UPL)? How might paralegals violate state statutes prohibiting UPL? What types of tasks can legally be performed by paralegals?

■ ETHICS QUESTIONS

1. Norma Sollers works as a paralegal for a small law firm. She is a trusted, experienced employee who has worked for the firm for twelve years. One morning, Linda Lowenstein, one of the attorneys, calls from her home and asks Norma to sign Linda's name to a document that must be filed with the court that day. Norma had just prepared the final draft of the document and had placed it on Linda's desk for her review and signature. Linda explains to Norma that because her child is sick, she does not want to leave home to come into the office. Norma knows that she should not sign Linda's name—only the client's attorney can sign the document. She mentions this to Linda, but Linda says, "Don't worry. No one will ever know that you signed it instead of me." How should Norma handle this situation?

2. The law firm of Dover, Cleary and Harper decides to store all of its data in the cloud and enters into a contract with Cloud Service Provider for data storage. The firm does not mention its conversion to cloud storage to any of its clients. Six months later an employee of the Cloud Service Provider notices that one of the firm's clients, a local celebrity, has serious financial problems and broadcasts this fact on Facebook, causing significant embarrassment to the client. The client is able to track the disclosure of her confidential information on Facebook to Cloud Service Provider, which obtained the client's file from Dover, Cleary and Harper. Is the law firm guilty of an ethical violation?

■ PRACTICE QUESTIONS AND ASSIGNMENTS

1. In which of the following instances may confidential client information be disclosed?

   a. The client in a divorce case threatens to hire a hit man to kill her husband because she believes that killing her husband is the only way that she can stop him from stalking her. It is clear that the client intends to do this.

   b. A former client sues her attorney for legal malpractice in the handling of a breach-of-contract case involving her cosmetics home-sale business. The attorney discloses that the client is having an affair with her next-door neighbor, a fact that is unrelated to the malpractice case or the breach-of-contract case.

2. Using the material presented in the chapter on conflicts of interest, determine which type of conflict of interest is presented in the situations below:

   a. A lawyer has a case pending before the state supreme court, advocating that divorced parents must obtain court permission for their children to move more than 300 miles from the other parent. The same lawyer takes a case for a client who wants to move 700 miles from the other parent, and he argues that the court does not need to grant permission. This case will likely end up before the state supreme court.

   b. Melissa is an attorney with a criminal law practice. She has a big case in which her client was convicted of violating the state's recently enacted medical marijuana law, and she is appealing his conviction to the state supreme court. Tom, her husband, is a paralegal who works for the state attorney's office and has been assigned to gather research opposing the brief that Melissa filed on behalf of her client.

   c. Attorney Sam prepares a will for a client; the will leaves the client's vacation home to Sam.

   d. A new client brings a case to attorney Mark and asks Mark to represent him. The case would require Mark to sue a former client whom he previously defended on the same issue.

3. Which of the following actions should you take as a paralegal to avoid charges of engaging in the practice of law?

   a. Include the title "paralegal" when signing letters and e-mails.

   b. Introduce yourself without using your title in meetings with clients.

   c. Include the title "paralegal" on your business cards.

   d. Disclose your status as a paralegal when communicating with a court.

4. Matthew Hinson is a legal technician. He provides divorce forms and typing and filing services to the public at very low rates. Samantha Eggleston uses his services. She presents him with her completed forms, but she has one question: How much will she be entitled to receive in monthly child-support payments? How may Matthew legally respond to this question?

5. A paralegal experienced in employment discrimination law was hired by an attorney to develop a practice requiring appearances before both the state discrimination agency and the EEOC. The paralegal had previously advocated for clients before this state agency as permitted by state law. The attorney had no experience with employment discrimination cases. The attorney's clients were charged contingency fees, with the attorney

receiving two-thirds of the fees and the paralegal one-third. The paralegal solicited clients and handled their cases without supervision, to the extent of having more than forty cases pending before the state agency. The paralegal also removed cases from the agencies and refiled them in the courts using the attorney's name and bar license without seeking the attorney's approval for doing so. Using the material in the chapter, what ethical violations did the paralegal commit? Did the attorney violate any ethical duties?

6. According to this chapter's text, which of the following tasks can a paralegal legally perform?

a. Provide legal advice to clients in the course of helping them prepare divorce pleadings.

b. Interview a witness to a car accident.

c. Represent a client in court.

d. Set legal fees.

e. Work as a freelance paralegal for attorneys.

f. Work as a legal technician providing legal services directly to the public.

⬛ GROUP PROJECT

This project involves the review of your state's version of one of the ethical rules of competence, conflict of interest, or client confidentiality as assigned by your instructor. Students one, two, and three will locate your state's version of the rule using online sources, your school's library, or a local law library. They will also summarize the assigned sections of the rule and will determine which rule is the law in your state. Student four will compare the summarized sections of the state rule to the ABA Model Rule discussed in this chapter and will present the comparison to the class.

⬛ INTERNET PROJECTS

1. Access your state's rules online to learn the requirements for becoming licensed to practice law in your state. In addition, find out how your state defines the unauthorized practice of law. Do your state's rules differ from the requirements mentioned in the text? If so, how?

2. Go to **www.legalzoom.com** and click on "LLC." Generally, what product(s) and guarantee(s) does LegalZoom provide?

a. What legal services are offered at the three different pricing options?

b. Describe how an LLC is created by LegalZoom. Is any information given about whether an attorney files the documents with the state or creates a company-specific operating agreement?

c. Does LegalZoom provide any information on how to choose between an LLC or a corporation as the appropriate organizational form for a customer's business? What services or guidance is provided to customers who do not elect to purchase the package offering attorney consultation?

d. Review the material in the chapter on software as it relates to the unauthorized practice of law (UPL). Is LegalZoom providing forms or legal advice? Is LegalZoom engaging in UPL? Why or why not?

e. Do an Internet search on "lawsuits against LegalZoom." Summarize your results in one paragraph.

⬛ END NOTES

1. Title 2 of the Texas Government Code, Section 81.101.

2. *Faretta v. California*, 422 U.S. 806 (1975).

3. *Oregon State Bar v. Smith*, 942 P.2d 793 (1997).

4. This law is codified in California Business and Professions Code, Sections 6400–6416.

5. *In re Nolo Press/Folk Law, Inc.*, 991 S.W.2d 768 (1999).

6. Texas Government Code Section 81.101(c) (Vernon Supp. 2000).

CHAPTER 5

Sources of American Law

CHAPTER OBJECTIVES

After completing this chapter, you will know:

- The meaning and relative importance in the American legal system of case law, constitutional law, statutory law, and administrative law.

- How English law influenced the development of the American legal system.

- What the common law tradition is and how it evolved.

- The difference between remedies at law and equitable remedies.

- Some of the terms that are commonly found in case law.

- How national law and international law differ and why these bodies of law sometimes guide judicial decision making in U.S. courts.

Introduction

The first English colonists brought the law of England with them to the New World. Over time, American law developed its own unique characteristics. As Americans adopted the law in their new environment and as the nation grew, they absorbed ideas from the Spanish, French, and Mexican legal systems. We open this chapter with a discussion of the nature of law and then examine traditional law and its significance in the American legal system. Next, we focus on other sources of American law, including constitutional, statutory, and administrative. We also explain how the law of other countries and international law affect decision making in American courts. Another major part of the American legal structure—the court system—will be examined in Chapter 6.

The Framework of American Law

The law means different things to different people. Before beginning your study of American law, it is useful to have an understanding of what law is and some of the different approaches to law that influence courts' decisions. These topics are covered in the following subsections.

What Is the Law?

law
A body of rules of conduct established and enforced by the controlling authority (the government) of a society.

How a person defines *law* frequently depends on the person's views on morality, ethics, and truth. Generally, we define law as a body of rules of conduct established and enforced by the government of a society. These "rules of conduct" may consist of written principles of behavior, such as those established by ancient societies. They may be set forth in a comprehensive code, as used in many European nations. They may consist of a combination of legislatively enacted statutes and court decisions, as in the United States. Regardless of how the rules are created, they establish rights, duties, and privileges for the citizens they govern.

One of the most important functions of law in any society is to provide stability, predictability, and continuity so that people can arrange their affairs. If a democratic society is to be credible, its citizens must be able to determine what is legally right and wrong.

> **EXAMPLE 5.1** Citizens must know what penalties will be imposed on them if they commit wrongful acts. If people suffer harm as a result of others' wrongful acts, they need to know whether and how they can receive compensation for their injuries.

By setting forth the rights, obligations, and privileges of citizens, the law enables people to go about their business and personal lives with confidence and a certain degree of predictability.

Primary Sources of American Law

primary source of law
In legal research, a document that establishes the law on a particular issue, such as a case decision, legislative act, administrative rule, or presidential order.

American law has numerous sources. Primary sources of law, or sources that establish the law, include the following:

1. Case law and common law doctrines.
2. The U.S. Constitution and the constitutions of the various states.
3. Statutes—including laws passed by Congress, state legislatures, and local governing bodies.
4. Regulations created by administrative agencies, such as the U.S. Food and Drug Administration (FDA) or state insurance commissions.

We describe each of these important sources of law in the following pages. Note that treaties with other nations are also a primary source of law, although most legal practitioners do not deal with them directly but instead retain an attorney from the foreign jurisdiction to assist. We discuss international law near the end of the chapter.

Secondary sources of law are books and articles that summarize, synthesize, and explain the primary sources of law. Examples include legal encyclopedias, treatises, articles in law reviews, and compilations of law, such as the *Restatements of the Law* (discussed later in this chapter). Courts often refer to secondary sources of law for guidance in interpreting the primary sources of law discussed here. They are also useful research tools that aid in locating primary sources.

secondary source of law
In legal research, any publication that indexes, summarizes, or interprets the law, such as a legal encyclopedia, a treatise, or an article in a law review.

Case Law and the Common Law Tradition

An important source of law consists of the decisions issued by judges in cases that come before the courts. Lawyers call this case law. As mentioned earlier, because of our colonial heritage, much American law is based on the English legal system. Our reliance on reported court decisions is a key part of our English heritage.

case law
Rules of law announced in court decisions.

The English common law is a body of general rules applied by the courts. In deciding common law cases, judges attempt to be consistent by basing decisions on principles from earlier cases. By doing this, they seek to ensure that they decide similar cases in similar ways. Each decision becomes part of the law on the subject and serves as a legal precedent. Later cases that involve similar legal principles or facts are decided with reference to precedents.

common law
A body of law developed from custom or judicial decisions in English and U.S. courts and not by a legislature.

precedent
A court decision that furnishes authority for deciding later cases in which similar facts are presented.

The Doctrine of *Stare Decisis*

The practice of deciding new cases with reference to former decisions, or precedents, is a cornerstone of the English and American judicial systems. It forms a doctrine called *stare decisis*[1] ("to stand by things decided"). Under this doctrine, judges are obligated to follow the precedents established by their own courts or by higher courts in their jurisdictions (the areas over which they have authority—see Chapter 6). These controlling precedents are referred to as binding authorities.

A binding authority is a source of law that a court must follow when deciding a case. Binding authorities include constitutions, statutes, and regulations that govern an issue being decided, as well as court decisions that are controlling precedents within the jurisdiction. When no binding authority exists, courts will often review persuasive precedents, which are precedents decided in similar cases in other jurisdictions. The court may either follow or reject persuasive precedents, but these decisions are entitled to respect and careful consideration.

stare decisis
The doctrine of precedent, under which a court is obligated to follow earlier decisions of that court or higher courts within the same jurisdiction. This is a major characteristic of the common law system.

binding authority
Any source of law that a court must follow when deciding a case. Binding authorities include constitutions, statutes, and regulations that govern the issue being decided, as well as court decisions that are controlling precedents within the jurisdiction.

persuasive precedent
A precedent decided in another jurisdiction that a court may either follow or reject but that is entitled to careful consideration.

The doctrine of *stare decisis* helps the courts be more efficient because if other courts have carefully reasoned through similar cases, their legal reasoning and opinions can serve as guides. *Stare decisis* also makes the law more stable and predictable. If the law on a given subject is well settled and there are numerous precedents, someone wishing to bring a case is likely to be told by an attorney how the law will resolve the matter.

Departures from Precedent

Sometimes a court will depart from the rule of precedent. If a court decides that a precedent is wrong or that technological or social changes have made the precedent inappropriate, the court might overrule the precedent. These cases often receive a great deal of publicity.

EXAMPLE 5.2 In *Brown v. Board of Education of Topeka*,[2] decided in 1954, the United States Supreme Court expressly overturned prior precedent when it held that separate schools for whites and African Americans, which had been upheld as constitutional in previous cases, were in violation of the Constitution. The Supreme Court's departure from precedent in *Brown* received tremendous publicity as people began to realize the impact of this change in the law. It helped encourage the civil rights movement, which included legal challenges to existing procedures.

IN THE OFFICE

DAILY CLEANUP

A neat office is important. A messy desk presents a less-than-professional appearance. But, more importantly, staying neat forces us to stay organized. When papers are piled up on a desk or in a file cabinet, files might be lost even though we may not realize it. The only work item that should be on a desk is what you are working on that day. At the end of every day, the desk should be cleared.

As a part of that, all papers must be filed in their proper files (and copies made if they are needed). Don't presume you will do it tomorrow. Have everything put away where it belongs so you can start fresh the next workday. Most legal documents are confidential and should be put away except when being worked on so they are unlikely to be seen by unauthorized parties.

Cases of First Impression

Sometimes, there is no precedent on which to base a decision, as when a case involves a new technology. (See this chapter's *Technology and Today's Paralegal* feature on the facing page for a case of this kind involving the right to access videos made from police cars.)

case of first impression
A case presenting a legal issue that has not yet been addressed by a court in a particular jurisdiction.

public policy
A governmental policy based on widely held societal values.

remedy
The means by which a right is enforced or the violation of a right is prevented or compensated for.

court of law
A court in which the only remedies were things of value, such as money. Historically, in England, courts of law were different from courts of equity.

remedy at law
A remedy available in a court of law. Money damages and items of value are awarded as a remedy at law.

remedy in equity
A remedy allowed by courts in situations where remedies at law are not appropriate. Remedies in equity are based on rules of fairness, justice, and honesty.

court of equity
A court that decides controversies and administers justice according to the rules, principles, and precedents of equity.

EXAMPLE 5.3 A New Jersey court had to decide whether a surrogate-parenting contract should be enforced against the wishes of the surrogate parent (the birth mother).[3] This was the first such case to reach the courts, and there was no precedent in any jurisdiction to which the court could look for guidance. (Note: The court invalidated the contract, but upheld the original agreement by treating it as a child custody case and awarded custody to the parents who hired the surrogate.)

Cases with no precedents are called cases of first impression. In these cases or when precedents conflict, courts may consider a number of factors, including legal principles and policies underlying previous court decisions or existing statutes, fairness, social values and customs, public policy (a governmental policy based on widely held societal values), and data and concepts drawn from the social sciences. Which of these sources receives the greatest emphasis will depend on the nature of the case being considered and the particular judge hearing the case.

Judges try to be free of personal bias in deciding cases. Each judge, however, has a unique personality, values or philosophical leanings, personal history, and intellectual attributes—all of which frame the decision-making process.

Remedies at Law versus Remedies in Equity

The early English courts could grant only limited remedies. If one person wronged another in some way, the court could award as compensation land, items of value, or money. The courts that awarded these things became known as courts of law, and the three remedies awarded by these courts became known as remedies at law.

This system helped to standardize the ways in which disputes were settled, but parties who wanted a remedy other than economic compensation could not be helped. Sometimes these parties petitioned the king for relief. Most petitions were decided by an adviser to the king, called a *chancellor*, who was said to be the "keeper of the king's conscience." When the chancellor thought that the claim was a fair one for which there was no adequate remedy at law, he would fashion a different remedy, called a remedy in equity. In this way, a new body of rules and remedies came into being and eventually led to the establishment of formal courts of chancery, or courts of equity.

TECHNOLOGY AND TODAY'S PARALEGAL

CASES OF FIRST IMPRESSION AND POLICE VIDEOS

The evolution of technology means courts must deal with new issues that lead to cases of first impression. Here, we look at an Ohio case involving the right to access videos made in police cars. The question raised was whether a citizen could require the police to provide access to videos made from police cars when officers stop drivers for suspected violations.[a]

Cases involving the use of new technology can raise novel questions.

DO CITIZENS HAVE RIGHT OF ACCESS TO POLICE VIDEOS?

Miller works with a group in Ohio that is opposed to alleged abuse of government power. To help further the group's goals, Miller often makes public records requests to bring light to government waste or abuse.

Ohio Highway Patrol Officer Westhoven pulled over Ruberg, who was driving 72 mph in a 45–mph zone. The officer noticed that Ruberg's eyes were red, and he detected the smell of alcohol. Sobriety tests indicated that Ruberg was under the influence. A Breathalyzer test showed her blood-alcohol level to be .116, well above the legal limit. She was arrested and charged with driving under the influence.

The arrest was captured on video by the officer's dashboard camera. Miller requested various documents related to the arrest, along with a copy of Ruberg's arrest video. The Highway Patrol refused to comply because the requested items were being used in an ongoing criminal investigation of Ruberg.

Miller brought a *mandamus* action at the Ohio Court of Appeals (*mandamus* is a request that a superior court require a lower-level official to perform a public duty properly.) Miller asked the court to force the Highway Patrol to provide the documents he requested. The court dismissed his request. Miller appealed to the Ohio Supreme Court, contending that he was entitled to relief. That court held that the Highway Patrol had failed to properly consider Miller's request but did not determine if he had the right to have a copy of the video. The case was sent back (remanded) to the Court of Appeals for further consideration.

a. *State v. Ohio State Highway Patrol*, 14 N.E.3d 396 (Ct. App., Ohio, 2014).

REVIEW OF CASE OF FIRST IMPRESSION

The court was required by the state supreme court to review the withheld records and determine if they fell within the "confidential law enforcement investigatory record" exception to the Public Records Act. The request for the video was an issue that had not been raised before, so it was a matter of first impression.

The Court of Appeals explained that the law favors release of government documents to citizens who request them. However, when a law enforcement matter is under investigation, materials related to the investigation may be withheld. Citing earlier decisions relating to materials withheld from release, the court held that the portion of the video related to the "traffic stop, detention, and arrest" of Ruberg were part of the criminal investigation performed by the officer, so it was not subject to public access until the legal matter was resolved.

RESEARCHING CASES OF FIRST IMPRESSION

New technology poses new issues for the courts in adapting traditional legal principles to novel situations. Your approach to research thus needs to be flexible. First, see if there is existing law that the judge might determine should apply to your case (or that your supervising attorney can argue should apply). This is important given that new technologies have forced the courts to adapt existing law to meet the needs of modern society. Second, look to see if any other court (in a different state or district, for example) has considered a similar legal issue and what that court concluded. Although cases decided in other jurisdictions are not binding, courts often look at how other courts have handled an issue when deciding matters of first impression.

TECHNOLOGY TIP

Generally, when researching cases of first impression, you will need to broaden the scope of your search of the sources of law. A wise paralegal will be creative and adopt a research strategy aimed at discovering which laws *may* apply and which laws *should* apply given the specific facts of the case.

Equity is the branch of law, founded on what might be described as notions of justice and fair dealing, that seeks to supply a remedy when there is no adequate remedy available at law. Once the courts of equity were established, plaintiffs could bring claims in either courts of law (if they sought money damages) or courts of equity (if they sought equitable remedies). Plaintiffs had to specify whether they were bringing an "action at law" or an "action in equity," and they chose their courts accordingly. Only one remedy could be granted for a particular wrong. Today, the separate courts have been combined and both types of remedies can be sought. (See Exhibit 5.1 below.)

Equitable Principles and Maxims

equitable principles and maxims
Propositions or general statements of rules of law that are frequently involved in equity jurisdiction.

Courts in the United States can award both legal and equitable remedies, so plaintiffs may request both equitable and legal relief in the same case. Whenever a court orders a party to do or not do something as part of a remedy, such as to stop a discriminatory practice, it is providing an equitable remedy. Yet judges continue to be guided by equitable principles and maxims when deciding whether to grant equitable remedies. *Maxims* are propositions or general statements of rules of law that courts often use in arriving at a decision. Some of the most influential maxims of equity are:

- Whoever seeks equity must do equity. (Anyone who wishes to be treated fairly must treat others fairly.)

- Equity requires clean hands. (The plaintiff must have acted fairly and honestly.)

- Equity will not suffer a right to exist without a remedy. (Equitable relief will be awarded when there is a right to relief and there is no adequate legal remedy.)

- Equity values substance over form. (It is more concerned with fairness and justice than with legal technicalities.)

- Equity aids the vigilant, not those who sleep on their rights. (Individuals who fail to assert their legal rights within a reasonable time will not be helped.)

Doctrine of Laches

laches
An equitable doctrine that bars a party's right to legal action if the party has neglected for an unreasonable length of time to act on his or her rights.

The last maxim listed above has evolved into the equitable doctrine of laches to encourage people to bring lawsuits while the evidence is still fresh. The idea is that if a party waits too long, the party has "slept on his rights" and lost the ability to bring a claim. What constitutes a reasonable time depends on the circumstances of the case.

EXAMPLE 5.4 The Nature Conservancy (TNC) contracted to buy land from Wilder Corporation. Wilder promised there were no storage tanks on the property. Six years later, having discovered such tanks, TNC sued. Wilder claimed that laches barred the suit—TNC had waited too long to sue. The appeals court held that laches did not apply, as there was no unreasonable delay by TNC in bringing the litigation.[4]

The time period for pursuing a particular claim against another party is now usually fixed by a statute of limitations (see Chapter 3 on page 64). After the time allowed under the statute of limitations has expired, further action on that claim is barred. (See *Ethics Watch* on the next page.)

For civil wrongs (torts), the statute of limitations varies, typically ranging from two to five years. For contracts involving the sale of goods, it is normally four years. For

EXHIBIT 5.1

Procedural Differences between an Action at Law and an Action in Equity

Procedure	Action at Law	Action in Equity
Decision	By judge or jury	By judge (no jury)
Result	Judgment	Decree
Remedy	Monetary damages	Injunction or decree of specific performance

criminal prosecutions, the duration is related to the seriousness of the offense. For example, the statute of limitations for petty theft (the theft of an item of insignificant value) may be a year, while the statute of limitations for armed robbery might be twenty years. For the most serious crimes involving first degree murder, there is no statute of limitations.

Equitable Remedies

As mentioned previously, equitable remedies are normally granted only if the court concludes that the remedy at law (monetary damages) is inadequate. The most important equitable remedies—specific performance and injunction—are discussed here and will be discussed further in Chapter 15.

SPECIFIC PERFORMANCE.   A judge's decree of specific performance is an order to do what was promised. This remedy was, and still is, generally only available in the United States when the dispute before the court concerns a contractual transaction involving something unique for which money damages are inadequate. By contrast, many European countries routinely allow a decree of specific performance. The parties to complex contracts also regularly include provisions in their contracts allowing each to seek it against the other in case of breach.

Contracts for the sale of goods that are readily available on the market rarely qualify for specific performance. Monetary damages ordinarily are adequate in such situations because substantially identical goods can be bought or sold in the market.

If the goods are unique, however, a court of equity may grant specific performance. For example, paintings, sculptures, and rare books and coins are so unique that money damages will not enable a buyer to obtain substantially identical substitutes in the market. Similarly, it is sometimes allowed in cases involving the sale of a business. The same principle applies to disputes relating to interests in land because each parcel is unique.

specific performance
An equitable remedy requiring the performance that was specified in a contract; usually granted only when money damages would be an inadequate remedy and the subject matter of the contract is unique (for example, real property).

ETHICS WATCH

THE STATUTE OF LIMITATIONS AND THE DUTY OF COMPETENCE

The duty of competence requires, among other things, that attorneys and paralegals be aware of the statute of limitations governing a client's legal matter. For example, if a client of your firm, a restaurant owner, wanted to sue a restaurant-supply company for breaking a contract for the sale of dishes, the first thing you should check is your state's statute of limitations covering contracts for the sale of goods. If the time period is about to expire, then you and your supervising attorney need to act quickly to make sure that the complaint (the document that initiates a lawsuit) is filed before the claim is time barred.

Of course, the attorney is responsible to the client, but it is normal for an attorney to rely on a paralegal to check such details. This example reflects the NFPA *Model Code of Ethics and Professional Responsibility*, Section 1.1(a), "A paralegal shall achieve competency through education, training, and work experience," and Section 1.1(c), "A paralegal shall perform all assignments promptly and efficiently."

Reprinted by permission of the National Federation of Paralegal Associations, Inc. (NFPA®). www.paralegals.org.

EXAMPLE 5.5 A party agreed to sell a piece of land to a buyer who hired engineers and architects to design a building suited for the land. Right before the transaction was to be completed, and for no clear reason, the seller refused to go through with the property transfer. The buyer may sue for specific performance, asking the court to require the sale to proceed, due to the time and expense in planning for use of the property.

Specific performance is rarely granted in cases involving personal services, but see *Developing Paralegal Skills* on the facing page for a practical example of how the issue arises.

INJUNCTION.　An **injunction** is a court order in equity directing the defendant to do or, more commonly, to refrain from doing a particular act. An injunction may be obtained to stop a neighbor from burning trash in his yard or to prevent an estranged husband from coming near his wife.

EXAMPLE 5.6 Jacqueline Kennedy Onassis asked a court to stop a photographer from stunts such as throwing a firecracker near her or getting someone to scream at her so he could get an unusual photograph to sell at a high price. The court agreed that money was not the issue and ordered the photographer to keep his distance and not to pull any tricks.

Persons who violate injunctions may be held in contempt of court and punished with a jail sentence or a fine.

injunction
A court decree ordering a person to do or to refrain from doing a certain act.

The Common Law Today

The common law—which consists of the rules of law announced in previous court decisions—plays a significant role in the United States. As with contracts and property, the rules governing tort law (civil wrongs) are largely common law. Even where there is a statute, court decisions often play an important role by clarifying ambiguous statutory language. Federal and state courts frequently must interpret and enforce constitutional provisions, statutes enacted by legislatures, and regulations created by administrative agencies.

To summarize and clarify common law rules and principles, the American Law Institute (ALI) has published a number of *Restatements of the Law*. The ALI, which was formed in the 1920s, is a group of highly regarded practicing attorneys, legal scholars, and judges. The *Restatements* generally summarize and explain the common law rules that are followed in most states with regard to a particular area of law, such as contracts or torts. Although the *Restatements* do not have the force of law unless adopted by a state's highest court, they are important secondary sources of legal analysis on which judges often rely in making their decisions. You will read more about the *Restatements of the Law* in Chapter 7, in the context of legal research.

The Terminology of Case Law

Throughout this text, you will encounter terms traditionally used to describe parties to lawsuits, case titles, and the types of decisions that judges write. Although details on how to research case law will be given in Chapter 7, it is worthwhile at this point to explain some of the terminology.

Case Titles

The title of a case, or the *case name*, indicates the names of the parties to the lawsuit. A case title, such as *Baranski v. Peretto*, includes only the parties' surnames, not their first names. The *v.* in the case title stands for *versus*, which means "against." In the trial court (the court in which a lawsuit is first brought and tried), Baranski is the plaintiff, so Baranski's name appears first in the case title.

DEVELOPING PARALEGAL SKILLS

REQUIREMENTS FOR SPECIFIC PERFORMANCE

Louise Lassen, a wealthy heiress, buys a painting from an artist in New York for $275,000. The artist agrees to ship the painting to Louise's home in Chicago within two weeks. After Louise returns home, she learns from the artist that he has changed his mind—he is no longer interested in selling the painting and is returning her payment.

Louise contacts the firm of Murdoch & Larson to have the contract enforced. Kevin Murdoch, one of the firm's partners, asks paralegal Ling Humboldt to assist him in determining whether the remedy of specific performance, which would require the artist to provide the painting, can be sought. Ling is to research case law on specific performance and prepare a research memorandum summarizing his results. Ling lets the attorney know that he will have the memorandum on the attorney's desk by the next morning.

CHECKLIST FOR ANALYZING A LEGAL PROBLEM

- Gather the facts involved in the problem.
- Determine whether unique or rare articles are involved.
- Find out what type of remedy the client wants.
- Determine whether a remedy at law, such as money damages, will compensate the client.
- Apply the law to the client's facts to reach a conclusion regarding the appropriate remedy.

If the case is appealed to a higher court for review, the appeals court sometimes places the name of the party appealing the decision first, so that the case may be called *Peretto v. Baranski*. Because some appeals courts retain the trial court order of names, it is often impossible to distinguish the plaintiff from the defendant just by looking at the title of a reported decision. You must read the facts of the case to identify the parties.

When attorneys or paralegals refer to a court decision, they give the title of the case and the case citation. The **citation** indicates the reports or reporters in which the case can be found (reports and reporters are volumes in which cases are published, or "reported").

citation
A reference that indicates where a particular constitutional provision, statute, reported case, or article can be found.

EXAMPLE 5.7 A citation to 251 Kan. 728 following a case name (*Tongish v. Thomas*) indicates that the opinion (the court decision) is found in volume 251 of the Kansas state court reports on page 728. You will read more about how to read case citations and locate case law in Chapter 7.

The Parties

The **parties** to a lawsuit are the plaintiff, who initiates (files) the lawsuit, and the defendant, against whom the lawsuit is brought. Lawsuits frequently involve multiple parties—that is, more than one plaintiff or defendant.

party
With respect to lawsuits, the plaintiff or the defendant. Some cases involve multiple parties (more than one plaintiff or defendant).

EXAMPLE 5.8 A consumer named Aiken, claiming to be injured by a product made by Toshiba that he purchased at Target, may sue both Toshiba and Target (the manufacturer and the retailer) to try to obtain compensation for injuries alleged to be caused by the product. The manufacturer and the retailer would be *co-defendants*. On appeal, the party asking for review is often called the *appellant* and the other party is called the *appellee*.

Why is the common law important even in areas that are primarily governed by statutory law?

© Pressmaster/www.Shutterstock.com.

Judges and Justices

The terms *judge* and *justice* usually mean the same and represent two designations given to judges in various courts. All members of the United States Supreme Court are referred to as justices. Justice is also the formal title usually given to judges of appeals courts, although this is not always the case. Different states use different terms. Justice is commonly abbreviated as J., justices as JJ, and Chief Justice as C.J. A Supreme Court case might refer to Justice Sotomayor as Sotomayor, J., or to Chief Justice Roberts as Roberts, C.J.

In a trial court, one judge hears a case. In an appeals court, normally a panel of three or more judges (or justices) sits on the bench to hear the appeal. Decisions reached by appeals courts are often explained in written court opinions.

Decisions and Opinions

opinion
A statement by the court setting forth the applicable law and the reasons for its decision in a case.

The opinion typically contains a brief procedural history of the case, a summary of the relevant facts, the court's reasons for its decision, the rules of law that apply, and the judgment. There are five types of opinions. When all judges or justices agree on an opinion, the opinion is written for the entire court and is called a *unanimous opinion*. When there is not a unanimous opinion, a *majority opinion* is written, explaining the views of the majority of the judges deciding the case. Sometimes a majority agrees on the result but not on the reasoning. The opinion joined by the largest number of judges, but less than a majority, is called a *plurality opinion*.

A judge who feels strongly about making or emphasizing a point that was not made in the majority opinion writes a *concurring opinion*. In that opinion, the judge agrees (concurs) with the decision given in the majority opinion but for different reasons. When an opinion is not unanimous, a judge who does not agree with the majority may write a *dissenting opinion*. The dissenting opinion may be important as it may form the basis of arguments used in the future to modify the law or even overrule the current majority opinion.

The Adversarial System of Justice

adversarial system of justice
A legal system in which the parties to a lawsuit are opponents, or adversaries, and present their cases in the light most favorable to themselves. The impartial decision maker (the judge or jury) determines who wins based on an application of the law to the evidence presented.

U.S. courts follow the adversarial system of justice, in which the parties act as adversaries, or opponents. Parties to a lawsuit come before the court as contestants, both sides presenting the facts of their cases in the light most favorable to themselves, in an attempt to win. The parties do not come to the courtroom with the idea of working out a compromise solution to their problems or of looking at the dispute from each other's point of view. Rather, they take sides, present their best case to the judge or jury (if it is a jury trial), and hope that the decision maker rules in their favor. Because both sides' positions are tested at trial, in theory the strongest case wins.

The Goal Is to Win

The role of the attorney is to discover and present the strongest legal argument on behalf of a client, regardless of personal feelings about the client or the client's case. Because of the adversarial nature of our system, you may be asked to work on cases that you do not believe in or for clients you do not like.

Constitutional Law

We turn next to other primary sources of law. The federal government and the states have separate written constitutions that set forth the general organization, powers, and limits of their respective governments. Constitutional law is the law made up of the text of a constitution and court decisions interpreting that text.

constitutional law
Law based on the U.S. Constitution and the constitutions of the states.

The Federal Constitution

The U.S. Constitution is often called the nation's highest law. This principle is set forth in Article VI of the Constitution, which states that the Constitution, laws, and treaties of the United States are "the supreme Law of the Land." This provision is commonly referred to as the supremacy clause. A law in conflict with the Constitution (including its amendments), no matter what its source, will be declared unconstitutional when challenged.

supremacy clause
The provision in Article VI of the U.S. Constitution that declares the Constitution, laws, and treaties of the United States "the supreme Law of the Land."

EXAMPLE 5.9 Congress is authorized by the Constitution to regulate trade with foreign nations. If a state passes a law to prohibit the import into the state of products from a particular country, or imposes taxes on imports, the state law would be unconstitutional, as it is in conflict with the Constitution.

The U.S. Constitution consists of seven articles. These articles, which are summarized in Exhibit 5.2 on the following page, set forth the powers of the three branches of government and the relationships among the three branches.

Constitutional Rights

Soon after the Constitution had been ratified by the states, the first Congress of the United States submitted amendments to the Constitution to the states for approval.

BILL OF RIGHTS. The first ten amendments, commonly known as the Bill of Rights, were adopted in 1791 and provide protections for individuals—and in some cases, business entities—against various types of government interference. Summarized below are the protections mentioned by the Bill of Rights. The full text of the Constitution, including its amendments (there are now twenty-seven), is presented in Appendix I.

Bill of Rights
The first ten amendments to the U.S. Constitution.

1. The First Amendment guarantees the freedoms of religion, speech, and the press and the rights to assemble peaceably and to petition the government.
2. The Second Amendment guarantees the right to keep and bear arms.
3. The Third Amendment prohibits, in peacetime, the lodging of soldiers in any house without the owner's consent.
4. The Fourth Amendment prohibits unreasonable searches and seizures of persons or property.

EXHIBIT 5.2

The Articles of the
U.S. Constitution

Article I creates and empowers the legislature. It provides that Congress is to consist of a Senate and a House of Representatives and fixes the composition of each house and the election procedures, qualifications, and compensation for senators and representatives. Article I also establishes the procedures for enacting legislation and the areas of law in which Congress has the power to legislate.

Article II establishes the executive branch, the process for electing and removing a president from office, the qualifications to be president, and the powers of the president.

Article III creates the judicial branch and authorizes the appointment, compensation, and removal of judges. It also sets forth the jurisdiction of the courts and defines *treason*.

Article IV requires that all states respect one another's laws. It requires each state to give citizens of other states the same rights and privileges it gives its own citizens. It requires that persons accused of crimes be returned to the state in which the crime was committed.

Article V governs the process for amending the Constitution.

Article VI establishes the Constitution as the supreme law of the land. It requires that every federal and state official take an oath of office promising to support the Constitution. It specifies that religion is not a required qualification to serve in any federal office.

Article VII required the consent of nine of the original thirteen states to ratify the Constitution.

5. The Fifth Amendment guarantees the rights to indictment by grand jury and to due process of law and prohibits compulsory self-incrimination and double jeopardy. (This will be discussed in Chapter 13, which deals with criminal law and procedures.) The Fifth Amendment also prohibits the taking of private property for public use without just compensation.

6. The Sixth Amendment guarantees the accused in a criminal case the right to a speedy and public trial by an impartial jury and the right to counsel. The accused has the right to cross-examine opposing witnesses and to solicit testimony from favorable witnesses.

7. The Seventh Amendment guarantees the right to a trial by jury in a civil case involving at least twenty dollars.[5]

8. The Eighth Amendment prohibits excessive bail and fines, as well as cruel and unusual punishment.

9. The Ninth Amendment establishes that the people have rights in addition to those specified in the Constitution.

10. The Tenth Amendment establishes that powers neither delegated to the federal government nor denied to the states are reserved for the states.

APPLICATION TO STATE GOVERNMENTS.   Originally, the Bill of Rights limited only the powers of the national government. That changed after the adoption of the Fourteenth Amendment to the Constitution. That amendment, passed in 1868 after the Civil War, provides in part: "No State shall . . . deprive any person of life, liberty, or property, without due process of law." The Supreme Court defines various rights and liberties guaranteed in the national Constitution as "due process of law," which is required of state governments under the Fourteenth Amendment. Today, most of the rights in the Bill of Rights—such as the freedoms of speech and religion guaranteed by the First Amendment—apply to state governments as well as to the national government.

The Courts and Constitutional Law

The rights secured by the Bill of Rights are not absolute. The principles outlined in the Constitution are given form and substance by the courts. Courts often have to balance the rights and freedoms stated in the Bill of Rights against other rights, such as the right to be free from the harmful actions of others. Ultimately, it is the United States Supreme Court, as the final interpreter of the Constitution that gives meaning to constitutional rights and determines their boundaries.

COURTS BALANCE THE RIGHT TO FREE SPEECH.   An instance of how the courts must balance the rights and freedoms granted by the Constitution can be found by looking at our right to free speech. Even though the First Amendment guarantees the right to free speech, we are not, in fact, free to say anything we want.

EXAMPLE 5.10 In interpreting the meaning of the First Amendment, the Supreme Court has been clear that certain speech will not be protected. Speech that harms the good reputation of another, for instance, is commonly considered to be a tort, or civil wrong. If the speaker is sued, she may be ordered by a court to pay damages to the harmed person (as you will read in Chapter 14).

FREE SPEECH AND THE INTERNET.   The Internet raised new issues for the courts in determining how to apply the protections conferred by the Constitution, particularly with respect to free speech. For example, the Supreme Court ruled that obscene speech, though difficult to define, is not entitled to complete First Amendment protection. Regulating obscene online speech has proved to be difficult.

EXAMPLE 5.11 Congress attempted to prohibit online obscenity in the Communications Decency Act (CDA), which made it a crime to make available to minors online any "obscene or indecent" message.[6] Civil rights groups claimed the CDA was an unconstitutional restraint on speech. The Supreme Court held that portions of the act were unconstitutional in *Reno v. American Civil Liberties Union*.[7] Congress then passed the Child Online Protection Act (COPA).[8] That law was struck down by a federal appeals court as being unconstitutional because it was too vague.[9] The Supreme Court agreed with that ruling.[10]

State Constitutions

Each state has a constitution that sets forth the general organization, powers, and limits of the state government. The Tenth Amendment to the U.S. Constitution, which defines the powers and limitations of the federal government, reserves all powers not granted to the federal government to the states. Unless they conflict with the U.S. Constitution, state constitutions are supreme within the states' border, so they are important sources of law. Many state constitutions are much more detailed than the federal Constitution; Alabama's is 40 times longer than the U.S. Constitution.

Statutory Law

Statutes, which are laws enacted by legislative bodies at any level of government, make up a major source of law. The body of written laws created by the legislature is generally referred to as statutory law.

statute
A written law enacted by a legislature under its constitutional lawmaking authority.

statutory law
The body of written laws enacted by the legislature.

Federal Statutes

Federal statutes are laws that are enacted by the U.S. Congress. As mentioned, any law—including a federal statute—that violates the U.S. Constitution will be struck down. Areas of federal statute law include protection of intellectual property rights (see Chapter 15), regulation of the purchase and sale of corporate stock (see Chapter 18), prohibition of employment discrimination (see Chapter 18), protection of the environment (see Chapter 19), and protection of consumers (discussed in Chapter 14). As is discussed in the *Featured Contributor* box on pages 134 and 135, paralegals must know how to use a variety of legal sources to research federal, state, and local statutes pertaining to a given case.

The Federal Government's Constitutional Authority to Enact Laws

federal system
The system of government established by the Constitution, in which the national government and the state governments share sovereign power.

In the federal system of government established by the Constitution, the national government (usually called the federal government) and the state governments *share* sovereign power. The Constitution specifies, however, that certain powers can be exercised only by the national government. For example, the national government is authorized to regulate domestic and foreign commerce (trade).

The president of the United States is the nation's chief executive and commander in chief of the armed forces. And, as already noted, the Constitution makes clear that laws made by the national government take priority over conflicting state laws. At the same time, the Constitution provides for certain states' rights, including the right to control commerce within state borders and to exercise powers to protect public health, safety, morals, and general welfare.

To protect citizens from the national government using its power arbitrarily, the Constitution divided the national government's powers among three branches:

- The legislative branch, or Congress, which makes the laws.

- The executive branch, which enforces the laws.

- The judicial branch, which interprets the laws.

checks and balances
A system in which each of the three branches of the national government—executive, legislative, and judicial—exercises a check on the actions of the other two branches.

Each branch performs a separate function, and no branch may exercise the authority of another branch. Each branch has some power to limit the actions of the other branches. Congress, for example, can enact legislation relating to spending and commerce, but the president can veto that legislation. The executive branch is responsible for foreign affairs, but treaties with foreign governments require approval by the Senate. Although Congress determines the jurisdiction of the federal courts, the federal courts have the power to hold acts of the other branches of the federal government unconstitutional. With this system of checks and balances, no one branch of government should accumulate too much power.

The Federal Lawmaking Process

Each law passed by Congress begins as a *bill*, which may be introduced either in the House of Representatives or in the Senate. Often, similar bills are introduced in both chambers of Congress. In either the House or the Senate, the bill is referred to a committee and its subcommittees for study, discussion, hearings, and rewriting. If the committee does not approve the bill, it "dies" and goes no further. If approved by the committee, it is scheduled for debate by the full House or Senate. Finally, a vote is taken, and the bill is passed or defeated. If the two chambers pass similar, but not identical, bills, a *conference committee* is formed to write a compromise bill, which must then be approved by both chambers before it is sent to the president to sign. Once the president signs the bill, it becomes law.

During the legislative process, bills are identified by a number. A bill in the House of Representatives is identified by a number preceded by "HR" (such as HR 212). In the

Senate, the bill's number is preceded by an "S" (such as S 212). When both chambers pass the bill and it is signed into law by the president, the statute is initially published in the form of a *slip law*. The slip law is assigned a public law number, or P.L. number (such as P.L. 5030).

At the end of the two-year congressional term, or session, the statute is published in the term's *session laws*, which are collections of statutes contained in volumes and arranged by year or legislative session. The statute is included in the *United States Code*, in which all federal laws are codified (systematized, or arranged in topical order). You may need to locate a statute by bill number, public law number, or U.S. Code section number in the course of your research. (See Chapter 7 for further details on federal statutes.)

public law number
An identification number assigned to a statute.

State Statutes

State statutes are laws enacted by state legislatures. Any state law that is found by a court to conflict with the U.S. Constitution or with the state's constitution will be deemed unconstitutional. State statutes include state laws governing real property and insurance (see Chapter 16), estates and family law (discussed in Chapter 17), the formation of corporations and other business entities (see Chapter 18), and certain crimes (see Chapter 13), along with state versions of the Uniform Commercial Code (to be discussed shortly).

Conflicts between Federal and State Laws

If a state statute conflicts with a federal statute, the state law is invalid. Because some powers are shared, however, it is necessary to determine which law governs in a particular circumstance. *Concurrent powers* are those shared by the federal government and the states, such as the power to impose taxes or to establish courts.

Preemption occurs when Congress chooses to act exclusively in a concurrent area. In this circumstance, a valid federal law or regulation in the preempted area takes precedence over a conflicting state or local law. Often, it is not clear whether Congress, in passing a law, intended to preempt an entire area of law. In these situations, the courts must determine Congress's intention. No single factor determines whether a court will find preemption. Congress has recognized that the states regulate some areas of business, such as insurance. In those areas, Congress generally does not preempt state law. As the *Developing Paralegal Skills* feature on page 136 discusses, federal preemption of state law can be a critical issue.

preemption
A doctrine under which a federal law preempts, or takes precedence over, conflicting state and local laws.

The State Lawmaking Process

When passing laws, state legislatures follow procedures similar to those followed in Congress. All of the states except one have bicameral (two-chamber) legislatures (Nebraska has a unicameral, or one-chamber, legislature). Bills may be introduced in either chamber, or both chambers, of the legislature. As in the U.S. Congress, if the two chambers pass bills that differ from one another in any respect, a conference committee works out a compromise, which must then be approved by both chambers before being sent to the state's governor to sign into law. State constitutions often impose additional restrictions on state legislatures beyond what the federal constitution imposes on Congress. For example, many state legislatures operate under a state constitutional "single subject rule" which requires that each piece of legislation address only one subject, while Congress is free to combine multiple topics within a single bill.

Local Ordinances

Statutory law also includes local governments' ordinances. An ordinance is an order, rule, or law passed by a city, county, or special district government to govern matters not covered by federal or state law. As state governments create local governments,

ordinance
An order, rule, or law enacted by a municipal or county government to govern a local matter as allowed by state or federal legislation.

FEATURED CONTRIBUTOR

SOURCES OF LAW

John D. DeLeo, Jr.

BIOGRAPHICAL NOTE

John D. DeLeo, Jr. earned a B.A. from Penn State University and a law degree from Loyola of New Orleans College of Law. He is licensed to practice law in Louisiana and Pennsylvania. For the past 25 years, DeLeo has served as a professor and director of the Legal Studies Program at Central Penn College in Summerdale, PA, where he was Faculty Member of the Year for 1990, 1993 and 2005. He is the author of *The Student's Guide to Understanding Constitutional Law*; *Administrative Law*; and co-author of *The Pennsylvania Paralegal*, published by Delmar Cengage Learning.

SOURCES OF LAW

Imagine that authorities have quarantined one of your firm's clients because it is alleged that he or she was exposed to Ebola and thus poses a health risk to the public. What can be done? You are asked to do the legal research and draft a memo that gives the attorney options in assisting the client. You will learn the mechanics of doing research and finding sources of law in your legal research classes. For now, let's take a look at the *kinds* of legal sources that can give you answers.

The Constitution

The Constitution is the supreme law of the land, and all federal, state and local officials must operate with its bounds. The Constitution consists of seven articles that comprise the original text, in addition to the Bill of Rights (the first ten amendments) plus seventeen other amendments. The Constitution

is the source of many rights such as freedom of speech, due process, and equal protection. All states also have their own constitutions.

Statutes

Congress and state governments pass statutes that may add to the rights found in the Constitution and state constitutions. The Civil Rights Act of 1964 that outlawed discrimination based on race, and national origin is one example. States pass statutes that control within state borders.

Judicial Rulings/Common Law

Courts from the United States Supreme Court on down to state courts interpret statutes and base their rulings on a body of common law known as judge-made law. For example, the law related to contracts has been developed by judges in the process of deciding cases.

ordinances may not violate the state or federal Constitution, or go beyond what is allowed by state law. Local ordinances often have to do with land use (zoning ordinances), building and safety codes, construction and appearance of housing, and other matters affecting a local area. Persons who violate ordinances may be fined, jailed, or both.

Uniform Laws

Many areas of state law vary from state to state. The differences were particularly notable in the 1800s, when conflicting statutes created problems for the rapidly developing trade among the states. To counter these problems, a group of legal scholars and lawyers formed the National Conference of Commissioners on Uniform State Laws (NCCUSL) in 1892 to draft uniform statutes for adoption by the states.

Executive Orders

An executive order is issued by the president or governor directing an agency to follow a certain policy. Such orders do not require legislative approval.

Rules or Regulations

Federal and state agencies issue regulations—policies that implement and enforce a statute. For example, in the area of environmental law, Congress might pass a statute that directs the Environmental Protection Agency (EPA) in general terms to "clean up the air." The EPA then issues regulations that ban or limit various emissions.

Now, let's look at how these sources could be useful to you in researching the issue at hand.

> " ... a paralegal needs to know many sources to be an effective researcher."

The Constitution

A government may only quarantine individuals within the bounds of the Constitution and the constitution of the respective state. Individuals who are detained can file a writ of *habeas corpus* under Article I, Sec. 9 of the Constitution to challenge the legality of their detention. States have primary authority for containing infectious diseases within their borders based on state "police power" derived from the Tenth Amendment to the Constitution.

Statutes

Congress passed the Public Health Service Act to prevent the entry and spread of communicable diseases from foreign countries into the United States and between states. States also pass laws designed to protect citizens from communicable diseases. An example of a state statute is one passed by Maine to deal with disease outbreaks (22 M.R.S. Section 811(3)). This statute authorizes a court to "make such orders as it deems necessary to protect other individuals from the dangers of infection."

Judicial Rulings/Common Law

An American nurse treated patients with Ebola in West Africa. She then returned to New Jersey, where she was quarantined for three days before returning to her home in Maine. A state judge in Maine, pursuant to 22 M.R.S. Section 811(3), issued an order specifying the limits on her activity during the 21-day incubation period. The United States Supreme Court has recognized the power of states to quarantine individuals to prevent the spread of infectious diseases.

Executive Orders

Federal Executive Order 13295 lists the communicable diseases for which individuals can be subject to quarantine. These diseases are cholera, diphtheria, infectious tuberculosis, plague, smallpox, yellow fever, viral hemorrhagic fevers (including Ebola), SARS, and influenza viruses.

Rules or Regulations

The Public Health Service Act grants the secretary of Health and Human Services the authority to make and enforce regulations "to prevent the introduction, transmission, or spread of communicable diseases from foreign countries into the States or possessions, or from one State or possession into any other State or possession." The authority for carrying out these functions on a daily basis has been delegated to the Centers for Disease Control and Prevention. State health agencies also issue regulations to control the spread of infectious diseases.

As this example shows, a paralegal needs to be familiar with many legal sources to be an effective researcher. By knowing where to look and casting a wide net in your research, you will be in a position to provide answers for your attorney and serve the best interests of the firm's client.

The NCCUSL continues to issue uniform statutes, often in conjunction with the American Law Institute.

Adoption of uniform laws is a state matter, and a state may reject all or part of proposed uniform laws or rewrite them as the state legislature wishes. Hence, even when a uniform law is adopted in many states, the laws may not be entirely "uniform." Once adopted by a state legislature, a uniform act becomes a part of the statutory law of that state.

EXAMPLE 5.12 A uniform law that has been adopted (at least in part) by all states is the Uniform Commercial Code (UCC) (discussed in Chapter 15). First published in 1962, it provides a set of rules governing commercial transactions and sales contracts. It helps harmonize terms of sales across state lines and sets rules for bank checks and other standard financial instruments.

DEVELOPING PARALEGAL SKILLS

STATE VERSUS FEDERAL REGULATION

Stephanie Wilson works as a paralegal in the legal department of National Pipeline, Inc., whose business is transporting natural gas to local utilities, factories, and other sites around the country. Last month, one of National's pipelines, which ran under a residential street in Minneapolis, Minnesota, exploded, resulting in several injuries and one death.

The federal government has regulated pipeline safety and maintenance since 1968, under the Natural Gas Pipeline Safety Act. As a result of the explosion, the state of Minnesota wants to regulate pipeline safety as well. Stephanie's boss, the general counsel of the company, and several other executives believe that the federal act preempts this field of law, preventing the state from enacting another layer of safety legislation. Stephanie is assigned the task of researching the statute and relevant case law to determine if the federal law does in fact preempt the state's regulation.

TIPS FOR DETERMINING FEDERAL PREEMPTION

- Read through the statute to see if it expressly states that Congress intended to preempt (or not) the relevant field (in this case, pipeline safety).

- If there is no express provision, look for indications that Congress has impliedly occupied the field: Is the federal regulatory scheme pervasive? Is federal occupation of the field necessitated by the need for national uniformity? Is there a danger of conflict between state laws and the administration of the federal program?

- Locate and read cases discussing the issue of federal preemption in this area. Brief any cases that are relevant to this issue. (See Chapter 7 for instructions on how to brief a case.)

Administrative Law

administrative law
A body of law created by administrative agencies in the form of rules, regulations, orders, and decisions in order to carry out their duties and responsibilities.

administrative agency
A federal or state government agency established to perform a specific function. Administrative agencies are authorized by legislative acts to make and enforce rules relating to the purpose for which they were established.

Another important source of American law is administrative law. It consists of the rules, orders, and decisions of administrative agencies. An administrative agency is a federal, state, or local government agency established to perform a specific function, such as the regulation of food sold to consumers. Rules issued by administrative agencies affect most aspects of a business's operation, including the firm's financing, its hiring and firing procedures, its relations with employees and unions, and the way it manufactures and markets its products.

At the federal level there are many administrative agencies with a variety of missions.

EXAMPLE 5.13 The federal Environmental Protection Agency enforces federal environmental laws and oversees state environmental regulations. The states are authorized to customize regulations and enforce them at the state level. The Securities and Exchange Commission regulates purchases and sales of securities (corporate stocks and bonds). Congress has limited the ability of the state courts to handle many aspects of federal securities laws.

Some state administrative agencies work with a federal agency to regulate an area. State environmental agencies, as noted, play important roles in implementing regulations issued by the federal EPA. Other state agencies, such as those dealing with workers' compensation, mostly operate under state law. Just as federal statutes take precedence over conflicting state statutes, so do federal agency regulations take precedence over conflicting state regulations. Because the rules of state and local agencies vary widely, we focus here exclusively on federal administrative law.

Agency Creation

Because Congress cannot possibly oversee the implementation of all the laws it enacts, it delegates such tasks to others, particularly when the issues relate to technical areas, such as air and water pollution. Congress creates an administrative agency by passing enabling legislation, which specifies the name, composition, purpose, and powers of the agency being created.

enabling legislation
A statute enacted by a legislature that authorizes the creation of an administrative agency and specifies the name, purpose, composition, and powers of the agency being created.

EXAMPLE 5.14 The Federal Trade Commission (FTC) was created in 1914 by the Federal Trade Commission Act. This act prohibits unfair and deceptive trade practices. It also describes the procedures the agency must follow to charge persons or organizations with violations of the act, and it provides for judicial review (review by the courts) of agency orders. The act also grants the agency powers to "make rules and regulations for the purpose of carrying out the Act," to conduct investigations of business practices, to obtain reports from interstate corporations concerning their business practices, to investigate possible violations of the act, to publish findings of its investigations, and to recommend new legislation. The act empowers the FTC to hold trial-like hearings and to adjudicate certain kinds of trade disputes that involve FTC regulations.

adjudicate
To resolve a dispute using a neutral decision maker.

Note that the FTC's grant of power incorporates functions associated with the legislative branch of government (rulemaking), the executive branch (investigation and enforcement), and the judicial branch (adjudication). Taken together, these functions constitute *administrative process*.

Rulemaking

One of the major functions of an administrative agency is rulemaking—creating or modifying rules or regulations. The Administrative Procedure Act imposes procedural requirements that agencies must follow in their rulemaking and other functions.

rulemaking
The actions undertaken by administrative agencies when formally adopting new regulations or amending old ones.

The most common rulemaking procedure involves three steps:

1. The agency must give public notice of the proposed rulemaking proceedings, must announce where public hearings will be held, and must convey the subject matter of the proposed rule. The notice must be published in the *Federal Register*, a daily online publication of the U.S. government.

2. Following this notice, the agency must allow time for interested parties to comment in writing on the proposed rule. After the comments have been reviewed, the agency takes them into consideration when drafting the final version of the regulation.

3. The last step is the writing of the final rule and its publication in the *Federal Register*. (See Chapter 7 for an explanation of how to find agency regulations.)

Investigation and Enforcement

Many agencies have both investigatory and prosecutorial powers. When conducting an investigation, an agency can request that individuals or organizations hand over specific papers, files, or other documents. Firms subject to regulations often must file reports on a regular basis, including reports of violations. Agencies may conduct on-site inspections. Sometimes, a search of a home, an office, or a factory is the only way to obtain evidence needed to prove a regulatory violation.

EXAMPLE 5.15 The Environmental Protection Agency employs special agents, authorized to carry firearms, who investigate environmental crimes such as illegal dumping of untreated wastewater into a sewer system or disposing of toxic wastes in a municipal landfill.

After investigating a suspected rule violation, an agency may take administrative action against an individual or a business. Most actions are resolved through negotiated settlements, without the need for formal adjudication. If a settlement cannot be reached, the agency may issue a formal complaint against the suspected violator, and the case may proceed to adjudication.

Adjudication

administrative law judge (ALJ)
One who presides over an administrative agency hearing and who has the power to administer oaths, take testimony, rule on questions of evidence, and make determinations of fact.

Agency adjudication usually involves a trial-like hearing before an administrative law judge (ALJ). The ALJ presides over the hearing and has the power to administer oaths, take testimony, rule on questions of evidence, and make determinations of fact. Although the ALJ works for the agency prosecuting the case, he or she is required by law to be an unbiased adjudicator (judge). Hearing procedures vary from agency to agency. They may be informal meetings conducted at a table in a conference room, or they may be formal hearings resembling trials. Some agencies allow paralegals to represent clients at these hearings.

After the hearing, the ALJ issues a decision. The ALJ may compel the charged party to pay a fine or may prohibit the party from carrying on a certain activity. Either side may appeal the ALJ's decision through an internal agency review process. Once the agency has completed its procedures, a dissatisfied party may appeal to a federal court. If no party appeals the case, or if the commission and the court decline to review the case, the ALJ's decision becomes final.

National and International Law

Because business and other activities are increasingly global in scope, many cases now brought before U.S. courts relate to issues involving foreign parties or governments. The laws of other nations and international doctrines or agreements may affect the outcome of these cases. Many paralegals, particularly those who work for law firms with clients operating in foreign countries, may need to become familiar with the legal systems of other nations during the course of their careers.

For example, if you work in a firm in Arizona, California, New Mexico, or Texas, you may assist in the representation of clients who are citizens of Mexico. In this situation, you will want to have some familiarity with Mexican law and any international agreements that regulate U.S.-Mexican relations, such as the North American Free Trade Agreement (NAFTA).

National Law

national law
Law that relates to a particular nation (as opposed to international law).

The law of a particular nation is referred to as national law. Broadly speaking, however, there are two types of legal systems used by the various countries of the world. We have already discussed one of these systems—the common law system of England and the United States. Generally, countries that were once colonies of Great Britain retained parts of their English common law heritage after they achieved their independence.

civil law system
A system of law based on a code rather than case law, often originally from the Roman Empire; the predominant system of law in the nations of continental Europe and the nations that were once their colonies.

In contrast to Great Britain and the common law countries, most European nations base their legal systems on Roman *civil law*, or "code law." The term *civil law*, as used here, refers not to civil as opposed to criminal law but to *codified law*—which is an ordered grouping of legal principles enacted into law by a legislature or governing body. In a civil law system, the primary source of law is a statutory code, and case precedents are not judicially binding, as they normally are in a common law system. This is not to say that precedents are unimportant in a civil law system. Judges in such systems do refer to previous decisions as sources of legal guidance. The difference is that judges in a civil law system are not obligated to follow precedent to the extent that judges in a common law system are; in other words, the doctrine of *stare decisis* does not apply.

Today, the civil law system is followed in most of the continental European countries, as well as in the Latin American, African, and Asian countries that were once colonies of the continental European nations. China, Japan, and Thailand also have civil law systems. Ingredients of the civil law system are also found in the Islamic courts of predominantly Muslim countries. In the United States, the state of Louisiana, because of its historical ties to France, has in part a civil law system. The legal systems of Puerto Rico, Québec, and Scotland also have elements of a civil law system.

International Law

Relationships among countries are regulated to an extent by international law. International law can be defined as a body of written and unwritten laws observed by independent nations and governing the acts of individuals as well as governments. The key difference between national law and international law is the fact that national law can be enforced by government authorities, whereas international law is enforced primarily for reasons of courtesy or expediency.

In essence, international law is the result of attempts to reconcile the need of each nation to be the final authority over its own affairs with the desire of nations to benefit economically from trade and good relations with one another. Although no independent nation can be compelled to obey a law external to itself, nations can and do voluntarily agree to be governed in certain respects by international law for the purpose of facilitating international trade and commerce and civilized discourse.

international law
The law that governs relations among nations. International customs and treaties are generally considered to be two of the most important sources of international law.

Treaties

Traditional sources of international law include the customs that have been historically observed by nations in their dealings with one another. Other sources are treaties and international organizations and conferences. A treaty is an agreement between two or more nations that creates rights and duties binding on the parties to the treaty, just as a private contract may be used to create rights and duties binding on the parties to the contract. To give effect to a treaty, the supreme power of each nation that is a party to the treaty must ratify it. For example, the U.S. Constitution requires approval by two-thirds of the Senate before a treaty executed by the president will be binding on the U.S. government.

Bilateral agreements, as their name implies, occur when two nations form an agreement that will govern their relations with each other. *Multilateral agreements* are formed by several nations. The European Union, for example, which regulates commercial activities among its European member nations, is the result of a multilateral treaty. Other multilateral agreements have led to the formation of regional trade associations.

treaty
An agreement, or compact, formed between two independent nations.

EXAMPLE 5.16 In 1993 Congress approved the North American Free Trade Agreement (NAFTA), which includes Canada, Mexico, and the United States. It gradually eliminated many of the trade barriers among those nations. Its legal texts are provided in English, French, and Spanish at **www.nafta-sec-alena.org**.

International Organizations

International organizations play an important role in the international legal arena. They adopt resolutions, declarations, and other types of standards that often require a particular behavior of nations. The General Assembly of the United Nations, for example, has adopted numerous resolutions and declarations that embody principles of international law and has sponsored conferences that have led to the formation of international agreements. The United States is a member of more than one hundred multilateral and bilateral organizations, including at least twenty through the United Nations.

KEY TERMS AND CONCEPTS

adjudicate   137

administrative agency   136

administrative law   136

administrative law
   judge (ALJ)   138

adversarial system of justice   128

Bill of Rights   129

binding authority   121

case law   121

case of first impression   122

checks and balances   132

citation   127

civil law system   138

common law   121

constitutional law   129

court of equity   122

court of law   122

enabling legislation   137

equitable principles
   and maxims   124

federal system   132

injunction   126

international law   139

laches   124

law   120

national law   138

opinion   128

ordinance   133

party   127

persuasive precedent   121

precedent   121

preemption   133

primary source of law   120

public law number   133

public policy   122

remedy   122

remedy at law   122

remedy in equity   122

rulemaking   137

secondary source of law   121

specific performance   125

stare decisis   121

statute   131

statutory law   131

supremacy clause   129

treaty   139

Chapter Summary / Sources of American Law

THE FRAMEWORK OF AMERICAN LAW

1. *What is the law?*—The law has been defined in many ways, but all definitions rest on the assumption that law consists of a body of rules of conduct established and enforced by the controlling authority (the government) of a society.

2. *Primary sources of American law*—There are four primary sources of American law: the common law doctrines developed in cases; the U.S. Constitution and the constitutions of various states; statutory law, including laws passed by Congress, state legislatures, and local governing bodies; and regulations created by administrative agencies.

CASE LAW AND THE COMMON LAW TRADITION

Case law consists of the decisions issued by judges in cases that come before the court. Case law evolved through the common law tradition, which originated in England and was adopted in America during the colonial era.

1. *The doctrine of* stare decisis—*Stare decisis* means "to stand by things decided" and is the doctrine of precedent, which is a major characteristic of the common law system. Under this doctrine, judges must follow the earlier decisions of their courts or a higher court within their jurisdiction if the same points arise again in litigation.

   a. A court will depart from precedent if the court decides that the precedent should no longer be followed because the earlier ruling was incorrect or does not apply in view of changes in the social or technological environment.

   b. If no precedent exists, the court considers the matter as a case of first impression and looks to other areas of law and public policy for guidance.

2. *Remedies at law versus remedies in equity*—Historically in England, two types of courts emerged: courts of law and courts of equity. Courts of law granted remedies at law (such as money damages). Courts of equity arose in response to the need for other types of relief. In the United States today, the same court can typically grant either legal or equitable remedies.

3. *Remedies in equity*—Remedies in equity, which are normally available only when the remedy at law (money damages) is inadequate, include the following:

   a. **SPECIFIC PERFORMANCE**—A court decree ordering a party to perform a contractual promise.

   b. **INJUNCTION**—A court order directing someone to do or refrain from doing a particular act.

4. *The common law today*—The common law governs all areas of law not covered by statutory law. As the body of statutory law grows to meet different needs, the common law covers fewer areas. Even if an area is governed by a statutory law, however, the common law plays an important role because statutes are interpreted and applied by the courts, and court decisions may become precedents that must be followed by lower courts within the jurisdiction.

5. *The terminology of case law*—

   a. **CASE TITLES**—A case title consists of the surnames of the parties, such as *Baranski v. Peretto.* The citation itself (such as 12 P.3d 385) indicates the volume and page number of the reporter in which the case can be found.

   b. **PARTIES**—The plaintiff or the defendant. Some cases involve multiple parties—that is, more than one plaintiff or defendant.

   c. **JUDGES AND JUSTICES**—These terms are often used synonymously. Usage of the terms varies among courts. The term *justice* is traditionally used to designate judges who sit on the bench of a supreme court.

   d. **DECISIONS AND OPINIONS**—A document containing the court's reasons for its decision, the rules of law that apply, and the judgment. If the opinion is not unanimous, a majority opinion—reflecting the view of the majority of judges or justices—will be written. Concurring and dissenting opinions may also be written.

6. *The adversarial system of justice*—American courts, like English courts, follow a system of justice in which the parties to a lawsuit are opponents, or adversaries, and present their cases in the light most favorable to themselves. The impartial decision maker (the judge or jury) then determines who wins and who loses based on the evidence presented.

CONSTITUTIONAL LAW

Constitutional law is based on the provisions in the U.S. Constitution and the state constitutions. The U.S. Constitution creates and empowers the three branches of government, sets forth the relationship between the states and the federal government, and establishes procedures for amending the Constitution.

1. *The federal Constitution*—The U.S. Constitution is the supreme law of the land. A law in violation of the Constitution or one of its amendments, no matter what its source, will be declared unconstitutional and will not be enforced. A state constitution, so long as it does not conflict with the U.S. Constitution, is the supreme law within the state's borders.

2. *Constitutional rights*—The first ten amendments to the federal Constitution are known as the Bill of Rights.

These amendments embody a series of protections for individuals—and in some instances, business entities—against certain government actions. The Bill of Rights limited only the powers of the federal government. After the Fourteenth Amendment was passed, the Supreme Court applied the protections of the Bill of Rights against state government actions.

3. *The courts and constitutional law*—The rights secured by the Constitution are interpreted and defined by the courts, especially the United States Supreme Court.

4. *State constitutions*—Each state has a constitution that defines and limits the powers of state government. Most state Constitutions are much more detailed than the U.S. Constitution.

STATUTORY LAW

Statutory law consists of all laws enacted by the federal Congress, a state legislature, a municipality, or some other governing body.

1. *Federal statutes*—Laws passed by Congress are *statutes.* Congress has power over areas declared in the Constitution to be within federal jurisdiction. The power of Congress is subject to checks and balances as the judicial branch interprets the laws and the executive branch helps to enforce the laws.

Public laws must pass both branches of Congress and then be signed by the president to become part of the U.S. Code.

2. *State statutes*—Laws enacted by state legislatures under the powers granted by the state constitution. If a state statute conflicts with federal law, it will be stricken as unconstitutional, as federal law preempts state law.

3. *Local ordinances*—Laws passed by local governing units (cities and counties) are called *ordinances*. Such laws may not violate either the federal or state constitution or conflict with laws at the state or federal levels.

4. *Uniform laws*—While laws vary in detail from state to state, many states have adopted uniform statutes, such as the Uniform Commercial Code, to reduce confusion as businesses operate across state lines.

ADMINISTRATIVE LAW

Administrative law consists of the rules, regulations, and decisions of administrative agencies at all levels of government.

1. *Agency creation*—Congress creates administrative agencies by passing enabling legislation, which specifies the name, function, and powers of the agency created.

2. *Administrative process*—Administrative agencies exercise three basic functions:

   a. **RULEMAKING**—Agencies make rules governing activities within the areas of their authority. Typically, rulemaking procedure involves publishing notice of the proposed rulemaking, allowing a comment period, and then drafting the final rule.

   b. **INVESTIGATION AND ENFORCEMENT**—Agencies conduct investigations of regulated entities to gather information and to monitor compliance with agency rules. When an entity fails to comply with agency rules, the agency can take administrative action. Most violations are resolved by negotiated settlements.

   c. **ADJUDICATION**—If a settlement cannot be reached, the agency may issue a formal complaint and an administrative law judge (ALJ) conducts a hearing and decides the issue. Either party can appeal the ALJ's order to the board or commission that governs the agency if dissatisfied. Most agency decisions can also then be appealed to a court.

NATIONAL AND INTERNATIONAL LAW

1. *National law*—The law of a particular nation. National law differs from nation to nation because each country's laws have evolved from that nation's unique customs and traditions. Most countries have one of the following types of legal systems:

   a. **THE COMMON LAW SYSTEM**—Great Britain was the originator of common law. Countries that were once colonies of Great Britain retained at least part of their English common law heritage after achieving independence. Under the common law, case precedents are judicially binding.

   b. **THE CIVIL LAW SYSTEM**—Many of the continental European countries and the nations that were formerly their colonies have civil law systems. Civil law (or code law) is a grouping of legal principles enacted into law by a governing body. The primary source of law is a statutory code. Although important, case precedents are not judicially binding. Judges focus on the code.

2. *International law*—A body of laws that governs relationships among nations. International law allows nations to enjoy good relations with one another and to benefit economically from international trade. Sources include international customs developed over time, treaties among nations, and international organizations.

■ QUESTIONS FOR REVIEW

1. Define law. What are the primary sources of American law?

2. Why is the doctrine of *stare decisis* the cornerstone of American common law, and what is its relationship to binding authority? May courts depart from precedent? What is a case of first impression?

3. What remedies were originally available from courts of law? Courts of equity? How did courts of equity evolve? Are the courts of law and equity still separate?

4. What is a statute? How is statutory law created? What is the difference between a statute and an ordinance? What happens when a state statute conflicts with a federal statute?

5. What is the supremacy clause and where is it located? Briefly summarize each article of the Constitution. What is the Bill of Rights?

■ ETHICS QUESTION

Paralegal Carlos is asked by his supervising attorney to do some research. Carlos is to review a new state statute exempting certified, ill persons from prosecution for medical marijuana use, in order to find out what the requirements are for becoming a certified medical marijuana user. Carlos looks up the relevant state statute and finds the requirements. He conveys this information to John, his supervising attorney. Carlos has neglected to research the federal drug laws and fails to tell the attorney that there is not an exemption for the medical use of marijuana under federal law. The attorney, relying on Carlos's conclusion, advises the client that once she is a certified medical user, she will be exempt from prosecution. Have John and Carlos violated any ethical rules? Explain.

■ PRACTICE QUESTIONS AND ASSIGNMENTS

1. In the following hypothetical situations, identify the remedy being sought and whether it is a remedy at law or a remedy in equity:

   a. Brianna files a petition with the court. She is seeking compensation from Travis, who failed to deliver new furniture as promised.

   b. Juan sues Bob, seeking to be compensated for the cost of replacing several new trees that Bob's dog destroyed.

   c. Laurie seeks to have a contract enforced for the sale of an antique Mercedes automobile.

   d. Sam files a petition seeking to prevent the electric company from cutting down a large tree on his property.

2. Identify the type of law (common law, constitutional law, statutory law, or administrative law) that applies in each of the following scenarios:

   a. LaToya strongly disagrees with the U.S. government's decision to declare war on a foreign country. She places an antiwar sign in the window of her home. The city passes an ordinance that bans all such signs.

   b. An official of the state department of natural resources learns that the Ferris Widget Company has violated the state's Hazardous Waste Management Act. The official issues a complaint against the company for not properly handling and labeling its toxic waste.

   c. Mrs. Sams was walking down a busy street when two teenagers on skateboards crashed into her because they were racing and not watching where they were going. As a result of the teenagers' conduct, Mrs. Sams broke her hip, and according to her doctor, she will never walk normally again. Mrs. Sams's attorney files suit against the teenagers for damages.

   d. Joseph Barnes is arrested and charged with the crime of murder.

3. Look at the U.S. Constitution in Appendix I of this text. Identify the amendment and quote the relevant language in the Bill of Rights that gives U.S. citizens the following rights and protections:

   a. The right to freedom of the press.

   b. Protection from excessive bail and fines.

   c. Protection against self-incrimination.

   d. The right to counsel in criminal prosecutions.

   e. The right to keep and bear arms.

4. Identify the constitutional amendment being violated in the following hypothetical situations:

   a. A state imposes the death penalty on a 17-year-old.

   b. The federal government suppresses political speech based on the speaker's identity as a corporation.

   c. The police decide that because a house is located in a poor neighborhood, it must be a crack house. The police burst in, tear the house apart looking for drugs, and find nothing.

   d. A local government bans handgun possession in the home.

■ GROUP PROJECT

This chapter describes uniform laws that were created to alleviate conflicting laws that hindered rapidly developing trade among the states. One such uniform law that was created was the Uniform Commercial Code (UCC), a core provision of which regulates the sales of goods. Trade problems also arose among nations. For this project, the group should search the Internet to locate a uniform international law similar to the UCC. Student one will research the source of law to determine what entity created it and what form the law takes (case law, statutory law, treaty, etc.). Student two will research the law and provide an overview of its main provisions. Student three will research the role of the U.S. government and U.S.-based businesses: how they are, or are not, governed by this law and why. Student four will prepare a two-page written summary of this particular law on behalf of the group and submit it to the instructor.

INTERNET PROJECT

1. Go to Google Scholar at **www.scholar.google.com**. Search for the United States Supreme Court case *Riley v. California* in the search box. Select "case law" right below the search box. Click on the opinion and answer these questions:

   a. What is the citation to the case? What does each item in the citation refer to?

   b. Which justice wrote the opinion?

   c. List all the names above the name of the justice who authored the opinion.

   d. The opinion begins immediately following the name of the justice who wrote the opinion. What issue did the Court address in this case?

   e. Press the Control and F keys on your keyboard simultaneously. In the search box that opens, type the words "it is so ordered." What did the Supreme Court decide and why?

   f. Did any justice write a concurring or dissenting opinion? If so, which one(s)?

END NOTES

1. Pronounced *stahr-ee dih-si-ses.*
2. 347 U.S. 483, 74 S.Ct. 686, 98 L.Ed. 873 (1954).
3. *In re Baby M*, 217 N.J.Super. 313, 525 A.2d 1128 (1987).
4. *Nature Conservancy v. Wilder Corporation of Delaware*, 656 F.3d 646 (2011).
5. Twenty dollars was forty days' pay for the average person when the Bill of Rights was written.
6. 47 U.S.C. Section 223(d)(1)(B). Specifically, the CDA prohibited any obscene or indecent message that "depicts or describes, in terms patently offensive as measured by contemporary community standards, sexual or excretory activities or organs."
7. 521 U.S. 844, 117 S.Ct. 2329, 138 L.Ed.2d 874 (1997).
8. 47 U.S.C. Section 231. COPA made it a criminal act to post "material that is harmful to minors" on the Web.
9. *American Civil Liberties Union v. Mukasey*, 534 F.3d 181 (3d Cir. 2008).
10. *Cert.* denied, 129 S.Ct. 1032 (2009).

CHAPTER 6

The Court System and Alternative Dispute Resolution

CHAPTER OBJECTIVES

After completing this chapter, you will know:

- The requirements that must be met before a lawsuit can be brought in a particular court by a particular party.

- The difference between jurisdiction and venue.

- The types of courts that make up a typical state court system and the different functions of trial courts and appellate courts.

- The organization of the federal court system and the relationship between state and federal jurisdiction.

- How cases reach the United States Supreme Court.

- The ways in which disputes can be resolved outside the court system.

Introduction

As explained in Chapter 5, American law is based on the case decisions and legal principles that form the common law, the federal and state constitutions, statutes passed by federal and state legislatures, administrative law, and, in some instances, the laws of other nations and international law.

Paralegals need to understand the different types of courts in the American system. There are fifty-two court systems—one for each of the fifty states, one for the District of Columbia, and the federal system. There are many similarities among these systems, but there are differences as well.

In the first part of this chapter, we examine the structure of the American courts. In addition to the public courts, there is also a system of private dispute resolution mechanisms. Because of the costs, in time and money, and the publicity that can come from court trials, many parties use these alternative methods of dispute resolution to resolve disputes outside of court. In some cases, parties are required by the courts to try to resolve their disputes by one of these methods. In the second part of this chapter, we provide an overview of these alternative methods of dispute resolution and the role that attorneys and paralegals play in facilitating them.

Judicial Requirements

Before a lawsuit can be brought before a court, certain requirements must be met. We begin with these important requirements and some of the key features of the American system of justice.

Standing to Sue

standing to sue
A sufficient stake in a controversy to justify bringing a lawsuit. To have standing to sue, the plaintiff must demonstrate an injury or a threat of injury.

To bring a lawsuit before a court, a party must have standing to sue—a sufficient "stake" in a matter to justify seeking relief through the court system. In other words, a party must have a legally protected, genuine interest at stake in the litigation to have standing. The party bringing the lawsuit must have suffered a legally recognized harm as a result of the action about which he or she complained.

> **EXAMPLE 6-1** Assume that a friend of one of your firm's clients was injured in a car accident caused by defective brakes. The client's friend would have standing to sue the automobile manufacturer for damages. Your firm's client, who feels horrible about the accident and is angry about it, would not have standing because the client was not injured and has no legally recognizable stake in the controversy.

Note that in some cases, a person has standing to sue on behalf of another person.

> **EXAMPLE 6-2** Suppose that a child suffered serious injuries as a result of a defectively manufactured toy. Because the child is a minor, a lawsuit could be brought on his behalf by the child's parent or legal guardian.

Standing to sue also requires that the controversy at issue be justiciable. A justiciable[1] controversy is one that is real and substantial, as opposed to hypothetical.

justiciable controversy
A controversy that is real and substantial, as opposed to hypothetical or academic.

> **EXAMPLE 6-3** Suppose a child's parents learned through news reports that a toy they purchased was defective and had injured some children. The parents could not sue on the ground that they feared the toy could cause injury. The issue would become justiciable only if their child had actually been injured due to a defect in the toy. The parents could not ask the court to determine what damages might be obtained if their child were to be injured, because that would be a hypothetical question.

Types of Jurisdiction

In Latin, *juris* means "law," and *diction* means "to speak." Thus, "the power to speak the law" is the literal meaning of the term jurisdiction. Before any court can hear a case, it must have jurisdiction over the person against whom the suit is brought or over the property involved in the suit as well as over the subject matter.

jurisdiction
The authority of a court to hear and decide a specific case.

Jurisdiction over Persons

Generally, a court can exercise personal jurisdiction (*in personam* jurisdiction) over residents of a certain geographic area. A state trial court, for example, normally has jurisdictional authority over residents within the state or within a particular area of the state, such as a county or district. A state's highest court (often called the state supreme court[2]) has jurisdictional authority over all residents within the state.

Under the authority of a long arm statute, a state court can exercise personal jurisdiction over nonresident defendants based on activities that took place within the state. Before a court can exercise jurisdiction over a nonresident under a long arm statute, though, it must be demonstrated that the nonresident had sufficient contacts (*minimum contacts*) with the state to justify the jurisdiction.

long arm statute
A state statute that permits a state to obtain jurisdiction over nonresidents. The nonresidents must have certain "minimum contacts" with that state for the statute to apply.

EXAMPLE 6-4 If a California citizen caused an injury in a car accident in Arizona, an Arizona state court usually could exercise jurisdiction over the California citizen in a suit by the Arizona victim. Similarly, a state may exercise personal jurisdiction over a nonresident defendant who is sued for breaching a contract that was formed within that state.

For corporations, the minimum-contacts requirement boils down to whether the corporation does business in the state.

EXAMPLE 6-5 A Maine corporation that has a branch office or warehouse in Georgia has sufficient minimum contacts with the state to allow a Georgia court to exercise jurisdiction over the Maine corporation. If, however, someone from Georgia is injured while on a guided fishing trip in Maine and claims that personnel from the Maine fishing company caused the injury, suit could not be brought in a Georgia court if the Maine company does no business in Georgia. A Georgia court could not exercise jurisdiction.

A state court may also be able to exercise jurisdiction over a corporation in another country if it can be demonstrated that the alien (foreign) corporation has met the minimum-contacts test.

EXAMPLE 6-6 A Chinese corporation markets its products through an American distributor. As the corporation knew its products would be distributed throughout the United States, it could be sued in any state by a plaintiff injured by one of the products.

Jurisdiction over Property

A court can also exercise jurisdiction over property that is located within its boundaries even if the parties involved in the suit do not. This kind of jurisdiction is known as *in rem* jurisdiction, or "jurisdiction over the thing."

EXAMPLE 6-7 A dispute arises over ownership of a boat docked in Fort Lauderdale, Florida. Ownership is claimed by residents of both Ohio and Nebraska. A Florida court normally cannot exercise personal jurisdiction, but in this situation, a lawsuit concerning the boat could be brought in a Florida state court on the basis of the court's *in rem* jurisdiction.

Jurisdiction over Subject Matter

Jurisdiction over subject matter is another factor in the cases a certain court can hear, such as civil or criminal cases, or cases involving bankruptcy, probate, or torts. In both the state and federal court systems, there are courts of *general jurisdiction* and courts of *limited jurisdiction*. The basis for the difference is the subject matter of cases heard. A probate court—a state court that handles only matters relating to the transfer of a person's assets and obligations on that person's death—is a court with limited subject-matter jurisdiction. A federal court of limited subject-matter jurisdiction is a bankruptcy court. Bankruptcy courts handle only proceedings governed by bankruptcy law (covered in Chapter 19). In contrast, a court of general jurisdiction can decide a wide array of cases.

The subject-matter jurisdiction of a court is usually defined in the statute creating the court. In both the state and federal court systems, a court's subject-matter jurisdiction can be limited not only by the subject of the lawsuit but also by the amount in controversy, by whether the case is a felony (serious crime) or a misdemeanor (less serious crime), or by whether the proceeding is a trial or an appeal.

Original and Appellate Jurisdiction

The distinction between courts of original jurisdiction and courts of appellate jurisdiction normally lies in whether the case is being heard for the first time or not. Courts having original jurisdiction are called courts of the first instance and are usually trial courts—that is, courts in which lawsuits begin, trials take place, evidence is presented, and a decision is rendered.

In the federal court system, the *district courts* are trial courts. In a few instances, such as appeals of agency rules, the court of original jurisdiction is a federal court of appeals. There are a few rare instances in which cases begin in the United States Supreme Court. In the state court systems, the trial courts are known by different names for historical reasons. For example, New York's trial courts are confusingly known as the "Supreme Court," and its highest court as the "Court of Appeals."

Courts having appellate jurisdiction act as reviewing courts, or appellate courts (courts of appeal). In general, cases can be brought to them only on appeal from an order or a judgment of a trial court or other lower court.

Jurisdiction of the Federal Courts

Because the federal government is a government of limited powers, the jurisdiction of the federal courts is also limited. Article III of the U.S. Constitution establishes the boundaries of federal judicial power. Section 2 of Article III states that "the judicial Power shall extend to all Cases, in Law and Equity, arising under this Constitution, the Laws of the United States, and Treaties made, or which shall be made, under their Authority."

Federal Questions

Whenever a plaintiff's cause of action is based, at least in part, on the U.S. Constitution, a treaty, or a federal law, then a federal question arises, and the federal courts have subject-matter jurisdiction. Any lawsuit involving a federal question can originate in a federal district (trial) court.

EXAMPLE 6-8 J-H Computers, a California company, sues Ball Computers, a Texas company, for patent infringement. J-H claims that some parts Ball used in its new computers are based on J-H inventions. J-H contends that Ball has used its protected patents without permission. Because patent law is federal law and the federal courts have exclusive jurisdiction over such suits, J-H must file suit against Ball in federal court.

---

probate court
A court having jurisdiction over proceedings concerning the settlement of a person's estate.

bankruptcy court
A federal court of limited jurisdiction that hears only bankruptcy proceedings.

original jurisdiction
The power of a court to take a case, try it, and decide it.

trial court
A court in which cases begin and in which questions of fact are examined.

appellate jurisdiction
The power of a court to hear and decide an appeal; the authority of a court to review cases that have already been tried in a lower court and to make decisions about them without holding a trial.

appellate court
A court that reviews decisions made by lower courts, such as trial courts; a court of appeals.

federal question
A question that pertains to the U.S. Constitution, acts of Congress, or treaties. It provides a basis for jurisdiction by the federal courts as authorized by Article III, Section 2, of the Constitution.

Diversity Jurisdiction

Federal district courts can also exercise original jurisdiction over cases involving diversity of citizenship. Such cases may arise between (1) citizens of different states, (2) a foreign country and citizens of a state or of different states, or (3) citizens of a state and citizens or subjects of a foreign country. The amount in controversy must be more than $75,000 before a federal court can take jurisdiction in such cases. For purposes of diversity-of-citizenship jurisdiction, a corporation is a citizen of the state in which it is incorporated and of the state in which its principal place of business is located.

EXAMPLE 6-9 Ramirez, a citizen of Florida, was walking near a street in Miami when a box fell off a passing truck and hit and seriously injured her. She incurred medical expenses and could not work for six months. She wants to sue the trucking firm for $500,000 in damages. The firm's headquarters are in Georgia, although the company does business in Florida. Ramirez could bring suit in a Florida court because she is a resident of Florida, the trucking firm does business in Florida, and that is where the accident occurred. She could also bring suit in a Georgia court, because a Georgia court could exercise jurisdiction over the trucking firm, which is headquartered in that state. She could also sue in a federal court because the requirements of diversity jurisdiction have been met—the lawsuit involves parties from different states, and the amount in controversy (the damages Ramirez is seeking) exceeds $75,000.

When a case is based on a federal question, a federal court will apply federal law. In a case based on diversity of citizenship, however, a federal court will normally apply state law. This is because cases based on diversity of citizenship generally do not involve claims based on federal law.

Exclusive versus Concurrent Jurisdiction

When both federal and state courts have the power to hear a case, as is true in suits involving diversity of citizenship (such as Ramirez's case described in *Example 6-9*), concurrent jurisdiction exists. When cases can be tried only in one or the other, exclusive jurisdiction exists. Federal courts have exclusive jurisdiction in cases involving federal crimes, bankruptcy, patents, trademarks, and copyrights; in most class-action lawsuits;[3] and in suits against the United States. States also have exclusive jurisdiction in certain subject matters—for example, in divorce and adoptions.

The concepts of concurrent and exclusive jurisdiction are illustrated in Exhibit 6.1 on the following page. Some matters, such as bankruptcy law, are under the exclusive jurisdiction of the federal courts. Other matters, such as banking regulation, can fall under state or federal jurisdiction, whereas corporate law falls under state jurisdiction.

When concurrent jurisdiction exists, a party has a choice of whether to bring a suit in a federal or a state court. As described in *Developing Paralegal Skills* on page 151, the party's lawyer will consider several factors in counseling the party. The lawyer may prefer to litigate the case in a state court, perhaps because of familiarity with the state court's procedures, or in federal court because the docket is known to be less crowded. Other considerations include the law in an available jurisdiction, how that law has been applied in the jurisdiction's courts, and what the results have been in that jurisdiction.

Jurisdiction in Cyberspace

The Internet makes it easier to interact with people in other jurisdictions. As discussed, for a court to compel a defendant to come before it, there must be at least minimum contacts with the jurisdiction within which the court sits—such as the presence of a company's salesperson within the state. Are there sufficient minimum contacts if the only connection to a jurisdiction is an ad on the Web originating from a remote location?

diversity of citizenship
Under the Constitution, a basis for federal district court jurisdiction over a lawsuit between (1) citizens of different states, (2) a foreign country and citizens of a state or states, or (3) citizens of a state and citizens of a foreign country. The amount in controversy must be more than $75,000 before a federal court can exercise jurisdiction in such cases.

concurrent jurisdiction
Jurisdiction that exists when two different courts have the power to hear a case. For example, some cases can be heard in either a federal or a state court.

exclusive jurisdiction
Jurisdiction that exists when a case can be heard only in a particular court, such as a federal court.

docket
The list of cases entered on the court's calendar and scheduled to be heard by the court.

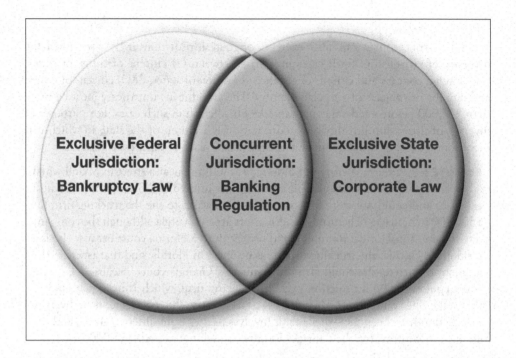

EXAMPLE 6-10 Tom, who lives in Idaho, orders $20,000 worth of merchandise from Juanita's On-Line, a New Mexico company that operates on the Internet. After paying for and receiving the merchandise, Tom claims Juanita's goods are not of the quality described on the company's website. Tom sues Juanita's in state court in Idaho. Does the Idaho state court have jurisdiction over the matter? Yes. The company offers to sell goods around the country, and it did make a sale to Tom, so it has sufficient contacts with Idaho to give Idaho courts jurisdiction.

The "Sliding-Scale" Standard

To cope with the challenges to jurisdiction analysis posed by doing business over the Internet, the courts use a "sliding-scale" standard for determining when the exercise of jurisdiction over an out-of-state party is proper. The courts have identified three types of Internet business contacts: (1) substantial business conducted over the Internet (with contracts or sales, for example), (2) some interactivity through a website, and (3) passive advertising. Jurisdiction is proper for the first category, is improper for the third, and may or may not be appropriate for the second—that is an area of law still evolving.

International Jurisdictional Issues

Because the Internet is global, international jurisdictional issues arise. What seems to be emerging is a standard that echoes the requirement of minimum contacts applied by the U.S. courts. Courts in many nations indicate that minimum contacts—such as doing business within the jurisdiction—are enough to compel a defendant to appear and that the defendant's physical presence is not required for the court to exercise jurisdiction. The effect is that a company may have to comply with the laws of any jurisdiction in which it has Internet-based customers. This has been a problem for online auction sites such as eBay, because countries have different rules on what may be offered for sale. Germany, for example, prohibits advertising Nazi memorabilia.

EXAMPLE 6-11 A Minneapolis company requested bids from cell phone makers. A firm in Singapore won the bid to supply the phones. Discussions between the companies took place by e-mail, telephone, and fax. The Singapore supplier delivered the goods to the buyer at the port in Singapore for shipment. When the phones arrived

DEVELOPING PARALEGAL SKILLS

CHOICE OF COURTS: STATE OR FEDERAL?

Susan Radtke, a lawyer specializing in employment discrimination, and her legal assistant, Joan Dunbar, are meeting with a new client who wants to sue her former employer for gender discrimination. The client complained to her employer when she was passed over for a promotion. She was fired, she claims, in retaliation for her complaint. The client appears to have a strong case, because several of her former co-workers have agreed to testify that they heard the employer say that he would never promote a woman to a managerial position.

Because both state and federal laws prohibit gender discrimination, the case could be brought in either state or federal court. The client tells Susan that she wants her to decide whether the case should be filed in a state or federal court. Joan will be drafting the complaint, so Susan and Joan discuss the pros and cons of filing the case in each court. Joan reviews a list of considerations with Susan.

TIPS FOR CHOOSING A COURT

- Review the jurisdiction of each court.
- Evaluate the strengths and weaknesses of the case.
- Evaluate the remedy sought.
- Evaluate the population from which the jury will be selected in each court.
- Evaluate the likelihood of winning in each court.
- Evaluate the length of time it will take each court to decide the case.
- Review the costs and procedural rules involved in filing in each court.
- Evaluate the types of discovery available in each court.
- Evaluate the personalities and records of the judges sitting in each court.

in Minneapolis, the buyer claimed they did not meet the terms of the contract and sued the Singapore firm. Did the federal court in Minnesota have jurisdiction over the Singapore company? No, the Singapore supplier had no business presence in the U.S. It sold the goods to the Minneapolis company in Singapore over the Internet, so the Minneapolis company would have to file suit in a Singapore court.

Venue

While jurisdiction has to do with whether a court has authority to hear a case, venue[4] is concerned with the most appropriate location for a trial. For example, two state courts may both have the authority to exercise jurisdiction over a case, but it may be more appropriate or convenient to hear the case in one court because all the witnesses live near there.

> **venue**
> The geographic district in which an action is tried and from which the jury is selected.

The concept of venue reflects the policy that a court trying a suit should be in the geographic area (usually the county) in which the parties involved in the lawsuit reside or in which the incident leading to the lawsuit occurred. Pretrial publicity or other factors may require a change of venue to another community, especially in criminal cases in which the defendant's right to a fair and impartial jury has been impaired.

EXAMPLE 6-12 A bomb was set off at a federal building in Oklahoma City, killing 168 persons and injuring hundreds of others. Timothy McVeigh was indicted in connection with the bombing and scheduled for trial in an Oklahoma federal court. The defense attorneys argued—and the court agreed—that McVeigh could not receive a fair trial in Oklahoma because an impartial jury could not be chosen. Although the federal court in Oklahoma had jurisdiction, the court ordered a change of venue to a federal court in Denver for trial.

Judicial Procedures

From beginning to end, litigation follows specifically designated procedural rules. As the *Technology and Today's Paralegal* feature on page 154 discusses, courts are increasingly moving to fulfill procedure via electronic processes.

The general procedural rules for federal civil court cases are set forth in the Federal Rules of Civil Procedure. For criminal cases they are in the Federal Rules of Criminal Procedure. Each federal court also has its own local rules. State rules, which are often similar to the federal rules, vary from state to state, and even from court to court within a given state. Rules of procedure also differ in criminal and civil cases. Paralegals who work for trial lawyers need to be familiar with the procedural rules of the relevant courts (this includes complying with deadlines—see the *In the Office* feature below). Because judicial procedures will be examined in detail in Chapters 10 through 13, we do not discuss them here.

State Court Systems

Each state has its own system of courts, and no two state systems are the same. As Exhibit 6.2 on the facing page indicates, there may be several levels, or tiers, of courts within a state court system: (1) state trial courts of general jurisdiction and limited jurisdiction, (2) appellate courts, and (3) the state's highest court (often called the state supreme court). Judges in the state court system are sometimes elected by the voters for a specified term; in other states they are appointed.

Generally, any person who is a party to a lawsuit has the opportunity to plead the case before a trial court and then, if she loses, appeal to at least one level of appellate court. Finally, if a federal statute or federal constitutional issue is involved in the decision of a state supreme court, that decision may be further appealed to the United States Supreme Court.

Trial Courts

Trial courts are what their name implies—courts in which trials are held and testimony taken. You will read about trial procedures in Chapter 12, where we follow a hypothetical

IN THE OFFICE

WATCH THOSE DEADLINES!

One of the paralegal's most important responsibilities is making sure that court deadlines are met. Suppose that your supervising attorney asks you to file with the court a motion to dismiss, which is a document requesting the court to dismiss a lawsuit for a specific reason. You know that the deadline for filing the motion is in three days. After you prepare the document and have it reviewed by your attorney, you put it in the client's file. You plan to deliver the motion to the court the next day.

As soon as you get to work the next morning, you are called to help with a rush matter on another case. Busy

with that, you forget about the motion to dismiss until the next week. Too late! Court deadlines are hard rules. To prevent such things from happening, *always* enter every deadline on the office calendaring system, and *always* check your calendar several times a day no matter what else is happening. Missed deadlines can be the basis for malpractice suits by clients against attorneys. If you are using electronic filing, as some courts now require, be sure to allow time for technical difficulties and have a backup plan ready if computer problems occur.

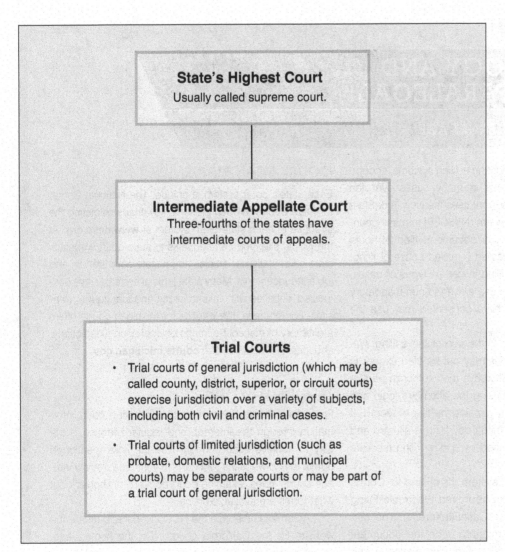

EXHIBIT 6.2
Levels in a State Court System

case through the various stages of a trial. (The *Technology and Today's Paralegal* feature on the following page explains some of the changes occurring in the courts as they adapt to Web-based tools.)

Briefly, a trial court is presided over by a judge, who controls the proceedings and issues a decision on the matter before the court. If the trial is a jury trial (many are held without juries), the jury decides the outcome of factual disputes, and the judge issues a judgment based on the jury's conclusion. During the trial, the attorney for each side introduces evidence (such as relevant documents, exhibits, and testimony of witnesses) in support of his or her client's position. Each attorney is given an opportunity to cross-examine witnesses and challenge evidence offered by the opposing party.

General Jurisdiction Courts

State trial courts have either general or limited jurisdiction. Trial courts that have general jurisdiction as to subject matter may be called county, district, superior, or circuit courts.[5] State trial courts of general jurisdiction have jurisdiction over a wide variety of subjects, including both civil disputes (such as landlord-tenant matters or contract claims) and criminal prosecutions. In some states, trial courts of general jurisdiction may hear appeals from courts of limited jurisdiction.

TECHNOLOGY AND TODAY'S PARALEGAL

COURTS IN THE INTERNET AGE

Courts are increasingly adopting e-filing systems, accepting and serving documents in many cases over the Internet. For example, New York uses the New York State Courts Electronic Filing System (NYSCEF) in many counties. Cases can be initiated or documents filed 24 hours a day. The system provides an e-mailed notice of filing. Some counties require e-filing in certain types of cases. Attorneys must consent to use e-filing in non-mandatory cases. Only parties who have consented may use the system.

Once a party agrees to the use of the e-filing system for a case, hard copies may not be filed except in unusual circumstances. Attorneys may authorize paralegals to e-file a document using the attorney's login and password, but the attorney remains the filer of record. If the system breaks down, hard copy filing is allowed and many deadlines are extended by a day. Filing fees are paid by credit card.

Texas has a different system. Its eFiling for Courts system requires use of an approved Electronic Filing Service Provider (such as CaseFileXpress). The service provider e-mails a receipt. Once the document is accepted by a court, a confirmation message and file-stamped copy are e-mailed to the filing attorney. Texas also allows "eService" of documents for cases in which parties have consented to it. Unlike in New York, both the state website and the service providers charge fees in Texas. The average cost is about $10 per document.

Systems such as those used in Texas and New York are becoming increasingly common as courts move to more efficient document-handling procedures. Paralegals need to become familiar with software such as Adobe Acrobat that produces PDF files suitable for e-filing.

COURT STRUCTURES

Each state's court system is unique. The National Center for State Courts (NCSC) presents flowcharts depicting the structure of each state court system at **www.ncsc.org**. At the NCSC site, you can find links to state court websites, state court statistics, articles about state court trends, and job announcements. Many state judicial systems have centralized websites with links to circuit and trial courts' websites. For example, the website for Michigan courts offers a directory of trial courts, maps of local court jurisdictions, and local trial court links at **courts.michigan.gov**.

TECHNOLOGY TIP

Paralegals should be comfortable gathering court information through the Internet, and regular practice is the way to achieve such comfort. Use the links mentioned above to find websites for courts in your area, review various courts' rules, examine court dockets, and check out what forms are available online.

As an example, use the NCSC website to locate the website for the California courts. (On the home page, select "Information & Resources," then "Browse by State," then "Court Web Sites.") At the California site, browse the docket for the California Supreme Court. A paralegal should be comfortable finding, filling out, and submitting court forms online. Click on "Forms & Rules" from the menu at the top of the California Courts home page at **www.courts.ca.gov**, read the instructions, choose a form from the list, and fill out the form. Then search the website to locate the specific procedures that are required for filing the documents with the court. You will find valuable court information through such exercises and be on the road to becoming the technology expert of your legal team.

Limited Jurisdiction Courts

Courts with limited subject-matter jurisdiction are often called "inferior" trial courts or minor courts. Courts of limited jurisdiction include:

- Small claims courts that hear only civil cases involving claims of less than a certain amount, such as $5,000;
- Domestic relations courts that handle only divorce actions, paternity suits, and child-custody and support cases;

- Municipal courts that mainly handle traffic violations; and
- Probate courts that handle the administration of wills, estate-settlement problems, and related matters.

Appellate, or Reviewing, Courts

After a trial, the parties have the right to file an appeal to a higher court if they are unsatisfied with the trial court's ruling. Practically speaking, parties are unlikely to file an appeal unless a reversible error was committed by the trial court that would cause the appellate court to overturn the trial court's decision. A reversible error is a legal error at the trial court level that is significant enough to have affected the outcome of the case. For example, the judge may have given improper instructions about the law to the jury. Usually, appellate courts do not look at questions of *fact* (such as whether a party did, in fact, commit a certain action) but at questions of *law* (whether the trial judge applied the law properly to the facts established at trial). Only a judge, not a jury, can rule on questions of law.

Appellate courts normally defer to a trial court's findings on questions of fact because the trial court judge and jury were in a better position to evaluate testimony by directly observing witnesses' gestures, demeanor, and nonverbal behavior during the trial. When a case is appealed, an appellate panel of three or more judges reviews the record (including the written transcript of the trial) of the case on appeal, but the record does not include such nonverbal elements.

reversible error
A legal error at the trial court level that is significant enough to have affected the outcome of the case. It is grounds for reversal of the judgment on appeal.

Intermediate Appellate Courts

A majority of states have intermediate appellate courts (IAC), or courts of appeals. The subject-matter jurisdiction of these courts is limited to hearing appeals. Usually, IACs review the records, read appellate briefs filed by the parties, and listen to the oral arguments presented by the parties' attorneys. Then the panel of judges renders (issues) a decision. If a party is unsatisfied with the IAC's ruling, that party can appeal to the highest state court.

Highest State Courts

The highest appellate court in a state is usually called the supreme court but may be called by some other name. For example, both Maryland and New York, as previously mentioned, refer to the highest state court as the court of appeals. Texas and Oklahoma have two high courts, one for civil cases and one for criminal cases. The decisions of each state's highest court on all questions of state law are final. Only when issues of federal law are involved can a decision made by a state's highest court be reviewed by the United States Supreme Court.

The Federal Court System

The federal court system is basically a three-level model consisting of (1) U.S. district courts (trial courts of general jurisdiction) and various courts of limited jurisdiction, (2) U.S. courts of appeals (intermediate courts of appeals), and (3) the United States Supreme Court. Exhibit 6.3 on the next page shows the organization of the federal court system.

According to Article III of the U.S. Constitution, there is only one national Supreme Court. All other courts in the federal system are considered "inferior." Congress has the power to create inferior courts. The courts that Congress has created include the district courts and courts of limited jurisdiction, as well as the U.S. courts of appeals.

Unlike state court judges, who are often elected, federal court judges—including the justices of the United States Supreme Court—are appointed by the president of the United States and confirmed by the U.S. Senate. Federal judges receive lifetime appointments (because under Article III they "hold their Offices during good Behavior").

EXHIBIT 6.3
The Organization of the Federal Court System

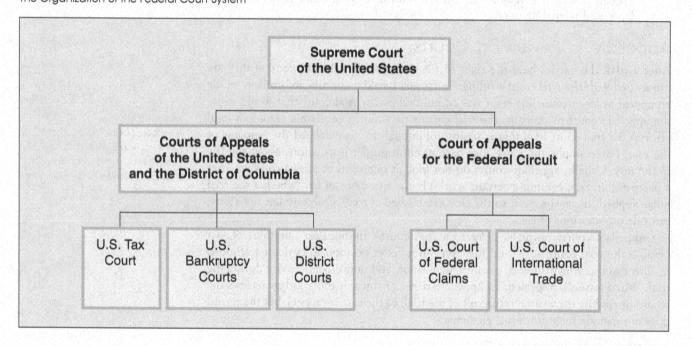

U.S. District Courts

At the federal level, the trial court of general jurisdiction is the district court. There is at least one federal district court in every state. The number of judicial districts varies over time, owing to population changes and caseloads. Currently, there are ninety-four judicial districts.

U.S. district courts have original jurisdiction in matters of federal law. There are other trial courts with original but special (or limited) jurisdiction, such as the federal bankruptcy courts and others shown in Exhibit 6.3 above. The *Developing Paralegal Skills* feature on page 158 discusses some considerations in federal jurisdiction.

U.S. Courts of Appeals

As seen in Exhibit 6.4 on the facing page, in the federal court system, there are thirteen U.S. courts of appeals—also referred to as U.S. circuit courts of appeals. The federal courts of appeals for twelve of the circuits (including the District of Columbia Circuit) hear appeals from the federal district courts located within their respective judicial circuits. The court of appeals for the thirteenth circuit, called the Federal Circuit, has national appellate jurisdiction over certain types of cases, such as cases involving patent law and cases involving contract claims against the U.S. government.

A party who is dissatisfied with a federal district court's decision on an issue may appeal that decision to the relevant federal circuit court of appeals. The judges on the court review decisions made by trial courts for any errors of law. The judges generally defer to a district court's findings of fact. The decisions of the circuit courts of appeals are final in most cases, but review by the United States Supreme Court is possible.

The United States Supreme Court

The highest level of the federal court system is the United States Supreme Court, composed of nine justices. Although the Supreme Court has original, or trial, jurisdiction in rare instances (set forth in Article III, Section 2, of the Constitution—see Appendix I), most of its work is as an appeals court. The Supreme Court can review any case decided

EXHIBIT 6.4

Boundaries of the U.S. Courts of Appeals and U.S. District Courts

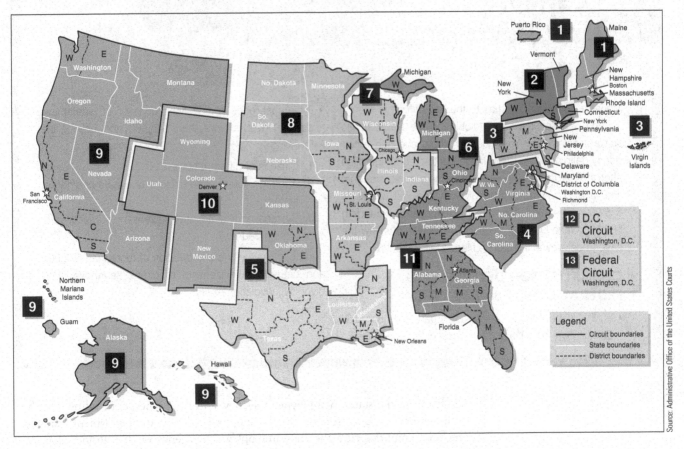

Source: Administrative Office of the United States Courts

by any of the federal courts of appeals, and it also has appellate authority over some cases decided in the state courts.

How Cases Reach the Supreme Court

There is no absolute right of appeal to the United States Supreme Court. Thousands of cases are filed with the Supreme Court each year, but it hears only about eighty cases each year.

To bring a case before the Supreme Court, a party requests the Court to issue a writ of *certiorari*. A writ of *certiorari*[6] is an order issued by the Supreme Court to a lower court requiring it to send the record of the case for review. The Court will issue a writ only if at least four of the nine justices vote to do so. The vast majority of petitions for writs are denied. A denial is not a decision on the merits of a case, nor does it indicate agreement with the lower court's opinion. It simply means that the Supreme Court declines to grant the request (petition) for appeal.

Types of Cases Reviewed by the Supreme Court

Typically, petitions are granted by the Court in cases that raise constitutional questions or where lower court decisions conflict with other state or federal courts' decisions. Similarly, if federal appellate courts issue inconsistent opinions on an issue, the Supreme Court may review a case involving that issue and generate a decision to settle the issue.

EXAMPLE 6-13 Suppose an employer fires an employee who refuses to work on Saturdays for religious reasons. The fired employee applies for unemployment

writ of *certiorari*

A writ from a higher court asking a lower court to send it the record of a case for review. The United States Supreme Court uses *certiorari* to review most of the cases it decides to hear.

DEVELOPING PARALEGAL SKILLS

FEDERAL COURT JURISDICTION

Mona, a new client, comes to the law offices of Henry, Jacobs & Miller in Detroit, Michigan. She wants to file suit against a New York hospital where she had emergency gallbladder surgery. Mona contracted an infection after the surgery and nearly died. She was so sick that she missed several months of work and lost wages of $18,000. She also has medical expenses exceeding $60,000. Jane Doyle, a paralegal, is asked to review the case to determine if it can be filed in federal court.

CHECKLIST FOR DETERMINING FEDERAL COURT JURISDICTION

- Is the case based, at least in part, on the U.S. Constitution, a treaty, or other question of federal law?

- If the case does not involve a question of federal law, does it involve more than $75,000 and one of the following:
  1. Citizens of different states?
  2. A foreign country and citizens of a state or different states?
  3. Citizens of a state and citizens or subjects of a foreign country?

If the case involves a combination of more than $75,000 and one of the citizenship requirements above, then diversity jurisdiction exists.

---

benefits from the state unemployment agency, and the agency, concluding that the employer had good reason to fire the employee, denies unemployment benefits. The fired employee sues the state unemployment agency on the ground that the employee's right to freely exercise her religion—a constitutional right—was violated. The case is ultimately appealed to a state supreme court, which decides the issue in a way contrary to several recent federal appellate courts' interpretations of freedom of religion in the employment context. If the losing party petitions the Supreme Court for a writ of *certiorari*, the Court is more likely to grant the petition and review the case than if all lower court decisions were consistent.

Alternative Dispute Resolution

alternative dispute resolution (ADR)
The resolution of disputes in ways other than those involved in the traditional judicial process. Negotiation, mediation, and arbitration are forms of ADR.

Litigation is expensive, adversarial, and time consuming. For these and other reasons, more and more individuals are turning to alternative dispute resolution (ADR) as a means of settling their disputes.

Methods of ADR range from neighbors sitting down over a cup of coffee in an attempt to work out their differences to multinational corporations agreeing to resolve a dispute through a formal hearing before a panel of experts. The great advantage of ADR is its flexibility. Normally, the parties themselves decide the method that will be used to settle the dispute, what procedures will be used, and whether the decision reached (either by themselves or by a neutral third party) will be legally binding or not.

About 95 percent of cases are settled before trial, often through some form of ADR. Indeed, over half of the states either require or encourage parties to undertake ADR (usually mediation) prior to trial. Several federal courts have instituted ADR programs as well. Here, we examine various forms of ADR. Keep in mind that new methods of ADR—and variations of existing methods—are being devised. Additionally, ADR services are now being offered via the Internet. Paralegals who develop expertise in the area of ADR can expand their career opportunities (by becoming mediators, for example). Paralegals can

DEVELOPING PARALEGAL SKILLS

TO SUE OR NOT TO SUE

Millie Burke, a paralegal, works for a sole practitioner. She has just been asked by the firm's owner, attorney Jim Wilcox, to draw up a checklist. It is to consist of questions that clients should consider before initiating a lawsuit. Wilcox wants to have the checklist on hand when he first interviews clients who come to him for advice on whether to bring a lawsuit or to settle a dispute by some alternative means. Burke drafts a checklist for Wilcox's review.

CHECKLIST FOR DECIDING WHETHER TO SUE

• Now that you have a rough idea of what it might cost to litigate your dispute, are you still interested in pursuing a trial? If so, you will need to pay a retainer now from which I will draw the initial filing fees and court costs. You will also need to sign an agreement that you will pay me hourly rates if the costs exceed the amount of the retainer.

• What is your goal for the litigation? What do you want to accomplish? What could the other party do to settle the case now?

• Do you have the time and patience to follow a court case through the judicial system, even if it takes several years?

• Is there a way to settle your grievance without going to court? Even if the settlement is less than you think you are owed, you may be better off settling now for the smaller figure. An early settlement will save the cost of litigation and prevent the time loss and frustration associated with litigation.

• Can you use some form of alternative dispute resolution (negotiation, mediation, or arbitration) to settle the dispute? Before you say no, let's review these dispute-settlement methods and discuss the pros and cons of each alternative. Is it important for you to be able to work with or have a relationship with the other party after the case is resolved?

also help attorneys to clarify the issues for clients who must decide whether to take a case to court or choose ADR, as described in *Developing Paralegal Skills* above.

Negotiation

Negotiation is one alternative means of resolving disputes. Attorneys frequently advise their clients to try to negotiate a settlement of their disputes voluntarily before they proceed to trial. During pretrial negotiation, the parties and/or their attorneys may meet to see if a mutually satisfactory agreement can be reached.

negotiation
A process in which parties attempt to settle their dispute voluntarily, with or without attorneys to represent them.

EXAMPLE 6-14 Assume that Katherine Baranski is suing Tony Peretto. He ran a stop sign and crashed into Baranski's car, causing her to suffer injuries and damages exceeding $100,000. After pretrial investigations into the matter, both parties realize that Baranski will likely win the suit. Peretto's attorney may make a settlement offer on behalf of Peretto. Baranski may be willing to accept a settlement offer for an amount lower than the amount of damages claimed in her complaint to avoid the time, trouble, expense, and uncertainty involved in taking the case to trial.

To facilitate an out-of-court settlement, Baranski's attorney may ask his paralegal to draft a letter to Baranski pointing out the strengths and weaknesses of her case against Peretto, the ADR options for settling the case before trial, and the advantages and disadvantages associated with each ADR option. Additionally, the paralegal may be asked to draft a letter to Peretto's attorney indicating the strengths of Baranski's case against him and the advantages to Peretto of settling the dispute out of court.

EXHIBIT 6.5
A Sample
Settlement Agreement

SETTLEMENT AGREEMENT

THIS AGREEMENT is entered into this twelfth day of May, 2017, between Katherine Baranski and Tony Peretto.

WITNESSETH

WHEREAS, there is now pending in the U.S. District Court for the District of Nita an action entitled *Baranski v. Peretto,* hereinafter referred to as "action."

WHEREAS, the parties hereto desire to record their agreement to settle all matters relating to said action without the necessity of further litigation.

NOW, THEREFORE, in consideration of the covenants and agreements contained herein, the sufficiency of which is hereby mutually acknowledged, and intending to be legally bound hereby, the parties agree as follows:

1. Katherine Baranski agrees to accept the sum of seventy-five thousand dollars ($75,000) in full satisfaction of all claims against Tony Peretto as set forth in the complaint filed in this action.

2. Tony Peretto agrees to pay Katherine Baranski the above-stated amount, in a lump-sum cash payment, on or before the first day of July, 2017.

3. Upon execution of this agreement and payment of the sum required under this agreement, the parties shall cause the action to be dismissed with prejudice.

4. When the sum required under this agreement is paid in full, Katherine Baranski will execute and deliver to Tony Peretto a release of all claims set forth in the complaint filed in the said action.

Katherine Baranski
Katherine Baranski

Tony Peretto
Tony Peretto

Sworn and subscribed before me this twelfth day of May, 2017.

Leela M. Shay
Leela M. Shay
Notary Public
District of Nita

settlement agreement
An out-of-court resolution to a legal dispute, which is agreed to by the parties in writing. A settlement agreement may be reached at any time prior to or during a trial.

As a result of pretrial negotiations, such as those just described, a settlement agreement may be reached. In a settlement agreement, one party gives up the right to initiate or continue litigation in return for a sum to be paid by the other party. Exhibit 6.5 above shows an example of a settlement agreement. Settlements must usually be approved by the court, and if a party does not live up to its agreement, that can be the basis for a lawsuit to enforce the settlement.

A paralegal mediates a dispute by emphasizing the common ground shared by the parties as she proposes possible solutions. Is mediation binding on both parties? Why or why not?

© NotarYes/www.Shutterstock.com.

Mediation

Another alternative to a trial is mediation. In the mediation process, the parties attempt to negotiate an agreement with the assistance of a neutral third party, a mediator. In mediation, the mediator typically talks with the parties separately and often jointly. The mediator emphasizes points of agreement, helps the parties evaluate their positions, and proposes solutions. The mediator, however, does not make a binding decision on the matter being disputed.

The parties may select a mediator on the basis of expertise in a particular field or a reputation for fairness and impartiality. The mediator need not be a lawyer. The mediator may be one person, such as a paralegal, an attorney, or a volunteer from the community, or a panel of mediators may be used. Usually, a mediator charges a fee, which can be split between the parties. Many state and federal courts require that parties mediate disputes before being allowed to resolve the disputes through trials. In this situation, the mediators may be appointed by the court.

mediation
A method of settling disputes outside of court by using the services of a neutral third party, who acts as a communicating agent between the parties; a method of dispute settlement that is less formal than arbitration.

A Nonadversarial Forum

Mediation is not adversarial in nature, as lawsuits are. In litigation, the parties "do battle" with each other in the courtroom, while the judge serves as the neutral referee. The adversarial nature of the trial process may inflame tensions between the parties. Because of its nonadversarial nature, the mediation process tends to reduce the hostility between the parties and may allow them to resume their former relationship. For this reason, mediation is often the preferred form of ADR for disputes involving businesses, family members, or other long-term relationships.

EXAMPLE 6-15 Suppose two business partners have a dispute over how the profits of their firm should be distributed. If the dispute is litigated, the parties will be adversaries, and their attorneys will emphasize how the parties' positions differ, not what they have in common. In contrast, if the dispute is mediated, the mediator emphasizes common ground shared by the partners and helps them work toward agreement. If the partners wish to do business together after the case is over, mediation will be preferred to litigation.

FEATURED CONTRIBUTOR

WHY MEDIATION MAY BE THE BEST LEGAL ALTERNATIVE

P. Darrel Harrison

BIOGRAPHICAL NOTE

P. Darrel Harrison is a trained mediator who holds an MBA in organizational development and a JD degree. He is an instructor and the program director for the ABA-approved paralegal program at San Diego Miramar College. Mr. Harrison is also vice president and chief grievance/arbitration officer for the San Diego Chapter of the American Federation of Teachers (AFT), Local 1931. He was appointed as a board member to the Mayor's Citizen Review Board, which reviews citizen complaints filed against the San Diego Police Department.

Litigated cases can be costly. Mediation is a cost-effective method of resolving many disputes because it avoids the expense of going to court. Mediation is satisfying because it allows a client the ability to negotiate an outcome based on compromise rather than a simple win or loss in court.

Mediation is a process for resolving conflicts, in which a neutral, skilled mediator assists the parties to discuss and negotiate their issues and reach a mutually acceptable resolution.

Because many state and federal courts around the United States have provided alternative dispute resolution services, various forms of mediation specialties have developed over

the years, such as Parent/Teen Mediation, Family Mediation, Business Mediation, Employment Mediation, Elder Care Mediation, and Guardianship Mediation, to name a few.

THE MEDIATION PROCESS

Despite the specialty areas, mediation basics are universally applied. First there must be willing participants. The commitment to mediation creates an atmosphere of good faith and the positive momentum that leads to a negotiated conclusion.

Once the parties have joined the process, it is essential that the mediator—the neutral third party—has the ability to engage

Paralegals as Mediators

Because a mediator need not be a lawyer, this field is open to paralegals who acquire appropriate training and expertise. If you are interested in becoming a mediator, you can check with your local paralegal association or with one of the national paralegal associations to find out how you can pursue this career goal. You can also check with a county, state, or federal court in your area to see how to qualify as a mediator for court-referred mediation (to be discussed shortly).

Generally, any paralegal aspiring to work as a mediator must have excellent communication skills. This is because, as a mediator, it will be your job to listen carefully to each party's complaints and communicate possible solutions to a dispute in a way that is not offensive to either party. (See this chapter's *Featured Contributor* article above for further details on the functions performed by mediators and the role played by paralegals in the mediation process.)

Arbitration

arbitration
A method of settling disputes in which a dispute is submitted to a disinterested third party (other than a court), who issues a decision that may or may not be legally binding.

A more formal method of ADR is arbitration, in which an arbitrator hears a dispute and determines the outcome. The key difference between arbitration and the forms of ADR just discussed is that in arbitration, the third party hearing the dispute makes the decision for the parties—a decision that will usually be legally binding. In negotiation and mediation, in contrast, the parties decide for themselves, although a third party the parties and help navigate them through the issues to come to a common solution. Unlike arbitration, where the intermediary listens to the arguments of both sides and makes a decision for the disputants, a mediator assists the parties to develop a solution themselves.

Although mediators may provide ideas or even formal proposals for settlement, the mediator is primarily a "process person." The mediator helps the parties define the agenda, identify and reframe the issues, communicate more effectively, find areas of common ground, negotiate fairly, and reach an agreement. A successful mediation has an outcome that is accepted and owned by the parties themselves.

THE MEDIATOR'S SKILLS

No license is required to be a mediator, but nonprofit organizations and universities offer certificates and degrees for mediation training. The National Conflict Resolution Center (NCRC) headquartered in San Diego, California, provides a training program for paralegals, attorneys, mental health professionals, managers, educators, law enforcement professionals, and others who want to complete the certification or credentialing process.

Training programs note that a successful mediator:

- is a good listener,
- has the discipline to resist taking sides,
- can comprehend facts and repeat them accurately,
- is diligent in keeping the parties engaged at all times, and

> " ... mediation basics are universally applied."

- possesses the writing skills needed to draft the final agreement.

Additionally, mediators must be diplomatic and use persuasion to get people to soften hard-line positions. Although many mediators are highly trained and experienced, many are not full-time mediators. They work in a variety of professions.

WHEN AND HOW TO ENGAGE A MEDIATOR

If your firm's client is engaged in a dispute with another party and is considering litigation:

- It may help to give the other party information about mediation. Provide a link to a mediator's website for information about the process.
- Consider asking the other party to suggest a mediator to help resolve the dispute.
- Some mediators will call the other side, explain mediation to them, and encourage them to mediate the dispute.
- You can ask the other side to mediate your dispute *before* or *after* a case is filed.

Preparing for mediation is a lot like preparing to go to a court hearing. Identify and organize the facts relevant to the dispute and make sure you know the facts that support the other side, too. If the parties are willing, and the mediator provides good facilitation skills, the benefits of the process and outcome can far outweigh the cost and stress of litigation.

---

assists them. In a sense, the arbitrator acts as a private judge, even though the arbitrator is not required to be a lawyer. In some instances a panel of experts arbitrates disputes.

Arbitration can resemble a trial, although the procedural rules are much less restrictive than those governing litigation. In the typical format, the parties present facts and arguments to the arbitrator and describe the outcome they want. Witnesses may be called but the format is less formal than in court. The arbitrator then issues a decision.

Depending on the parties' circumstances and preferences, the arbitrator's decision may or may not be legally binding on the parties. In nonbinding arbitration, the parties submit their dispute to a third party but remain free to reject the third party's decision. Nonbinding arbitration is more similar to mediation than to binding arbitration. As will be discussed later in this chapter, ADR mandated by the courts is not binding on the parties. If, after mandated arbitration, the parties are not satisfied with the results, they may insist on litigation in court. It is rare to be able to appeal the results of binding arbitration.

Arbitration Clauses and Statutes

Commercial matters are often submitted to arbitration both for speed and because the parties may wish to preserve their relationship. When a dispute arises, parties can agree to settle their differences through binding arbitration rather than through the court system.

EXAMPLE 6-16 A building is being built for $20 million. As construction proceeds, issues arise that are not covered in the details of the original plans. Extra expense will be incurred. Rather than stop work and negotiate a change to the contract, it is common for the parties to have agreed in the original contact to resolve such issues through binding arbitration when the job is done. The arbitrator is likely be an experienced contractor who understands construction process and expenses.

CONTRACTUAL OBLIGATION. Disputes are often arbitrated because of an arbitration clause in a contract agreed to before the dispute arose. For example, most checking accounts have an arbitration clause in the contract when the checking account was opened. An arbitration clause provides that any disputes arising under the contract will be resolved by arbitration and usually explains how the arbitration will be handled. For example, an arbitration clause in a contract for the sale of goods might provide that "any controversy or claim arising under this contract will be referred to arbitration before the American Arbitration Association."[7] Most international business contracts require arbitration, often in an international business center such as London or Stockholm.

STATUTORY BACKING. Most states have statutes (often based on the Uniform Arbitration Act) under which arbitration clauses will be enforced, and some state statutes compel arbitration of certain disputes, such as those involving public employees. At the federal level, the Federal Arbitration Act (FAA) enforces arbitration clauses in contracts involving interstate commerce. Because of the wide scope of the commerce clause in the Constitution, even business activities that have only minimal effects on commerce between two or more states are considered interstate commerce. Thus, arbitration agreements involving business transactions usually fall under the FAA.

The FAA does not establish a set arbitration procedure. The parties must agree on the manner of resolving their disputes. The FAA provides only that if the parties have agreed to arbitrate disputes arising in relation to their contract, through an arbitration clause, the arbitration clause will be enforced by the courts. In other words, arbitration must take place. There is no right to file suit in court.

The Arbitration Process

The first step in the arbitration process is the submission agreement, in which the parties agree to submit their dispute for arbitration. If an arbitration clause was included in a contract, the clause serves this function so the complaining party can file with the arbitrator to begin the process. Most states require that an agreement to submit a dispute to arbitration must be in writing. The submission agreement typically identifies the parties, the nature of the dispute, the monetary amounts in the dispute, the place of arbitration, and the powers that the arbitrator will exercise. Frequently, the agreement includes a signed statement that the parties intend to be bound by the arbitrator's decision.

THE HEARING. The next step in the process is the *hearing*. Normally, the parties agree prior to arbitration—in an arbitration clause or in a submission-to-arbitrate agreement—on the procedural rules that govern the proceedings. This includes the method to be used to select an arbitrator or a panel of arbitrators. In a typical hearing, the parties begin as they would at a trial by presenting opening arguments and stating what remedies should or should not be granted. In some cases, the matter is handled entirely by submitting documents online. No in-person contact with the arbitrator may be needed.

After the opening positions are established, evidence is presented. Witnesses may be called and examined by both sides. Once all evidence has been presented, the parties give their closing arguments. Although arbitration is in some ways similar to a trial, the rules (such as those regarding what kinds of evidence may be introduced) are usually much less restrictive than those involved in formal litigation.

arbitration clause
A clause in a contract providing that, in case of a dispute, the parties will determine their rights through arbitration rather than the judicial system.

submission agreement
A written agreement to submit a legal dispute to an arbitrator or arbitrating panel for resolution.

THE AWARD.   After each side has had an opportunity to present its case, the arbitrator reaches a decision. The decision of the arbitrator is called an award, even if no monetary award is conferred as a result of the proceedings. The award is usually announced within thirty days of the close of the hearing. In most instances, the arbitrator does not give a written explanation for the decision.

award
In the context of ADR, the decision rendered by an arbitrator.

A paralegal may become involved in preparations for arbitration, just as in preparing for a trial. The paralegal will assist in obtaining and organizing evidence relating to the dispute, may interview witnesses and prepare them for the hearing, and generally will help with other tasks commonly undertaken prior to a trial (see Chapter 10).

The Role of the Courts in Prearbitration

The role of the courts in arbitration is limited. One important role is at the prearbitration stage. When a dispute arises as to whether the parties have agreed in an arbitration clause to submit a particular matter to arbitration, one party may file suit to force arbitration. The court before which the suit is brought will not decide the underlying substantive controversy but must decide whether the dispute is *arbitrable*—that is, whether the matter is one capable of being resolved through arbitration and whether the parties have actually agreed to the arbitration.

EXAMPLE 6-17 Suppose that a dispute involves a claim of employment discrimination on the basis of age. If the issue of arbitrability reaches a court, the court will have to decide whether the Age Discrimination in Employment Act (which protects persons forty years of age and older against employment discrimination on the basis of age) permits such claims brought under this act to be arbitrated.

COMPEL ARBITRATION.   If the court finds that the subject matter in controversy is covered by an arbitration agreement, then a party is likely to be compelled to arbitrate the dispute. Even when a claim involves a violation of a statute passed to protect a certain class of people, such as a statute prohibiting age discrimination against employees in the workplace, a court may determine that the parties must nonetheless abide by their agreement to arbitrate the dispute.

EXAMPLE 6-18 In the employment discrimination *Example 6-17*, suppose the "agreement to arbitrate" is a paragraph in a 300-page employee handbook. The court will have to decide whether there was actually an agreement between the parties to arbitrate their disputes. Generally courts expect arbitration agreements to be clearly stated.

Usually, a court will allow the claim to be arbitrated if the court, in interpreting the statute, can find no legislative intent to the contrary and the parties clearly agreed to arbitration.

FAIRNESS ISSUE.   The courts will not compel arbitration if the arbitration rules and procedures are inherently unfair to one of the parties.

EXAMPLE 6-19 Suppose that an employer's arbitration agreement with an employee states that the employer establishes the rules for the arbitration. In this situation, the court is likely to conclude that the rules are unfair and thus refuse to enforce the arbitration agreement.

The Postarbitration Role of the Courts

Courts may play a role at the postarbitration stage. After arbitration produces an award, one party may appeal the award or may seek a court order compelling the other party to comply with the award. The general view is that because the parties were free to frame the issues and set the powers of the arbitrator at the outset, they cannot complain about the result. An arbitration award may be set aside, however, if the award resulted from the arbitrator's misconduct or "bad faith," or if the arbitrator exceeded his or her powers in arbitrating the dispute. Setting aside an award does not happen very often. Courts generally enforce arbitration awards and will order payment to be made if the losing party fails to pay.

Other ADR Forms

The three forms of ADR just discussed have been the most commonly used forms to date. In recent years, a variety of new types of ADR have emerged. Some of them combine elements of mediation and arbitration. For example, in binding mediation, a neutral mediator tries to facilitate agreement between the parties, but if no agreement is reached, the mediator issues a legally binding decision on the matter. In one version of this approach, known as mediation arbitration (med-arb), an arbitrator first attempts to help the parties reach an agreement, just as a mediator would. If no agreement is reached, then formal arbitration is undertaken, and the arbitrator issues a legally binding decision.

Another ADR form is referred to as "assisted negotiation" because it involves a third party in what is essentially a negotiation process. For example, in early neutral case evaluation, the parties select a neutral third party (generally an expert in the subject matter of the dispute) to evaluate their respective positions. The parties explain their positions to the case evaluator however they wish. The case evaluator then assesses the strengths and weaknesses of the parties' positions, and this evaluation forms the basis for negotiating a settlement.

The mini-trial is a form of assisted negotiation that is often used by business parties. In a mini-trial, each party's attorney briefly argues the party's case before representatives of each firm who have the authority to settle the dispute. Typically, a neutral third party (usually an expert in the area being disputed) acts as an adviser. If the parties fail to reach an agreement, the adviser renders an opinion as to how a court would likely decide the issue. The proceeding assists the parties in determining whether they should negotiate a settlement of the dispute or take it to court. It is a useful way for the parties to assess the strength of each side's case.

Collaborative Law

Still another method of resolving disputes is the collaborative law approach, which is increasingly being used during marital separation procedures. In *collaborative law*, both parties, their attorneys, and any professionals working with the parties agree to meet to resolve all of their issues without litigation. Sometimes a single attorney handles the matter for both sides. The lawyers act as negotiators and communication moderators while advising their clients about their legal rights, entitlements, and obligations. Both parties promise to take a reasoned stand on every issue, to keep discovery cooperative and informal, and to work together to craft an agreement. Any abusive communications are identified, discussed, and eliminated.

Because the attorneys agree not to take part in any litigation that may occur if an agreement is not reached, the attorneys focus only on settlement rather than on preparing documents or presentations for court. If either party seeks court intervention, all attorneys must withdraw from representation. The Uniform Collaborative Law Act, written by the Uniform Law Commission, has been adopted in about a dozen states.

Court-Referred ADR

Today, most states require or encourage parties to undergo mediation or arbitration prior to trial. Generally, when a trial court refers a case for arbitration, the arbitrator's decision is not binding on the parties. If the parties do not agree with the arbitrator's decision, they can go forward with the lawsuit.

binding mediation
A form of ADR in which a mediator attempts to facilitate agreement between the parties but then issues a legally binding decision if no agreement is reached.

early neutral case evaluation
A form of ADR in which a neutral third party evaluates the strengths and weaknesses of the disputing parties' positions; the evaluator's opinion forms the basis for negotiating a settlement.

mini-trial
A private proceeding that assists disputing parties in determining whether to take their case to court. Each party's attorney briefly argues the party's case before the other party and (usually) a neutral third party, who acts as an adviser. If the parties fail to reach an agreement, the adviser issues an opinion as to how a court would likely decide the issue.

The types of court-related ADR programs in use vary widely. In some states, such as Missouri, ADR is completely voluntary. In other states, such as Minnesota, parties are required to undertake ADR before a court will hear their cases. Some states offer a menu of options. Other states, including Florida (which has a statewide, comprehensive mediation program), offer only one alternative.

Courts experiment with a variety of ADR alternatives to speed up justice and reduce its cost. Some federal and state courts now hold summary jury trials (SJTs), in which the parties present their arguments and supporting evidence (other than witness testimony—witnesses are not called in an SJT). The jury renders a verdict, but unlike the verdict in an actual trial, the jury's verdict is not binding. The verdict acts as a guide to both sides in reaching an agreement during mandatory negotiations that immediately follow the SJT. If no settlement is reached, both sides have the right to a full trial later.

summary jury trial (SJT)
A settlement method in which a trial is held but the jury's verdict is not binding. The verdict acts as a guide to both sides in reaching an agreement during mandatory negotiations that follow the trial. If a settlement is not reached, both sides have the right to a full trial later.

Other alternatives being employed by the courts include summary procedures for commercial litigation and the appointment of special masters to assist judges in deciding complex issues.

Providers of ADR Services

ADR services are provided by both government agencies and private organizations. A major provider of ADR services is the American Arbitration Association (AAA). Most of the nation's largest law firms are members of this nonprofit association. Hundreds of thousands of disputes are submitted to the AAA for resolution each year in the United States and internationally. Cases brought to the AAA are heard by an expert or a panel of experts in the area relating to the dispute and are usually settled quickly. Generally, about half of the panel members are lawyers. To cover its costs, the AAA charges a fee, paid by the party filing the claim. In addition, each party to the dispute pays a specified amount for each hearing day. An additional fee is charged for cases involving personal injuries or property loss.

American Arbitration Association (AAA)
The major organization offering arbitration services in the United States.

Many for-profit firms around the country also provide ADR services. Some firms hire retired judges to conduct arbitration hearings or assist parties in settling their disputes. Private ADR firms normally allow the parties to decide on the date of the hearing, the presiding judge, whether the judge's decision will be legally binding, and the site of the hearing—which may be a conference room, a law school office, or a leased courtroom. The judges follow procedures similar to those of the federal courts and use similar rules. Usually, each party to the dispute pays a filing fee and a designated fee for a hearing session or conference.

As mentioned, courts also have ADR programs in which disputes are resolved by court-appointed attorneys or paralegals who are qualified to act as arbitrators or mediators in certain types of disputes. Paralegals have found that becoming a mediator or an arbitrator is an especially rewarding career option. See the *Ethics Watch* feature on the following page regarding the paralegal's role in ensuring that the arbitration process is proper.

Online Dispute Resolution

A number of companies and organizations offer online dispute resolution (ODR) via the Internet. Disputes resolved in online forums often involve disagreements over the right to use a certain website address or disputes involving sales over the Internet. Those who do business online (and the attorneys who represent them) should be aware of this ADR option.

online dispute resolution (ODR)
The resolution of disputes with the assistance of an organization that offers dispute resolution services via the Internet.

Most online forums do not automatically apply the law of a specific jurisdiction but use general, universal legal principles. As with traditional methods of dispute resolution, a party normally may appeal to a court at any time. Negotiation, mediation, and arbitration services are all available to disputants over the Internet.

Several firms offer online forums for negotiating monetary settlements. Typically, one party files a complaint, and the other party is notified by e-mail. Password-protected

ETHICS WATCH

POTENTIAL ARBITRATION PROBLEMS

When individuals and businesses prefer to arbitrate disputes rather than take them to court, they include arbitration clauses in their contracts. These clauses specify who or what organization will arbitrate the dispute, where the arbitration will take place, and what law will apply. To safeguard a client's interests when drafting and reviewing arbitration clauses in contracts, the careful paralegal will be alert to the possibility that those who arbitrate the dispute might not be truly neutral or that the designated place of arbitration may pose a great inconvenience and expense for the client. The paralegal should call any such problems to his or her supervising attorney's attention. The attorney can then discuss the problem with the client and help the client negotiate a more favorable arbitration clause.

This level of care is necessary to be consistent with the NFPA *Model Code of Ethics and Professional Responsibility*, Section 1.6(a): "A paralegal shall act within the bounds of the law, solely for the benefit of the client." It is also consistent with the ABA *Model Guidelines for the Utilization of Paralegal Services*. The *Guidelines* state that lawyers may assign legal work to paralegals, but the lawyers remain responsible for the work product. Hence, paralegals should be sure their work is reviewed by supervising attorneys. Paralegals may not perform work for attorneys that may only be performed by licensed attorneys by the rules of a court, the bar association, a statute, or other controlling authority.

Reprinted by permission of the National Federation of Paralegal Associations, Inc. (NFPA®), www.paralegals.org.

access to the online forum site is made available. Fees are generally low (often 2 to 4 percent, or less, of the disputed amount). The parties can drop the negotiations at any time. For example, the Web-based firm Smartsettle offers a unique blind-bidding system to help resolve disputes. Given the rapid advances in online services, more creative, lower-cost dispute resolution methods will be devised.

KEY TERMS AND CONCEPTS

alternative dispute resolution (ADR) 158

American Arbitration Association (AAA) 167

appellate court 148

appellate jurisdiction 148

arbitration 162

arbitration clause 164

award 165

bankruptcy court 148

binding mediation 166

concurrent jurisdiction 149

diversity of citizenship 149

docket 149

early neutral case evaluation 166

exclusive jurisdiction 149

federal question 148

jurisdiction 147

justiciable controversy 146

long arm statute 147

mediation 161

mini-trial 166

negotiation 159

online dispute resolution (ODR) 167

original jurisdiction 148

probate court 148

reversible error 155

settlement agreement 160

standing to sue 146

submission agreement 164

summary jury trial (SJT) 167

trial court 148

venue 151

writ of *certiorari* 157

JUDICIAL REQUIREMENTS

1. *Standing to sue*—A legally protected and real interest in a matter sufficient to justify seeking relief through the court system. The controversy at issue must also be a justiciable controversy—one that is real and substantial, not hypothetical.

2. *Types of jurisdiction*—Before a court can hear a case, it must have jurisdiction over the person against whom the suit is brought (*in personam* jurisdiction) or the property involved in the suit (*in rem* jurisdiction), as well as jurisdiction over the subject matter.

   a. **JURISDICTION OVER PERSONS AND PROPERTY**—Courts have jurisdiction over persons, including businesses, who reside in the geographic area of the court. Businesses that have a certain level of minimum contacts in a state will be subject to court jurisdiction under a long arm statute. Courts also have jurisdiction over property located within the boundaries of the court.

   b. **JURISDICTION OVER SUBJECT MATTER**—Limited jurisdiction exists when a court is limited to a specific subject matter, such as probate or divorce. General jurisdiction exists when a court can hear any kind of case. State and federal statutes often define the power of courts to hear matters relating to statutory law.

   c. **ORIGINAL AND APPELLATE JURISDICTION**—Courts that have authority to hear a case for the first time (trial courts) have original jurisdiction. Courts of appeals, or reviewing courts, have appellate jurisdiction; generally, these courts do not have original jurisdiction.

3. *Jurisdiction of federal courts*—Is limited to powers of the national government that arise from the Constitution.

   a. **FEDERAL QUESTIONS**—Jurisdiction exists in federal court when a federal question is involved (when the plaintiff's cause of action is based, at least in part, on the U.S. Constitution, a treaty, or a federal law).

   b. **DIVERSITY JURISDICTION**—May arise for a federal court when a case involves diversity of citizenship (as in disputes between citizens of different states, between a foreign country and citizens of a state or states, or between citizens of a state and citizens of a foreign country) and the amount in controversy exceeds $75,000.

   c. **EXCLUSIVE VERSUS CONCURRENT JURISDICTION**—Concurrent jurisdiction exists when two different courts have authority to hear the same case. Exclusive jurisdiction exists when only state courts or only federal courts have authority to hear a case.

4. *Jurisdiction in cyberspace*—Because the Internet does not have physical boundaries, traditional jurisdictional concepts are applied to develop standards to determine when jurisdiction over a website owner or operator in another state is proper.

5. *Venue*—Venue has to do with the most appropriate location for a trial, which is usually the geographic area where the event leading to the dispute took place or where the parties reside.

6. *Judicial procedures*—Rules of procedure prescribe the way in which disputes are handled in the courts. The Federal Rules of Civil Procedure govern all civil litigation in federal courts. Each state has its own procedural rules (often similar to the federal rules), and each court within a state has specific court rules that must be followed.

STATE COURT SYSTEMS

1. *Trial courts*—Courts of original jurisdiction, in which legal actions are initiated. State trial courts have either general jurisdiction or limited jurisdiction.

2. *Appellate, or reviewing, courts*—After a trial there is a right of appeal in the federal and state court systems. The focus on appeal is for reversible errors in law at trial.

   a. **INTERMEDIATE APPELLATE COURTS**—Many states have intermediate appellate courts that review the proceedings of the trial courts; generally, these courts do not have original jurisdiction. Appellate courts ordinarily examine questions of law and procedure while deferring to the trial court's findings of fact.

   b. **HIGHEST STATE COURTS**—Each state has a supreme court, although it may be called by some other name. Decisions of the state's highest court are final on all questions of state law. If a federal question is at issue, the case may be appealed to the United States Supreme Court.

THE FEDERAL COURT SYSTEM

1. *U.S. district courts*—The federal district court is the equivalent of the state trial court. The district court exercises general jurisdiction over claims arising under federal law or based on diversity of citizenship. Federal courts of limited jurisdiction include the U.S. Tax Court, the U.S. Bankruptcy Court, and the U.S. Court of Federal Claims.

2. *U.S. courts of appeals*—There are thirteen intermediate courts of appeals (or circuit courts of appeals) in the federal court system. Twelve of the courts hear appeals from the district courts within their circuits. The thirteenth court has national appellate jurisdiction over certain cases, such as patent law and those in which the U.S. government is a defendant.

3. *United States Supreme Court*—The United States Supreme Court is the highest court in the land and the final arbiter of the Constitution and federal law. There is no absolute right of appeal to the Supreme Court, and only a fraction of the cases filed with the Court each year are heard.

   a. **HOW CASES REACH THE SUPREME COURT**—The Supreme Court has original jurisdiction in a few cases, but it functions primarily as an appellate court. It accepts a tiny fraction of the appeals made to it when at least four justices agree to issue a *writ of certiorari* requiring the lower court to send it the record of the case for review.

   b. **TYPES OF CASES REVIEWED**—As a rule, only petitions that raise constitutional questions are granted. The Court may also review matters where the lower courts are split in their interpretation of a legal issue.

ALTERNATIVE DISPUTE RESOLUTION

The costs and time-consuming character of litigation, as well as the public nature of court proceedings, have caused many to turn to various forms of alternative dispute resolution (ADR) for settling disagreements. The methods of ADR include the following:

1. *Negotiation*—The simplest form of ADR, in which the parties come together, with or without attorneys to represent them, and try to reach a settlement without the involvement of a third party.

2. *Mediation*—A form of ADR in which the parties reach an agreement with the help of a neutral third party, called a mediator, who proposes solutions and emphasizes areas of agreement.

3. *Arbitration*—The most formal method of ADR, in which the parties submit their dispute to a neutral third party, the arbitrator (or panel of arbitrators), who issues a decision. The decision may or may not be legally binding, depending on the circumstances.

   a. **ARBITRATION CLAUSES AND STATUTES**—Arbitration clauses that are agreed on in contracts require the parties to resolve their disputes in arbitration (rather than in court). Federal and state laws encourage the courts to uphold arbitration agreements.

   b. **THE ARBITRATION PROCESS**—A submission agreement is given to the arbiter to outline the dispute. A hearing is held before a single arbiter or a panel so both sides may present facts and arguments. After proceedings less formal than in a court, an award is issued to declare the results of the matter.

   c. **ROLE OF THE COURTS IN PREARBITRATION**—A court may be asked to determine if a matter is, in fact, subject to arbitration rather than a court proceeding.

   d. **POSTARBITRATION ROLE OF THE COURTS**—Awards, even when binding, may be appealed to the courts for review. The court's review is much more restricted than an appellate court's review of a trial court record.

4. *Other ADR forms*—These include binding mediation, mediation arbitration, early neutral case evaluation, mini-trials; generally, these are forms of "assisted negotiation."

5. *Collaborative law*—A form of ADR in which both parties, their attorneys, and any professionals working with the parties meet to resolve their issues without litigation. The lawyers act as negotiators and communication moderators while advising their clients about their legal rights, entitlements, and obligations. If either party seeks court intervention, both attorneys must withdraw from representation.

6. *Court-referred ADR*—In some jurisdictions, courts require parties to undergo some form of ADR so as to help resolve disputes prior to trial. One form for more complicated matters is the summary jury trial, where a jury hears a shortened form of a full trial and issues a nonbinding verdict.

7. *Providers of ADR services*—The leading nonprofit provider of ADR services is the American Arbitration Association. Many for-profit firms also provide ADR services domestically and internationally.

8. *Online dispute resolution*—A number of organizations and firms offer negotiation and arbitration services through online forums. These forums have been a practical alternative for the resolution of disputes over the right to use a certain website address or the quality of goods purchased over the Internet.

QUESTIONS FOR REVIEW

1. Define *jurisdiction*. Define *venue*. What is the difference between personal jurisdiction and subject-matter jurisdiction? What is a long arm statute?

2. Describe the types of cases over which federal courts exercise jurisdiction.

3. How do original and appellate jurisdictions differ? The relationship between state and federal jurisdiction is an example of what type of jurisdiction?

4. How do the functions of a trial court differ from the functions of an appellate court?

5. Describe the procedure for cases to reach the United States Supreme Court.

6. Describe the various methods of alternative dispute resolution.

ETHICS QUESTION

Aaron is a paralegal with a law firm that specializes in intellectual property law. Aaron's supervising attorney asks him to e-mail a letter to the client that the attorney has prepared. The letter and its attachments discuss a patent application and contain drawings and plans for a heated steering wheel that the client plans to sell to automobile manufacturers. Aaron does so without encrypting the letter or the attachments, which contain confidential information. A temporary employee working at the client's office accesses the unencrypted e-mail and steals the information. Have any ethical rules been violated by Aaron or by his supervising attorney? If so, which rules? What could Aaron and his supervising attorney have done differently to better protect the client's interests?

PRACTICE QUESTIONS AND ASSIGNMENTS

1. Identify each of the following courts. If not indicated, specify whether it is a state or federal court.

   a. This state court has general jurisdiction over civil and criminal cases and takes testimony from witnesses and receives evidence.

   b. This court has appellate jurisdiction and is part of a court system that is divided into geographic units called *circuits*.

   c. This state court only hears issues related to divorce and custody matters. It has original jurisdiction.

   d. This court can exercise federal question and diversity-of-citizenship jurisdiction, and receives testimony and other evidence.

   e. The decisions of this state court are usually final. It is the highest appellate court within its court system.

   f. This federal court has nine justices. It has original jurisdiction over several types of cases but functions primarily as an appellate court. There is no automatic right to appeal to this court.

2. Look at Exhibit 6.4 on page 157 and answer these questions:

   • How many federal circuits are there?

   • In which federal circuit is your state located?

   • How many federal judicial districts are located in your state? In which federal district is your community located?

3. Marcella, who is from Toledo, Ohio, drives to Troy, Michigan, and shops at a popular mall. When leaving the parking lot, Marcella runs a red light while texting and causes an accident resulting in personal injuries to the driver of the other vehicle. On what basis could a Michigan court obtain jurisdiction over Marcella? If the damages in the lawsuit exceed $75,000, could a federal court in Michigan have jurisdiction over this case? On what jurisdictional basis? What type of jurisdiction would exist if both the courts of the state of Michigan and the federal court have jurisdiction over this case? Discuss the other types of jurisdiction the court may have in this case (such as *in personam* jurisdiction, *in rem* jurisdiction, subject-matter jurisdiction, limited jurisdiction, general jurisdiction, original jurisdiction, appellate jurisdiction, concurrent jurisdiction, and exclusive jurisdiction).

4. Using the materials presented in the chapter, identify the following methods of alternative dispute resolution:

   a. The parties to a divorce meet with a neutral third party who emphasizes points of agreement and proposes solutions to resolve their dispute. After several hours, the parties reach a compromise.

   b. The parties to a contract dispute submit it to a neutral third party for a legally binding resolution. The neutral third party is not a court.

   c. The plaintiff and defense attorneys in a personal-injury case propose settlement figures to one another and their clients in an effort to resolve the lawsuit voluntarily.

d. The attorneys from the personal-injury example above are able to reach an acceptable settlement figure of $100,000. They draft an agreement whereby the plaintiff gives up her right to sue in exchange for a payment of $100,000 by the defendant.

e. A commercial dispute involving $95,000 in damages is filed in a federal court. The judge requires the parties' attorneys to present their arguments and supporting evidence, excluding witnesses, to the jury. The jury then renders a nonbinding verdict. Once the nonbinding verdict is rendered, the parties reach a settlement.

■ GROUP PROJECT

As a group, diagram your state court system by going to the National Center for State Courts website at: **http://www. ncsc.org/Information-and-Resources/Browse-by-State. aspx**. Under "Browse by State," click on "Court Web Sites" and select your state.

Students one and two will locate the state's trial courts and describe the jurisdiction of each one. Courts of limited jurisdiction, such as probate and divorce courts, should be included along with the trial courts of general jurisdiction. Students will create a document with a diagram showing the various levels of trial courts, as well as the subject matter jurisdiction of each one.

Student three will describe the state's intermediate appellate court and the types of appeals it hears. This information should be added to the diagram created by students one and two.

Student four will research the state's highest appellate court, list the types of appeals it accepts, and outline the basic procedure for filing an appeal with this court. This information should be added to the diagram created by the other students.

Each group will submit its court diagram to the instructor.

■ INTERNET PROJECT

1. The American Arbitration Association (AAA) is the largest provider of alternative dispute resolution services in the country. To learn more about ADR procedures, go to **www.adr.org**, the home page for the American Arbitration Association. Browse through the site's offerings and find the answers to the following questions:

a. What types of services does the AAA offer? Does the AAA engage in arbitration outside the United States?

b. Describe the steps in filing a case online.

c. Locate the form for filing a consumer demand for a non-California arbitration. Make a list of the different categories of information that the form requires. Attach a copy of the form to your assignment.

d. What are the fees to file a consumer case with the AAA? Which party pays more in a consumer arbitration, a consumer or a business?

■ END NOTES

1. Pronounced jus-*tish*-a-bul.

2. A state's highest court is often referred to as the state supreme court, but there are exceptions. For example, in New York, what is called the supreme court is a trial court.

3. Under the Class Action Fairness Act (CAFA) of 2005, it is likely that most class-action lawsuits will not qualify for state court jurisdiction.

4. Pronounced *ven*-yoo.

5. The name in Ohio is Court of Common Pleas; the name in New York is Supreme Court; the name in Florida, Illinois, and Missouri is Circuit Court.

6. Pronounced sur-shee-uh-*rah*-ree.

7. As discussed later in the chapter, the American Arbitration Association is a leading provider of arbitration services in the United States.

Legal Procedures and Paralegal Skills

Legal Research and Analysis

CHAPTER OBJECTIVES

After completing this chapter, you will know:

- How primary and secondary sources of law differ and how to use each of these types of sources in the research process.

- How court decisions are published and how to read case citations.

- How to analyze case law and summarize, or brief, cases.

- How federal statutes and regulations are published and the major sources of statutory and administrative law.

- How to interpret statutory law and understand what kinds of resources are available for researching the legislative history of a statute.

Introduction

Legal research is a central and fascinating part of paralegal work. It is interesting to read the actual words of a court's opinion on a legal question or the text of a statute. Additionally, paralegals acquire firsthand knowledge of the law and how it applies to people and events. The ability to conduct research thoroughly yet efficiently enhances a paralegal's value to the legal team.

You may be asked to perform a variety of research tasks. Some tasks will be simple, such as locating and printing a court case. Other tasks may take days or weeks to complete. In all but the simplest tasks, legal research overlaps with legal analysis. To find relevant case law you need to be able to analyze the cases you find to ensure that they are on point. As the Featured Contributor discusses on page 176, you want to think carefully about the questions to be addressed in approaching a case.

Many paralegals conduct research without entering a law library. Westlaw and Lexis are the leading providers of online research services for legal professionals needing access to legal documents. Many free sources also can be located via Google and other search engines. (See Chapter 8 for a discussion of online legal research.) Regardless of how or where you conduct legal research, it is essential to know what sources to consult for different types of information.

Researching Case Law—
The Preliminary Steps

To illustrate how to research case law, we use a hypothetical case. One of your firm's clients, Trent Hoffman, is suing Better Homes Store for negligence. During the initial client interview, Hoffman explained to your supervising attorney and you that he had gone to the store to buy a large mirror. As he was leaving the store through a side entrance, carrying the mirror, he ran into a large pole just outside the door. He did not see the pole because the mirror blocked his view. When he hit the pole, the mirror broke, and a piece of glass went into his left eye, causing permanent loss of eyesight. Hoffman claims that the store was negligent in placing a pole so close to the door and wants to sue the store for millions of dollars in damages.

You have done a preliminary investigation and have obtained evidence supporting Hoffman's account of the facts. Your supervising attorney now asks you to research case law to find other cases with similar fact patterns and see what the courts decided. Before you begin, you need to define the issue to be researched and determine your research goals. We look now at these two preliminary steps in researching case law.

Defining the Issue

In defining the legal issue that you need to research, your first task is to examine the facts of Hoffman's case to determine the nature of the legal issue involved. (An example is provided in *Developing Paralegal Skills* on page 178.) Based on his description of the circumstances (verified through your preliminary investigation) and on his allegation that Better Homes Store should not have placed a pole just outside one of the store's entrances, you know that the legal issue relates to the tort of negligence and premises liability. As a starting point, you should therefore review what you know about negligence theory.

Background Research

If you are unfamiliar with negligence law or premises liability for merchants, you can start by doing background research to familiarize yourself with the topic, as described in the section on legal encyclopedias later in this chapter.

FEATURED CONTRIBUTOR

IS THE GLASS HALF FULL?

Judith Mathers Maloney

BIOGRAPHICAL NOTE

Judith Mathers Maloney is an attorney licensed in New York State. Her practice focuses on contracts, alternative dispute resolution, and civil litigation. She is director of paralegal studies, an adjunct professor, and advisor to the moot court team at Molloy College in Rockville Centre, New York. She is a member of the American Bar Association, the Nassau County Bar Association, and the board of the American Association for Paralegal Education (AAfPE), serving as director of the northeast region.

Mathers Maloney has been involved in the legal education field at the undergraduate and graduate levels for two decades. She co-authored a publication on litigation practice under New York State law and reviews texts and manuscripts on paralegal studies topics. She has developed courses for both the traditional and hybrid classroom.

Legal analysis connects the research students engage in with the written document they produce. It is also a stumbling block for many students. Analysis forces an objective interpretation of facts and requires the ability to support the chosen argument with primary law. For students, it is often difficult to move from "I think" to "the law states." A simple way to focus paralegal students on the concept is to ask them to look at the problem in context and determine which facts are significant. Arguments need to be properly constructed and thoroughly supported.

Ask the question, "Is that glass of water half full or half empty?" It seems simple and elicits an easy answer. Depending on your point of view, the answer can go either way and still be "right." However, if we subject this seemingly simple question and answer to the type of rigorous legal analysis that we require of legal professionals, the results can be less obvious.

THE FACTUAL QUESTION

The first step in legal research and analysis, before we ever get to the "answer," is to sort through the facts and analyze the

The tort of negligence (discussed in Chapter 14 in detail) is defined as the failure to exercise reasonable care. To succeed in a negligence action, a plaintiff must establish four elements:

1. The defendant had a duty of care to the plaintiff.
2. The defendant breached that duty.
3. The plaintiff suffered a legally recognizable injury.
4. The injury was caused by the defendant's breach of the duty of care.

Focus on the Legal Issues

These elements help you determine the issue that needs to be researched. There is little doubt that the third requirement has been met—Hoffman's loss of sight is a legally recognizable injury for which he can be compensated—if he succeeds in proving the other three elements of negligence. Proving the fourth element, causation, depends largely on proving the first two elements. You will therefore focus your research on the first two elements. Specifically, you need to answer the following questions:

- Did Better Homes Store owe a duty of care to its customer, Hoffman? You might phrase this question in more general terms: Do business owners owe question. In our example, we would determine what information is critical to the analysis.

For example:

- Is the question about materials? If so, we need to determine if the "glass" is really glass, or is it plastic, acrylic, or some other transparent substance.

- Is the question about what is in the glass? If so, we need to determine if the "water" is water or some other clear liquid.

- Is the question about measurement? Do we need to measure the volume of the glass and the amount of water in it to determine if it is filled exactly halfway?

To answer those factual questions, we need to test the materials and determine the composition or measurement through established scientific practice. The paralegal student can follow this example, understanding that the first steps in analysis are to identify the salient facts of a client's case and research the primary law assumed to be applicable.

> "Analysis forces an objective interpretation of facts …"

THE ANSWER

When, and only when, all factual questions have been fully analyzed do we move toward the answer. We have gathered all of the information we can. That is, we know that the volume of liquid in the container is exactly half of the volume of the container, the liquid is water, and the container is made of acrylic. Now we look at the context in which the answer is required and translate it into legal form.

For example:

- In a pleading, the answer could be to admit that the glass is half full and deny knowledge or information as to any other part of the allegation.

- At a deposition, the answer to the question about whether the glass is half full or half empty could be "both" or an even more disingenuous "yes."

The point of this exercise is to show that in legal analysis, words matter. A huge difference exists between a statute that imposes strict liability and one that imposes liability for only "knowing" violations. For the defendant, it may be the difference between incarceration and freedom.

It is critical for every member of the legal team to understand the importance of precise expression. Legal analysis, done right, is a team sport. A clear, precise question will result in a more focused and useful answer—one that responds to the exact issues that exist in the particular case. Take time to focus on the factual question. Do we care if the glass is glass, or the water is water, or is the focus only on the amount in the glass? The team can then concentrate on what is important and use the right tools—a measuring cup if volume is important, or a microscope if we must determine composite materials.

Ensuring precision of expression in questions and answers is an everyday part of the legal team's analysis. It has a considerable effect on the likelihood that, at the conclusion of the case, the client's glass will be objectively full.

a duty of care to business invitees—customers and others invited onto their premises?

- If so, what is the extent of that duty, and how is it measured? In other words, are business owners always liable when customers are injured on their premises or must some condition be met before merchants are liable? Must a customer's injury be a *foreseeable* consequence of a condition on the premises, such as the pole right outside the store's door, for the merchant to be liable for the injury?

- If the injury must be a foreseeable consequence of a condition, would a court find that Hoffman's injury in this case was a foreseeable consequence of the pole's placement just outside the store's door?

These are the issues you need to research. Notice that there is more than one issue. This is common in legal research—only rarely will you be researching a single legal issue.

business invitee
A person, such as a customer or client, who is invited onto business premises by the owner of those premises for business purposes.

Determining Your Research Goals

Once you have defined the issues to be researched, you will be in a better position to determine your research goals. Remember that you are working on behalf of a client, who is paying for your services (see the *In the Office* feature on page 180). Your overall

DEVELOPING PARALEGAL SKILLS

DEFINING THE ISSUES TO BE RESEARCHED

Federal agents observed David Berriman in his parked car talking on his cell phone. Other cars were seen driving up to Berriman's car and stopping. The drivers received brown paper bags in exchange for money. The agents then questioned Berriman, and his car was searched. Cocaine was found in the car. He was arrested for transporting and distributing cocaine, and the police took his car and cell phone. His lawyer is arguing that the government agents did not have the authority to seize the car and cell phone and force him to forfeit this property.

Natalie Chen, a legal assistant with the U.S. attorney's office, has been assigned to research the federal statutes and cases on this issue. Natalie can begin her research project only if she first frames the issues critical to the case. She must thoroughly review the case to determine what specific issues need to be researched. Using a checklist method, she breaks the facts of the case down into five categories and inserts the relevant facts from her assignment. Now Natalie is ready to begin her research.

CHECKLIST FOR DEFINING RESEARCH ISSUES

- **Parties:** Who are the people involved in the action or lawsuit?

- **Places and things:** Where did the events take place, and what items are involved in the action or lawsuit?

- **Basis of action or issue:** What is the legal claim or issue involved in the action or lawsuit?

- **Defenses:** What legal justification did the police have for seizing David's car and cellular phone? Will this justification still exist if David is found not guilty of the underlying charges, or will the police be required to return the forfeited property?

- **Relief sought:** What is the legal remedy or penalty sought in the case?

---

goal is to find legal support for Hoffman's claim, but you must also locate legal authority that could be a problem for his claim. To do so, you want to find cases on point and cases that are binding authority. Depending on what you find, you may also need to look for persuasive authorities.

Cases on Point

case on point
A case involving factual circumstances and issues that are similar to those in the case being researched.

One goal is to find cases on point in which the court held for the plaintiff. A **case on point** is one involving fact patterns and legal issues similar to those in the case you are researching. For Hoffman's negligence claim, a case on point would be one in which the plaintiff alleged that he was injured while on a store's premises because of a dangerous condition on the premises.

The ideal case on point would be one in which all four elements (the parties, the circumstances, the legal issues involved, and the remedies sought by the plaintiff) are as similar as possible to those in your case. Such a case is called a case on "all fours." Here, a **case on "all fours"** would be a case in which the plaintiff-customer did not expect a condition (such as an obstacle in her path) to exist and was prevented from seeing the condition by some action that a customer would reasonably undertake (such as carrying an item out of a store). The parties and the circumstances of the case would thus be similar to those in Hoffman's case. In addition, the plaintiff would have sustained a permanent injury, as Hoffman did, and sought damages for negligence.

case on "all fours"
A case in which all four elements (the parties, the circumstances, the legal issues involved, and the remedies sought) are very similar to those in the case being researched.

Binding Authorities

Another research goal is to find cases that are binding authorities. As discussed in Chapter 5, a *binding authority* is one that the court must follow in deciding an issue. A

Although today most legal research is carried out using online resources, some paralegals still consult printed legal volumes when conducting legal research. How could you use printed resources to confirm some of your online research results?

© Blend Images/www.Shutterstock.com.

binding authority may be a statute, regulation, or constitution that governs the issue, or it may be a previously decided court case that is controlling in your jurisdiction.

BE ON POINT.   For a case to serve as binding authority, it must be on point and must have been decided by a higher court in the same jurisdiction.

SOURCE OF PRECEDENT.   A lower court is bound to follow the decisions by a higher court in the same jurisdiction. An appellate court's decision in a case involving facts and issues similar to a case brought in a trial court in the same jurisdiction would thus be a binding authority. A higher court is not required to follow an opinion written by a lower court in the same jurisdiction. When you are performing research, as in the Hoffman case, look for cases on point decided by the highest court in your jurisdiction, because those cases carry the most weight.

State courts generally have the final say on state law, and federal courts have the final say on federal law. Thus, except in deciding an issue that involves federal law, state courts do not have to follow the decisions of federal courts. In deciding issues that involve federal law, state courts must abide by the decisions of the United States Supreme Court or the U.S. Courts of Appeals if the Supreme Court has not ruled on the matter. In diversity cases, federal courts must follow the relevant state courts' rulings on matters of state law.

IN THE OFFICE

EFFICIENCY IN RESEARCH

Attorneys have a duty to charge their clients reasonable fees. As a paralegal, you help fulfill this duty by working efficiently so as to minimize the number of hours you spend working on the client's matter. Legal research can be extremely time consuming, as every paralegal knows. To reduce the time spent researching an issue, start your quest with a clear idea of your research task. After all, your time is expensive not only for the client (who pays for it), but also for your supervising attorney (who may need your assistance on other cases as well).

By knowing as precisely as possible what the goal of your research is, you can reach that goal more quickly and thus better serve the interests of both the client and your supervising attorney.

Published and Unpublished Opinions

Some court opinions are "published," while others, despite being available in commercial databases such as Westlaw, Lexis, and Bloomberg Law, may be "unpublished." This distinction is important. A published decision has been declared, by the court that issued it, to be binding precedent. For example, California defines published opinions as "certified for publication or ordered published and may be cited or relied on by courts and parties." A published decision appears in the official reporter. For example, decisions of the Supreme Court of California are published in *California Reports (Cal.)*, and decisions of the California Courts of Appeal are published in *California Appellate Reports (Cal. App.)*. Other "unofficial" reporters, such as West's *California Reporter (Cal. Rptr.)*, publish decisions from both supreme and appellate courts. West's *Pacific Reporter (P.)* publishes only California Supreme Court decisions. Note that half the states do not publish official reporters, so the West reports, although "unofficial," are relied upon in those states.

UNPUBLISHED OPINIONS CAN SOMETIMES BE CITED. An unpublished decision is generally *not* binding precedent, but may be both persuasive to a court and indicative of how a court is likely to rule in the future. The terminology can be confusing. Opinions appearing in West's *Federal Appendix* reporter are considered unpublished and are often not citable as precedent, but they do appear in a reporter that lawyers and paralegals can cite.

LOOK FOR STATEMENT BY THE COURT. Sometimes unpublished opinions include a statement noting that they are not formally published. For example, the federal Second Circuit Court of Appeals provides that its unpublished "summary disposition" opinions "shall not be cited or otherwise used before this or any other court." In contrast, the federal District of Columbia Circuit Court of Appeals allows citation of its unpublished opinions.

Many courts issue large numbers of unpublished decisions. Each court has its own rules about the citation of unpublished decisions. Some courts forbid citing these decisions. Others require that an attorney citing an unpublished opinion note that it is not published, or perhaps provide the court and opposing counsel with a copy of the opinion. Be sure to check the rules of the jurisdiction in which a legal document is going to be filed to ensure that any reference to an unpublished decision is done properly.

For example, California defines unpublished opinions as "opinions not certified for inclusion in the Official Reports that are not generally citable as precedent."

California has a practice of "depublishing" appellate court opinions that its supreme court dislikes. When citing California appellate decisions, it is thus important to verify that they have not been depublished.

Persuasive Authorities

A persuasive authority is not binding on a court. In other words, the court is not required to follow that authority in making its decisions. Examples of persuasive authorities include:

- Persuasive precedents—previous court opinions from other jurisdictions.

- Legal periodicals, such as law reviews, in which the issue at hand is discussed by legal scholars.

- Encyclopedias summarizing legal principles or concepts relating to a particular issue.

- Legal dictionaries that describe how the law has been applied in the past.

Often, a court refers to persuasive authorities when deciding a *case of first impression*, which is a case involving an issue that has never been specifically addressed by that court before. For example, if in researching Hoffman's claim you find that no similar cases have ever reached a higher court in your jurisdiction, you will look for similar cases decided by courts in other jurisdictions. Decisions by these courts may help guide the court deciding Hoffman's case. Your supervising attorney will want to know about these persuasive authorities so that she can present them to the court for consideration.

persuasive authority
Any legal authority, or source of law, that a court may look to for guidance but on which it need not rely in making its decision. Persuasive authorities include cases from other jurisdictions, discussions in legal periodicals, and so forth.

Finding Relevant Cases

When conducting legal research, distinguish between two basic categories of legal sources: primary sources and secondary sources. As discussed in Chapter 5, *primary sources of law* include court decisions, statutes enacted by legislative bodies, rules and regulations created by administrative agencies, presidential orders, and generally any documents that *establish* the law. *Secondary sources of law* consist of books and articles that summarize, systematize, compile, explain, and interpret the law.

Generally, when beginning research projects, paralegals use secondary sources of law to help them find relevant primary sources and to educate themselves on topics of law with which they are unfamiliar. For this reason, secondary sources of law are often referred to as *finding tools*. For the Hoffman claim, how can you find cases on point and binding authorities on this issue? American case law consists of millions of court decisions, and more than forty thousand new decisions are added each year. Finding relevant precedents would be a terrible task if not for secondary sources of law that classify decisions according to subject. Two important finding tools that are helpful in researching case law are legal encyclopedias and case digests, which we describe next. We also look at some other secondary sources that may be helpful.

Legal Encyclopedias

In researching Hoffman's claim, you might look first at a legal encyclopedia to learn more about negligence and the duty of care that businesses owe to business invitees. A popular legal encyclopedia is *American Jurisprudence*, Second Edition, commonly referred to as *American Jurisprudence 2d* or, more briefly, as *Am. Jur. 2d*. (An excerpt from this encyclopedia is shown in Exhibit 7.1 on the following page. It is also available online from Westlaw and LexisNexis.)

Major Legal Encyclopedias

American Jurisprudence covers hundreds of topics in more than 140 volumes. It is good to consult when you are unfamiliar with a topic being researched. The topics are

EXHIBIT 7.1

Excerpt from *American Jurisprudence 2d*

PREMISES LIABILITY

by

Irwin J. Schiffres, J.D. and Sheila A. Skojec, J.D.

Scope of topic: This article discusses the principles and rules of law applicable to and governing the liability of owners or occupants of real property for negligence causing injury to persons or property by reason of defects therein or hazards created by the activities of such owners or occupants or their agents and employees. Treated in detail are the classification of persons injured as invitees, licensees, or trespassers, and the duty owed them, as well as the rules applicable in those jurisdictions where such status distinctions are no longer determinative of the duty owed the entrant; the effect of "recreational use" statutes on the duty owed persons using the property for such purposes; the greater measure of duty owed by the owner to children as compared to adult licensees and trespassers, including the attractive nuisance doctrine; and the specific duties and liabilities of owners and occupants of premises used for business or residential purposes. Also considered is the effect of the injured person's negligence on the plaintiff's right to recover under principles of contributory or comparative negligence.

Federal aspects: One injured on premises owned or operated by the United States may seek to recover under general principles of premises liability discussed in this article. Insofar as recovery is sought under the Federal Torts Claims Act, see 35 Am Jur 2d, FEDERAL TORTS CLAIMS ACT § 73.

Treated elsewhere:

Mutual obligations and liabilities of adjoining landowners with respect to injuries arising from their acts or omissions, see 1 Am Jur 2d, ADJOINING LANDOWNERS AND PROPERTIES §§ 10, 11, 28 et seq., 37 et seq.

Liability for the acts or omissions of the owners or occupants of premises abutting on a street or highway which cause injury to those using the way, see 39 Am Jur 2d, HIGHWAYS, STREETS, AND BRIDGES §§ 517 et seq.

Liability for violation of building regulations, see 13 Am Jur 2d, BUILDINGS §§ 32 et seq.

Liability of employer for injuries caused employees on the employer's premises, see 53 Am Jur 2d, MASTER AND SERVANT §§ 139 et seq.

Liability for injuries caused by defective products on the premises, see 63 Am Jur 2d, PRODUCTS LIABILITY

Respective rights and liabilities of a landlord and tenant where one is responsible for an injury suffered by the other, or by a third person, on leased premises or on premises provided for the common use of tenants, see 49 Am Jur 2d, LANDLORD AND TENANT §§ 761 et seq.

Liability of a receiver placed in charge of property for an injury sustained thereby or thereon by someone other than the persons directly interested in the estate, see 66 Am Jur 2d, RECEIVERS § 364

Duties and liabilities of occupiers of premises used for various particular types of businesses or activities, see 4 Am Jur 2d, AMUSEMENTS AND EXHIBITIONS §§ 51 et seq.; 14 Am Jur 2d, CARRIERS §§ 964 et seq.; 38 Am Jur 2d, GARAGES, AND FILLING AND PARKING STATIONS §§ 81 et seq.; 40 Am Jur 2d, HOSPITALS AND ASYLUMS § 31; 40 Am Jur 2d, HOTELS, MOTELS, AND RESTAURANTS §§ 81 et seq.; 50 Am Jur 2d, LAUNDRIES, DYERS, AND DRY CLEANERS §§ 21, 22; 54 Am Jur 2d, MOBILE HOMES, TRAILER PARKS, AND TOURIST CAMPS § 17; 57 Am Jur 2d, MUNICIPAL, COUNTY, SCHOOL, AND STATE TORT LIABILITY; AND 59 Am Jur 2d, PARKS, SQUARES, AND PLAYGROUNDS §§ 43 et seq.

Duties and liabilities with respect to injuries caused by particular agencies, such as

317

presented alphabetically, and each topic is divided into subtopics describing rules of law that have emerged from generations of court decisions. The encyclopedia also provides cross-references to specific court cases, statutory law, and relevant secondary sources of law. Additionally, each volume includes an index; a separate index covers the entire encyclopedia.

Traditional printed volumes are kept current through supplements called pocket parts. Pocket parts, so named because they slip into a pocket (sleeve) in the front or back of the volume, contain changes and additions to various topics and subtopics. Updates to the online services are added regularly. Online services such as Westlaw and Lexis include the date of the most recent update of particular statutory and regulatory provisions. When a legislature or Congress is in session, it is necessary to check more than one online database to get the most up-to-date information on a statutory provision.

pocket part

A pamphlet containing recent cases or changes in the law that is used to update legal encyclopedias and other legal authorities. It is called a "pocket part" because it slips into a pocket, or sleeve, in the front or back binder of the volume.

A similar encyclopedia is *Corpus Juris Secundum*, or *C.J.S.* This encyclopedia also provides detailed information on most areas of the law and includes indexes for each volume as well as for the entire set. Its 164 volumes (plus 5 index volumes and 11 table of cases volumes) cover 433 topics, which are presented alphabetically and divided into subtopics. Like *American Jurisprudence*, this encyclopedia is available on Westlaw.

Other Sources

Still another tool is *Words and Phrases*, which offers definitions and interpretations of legal terms and phrases. Each term or phrase in this 132-volume set is followed by brief summary statements from federal or state court decisions in which the word or phrase has been interpreted or defined. The summary statements also indicate the names of the cases and the reporters in which they can be located. Reporters are publications containing the actual text of court cases, as will be discussed later.

When beginning your research into the Hoffman claim, you could use any of these secondary sources, or finding tools, to familiarize yourself with the topic of premises liability and lead you to the primary sources (cases) that you need to read and analyze. You can also search some free online sources, such as FindLaw (**lp.findlaw.com**) or Justia US Law (**law.justia.com**) for ideas. Sources may be searched for such terms as *premises liability*, *business invitees*, and *duty of care*. Remember, though, that legal encyclopedias do not include specific rules of law from your state, which you will need to locate.

reporter
A book in which court cases are published, or reported.

Case Digests

In researching Hoffman's case, you might want to check a case digest as well as a legal encyclopedia for references to relevant case law. Digests, which are produced by various publishers, are helpful research tools because they provide indexes to case law—from the earliest recorded cases through the most current opinions. Case digests arrange topics alphabetically and provide information to help you locate referenced cases, but they do not offer the detail found in legal encyclopedias. Digests are available in both hard copy and online. The online versions are usually included in legal databases such as Westlaw and Lexis. (There are also some free online digests that may be worth searching.)

digest
A compilation in which brief summaries of court cases are arranged by subject and subdivided by jurisdiction and court.

Collected under each topic heading in a case digest are annotations. Annotations are comments, explanatory notes, or case summaries. In case digests, annotations consist of very short statements of relevant points of law in reported cases. The digests published by West offer the most comprehensive system for locating cases by subject matter. Exhibit 7.2 on the following page shows some excerpts from one of West's federal digests on the standard of care that is owed to an invitee.

annotation
A brief comment, an explanation of a legal point, or a case summary found in a case digest or other legal source.

The West Key-Number System

West's key-number system has simplified the task of researching case law. The system divides all areas of American law into specific categories, or topics, arranged in alphabetical order. The topics are further divided into many subtopics, each designated by a key number, which is accompanied by the West key symbol: 🔑. You can see the use of this key symbol in Exhibit 7.2. Exhibit 7.3 on page 185 shows some of the key numbers used for other subtopics under the general topic of negligence.

key number
A number (accompanied by the symbol of a key) corresponding to a specific topic within West's key-number system to facilitate legal research of case law.

USING KEY NUMBERS.   The key-number system organizes millions of case summaries under specific topics and subtopics. In researching the Hoffman claim, suppose that you locate a negligence case on point decided by a court in your state five years ago. Your goal is to find related—and perhaps more recent—cases that support Hoffman's claim. Here is how the key-number system can help. When you read through any case in a West's case reporter, you will find a series of headnotes before the court's actual opinion. Each headnote summarizes one aspect of the opinion. West editors create each headnote and assign it to a particular topic with a key number.

headnote
A note, usually a paragraph long, near the beginning of a reported case summarizing the court's ruling on an issue.

EXHIBIT 7.2

Excerpt from *West's Federal Practice Digest 4th* on Negligence

---

77A F P D 4th—173

NEGLIGENCE ☞ 1037(4)

For references to other topics, see Descriptive-Word Index

E.D.Mich. 1998. Under Michigan law, a property owner is not an absolute insurer of the safety of invitees.

Meyers v. Wal-Mart Stores, East, Inc., 29 F.Supp.2d 780.

E.D.Mich. 1995. under Michigan law, property owner is not insurer of safety of invitees.

Bunch v. Long John Silvers, Inc., 878 F.Supp. 1044.

E.D.Mich. 1994. Under Michigan law, property owner is not insurer of safety of invitees.

Dose v. Equitable Life Assur. Soc., 864 F.Supp. 682.

E.D.N.C. 1993. Premises owner does not automatically insure safety of invitees and is not liable in absence of negligence.

Faircloth v. U.S., 837 F.Supp. 123.

E.D.Va. 1999. Under Virginia law, owner of premises is not insurer of his invitees safety; rather, owner must use ordinary care to render premises reasonably safe for invitee's visit.

Sandow-Pajewski v. Busch Entertainment Corp., 55 F.Supp.2d 422.

☞ **1037(4). Care required in general.**

C.A.7 (Ill.) 1986. Under Illinois law, landowner is liable for physical harm to his invitees caused by condition on his land: where landowner could by exercise of reasonable care have discovered condition; where landowner should realize that condition involves unreasonable risk to harm to invitees; where landowner should expect that invitees will not discover danger or will fail to protect against it; and where landowner fails to exercise reasonable care to protect invitees.

Higgins v. White Sox Baseball Club, Inc., 787 F.2d 1125.

C.A.7 (Ind.) 1994. Under Indiana law, landowner's duty to invitee while that invitee is on premises is that of reasonable care.

Salima v. Scherwood South, Inc., 38 F.3d 929.

Under indiana law, landowner is liable for harm caused to invitee by condition on land only if landowner knows of or through exercise of reasonable care would discover condition and realize that it involves unreasonable risk of harm to such invitees, should expect the invitee will fail to discover or realize danger or fail to protect against it, and fails to exercise reasonable care in protecting invitee against danger.

Salima v. Scherwood South, Inc., 38 F. 3d 929.

Under Indiana law, landowner is not liable for harm caused to invitees by conditions whose

For cited U.S.C.A. sections and legislative hist

danger is known or obvious unless landowner could anticipate harm despite obviousness.

Salima v. Scherwood South, Inc., 38 F.3d 929.

C.A.6 (Mich.) 1998. Under Michigan law, where invitor has reason to expect that, despite

NEGLIGENCE

77A F P D 4th—542

XVI. DEFENSES AND MITIGATING CIRCUMSTANCES.—Continued.

570. _____ Professional rescuers; "firefighter's rule."
575. Imputed contributory negligence.

XVII. PREMISES LIABILITY.

(A) IN GENERAL.

☞ 1000. Nature.
1001. Elements in general.
1002. Constitutional, statutory and regulatory provisions.
1003. What law governs.
1004. Preemption.

(B) NECESSITY AND EXISTENCE OF DUTY.

☞ 1010. In general.
1011. Ownership, custody and control.
1012. Conditions known or obvious in general.
1013. Conditions created or known by defendant.
1014. Foreseeability.
1015. Duty as to children.
1016. _____ In general.
1017. _____ Trespassing children.
1018. Duty to inspect or discover.
1019. Protection against acts of third persons in general.
1020. Duty to warn.
1021. Duty of store and business proprietors.
1022. _____ In general.
1023. _____ Duty to inspect.
1024. _____ Protection against acts of third persons.
1025. Duty based on statute or other regulation.

(C) STANDARD OF CARE.

☞ 1030. In general.
1031. Not insurer or guarantor.
1032. Reasonable or ordinary care in general.
1033. Reasonably safe or unreasonably dangerous conditions.
1034. Status of entrant.
1035. _____ In general.
1036. _____ Care dependent on status.
1037. _____ Invitees.
    (1). In general.
    (2). Who are invitees.
    (3). Not insurer as to invitees.
    (4). Care required in general.
    (5). Public invitees in general.
    (6). Implied invitation.
    (7). Persons working on property.
    (8). Delivery persons and haulers.
1040. _____ Licensees.
    (1). In general.
    (2). Who are licensees.

EXHIBIT 7.3

Subtopics and Key
Numbers in a West Digest

NEGLIGENCE

SUBJECTS INCLUDED

General civil negligence law and premises liability, including duty, standards of care, breach of duty, proximate cause, injury, defenses, and comparative fault, whether based on the common law or statute, as well as procedural aspects of such actions

General civil liabilities for gross negligence, recklessness, willful or wanton conduct, strict liability and ultrahazardous instrumentalities and activities

Negligence liabilities relating to the construction, demolition and repair of buildings and other structures, whether based on the common law or statute

General criminal negligence offenses and prosecutions

SUBJECTS EXCLUDED AND COVERED BY OTHER TOPICS

Accountants or auditors, negligence of, see ACCOUNTANTS ☞8,9

Aircraft, accidents involving, see AVIATION ☞141–153

Attorney's malpractice liability, see ATTORNEY AND CLIENT ☞105–129.5

Banks, liabilities of, see BANKS AND BANKING ☞100

Brokers, securities and real estate, liabilities of, see BROKERS

Car and highway accidents, see AUTOMOBILES

Common carriers, liabilities to passengers, see CARRIERS

Domestic animals, injuries by or to, see ANIMALS

Dram Shop liability and other liabilities for serving alcohol, see INTOXICATING LIQUORS ☞282–324

* * * *

For detailed references to other topics, see Descriptive-Word Index

Analysis

I. **IN GENERAL,** ☞200–205.

II. **NECESSITY AND EXISTENCE OF DUTY,** ☞210–222.

III. **STANDARD OF CARE,** ☞230–239.

IV. **BREACH OF DUTY,** ☞250–259.

V. **HEIGHTENED DEGREES OF NEGLIGENCE,** ☞272–276.

VI. **VULNERABLE AND ENDANGERED PERSONS; RESCUES,** ☞281–285.

VII. **SUDDEN EMERGENCY DOCTRINE,** ☞291–295.

VIII. **DANGEROUS SITUATIONS AND STRICT LIABILITY,** ☞301–307.

FINDING WHAT YOU NEED. Key numbers correlate the headnotes in cases to the topics in digests and can be useful in finding cases on a particular subject. Once you find the key number in a case that discusses the issue you are researching, you can find every other case in your state that discusses the same issue. You go to the West case digest and locate the particular key number and topic. Beneath the key number, the digest provides case summaries, titles, and citations to cases discussing the issue in the area covered by the digest. When you find a case that seems on point, you know where to find it because you have the citation. (In the next chapter, we will see how this works using *KeyCite* offered by West and *Shepard's* offered by Lexis.)

Types of Digests

As mentioned, West offers a comprehensive system of digests. West publishes digests of both federal court opinions and state court opinions, as well as regional digests and digests that correspond with its reporters covering specialized areas, such as bankruptcy. For example, the *Supreme Court Digest* corresponds to decisions published in West's *Supreme Court Reporter*.

Other sources, available online and sometimes free, publish various digests (for example, **lawdigest.uslegal.com**). Some digests are specific to individual states. Note that other publishers' digests do not use the key-number system.

Annotations: *American Law Reports*

The *American Law Reports* (ALR) and *American Law Reports Federal* (ALR Fed), published by West, are also useful resources for legal researchers. These multivolume sets present the full text of selected cases in many areas of the law. They are helpful in finding cases from jurisdictions around the country with similar facts and legal issues.

There are six different series of *American Law Reports* covering case law since 1919. The first and second series contain separate digests that provide references to cases and also have word indexes to assist the researcher in locating specific areas. The remaining sets of ALR volumes use a different approach, called a *Quick Index*, which lets the user access cases and information on a particular topic. The cases in these reporters are followed by annotations—that is, references to articles that explain or comment on the specific issues involved in the cases. These reporters can be a good source to turn to for an overview of a specific area of law or current trend in the law.

When using any of the volumes of ALR, be sure to update your results. ALR annotations are periodically updated by the addition of relevant cases. For the first series, the annotations are updated in a set of books called the *ALR Blue Book of Supplemental Decisions*. The second series is updated in the *ALR, 2d, Later Case Service*, and the remaining series are made current by pocket-part supplements located in the front of each volume. In addition, you can consult the annotation history table at the end of the Quick Index to see whether any new annotations supplement or change an earlier annotation. (Of course, most of these services are now available online.)

Other Secondary Sources

A number of other secondary sources are useful in legal research. We look here at three of these sources: treatises, *Restatements of the Law*, and legal periodicals. Like other secondary sources of law, these sources do not have the force of law. Nevertheless, they are important sources of legal analysis and opinion and are often cited as persuasive authorities.

Treatises

treatise
In legal research, a work that provides a systematic, detailed, and scholarly review of a particular legal subject.

hornbook
A single-volume scholarly discussion, or treatise, on a particular legal subject.

A **treatise** is a scholarly work by a law professor or other legal professional that treats a particular subject systematically and in detail. Some treatises are published in multivolume sets, while others are contained in a single book.

Single-volume treatises that synthesize the basic principles of a given legal area are known as **hornbooks**. Some hornbooks are available online. These texts are useful to paralegals to familiarize themselves with a particular area of the law, such as torts or contracts. For example, in researching the issues in Hoffman's negligence case, you might want to locate the treatise entitled *Prosser and Keeton on the Law of Torts*, Fifth Edition, which is included in West's Hornbook Series, and read the sections on negligence. (Exhibit 7.4 on the facing page shows the book open to the chapter on defenses to negligence.) Hornbooks such as *Prosser and Keeton on the Law of Torts* present many examples of case law and references to cases that may be helpful to a researcher.

Restatements of the Law

The *Restatements of the Law* are also a helpful resource, and one on which judges often rely as a persuasive authority when making decisions. They are available on Lexis and

Westlaw. There are *Restatements* in the areas of contracts, torts, agency, trusts, property, restitution, security, judgments, and conflict of laws. Each section in the *Restatements* contains a statement of the principles of law that are generally accepted by the courts or embodied in statutes, followed by a discussion of those principles. The discussions present cases as examples and also discuss variations.

Legal Periodicals

Legal periodicals, such as law reviews and law journals, are secondary sources that can be helpful. If an article in a legal periodical deals with the specific area that you are researching, the article will likely include footnotes citing cases relating to the topic. These references can save you hours of research time in finding relevant case law.

EXHIBIT 7.4

A Page from the *Hornbook on the Law of Torts*

Chapter 11

NEGLIGENCE: DEFENSES

Table of Sections

Sec.
65. Contributory Negligence.
66. Last Clear Chance.
67. Comparative Negligence.
68. Assumption of Risk.

§ 65. Contributory Negligence

The two most common defenses in a negligence action are contributory negligence and assumption of risk. Since both developed at a comparatively late date in the development of the common law,[1] and since both clearly operate to the advantage of the defendant, they are commonly regarded as defenses to a tort which would otherwise be established. All courts now hold that the burden of pleading and proof of the contributory negligence of the plaintiff is on the defendant.[2]

Contributory negligence is conduct on the part of the plaintiff, contributing as a legal cause to the harm he has suffered, which falls below the standard to which he is required to conform for his own protection.[3] Unlike assumption of risk, the defense does not rest upon the idea that the defendant is relieved of any duty toward the plaintiff. Rather, although the defendant has violated his duty, has been negligent, and would oth-

---

§ 65

1. The earliest contributory negligence case is Butterfield v. Forrester, 1809, 11 East 60, 103 Eng.Rep. 926. The first American case appears to have been Smith v. Smith, 1824, 19 Mass. (2 Pick.) 621. Assumption of risk first appears in a negligence case in 1799. See infra, § 68 n. 1.

2. E.g., Wilkinson v. Hartford Accident & Indemnity Co., La.1982, 411 So.2d 22; Moodie v. Santoni, 1982, 292 Md. 582, 441 A.2d 323; Addair v. Bryant, 1981, ___ W.Va. ___, 284 S.E.2d 374; Pickett v. Parks, 1981, 208 Neb. 310, 303 N.W.2d 296; Hatton v. Chem-Haulers, Inc., Ala.1980, 393 So.2d 950; Sampson v. W. F. Enterprises, Inc., Mo.App.1980, 611 S.W.2d 333; Howard v. Howard, Ky.App.1980, 607 S.W.2d 119; cf. Reuter v. United States, W.D.Pa.1982, 534 F.Supp. 731 (presumption that person killed or suffering loss of memory was acting with due care).

Illinois and certain other jurisdictions held to the contrary for some time. See West Chicago Street Railroad Co. v. Liderman, 1900, 187 Ill. 463, 58 N.E. 367; Kotler v. Lalley, 1930, 112 Conn. 86, 151 A. 433; Dreier v. McDermott, 1913, 157 Iowa 726, 141 N.W. 315. See Green, Illinois Negligence Law II, 1944, 39 Ill.L.Rev. 116, 125–130.

3. Second Restatement of Torts, § 463. See generally, Malone, The Formative Era of Contributory Negligence, 1946, 41 Ill.L.Rev. 151; James, Contributory Negligence, 1953, 62 Yale L.J. 691; Bohlen, Contributory Negligence, 1908, 21 Harv.L.Rev. 233; Lowndes, Contributory Negligence, 1934, 22 Geo.L.J. 674; Malone, Some Ruminations on Contributory Negligence, 1981, 65 Utah L.Rev. 91; Schwartz, Contributory and Comparative Negligence: A Reappraisal, 1978, 87 Yale L.J. 697; Note, 1979, 39 La.L.Rev. 637.

451

The Case Reporting System

The primary sources of case law are the cases themselves. Once you have learned which cases are relevant to the issue you are researching, you need to find the cases and examine the court opinions.

Assume, for example, that in researching Hoffman's case, you learn that your state's supreme court issued a decision a few years ago on a case with a similar fact pattern. In that case, the state supreme court upheld a lower court's judgment that a retail business owner had to pay damages to a customer who was injured on the store's premises when carrying a large item. You know that the state supreme court's decision is a binding authority, and, to your knowledge, the decision has not been overruled or modified. Therefore, the case will likely provide weighty support to your attorney's arguments in support of Hoffman's claim.

At this point, however, you have only read about the case in secondary sources. To locate the case itself and make sure it is applicable (the *Ethics Watch* below explains why this is important), you must understand the case reporting system and the legal "shorthand" employed in referencing court cases.

ETHICS WATCH

USING SECONDARY SOURCES

When rushing to meet a deadline, you may be tempted to avoid a critical step in the research process—checking primary sources. For example, suppose a firm's client complains that a publisher of his novels is now publishing the novels online, as e-books. The client wants to know if online publication is copyright infringement. At issue is whether the publisher, which has the right to publish the printed texts, also has the right to publish the books online. An attorney for the firm asks Sarah, a paralegal, to research case law to see how the courts have dealt with this issue.

Sarah has just read an article in a law journal about a similar case recently decided by the United States Supreme Court. Without taking the time to read the case itself, she relies on the author's conclusions in the article. She prepares a memo to the attorney presenting her "research" results.

Based on Sarah's memo, the attorney advises the client that the publisher had no right to publish the client's works online. The client decides to sue the publisher. Later, during more extensive pretrial research, Sarah reads the case. Unfortunately for her (and the client and the attorney), the author of the article did not discuss an important qualification made by the Court in its ruling relating to the terms of the publishing contract. The Court's decision does not apply to the client's situation, and the case is not a binding authority.

While the attorney is responsible for the work product for the client, Sarah's failure to rely on primary sources is likely seen as a failure to produce competent work. Such a failure could injure the position of the client and violate the NFPA Model Disciplinary Rule 1.1, "A paralegal shall achieve and maintain a high level of competence."

State Court Decisions and Reporters

Written decisions of state appellate courts are published chronologically in volumes called *reports* or *reporters*, which are numbered consecutively. State appellate court decisions are found in the state reporters of that particular state. The reporters may be either the "official" reporters, designated as such by the state legislature, or "unofficial" reporters, published by West. Although some states still have official reporters (and a few states, such as New York and California, have more than one official reporter), many states have eliminated their own official reporters in favor of West's National Reporter System, discussed next. Most state trial court decisions are not published.

Regional Reporters

State court opinions also appear in regional units of West's National Reporter System. Many lawyers and libraries have the West reporters because they report cases more quickly and are distributed more widely than the state-published reports.

The National Reporter System divides the states into the following geographic areas: *Atlantic* (A., A.2d, or A.3d), *South Eastern* (S.E. or S.E.2d), *North Eastern* (N.E. or N.E.2d), *North Western* (N.W. or N.W.2d), *Pacific* (P., P.2d, or P.3d), *South Western* (S.W., S.W.2d, or S.W.3d), and *Southern* (So., So.2d, or So.3d). The 2d and 3d in the abbreviations refer to *Second Series* and *Third Series*. The states included in each of these regional divisions are indicated in Exhibit 7.5 on the following page, which illustrates West's National Reporter System. The names of the areas may not be the same as what we commonly think of as a geographic region. For example, the *North Western* reporter does not include the Pacific Northwest but includes Iowa, which people do not think of as being in the Northwest. Similarly, Oklahoma is in the Pacific Reporter.

Citation Format

To locate a case, you must know where to look. After a decision has been published, it is normally referred to (cited) by the name of the case, the volume number and the abbreviated name of the book in which the case is located, the page number on which the case begins, and the year. In other words, there are five parts to a standard citation:

Case name	Volume number	Name of book	Page number	(Year)

This format is used for every citation regardless of whether the case is published in an official state reporter or a regional reporter (or both). When more than one reporter is cited for the same case, each reference is called a parallel citation and is separated from the next citation by a comma. The first citation is to the state's official reporter (if there is one), although the text of the court's opinion will be the same (parallel) at any of the listed locations.

AN EXAMPLE. To illustrate how to find case law from citations, suppose you want to find the following case: *Goldstein v. Lackard*, 81 Mass.App.Ct. 1112, 961 N.E.2d 163 (2012). You can see that the opinion in this case can be found in Volume 81 of the official *Massachusetts Appellate Court Reports*, beginning on page 1112. The parallel citation is to Volume 961 of the *North Eastern Reporter, Second Series*, at page 163. In some cases, additional information may appear in parentheses at the end of a citation, usually indicating the court that heard the case (if that information is not clear from the citation alone). Exhibit 7.6 on pages 192 and 193 further illustrates how to read case citations.

PROPER FORM. When conducting legal research, you should write down the citations to the cases or other legal sources that you have consulted, quoted, or want to refer to in a written summary of your research results. Several guides have been published on how to cite legal sources.

citation
In case law, a reference to a case by the name of the case, the volume number and name of the reporter in which the case can be found, the page number on which the case begins, and the year. In statutory and administrative law, a reference to the title number, name, and section of the code in which a statute or regulation can be found.

parallel citation
A second (or third) citation for a given case. When a case is published in more than one reporter, each citation is a parallel citation to the other(s).

EXHIBIT 7.5

West's National Reporter System—Regional and Federal

Regional Reporters	Coverage Beginning	Coverage
Atlantic Reporter (A. or A.2d)	1885	Connecticut, Delaware, Maine, Maryland, New Hampshire, New Jersey, Pennsylvania, Rhode Island, Vermont, and District of Columbia.
North Eastern Reporter (N.E. or N.E.2d)	1885	Illinois, Indiana, Massachusetts, New York, and Ohio.
North Western Reporter (N.W. or N.W.2d)	1879	Iowa, Michigan, Minnesota, Nebraska, North Dakota, South Dakota, and Wisconsin.
Pacific Reporter (P., P.2d, or P.3d)	1883	Alaska, Arizona, California, Colorado, Hawaii, Idaho, Kansas, Montana, Nevada, New Mexico, Oklahoma, Oregon, Utah, Washington, and Wyoming.
South Eastern Reporter (S.E. or S.E.2d)	1887	Georgia, North Carolina, South Carolina, Virginia, and West Virginia.
South Western Reporter (S.W., S.W.2d, or S.W.3d)	1886	Arkansas, Kentucky, Missouri, Tennessee, and Texas.
Southern Reporter (So. or So.2d)	1887	Alabama, Florida, Louisiana, and Mississippi.

Federal Reporters		
Federal Reporter (F., F.2d, or F.3d)	1880	U.S. Circuit Court from 1880 to 1912; U.S. Commerce Court from 1911 to 1913; U.S. District Courts from 1880 to 1932; U.S. Court of Claims (now called U.S. Court of Federal Claims) from 1929 to 1932 and since 1960; U.S. Court of Appeals since 1891; U.S. Court of Customs and Patent Appeals since 1929; and U.S. Emergency Court of Appeals since 1943.
Federal Supplement (F.Supp. or F.Supp.2d)	1932	U.S. Court of Claims from 1932 to 1960; U.S. District Courts since 1932; and U.S. Customs Court since 1956.
Federal Rules Decisions (F.R.D.)	1939	U.S. District Courts involving the Federal Rules of Civil Procedure since 1939 and Federal Rules of Criminal Procedure since 1946.
Supreme Court Reporter (S.Ct.)	1882	U.S. Supreme Court since the October term of 1882.
Bankruptcy Reporter (Bankr.)	1980	Bankruptcy decisions of U.S. Bankruptcy Courts, U.S. District Courts, U.S. Courts of Appeals, and U.S. Supreme Court.
Military Justice Reporter (M.J.)	1978	U.S. Court of Military Appeals and Courts of Military Review for the Army, Navy, Air Force, and Coast Guard.

NATIONAL REPORTER SYSTEM MAP

Legend:
- Pacific
- North Western
- South Western
- North Eastern
- Atlantic
- South Eastern
- Southern

Traditionally, the most widely used guide has been *The Bluebook: A Uniform System of Citation*, published by the Harvard Law Review Association. This book explains the proper format for citing cases, statutes, constitutions, regulations, and other legal sources. It is a good idea to memorize the basic format for citations to cases and statutory law because these legal sources are frequently cited in legal writing.

An alternative guide is a booklet entitled *ALWD Citation Manual: A Professional System of Citation*, which is published by the Association of Legal Writing Directors. Legal practitioners should check the rules of their jurisdiction for guidelines on the proper format for citations in documents submitted to a court.

Federal Court Decisions

Court decisions from the U.S. district courts (federal trial courts) are published in West's *Federal Supplement* (F.Supp. or F.Supp.2d), and opinions from the courts of appeals are reported in West's *Federal Reporter* (F., F.2d, or F.3d). These are both unofficial reporters (there are no official reporters for these courts). Both the *Federal Reporter* and the *Federal Supplement* incorporate decisions from specialized federal courts. West also publishes separate reporters, such as its *Bankruptcy Reporter*, that contain decisions in certain specialized fields under federal law. All of these reporters are published online.

United States Supreme Court Decisions

Opinions from the United States Supreme Court are published in several reporters, including the *United States Reports*, West's *Supreme Court Reporter*, and the *Lawyers' Edition of the Supreme Court Reports*, each of which we discuss below. A sample citation to a Supreme Court case is also included in Exhibit 7.6 on the bottom of the next page. Note that there is free access to Supreme Court materials at the Court's website and also at Oyez (**www.oyez.org**).

The *United States Reports*

The *United States Reports* (U.S.) is the official edition of decisions of the United States Supreme Court for which there are written opinions. Published by the federal government, the series includes reports of Supreme Court cases dating from the August term of 1791. Soon after the Supreme Court issues a decision, the U.S. Government Printing Office publishes the official slip opinion. (It is published online more quickly at the Supreme Court's website. Go to **www.supremecourt.gov**, and select "Opinions," then "Latest Slip Opinions.") The slip opinion is the first authoritative text of the opinion and is later printed in what the Supreme Court notes is the "official version." The full text of all opinions is on the Court's website.

slip opinion
A judicial opinion published shortly after the decision is made and not yet included in a case reporter or advance sheets.

After a number of slip opinions have been issued, the advance sheets of the official *United States Reports* appear. These are issued in pamphlet form to provide a temporary resource until the official bound volume is finally published.

The *Supreme Court Reporter*

Supreme Court cases are also published in West's *Supreme Court Reporter* (S.Ct.), which is an unofficial edition of Supreme Court opinions dating from the Court's term in October 1882. In this reporter, the case report—the formal court opinion—is preceded by a syllabus (summary of the case) and headnotes with key numbers (used throughout the West reporters and digests) prepared by West editors. This reporter, like the others, can be accessed through online legal search services, as discussed later in the chapter.

syllabus
A brief summary of the holding and legal principles involved in a reported case, which is followed by the court's official opinion.

The *Lawyers' Edition of the Supreme Court Reports*

The *Lawyers' Edition of the Supreme Court Reports* (L.Ed. or L.Ed.2d) is an unofficial edition of the entire series of the Supreme Court reports containing many decisions not reported in early official volumes. It is published on LexisNexis. The advantage offered to the legal researcher by the *Lawyers' Edition* is its research tools. In its second series,

EXHIBIT 7.6
How to Read Citations

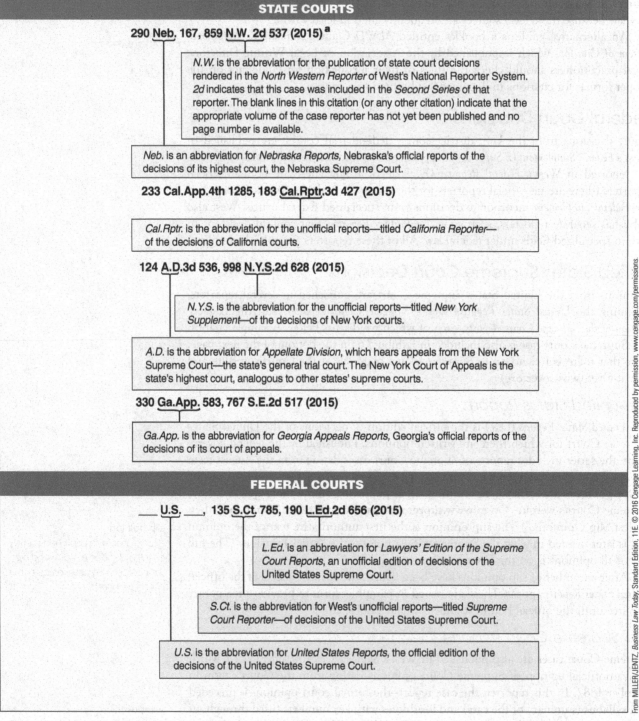

a. The case names have been deleted from these citations to emphasize the publications. It should be kept in mind, however, that the name of a case is as important as the specific page numbers in the volumes in which it is found. If a citation is incorrect, the correct citation may be found in a publication's index of case names. In addition to providing a check on errors in citations, the date of a case is important because the value of a recent case as an authority is likely to be greater than that of older cases from the same court.

EXHIBIT 7.6

How to Read Citations—Continued

FEDERAL COURTS (Continued)

775 F.3d 1172 (9th Cir. 2015)

9th Cir. is an abbreviation denoting that this case was decided in the U.S. Court of Appeals for the Ninth Circuit.

___ F.Supp.3d ___ 2015 WL 273140 (N.D.Cal. 2015)

N.D.Cal. is an abbreviation indicating that the U.S. District Court for the Northern District of California decided this case.

WESTLAW® CITATIONS[b]

2015 WL 358246

WL is an abbreviation for Westlaw. The number 2015 is the year of the document that can be found with this citation in the Westlaw database. The number 358246 is a number assigned to a specific document. A higher number indicates that a document was added to the Westlaw database later in the year.

STATUTORY AND OTHER CITATIONS

18 U.S.C. Section 1961(1)(A)

U.S.C. denotes *United States Code*, the codification of *United States Statutes at Large.* The number 18 refers to the statute's U.S.C. title number and 1961 to its section number within that title. The number 1 in parentheses refers to a subsection within the section, and the letter A in parentheses to a subsection within the subsection.

UCC 2–206(1)(b)

UCC is an abbreviation for *Uniform Commercial Code.* The first number 2 is a reference to an article of the UCC, and 206 to a section within that article. The number 1 in parentheses refers to a subsection within the section, and the letter b in parentheses to a subsection within the subsection.

***Restatement (Third) of Torts,* Section 6**

Restatement (Third) of Torts refers to the third edition of the American Law Institute's *Restatement of the Law of Torts.* The number 6 refers to a specific section.

17 C.F.R. Section 230.505

C.F.R. is an abbreviation for *Code of Federal Regulations*, a compilation of federal administrative regulations. The number 17 designates the regulation's title number, and 230.505 designates a specific section within that title.

b. Many court decisions that are not yet published or that are not intended for publication can be accessed through Westlaw, an online legal database.

it precedes each case report with a summary of the case and discusses in detail selected cases of special interest to the legal profession. Also, the *Lawyers' Edition* is the only reporter of Supreme Court opinions that provides summaries of the briefs presented by counsel.

Analyzing Case Law

Attorneys often rely heavily on case law to support a position or argument. One of the difficulties all legal professionals face in analyzing case law is the length and complexity of many court opinions. While some opinions may be only two or three pages long, others can be a hundred pages. Understanding the components of a case—that is, the basic format in which cases are presented—can simplify your task of reading and analyzing case law. Over time, as you acquire experience, case analysis becomes easier. This section focuses on how to read and analyze cases, as well as how to summarize, or *brief*, a case.

The Components of a Case

Reported cases have different parts, and you should know why each part is there and what information it communicates. To illustrate the various components of a case, we present an annotated sample court case in Exhibit 7.7 starting on the facing page. This exhibit shows an actual case that was decided by a California court of appeal.

Important sections, terms, and phrases in the case are defined or explained in the margins. You will also note that triple asterisks (* * *) frequently appear in the exhibit. The triple asterisks indicate that we have deleted a few words or sentences from the opinion for the sake of readability or brevity. If the asterisks appear between paragraphs, then one or more paragraphs have been deleted. Also, when the opinion cites another case or legal source, the citation to the referenced case or source has been omitted to save space and to improve readability.

Following Exhibit 7.7, we discuss the various parts of a case. As you read through the descriptions of these parts, refer to the exhibit, which illustrates most of them. Remember, though, that the excerpt presented in Exhibit 7.7, because it has been pared down for illustration, may be much easier to read than many court opinions that you will encounter.

Case Title

The title of a case indicates the names of the parties to the lawsuit, and the *v.* in the case title means *versus*, or "against." In the trial court, the plaintiff's last name appears first, and the second name is the defendant's. If the case is appealed, however, the appellate court will sometimes place the name of the party appealing the decision first, so the parties' names may be reversed. One must carefully read the facts of each case to identify the roles of the parties.

Case Citation

Typically, the citation to the case is found just above or just below the case title (and often at the tops of consecutive printed or online pages). If the citation appears on Westlaw and one of the parallel citations is not yet available, the citation may include underlined spaces for the volume and page numbers to be filled in once they become available (such as "___ U.S. ___").

Docket Number

The docket number immediately follows the case title. The court clerk assigns a docket number when a case is initially filed. The number serves as an identifier for all papers submitted in connection with the case. A case published in a reporter should not be cited by its docket number, but the number may serve as a tool in obtaining background information on the case.

EXHIBIT 7.7

A Sample Court Case

This section contains the case citation—the name of the case, the name of the court that heard the case, the year of the court's decision, and the reporter in which the court's decision can be found. →	The People, Plaintiff and Respondent, v. Viktors Andris Rekte, Defendant and Appellant. Court of Appeal, Fourth District, Division 2, California 232 Cal.App.4th 1237, 181 Ca.Rptr.3d 912 (2015)
The *docket number* assigned by court. →	E060272
The *syllabus*—a brief summary of proceedings. Some reported cases provide more detail than is seen here. →	Appeal from the Superior Court of Riverside County. William A. Anderson, Temporary Judge. (Pursuant to Cal. Const., art. VI, § 21.) Reversed. (Super.Ct.Nos. APP1300118 & RR182259VR).
Names of counsel for the parties. →	D. Scott Elliot for Defendant and Appellant. Gregory P. Priamos, City Attorney, Kristi J. Smith and Rosemary Koo, Deputy City Attorneys, for Plaintiff and Respondent.
Name of the member of the Court of Appeal who authored the opinion of the court. →	Ramirez, P.J.
Brief summary provided by the court. →	Viktors Rekte received a citation by mail for a violation of Vehicle Code, section 21453, subdivision (a), for failing to stop at a red light, based on a photograph taken pursuant to the Automated Traffic Enforcement System (ATES). At trial, the court overruled in limine objections to the admission of the photographic evidence on foundational grounds. Thereafter, defendant presented expert testimony to rebut the presumption of the reliability of the photographic evidence due to noncompliance with the California Manual on Uniform Traffic Control Devices (MUTCD or Manual). The trial court found defendant guilty of the offense. Defendant appealed to the Appellate Division of the Riverside County Superior Court, arguing, among other things, that the presumptions established by Evidence Code sections 1552 and 1553, affecting the burden of producing evidence, were rebutted. The Appellate Division affirmed the judgment and subsequently certified the matter for transfer to this court. We reverse.
The court divides the opinion into parts, beginning with the Background. It covers the facts developed at trial and the ruling of the lower courts. (An *in limine* motion requests the trial judge to exclude certain evidence as improperly gathered.) →	BACKGROUND Prior to the commencement of trial, defendant made an in limine motion to exclude the photographic and video evidence on grounds: (1) the yellow light interval did not conform with the standards required by the MUTCD; (2) the

Continued

EXHIBIT 7.7

A Sample Court Case—Continued

defendant was not provided with pretrial discovery of the video clip upon which the ATES citation was based; and (3) the geometry of the intersection and placement angles of the ATES equipment and traffic signals obscured the view of a substantial portion of the traffic signal light.

The trial court denied the in limine motion. Defendant also objected to the foundational statement and introduction of the evidence of the videotape, or the declarations of any Redflex employee, which objections were overruled. The matter proceeded to trial with Operator Teagarden appearing on behalf of the City of Riverside. Operator Don Teagarden is a retired Riverside Sheriff's Department deputy. Since May 2010, he has been employed by the Riverside Police Department to review violations of the Automated Traffic Enforcement System (ATES). The automated camera system captures drivers who enter an intersection while facing a red traffic light. The system is triggered when a car goes through a red light while driving at least 15 miles per hour. The ATES system was installed and maintained by Redflex Traffic Systems (Redflex).

The system takes a series of still photographs and a 12-second video, depicting the elements of the violation. The images are transmitted electronically to the Redflex office in Phoenix, where they are reviewed by Redflex personnel. Redflex then sends a compact disc with the images and the 12-second video on it to the Riverside Police Department, where Operator Teagarden reviews them. Digitally printed on the photographic image is information relative to the date, time, location, vehicle speed, and how long the signal light had been in the red at the time the photograph was taken. Although Operator Teagarden did not personally test the sequence, he testified that the yellow phases met or exceeded the minimum "recommendations" established by the California Department of Transportation (CalTrans).

* * *

On cross-examination, Operator Teagarden acknowledged he could not tell if the monthly inspections of the equipment conducted by Redflex included verification of the time intervals for the signal lights, and did not know if anyone employed by the City of Riverside checked to make sure the system was calibrated properly.

The defense presented expert testimony by engineer Sean Stockwell, who visited the location of the infraction on more than one occasion, before and after the date of the offense, to time the yellow light interval. To time the interval, Stockwell took four video clips of the changing traffic signals, which he uploaded onto a

EXHIBIT 7.7

A Sample Court Case—Continued

video program on his computer, in order to get a time index. On each occasion, using the software indexing capability, the yellow light interval was found to be 3.5 seconds, plus or minus 0.07 seconds, which is less than the 3.6 second minimum interval required by the MUTCD.

* * *

When the case was closed to evidence, the defense argued for dismissal because the geometry of the intersection and placement of the signals requires the driver to look away from his or her direction of travel in order to see the light, and because the yellow light interval was less than the mandated 3.6 seconds, demonstrating that the equipment was not functioning properly and the evidence was unreliable. The court found beyond a reasonable doubt that defendant violated Vehicle Code section 21453, subdivision (a) and imposed a fine of $490.00. Defendant appealed to the Appellate Division of the Riverside County Superior Court. On November 20, 2013, the appellate division affirmed the judgment on the infraction.

On December 4, 2013, defendant applied for certification to transfer the matter to this court. On December 19, 2013, the Appellate Division of the Riverside County Superior Court granted that request.

> Major section that reviews the issues raised on appeal and explains the reasoning of the court for its decision. More complex cases often have more sections in the decision.

DISCUSSION

Defendant raises three issues on appeal: (1) whether the trial court committed error by referring to *People v. Gray* (2011) 199 Cal.App.4th Supp. 10, 131 Cal.Rptr.3d 220 (*Gray*), review granted June 20, 2012, S202483 [superseding opinion filed March 13, 2014, *People v. Gray* (2014) 58 Cal.4th 901, 168 Cal.Rptr.3d 710, 319 P.3d 988]; (2) whether the trial court committed error in applying Evidence Code sections 1552 and 1553; and (3) whether the trial court committed error relating to the burden of proof in infraction cases.

The first issue involves the trial court's reference to a case pending review that has now been superseded by a subsequent opinion of the California Supreme Court. The second and third issues, which are interrelated and involve the burden of producing evidence, are issues of first impression. Because these issues are so intertwined, we will deal with them as one issue.

* * *

The appellate decision in *Gray* involved a limited issue: whether the local jurisdiction failed to comply with Vehicle Code section 21445.5 (regarding the requirement of posting warning notices for 30 days before issuing citations upon

Continued

EXHIBIT 7.7
A Sample Court Case—Continued

commencement of the ATES program). The trial court's reference to that decision, whether published or not, was irrelevant to the issues posited by defendant at trial: whether the evidence lacked sufficient foundation to be admissible, and whether the equipment was properly calibrated where it recorded a yellow light interval of 3.65 seconds, in the face of expert testimony that the actual interval was only 3.5 seconds. Thus, any reliance by the trial court on that decision was harmless error.

* * *

The trial court mistakenly believed the *Gray* decision related to the admissibility of the digital photographs produced by an ATES camera over objections similar to those raised by defendant here. * * * The trial court's erroneous reliance on *Gray*, after review had been granted in that case, was harmless. * * *

Defendant argues that the court erred in applying Evidence Code Sections 1552 and 1553, respecting the information depicted in the records of Redflex Traffic Systems, consisting of the traffic citation, the 12-second video, and several still pictures of the vehicle with computer data imprinted at the top of the photographs. In this respect, defendant argues that the presumptions embodied in Evidence Code sections 1552 and 1553 were improperly viewed as presumptions affecting the burden of proof, rather than presumptions affecting the burden of producing evidence. We agree.

We begin by noting that our Supreme Court has recently ruled on the admissibility of Automated Traffic Enforcement System (ATES) evidence over defense objections based hearsay and lack of authentication. In *Goldsmith*, the court held that the trial court did not err in admitting the ATES evidence because the presumptions of authenticity provided by Evidence Code sections 1552 and 1553 supported a finding, in the absence of contrary evidence, that the printed versions of ATES images and data were accurate.

* * *

Evidence Code sections 1552 and 1553 provide a presumption for both the existence and content of computer information and digital images that the printed versions purport to represent, and establish, preliminarily, that a computer's print function has worked properly. (*Goldsmith, supra,* 59 Cal.4th at p. 269, 172 Cal.Rptr.3d 637, 326 P.3d 239.) They may support a finding that, in the absence of contrary evidence, the printed versions of ATES images and data are accurate representations of the images stored in the ATES equipment. *(Ibid.)*

* * *

EXHIBIT 7.7

A Sample Court Case—Continued

Here, the defendant undermined the presumptions created by Evidence Code sections 1552 and 1553. He produced expert testimony and evidence that the printed representation of computer generated information (Evid.Code, § 1552) and the video or digital images admitted into evidence (Evid.Code, § 1553) were inaccurate and unreliable. An inadequate yellow light interval renders a safe stop impossible, and constitutes an emergency justifying the entry into an intersection when the signal turns red. (*People v. Ausen* (1940) 40 Cal.App.2d Supp. 831, 835, 105 P.2d 321.) The burden of producing evidence shifted to the city once the presumption was rebutted, but the expert's testimony and opinions were not refuted. Because the digital images were previewed by Redflex before being forwarded to the Riverside Police Department, and because digital images are susceptible to manipulation, it was incumbent upon the City to introduce evidence that the printed representations were accurate. (See *People v. Beckley* (2010) 185 Cal.App.4th 509, 515–516, 110 Cal.Rptr.3d 362.) Otherwise, the images were inadmissible because they were not properly authenticated. Thus, the question of guilt should have been determined *without* the photographic evidence. Without that evidence, there was no reliable evidence of a violation of Vehicle Code section 21453, subdivision (a).

* * *

The sole evidence presented to the trier of fact in the present case consisted of photographs, initially presumed to be reliable, but which presumption was rebutted. As a result, the foundational requirement of authentication was lacking. Operator Teagarden was not a percipient witness to the violation. As a matter of law, without the photographic evidence, there is insufficient evidence to support the judgment.

* * *

At oral argument, the People argued that if reversal is required because evidence was erroneously admitted at trial, double jeopardy is not implicated and the proper remedy is to remand for retrial. (*People v. Llamas* (1997) 51 Cal.App.4th 1729, 1741, 60 Cal.Rptr.2d 357.) Remand for retrial is not a viable option where the inadmissible evidence was the *sole* evidence of guilt.

Because the prosecution did not produce reliable evidence of the offense, the judgment must be reversed.

Conclusion of the Court of Appeal. → DISPOSITION

The judgment is reversed.

Cases appearing in slip-opinion form (decisions that have been decided but not yet published in a reporter) are usually identified, filed, and cited by docket number. After publication of the decision, the docket number may continue to serve as an identifier for appellate records and briefs (appellate briefs will be discussed in Chapter 9). There may be changes to correct typographical mistakes made between the initial slip opinion and the reported decision, or the court may change its mind on a matter of substance and withdraw the opinion. Always check to see whether there is a later, reported version of a slip opinion you find during your research to ensure you are citing the correct version of the opinion.

Dates Argued and Decided

An important component of a case is the date on which the court decided it. Usually, the date of the decision immediately follows the docket number. In addition to the date of the court's decision on the matter, the date on which the case was argued before the court (in appellate court cases) may also be included.

Syllabus

Following the docket number is the *syllabus*—a brief synopsis of the facts of the case, the issues analyzed by the court, and the court's conclusion. In official reporters, the courts usually prepare the syllabi. In unofficial reporters, the publishers of the reporters usually prepare them. The syllabus is often a helpful research tool. It provides an overview of the case and points out legal issues discussed by the court. In a few states, such as Ohio, the official syllabus has precedential value. In most states, the syllabus is not binding. In all cases, keep in mind that reading the syllabus is not a substitute for reading the case if the case is relevant.

Headnotes

Unofficial reporters, such as those published by West, often make extensive use of case *headnotes*. As discussed earlier, headnotes are short paragraphs that highlight and summarize specific rules of law mentioned in the case. In reporters published by West, they are correlated to the comprehensive West key-number system. In Exhibit 7.7, the headnotes were deleted for reasons of space.

Names of Counsel

The published report of the case usually contains the names of the lawyers (counsel) representing the parties. The attorneys' names are typically found just following the syllabus (and headnotes, if any).

Name of Judge or Justice Authoring the Opinion

The name of the judge or justice who authored the opinion in the case will also be included in the published report of the case, just before the court's opinion. In some cases, instead of the name of a judge or justice, the decision will be authored *per curiam* (Latin for "by the court"), which means that the opinion is that of the whole court, or the majority of the court, and not the opinion of any one judge or justice. Sometimes the phrase is used to indicate that the chief justice or presiding judge wrote the opinion. The phrase also may be used for an announcement of a court's disposition of a case that is not accompanied by a written opinion.

Opinion

The term *opinion* is often used loosely to refer to a court case or decision. In fact, the term has a precise meaning. The opinion of the court contains the analysis and decision of the judge or judges who heard and decided the case. Most opinions contain a brief statement of the facts of the case, a summary of the legal issues raised by the facts, and the remedies sought by the parties.

In appellate court cases, the court summarizes the errors of the lower court, if any, and the impact of these errors on the case's outcome. The main body of the opinion is the application of the law to the particular facts. The court often mentions case precedents, relevant statutes, and administrative rules to support its reasoning. Additionally, court opinions may contain discussions of policy and other factors that clarify the reason for the court's decision. The various kinds of opinions that may be issued by an appeals court are noted in Exhibit 7.8 below.

The Court's Conclusion

In the opinion, the judges indicate their conclusion, or decision, on the issue or issues before the court. If several issues are involved, as often happens, there may be a conclusion at the end of the discussion of each issue. Often, at the end of the opinion, the conclusions are briefly summarized.

An appellate court also specifies what the *disposition* of a case should be. If the court agrees with a lower court's decision, it will *affirm* that decision, which means that the decision of the lower court remains unchanged. If the appellate court concludes that the lower court erred in its interpretation of the law, the court may *reverse* the lower court's ruling.

Sometimes an appellate court concludes that further factual findings are necessary or that a case should be retried and a decision made that is consistent with the appellate court's conclusions of law. Then, the appellate court will *remand* the case to the lower court for further proceedings consistent with its opinion. In the sample case presented in Exhibit 7.7 on pages 195 through 199, a California court of appeal reversed the decisions of lower courts.

Analyzing Cases

When you are researching case law, your main focus should be on the opinion—the words of the court itself. Some opinions are easier to understand than others. Some judges write more clearly than others. You may need to reread a case (or a portion of a case) to understand what is being said, why it is being said at that point in the case, and what the judge's legal reasoning is.

EXHIBIT 7.8

Types of Appellate
Court Decisions

Concurring: When one or more judges deciding a case agree with the decision of the majority, they may provide different reasons to support the decision or wish to emphasize a particular point.

Dissenting: When one or more judges disagree with the decision of the majority, the dissenters may write an explanation of why the result should have been different. These can be important as persuasive authority later should the holding in the case be limited or overturned. They are also important as signals that the law in a particular area may not be completely settled.

Majority: An opinion that represents the views of the majority of the judges who decide a case, either affirming or reversing the decision of the lower court.

Memorandum: An opinion in a case that does not create precedent.

Plurality: When there is no single opinion that receives the support of a majority of the judges on a court, the plurality is the opinions receiving the most votes. This often happens when a majority agrees on the outcome but for incompatible reasons.

Unanimous: When all judges on a court (or the panel of judges assigned to hear an appeal) agree on the legal reasoning and decision.

Some cases contain several pages describing facts and issues of previous cases and how those cases relate to the one being decided by the court. You might want to reread these discussions several times to distinguish between comments made in the previous case and comments that are being made about the case at bar (before the court).

Look for Guideposts in the Opinion

Often, the judge writing the opinion provides some guideposts, perhaps by indicating sections and subsections within the opinion by numbers, letters, or subtitles. Note that in Exhibit 7.7 on pages 195 through 199, subheadings are used to divide the opinion into basic sections. Scanning through the opinion for these types of indicators can help orient you to the opinion's format.

In cases that involve dissenting or concurring opinions, make sure that you identify these opinions so that you do not mistake one of them for the majority opinion. You can scan through the case a time or two to identify its components and then read the case (or sections of the case) until you understand the facts and procedural history of the case, the issues involved, the applicable law, the legal reasoning of the court, and how the reasoning leads to the court's conclusion on the issues.

Distinguish the Court's Holding from *Dicta*

holding
The binding legal principle, or precedent, that is drawn from the court's decision in a case.

dicta
A Latin term referring to nonbinding (nonprecedential) judicial statements that are not directly related to the facts or issues presented in the case and thus are not essential to the holding.

When analyzing cases, you should determine which statements of the court are legally binding and which are not. Only the holding (the legal principle to be drawn from the court's decision) is binding. Other views expressed in the opinion are referred to as dicta and are not binding.

Dicta is the plural of *dictum*. *Dictum* is an abbreviated form of the Latin term *obiter dictum*, which means "a remark by the way." *Dicta* are statements made in a decision that go beyond the facts of the case or that do not directly relate to the facts or to the resolution of the issue being addressed. *Dicta* include comments used by the court to illustrate an example and statements concerning a rule of law not essential to the case. You can probably assume that statements are *dicta* if they begin with "If the facts were different" or "If the plaintiff had . . ." or some other "if/then" phrase.

Summarizing and Briefing Cases

briefing a case
Summarizing a case. A case brief gives the full citation, the factual background and procedural history, the issue or issues raised, the court's decision, the court's holding, and the legal reasoning on which the court based its decision. It may also include conclusions or notes concerning the case made by the one briefing it.

After you have read and analyzed a case, you may decide that it is on point and that you want to include a reference to it in your research findings. If so, you will summarize in your notes the important facts and issues in the case, as well as the court's decision, or holding, and the reasoning used by the court. This is called briefing a case.

There is a fairly standard procedure for briefing court cases. First, read the case opinion carefully. When you feel you understand the case, begin to prepare the brief. Typically, a brief presents the essentials of the case under headings such as those listed below. Many researchers conclude their briefs with an additional section in which they note their own comments or conclusions about the case.

1. **Citation.** Give the full citation for the case, including the name of the case, the date it was decided, and the court that decided it.

2. **Facts.** Briefly indicate (a) the reasons for the lawsuit (who did what to whom) and (b) the identity and arguments of the plaintiff(s) and defendant(s).

3. **Procedure.** Indicate the procedural history of the case in a sentence or two. What was the lower court's decision? What did the appellate court do (affirm, reverse, remand)? How did the matter arrive before the present court?

4. **Issue.** State, in the form of a question, the essential issue before the court. If more than one issue is involved, you may have two—or even more—questions.

5. **Decision.** Indicate here—with a "yes" or "no," if possible—the court's answer to the question (or questions) that you noted in the *Issue* section.

6. **Reasoning**. Summarize as briefly as possible the reasons given by the court for its decision (or decisions) and the case or statutory law relied on by the court in arriving at its decision.

7. **Holding**. State the rule of law for which the case stands.

Exhibit 7.9 on the following page presents a briefed version of the sample court case presented in Exhibit 7.7. This brief illustrates the typical format used in briefing cases.

IRAC: A Method for Briefing Cases

Besides the example just provided, another standard format for briefing cases is called the *IRAC method*, referring to *issue, rule, application,* and *conclusion.* This method, which will be discussed more in Chapter 9, involves the following steps:

1. First, decide what legal *issues* are involved in the case. For the case presented in Exhibit 7.7 on pages 195 through 199, these are identified under "Issues" in the case briefing in Exhibit 7.9 on the following page.

2. Next, determine the *rule of law* that applies to the issues. In Exhibit 7.9, the rule of law is discussed under "Reasoning."

3. After identifying the applicable law, determine the *application* of the law to the facts of the case. In Exhibit 7.9, the "Holding" section deals with the court's application of the law.

4. Finally, draw a *conclusion.* Exhibit 7.9 calls that the "Decision." It is the determination of the court after it has applied the law to the case.

Different lawyers and law offices have different preferences for the format to be used in briefing cases. What is most important is accuracy in explaining the key facts, the issues under consideration, the rule of law or legal reasoning used by the court, the application of the law, and the conclusion resulting from that application.

Researching Constitutional and Statutory Law

To this point, we have been discussing case law, which is sometimes called *judge-made* law because it is made by the judges in the state and federal court systems. Judge-made law is also known as the common law, as explained in Chapter 5. Another primary source of law is *statutory law*—the statutes and ordinances enacted by legislative bodies, such as the U.S. Congress, state legislatures, and town governments.

Congress draws its authority to enact federal legislation from the U.S. Constitution. A state legislature draws its authority from the state constitution. In some legal disputes, the constitutionality of a statute or government action may be an issue. In such instances, you may have to go behind the statutes to the relevant constitution, so we look at constitutional law before going into detail about statutes.

Finding Constitutional Law

The federal government and all states have constitutions describing the powers, responsibilities, and limitations of the branches of government. Constitutions, especially state constitutions, are amended over time. All are available online.

A key source of federal constitutional law is *The Constitution of the United States of America,* published under the authority of the U.S. Senate and available through the Library of Congress (available at **congress.gov**). It includes the U.S. Constitution, annotations concerning United States Supreme Court decisions interpreting the Constitution, and a discussion of each provision, including background information on its history and interpretation.

The People v. Rekte

232 Cal.App.4th 1237, 181 Cal.Rptr.3d 912 (Ct. App., Calif., 2015)

FACTS   Defendant Rekte was cited for failing to stop at a red light. His action was not observed by an officer but by an automated video system that provided photographic evidence. The information captured in the videos is sent by the system operator, in Arizona, to the local police department that issues the ticket based on a review of the video. The police department could not confirm when the system was last checked for accuracy to be sure it allowed drivers at least 3.6 seconds of yellow light.

PROCEDURE   Rekte hired an expert who testified that the yellow light operated for only 3.5 seconds in some instances. Rekte argued that the video evidence should be excluded. The trial court rejected that argument and allowed the ticket for $490 to stand. Rekte appealed.

ISSUES   Rekte raised three issues. (1) The trial court committed error by referring to *People v. Gray*, a California Supreme Court decision; (2) the trial court committed error in applying Evidence Code Sections 1552 and 1553; and (3) the trial court committed error related to the burden of proof.

DECISION   The three issues raised by the defendant are intertwined and will be treated as one issue. Reference by the court to *People v. Gray* was harmless. However, the lower courts misinterpreted Evidence Code sections 1552 and 1553.

REASONING   *People v. Gray* was depublished by the California Supreme Court, so may not be cited as evidence. Moreover, the issue in that case is not related to the issue here, so is irrelevant to the holding. Evidence Code sections 1552 and 1553 were improperly viewed as presumptions affecting the burden of proof, rather than presumptions affecting the burden of producing evidence. The prosecution bears the burden of proving the evidence—in this case the accuracy of the video system. Defendant's expert cast doubt on the validity of that evidence and the prosecutor did not overcome that evidence.

HOLDING   Reversed. The conviction rested entirely on the video evidence, the validity of which was not established.

Additional constitutional sources are found in the *United States Code Annotated* and the *United States Code Service*, which contain the text of the Constitution and its amendments as well as citations to cases discussing particular constitutional provisions. We discuss these publications shortly, and they are available online. Annotated state codes provide a similar service for state constitutions. State constitutions are usually included in the publications containing state statutes.

Finding Statutory Law

Some statutes supplement the common law, while other statutes replace it. State legislatures and the U.S. Congress have broad powers to establish law. If a common law principle conflicts with a statutory provision, the statute will normally take precedence. Additionally, a legislature may create statutes that deal with issues, such as age discrimination, that are not covered by the common law.

Statutes are often published in compilations called codes, which arrange materials by topic. Familiarize yourself with the dates the relevant legislature is in session, as you will want to investigate whether or not the statute in question has been amended. Online legal research services such as Westlaw and Lexis include a note about how up-to-date their coverage is. Printed services are also available.

code
A systematic and topically organized presentation of laws, rules, or regulations.

Federal Statutes

Federal statutes are contained in the *United States Code,* or *U.S.C.* This official compilation of federal statutes is published by the U.S. government and is updated annually. The U.S.C. is divided into titles (topics) as seen in Exhibit 7.10 on the following page.

For example, laws relating to commerce and trade are in Title 15. Laws concerning the judiciary and judicial procedures are in Title 28. Titles are divided into chapters (sections) and subchapters. A citation to the U.S.C. includes title and section numbers. Thus, a reference to "28 U.S.C. Section 1346" means that the statute can be found in Section 1346 of Title 28. "Section" may also be designated by the symbol §, and "Sections" by §§.

NAMES OF STATUTES.   Statutes are listed in the U.S.C. by their official names. Many legislative bills enacted into law are commonly known by a popular name, however. Some have descriptive titles reflecting their purpose. Others are named after their sponsors.

Sometimes a researcher may know the popular name of a legislative act but not its official name. In this situation, the researcher can consult the U.S.C. volume entitled *Popular Name Table,* which lists statutes by their popular names. For example, suppose you have learned that the Landrum-Griffin Act governs an issue that you are researching. This is the popular name for the act, not the official name. You can consult the *Popular Name Table* to find the act's official title, which is the Labor-Management Reporting and Disclosure Act of 1959. In online searches you would want to use both names.

UNOFFICIAL VERSIONS OF U.S. CODE.   There are also two unofficial versions of the federal code, each of which contains additional information that is helpful to researchers. West's *United States Code Annotated* (U.S.C.A.) contains the full text of the U.S.C., the U.S. Constitution, the Federal Rules of Evidence, and other rules, including the Rules of Civil Procedure and the Rules of Criminal Procedure. This set of approximately two hundred volumes includes historical notes relating to the text of each statute, along with any amendments to the act. Annotations offer additional assistance by listing cases that have analyzed, discussed, or interpreted the particular statute.

The other unofficial version of the code is the *United States Code Service* (U.S.C.S.), also published by West. The U.S.C.S. and the U.S.C.A. provide somewhat different research tools. For example, the U.S.C.S. contains references and citations to some sources, such as legal periodicals and the legal encyclopedia *American Jurisprudence,* that are not included in the U.S.C.A. Both codes are available on Westlaw and Lexis.

State Statutes

State codes follow the U.S.C. pattern of arranging statutes by subject. Depending on the state, they may be called codes, revisions, compilations, consolidations, general statutes, or statutes.

In some codes, subjects are designated by number. In others, they are designated by name. For example, "13 Pennsylvania Consolidated Statutes Section 1101" means that the statute can be found in Section 1101 of Title 13 of the Pennsylvania code. "California Commercial Code Section 1101" means that the statute can be found in Section 1101 under the heading "Commercial" in the California Code. Abbreviations may be used. For example, "13 Pennsylvania Consolidated Statutes Section 1101" may be abbreviated to "13 Pa.C.S. § 1101," and "California Commercial Code Section 1101" may be abbreviated to "Cal. Com. Code § 1101."

In many states, official codes are supplemented by annotated codes published by private publishers. Annotated codes follow the numbering scheme set forth in the official state code but provide outlines, explanations, and indexes to assist in locating information. These codes also provide references to case law, legislative history sources, and other documents in which the statute has been considered or discussed.

EXHIBIT 7.10

Titles in the *United States Code*

TITLES OF UNITED STATES CODE

*1. General Provisions.

2. The Congress.

*3. The President.

*4. Flag and Seal, Seat of Government, and the States.

*5. Government Organization and Employees; and Appendix.

†6. [Surety Bonds.]

7. Agriculture.

8. Aliens and Nationality.

*9. Arbitration.

*10. Armed Forces; and Appendix.

*11. Bankruptcy; and Appendix.

12. Banks and Banking.

*13. Census.

*14. Coast Guard.

15. Commerce and Trade.

16. Conservation.

*17. Copyrights.

*18. Crimes and Criminal Procedure; and Appendix.

19. Customs Duties.

20. Education.

21. Food and Drugs.

22. Foreign Relations and Intercourse.

*23. Highways.

24. Hospitals and Asylums.

25. Indians.

26. Internal Revenue Code.

27. Intoxicating Liquors.

*28. Judiciary and Judicial Procedure; and Appendix.

29. Labor.

30. Mineral Lands and Mining.

*31. Money and Finance.

*32. National Guard.

33. Navigation and Navigable Waters.

‡34. [Navy.]

*35. Patents.

36. Patriotic Societies and Observances.

*37. Pay and Allowances of the Uniformed Services.

*38. Veterans' Benefits.

*39. Postal Service.

40. Public Buildings, Property, and Works.

41. Public Contracts.

42. The Public Health and Welfare.

43. Public Lands.

*44. Public Printing and Documents.

45. Railroads.

*46. Shipping; and Appendix.

47. Telegraphs, Telephones, and Radiotelegraphs.

48. Territories and Insular Possessions.

*49. Transportation; and Appendix.

50. War and National Defense; and Appendix.

*This title has been enacted as law. However, any Appendix to this title has not been enacted as law.
†This title was enacted as law and has been repealed by the enactment of Title 31.
‡This title has been eliminated by the enactment of Title 10.

Page III

Source: The United States Code.

Analyzing Statutory Law

Because of the tremendous growth in statutory and regulatory law in the last century, statutes and administrative agency regulations often govern the legal issues dealt with by attorneys. Paralegals must understand how to interpret and analyze this body of law. Although we use the terms *statute* and *statutory law* in this section, the following discussion applies to regulations issued by administrative agencies.

Two Steps in Statutory Analysis

To determine how well a statute applies to the legal issues in your case, you must understand the statute. The first step in statutory analysis is therefore to read the language of the statute.

As with court cases, some statutes are more difficult to read than others. Some are extremely wordy, lengthy, or difficult to understand for some other reason. By carefully reading a statute, however, you can usually determine:

- the reasons for the statute's enactment,
- the date on which it became effective,
- the class of parties to which the statute applies,
- the kind of conduct regulated by the statute, and
- the circumstances in which that conduct is prohibited, required, or permitted.

You can also learn whether the statute allows for exceptions and, if so, in what circumstances.

The second step in statutory analysis is to interpret the meaning of the statute. Generally, when trying to understand the meaning of statutes, you should do as the courts do. We therefore now look at some of the techniques used by courts when faced with the task of interpreting the meaning of a given statute or statutory provision. Some practical tips for reading statutes are provided in the *Developing Paralegal Skills* feature below.

DEVELOPING PARALEGAL SKILLS

READING STATUTORY LAW

Statutes are a major source of law at both the state and federal level. Being able to read statutes properly is a crucial skill for paralegals (and lawyers!). Reading and understanding a statute, however, is not the same as reading a court decision. It takes application of special techniques (called principles of statutory interpretation) to properly interpret a statute. Here are five of the most important principles:

1. **The Plain Meaning Rule.** If the language of a statute is clear, the court applies the language as written. While this rule seems obvious and easy to employ, it is not, because courts and agencies often stumble over how to interpret particular words in a statute.

2. **Read a Statute as a Whole.** Provisions in different parts of a statute should be interpreted to fit together, not conflict. As a result, to understand a statute, you must look at all of the statute, not just a single section. A good first step is to skim the statute quickly, noting the organizational structure, location of definition sections, and other key elements.

3. **Statutory Definitions Govern.** When a statute includes a specific definition, or an area of law uses a word as a term of art, that meaning will be used in interpreting the statute. Dictionary definitions are guides when there is no statutory definition, but dic-

tionaries differ and the meaning of words can shift over time.

The United States Supreme Court has relied on dictionaries in hundreds of cases. You should check to see if a particular dictionary is recognized as authoritative by the court involved and should use an edition of the dictionary that was current at the time legislation was drafted. *Just doing an Internet search of a word is not acceptable research technique.*

4. **Distinguish between "and" and "or."** When a list of requirements in a statute uses "and," all of the things in the list must be satisfied. When the list in a statute uses "or," only one of the items in a list must be satisfied.

5. **"Shall" does not mean "may" and "may" does not mean "shall."** When a statute uses the word "shall," it will be interpreted as requiring a particular action. When a statute uses the word "may," it will be interpreted as allowing discretion.

Like any area of the law, learning how to do statutory interpretation takes practice and effort. The most important concept to remember is that you must read statutes carefully and look at the entire statute, not just one provision.

Previous Judicial Interpretation

Researching statutory law means researching case law to see how the courts have interpreted and applied statutory provisions. As discussed, courts are obligated to follow the precedents set by higher courts in their jurisdictions. A statutory interpretation made by a higher court must be accepted as binding by lower courts in the same jurisdiction. You can find citations to court cases relating to specific statutes by referring to annotated versions of state or federal statutory codes, such as the U.S.C.A., in print and online.

Legislative Intent

Another factor in statutory interpretation is learning the intent of the legislature. A court determines the meaning of the statute by attempting to find out why the legislators chose to word the statute as they did or, more generally, what the legislators sought to accomplish by enacting the statute. To learn the intent of the legislators who wrote a particular law, it is often necessary to investigate the legislative history of the statute. This can be done by researching such sources as committee reports and records of official hearings and other proceedings.

Committee Reports

Committee reports are the most important source of legislative history. Congressional committees produce reports for each bill, and these reports often contain the full text of the bill, a description of its purpose, and the committee's recommendations. Several tables are also included to set out dates for certain actions. The dates help the researcher locate floor debates and committee testimony in the *Congressional Record* and other publications. Committee reports are published according to a numerical series and are available through the U.S. Government Printing Office, which is accessible online.

Other Sources of Legislative History

The two tools most frequently used in conducting research on legislative history are the *United States Code Congressional and Administrative News* (U.S.C.C.A.N.) and the **congress.gov** site.

The U.S.C.C.A.N., a West publication, contains reprints of statutes and sections describing the statutes' legislative history, including committee reports. Statutes in the U.S.C.A. are followed by notations directing the researcher to the corresponding legislative history in the U.S.C.C.A.N. The site **congress.gov** provides access to committee reports, the text of Congressional bills, and the *Congressional Record*, which is published daily while Congress is in session. This publication contains the text of congressional debates and proceedings.

While our focus here has been on existing statutes and related materials, there are times when we need to know what may be coming. Resources devoted to new developments are reviewed in *Technology and Today's Paralegal* on the facing page.

Researching Administrative Law

Administrative rules and regulations constitute a growing source of American law. As discussed in Chapter 5, Congress frequently delegates authority to administrative agencies through enabling legislation. For example, in 1914 Congress passed the Federal Trade Commission Act, which established the Federal Trade Commission, or FTC. The act gave the FTC the authority to issue and enforce rules and regulations relating to unfair and deceptive trade practices in the United States. There are, of course, many other federal administrative agencies. The orders, regulations, and decisions of such agencies are legally binding and, as such, are primary sources of law.

TECHNOLOGY AND TODAY'S PARALEGAL

LOOKING AHEAD

Every day, it seems, legislatures propose or pass new laws, administrative agencies propose or issue new regulations, and new cases begin to work their way through the court system. A few of these may reach the nation's highest court. As a paralegal, you can perform a valuable service for your supervising attorney by keeping up with new developments in the legal arena or in your specialty area.

WHAT NEW FEDERAL STATUTES ARE LIKELY TO BE ENACTED?

You can keep up to date on what bills are pending in Congress by subscribing to e-newsletters published by law firms, think tanks, and interest groups.

Washington-based think tanks often follow specific areas, and their e-newsletters and blogs include useful information on the progress of pending legislation. There are no guarantees that the information on such sites is up to date or accurate, so be careful to read the actual legislation rather than relying on a third-party account. Law firms with specific practice areas also monitor legislation. Use a legal directory to identify major Washington firms in the practice area you are interested in and then explore the firms' websites for free newsletters. Finally, as noted previously, the Library of Congress's website tracks pending legislation. Web searches (using a service such

as Google or Yahoo!) can also help you spot the mention of legislative proposals in the news media.

ARE ANY NEW UNIFORM LAWS BEING DEVELOPED?

To find out about new uniform laws being developed by the National Conference of Commissioners on Uniform State Laws (NCCUSL), you can visit its website at **www.nccusl.org**. There, you will find the text of all uniform acts, including every draft of the final uniform act. You can also find out which states have adopted an act and which states have legislation pending, as well as the status of the legislation.

TECHNOLOGY TIP

You can find out what cases are pending before the Supreme Court from online sources. For example, at **www.oyez.org**, you will find a list of cases that the Supreme Court has heard recently or is scheduled to hear in the current term. If you are aware of a case pending before the Court or want to search for cases on a particular issue, you can find the case name and a brief description at this site. That way you will know if it is relevant to your search. All details of cases, including briefs, can be found at **www.supremecourt.gov**, as well as through online research services, including Westlaw and Lexis.

The *Code of Federal Regulations* (C.F.R.) is a government publication containing all federal administrative agency regulations. The regulations are compiled from the *Federal Register*, a daily government publication consisting of executive orders and administrative regulations, in which regulations are first published.

The C.F.R. uses the same titles as the *United States Code*. This subject-matter organization allows the researcher to determine the section in the C.F.R. in which a regulation will appear. Each title of the C.F.R. is divided into chapters, subchapters, parts, and sections.

The C.F.R. is revised and formally republished four times a year. Recent regulations appear in the *Federal Register* until they are incorporated into the C.F.R. The online version is updated continuously and is available at the Government Printing Office's website (**www.gpo.gov/fdsys**).

KEY TERMS AND CONCEPTS

Chapter Summary / Legal Research and Analysis

RESEARCHING CASE LAW—THE PRELIMINARY STEPS

1. *Defining the issue*—The first step in research is to identify the legal question, or issue, to be researched. Often, more than one issue is involved.

2. *Determining your research goals*—In researching case law, the goal is to find cases that are on point and are binding authorities. Binding authorities are all legal authorities (statutes, regulations, constitutions, and cases) that courts must follow in making their decisions. Courts are not bound to follow persuasive authorities (such as cases decided in other jurisdictions), although courts often consider such authorities, particularly when deciding cases of first impression.

FINDING RELEVANT CASES

Primary sources of law include all documents that establish the law, including court decisions, statutes, regulations, constitutions, and presidential orders. *Secondary sources of law* are publications written about the law, such as legal encyclopedias, digests, treatises, and periodicals.

1. *Legal encyclopedias*—Legal encyclopedias provide detailed summaries of legal rules and concepts and are useful for finding background information on issues being researched. These books arrange topics alphabetically and contain citations to cases and statutes relating to the topic. Two popular legal encyclopedias are *American Jurisprudence, Second Edition (Am. Jur. 2d)*, and *Corpus Juris Secundum (C.J.S.)*. A third encyclopedia, *Words and Phrases*, covers legal terms and phrases and cites cases in which the terms or phrases appear.

2. *Case digests*—Digests are compilations in which brief summaries of court cases are arranged by subject and subdivided by jurisdiction and court. They are major secondary sources of law and helpful finding tools. Digests using the West system of topic classification and key numbers provide cross-references to other West publications. Digests arrange topics alphabetically with annotations to cases on each topic but are not as detailed as encyclopedias.

1. *Annotations: American Law Reports*—The *American Law Reports* are multivolume sets that present leading cases, each followed by an annotation that discusses the key issues in the case and that refers the researcher to other sources on the issues.

2. *Other secondary sources*—Other secondary sources include treatises, which are scholarly publications that discuss specific areas of law. They summarize, evaluate, or interpret the law, either in a single volume or in multivolume sets. Hornbooks are single-volume treatises. *Restatements of the Law* are respected scholarly compilations of the common law. They present particular cases as examples. Legal periodicals, such as law reviews, contain articles on specific areas of law.

THE CASE REPORTING SYSTEM

The primary sources of case law are the cases themselves. Cases are published in various case reporters.

1. *State court decisions and reporters*—Most state trial court decisions are not published in printed volumes.

State appellate court (including supreme court) opinions are normally published in official state reporters. Many states eliminated their own reporters in favor of West's National Reporter System, which reports state cases in its regional reporters. To locate a case in a reporter, you use the case citation. There are five parts: the case name, the volume number, the abbreviated name of the book (volume), the page number on which the decision begins, and the year the case was decided. A parallel citation may appear after the first citation when the case is reported in more than one reporter.

2. *Federal court decisions*—Federal trial court opinions are published unofficially in West's *Federal Supplement,* and opinions from the federal circuit courts of appeals are published in West's *Federal Reporter.*

3. *United States Supreme Court decisions*—Supreme Court opinions are published officially in the *United States Reports,* published by the federal government, and unofficially in West's *Supreme Court Reporter* and the *Lawyers' Edition of the Supreme Court Reports.*

ANALYZING CASE LAW

Case law is often relied upon to support positions taken in court.

1. *Components of a case*—Reported cases contain more information than just the court's decision. Typically, case formats include the following components:

   - The case title (usually plaintiff versus defendant);

   - The name of the court that decided the case;

   - The case citation;

   - The docket number assigned by the court;

   - The dates on which the case was argued and decided;

   - The syllabus (a brief summary of the facts, issues, and ruling);

   - The headnotes (short paragraphs that summarize the rules of law discussed in the case; in West's reporters, headnotes correlate with the key-number system);

   - The names of counsel;

   - The name of the judge who authored the opinion;

   - The opinion (the court's own words on the matter); and

   - The conclusion (holding, ruling).

2. *Analyzing cases*—Legal professionals often brief, or summarize, the cases they research. Knowing how to read, analyze, and summarize cases makes it easier to compare cases and bring together research results accurately and efficiently. One must distinguish holdings from *dicta.*

3. *Summarizing and briefing cases*—Although the format of briefs varies, the following headings are typical: citation, facts, procedure, issue, decision, reasoning, and holding.

4. *IRAC: A method for briefing cases*—Another format for briefing cases is IRAC, which refers to issue, rule, application, and conclusion.

RESEARCHING CONSTITUTIONAL AND STATUTORY LAW

Statutory and constitutional law are primary sources of law. Statutes are based on the constitutional authority of a legislature to enact laws in particular areas.

1. *Finding constitutional law*—The U.S. Constitution can be found in a number of publications, including *The Constitution of the United States of America.* Annotated versions of state constitutions are also available.

2. *Finding statutory law*—Bills and ordinances passed by legislative bodies (federal, state, and local) become statutory law. Statutes are eventually published in codes, which are updated by supplemental pocket parts and loose-leaf services and are also available online. Federal laws are published officially in the *United States Code* (U.S.C.). The U.S.C. organizes statutes into subjects, or titles, and divides titles into chapters (sections) and subchapters. The *United States Code Annotated (U.S.C.A.)* and the *United States Code Service (U.S.C.S.)* are unofficial publications of federal statutes. They are useful because they provide annotations (comments) and citations to other resources. State codes follow the U.S.C. pattern of arranging statutes by subject. They may be called codes, revisions, compilations, general statutes, or statutes. In many states, official codes are supplemented by annotated codes published by private publishers.

ANALYZING STATUTORY LAW

Statutory law is often difficult to understand, so careful reading and rereading are often required to understand the meaning.

1. *Previous judicial interpretation*—To interpret statutory law, one can turn to several helpful guidelines, including how courts have interpreted the statutes in previous holdings.

2. *Legislative intent*—The legislative history of a statute can reveal what the legislature intended a statute to accomplish in practice and thus help to establish the relevance of the statute to the issue being researched. Sources include transcripts of committee reports and hearings, transcripts of congressional proceedings, and the wording of statutes as first published.

RESEARCHING ADMINISTRATIVE LAW

Regulations issued by federal administrative agencies are primary sources of law. Agency regulations are published in the *Code of Federal Regulations (C.F.R.)*. The C.F.R. follows a format similar to that of the *United States Code (U.S.C.)*, and the subject classifications (titles) of the C.F.R. correspond to the titles in the U.S.C.

QUESTIONS FOR REVIEW

1. What is binding authority? Persuasive authority?

2. What is the difference between a case on point and a case on "all fours"? Why is finding either of these important when researching case law?

3. What is the definition of a primary source of law? A secondary source of law? How are these sources used in legal research?

4. List and identify the various parts of a case citation. How do citations help you locate a case?

5. List and briefly describe the components of a reported case. Which part should you focus on when analyzing a case? How do you brief a case? What is the purpose of briefing a case? What should be included in a case brief?

6. Describe how statutes are published. What is the name of the official code containing the statutes of the U.S. government? What are the parts of a statute's citiation?

ETHICS QUESTION

Krystee Connolly, a paralegal in a litigation firm, has finished reading a brief that the opposing side submitted to the court in support of a motion for summary judgment. In the brief, she notices a citation to a state supreme court case of which she is unaware. Krystee is experienced in the field and keeps current with new cases as they are decided. She wants to look at the case because it gives the other side a winning edge, so she checks in case digests and state encyclopedias, as well as on Westlaw. Krystee also checks the state supreme court's website and sees no record of such a case. She asks the legal assistant for the opposing counsel to give her a copy of the case. When she does not receive it, she decides that the case is probably fictional. What should Krystee do?

PRACTICE QUESTIONS AND ASSIGNMENTS

1. Identify the case name, volume number, reporter abbreviation, page number, and year of decision for each of the following case citations, including the parallel citations:

   a. *Towe v. Sacagawea, Inc.*, 246 Or.App. 26, 264 P.3d 184 (2011).

   b. *Miranda v. Arizona*, 384 U.S. 436, 86 S.Ct. 1602, 16 L.Ed.2d 694 (1966).

2. Identify the title number, code abbreviation, and section number for the following statutory citations:

a. 42 U.S.C. Section 1161(a).

b. 20 C.F.R. 404.101(a).

3. Ana returns home from a business trip to find that her house has been ransacked. Her former boyfriend, Jason, had a key, but when they broke up he returned it. Ana's neighbors tell her that someone matching Jason's description stayed at Ana's house while she was away and had a loud party one night. Ana's food has been taken, several pieces of her furniture have been broken, her bed was slept in, and the house is such a mess that it will require professional cleaning. Ana has come to your firm for legal advice on pursuing a claim against Jason. Using the *Developing Paralegal Skills* feature, *Defining the Issues to Be Researched* on page 178, create a checklist for defining the research issues for the case of *Ana v. Jason*.

4. Ms. Consumer bought a weight-loss tea, advertised as "the dieter's secret weapon," that guaranteed weight loss of 17 pounds and 16 percent of body fat in just 12 weeks without diet or exercise. This offer was appealing because Ms. Consumer's job and family commitments left her with no time to exercise. In addition, her doctor was concerned about her cholesterol and blood sugar levels and told her she needed to lose 25 pounds. Ms. Consumer learned about the product, Healthtea, on a national TV show. While being interviewed, the owner of the company claimed that his product was backed by a clinical study. Ms. Consumer decided to purchase the required minimum six-month supply at a cost of $100 a month. After using the tea for six months, Ms. Consumer had lost only three pounds. She seeks legal counsel because she feels she was taken advantage of and wants to prevent Healthtea from continuing to make false claims. She would also like to get her money back, but that is not her primary concern.

The federal government and many states have laws and agencies that protect consumers from unfair and deceptive business practices. In this assignment we will review a secondary source pertaining to consumer protection laws and government agencies to see how they could help Ms. Consumer.

a. Begin by analyzing the facts. Make a list of relevant legal terms to look up in an index.

b. Select a secondary legal resource—such as *American Jurisprudence*, *Corpus Juris Secundum*, or *American Law Reports*—to use in your research. Record the name of the source. Consult the general index volumes.

c. List the index topics and citations from the general index volumes under which you found relevant information. (If you have difficulty locating rel-

evant information, try checking the topic indexes in the individual volumes.) Many primary and secondary sources have tables of abbreviations near the front of the book (or on the website) that you should consult about the meaning of abbreviations.

d. Look up these citations in the individual volumes of the secondary sources to find an answer to Ms. Consumer's legal issues. According to the secondary source, what rights does Ms. Consumer have against Healthtea? What action(s) can Ms. Consumer take to stop Healthtea from selling its product? Can Ms.Consumer recover any money?

e. List the citations to the volumes, topics, and sections where you found the possible answers. Be sure to check the pocket part for the most current citations if you use printed resources.

5. After you have analyzed the facts of Ms. Consumer's legal dilemma, made a list of legally and factually relevant terms, and reviewed a secondary source as described in the preceding question, can you find a citation to the federal law governing this topic? If so, locate the volume needed in the federal statutes. If not, use an index to an annotated version of the federal statutes in order to look up the relevant terms that will help you locate the statute volume. Then do the following:

a. Go to the volume of the statute containing the cited sections and read those sections. Have you located any additional information in the statute to help resolve Ms. Consumer's legal problem?

b. Does your research on relevant federal statutes lead you to the same conclusions you arrived at by using the secondary source? If not, how did your results differ? Under what topics did you look in each phase of your research?

6. Using the annotated version of the federal statutes, look for relevant case law annotations on Ms. Consumer's legal problem in the notes of decisions following the relevant statutory section. If there is not an annotated version of the federal statutes in your library, if no cases appear there, or if you want to learn to use another source, use a federal digest. Once you find relevant case annotations, you will want to locate the cases that interpret the statute and are as similar to Ms. Consumer's situation as possible.

a. Write down the citations to no more than three relevant cases. Now look up those cases in the case reporters.

b. Read through the summary and headnotes of each case. Do the cases still appear to be relevant? If not, go back to the annotated statute or digest and look for more relevant cases.

c. What did you find? Did the courts' application of the statute change your answer to the legal problem facing Ms. Consumer?

d. How would you update the case law that you located to make sure that it was still current law?

7. If you concluded that Ms. Consumer should pursue a state law remedy, research the answer to Ms. Consumer's problem in your state's law. Provide the citations to the relevant state statute sections and no more than three cases explaining Ms. Consumer's legal rights and the action she should take under state law to prevent Healthtea from selling its product. Based on your findings, is Ms. Consumer likely to recover any money?

GROUP PROJECT

This project will involve creating a case brief of the *People v. Rekte* case in Exhibit 7.7 on pages 195 through 199.

Student one will write the facts section of the case brief. Student two will write the procedure section of the case brief. Student three will write the issues and answers section and the holding. Student four will write the reasoning section.

The group members will then compare the brief that they have prepared to the sample case brief in Exhibit 7.9 on page 204 and will critique their brief by making a list of the differences between their case brief and the sample case brief.

INTERNET PROJECTS

1. Run a Google search for law libraries in your area that are open to the public. Make arrangements to visit a law library. If tours of the library are offered, try to take a tour.

2. Go to the Cornell University Law School's Legal Information Institute website at **www.law.cornell.edu**. Browse through the page that opens, and then answer the following questions:

a. Scroll down to "Legal Resources." What types of primary sources can you access? Are there any secondary sources that are accessible from this page?

b. Under "Legal Resources" click on "Wex legal encyclopedia" and answer these questions:

- What is Wex?
- Locate the definition of a motion *in limine* and record it.
- Explain why a motion *in limine* was used in *People v. Rekte* (see Exhibit 7.7 on pages 195 through 199).

c. Go to **www.law.cornell.edu/citation**. On the left side of the page, click on examples of judicial opinions and scroll down to state case citations. Click on your state. How do your state's case citations compare to the five parts of a standard citation depicted on page 189? Are parallel citations required? Print the Web page containing your state's case citation examples and rules.

CHAPTER 8

Online Legal Research

CHAPTER OUTLINE

Introduction

Free Legal Resources
on the Internet

Lexis and Westlaw

Alternative Legal
Research Sources

Conducting Online Research

CHAPTER OBJECTIVES

After completing this chapter, you will know:

- Strategies for planning and conducting research on
  the Internet.

- How you can find people and investigate companies
  using Internet search tools.

- How to find some of the best legal resources available
  on the Internet.

- The advantages of the major fee-based online
  programs.

Introduction

Online services and databases have improved the ability of paralegals to do high-quality legal research. As you learned in Chapter 7, thorough and up-to-date legal research requires access to a huge volume of source materials, including state and federal court decisions and statutory law. Today, attorneys and paralegals can access most of these materials online.

An obvious advantage of online research is that you can locate, download, and print court cases, statutory provisions, and other legal documents quickly without leaving your desk. Another advantage is that new case decisions and changes in statutory law are entered almost immediately into certain online legal databases, especially Westlaw and Lexis. This means that you can find out quickly whether a case decided three months ago is still "good law" today.

In this chapter, we describe various forms of online research. By the time you read the chapter, some of what we say will have changed, particularly with respect to Internet resources. Some of these resources may have improved, others may have been removed, and new ones may have been added. (See this chapter's *Featured Contributor* article on pages 218 and 219 for tips on conducting research online.) The general approach to conducting research online will not have altered, however. If you master the basic principles of online research discussed in this chapter, you will be able to conduct research on the Internet no matter how much its content changes. The fee-based Lexis and Westlaw services are the dominant legal research resources on the Internet, and we discuss them later in the chapter. First, we consider some free online services.

Free Legal Resources on the Internet

Most public documents, such as statutes and cases, are available to the public. If these documents are on the Internet, they may be accessible through various websites, but some sites have evolved to maintain lead positions in legal research. Here, we look at leading free legal information sites. Later we look at subscription-based sites.

As a general rule, you must know that case law sources are reliable. Commercial databases, such as Westlaw and Lexis, have their content verified but can be expensive,

Expanded online access to legal resources has changed the nature of legal research. Today, paralegals conduct most of their legal research online. How does online legal research benefit your clients?

so free sources are important to save your and your clients' resources. But you must be sure the sites you use for legal analysis are trustworthy.

General Legal Resources

There are several commonly used legal sites for those who are not using fee-based services. The Justia site (**justia.com**) and FindLaw for Legal Professionals (**lp.findlaw.com**) provide access to a massive amount of legal information, such as case law, codes, law reviews, and other legal materials broken down by topics of legal practice areas. The Legal Information Institute (LII) at Cornell University Law School (**law.cornell.edu**) is another major legal resource site. Besides legal documents, this site provides other useful information, such as a guide to legal citations (**law.cornell.edu/citation**), a legal encyclopedia (a good place to start a project), and a dictionary of legal terms (**law.cornell.edu/wex**).

The Washburn University Law School maintains a popular site at **washlaw.edu**. As you will see, it has a plain, no-nonsense menu that provides easy access to certain categories of legal information. Another helpful research portal is **lawhelp.org**. This site is particularly useful when searching for legal information for a specific state. For example, **texaslawhelp.org** provides a sample landlord-tenant agreement for the state of Texas. As the *Developing Paralegal Skills* feature on page 220 notes, one needs to think about the accuracy of websites used in legal research.

Specific Legal Resources

Besides the general sites just mentioned, which offer access to a broad range of resources, many websites provide legal information within specific areas. We discuss just a sampling here.

Secondary Sources of Law

The savvy legal researcher realizes that consulting a relevant secondary source at the beginning of a research project may save time and effort, as the source should provide a good overview of the law in an area and point to leading cases and issues. Many secondary sources, such as commercially published legal encyclopedias and treatises, are not likely to be found on the Web for free. However, an increasing number of law review articles are published free on the Internet by the law review's institution.

Individual law review articles are not organized by topic. One volume of a law journal may include articles on topics ranging from changes in the laws of bankruptcy litigation to the theoretical property laws of space. Therefore, without a citation to a specific law review article, you must search by topic in order to find articles on point.

Google Scholar (**scholar.google.com**) indexes the content of databases that make themselves available to Google. Although not comprehensive, Google Scholar is easy to use and free. Selecting "Articles" under the search box will enable you to search by key words, author, publisher, and date.

Google Scholar also provides multiple ways to build off of an initial search. If an article looks relevant to the original search query, the "Cited By" and "Related Articles" hyperlinks beneath the article can be useful in leading you to other sources. The "Cited By" option provides a similar function to Lexis's Shepard's or West's KeyCite, as it allows you to scan article footnotes to find the sources from which the author derived his or her information. "Cited By" helps discover relevant articles that were written after the publication of the current search result.

Court Opinions

More than a century's worth of United States Supreme Court opinions are available on FindLaw (**lp.findlaw.com**), and several decades' worth are available through LII at Cornell Law School. You can also find the Supreme Court's opinions on its website (**supremecourt.gov**). Archived audio recordings and text of Supreme Court oral

FEATURED CONTRIBUTOR

TIPS FOR DOING ONLINE LEGAL RESEARCH

Matt Cornick

BIOGRAPHICAL NOTE

Matthew S. Cornick is a graduate of SUNY at Buffalo and the Emory University School of Law. He has been teaching legal research, law office technology, and introduction to law and ethics to paralegal students for over twenty-five years. He frequently speaks to paralegal associations and law firms on the topic of technology in the law office. Cornick has served on the Approval Commission to the American Bar Association's Standing Committee on Paralegals. He is the author of *Using Computers in the Law Office*, Seventh Edition (Cengage Learning).

TIPS FOR DOING ONLINE LEGAL RESEARCH

Online legal research can make research easier, more efficient, and more thorough. But for some students, and some practicing legal professionals, online legal research offers the prospect of the inherent difficulties of legal research combined with the frustration of working with computers. I have been in your shoes, and I can assure you that everything is

going to be all right. In that spirit, here is some advice for completing your online legal research with a minimum of hassle and distress.

1. **Think before you begin the research.** Much of the frustration that students feel when researching online is due to the lack of proper preparation. Make sure you know precisely which terms you will use in your search query.

arguments from 1955 onward are found on the Oyez Project (**oyez.org**). Federal appeals courts began to place opinions on the Internet in the early 1990s. For information about federal courts and cases they release, see **uscourts.gov**. FindLaw also provides access to federal district courts, as well as to state courts and other state bodies.

In addition to its article-search capability, Google Scholar began indexing its collection of searchable case law in 2009. Since then, Google Scholar has built a vast, yet incomplete, collection of federal and state case law. Hence, the "Cited By" hyperlink provides a similar function to Shepard's or KeyCite. While Google Scholar's citation function is not as complete or easy to navigate as Lexis's or Westlaw's commercial citators, Google still provides a free and easy-to-use starting point for researching unfamiliar areas of the law. Regardless of which search tool you use, remember some of the tips covered in *Technology and Today's Paralegal* on page 221.

Dockets

Justia (**dockets.justia.com**) provides a way to search for information included in case dockets of lawsuits recently filed in federal court. State court dockets are usually located on each state court's website. For example, if you are looking for a recent motion filed in the Florida Supreme Court, you can search the dockets on Florida's state court site, **flcourts.org**.

Federal Law Starting Points

USA.gov (**usa.gov**), the official portal to U.S. government information, provides links to every branch of the federal government. The A–Z List of Agencies on that site provides helpful links to federal agencies. The U.S. Government Printing Office Federal Digital

Prepare a list of alternative terms. For example, if you are researching an issue relating to divorce, it might be found under "Divorce" or "Dissolution" or "Marriage, Termination of" or "Husband and Wife."

2. **There is no need to reinvent the wheel.** By searching in legal encyclopedias, law journals, treatises, and the like, you can tap into a world of useful information. This is especially true if you review the footnotes. This is where you will find specific references to cases, statutes, and administrative regulations.

3. **Both Westlaw and Lexis offer online training lessons.** Westlaw offers a free certification program (it does not require access to Westlaw) at **http://training.westlaw.com/ paralegal**.

4. **There is more to online legal research than Westlaw, Lexis, and other similar services.** For example, Google now offers the ability to research case law using Google Scholar (**scholar.google.com**).

5. **When using online legal research services, time may literally be money.** Make sure you know whether the tool you plan to use permits unlimited use or charges by the minute. While in paralegal school, you may have free access to Westlaw or Lexis.

Rest assured, in the real world there is no "free access." Make sure you have permission to use Westlaw or Lexis and keep an eye on the clock. Use common sense; do not use $500 worth of time to solve a $100 problem.

6. **Keep your skills current.** Westlaw is now WestlawNext; Lexis is now Lexis Advance. These new versions make online legal research even more intuitive.

7. **Keep track of your research.** Making mistakes during legal research is unavoidable. Making the same mistakes twice (or more) is completely avoidable. Making a list of all the cases, statutes, articles, and other sources you have reviewed will save you time and aggravation.

8. **Perhaps the most valuable online legal research skill you can develop is the ability to cite check primary authorities.** Be sure you take the time in school to gain the expertise employers will value. Here is an online resource you may find useful: **law.cornell.edu/citation**.

9. **Know when to walk away.** Once you start seeing the same cases and statutes over and over again, you have probably found everything worth finding.

10. **Don't worry.** You are not going to break the Internet. Make mistakes, but learn from them.

> " ... everything is going to be all right ... You are not going to break the Internet."

System (**gpo.gov/fdsys**) provides links to the *Code of Federal Regulations, the Congressional Record,* the *Federal Register,* all bills introduced in Congress, the *United States Code,* and other government publications. The Library of Congress's site, **www.congress.gov**, provides a daily congressional digest, a link to the Law Library of Congress, and the full text of laws passed by Congress, as well as summaries of bills. This site is a good place to find information about the status of a bill before Congress. The U.S. Department of Justice (**justice.gov**) provides information on federal criminal prosecutions and the enforcement of the federal laws of civil rights, employment discrimination, and immigration.

Federal Legislative Home Pages

The U.S. House of Representatives website at **house.gov** provides links to representatives' roll-call votes, the Congressional schedule, current debates on the House floor, and websites of representatives. The U.S. Senate site (**senate.gov**) hosts a Virtual Reference Desk with links to more than sixty topics pertaining to the Senate's history and operations. The site also displays roll-call votes, information about recent legislative activity, and links to sites of senators.

Business Information

The U.S. Department of Commerce (**commerce.gov**) provides a wealth of business and economic statistical data and other information. The U.S. Patent and Trademark Office provides many resources regarding patents and trademarks at **uspto.gov**. Information on copyrights and a searchable database of copyright records is provided by the U.S. Copyright Office at **copyright.gov**. The Equal Employment Opportunity Commission

DEVELOPING PARALEGAL SKILLS

INTERNET-BASED RESEARCH

Many legal materials are available on the Internet, with both fee-based (Westlaw, Lexis, Loislaw, Fastcase, Casemaker, VersusLaw) and free (Cornell Law School's Legal Information Institute, Google Scholar) services providing court opinions, statutes, and agency materials. Courts, legislatures, and agencies also operate their own websites, which are often useful resources. Interest groups and law firms maintain specialized collections of key materials as well.

With all that information at your fingertips, often the most important problem is winnowing it down to what is really useful. Here are five questions you should ask about any legal resource you find on the Internet.

- Who created it, and why did they post it on the Internet? Does the information come from a neutral source or an interest group? From someone with experience and credentials or a crank? Before you rely on the results of a Web search, check to make sure your results have a legitimate pedigree.

- Is it accurate? Joe's Legal Blog may be fun to read, but has Joe accurately reproduced a court opinion or statute? It is always best to check unofficial materials against either an official Web resource or a commercial service that certifies the accuracy of its materials.

A medical study on cancer from a respected hospital's site may be more reliable than a similar report you find on a blog.

- Is it up to date? Last year's brilliant website on employment law in Illinois might be wrong if there has been a new statute, regulation, or case since it was posted. Attorneys are always concerned with the currency of the information they're reading.

- Is it easy to use? Many court websites are harder to use than commercial services such as Westlaw. It may save your client a few dollars in search costs, but if it takes you twice as long to find the information, the total bill won't be any less.

- What is the coverage? Does the resource cover material only up to a certain date? Can you tell easily? How can you get the most up-to-date information? Your clients are paying for your expertise in research. You must be able to deliver a comprehensive answer to them.

One of the most important skills you must have as a paralegal is the ability to do quality legal research. Your clients and your employer deserve your best efforts, so always make sure you use the best research tools to obtain the most accurate information.

(EEOC) posts information on employment discrimination, EEOC regulations, and enforcement at **eeoc.gov**.

Numerous resources to help in forming, financing, and operating small businesses are offered by the Small Business Administration at **sbaonline.sba.gov**. The Securities and Exchange Commission maintains public companies' electronic filings at **sec.gov** (see the Filings menu for a link to its EDGAR database, which will be described later in this chapter). FedStats (**fedstats.sites.usa.gov**) provides access to the statistical information compiled by federal agencies, including information about population, crime statistics, and income.

Other Resources

When you are first looking into an issue, you can check **LLRX.com** for discussions or research guides that relate to your topic. LLRX provides information on a wide range of Internet research resources for legal professionals and links to hundreds of forms. If you are researching an area of law and want to know what the most relevant books and websites are for that subject, try Zimmerman's Research Guide (**law.lexisnexis.com/ infopro/zimmermans**).

TECHNOLOGY AND TODAY'S PARALEGAL

STOPPING PROBLEMS BEFORE THEY START

Legal research is easier than ever, thanks to Internet-based research tools. You can quickly find a long list of cases through online databases. But research requires more than turning on a computer, connecting to Lexis or Westlaw, and pressing "print." Your attorneys need *relevant* cases, and it takes skill to winnow a list of search results down to the important cases. Moreover, technical problems can disrupt even a careful research strategy, and there are budget constraints to consider, so here are some tips to help deal with the realities of life as a legal researcher.

Rule 1: Never put off research to the last minute. What seems like a simple research question can turn out to be complicated. Your server may fail at a crucial time. Be prepared—if your firm's Internet connection goes out, don't panic. Know how to switch your research to a smartphone or tablet Internet connection. Nearby alternative locations are often available, from libraries to coffee shops. And always start your research early enough to allow for being thorough, as well as following up on unexpected leads you discover.

Rule 2: Be familiar with low-cost and free alternatives to commercial legal research databases. Westlaw and Lexis are great tools, but sometimes clients cannot afford the cost of their use. **LLRX.com** provides free access to court rules and forms as well as links to useful sources of legal information on the Web. As we see numerous times throughout this text, Cornell Law School's Legal Information Institute (LII) has free and reliable access to court opinions, statutes, and more. Google Scholar (**scholar.google.com**) allows researchers to run keyword searches for cases and legal articles. These resources can help you get research done on the cheap. But keep in mind that "cheap" is not always less expensive. If you spend twice as long on research from a free site as you would on a paid site, the "free" one may be more expensive in the long run.

Rule 3: Have a backup system and use it. Make sure you regularly archive your research on a server or other location. Your firm will likely have a backup system for computers. Find out how it works and what steps you need to take to keep your research files securely backed up. Your work should be regularly backed up during the day in case your computer crashes. If your firm allows it, use a cloud backup service to ensure key materials are also stored off-site—but make sure the cloud service offers adequate security. Be equally sure you are not putting sensitive materials on portable media, such as a flash drive, that could be lost.

Rule 4: Download and archive. Don't rely on being able to find that crucial document on the Web again. Websites vanish, are reorganized, and change their content. Download and store crucial information on your computer or print it out, but make sure you can find what you need quickly. Tools such as X1 (**x1.com**), Copernic Desktop Search (**desktop.copernic.com**), and Instant File Find (**popusoft.com**) make finding files stored on your computer quick and easy. Free-form databases, such as **DEVONthink** (for Macs) or **askSam** (for both PCs and Macs), allow you to create sets of information of varied materials for quick retrieval. Free browser extensions such as Zotero (**zotero.org**) and Evernote (**evernote.com**) allow you to save documents and Web clippings to a cloud-based personal account accessible from any computer. Find a tool that works for you and master it.

Rule 5: Plan ahead. As you plan your work on a case, think about what resources you must have to accomplish each task. What documents will you need so you can keep working on the project if your office is closed? Are there any things that cannot be done off-site? Do you have all the relevant passwords and login information needed to access websites to continue researching off-site? Which deadlines are coming up?

TECHNOLOGY TIP

As a paralegal, you will likely be working on projects where a missed deadline can mean that your client loses her case. Making sure you can respond to the challenges of everything from malfunctioning technology to natural disasters is a crucial part of your job.

Many law libraries create research guides on different topics of law. Georgetown University Law Library maintains an extensive collection of up-to-date research guides (**www.law.georgetown.edu/library/research/guides/**). These guides provide a comprehensive overview of sources to consult in your research. Each guide lists relevant primary and secondary sources, books, Internet resources, and electronic resources that the school's library can access.

A state library's research guide is also a great place to find an extensive list of state resources. For example, the New York State Library has a useful guide for researching legislative history for a New York law at **www.nysl.nysed.gov/leghist**. The Maurer School of Law at Indiana University maintains a site that provides links to legislative materials for all states, as well as information on many other legal topics (**www.law.indiana.edu/lawlibrary/research/guides/index.shtml**).

Lexis and Westlaw

Most legal researchers use Lexis and Westlaw (Lexis is part of LexisNexis Group and is supplemented by Lexis Advance; Westlaw, owned by Thomson Reuters, was replaced by WestlawNext in 2015, so we use the respective terms interchangeably). They are the dominant fee-based providers in the legal research business. The services are comprehensive, and once you become familiar with them, they are user friendly. Subscribers pay for the use of these services, and they are expensive. Different law firms pay different rates depending on their contracts with the providers.

We will review several other online sites, in part because the use of those services can reduce the amount of time spent on Westlaw or Lexis and thereby keep down research costs. Doing initial work on free sites and organizing materials in advance will enable you to be more efficient in the use of these costly resources. Your employer will set the rules for use of the fee-based research sites so you will know what is expected.

While we focus on Lexis and Westlaw, lower-cost competitors are making inroads. Competitors get a share of the market by offering lower prices for similar, if less comprehensive, services. After examining Westlaw and Lexis, we discuss some of these alternatives.

Westlaw and Lexis both include searchable versions of federal and state cases, statutes, and regulations. Additionally, they both contain many law reviews, treatises, legal encyclopedias, legal forms, public records, newspapers and magazines, and other sources. Both services are particularly popular for their *KeyCite* and *Shepard's* citator services (discussed below). Westlaw's key-number service, which arranges the issues in case law into categories, is a fundamental part of many legal research projects, as we discussed in the previous chapter. *KeyCite* builds upon that service.

Accessing Westlaw or Lexis

A subscriber can access Westlaw (WestlawNext) and Lexis (Lexis Advance) via **www.westlaw.com** and **www.lexis.com**, respectively. The opening pages are seen in Exhibits 8.1 and 8.2 on the facing page. To use most of the legal research tools offered by these services, you must subscribe to them and obtain a password. Once you have a password, when you sign on to the service, a welcome page is displayed. You can then begin your research. You can conduct a search, check citations, review documents related to a case or topic, set up alerts, and track previous research trails.

Conducting a Search

Veteran users of either Westlaw or Lexis know how much the look of both databases has changed over the past decade. With the rise in Google's popularity, many databases have simplified their user interfaces to incorporate a single, Google-like search box.

Regardless of the change in appearance, Westlaw and Lexis still allow subscribers to locate documents using various search-and-browse methods. If you have the citation for

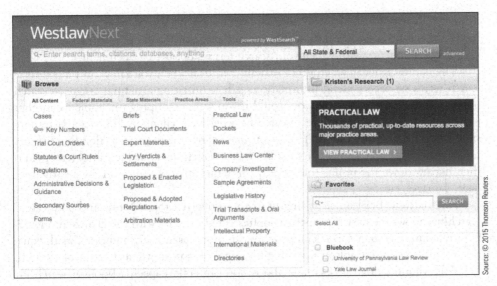

Source: © 2015 Thomson Reuters.

EXHIBIT 8.1

Opening Screen of WestlawNext

a document, such as a court case or statute, you can enter the number and quickly call up the document. If you do not know the citation number, you can search according to legal topic, by case or party name, or by publication.

Although a single search box looks easier to use than the former method, this type of searching comes with its own advantages and disadvantages. Simply typing a few key words in the search box will yield results from all databases your firm can access. Casting a wide search net can be helpful when you are unsure of the precise phrasing of a legal term or simply want to see what kinds of cases or secondary sources discuss a particular legal concept. A disadvantage of this approach is that unless you narrow your search to only a few databases, searches conducted through the main search bar can easily turn up thousands of documents. Not only does wading through a long list of results become overwhelming and time consuming, but it can also rack up hefty charges for a firm that does not pay a flat-rate subscription for either Westlaw or Lexis.

Additionally, both Westlaw and Lexis have the single search box set to interpret your query as a natural language search, which means you can type a phrase, sentence, or question to indicate what you are looking for. This method is in contrast to the more traditional Boolean searching approach in which key words are joined by "operator

EXHIBIT 8.2

Opening Screen of Lexis Advance

Source: © 2015 LexisNexis.

words" such as *and*, *not*, and *or* that serve to tailor the results. Natural language searching uses the database's own unique algorithm that ranks document relevance on factors such as the frequency with which your search terms appear in a document.

The natural language method of searching is ideal when you know only a few basic search terms or need general information. When initiating a natural language search query, use the same terms that you would if you were describing this topic to another person. For example, if you are researching whether a client in Louisiana is responsible when his dog bites another dog, you may search for the terms "dog bite liability Louisiana." Note that a researcher could enter a search query at the initial screen, and then narrow down the results that appear on the left side of the screen by jurisdiction, date, damages, etc.

Alternatively, Boolean searching, sometimes referred to as "terms and connector" searching, allows the user to construct sophisticated searches with less chance of including irrelevant documents. Boolean searches can often resemble complicated math equations. This is because Boolean searching uses symbols and shortcuts to control a search.

Following the dog bite example above, you can craft a specific Boolean search for the same query to weed out irrelevant results. A Boolean search for "(("dog bite" & liability) /p Louisiana) & DA(aft 12-31-1990)" reads that you are searching for any variation of the phrase "dog bite." This includes "dog bites," "dog biting," etc. Additionally, results must include the words "dog bite" and "liability" within the same paragraph as "Louisiana." These results are further narrowed down by defining the date range. Adding "DA" to the query shows that you only want results dated after December 31, 1990. Notice how this form of tailored searching provides much more control over initial search results.

To craft Boolean searches, find the advanced search button located on both Lexis's and Westlaw's homepage (see Exhibit 8.3 for a Westlaw Boolean search). There you will find lists of shortcuts to assist you in crafting your search. You will find a more detailed description of searching styles under "Search Methods" later in this chapter.

Checking Citations

All paralegals should become familiar with citators. A citator provides a list of legal references that have cited or interpreted a case, statute, or regulation. A *case citator* provides, in addition, a history of the case. The primary purpose of a case citator is to determine the validity of a case. Secondarily, the purpose is to locate additional sources. A

citator
A book or online service that provides the history and interpretation of a statute, regulation, or court decision and a list of the cases, statutes, and regulations that have interpreted, applied, or modified a statute or regulation.

EXHIBIT 8.3
Westlaw Advanced
Search Screen Shot

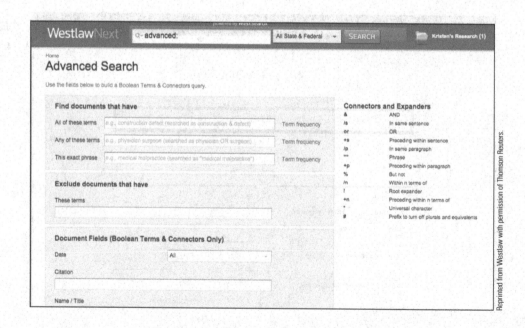

case decided a year or two ago may now be "bad law" if it has been reversed or modified on appeal. A statute may have been amended or held unconstitutional after its passage by a legislature. So whether you are looking at cases, regulations, or statutes, you want to know if your findings are up to date and considered "good law."

The tools provided by *KeyCite* and *Shepard's* allow you to access updated law within seconds. As emphasized in Chapter 7, a crucial part of legal research is making sure your findings are accurate and up to date. If your supervising attorney is preparing for trial, for example, the attorney will want to base a legal argument on current authorities. A precedential case that may have been good law last month may not remain so today.

Both Westlaw and Lexis provide online citators. In Lexis, the primary citator is *Shepard's*. Westlaw provides a similar service, *KeyCite*. For practical purposes, you can think of *Shepard's* and *KeyCite* as performing much the same functions. The *Developing Paralegal Skills* feature below discusses some extra points about *KeyCite*.

Shepard's Citations

Shepard's Citations is available both in print and online. Most libraries and law firms no longer subscribe to the print citators; most attorneys prefer to use the online version.

Information Provided by *Shepard's* and *KeyCite*

Paralegals use *Shepard's* and *KeyCite* citators to accomplish several research objectives:

- **Parallel citations**—On occasion, a court's opinion may be published in several different sets of books. Cases that have multiple citations are referred to as having parallel citations. Both *Shepard's* and *KeyCite* list those parallel citations.

KeyCite
An online citator on Westlaw that can trace case history, retrieve secondary sources, categorize legal citations by legal issue, and perform other functions.

Shepard's
An online citator on LexisNexis that provides a list of all the authorities citing a particular case, statute, or other legal authority.

DEVELOPING PARALEGAL SKILLS

CITE CHECKING ON WESTLAW

Katia, a paralegal, needs to check a citation quickly for a case from the court of appeals to see if it is still good law. Her supervising attorney wants to use the case in a brief that must be filed within a few hours. Katia accesses Westlaw. She enters her password and client-identifying information. Once she has gained access, she enters the case citation in the main search box. The search turns up a red flag in the top left corner, which means that at least part of the case has been reversed or overruled and is no longer good law.

Katia clicks on the red flag, which takes her to the decision in which the case was reversed or overruled. It turns out that part of the case was reversed on grounds that were not related to the rule of law for which her supervising attorney wants to cite the case. Katia and her supervisor can use the case in their brief after all, because the issue they are researching is still good law.

TIPS FOR USING *KEYCITE*

- A red flag means that a case has been reversed or overruled for at least one point of law and must be reviewed.
- A yellow flag means that the case has been questioned or criticized and should be checked.
- Never cite a case without verifying that it is still good law.
- Always read a citing case (discussed on the next page) to find out why your case has a red or yellow flag, and to determine what issue in your case has been questioned, reversed, or overruled. A red flag doesn't always mean that the entire case has been reversed. The case may provide the support you need for a particular issue.

citing case
A case listed in a citator, which cites the case being researched.

- **Other cases**—When you check a case or other law in a citator, you will find a list of cases. These are citing cases; that is, they are cases that cite the case you looked up in the citator ("the cited case"). Because they are citing the case you are researching, these citing cases may deal with the same issue, and therefore may be of interest to an attorney.

- **References to periodicals, treatises, and *American Law Reports* annotations**—If you are researching a case on point, *Shepard's* and *KeyCite* may include references to periodicals and treatises that cite that case. A book or article that references the cited case may provide a valuable discussion of the issues in the cited case, as well as referring to other, related cases.

- **Case history**—As mentioned, the citators provide a history of the cited case. For example, they will tell you if the decision in your case on point has been overturned on appeal (or if any further action has been taken).

Use of Symbols

Shepard's uses an elaborate abbreviation system to provide information on how the cited case has been used or treated in the citing case. See Exhibit 8.4 on the facing page for a list of the abbreviations. For example, if the ruling in the cited case has been followed by a citing case, the symbol *f* (for "followed") will appear. So if a paralegal is Shepardizing a state appellate court opinion (the cited case) and finds that a subsequent appellate court (citing case) has followed the decision in the cited case being Shepardized, the symbol *f* will appear before the citation to the citing case.

Both online citators use a series of color-coded symbols to indicate a law's status. Red stop signs or flags next to a case name, for instance, will indicate that the case is no longer good law for at least one of its points. A yellow stop sign or flag will indicate that a case has been questioned, distinguished, or criticized by a later court decision. Online user guides that explain more about the symbols used in *KeyCite* and *Shepard's* are available from Westlaw and Lexis.

You can use *Shepard's* or *KeyCite* for almost any legal citation. If you have a regulation, a law review article, or a code section, you can always use a citator to try to find other materials that cite it. If, for instance, you are trying to interpret a code section, you might want to look at the materials that cite it in order to get an idea of how courts have interpreted the code.

Selecting Databases

The legal research materials available through Westlaw and Lexis draw from thousands of databases. As discussed above, searching in the main search box on Lexis's or Westlaw's homepage yields results from every one of these databases. As a result, paralegals often need to limit their searches to specified databases. On Westlaw, you can find specific databases in multiple ways. The first is simply searching for that database in the main search bar. For example, by just entering "tax" into the search bar, a dropdown menu will reveal suggestions of databases. If you would rather drill down into specific databases based on a broad topic or resource type, you can browse databases by federal and state material, practice areas of law, and tools.

Note that Westlaw still recognizes database identifiers, which were a common shortcut used to direct searches into a particular database. For example, you can start your search by trying "ca-cs" to direct Westlaw to search all California cases. However, with a move toward natural language searching, you can also use key words to find recommended databases.

Lexis functions similarly to Westlaw when navigating through databases. You can search for the database in the main search box, as well as browsing databases by topics and sources (see Exhibit 8.5 on page 228). To browse a database, use the "Browse" button at the top of the window. For example, suppose your supervising attorney has asked

EXHIBIT 8.4

Abbreviations Used
in *Shepard's*

ABBREVIATIONS—ANALYSIS

History of Case

a	(affirmed)	Same case affirmed on rehearing.
cc	(connected case)	Different case from case cited but arising out of same subject matter or intimately connected therewith.
m	(modified)	Same case modified on rehearing.
r	(reversed)	Same case reversed on rehearing.
s	(same case)	Same case as case cited.
S	(superseded)	Substitution for former opinion.
v	(vacated)	Same case vacated.
US cert den		*Certiorari* denied by U.S. Supreme Court.
US cert dis		*Certiorari* dismissed by U.S. Supreme Court.
US reh den		Rehearing denied by U.S. Supreme Court.
US reh dis		Rehearing dismissed by U.S. Supreme Court.

Treatment of Case

c	(criticized)	Soundness of decision or reasoning in cited case criticized for reasons given.
d	(distinguished)	Case at bar different either in law or fact from case cited for reasons given.
e	(explained)	Statement of import of decision in cited case. Not merely a restatement of the facts.
f	(followed)	Cited as controlling.
h	(harmonized)	Apparent inconsistency explained and shown not to exist.
j	(dissenting opinion)	Citation in dissenting option.
L	(limited)	Refusal to extend decision of cited case beyond precise issues involved.
o	(overruled)	Ruling in cited case expressly overruled.
p	(parallel)	Citing case substantially alike or on all fours with cited case in its law or facts.
q	(questioned)	Soundness of decision or reasoning in cited case questioned.

you to research case law on the liability of tobacco-product manufacturers for cancer caused by the use of tobacco products. To investigate, you need to search the databases containing decisions from all state courts as well as from all federal courts. By working your way through the "Browse" menu on Lexis (as seen in Exhibit 8.5 on page 228) or Westlaw, you will be able to find the databases containing decisions from all state courts and all federal courts.

Search Methods

The Terms and Connectors Method

In a search employing terms and connectors, or Boolean searching, you use numerical and grammatical connectors to specify the relationships of the terms. For example, to find cases on the liability of tobacco products manufacturers for cancer caused by the use of those products, you could type the following terms and connectors in the query box:

liability /p cancer /s tobacco

This would retrieve all cases in which the term *liability* is in the same paragraph ("/p") as the term *cancer*, with the term *cancer* in the same sentence ("/s") as the term *tobacco*.

To restrict the scope of your search, you can add a field restriction. For example, you might want to retrieve only court opinions rendered after 2014. If you are using Westlaw, you could add the following to your query to restrict the search results to cases decided after 2014:

$$\& \ DA \ (12/31/2014)$$

Many other grammatical and numerical connectors can be used to efficiently search a database. These are listed in the instructions provided to Lexis and Westlaw subscribers.

Generally, when drafting queries, make sure your query is not too broad. If you entered just the term *liability*, for example, your search would be futile because so many thousands of documents contain that term. At the same time, you do not want your search to be so narrow that no cases will be retrieved.

EXHIBIT 8.5
Lexis Advance Browse

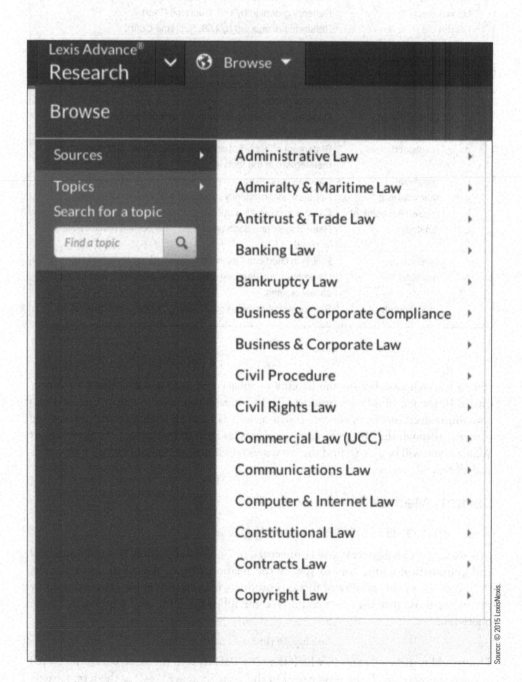

The Natural Language Method

As previously discussed, the natural language method allows you to type a description of an issue without the use of terms and connectors in order to retrieve the most relevant documents. In searching for cases relating to the topic in the previous example, your query might read as follows:

Is a tobacco manufacturer liable for cancer caused by the use of its products?

This query would retrieve the documents most closely matching your description. You could also write a query that consisted only of the most important key words:

tobacco manufacturer liable cancer products

Including synonyms in the search may sometimes be necessary to produce more comprehensive results.

Searching within Results

Often, once you have retrieved your search results, you would like to quickly locate certain key information. For example, suppose that your search resulted in a list of twenty cases relevant to your topic. At this point, Westlaw's "Search within Results" tool allows you to scan the documents in your search result for terms that were not included in your query.

Assume that your original request was, in natural language, "Is a tobacco manufacturer liable for cancer caused by the use of its products?" If you want to know whether "death" is discussed in any of your search-result documents, you can use the "Search within Results" tool. On Lexis, the "Focus" feature previously accomplished the same thing. However, Lexis recently redesigned its user interface and did not include this feature. Lexis may incorporate "Focus" searching again in the future.

When browsing through your search results, remember that the time you spend using the service online is costly. If you have found cases that appear to be on point,

ETHICS WATCH

FINDING ETHICS OPINIONS ON THE WEB

Suppose that your supervising attorney is defending a client in court, and the attorney learns that the client has given testimony that the attorney knows is false. What is the attorney's ethical responsibility in this situation? Should the attorney disclose the client's perjury to the court? Would this be a violation of the attorney-client privilege? Or suppose the attorney learns that the client intends to testify falsely in court. Must the attorney inform the court of the client's intention?

In such situations, the attorney may ask you to find out if the state bar association or the ABA has issued an ethical opinion on this issue. You can find this information by accessing **americanbar.org**, where the ABA posts summaries of its ethical opinions. The ABA also posts ethical opinions issued by state bar associations on its website. On the site, select "Resources for Lawyers" and then pick "Ethics & Professionalism."

you can download them for further study. Check with your supervisor before you print out or download materials so you know how charges are incurred for research materials.

Is Lexis or Westlaw Better?

Because Lexis and Westlaw compete head-on, they provide similar services. The formats are somewhat different, and there are differences in the specialty publications offered. Some users prefer one to the other, but that may be largely a matter of which program they have learned to use. Often, when asked which database is the best, the answer is always whichever service you can access.

In one survey, respondents said that legal researchers could switch between the systems and use *KeyCite* or *Shepard's* to accomplish the same tasks. So while Westlaw may have pulled ahead of Lexis as the dominant seller of premier online services, both do the task well. Respondents to the survey also noted that it is desirable to learn about other, less costly, programs. So we now turn to some of those offerings.

Alternative Legal Research Sources

Several other fee-based online programs offer services that are more limited but less expensive than those of Westlaw and Lexis. All take advantage of public-access databases, such as those for federal cases. Some have extra search features, usually for higher subscription fees. None is as comprehensive as Westlaw and Lexis, but each provides a lower cost alternative that can fulfill many research needs.

Bloomberg Law

While Lexis and Westlaw control a majority of the market for subscription-based online legal research services, Bloomberg Law, seen in Exhibit 8.6 below, has emerged as a popular alternative. Bloomberg offers primary legal content, court dockets, legal filings, and reports just like Westlaw and Lexis. However, Bloomberg Law also provides unique content such as the popular Bureau of National Affairs (BNA) law reports. Additionally, as Bloomberg Law is currently the underdog in the market, the service is priced more favorably than Lexis or Westlaw services.

EXHIBIT 8.6

Bloomberg Law Screenshot

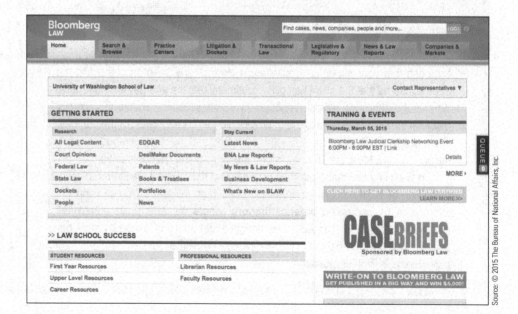

PACER

Public Access to Court Electronic Records (PACER) (**pacer.gov**) is an easy-to-use Internet service that allows users to obtain federal court cases and docket information from federal circuit, district, and bankruptcy courts. While PACER contains court opinions, its chief purpose is to provide a site where attorneys and other court personnel can view documents filed in federal litigation. A user might access PACER to view a complaint filed in a lawsuit in federal court.

Fastcase

Fastcase (**fastcase.com**) provides access to all Supreme Court decisions, federal appeals decisions back to 1924, and federal district court decisions back to 1932. For most research, that is adequate. Fastcase also has bankruptcy court decisions, as well as decisions of state supreme courts and appeals courts back to 1950. All federal and state statutes, constitutions, and administrative codes are included.

A unique feature of Fastcase is that it provides "Authority Check," which looks to see if a case is still good law and provides links to relevant cases. For an extra fee, a user can double-check by linking with *Shepard's* or *KeyCite*. Annual and monthly subscription fees are lower than those of Lexis and Westlaw, which has enhanced the system's popularity. Some state bar associations, such as those in Illinois and Ohio, have arranged for members to have access to Fastcase as part of membership, so it is becoming more widely used.

Loislaw

Loislaw (**loislaw.com**) is a part of Wolters Kluwer, a business and law publishing company. Loislaw has large federal and state case, statutory, and regulatory databases, but it also allows subscribers access to its specialized databases of secondary sources, including treatises and bar publications. Wolters Kluwer is the publisher of CCH, which publishes major tax treatises, and it owns Aspen Publishers, a provider of specialized treatises in various areas of law including bankruptcy, construction, employment, estates, family law, and tax.

When doing topical searches, Loislaw uses an application known as "Key Words in Context." This feature highlights the key words in your search documents, making it easier to review the documents by pinpointing the terms. Loislaw also offers "GlobalCite," a research citation tool. When you use this feature, you view the federal or state cases within the results of your search. GlobalCite also retrieves rules, regulations, treatises, and other documents that have cited a case or other document of interest. "LawWatch" is a feature that tracks trends in areas you have identified.

Casemaker

Similar to Fastcase, Casemaker Legal Research and CasemakerPRO (**casemakerx.com**) is provided by state bar associations to their members as a part of bar membership. Casemaker provides essentially the same set of federal and state case reports, statutes, and regulations as most other services. In some states, it provides state-specific documents, such as opinions of attorneys general, jury instructions, links to court forms, local federal court rules, and other helpful materials. Casemaker has been undergoing expansion of its services, so it is worth reviewing its latest capabilities.

VersusLaw

VersusLaw (**versuslaw.com**) is a low-cost service that includes Supreme Court and U.S. Court of Appeals cases and current federal district court cases, as well as state appellate court cases and cases of some specialized courts. A higher-level subscription plan includes federal district court opinions back to about 1950, along with state statutes and regulations. The highest-level plan includes the *United States Code* and the *Code of Federal Regulations* and provides added search features. VersusLaw has limited access to publications that are not in the public domain, so it primarily offers a reasonably priced means to access reported court cases and federal regulatory materials.

Conducting Online Research

As we have seen, the Internet offers many ways for paralegals to gather information while doing legal research. In addition to investigating the applicability of case law to clients' cases, paralegals often research other matters as well. They may need to locate people, gather information about companies, or conduct other practical, fact-based research into matters not directly related to legal issues. There are numerous online databases that make it possible to perform such research quickly and efficiently.

Your goal when conducting any online research is to find accurate, up-to-date information on the topic you are researching in a minimum amount of time. As anyone who has used the Internet knows, it is possible to spend hours navigating through cyberspace looking for specific information. Planning your research in advance and using a variety of research strategies, such as those discussed in this section, can help you achieve your goal of conducting thorough online research efficiently.

Plan Ahead—Analyze the Facts and Identify the Issues

Once you have been given a particular research project, you should plan your research steps before going online. The first step is to know what you are seeking. To avoid wasting time and money, outline your objectives clearly and be sure you understand your goals. To narrow the scope of your research, you may need to know the reason for the research or how the results will be used.

Online Research Strategies

Once online, you can use many strategies to find what you are looking for. We discuss some of those strategies here (see *Developing Paralegal Skills* on the facing page for tips on medical research).

Starting Points

Sometimes, a research session begins with one of the online directories or guides discussed earlier in this chapter. For example, if the object of your search is to find a law firm that practices in a specialized area of the law, start at the Martindale-Hubbell website (**martindale.com**). You can also search **legalhelp.org**.

A search engine can be used to compile a list of websites containing certain key words. Keep in mind the limitations of search engines, however. Your search may locate many irrelevant sources and may not lead you to every site that you would find helpful. In addition, different search engines will yield different results or order the results differently.

You may have to try several searches before you get to the right websites. Most search engines contain an advanced search feature that will help you refine your search. For instance, Google's advanced search will let you limit your search to particular phrases, eliminate unwanted words from your results, or find Web pages that were added to the Web after a particular date.

From the preliminary results of a general search, you can click on the links to the sites and determine which are useful. Many sites include their own links to other sources you may find helpful. Some websites attempt to collect links to all online resources about particular topics. These sites include directories, which were discussed earlier, as well as other sites, such as **usa.gov**, which provides links to federal offices and agencies.

DEVELOPING PARALEGAL SKILLS

MEDICAL RESEARCH ON THE INTERNET

Thom Shannon needs to locate information on bipolar disorder. Thom's supervising attorney is trying to prove that the defendant in a case has this mental condition. Thom runs a Google search on "bipolar disorder" and finds a reference to the Mayo Clinic's website (**mayoclinic.com**). He searches within the Mayo Clinic's site for articles describing this disorder. Thom finds several citations to articles, along with summaries of the articles, but the full text of the articles is not online. He goes to the library at the local medical school to obtain the full text of the articles for those he cannot find by Google Scholar or other search services.

TIPS FOR PERFORMING MEDICAL RESEARCH ONLINE

- Become familiar with medical terminology.
- Search the appropriate medical categories on the website.
- Locate appropriate articles and summaries.
- If the full text of the articles is not available online, go to the nearest medical school's library to obtain the articles.
- Make sure that your information is taken from a reputable website.

Discovering Available Resources

Despite your best intentions and attempts to focus your research, you may have to approach a project without a clear objective regarding what you need to find. Your initial research goal may be to discover the extent of resources available online, with your ultimate goal being to obtain more precise results.

CHECK THE LAW LIBRARIES. Keep in mind that there are several different approaches you can take to find legal resources on the Web. As noted before, many law school libraries provide subject guides to legal issues on their Web pages. These subject guides typically discuss the basic sources used for research in a particular field, and on occasion will provide information about the best approaches for researching particular issues. For instance, Georgetown Law Library has an extensive list of the major books available for a particular legal field in its online legal treatise finder (**www.ll.georgetown.edu/guides/treatisefinder.cfm**). Most law schools will have a guide to searching Google or another search engine for words such as *tax law treatise* or *tax law research* and will retrieve a list of relevant websites.

Zimmerman's Research Guide, discussed on page 220, provides information about the appropriate resources to consult when researching a particular legal issue. Many libraries provide access to their catalogs online (see, for example, the New York Public Library's website at **catalog.nypl.org** or Yale Law School's catalog at **morris.law.yale.edu**). You can search these catalogs on the Internet just as you would search them in the library. This can save the time that you otherwise might spend in a futile trip to the library. Often, you can arrange to have source material from a distant library delivered to a closer library or directly to you.

Usually, state university or state law libraries are open to the public. You may think the only value of entering a library to conduct research is the opportunity to look through printed materials. However, there are many benefits to researching within the confines of a library. The first is the ability to communicate your research needs to a reference librarian. Law librarians have expertise in navigating legal information and can quickly point out the best resource for your needs. Furthermore, many universities provide public access to their database subscriptions. If a pay wall blocks a resource you are looking for, it can be beneficial to check with your local library to see if you can access that resource on one of the library computers. Additionally, many public universities offer patrons limited access to databases in Westlaw and Lexis.

BLOGS.　　Another way to find out what resources are available is to begin with a blog. These can also be used to update your research. Millions of people generate blogs on a regular basis. A *blog*, short for "Weblog," is essentially an online journal. Some blogs are well established, while others disappear as the authors tire of them. Some of the best-recognized blogs in law include the general Am Law Daily (**amlawdaily.typepad.com**) and Legal Times (**legaltimes.typepad.com**). The American Bar Association's *ABA Journal* site maintains a list of legal blogs (**abajournal.com/blawgs**). The Law Library of Congress (**loc.gov/law**) has a searchable archive of law blogs arranged by subject.

Blogs can be useful in legal research because they often provide information about recent developments in an area of law and are typically written by law professors and attorneys. If, for instance, you had a problem that focused on a new issue in immigration law, you might want to check the ImmigrationProf Blog (**lawprofessors.typepad.com/immigration**) to see if the issue had been discussed there. Stanford Law School's Legal Research Plus blog (**legalresearchplus.com**) focuses on legal research skills and provides useful information about new research techniques and technology.

Browsing the Links

As you browse through the links that could be useful for your research, you will need to keep track of the websites you visit. Marking a site as a "Favorite" (Internet Explorer) or adding a "Bookmark" (Firefox, Safari, or Chrome) for the site is an electronic substitute for keeping a book on your desk. With these, you can create an automatic link to any point on the Web. Once you have added a bookmark, you can return to that site again without searching for it. For example, you might want an automatic link to the site at which you begin your research: a directory, a search engine, or a site that has many links that relate to what you need.

Narrowing Your Focus

Once you find a website that could be useful, you will probably need to zero in on specific data within that site. One way to do this, of course, is to use the links within the site.

Remember that your browser also has the ability to search a Web page that you are viewing. This can be particularly helpful when you are attempting to review a long document on the Web for a particular word or phrase. Assume that you found the text of a bill being considered by Congress at the Library of Congress's site (**congress.gov**), formally called "Thomas." Your browser's "Find" tool will let you search through that bill—which might be very lengthy—for a particular phrase. You might also use your find tool to search a company's document in the Electronic Data Gathering, Analysis, and Retrieval (EDGAR) database of the Securities and Exchange Commission (SEC) (go to **sec.gov/edgar.shtml** and select "Filings"). EDGAR is an indexed collection of documents and forms that public companies are required to file with the SEC.

Evaluating What You Find

After you have found what appears to be exactly what you are looking for, you need to consider its reliability and credibility. Ask yourself whether the source of the information is a primary, a secondary, or a tertiary source. Primary sources include company websites, experts, and persons with firsthand knowledge. For example, the inventor of a product would be a primary source for information about the invention.

Publicly filed documents are also primary sources. For example, the legal forms that companies are required to file with the Securities and Exchange Commission are good primary sources for the information that they contain (see the discussion of company investigations later in this chapter).

Secondary sources include books and periodicals (such as law journals, newspapers, and magazines) and their online equivalents that contain "secondhand" information.

Tertiary sources are any other sources that might be used in research (*tertiary* means "third" or "thirdhand"). It is always a good idea to find and interpret primary sources yourself before forming conclusions based on secondary or tertiary sources.

A researcher also needs to be aware of whether a source is reputable. A reputable source might be an organization that has established itself in a particular field. A less reputable source might be a personal, self-serving home page. Was the information placed on the Web by an organization that may be biased in a certain way? Some people providing information on the Internet may not even be who they represent themselves to be. Online resources are available to help you evaluate websites. For instance, the website of The Ohio State University Libraries includes an interactive tutorial and checklist for evaluating websites. You can access this tutorial by going to **liblearn.osu.edu/tutor/les1**.

Updating Your Results

Staying current with events in the law and in other areas that relate to your research is important. One way to confirm whether your research results represent the most recent data available is by going online. News sites abound on the Internet. There are general sites sponsored by news organizations, as well as sources such as Google's news search feature (**news.google.com**). Corporate press releases—both current and from archives—can be reviewed at PRNewswire's site, **prnewswire.com**. You can also subscribe to e-mailed newsletters and bulletins from various sites. FindLaw offers many free legal news e-mail services at **newsletters.findlaw.com**. Cornell Law School's Legal Information Institute will e-mail subscribers bulletins about Supreme Court cases and arguments.

It is very difficult to keep track of every new blog post published on a particular topic. Without subscribing to a listserv or RSS feed, staying up-to-date with current blogs or finding new blogs would require constant Internet searching. One way to keep on top of blogs and news about particular legal topics is to set up a Google Alert, (**google.com/alerts**), seen in Exhibit 8.7 on the next page. To set up an alert, it is best to have a Google account already. Using your e-mail address, you can then set up alerts for important key words that can arrive in your inbox daily. For example, if you set an alert for "property law" and "takings clause," you will receive a daily e-mail with all new websites or blogs that mention those terms.

Remember that after you have taken such pains to conduct exhaustive research, you do not want to lose your work. *In the Office* on the page 237 suggests ways to organize and keep track of your results.

Locating People and Investigating Companies

As mentioned earlier, paralegals often need to locate people or find information about specific companies, and the Internet can be especially useful in searching for this type of information. There are numerous search services. The comprehensive services charge for their searches.

Finding People

A paralegal may need to find particular persons to assist a lawyer in collecting debts, administering an estate, preparing a case for court, and so on. (We will discuss this topic more in Chapter 11.) Not all pubic record information can be found on the Internet, but search engines such as **Instant Checkmate** can be helpful. Despite this limitation, Web searches can be useful, and they can also be cheaper and faster than going to a government office or a library. Sometimes, using a commercial locator service or database can also be less costly than a trip out of the office to the local courthouse or state archives.

EXHIBIT 8.7
Google Alert Screenshot

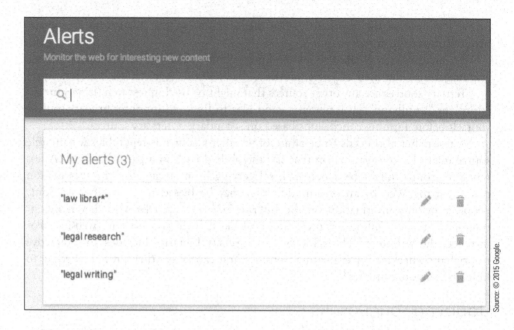

BROAD SEARCHES.   On the Web, a researcher can run a broad search with a general search engine such as Yahoo!, Bing, or Google. A researcher might also narrow the focus of a search to, for example, all U.S. telephone books. There are several phone book websites, such as **whitepages.com**. Some of these sites, such as the Yahoo People Search at **people.yahoo.com**, provide e-mail addresses. Some include business listings (for example, **www.superpages.com**). Some can conduct a reverse lookup search with a telephone number or an e-mail address to reveal a name and a street address (for example **ZabaSearch.com**).

NARROW SEARCHES.   If you know something about a person, such as an employer or a profession, you can use that information to narrow the search. For example, if you are looking for an attorney, you can link to the *West Legal Directory* in Westlaw, a comprehensive compilation of lawyers in the United States, or conduct a free search on **lawyers.findlaw.com**. The Martindale-Hubbell directory also provides attorneys' contact information.

If you are looking for a professor at a particular university or an employee at a certain company, you can often search the staff directory of the school or business firm online. LinkedIn, a social media site for networking professionals, is also a great tool to find personal profiles of professors, experts, or lawyers.

SPECIALTY SEARCH TOOLS.   With the right database, you can verify a person's business license, access information about a federal prison inmate, and find a military member or veteran. (For the latter, see **www.gisearch.com**.) Information can also be obtained about persons who contribute to federal election campaigns (see Political Money Line at **politicalmoneyline.com**). Adoptees and their birth parents can be located through databases such as **www.adoption.com** and **www.omnitrace.com**. For genealogy searches, there are huge databases of facts about family trees and historical events (see, for example, **ancestry.com**). Many local tax assessors' databases (see, for instance, the Mobile, Alabama, County Revenue Office's site at **mobilecopropertytax.com**) provide information about local property owners and property values.

FEE-BASED SEARCHES.   Some commercial services provide access to their information for a price. For example, possible aliases, home value and property ownership, bankruptcies, tax liens, and small claims civil judgments can be searched through US Search at **ussearch.com**. Through a service with access to states' incorporation data and other information, people can be located based on their ownership interest in business organizations.

IN THE OFFICE

PROTECT AND ORGANIZE YOUR RESEARCH RESULTS

Almost all work is now stored in computer files. For security, a computer should be connected to an external hard drive in case the computer crashes. Offices should also have secure off-site backup systems so copies of files can be accessed in case of fire. Many firms organize files by specific practice area, such as personal-injury litigation. Within a given area, there may be files for clients' cases, research by topic, memoranda of law, and so forth.

Besides following procedure about filing and backup, make sure your computer is well organized so your supervisor could go into it and find files if necessary. Files are a law firm's work products, not your personal property, so they should always be professionally maintained.

Real property records, bankruptcy filings, and documents relating to court dockets, lawsuits, and judgments can be searched through such sites as KnowX at **knowx.com**.

Social Security numbers can also be verified through the Veris database at **veris.info**. Similarly, the public records databases on Westlaw and Lexis can provide a great deal of background information, such as past addresses, marriage and divorce records, criminal history and arrest records, professional licenses, and other such information. Social Security numbers can be verified through these sites as well.

Investigating Companies

Lawyers often need to know about their clients' companies and the companies of their clients' competitors. For example, if a client has suffered an injury caused by a defectively designed product, a lawyer will need to identify the defendant manufacturer, find out whether the manufacturer is a subsidiary of a larger company, and learn the defendant's address. If a client wants to acquire or invest in a particular business firm, research into the firm's background may be vital. There are many ways to find some of this information on the Web.

FINDING COMPANY NAMES AND ADDRESSES.   A researcher can run a search using a telephone number to find a company's name and address (for example, see **superpages.com**). Without a telephone number, a company's name and address can be found with the help of a directory that searches by industry and state (see **switchboard.com**, for example). A search with such a directory can also help determine whether a specific firm name is in use anywhere in the United States. You can find out who owns a domain name by using the domain lookup tool at **whois.com** and other such service providers.

UNCOVERING DETAILED INFORMATION ABOUT COMPANIES.   You can find company information on company websites, which may contain annual reports, press releases, and price lists. Some companies put their staff directories online.

Information about publicly held companies may be available through the sites of government agencies. For example, the Securities and Exchange Commission (SEC) regulates public companies and requires them to file documents and forms reporting certain information. This material can be accessed through the SEC's EDGAR database, as already mentioned.

Other information about public companies can be found at free sites as well as fee-based sites. Some free sites provide data on the companies and links to the companies' home pages and other sources of information, such as news articles. The *Wall Street Journal*, at **wsj.com**, often includes archives of information that may span decades and may cover companies in other countries. Some of this information is free; some must be purchased.

ADDITIONAL SOURCES.   Another source of both free and for-a-fee information on public companies is **corporateinformation.com**. The BizTech Network maintains **brint.com**, which provides extensive links to U.S. and international businesses. The newspaper databases on Westlaw and Lexis are good sources of information about companies featured in the media.

Data on privately held companies is more difficult to find because these firms are not subject to the SEC's disclosure requirements. Much of the information available includes only what the companies want to reveal. There are a few sites that compile some data on private companies, associations, and nonprofit organizations. For example, Hoover's (**hoovers.com**), a Dun & Bradstreet company, provides brief profiles of many companies, with links to other sites, including search engines. For a fee, Hoover's will provide expanded profiles. Many of the Hoover's databases are available through Lexis.

There are many guides to online business research available through the Web. A search on Google or Yahoo! for a phrase such as *business research guide online* will retrieve many of them.

Associations and Organizations

When gathering information about a person or a company, you may find it useful to check various professional organizations and associations. The Internet Public Library provides lists of associations by category at **ipl.org** (select "Special Collections" and then "Associations on the Net"). Access to lists of many nonprofit organizations can be found at **idealist.org**. As the review of sources indicates, paralegals are increasingly sophisticated at Internet-based searches to track down needed information efficiently. The rapid evolution of technology also means better opportunities in law firms for paralegals who stay on top of the latest tools.

KEY TERMS AND CONCEPTS

citator   224
citing case   226

KeyCite   225

Shepard's   225

Chapter Summary / Online Legal Research

FREE LEGAL RESOURCES ON THE INTERNET

A great deal of legal information, especially public documents such as statutes and cases, is accessible through free Internet sites.

1. *General legal resources*—Some free legal sites act as portals, giving access to a broad range of free information. Major sites include FindLaw and Justia. Another is the Legal Information Institute at Cornell University Law School. Other law schools provide research source assistance, too.

2. *Specific legal resources*—Secondary sources are generally not found at free sites. However, an increasing number of law review articles are available. One can also find court opinions and various other legal resources at free sites.

3. *Federal law starting points*—All federal government organizations have Internet sites.

LEXIS AND WESTLAW

For serious legal research, legal professionals often use online commercial legal research services, particularly Lexis and Westlaw.

1. *Accessing Westlaw or Lexis*—Subscribers to these fee-based services can access the services' databases.

2. *Conducting a search*—Lexis and Westlaw provide users with access to an extensive collection of legal, business, and other resources. Using these services, paralegals can access specific documents, update the law, and search hundreds of databases.

3. *Checking citations*—For citation checking, Lexis provides *Shepard's Citations* and Westlaw provides *KeyCite*. Both services enable researchers to make sure their research results are still valid. Both Lexis and Westlaw allow users to search databases with queries using terms and connectors or natural language.

4. *Shepard's Citations*—Previously, *Shepard's* citation work was done with the print version; most research is now done using the online edition. Both *Shepard's* and Westlaw's *KeyCite* enable checking the status of a case for citation purposes.

5. *Selecting a database*—Because of the mass of data found in many searches, researchers learn to restrict searches to specific databases to be more efficient and precise.

6. *Searching a database*—Within a given database, many searches can be done in natural language using terms and connectors that are peculiar to that database.

7. *Searching within results*—Westlaw and Lexis allow a researcher to keep refining results to zero in on relevant documents and cases.

8. *Is Lexis or Westlaw better?*—Both services offer similar features; researchers tend to develop personal preferences.

ALTERNATIVE LEGAL RESEARCH SOURCES

Since Westlaw and Lexis are costly to use, less expensive and less comprehensive alternatives have become more popular. Examples include Bloomberg Law, PACER, Fastcase, Loislaw, Casemaker, VersusLaw, and Google Scholar. Such services may be adequate for some projects and may also be used for preliminary research.

CONDUCTING ONLINE RESEARCH

Searching can be costly in time and access fees, so paralegals must learn to become proficient in conducting extensive research as efficiently as possible. The following tips will help you as you learn to make full use of Internet resources:

1. *Plan ahead by analyzing the facts and identifying the issues*—To avoid wasting time, define what you are seeking and determine which sources are most likely to lead you to the desired results.

2. *Develop online research strategies*—Once online, you can use various search tools and other resources (such as listservs, newsgroups, and blogs) to locate information relevant to your topic. Often, researchers need to "browse the links" for a time before finding a site that is particularly relevant. Once you find a useful site, you can use your browser or the site's internal search tool to look for specific information within the site.

3. *Evaluate what you find*—In evaluating your research results, it is especially important to consider the reliability of any information obtained online. Discriminate among primary sources, secondary sources, and tertiary sources.

4. *Update your results*—To update results, you can access online news sites to look for articles or press releases concerning recent developments in the area you are researching.

5. *Locate people and investigate companies*—Paralegals often engage in online research to locate people and obtain their contact information, and to gather data about companies. Sometimes, a person can be located through a broad search of the Web using a search engine such as Yahoo!. Narrow searches can be conducted by accessing—for free or for a fee—specialized databases, such as compilations of physicians, lawyers, or expert witnesses. Searches for persons may also be conducted based on defining characteristics such as place of employment. Numerous online sites contain information about both private and public companies.

QUESTIONS FOR REVIEW

1. What questions should you ask yourself before going online to perform legal research?

2. List five free legal resources that can be accessed via the Internet.

3. What kinds of legal resources can be accessed at various government sites?

4. What is *KeyCite*? How can Westlaw be used to stay current on the law? Does Lexis have an online citator? Describe two ways in which you can search databases on Lexis and Westlaw.

5. List and briefly describe the dominant fee-based online legal research database services. Do the same for the alternative online legal research databases.

ETHICS QUESTION

1. Tony is doing research for his supervising attorney to include in a brief that has to be filed with the court of appeals by 5 P.M. today. He finds a case that is on point and provides the exact support needed for their argument. In his haste to summarize the case and get it into the brief, Tony fails to update the case using *Shepard's* or *KeyCite*. As a result, he does not inform the attorney that the case was reversed on appeal and is no longer good law. What ethical rule has Tony violated? What impact might Tony's neglect have on the client's case? On Tony's supervising attorney?

PRACTICE QUESTIONS AND ASSIGNMENTS

1. Go to **usa.gov** and locate the website for the Federal Trade Commission (FTC). Click on the link to the FTC site. Answer the following questions about weight-loss products:

  a. Where would you go to file an online complaint with the FTC about a weight-loss product? Paste the Web link to the complaint form into your assignment.

  b. What information does the FTC complaint form ask you to provide about health and fitness complaints? List what is asked for under "complaint details."

  c. Does the FTC website provide information on what consumers can expect once a consumer complaint has been filed?

  d. What suggestions does the website offer to consumers trying to get their money back?

  e. Does the website feature any articles or reports about the FTC pursuing companies providing deceptive weight-loss products? If so, what is the current status or outcome of such efforts? Print a copy of a relevant article and attach it to your assignment.

  f. Under "About the FTC," click on "What We Do" and then on "Enforcement Authority." Can and does the FTC take companies to court for using unfair and deceptive trade practices? If so, what remedies does it seek?

2. If you did the research assignment in the Chapter 7 *Practice Questions and Assignments* question 6 or 7, Shepardize one of the cases that you found, using *Shepard's* in print. Is the case still good law, or has it been reversed or overruled? How can you tell? How many citing cases are there? If you have access to Westlaw, Lexis, or any of the alternative legal research sites, update the same case using one of the online sources. Print out the results. Explain the differences between *Shepard's* print and online versions.

3. Do a Google Scholar search for articles about tobacco-products manufacturers' liability when cancer results from the use of their products. How many items did your search retrieve? Print the first two pages of your result to submit to your instructor.

4. You are working as a paralegal for a probate and estate planning law firm. One of the firm's clients died and now you have to locate all of the heirs. One is a 28-year-old nephew, whose last known address is a college dorm, according to the records that you have. This nephew was orphaned at the age of 17 when his parents died in a car accident, so there are no close relatives to help you find him. You reach an aunt who tells you that she believes the nephew is in graduate school in Chicago. Using the material on finding people, which websites would you use in your search to locate the missing nephew? If the free websites do not return any contact information for him, would you use fee-based sites? If so, which ones would you consult?

GROUP PROJECT

This project has you investigate the alternative legal research databases. Students one, two, and three will go online and find information about what state and federal case and statutory law databases, forms databases, citators, and other services are offered by Loislaw, Casemaker, VersusLaw, and Fastcase. Each student should write a summary of what is offered and describe the strengths and weaknesses for doing research with each one. Student four will collect and organize the summaries and present them to the class.

INTERNET PROJECTS

Using the facts and information in questions 4, 5, and 6 of Chapter 7 *Practice Questions and Assignments*, go to **law.cornell.edu**, click on "U.S. Code," and enter the citation to the Federal Trade Commission Act located in your research. Answer the following questions:

1. Are you able to locate a similar version of a state statute that provides legal protection similar to that of the Federal Trade Commission? If so, what remedy does it offer to Ms. Consumer?

2. Does the search retrieve case law on deceptive trade practices? If not, how do you locate case law from the U.S. district courts and courts of appeals for this statute? From the United States Supreme Court?

3. Does the case law you located in Question 2 have any effect on the applicability of the statute? Does it provide precedent that might be used by Ms. Consumer?

4. If you did Chapter 7 *Practice Questions and Assignments* questions number 4, 5, and 6 in the library, how do your search results from **law.cornell.edu** compare to your search results from the print sources? Which do you prefer and why?

CHAPTER 9

Legal Writing: Form and Substance

CHAPTER OUTLINE

CHAPTER OBJECTIVES

After completing this chapter, you will know:

- What to consider when accepting a writing assignment.

- What to consider when drafting a legal document.

- Some techniques for improving writing effectiveness.

- Guidelines for drafting effective paragraphs and sentences.

- The format for legal correspondence and the most common kinds of letters.

- How to write a legal memorandum.

Introduction

As a paralegal, you will likely draft a variety of documents, including letters, internal legal memoranda, and pleadings and motions. Legal writing is often closely related to legal research and analysis. Once your research identifies the law that governs an issue, you need to understand the law and, through legal analysis, determine how it applies to a client's case. And if your supervising attorney asks you to draft a memorandum, you will need to explicitly summarize your research and analysis in writing. Of course, many writing assignments are not directly related to legal research. For example, you would not need to do any research to write a letter to a client recapping recent developments in her or his case.

Many of the same writing principles apply regardless of the kinds of documents you draft. This chapter discusses (1) what to consider when receiving a writing assignment, (2) how to present a well-written product, and (3) the kinds of documents commonly prepared by paralegals.

Receiving a Writing Assignment

Before we discuss drafting different kinds of documents, we need to explain what to do when you receive a writing assignment.

When a supervising attorney gives you a writing assignment, you must learn the nature of the assignment, when it needs to be completed, and what kind of writing approach it calls for. We consider each in turn.

Understanding the Assignment

The practice of law can be hectic, and paralegals are often expected to research and write about issues within a short time. When you receive a writing assignment, make sure you understand its exact nature so that you can work as efficiently as possible. If you do not understand the assignment, you will likely waste time doing unnecessary work. Each project is a little different, and your approach varies depending on the kind of document you are drafting, the complexity of the subject matter, and the reader's needs. If you are uncertain about any aspect of the assignment, ask questions until the

Much of a paralegal's work involves legal writing, whether it be a research memorandum, a letter to a client, or a pleading or motion to be filed with a court. Excellent writing skills are a must for the professional paralegal. Assess your own writing skills. Think of ways that you can become a better writer and start putting them into practice now.

© eurobanks/www.Shutterstock.com

assignment is clear in your mind. As the old saying goes, there is no such thing as a stupid question.

Time Constraints and Flexibility

Knowing the deadline for a writing assignment and adhering to it is essential. Clients and supervising attorneys often need quick answers to questions, and you may need to file a document with a court by a specific date. Being late could have serious consequences.

Paralegals must be flexible and prepared to deal with changing circumstances. For example, you may discover an important issue in the middle of a trial or when a transaction is being finalized. Similarly, your supervising attorney may change an assignment because the client has charted a new course of action. If possible, budget extra time for the unexpected. You will be in a better position to take your work in new directions if necessary.

Writing Approaches

When you get an assignment, you must also determine what kind of writing approach is appropriate. Some documents call for objective analysis, meaning that you should present a balanced discussion of an issue or a neutral summary of facts. For a persuasive document you need to advocate for the client by presenting the law, issues, and facts in a favorable light.

A supervising attorney may ask you to consider whether certain clauses in two lease agreements create different legal obligations. Your assignment is not to argue that one agreement is better. Rather, you need to compare the documents objectively, pointing out which clauses lead to which obligations. Objective analysis may also be required when a document will help an attorney advise a client.

Clients often rely on their attorney to advise whether they have claims that justify filing suit. In such situations, the attorney may ask you to research the issue and draft a memorandum summarizing your analysis. Although you may be tempted to advocate for the client, it would be better to present an unbiased discussion. If the client has a weak claim, he or she should learn that before spending time and money on a hopeless lawsuit. You would not do the client any favors by predicting a favorable outcome that is ultimately unlikely.

If you are advocating for a client, in contrast, you need to write persuasively. For example, persuasive analysis is essential if you are drafting a motion asking a court to exclude certain evidence from a trial. When writing persuasively, you should present an analysis that clearly favors the client without misrepresenting the facts or the law.

Writing Well

Law is a communication-intensive profession, so writing is particularly important. For paralegals and attorneys, good writing skills go hand in hand with successful job performance. Some of your written work, such as correspondence, represents your employer to the outside world. Well-written documents reflect positively on your organization and enhance its reputation. See the *Developing Paralegal Skills* feature on the facing page for additional tips on quality document creation.

Tools for Writers

As you embark on your career, consider collecting a dictionary, a thesaurus, a style manual (such as *The Chicago Manual of Style*), and a book on proper English use (such as Strunk and White's *Elements of Style*). Those are tools common to all writers. Good *legal writing* benefits from using tools relevant to such work:

1. Legal writing requires accurate use of legal terminology. Words such as "trusts" or "consideration" have specific meanings that are not necessarily the same as

DEVELOPING PARALEGAL SKILLS

CREATING A USER-FRIENDLY DOCUMENT

Rianna Barnes works as a paralegal for a large law firm. A partner of the firm asks her to draft a policy on sexual harassment for a corporate client. The attorney gives Rianna several sheets of handwritten instructions and some notes on what the document should include. Rianna writes a draft and begins to proofread it.

She realizes that although she used plain English when possible and followed principles of good writing, the document is somewhat daunting in its appearance. She decides to add a series of headings and subheadings to break up the "fine print" and make the document more inviting to readers.

TIPS FOR CREATING A USER-FRIENDLY DOCUMENT

• Format the document attractively. For example, add enough margin space to make the text more inviting.

• Divide the document into sections with headings to make the organization immediately clear to the reader.

• Add subheadings to further divide large blocks of text. If you use subheadings, always create at least two.

• Make sure the relationships between sections and subsections are clear. You can often do this by drafting an introduction or using transitional sentences at the beginning of each section or subsection.

• Use short sentences, but do not overdo it. Too many short sentences in a row can make the writing choppy and interrupt the flow of the text.

• Use the active voice unless the situation calls for a passive construction (discussed on page 248).

• Use plain English whenever appropriate, especially when writing for readers who lack legal training.

• Be stylistically consistent. For example, do not hyphenate a phrase in one place but not others, and be sure to use the same line spacing between paragraphs throughout the document.

their meaning in ordinary speech. Use a legal dictionary regularly to ensure you have the right word. *Black's Law Dictionary* is the standard reference.

2. Legal writing has specific rules about how to refer to sources. These citation rules are quite complex, specifying everything from typeface to specific punctuation rules. The rules are set out in *The Bluebook: A Uniform System of Citation* (**legalbluebook.com**) and the Association of Legal Writing Directors' *Guide to Legal Citation* (**alwd.org**).

3. Legal writing requires clarity and organization. Legal writing guru (and editor of *Black's Law Dictionary*) Bryan Garner publishes *The Redbook: A Manual on Legal Style,* which provides detailed writing tips and numerous examples of model documents. One of Garner's tips is to read good writing (he recommends *The New Yorker* magazine, for example).

4. Legal writing requires specific organizational features. Some courts have explicit formats that must be followed, so you must learn any particular rules that apply. In general, appellate briefs typically must include a table of authorities, listing all sources cited and the page on which they are cited. Fortunately, electronic tools can both relieve the tedium of creating these reference lists and improve accuracy. Document-creation programs include tools to assist with citations. Specialized programs such as Best Authority and CiteIt! can help.

Next we consider elements needed to produce quality legal documents.

Choice of Format

A legal document's formatting can often be quite important. Rather than simply using your document-creation program's default settings for margin widths, paragraph indentations, line spacing, and so forth, you need to confirm that you are using the right formatting for the kind of document you are drafting. If you are drafting a document to be filed in court, you need to check the court's formatting rules, which are often available online. Your employer will probably also have special formats and even templates for other types of documents, such as letters and legal memoranda. If your employer has a format or template for the kind of document you are drafting, you should use it.

Write for Your Reader

Paralegals write for an audience. When you draft a legal document, you are writing for a judge, an attorney, a client, or a witness. To communicate information or ideas effectively, write with the reader's needs in mind. For example, you may use legal terms and concepts in a letter to an attorney, but those terms and concepts may confuse someone who lacks legal training. Similarly, a motion filed in court need not explain legal concepts in detail because your primary reader is the judge or the judge's clerk. A judge knows to follow a governing statute or a binding precedent of a higher court. Adding unnecessary background writing in such a document could distract or even annoy the judge, which will be unfavorable to your client's case.

In addition to the reader's legal knowledge, a paralegal should consider the reader's understanding of the subject matter. You cannot assume that the reader knows as much as you do, especially in cases involving complicated issues. You should normally assume that the reader lacks expertise in the area and is unfamiliar with the key facts and concepts. To help the reader, make the document understandable on its own terms. Be explicit about how everything fits together, leading the reader from Point A to Point B, from Point B to Point C, and so on. Write in a way that would have made sense to you before you began working on the matter.

Outline the Material

Once you know what you want to demonstrate, discuss, or prove to your reader, you must decide how to organize the material. Organization is essential to effective legal writing, so you should have a framework in mind before you begin writing. Most people find that writing is easier if they have an outline. For a simple writing assignment, you may need only to sketch an outline on a notepad. If you are drafting a complicated analysis of a legal issue, on the other hand, you may use a document creator to develop a detailed outline, complete with numbers, letters, and bullet points.

An outline helps you write more effectively and efficiently. Your first draft will be better organized, and you will spend less time moving material around.

When creating an outline, your first task is to decide the sequence in which topics should be discussed. Your goal is to organize the points you want to make in a logical fashion. Similar topics should be addressed together, and different topics should generally be addressed separately. Lawyers also often begin with their best points, especially when making arguments. As a matter of logic, however, you may need to work your way up to your best point by first establishing other things. As you outline, think about the advantages and disadvantages of different ways of organizing your information, paying special attention to the document's purpose and the reader's needs.

Organize the Material Logically

Once you begin writing, you need to divide the document into manageable blocks of information. As in an outline, similar topics should generally be addressed together. Also, when analyzing a topic that consists of several elements that must be proved, it is a good idea to address each element in the order in which the elements are required to be proved.

For example, in order to have a valid contract, there must be (1) an offer, (2) an acceptance, (3) an exchange of consideration, (4) legal subject matter, and (5) contractual capacity. As such, it would be logical to organize the material by first listing the elements to be proved and then analyzing each element in the order listed.

Purpose of a Paragraph

The most basic device for organizing ideas in a document is the paragraph. A paragraph is a group of sentences that develops a particular idea. A well-written paragraph often begins with a topic sentence that indicates what the paragraph is about. The paragraph's remaining sentences help develop the topic, leading the reader from one point to another. If a sentence does not relate to the topic of the paragraph, consider moving it to another paragraph or part of the document or simply deleting it.

When you write, be conscious of why and when you begin new paragraphs. In general, you should start a new paragraph whenever you begin discussing a new topic. If possible, however, you should also keep paragraphs relatively short. Long paragraphs are often hard to follow, and some topics are complicated enough that they deserve multiple paragraphs. As with outlining, you might try using different approaches to organization, seeing what works best given your writing objectives.

Be sure to take your reader with you as you move from one paragraph to another. Although the connections between paragraphs may be clear to you, they may not be clear to your reader. In places, you will need to provide transitional words and phrases to show the reader how different paragraphs relate to each other. Exhibit 9.1 below gives some examples of words and phrases that you can use to establish smooth transitions.

Use of Headings

In a long document, you may lead the reader through the discussion by adding descriptive headings and subheadings for different parts of the text. For example, if you are writing about a complex legal research project involving several issues, you may devote a separate section to each issue. You might make the document more reader friendly by providing an introductory "road map" that orients the reader by briefly identifying the issues. In places, you might also use bulleted or numbered lists to highlight key points or make complicated material more approachable. Try to write with the reader's needs in mind.

Proper Sequence

If your document discusses various events, it may help to arrange them chronologically — that is, in a time sequence. A chronologically structured discussion is often clearest,

chronologically
In a time sequence; naming or listing events in the time order in which they occurred.

EXHIBIT 9.1

Examples of Transitional Words and Phrases

1. **Indicating a series of ideas**
   first, second, third, next, then, finally

2. **Indicating a continuation of an idea**
   also, moreover, further, additionally

3. **Indicating a causal relationship**
   thus, therefore, hence, as a result, so, because

4. **Indicating a sequence of events**
   before, earlier, meanwhile, at the same time, next, later, then, afterward, eventually

5. **Indicating a contrast**
   although, however, nevertheless, in contrast, though

6. **Indicating a similarity**
   similarly, likewise, for the same reason

7. **Indicating a conclusion**
   in summary, in conclusion, to conclude, finally, in short

especially when you are describing a factual background leading to a lawsuit. You may also use chronological organization even when discussing legal issues. For example, you would probably need to structure a discussion chronologically if you are writing about how a particular rule has developed over time.

Write Effective Sentences

Most good writers prefer short, concrete sentences because they are easier to understand. Good writers write forcefully by using active verbs in place of nominalizations, which are verbs that have been transformed into nouns. For example, it is better to say "the plaintiff decided to settle" than "the plaintiff made a decision to settle." Similarly, you could change "make a statement" to "state," "take into consideration" to "consider," and "reach an agreement" to "agree." Strive to write concisely in every writing project. Wordy writing often obscures your points. Concise writing is clearer, more forceful, and more persuasive. See Exhibit 9.2 below for additional examples of how to write more concisely.

Active, Not Passive

Sentences are improved by using the active voice rather than the passive voice. The subject of an active-voice sentence is a person or thing that is *acting* ("The plaintiff filed a motion to exclude evidence"). The subject of a passive-voice sentence, in contrast, is a person or thing that is *being acted upon* ("A motion to exclude evidence was filed by the plaintiff"). The active voice is more direct and concise, and enlivens your writing by emphasizing who did what. In some cases you may use the passive voice to avoid referring to something inappropriate that your client may have done. For example, if your firm represents a defendant who has been accused of stealing a car, you may say "the car was stolen" instead of "the defendant allegedly stole the car."

Finally, it should go without saying, but be sure to write neatly. Typographical errors and punctuation mistakes reflect poorly on you, your employer, and the client. Here are some examples:

- *Incorrect:* The plaintiff should *of* told the defendant.

- *Correct:* The plaintiff should *have* told the defendant.

- *Incorrect:* *You're* hearing will be on December 15.

- *Correct:* *Your* hearing will be on December 15.

- *Incorrect:* The *plaintiffs* allegations are vague.

- *Correct:* The *plaintiff's* allegations are vague.

When proofreading, set aside time to check for basic writing mistakes. You must avoid them to produce acceptable, professional work.

EXHIBIT 9.2

Writing Concisely

Wordy	Concise
a period of five years	five years
as well as	and
at that point in time	then
due to the fact that	because
for the purpose of	for
in order to	to
in spite of the fact that	although
in the event that	if
it may be argued that	arguably
it seems probable that	probably
take into consideration	consider
whether or not	whether

Limit Legalese: Use Plain English

As discussed above, write with the reader's needs in mind. If you are writing for a person without legal training, minimize legalese, which consists of legal terms and phrases that may be unfamiliar to laypeople. Some novice legal writers assume that using legalese will impress the reader, but plain English will generally impress the reader more. When writing to someone without legal training, you should either define legal terms or avoid them altogether. For instance, you may refer to "*voir dire*" as simply "jury selection." You should generally avoid outdated words like "hereof," "therein," and "thereto."

Legal documents, especially contracts, also often contain a lot of unnecessary language. Consider a contractual provision that applies where a borrower makes a representation that is "false or erroneous or incorrect." What is the difference between being "false," being "erroneous," and being "incorrect"? These terms are interchangeable, and it is hard to imagine that something could be false without also being erroneous and incorrect. The contractual provision would achieve its intended purpose by applying only to false misrepresentations.

Although you should minimize legalese, you must also be careful to convey the right meaning. If you do not understand the purpose of specific language in a contract or pleading, ask your supervising attorney. For more information about writing in plain English, see the *Technology and Today's Paralegal* feature on the following page.

> **legalese**
> Legal language that is hard for the general public to understand.

Do Not Quote Heavily

Just as you should minimize legalese, you should limit quotations. Quotations can be effective if you use them sparingly, but numerous quotations create stylistic problems and rob a document of your voice and ideas.

When writing about the law, use quotations for the language that matters most and put everything else into your own words. If there is a statute on point, for example, you should probably quote it because its precise language matters. Similarly, you might quote a court's requirements for a claim or defense. But if the language itself does not matter, you should probably paraphrase it. Even when quoting an important rule, you usually need not quote the entire sentence. Instead, quote only the phrase or word that you want to emphasize, and weave it into your own sentence.

Avoid Sexist Language

Legal writing has traditionally used masculine pronouns to refer to both males and females, but there is a definite trend toward using gender-neutral language. Take special care to avoid sexist language in your own writing. For example, if you see a word with "man" or "men" in it (such as "policeman," "fireman," or "workmen's compensation"), use a gender-neutral substitute (such as "police officer," "firefighter," or "workers' compensation"). In the past few decades, writers have devised various ways to avoid sexist language, including the following:

- Use "he or she" rather than "he."
- Alternate between masculine and feminine pronouns.
- Make the noun plural so that a gender-neutral plural pronoun ("they," "their," or "them") can be used.
- Repeat the noun rather than using a pronoun.

Edit and Proofread Your Document

When you receive a writing assignment, budget time for editing and proofreading. Accuracy and precision are important for paralegal work, and a writer rarely turns out an error-free document on the first try. Proofreading helps you discover typographical errors, improve your document's organization, and confirm that the document says what it should. Do not expect your document-creation program's spell checker and grammar checker to catch everything. There is no substitute for printing out hard copies and reviewing them several times.

TECHNOLOGY AND TODAY'S PARALEGAL

ONLINE "PLAIN ENGLISH" GUIDELINES

The ability to write clearly and effectively is a valuable asset to any paralegal, because almost every paralegal's job requires writing. As mentioned elsewhere, clear and effective writing means keeping legalese—legal terminology typically understood only by legal professionals—to a minimum or even eliminating it entirely. The problem is how to convert traditional legal language into clear and understandable prose. Today's paralegals can find helpful instruction at many online locations on the art of writing in plain English.

GOVERNMENT PUBLICATIONS

The U.S. government publishes some of the best online plain English guides. *A Plain English Handbook,* put out by the Securities and Exchange Commission (SEC), is available at **sec.gov/pdf/handbook.pdf**. Although the handbook was intended to help individuals create clearer and more informative SEC disclosure documents, the booklet's guidelines apply generally. For guidelines on legal writing, see the Office of the Federal Register's booklet *Drafting Legal Documents* at **archives.gov**.

The U.S. government has an official website dedicated to the use of plain language (**plainlanguage.gov**) where you can find *Federal Plain Language Guidelines* and other helpful information.

GLOBAL CAMPAIGN FOR CLARITY

The plain English movement, which is fighting to have public information (such as laws) written in plain English, has received worldwide attention. A British organization called the Plain English Campaign is one of the most prominent groups in this movement. The Plain English Campaign has worked to promote the use of plain English in many nations, including the United States. You can find several helpful guides at its website (**plainenglishcampaign.com**), including *How to Write in Plain English* and *The A-Z of Alternative Words*. As businesses and the movement of people becomes ever more global, the ability to communicate clearly with non-native English speakers is critical in effective legal processes.

TECHNOLOGY TIP

Paralegals interested in improving their plain English writing skills have many Internet resources to which they can turn. The guides mentioned above provide practical information. In addition, paralegals can take online writing courses and use software programs that help edit writing.

Writing is a process, and good writers go through several drafts before filing a document in court or sending a letter to a client. When reviewing drafts, look for gaps in content. Confirm that points are fully developed and well organized, and ask yourself whether the document says what you intended. It is often helpful to read the document aloud or solicit feedback from someone who is unfamiliar with the case or topic. Another technique is to take a break and work on another project, then come back to review the document with fresh eyes.

When editing later drafts, pay attention to paragraph construction, sentence formation, word choice, and so forth. You might find it helpful to prepare a checklist to remind you of specific things to do or avoid—particularly if there is a required format for the kind of document you are drafting. Creating a polished product takes time, so spend time proofreading and revising. (Additional editing tips are offered in *Developing Paralegal Skills* on the facing page and in this chapter's *Featured Contributor* on pages 252 and 253.)

Take Advantage of Research and Writing Tools

Tools that assist in effective legal writing are continually coming on the market to improve accuracy and productivity. For example, Lexis for Microsoft Office is a legal drafting and review tool that runs within Word and Outlook. This tool is downloadable through Lexisnexis.com as an extension to Microsoft products. It requires a Lexis

DEVELOPING PARALEGAL SKILLS

EFFECTIVE EDITING

A supervising attorney asks paralegal Dixie Guiliano to draft a letter to an insurance company demanding it settle a dispute with a client. The client, Nora Ferguson, is an eighty-year-old woman who will never walk again because of a failed hip-replacement operation involving alleged malpractice by her surgeon. The attorney wants to settle the case out of court because of Nora's age and declining health.

Dixie creates the first draft using a settlement letter from another case as a sample. She then uses her document-creation program's spell-check and grammar-check features to look for errors. Dixie knows, however, that using these features is only a preliminary step in proofreading the document. She also knows that careful editing will improve the quality and persuasiveness of her letter.

TIPS FOR EDITING

- Always edit from a printed copy of the document. It is much easier to proofread and revise on paper than on a computer screen.

- If you use another document as a sample or if you cut and paste text from another document, double check that you have changed the names, dates, and other information accurately.

- Allow some time to pass (preferably a day) before editing the first draft so that you can review your writing more critically. Examine each draft in its entirety.

- Edit the content first. Ensure that the document is complete and says what you intended. Look for gaps in your reasoning. Make sure you have discussed all the points that you planned to discuss (including cases or statutes). Confirm that the document is well organized and progresses logically from one idea to another.

- Next, review for stylistic issues. Make sure the document is aimed at the appropriate audience and that you have omitted unnecessary words. Change passive voice into active voice, if possible. Make sure that the document is stylistically consistent.

- Check your grammar and spelling. For all sentences, confirm that verbs agree with subjects and that you use proper verb tenses. Check for punctuation problems with plurals, possessives, and commas.

Advance subscription and Windows operating system. Once installed, a LexisNexis ribbon appears in Word and Outlook.

The various buttons on the ribbon are useful when reading documents, but also when drafting legal documents. The "Get Cited Docs" button allows you to access all of the cited documents in a brief or memo, for example, and save them in virtual stacks as printable PDFs. You can also access *Shepard's* citation service to check the status of the cited laws and cases. Furthermore, this program gives you an efficient way to check *Bluebook* citations, automatically create a table of authorities, and check the accuracy of quotations.

Pleadings, Discovery, and Motions

Many paralegal writing tasks involve forms that must be submitted to courts or opposing counsel in connection with lawsuits or criminal prosecutions. These documents are covered in Chapters 10, 12, and 13. You can see those chapters for explanations and illustrations of specific pretrial forms (pleadings, discovery procedures, and pretrial motions) and for motions made during trials. Keep in mind that most documents submitted to courts should be written persuasively because they directly advocate for clients.

You should always know the rules of the specific court in which a document is being filed. If you cannot find a copy of a court's rules, ask your supervising attorney for help. It is critical that you use the correct formats and include all the right information.

FEATURED CONTRIBUTOR

TIPS FOR MAKING LEGAL WRITING EASIER

William Putman

BIOGRAPHICAL NOTE

William Putman received his Juris Doctor degree from the University of New Mexico School of Law and has been a member of the New Mexico Bar since 1975. For ten years, he was an instructor in the Paralegal Studies programs at Central New Mexico Community College in Albuquerque, New Mexico, and Santa Fe Community College in Santa Fe, New Mexico.

Putman is the author of the *Pocket Guide to Legal Writing* and the *Pocket Guide to Legal Research*. He also wrote the textbooks *Legal Analysis and Writing; Legal Research, Analysis, and Writing;* and *Legal Research.* He authored the legal writing column in *Legal Assistant Today* for two years and published several articles in that magazine on legal analysis and writing.

UNDERSTAND THE ASSIGNMENT

A legal-writing assignment may seem to be a daunting task. But all writing assignments are made easier if you answer some preliminary questions before you begin to conduct research or start writing.

What is the purpose of the assignment? An important step in the writing process is to be sure that you understand the task you have been assigned. If you have any questions concerning the general nature or specifics of the assignment, ask. Most attorneys welcome inquiries and prefer that a paralegal ask questions rather than proceed in a wrong direction. Misunderstanding the assignment can result in wasting a great deal of time performing the wrong task or addressing the wrong issue.

What type of legal writing (document) is required? Before you begin, determine what type of legal writing the assignment requires—a legal research memorandum, correspondence, the rough draft of a court brief, and so on. This is important because each type of legal writing serves a different function and has its own required elements and format.

Who is the audience? When assessing the requirements of an assignment, identify the intended audience. The intended reader may be a judge, an attorney, or a client. You should ensure that the writing meets the needs of that reader. A legal writing designed to inform a client or other layperson of the legal analysis of an issue is drafted differently than a writing designed to convey the same information to an attorney.

What are the constraints on the assignment? Most assignments have time and length constraints. Assignments usually have a time deadline. Typically, they should not exceed a certain number of pages. These constraints govern the amount of research you will conduct and require that you allocate sufficient time for both research and writing.

General Legal Correspondence

Paralegals often draft letters to clients, witnesses, opposing counsel, and others. Even when a message has already been conveyed orally to a party by phone or in person, you may write a letter confirming the discussion in writing. In fact, paralegals and lawyers often document communications. A letter helps prevent future problems by confirming that the conversation took place and resolving any ambiguities.

Most law firms and legal departments have official letterhead and stationery. The letterhead contains basic information about the firm or department, including its name, address, phone and fax numbers, and perhaps an e-mail address. Some law firms have more detailed letterhead that includes the names of partners or the locations of various offices. Always use your firm's or department's letterhead when representing your organization or writing a letter for an attorney. Put the correspondence's first page on letterhead paper and additional pages on plain, matching, numbered sheets.

What is the format for the type of document being prepared? Most law offices have rules or guidelines that govern the organization and format of most types of legal writing, such as case briefs, office memoranda, and correspondence. Courts have formal rules governing the format and style of briefs and other documents submitted for filing. Because the assignment must be drafted within the constraints of the required format, identify the format at the beginning of the process.

These preliminary questions are often overlooked or not given sufficient attention by beginning writers, resulting in headaches later. The task is made easier if you answer these questions.

SOME WRITING TIPS

Many paralegals assigned a legal-writing task find it difficult to make the transition from the research stage to the drafting stage. Here are some guidelines to help make the writing process easier.

Select the right time and place for your writing. Write during the time of day when you do your best work. For example, if you are a "morning person," write in the morning and save other tasks for later in the day. Also, make sure that the work environment is pleasant and physically comfortable. Have available all of the resources you will need—writing paper, a computer, research materials, and so on. Legal writing requires focus and concentration. Therefore, select a writing time and an environment that allow you to be as free from interruptions and distractions as possible.

Begin writing—do not procrastinate. Often, one of the most difficult steps in writing is starting to write. Do not put it off. The longer you put it off, the harder it will become to start your writing project. Start writing anything that has to do with the project. Do not expect what you start with to be great—just start. Once you begin writing, it will get easier.

Begin with a part of the assignment about which you feel confident. You do not have to write in the sequence of the outline. Write the easiest material first, especially if you are having trouble starting.

Do not try to make the first draft the final draft. The goal of the first draft should be to translate the research and analysis into organized paragraphs and sentences, not to produce a finished product. Just write the information in rough form. It is much easier to polish a rough draft than to try to make the first draft a finished product.

Do not begin to write until you are prepared. Do all the research and analysis before you begin to write. It is much easier to write a rough draft if you have completed the research and if the research is thorough.

If you become stuck, move to another part of the assignment. If you are stuck on a particular section, leave it. The mind continues to work on a problem when you are unaware of it. That is why solutions to problems often seem to appear in the morning. Let the subconscious work on the problem while you move on. The solution to the difficulty may become apparent when you return to the problem.

Establish a timetable. Break the project into logical units and allocate your time accordingly. This helps you avoid spending too much time on one section of the writing and running out of time. Do not become fanatical about the time schedule, however. You created the timetable, and you can break it. It is there as a guide to keep you on track and alert you to the overall time constraints.

> " All writing assignments are made easier if you answer some preliminary questions."

In this section, you will read about some common formats and types of legal correspondence. Keep in mind, though, that your employer will probably have its own forms, procedures, and requirements to follow.

General Format for Legal Correspondence

There are many types of legal correspondence, but most include the following components. See Exhibit 9.3 on the following page for a labeled example.

Date

Legal correspondence must be dated. The date appears below the official letterhead, and it should also be part of the file name on your computer. Typing the wrong date could have serious consequences, so make sure the date is right.

Dates serve important functions in legal matters. For example, the date of a letter may be critical to establish that someone had legal notice of a particular event.

EXHIBIT 9.3
Components of a Legal Letter

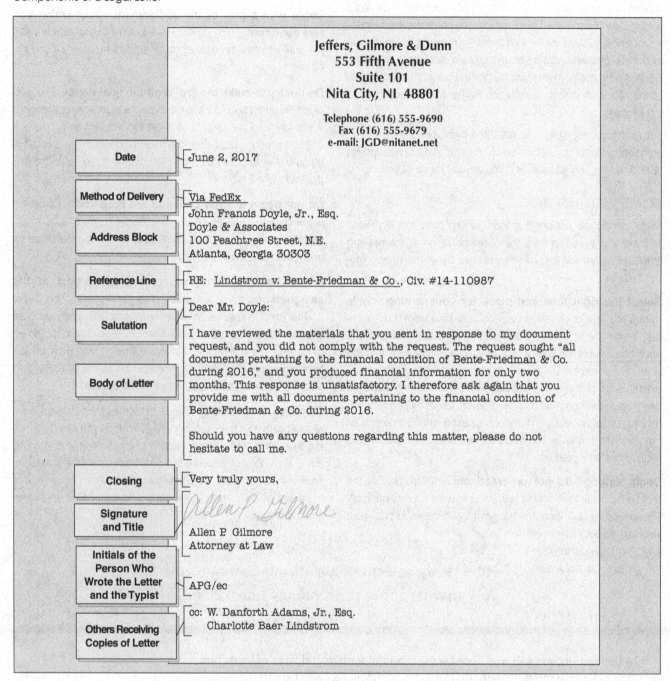

	Jeffers, Gilmore & Dunn **553 Fifth Avenue** **Suite 101** **Nita City, NI 48801** **Telephone (616) 555-9690** **Fax (616) 555-9679** **e-mail: JGD@nitanet.net**
Date	June 2, 2017
Method of Delivery	Via FedEx
Address Block	John Francis Doyle, Jr., Esq. Doyle & Associates 100 Peachtree Street, N.E. Atlanta, Georgia 30303
Reference Line	RE: Lindstrom v. Bente-Friedman & Co., Civ. #14-110987
Salutation	Dear Mr. Doyle:
Body of Letter	I have reviewed the materials that you sent in response to my document request, and you did not comply with the request. The request sought "all documents pertaining to the financial condition of Bente-Friedman & Co. during 2016," and you produced financial information for only two months. This response is unsatisfactory. I therefore ask again that you provide me with all documents pertaining to the financial condition of Bente-Friedman & Co. during 2016. Should you have any questions regarding this matter, please do not hesitate to call me.
Closing	Very truly yours,
Signature and Title	*Allen P Gilmore* Allen P Gilmore Attorney at Law
Initials of the Person Who Wrote the Letter and the Typist	APG/ec
Others Receiving Copies of Letter	cc: W. Danforth Adams, Jr., Esq. Charlotte Baer Lindstrom

Additionally, legal correspondence is normally filed chronologically. Without any record of the date, accurately filing a letter would be difficult if not impossible. As a general rule, place a date on every written item you create, including telephone messages, memos to file, and personal reminders.

Address Block and Method of Delivery

Below the date, you should give an **address block**. It indicates the name of the person to whom the letter is addressed. The address block should contain the person's name and title, and the name and address of the person's firm or place of business. If the letter is sent other than by U.S. mail, you should indicate the method of delivery in the line above the address block. If the letter is to be sent by FedEx, the line should read "Via

address block
The part of a letter that indicates to whom the letter is addressed. The address block is placed in the upper left-hand portion of the letter, above the salutation (and reference line, if one is included).

IN THE OFFICE

TIME MANAGEMENT

Many paralegals learn the hard way—through trial and error—that managing time effectively is an essential part of doing a good job. It is easy to forget that good writing takes time and that you may need to revise a document several times before you are satisfied with its quality.

When you receive a writing assignment, always give yourself enough time to revise and polish the final document. You have a duty to do the best work possible for your employer, your supervising attorney, and the client. To serve them well, you must manage your time effectively.

FedEx." Similarly, hand-delivered correspondence should say "By Hand Delivery," and fax communications can use the words "By Fax" or "By Facsimile." If a copy is sent as an attachment by e-mail, the communication should be in Portable Document Format (PDF) so it cannot be altered.

Reference Line and Salutation

Following the address block, a writer may include a **reference line** identifying the matter discussed in the letter. In a letter regarding a pending lawsuit, the reference line may contain the name of the case, its case file (or docket) number, and a brief notation about the nature of the dispute. Many attorneys also include the firm's file number for the case. In an informative letter (discussed below), the reference line may take the form of a title. For example, for a letter concerning the closing procedures for a financing transaction, the reference line may read "RE: Closing Procedures for ABC Company's $4,000,000 Financing Package."

Immediately below the reference line, you should provide the **salutation**, which is a greeting to the addressee. Because legal correspondence is a professional means of communication, you should generally call the person "Mr." or "Ms.," followed by the person's last name and a colon. Of course, it may be appropriate to address the person by his or her first name if you are writing to a friend or close acquaintance. Use your discretion to determine the appropriate level of formality. It is best to err on the side of being too formal.

reference line
The portion of the letter that indicates the matter to be discussed, such as "RE: Summary of Cases Applying the Family and Medical Leave Act of 1993." The reference line is placed just below the address block and above the salutation.

salutation
In a letter, the formal greeting to the addressee. The salutation is placed just below the reference line.

Body, Closing, and Signature

The main part of the letter is the body. The body's content varies depending on the letter's purpose, but it should always be written formally and communicate information effectively. If, for example, you are asking the recipient of your letter to respond in some way, be sure you are clear about what is expected and when a response is needed. A paralegal must carefully proofread all outgoing correspondence and confirm that it is accurate, well written, and free of grammatical and spelling errors. A carelessly written letter or e-mail reflects poorly on your employer and you.

The last part of the body typically consists of one or two concluding sentences. Final sentences are usually courteous statements, such as "Thank you for your time and attention to this matter" or "Should you have any questions or comments, please do not hesitate to contact me."

The last substantive part of a letter is the **closing**, which is followed by the writer's signature, name, and title. Closings in legal correspondence should be formal—for example, "Sincerely" or "Very truly yours." When you write a letter using your own signature, you should always include your title ("Paralegal") immediately after your name.

closing
In a letter, an ending word or phrase placed above the signature, such as "Sincerely" or "Very truly yours."

Similarly, you may include a line saying "Attorney at Law" when you write a letter to be signed by an attorney.

Types of Legal Letters

There are several types of legal correspondence, and each one serves a different purpose. The types of legal letters that you should be familiar with include informative letters, confirmation letters, opinion (or advisory) letters, and demand letters.

Informative Letters

informative letter
A letter that conveys information to a client, a witness, an adversary's counsel, or some other person regarding a legal matter (such as the date, time, place, and purpose of a meeting) or a cover letter that accompanies other documents being sent to a person or court.

An informative letter conveys information to another party. As a paralegal, you will likely write many such letters, and many will be to clients. You might write an informative letter to advise a client about recent developments in a case, to tell about an upcoming meeting or filing, to provide general background on a legal issue, or simply to break down the firm's bill. Write an informative letter so it is understandable to the client, given his or her education and experience.

Informative letters are also sent to opposing counsel and other parties. For example, law firms often send scheduling information to opposing counsel, witnesses, and other people involved in trials. Exhibit 9.4 below is a sample letter to a witness in an arbitration proceeding. An informative letter may also serve as a cover letter when you send someone documents.

Confirmation Letters

confirmation letter
A letter that summarizes an oral conversation to provide a permanent record of the discussion.

Paralegals also often write confirmation letters to communicate certain information. Confirmation letters differ, however, in that they mostly summarize conversations that

EXHIBIT 9.4
A Sample Informative Letter

Jeffers, Gilmore & Dunn
553 Fifth Avenue
Suite 101
Nita City, NI 48801

Telephone (616) 555-9690
Fax (616) 555-9679
e-mail: JGD@nitanet.net

June 25, 2017

Bernadette P. Williams
149 Snowflake Drive
Irving, TX 75062

RE: Kempf/Joseph Arbitration Proceedings

Dear Ms. Williams:

The arbitration will resume on Wednesday, August 6, 2017. Please arrive at the offices of the American Arbitration Association (the AAA) before 8:30 A.M. The offices of the AAA are located at 400 West Ferry Boulevard in Dallas. You will be called as a witness sometime before 12:00 noon.

Should you have any questions or concerns regarding your responsibilities as a witness, please do not hesitate to contact me.

Sincerely,

Elena Lopez

Elena Lopez
Paralegal

have already occurred. By providing attorneys with permanent records of conversations, confirmation letters safeguard against any misinterpretation or misunderstanding of what was said. If there is any disagreement about a conversation's details, an attorney can use a confirmation letter to support his or her account. See Exhibit 9.5 below for a sample confirmation letter.

Opinion Letters

The purpose of an opinion letter, or advisory letter, is to provide both information and advice. Unlike an informative letter, an opinion letter actually gives a legal opinion about the matter discussed. An attorney sending an opinion letter is required to provide a detailed analysis of the law and to bring the analysis to a definite conclusion that states a formal opinion.

An opinion letter may also advise a client about the legality of a course of action. An example of an opinion letter is seen on the following page in Exhibit 9.6. For example, a company planning to establish operations in a foreign country may seek a lawyer's opinion on whether certain conduct would be permissible. The attorney (or a paralegal) will research the issue and then draft an advisory letter to the client. Opinion letters are commonly quite long and include detailed explanations of how the law applies to the client. Sometimes, the attorney simply summarizes his or her conclusion in the opinion letter and attaches a detailed legal memorandum explaining the supporting law and analysis.

A firm's opinion letter reflects legal expertise and advice on which a client can rely. As discussed in the *Ethics Watch* feature on page 259, an attorney must sign an opinion

opinion (advisory) letter
A letter from an attorney to a client containing a legal opinion on an issue raised by the client's question or legal claim. The opinion is based on a detailed analysis of the law.

Jeffers, Gilmore & Dunn
553 Fifth Avenue
Suite 101
Nita City, NI 48801

Telephone (616) 555-9690
Fax (616) 555-9679
e-mail: JGD@nitanet.net

August 4, 2017

Pauline C. Dunbar
President
Minute-Magic Corporation
7689 Industrial Boulevard
San Francisco, CA 80021

RE: Purchase of real estate from C. C. Barnes, Inc.

Dear Ms. Dunbar:

As we discussed on the phone today, the Minute-Magic Corporation will purchase real estate located at 2683 Millwood Ave., Nita City, NI, from C. C. Barnes for $800,000. The purchase will be financed by a mortgage with Citiwide Bank at an interest rate of 5.5 percent.

I look forward to seeing you next week. If you have any questions or comments before then, please give me a call.

Very truly yours,

Allen P. Gilmore

Allen P. Gilmore
Attorney at Law

APG/ec

EXHIBIT 9.5
A Sample Confirmation Letter

letter. Should a client suffer a loss in a legal matter due to poor-quality legal advice or improper action by an attorney, the client may sue the firm for malpractice. An attorney's signature represents acceptance of responsibility for the document's content.

Demand Letters

demand letter
A letter in which one party explains its legal position in a dispute and requests that the recipient take some action, such as paying money owed.

Another basic type of letter is the demand letter. In a demand letter, one party explains its legal position in a dispute and demands that the recipient take some action. Typically, an attorney will send a demand letter before filing a lawsuit against a person or company. In fact, sending a demand letter may be required legal process, such as in many cases involving consumer-protection violations. Suppose your supervising attorney asks you to draft a letter demanding that a company pay a debt it owes to your firm's client. Your demand letter would summarize the relevant facts, demand payment by a certain date, and say that the client will sue if the company does not pay the debt.

Although a demand letter should be insistent and adversarial, it should not come across as unreasonable or harassing. After all, it seeks to accomplish something. For a sample demand letter, see Exhibit 9.7 on page 260. It covers the common situation of demanding that an adversarial party respond to a settlement offer in a lawsuit.

EXHIBIT 9.6
A Sample Opinion Letter

Jeffers, Gilmore & Dunn
553 Fifth Avenue
Suite 101
Nita City, NI 48801

Telephone (616) 555-9690
Fax (616) 555-9679
e-mail: JGD@nitanet.com

December 10, 2017

J. D. Joslyn
President and Chief Executive Officer
Joslyn Footwear, Inc.
700 Kings Avenue, Suite 4000
New City, NI 48023

Dear Ms. Joslyn:

After careful consideration, I have concluded that Joslyn Footwear, Inc., would risk significant liability by expanding into Latin American markets. The biggest problem concerns the proposed shoe-manufacturing plants. Due to their size, the plants would violate industrial regulations in Mexico, Uruguay, and Argentina.

The enclosed legal memorandum explains in detail how the law applies to your situation and the reasons for my conclusion. Please call me if you have any questions.

Very truly yours,

Allen P. Gilmore

Allen P. Gilmore
Attorney at Law

APG/ec

Enclosure

E-Mail Correspondence

Increasingly, legal professionals communicate by e-mail rather than by letter or telephone. E-mail often may be used for the same purposes as traditional correspondence with less formal content. For example, you might use e-mail to tell a client about recent case developments, to send copies of documents to a witness, or to confirm the details of a conversation. Nevertheless, it is still generally better to send hard copies of more formal legal documents, such as demand letters to opposing parties and formal opinion letters to clients. As always, follow your supervising attorney's preferences, being sure to include a standard confidentiality notice if your employer has one.

Most e-mails from a law office should be written formally. E-mails represent your employer and you to the outside world, and it should be presumed they never disappear. You should generally follow the same writing conventions that you would when drafting a letter. The salutation, for example, should generally address the recipient as "Mr." or "Ms.," and you should also write formally in the subject line, body, and closing. No

ETHICS WATCH

LETTERS AND THE UNAUTHORIZED PRACTICE OF LAW

As this text has stressed, engaging in the unauthorized practice of law is unlawful and unethical. To avoid liability for the unauthorized practice of law, never sign opinion or advisory letters with your own name, and when you sign other types of letters, always indicate your status as a paralegal. Even if you are sending a letter to a person who knows you well and knows that you are a paralegal, indicate your status on the letter itself. By doing so, you will prevent both potential confusion and potential legal liability. Even if your name and status are included in the letterhead, as some state laws allow, always type your title below your name as a precaution.

Here are some relevant rules and guidelines:

- NALA *Code of Ethics*, Canon 3: "A paralegal must not . . . give legal opinions or advice."

- NALA *Code of Ethics*, Canon 5: "A paralegal must disclose his or her status as a paralegal at the outset of any professional relationship with a client, an attorney, a court or administrative agency or personnel thereof, or a member of the general public."

- ABA *Model Guidelines* state that attorneys may not grant paralegals the authority to give legal opinions to clients.

- ABA *Model Guidelines* make clear that attorneys have a duty to be sure that clients and any other relevant parties, such as other lawyers, know that paralegals working with attorneys are not authorized to practice law.

- NFPA *Model Code of Ethics*, EC 1.7(a): "A paralegal's title shall clearly indicate the individual's status and shall be disclosed in all business and professional communications to avoid misunderstandings and misconceptions about the paralegal's role and responsibilities."

Reprinted by permission of the National Federation of Paralegal Associations, Inc. (NFPA®), www.paralegals.org.; Copyright 1975; Adopted 1975; Revised 1979, 1988, 1995, 2007. Reprinted with permission of NALA, the Association for Paralegals–Legal Assistants. Inquiries should be directed to NALA, 1516 S. Boston, #200, Tulsa, OK 74119, www.nala.org.

EXHIBIT 9.7

A Sample Demand Letter

Jeffers, Gilmore & Dunn
553 Fifth Avenue
Suite 101
Nita City, NI 48801

Telephone (616) 555-9690
Fax (616) 555-9679
e-mail: JGD@nitanet.com

June 13, 2017

Christopher P. Nelson, Esq.
Nelson, Johnson, Callan & Sietz
200 Way Bridge
Philadelphia, PA 40022

RE: *Fuentes v. Thompson*

Dear Mr. Nelson:

This morning, I met with my clients, Eduardo and Myrna Fuentes, the plaintiffs in the lawsuit against your client, Laura Thompson. Mr. and Mrs. Fuentes expressed a desire to withdraw their complaint and settle with Ms. Thompson. The Fuentes' settlement demand is $50,000, payable by certified check no later than July 15, 2017. We think that you and Ms. Thompson will find this offer quite reasonable. After all, given the strength of the Fuentes' claims, a jury award exceeding $200,000 is quite possible.

If you plan to take advantage of the Fuentes' settlement offer, please contact me by the close of business on Friday, June 20, 2017. If we do not hear from you by that date, we will assume that you have rejected our demand and we will proceed with litigation.

Very truly yours,

Allen P. Gilmore

Allen P. Gilmore
Attorney at Law

APG/ec

matter how short the e-mail, always proofread before clicking "send." As with letters, professionalism is highly important.

Also, before clicking on "send," reconfirm that the recipients are truly the ones who are supposed to receive the e-mail. It's easy to have added an incorrect recipient in the "To" line and in the "Cc" line (which comes from "carbon copy") or the "Bcc" line (which comes from "blind carbon copy").

The Legal Memorandum

A legal memorandum is prepared for internal use within a law firm, legal department, or other organization. Generally, a memo presents a thorough analysis of one or more specific legal issues.

As a paralegal, you may be asked to draft a legal memorandum for your supervising attorney. The attorney may need the memo for a number of reasons. For example, the attorney may be preparing an opinion letter or brief, either of which would require detailed legal analysis. To help your supervising attorney represent or advise a client more effectively, a memo should be thorough, well reasoned, and clearly written. Your primary reader is an attorney, so you need not explain basic legal concepts or define common legal terms. Instead, assume that your reader has general knowledge of the law but lacks expertise in the specific area you are discussing.

As with all legal documents, attention to detail is important. A memo must be accurate and neat. As the *Developing Paralegal Skills* feature below notes, you may be able to help improve the quality of documents drafted by attorneys.

Format

A legal memorandum must be well organized. There is no "right" way to structure a legal memo, but most are divided into sections that serve different purposes. The following sections are very common:

- a heading,
- the question(s) presented,
- brief answers to the questions presented,
- a statement of facts,
- a discussion of how the law applies to the facts, and
- a conclusion.

Of course, if your employer or supervising attorney prefers a particular format, you should follow it. Similarly, check for sample documents that your firm uses so that you can make use of them in preparing new memos.

Heading

The heading of a legal memorandum contains four types of information:

- The date on which the memo is submitted.

DEVELOPING PARALEGAL SKILLS

REVIEWING ATTORNEY-GENERATED DOCUMENTS

Ashana Carroll works as a paralegal for Jeremy O'Connell, a sole practitioner who owns a small general law practice. Jeremy frequently drafts motions and other legal documents because Ashana has her hands full with other writing tasks and general legal work. Typically, Jeremy e-mails his documents to Ashana, instructing her to send letters to recipients and file pleadings and motions in court. Ashana usually takes time to quickly review Jeremy's documents. Even though Jeremy has practiced law for years, Ashana occasionally finds errors in his documents, some of which could have serious consequences.

TIPS FOR REVIEWING AN ATTORNEY'S DOCUMENTS

- Confirm that all names and addresses are current and correct. The attorney may have forgotten that a client recently moved, for example, and mistakenly used an old address.

- If you are filing a document with a court, confirm that you have the most recent version of the court's rules. Court rules change, and it is important to ensure that the correct court rules are referenced in the document filed.

- Confirm that a document to be filed with a court complies with the court's rules concerning format, style, content, and deadlines. Also confirm that the document complies with the specific judge's preferences if you have them on file.

- Check with your supervising attorney if you have any question about how a particular document should be delivered.

EXHIBIT 9.8

Legal Memorandum—
Sample Heading

MEMORANDUM

DATE: August 6, 2017

TO: Allen P. Gilmore, Partner

FROM: Elena Lopez, Paralegal

RE: Neely, Raquel: Emotional Distress—File No. 00-2146
          Neely, Raquel, and D'andrea: Emotional Distress—File No. 00-2147

- The name of the person for whom the memo was prepared.
- The name of the person submitting the memo.
- A brief description of the matter, usually in the form of a reference line.

Exhibit 9.8 above illustrates a sample heading for a legal memorandum.

Questions Presented

The questions-presented section identifies the main legal issues that you discuss in the memorandum. Depending on how complicated the memo is, you may present one simple question or several more complicated questions. Often, a supervising attorney

EXHIBIT 9.9

Legal Memorandum—
Sample Statement of Facts

STATEMENT OF FACTS

Raquel Neely ("Neely") and her 11-year-old daughter, D'andrea Neely ("D'andrea"), seek advice in connection with possible emotional distress claims against Miles Thompson.

In October 2014, Neely and D'andrea moved from San Francisco to Union City, where Neely began working for an investment firm. At the firm, Neely worked for Thompson, and the two initially had a friendly, professional relationship. After about six months, however, their relationship soured when Thompson expressed romantic interest in Neely.

On April 1, 2016, Thompson visited Neely's house. D'andrea was home alone because Neely had gone to the grocery store, and Thompson invited D'andrea for a ride in his Corvette. Not knowing about her mother's problems with Thompson, D'andrea said yes. When Neely soon returned home to find D'andrea missing, she panicked and called the police.

Thompson drove D'andrea around Union City for approximately 30 minutes. During the drive, Thompson told D'andrea that her mother was a "selfish woman," that she did not care about her, and that she would leave her "once the right man comes along." As Thompson made his way back to Neely's house, an oncoming vehicle hit the car at the corner of Oak Street and Maple Road, where the Neelys live. According to the police report, Thompson had a high blood-alcohol level, indicating that he was drunk.

Neely heard the crash, ran outside, and approached Thompson's car. Neely then saw D'andrea bleeding profusely from head injuries, causing Neely to faint. She had to spend a day in Union City Hospital for extreme anxiety and trauma.

D'andrea spent two days in Union City Hospital, where she was kept under observation for possible internal injuries. D'andrea is also undergoing psychiatric therapy because of Thompson's comments. She is severely depressed and emotionally unstable, and she suffers from frequent nightmares.

QUESTIONS PRESENTED

I. Under California common law, may Raquel Neely recover for negligent infliction of emotional distress when she witnessed injuries to her daughter, D'andrea Neely, but was not herself hurt by the car accident that caused the injuries?

II. Under California common law, may D'andrea Neely recover against Miles Thompson for intentional infliction of emotional distress because he made statements to her that have made her emotionally unstable and have caused severe depression?

EXHIBIT 9.10

Legal Memorandum—
Sample Questions Presented

will identify the issues for you when asking you to write a memorandum. If so, you can use the attorney's request as a starting point for drafting this section of the memo.

Questions presented help bring the main issues into focus, and they should be case specific based on the facts. Each question should identify the governing law, briefly identify the issue, and explain the most important facts for that issue. See Exhibits 9.9 on the facing page and Exhibit 9.10 above for some examples.

Brief Answers

Brief answers respond to questions presented, and they should follow the same order. An answer's length will depend on the issue's complexity, but each answer should probably be only a few sentences long. Try to begin with a one- or two-word answer to the question, like "yes," "no," "probably," or "probably not." After giving a short answer, explain your reasoning in one to three sentences. Your goal is to give an overview of the discussion section, which will examine the issue in greater detail. See Exhibit 9.10 above for questions to be presented in the memo, and Exhibit 9.11 below for sample answers to those questions.

Statement of Facts

The statement of facts provides a factual background for the reader, focusing primarily on the facts that are relevant to the legal issues discussed in the rest of the memo. Facts are relevant if they have a bearing on your analysis, which will appear in the memo's discussion section. Therefore, you may consider writing the statement of facts after drafting the discussion section, even though the statement of facts will appear earlier in the final document. See which facts are important for your analysis, and then use them as a starting point for drafting the statement of facts. That approach also ensures that the statement of facts is thorough, so that the reader does not learn new details about the facts later in the memo.

BRIEF ANSWERS

I. Probably not. California courts require someone not injured physically to have been present at the scene of the injury-producing event at the time of the event. In this case, Neely did not witness the accident itself, merely the aftermath.

II. Probably. To recover for intentional infliction of emotional distress, a plaintiff must prove that the defendant (1) intended to cause emotional distress or was substantially certain it would result, (2) in fact caused severe emotional distress, and (3) engaged in outrageous conduct. In this case, all three requirements are probably satisfied.

EXHIBIT 9.11

Legal Memorandum—
Sample Brief Answers

STAY OBJECTIVE.   Like other parts of the memo, the statement of facts should be objective. This section should not present an argument for the client. Rather, it gives an objective, dispassionate summary of the key facts. You should never omit facts that are unfavorable to the client's case. To help the client, your supervising attorney needs to know everything.

IMPORTANCE OF ORGANIZATION.   The statement of facts must also be well organized. For example, you can help orient the reader by providing an introductory paragraph that briefly explains the client's issue, as in the sample statement of facts in Exhibit 9.9 on page 262. After a short introductory paragraph, you should explain the key facts in a logical order. For many memos, a chronological organization will work well, especially if the facts are relatively simple. If the facts are complicated, you might try a more topical organization that devotes separate paragraphs to various kinds of facts. Feel free to experiment with different ways of organizing and see what works best, given the subject matter and the reader's needs.

Discussion

The discussion section presents the writer's detailed analysis of how the law applies to the facts. Some memos address only one main issue, but many address multiple issues. If a memo discusses more than one issue, you may need to divide the discussion section into subsections. For example, if a memo discusses a client's potential claims for both negligent and intentional infliction of emotional distress, you may devote a separate subsection to each cause of action, providing a descriptive heading for each.

To be consistent, you should follow the discussion section's organization in other sections of the memo. Thus, if you address negligent infliction first in the discussion section, you should also address it first in the questions presented, brief answers, statement of facts, and conclusion sections.

The Heart of the Memorandum

The discussion section is the heart of a legal memorandum, and it should explicitly summarize both your research and analysis. A good memorandum should answer the following kinds of questions for each issue:

- What is the probability that the client will succeed? For example, does the client have a claim or defense?

- What law governs the issue?

- Is there a statute on point? If so, how does it apply to the client's case? Are the statute's requirements satisfied?

- Are there any cases on point? If so, how do they apply to the client's case? Are the court's rules satisfied? How is the client's case similar to the precedents? How does it differ?

Your analysis should be objective because the memo's purpose is to help an attorney represent or advise a client. The discussion section should candidly evaluate both the strengths and weaknesses of the client's position. If there is a problem with the client's position, you should address it. After all, the supervising attorney can deal with the problem much more effectively if he or she knows about it early on. Remember that your goal is to help the attorney.

IRAC

Like other kinds of legal writing, the discussion section must be well organized. You can keep the discussion clear by using IRAC, which stands for *issue, rule, application, conclusion*. As discussed in Chapter 7, IRAC is an organizational device that helps you present your analysis in a logical order. If you analyze multiple issues or rules of law you should probably present multiple IRACs for each rule you analyze. For each IRAC:

1. Identify the *issue*.

2. Explain the governing *rule*, which may come from statutory provisions, cases on point, or administrative agency regulations.

3. *Apply* the rule to the facts of the client's case.

4. State your *conclusion*.

Then repeat the process until all of the rules from various sources have been applied to the client's case.

Exhibit 9.12 below presents an excerpt from a simple discussion section that uses IRAC. The exhibit identifies the elements of IRAC for illustration purposes, but you would omit them, of course, from a memorandum to a supervising attorney. Also note

EXHIBIT 9.12

Legal Memorandum—
Sample Discussion (Excerpt
Using the IRAC Method)

DISCUSSION (Excerpt)

I. Negligent Infliction of Emotional Distress

Issue   The first issue is whether Neely can recover for negligent infliction of emotional distress because she witnessed injuries to her daughter D'andrea.

Rule   All the relevant events occurred in California, so California law governs this case. There is no statute on point, but California has rejected the "impact rule" that prevents a party from recovering when a plaintiff alleges emotional distress caused by merely witnessing a third party's injuries. 48 Cal.3d 644, 771 P.2d 814 (Cal. 1989) concerned a claim brought by a woman whose child was struck by a car. The mother did not see the accident, but saw her injured child unconscious and bleeding on the road when she arrived on the scene.

Under California's approach, a plaintiff must satisfy three elements to recover for negligent infliction of emotional distress based on injury to another person: (1) the plaintiff must be closely related to the victim; (2) the plaintiff must be present at the scene of the injury-producing event at the time it occurs and be contemporaneously aware that the injury is being caused; and (3) the plaintiff must suffer serious emotional distress as a result.

California adopted this rule, severely limiting the circumstances under which a negligent infliction claim could be brought, out of concern that an expanding "circle of liability" would result unless the law restricted who could bring such claims. 187 Cal.App.4th 926, 934–935, 114 Cal. Rptr.3d 661, 667 (Cal. App. 2 Dist. 2010). The California courts have held that "The merely negligent actor does not owe a duty the law will recognize to make monetary amends to all persons who have suffered emotional distress on viewing or learning about the injurious consequences of his conduct." 48 Cal.3d 664, 668, 257 Cal.Rptr. 865, 771 P.2d 814.

Application   In this case, Neely did not witness the car crash that injured D'andrea. Rather, she was inside her house when the accident occurred. The facts of her case are thus almost exactly identical to those in which the California Supreme Court rejected an analogous claim. Moreover, recent California court decisions cite approvingly and do not suggest any movement to relax the rule announced.

Conclusion   Because Neely did not witness the accident, she probably cannot recover for negligent infliction of emotional distress. The law is well settled in this area, and Neely is unlikely to prevail on that claim.

EXHIBIT 9.13

Legal Memorandum—
Sample Conclusion

CONCLUSION

Neely probably does not have a cause of action against Thompson for negligent infliction of emotional distress because she did not witness the accident that caused D'andrea's injuries. However, D'andrea probably has a cause of action for intentional infliction of emotional distress based on Thompson's outrageous comments to her about her mother and convincing her to ride in a car he was driving while drunk.

Neely might also pursue, on her own behalf, a claim that Thompson intentionally inflicted emotional distress by taking D'andrea from her home and making outrageous statements about her mother. I recommend that we talk to Neely about how Thompson's statements affected her. If it can be shown that Thompson intentionally or recklessly caused emotional distress, there may be a claim for Neely.

---

that the sample discussion provides citations to legal authorities for various points of law. As mentioned in Chapter 7, there are citation guides, including *The Bluebook: A Uniform System of Citation* and the *ALWD Citation Manual*. You should use the one that your supervising attorney prefers.

Conclusion

The conclusion is the culmination of the legal memo. The discussion section has examined the issues in detail, evaluating the strengths and weaknesses of the client's position. The conclusion is your opinion of how to resolve the issues. Exhibit 9.13 above gives an example.

The conclusion may acknowledge that research into a particular area bore little fruit. For example, there may be no cases on point addressing one of the issues. The conclusion may also inform the attorney that more facts are needed or suggest that a certain issue needs to be explored more fully. Finally, this section gives you an opportunity to make strategic suggestions. Paralegals should feel comfortable to recommend specific courses of action, especially after conducting a careful analysis. Your judgment will be helpful to your supervising attorney.

KEY TERMS AND CONCEPTS

Chapter Summary / Legal Writing: Form and Substance

RECEIVING A WRITING ASSIGNMENT

When receiving a writing assignment, a paralegal should learn the nature of the assignment, when the assignment is due, and what kind of writing approach should be used.

1. *Understanding the assignment*—Getting clear direction about an assignment is important so that you do not waste time working needlessly on something

or taking the wrong approach because you did not receive clear direction about the kind of assignment.

2. *Time constraints and flexibility*—Knowing and adhering to deadlines is essential. Some matters, such as those arising during a trial, will have to be addressed very quickly.

3. *Writing approaches*—Some documents, such as pretrial motions, are persuasive and require the writer to advocate for a particular position. Background material should generally be analytical and not be biased in favor of the client so that the case can be assessed objectively.

WRITING WELL

Good writing skills are essential for preparing legal documents. With experience and practice, you will improve your writing.

1. *Choice of format*—The document should be well organized and in the appropriate format. Most firms use specific templates, and courts often require certain formats in documents submitted to them.

2. *Write for your reader*—Tailor your writing for the intended reader. Documents written for a supervising attorney, a judge, and a client will each have a different style and varying levels of writing.

3. *Outline the material*—Create an outline before you begin writing. To help the reader follow the discussion, write effective paragraphs and provide transitions between ideas.

4. *Organize the material logically*—Large assignments should be broken into manageable blocks that can be organized in logical paragraphs. There should be headings between groups of paragraphs to help frame the presentation in an orderly sequence.

5. *Write effective sentences*—Draft short, concrete sentences with active verbs. Generally use the active voice, in which the sentence's subject is the actor, rather than the passive voice, in which the subject is being acted upon. Limit legalese—it is usually better to use plain English so the reader understands what is being said. Do not quote heavily, and use gender-neutral language.

6. *Edit and proofread your document*—Creating a polished product takes time, and you should spend much of that time proofreading and revising both on the computer and on hard copy. Confirm that the document is thorough, well organized, and neat.

PLEADINGS, DISCOVERY, AND MOTIONS

Paralegals often help draft litigation documents, which should almost always be persuasive. When drafting a document for court, always follow the court's rules concerning formatting and other issues.

GENERAL LEGAL CORRESPONDENCE

Paralegals frequently draft letters to clients, witnesses, opposing counsel, and others.

1. *Format*—Most firms and legal departments have preferred formats for legal correspondence. The first page of a letter is typically printed on the firm's letterhead. Letters should generally be formal in tone and include the following:

   a. The date.

   b. The address block and the method of delivery.

   c. The reference line (including case or file numbers when appropriate) and the salutation.

   d. The body of the letter, the closing, and the signature.

2. *Types of letters*—Paralegals commonly draft the following types of letters:

   a. Informative letters notify clients or others about something, or serve as cover letters when sending someone documents.

   b. Confirmation letters summarize oral conversations that have already occurred.

   c. Opinion letters convey a formal legal opinion about an issue or give formal advice. Only an attorney can sign an opinion letter.

   d. A demand letter explains a party's legal position in a dispute and demands that the recipient take some action, such as paying money owed.

THE LEGAL MEMORANDUM

A legal memorandum is a thoroughly researched analysis of one or more legal issues. A memo's purpose is to inform a supervising attorney about the strengths and weaknesses of a client's position.

1. *Format*—Generally, a legal memo includes the following sections:

   a. Heading

b. Questions presented

c. Brief answers

d. Statement of facts

e. Discussion and conclusion

2. *The heart of the memorandum*—The discussion section will clearly state your research and analysis objectively, summarizing strengths and weaknesses of a case and the relevant law.

3. *IRAC*—You can make your analysis of an issue clear by using the IRAC method, which stands for *issue, rule, application, conclusion.*

QUESTIONS FOR REVIEW

1. What are the three things you should consider when receiving a legal writing assignment?

2. Why is it important for paralegals to have good writing skills? What is the active voice? What is the passive voice? Why is it better to use the active voice in your legal writing?

3. List the components of a typical legal letter. What are the four types of letters discussed in this chapter? What is each letter's purpose?

4. How is a legal memorandum organized? List and describe its components. What is IRAC? How is IRAC used in a legal memorandum?

5. Should a memorandum be objective or persuasive? Why?

ETHICS QUESTION

A lawyer filed a complaint with a court that was badly drafted. After giving the lawyer an additional opportunity to correct and refile it, the court dismissed the complaint with prejudice (meaning that the complaint cannot be revised and refiled). One sentence in the complaint contained 345 words, and more than 20 other sentences contained over 100 words and were unintelligible. On appeal, the appellate court affirmed dismissal of the complaint with prejudice, issued an order to show cause to the attorney instructing him to explain to the court why he should not be barred from practicing law before the court, and directed the court clerk to send its opinion to the state ethics board. What ethics rules did the attorney violate? Would it make a difference if the attorney's writing problems were caused by a serious illness?

PRACTICE QUESTIONS AND ASSIGNMENTS

1. Proofread the following paragraph, circling all of the mistakes. Then rewrite the paragraph.

The defendent was arested and charge with drunk driving. Blood alcohol level of .15. He refused to take a breahalyzer test at first. After the police explained to him that he would loose his lisense if he did not take it, he concented. He also has a blood test to verify the results of the breathalyzer.

2. Prepare an informative letter to a client using the following facts:

The client, Dr. Brown, is being sued for medical malpractice and is going to be deposed on January 15, 2016, at 1:00 P.M. The deposition will take place at the law offices of Callaghan & Young.

The law office address is 151 East Jefferson Avenue, Cincinnati, Ohio. Ask Dr. Brown to call you to set up an appointment, so that you and your supervising attorney, Jeffrey Brilliant, can prepare Dr. Brown for the deposition.

3. Summarize the following hypothetical by applying the IRAC method:

Mr. Damien is a teacher at the Wabash Academy, a private boarding school. He has a twenty-one-year-old son, Dave, with bipolar affective disorder, formerly called manic depression, a mood disorder. While visiting Mr. Damien, Dave has repeatedly threatened members of the school community. On one occasion, Dave abducted the headmaster's sixteen-year-old daughter and attempted to have her admitted to a psychiatric hospital. Dave also made threatening phone calls to the headmaster. In one call, he claimed to have drained several quarts of his own blood from his body because he was not permitted to communicate with the headmaster's daughter. Mr. and Mrs. Damien refuse to prevent their son from visiting their home on the school's campus. As a result, the school has fired Mr. Damien. He claims that the termination of his employment violates the Americans with Disabilities Act (ADA) of 1990.

The ADA prohibits an employer from discriminating against a person because he or she is related to a person with disabilities. Under case law interpreting the ADA, however, employment is not protected if a disabled relative poses a direct threat to the health and safety of others.

4. If you did the research required by the *Practice Questions and Assignments* at the end of Chapter 7, prepare a legal memorandum summarizing Ms. Consumer's legal problem and her options for resolution. Be sure to use the IRAC method and include the statutory provisions and cases on point from your research.

■ GROUP PROJECT

In this assignment, students will document the benefits of using plain English in legal writing. To complete the assignment, refer to the Securities and Exchange Commission's *A Plain English Handbook* at **sec.gov/pdf/handbook.pdf**. (If you do not know what the Securities and Exchange Commission does, do an Internet search before doing this assignment.)

Student one will review the preface and describe the "unoriginal but useful" writing tip given by the author.

Student two will review Chapter 1 of the handbook and write a definition of a plain English document.

Student three will provide two pairs of "before" and "after" examples from Chapter 6 of the handbook showing how plain English improved sentences in SEC-disclosure documents.

Student four will summarize the information found by students one, two, and three, using their examples to describe the benefits of using plain English in legal documents.

■ INTERNET PROJECTS

1. Go to The Oatmeal website at **theoatmeal.com/comics/misspelling**.

   a. Explain the proper use of the following words:

   - The different spellings of the words that sound like *there*.

   - *Its* and *it's*.

   - *Then* and *than*.

   - *Affect* and *effect*.

   b. Click on the link to "Grammar" and find "How to Use an Apostrophe." Explain how an apostrophe is used with possessives.

CHAPTER 10

Civil Litigation: Before the Trial

CHAPTER OBJECTIVES

After completing this chapter, you will know:

• The basic steps involved in the civil litigation process and the types of tasks that may be required of paralegals during each step of the pretrial phase.

• What a litigation file is, what it contains, and how it is organized, maintained, and reviewed.

• How a lawsuit is initiated and what documents and motions are filed during the pleadings stage of the civil litigation process.

• What discovery is and what kinds of information attorneys and their paralegals obtain from parties to the lawsuit and from witnesses when preparing for trial.

Introduction

Every paralegal should be acquainted with the basic phases of civil litigation and the forms and terminology commonly used in the process. The paralegal plays an important role in helping the trial attorney prepare for and conduct a civil trial. Preparation involves a variety of tasks including:

- Carefully researching relevant law.
- Gathering and documenting evidence.
- Creating and organizing the litigation file.
- Meeting procedural requirements and deadlines for filing documents with the court.
- Preparing witnesses—persons asked to testify at trial—in advance and making sure they are available to testify during the trial.
- Preparing trial exhibits, such as charts, photographs, or video recordings.
- Making arrangements to have any necessary equipment, such as a video player, laptop, and projector, available for use at the trial.

witness
A person who is asked to testify under oath at a trial.

Paralegals' efforts are critically important in preparing for trial, and attorneys usually rely on paralegals to ensure that nothing has been overlooked.

The need for accuracy at even a simple civil trial requires that the paralegal be familiar with the litigation process and courtroom procedures. While we discuss the major elements of that process here, much expertise can be acquired only through hands-on experience. Attorneys may request that their paralegals assist them during the trial as well. In the courtroom, a paralegal performs numerous tasks. For example, the paralegal can locate documents or exhibits as they are needed. The paralegal can also observe jurors' reactions to statements made by attorneys or witnesses, check to see if a witness's testimony is consistent with sworn statements made by the witness before the trial, and give witnesses last-minute instructions outside the courtroom before they are called to testify.

In this chapter, you learn about the pretrial stages of a civil lawsuit, from the initial attorney-client meeting to the time of trial. In the next chapter, you will read about conducting investigations and interviews prior to trial. The *Featured Contributor* on pages 274 and 275 provides ideas about developing a plan.

Civil Litigation—A Bird's-Eye View

Although civil trials vary greatly in terms of complexity, cost, and detail, they share similar structural characteristics. They begin with an event that gives rise to the legal action, and (provided the case is not settled by the parties at some point during the litigation process—as most cases are) they end with the issuance of a judgment, the court's decision on the matter. In the process, the litigation itself may involve many twists and turns. Even though each case has its own "story line," most civil lawsuits follow some version of the course charted in Exhibit 10.1 on the following page.

judgment
The court's final decision regarding the rights and claims of the parties to a lawsuit.

Pretrial Settlements

In most cases, the parties reach a *settlement*—an out-of-court resolution of the dispute—before the case goes to trial. Lawsuits are costly in both time and money, and it is usually in the interest of both parties to settle the case out of court. Throughout the pretrial stage of litigation, the attorney will therefore attempt to help the parties reach a settlement. At the same time, the attorney and the paralegal must operate under the assumption that the case will go to trial, because all pretrial preparation must be completed prior to the trial date.

EXHIBIT 10.1

A Typical Case Flowchart

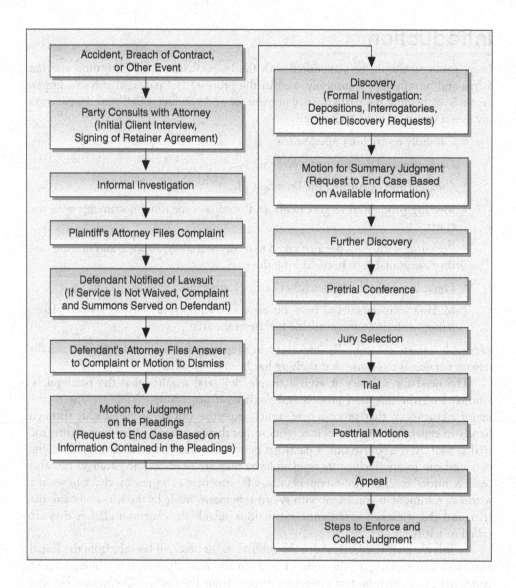

Procedural Requirements

Understanding and meeting procedural requirements are essential in the litigation process. These requirements are set out in the procedural rules of the court in which a lawsuit is brought. Civil trials held in federal district courts are governed by the Federal Rules of Civil Procedure (FRCP). These rules specify what must be done during the various stages of the federal civil litigation process. For example, Rule 4 of the FRCP describes the procedures that must be followed in notifying the defendant of the lawsuit.

Each state also has its own rules of civil procedure (which in many states are similar to the FRCP). In addition, many courts have their own rules of procedure that supplement the federal or state rules. The attorney and the paralegal must comply with all of the rules of procedure that apply to the specific court in which the trial will take place.

A Hypothetical Lawsuit

To illustrate the procedures involved in litigation, consider a hypothetical civil lawsuit. The case involves an automobile accident in which a car driven by Tony Peretto collided with a car driven by Katherine Baranski. Baranski suffered injuries and incurred substantial medical and hospital costs. She also lost wages for the five months in which she was unable to work. Baranski has decided to sue Peretto for damages. Because Baranski is the person bringing the lawsuit, she is the plaintiff. Peretto, because he must defend

Federal Rules of Civil Procedure (FRCP)

The rules controlling all procedural matters in civil trials brought before the federal district courts.

against Baranski's claims, is the defendant. The plaintiff and the defendant are referred to as the *parties* to the lawsuit, as discussed in Chapter 5. (Some cases involve several plaintiffs and/or defendants.)

The attorney for the plaintiff (Baranski) is Allen P. Gilmore. Gilmore is assisted by paralegal Elena Lopez. The attorney for the defendant (Peretto) is Elizabeth A. Cameron. Cameron is assisted by paralegal Gordon McVay. Throughout this chapter and the following two chapters, *Case at a Glance* features in the page margins remind you of the names of the participants in this lawsuit.

The Preliminaries

Katherine Baranski arranges to meet with Allen Gilmore, an attorney with the law firm of Jeffers, Gilmore & Dunn, to see if Gilmore will represent her in the lawsuit. Gilmore asks paralegal Elena Lopez to prepare the usual forms and information sheets, including a retainer agreement and a statement of the firm's billing procedures, and to bring them to the initial interview with Baranski. Gilmore also asks Lopez to run a conflicts check (see Chapter 4) to ensure that representing Baranski in this action will not create a conflict of interest.

The Initial Client Interview

Most often, the attorney—for several reasons—conducts an initial client interview. First, if attorney Gilmore is interested in taking on a new client, he will want to explain to the client the value of his services and those of his firm. Second, only an attorney can agree to represent a client. Third, only an attorney can set fees, and if Gilmore takes Baranski on as a client, fee arrangements will be discussed, and possibly agreed on, during the initial client interview. Finally, only an attorney can give legal advice, and the initial client interview may involve advising Baranski of her legal rights and options. In short, what transpires during the initial client interview normally falls under the umbrella of "the practice of law," and, as you read in Chapter 4, only attorneys are permitted to practice law.

Because attorney Gilmore and paralegal Lopez will be working together on the case, Gilmore asks Lopez to sit in on the interview. Gilmore wants Lopez to meet Baranski, become familiar with Baranski's claim, and perhaps make arrangements for follow-up interviews with Baranski should Gilmore take the case.

Collecting Facts

During the initial client interview, Katherine Baranski explains to attorney Gilmore and paralegal Lopez the facts of her case as she perceives them. Baranski tells them that Tony Peretto, who was driving a Dodge van, ran a stop sign and crashed into the driver's side of her Ford Fusion as she was driving through the intersection of Mattis Avenue and Thirty-eighth Street in Nita City, Nita. The accident occurred at 7:45 A.M. on August 4, 2016. Baranski has misplaced Peretto's address, but she knows that he lives in another state, the state of Zero.[1] Baranski claims that as a result of the accident, she has been unable to work for five months and has lost about $20,000 in wages. Her medical and hospital expenses total $95,000, and the damage to her car is estimated to be $15,000. Throughout the initial interview, Lopez takes notes to record the details of the case as relayed by Baranski.

Release Forms

Gilmore agrees to represent Baranski in the lawsuit against Peretto. He explains the fee structure to Baranski, and she signs the retainer agreement. Gilmore has Baranski sign forms authorizing him to obtain relevant medical, employment, and other records

FEATURED CONTRIBUTOR

CIVIL LITIGATION: BEFORE THE TRIAL

Loretta Calvert

BIOGRAPHICAL NOTE

Loretta Calvert graduated from NYU School of Law in 1998 and worked at Sullivan & Cromwell as a full-time associate doing complex commercial litigation. Ms. Calvert is the Paralegal Studies Director for Volunteer State Community College, an ABA-approved program. She has taken groups of students to Europe for research projects and produced DVDs with titles including *Dutch Cannabis Policy, Criminal Law in the UK,* and *Prostitution: An International Perspective*. She has presented at various conferences in the United States and served as the AAfPE president for 2012–2013.

For some paralegals working in litigation, this can be the fun part of pursuing a claim or defending a client. This idea may seem strange to you. "Fun?" you think. "A person's marriage, job, or freedom is at stake." Keep a careful distance in cases and remember that the client's problem is not your problem. Otherwise, you will be prone to burnout and stress. When representing a client, settlement is always possible at any time before, during, or after trial. However, many cases settle during this phase because of discovery. A paralegal who has taken the time to organize the client's case file and potential evidence dur-

ing the discovery phase helps the attorney decide what advice to give the client. I was once disappointed when a large case settled before trial. My supervising partner told me to be happy. The reason the case settled was because our litigation team did an excellent job during discovery.

DRAFTING COMPLAINTS

Now, when drafting a complaint there are two schools of thought. One, you throw everything in the complaint. Any reasonable claim that has some legal probability (remember, you can't put in

relating to the claim. (These *release forms* will be discussed in Chapter 11.) At the end of the interview, Gilmore asks Lopez to schedule a follow-up interview with Baranski. Lopez conducts that interview and obtains more details from Baranski about the accident and its consequences.

Preliminary Investigation

After Baranski leaves the office, attorney Gilmore asks paralegal Lopez to undertake a preliminary investigation to get as much information as possible concerning the facts of Baranski's accident. Sources of this information will include the police report of the accident, medical records, employment data, and eyewitness accounts of the accident.

You will read in Chapter 11 about the steps in investigating the facts of a client's case, so we will not discuss investigation here. Bear in mind that at this point in the pretrial process, the paralegal may engage in extensive investigation of the facts. Investigation is a key part of pretrial work, and facts discovered (or not discovered) by the investigator may play an important role in determining the outcome of the lawsuit.

Creating the Litigation File

Attorney Gilmore also asks paralegal Lopez to create a litigation file for the case. As the litigation progresses, Lopez will carefully maintain the file to make sure that such a frivolous claim; otherwise, you violate the rules) goes into the complaint in an effort to overwhelm the other side with volume. For example, on a tort claim you may have a clear assault and battery claim, but you throw in negligence just in case all the elements turn out not to be so clear on assault and battery.

The second option is to carefully select only the best claims, ones you know you will be able to establish all the elements on easily. For example, the client may have been discriminated against because of gender and race; however, most of the client's statements lean to gender issues. In that case, the attorney may decide to pursue only gender discrimination. Besides, you could try to amend a complaint later if circumstances change.

DISCOVERY

After the initial pleadings are out of the way, the parties will probably get down to discovery. This is the phase that makes or breaks a case because if you don't have the evidence to prove an element, you run the risk of losing at trial. Paralegals can use software to organize mounds of documentary evidence.

Electronic evidence grows every day in its importance, and there are more options to assist the legal team in gathering relevant evidence for use at trial. It is important to meet with the attorney and discuss how to organize all the evidence gathered from

document production, depositions, interrogatories, requests to admit, and subpoenas. If it is a large case, what software will you use? Who will have access to the database? How will items be keyed into the database? Does the firm need a third party provider to assist? If it is a small case, are standard files, binders, and boxes sufficient? What does the attorney prefer? Basically, you need a discovery plan.

A discovery plan allows you to make important decisions including:

- What sort of litigation hold to use so that important evidence is not destroyed by routine business practices;
- Whether to depose a witness or ask for documents first; and
- Whether metadata is important in the case to establish an element such as intent.

In a large case, one paralegal may focus on the privilege log while another paralegal is the database specialist. It is important that everyone on the team have the same instructions so that no matter who is reviewing a document, transcript, or other evidence, the item is receiving identical treatment in the way of coding and storage. There is creativity in the law, and this is the part where you have opportunities to creatively problem solve and use critical thinking skills to the advantage of the attorney.

> " ... discovery .... is the phase that makes or breaks a case ... "

items as correspondence, bills, research and investigation results, and all documents and exhibits relating to the litigation are in the file and arranged in an organized manner.

Organization

Each law firm or legal department has its own organizational scheme to follow when creating and maintaining client files. Recall from Chapter 3 that there are three goals of any law office filing system:

1. to preserve confidentiality,
2. to safeguard legal documents, and
3. to ensure that the contents of files can be easily and quickly retrieved when needed.

Usually it is the paralegal's responsibility to make sure that the litigation file is properly created and maintained.

As a case progresses through the litigation process, subfiles may be created for documents relating to the various stages. For example, at this point in the Baranski case, the litigation file contains notes taken during the initial client interview, the signed retainer agreement, and information and documents gathered by Lopez during her preliminary investigation of the claim. As the lawsuit progresses, Lopez makes sure that subfiles are created for documents relating to the pleadings and discovery stages (to be discussed

Litigation files can easily expand into thousands of documents. Part of the paralegal's job is to file and organize these documents in such a way that they can be quickly retrieved when needed. When might you wish to scan file documents and put them onto an external hard drive? How can you make sure that the external drive is secure?

shortly). Depending on the office filing system, the file folders for these subfiles may be color coded or numbered so that each subfile can be readily recognized and retrieved.

Many firms also scan documents and create electronic copies of the files. Lopez also prepares an index for each subfile to indicate the documents included. The index is placed at the front of the folder for easy reference.

Litigation Files

A properly created and maintained litigation file provides a comprehensive record of the case so that others in the firm can quickly acquaint themselves with the progress of the proceedings. Because well-organized files are critical to the success of any case, Lopez should take special care to properly maintain the file. The *Developing Paralegal Skills* feature on the facing page discusses file organization in more depth.

IN THE OFFICE

HACKING LEGAL FILES

Hackers work to steal information or destroy computer files. Protecting the privacy and security of client files, and all other office files, from hackers is a major concern. Security failures can affect a law firm's cases and its reputation. Large law firms usually have a specialist assigned to computer and Internet security. Smaller firms may be less formal, but the concerns are the same: Are files safe?

Is the transmission of files to courts safe from interception? Could a hacker destroy the contents of the firm's computers? Are files stored off site secure? While you are probably not a security expert, you should be aware of security for the computers you use and be sure to follow the procedures established by your firm.

DEVELOPING PARALEGAL SKILLS

FILE WORKUP

Once a litigation file has been created, the paralegal typically "works up" the file. In the Baranski case, after paralegal Lopez has completed her initial investigation into Baranski's claim, she reviews and summarizes the information she has amassed so far. This includes the information gathered through the initial and subsequent client interviews and any investigation that she has conducted.

Lopez also identifies areas that might require testimony of an expert witness. For example, if Baranski claimed that as a result of the accident she would always walk with a limp, Gilmore would want a medical specialist to give expert testimony to support the claim. (How to locate expert witnesses will be discussed in later chapters.) Lopez would prepare a list of potential experts for Gilmore to review.

Once Lopez has worked up the file, she prepares a memo to Gilmore summarizing the file. This memo provides him with factual information to decide which legal remedy or strategy to pursue, what legal issues need to be researched, and generally how to proceed with the case.

TIPS FOR PREPARING A FILE WORKUP MEMO

- Summarize the information that has been obtained about the case.
- Suggest a plan for further investigation in the case (reviewed in Chapter 11).
- Suggest additional information that might be obtained during discovery (discussed later in this chapter).
- Include a list of expert witnesses to contact, explaining which witnesses might be preferable, and why.

The Pleadings

The next step is for plaintiff Baranski's attorney, Gilmore, to file a complaint in the appropriate court. The complaint (called a *petition* in some courts) is a document that states the claims the plaintiff is making against the defendant. The complaint also contains a statement regarding the court's jurisdiction over the dispute and a demand for a remedy (such as money damages).

The filing of the complaint is the step that begins the formal legal action against the defendant, Peretto. The complaint is one of the pleadings, which inform each party of the claims made by the other and specify the issues (disputed questions) involved in the case. We examine here two basic pleadings—the plaintiff's complaint and the defendant's answer.

The complaint must be filed within the period of time allowed by law for bringing legal actions. The allowable period is fixed by state statutes of limitations (discussed in Chapter 5), and this period varies for different types of claims. For example, actions concerning breaches of sales contracts must usually be brought within four years. After the time allowed under a statute of limitations has expired, normally no action can be brought, no matter how strong the case was originally. For instance, if the statute of limitations covering the auto-negligence lawsuit that plaintiff Baranski is bringing against defendant Peretto allows two years for bringing an action, Baranski normally must initiate the lawsuit within that time or give up the possibility of suing Peretto for damages caused by the car accident.

complaint
The pleading made by a plaintiff or a charge made by the state alleging wrongdoing on the part of the defendant.

pleadings
Statements by the plaintiff and the defendant that detail the facts, charges, and defenses involved in the litigation.

Drafting the Complaint

The complaint itself may be no more than a few paragraphs long, or it may be many pages in length, depending on the complexity of the case. In the Baranski case, the complaint will probably be only a few pages long unless special circumstances require additional details. The complaint will include the following sections, each of which we discuss below:

- Caption.
- Jurisdictional allegations.
- General allegations (the body of the complaint).
- Prayer for relief.
- Signature.
- Demand for a jury trial.

Exhibit 10.2 on pages 280 and 281 shows a sample complaint.

Baranski's case is filed in a federal court, so the Federal Rules of Civil Procedure (FRCP) apply. If the case were filed in a state court, paralegal Lopez would need to review the appropriate state rules of civil procedure. The rules for drafting pleadings in state courts differ from the FRCP. The rules also differ from state to state and even from court to court within the same state. Lopez could obtain pleading forms from "form books" available in the law firm's files or library (or online) or from pleadings drafted previously in similar cases litigated by the firm.

The Caption

All documents submitted to the court or other parties during the litigation process begin with a caption. The caption is the heading, which identifies the name of the court, the title of the action, the names of the parties, the type of document, and the court's file number. Note that the court's file number may also be referred to as the case number or *docket number,* depending on the jurisdiction. (A docket is the official schedule of proceedings in lawsuits pending before a court.)

The caption for a complaint leaves a space for the court to insert the number that it assigns to the case. Courts typically assign the case a number when the complaint is filed. Any document subsequently filed with the court in the case will list the file, case, or docket number on the front page of the document. Exhibit 10.2 on the following pages shows how the caption will read in the case of *Baranski v. Peretto.*

Jurisdictional Allegations

Because attorney Gilmore is filing the lawsuit in a federal district court, he must include in the complaint an allegation that the federal court has jurisdiction to hear the dispute. (An allegation is an assertion, claim, or statement made by one party in a pleading that sets out what the party expects to prove to the court.) Recall from Chapter 6 that federal courts can exercise jurisdiction over disputes involving either a *federal question* or *diversity of citizenship.*

A federal question arises whenever a claim in a civil lawsuit relates to a federal law, the U.S. Constitution, or a treaty executed by the U.S. government. Diversity of citizenship exists when the parties involved in the lawsuit are citizens of different states and the amount in controversy exceeds $75,000. Because Baranski and Peretto are citizens of different states (Nita and Zero, respectively) and because the amount in controversy exceeds $75,000, the case meets the requirements for diversity-of-citizenship jurisdiction. Gilmore thus asserts that the federal court has jurisdiction on this basis, as illustrated in Exhibit 10.2 on the next page.

Certain cases, including those involving diversity of citizenship, may be brought in either a state court or a federal court. (This was discussed in the *Developing Paralegal*

docket
The list of cases entered on a court's calendar and thus scheduled to be heard by the court.

allegation
A party's statement, claim, or assertion made in a pleading to the court. The allegation sets forth the issue that the party expects to prove.

Skills feature in Chapter 6 on page 158.) Thus, an attorney in Gilmore's position can advise the client that there is a choice. Gilmore probably considered several factors when advising Baranski on which court would be preferable for her lawsuit. One issue is how long it would take to get the case to trial. Many courts are overburdened by their caseloads, and sometimes it can take years before a court will be able to hear a case. If Gilmore knows that the case could be heard two years earlier in the federal court than in the state court, that is an important factor to consider.

General Allegations (The Body of the Complaint)

The body of the complaint contains a series of allegations that set forth a claim for relief. In plaintiff Baranski's complaint, the allegations outline the factual events that gave rise to Baranski's claims.[2] The events are described in a series of chronologically arranged, numbered allegations so that the reader can understand them easily. As Exhibit 10.2 on page 279 shows, the numbers of the paragraphs in the body of the complaint continue the sequence begun in the section on jurisdictional allegations.

ADVOCATE THE PLAINTIFF'S POSITION. When drafting the complaint, Lopez acts as an advocate. She must present the facts forcefully to support and strengthen the client's claim. The recitation of the facts must demonstrate that defendant Peretto engaged in conduct that entitles plaintiff Baranski to relief. Even though she wants to present the facts in a light most favorable to Baranski, Lopez must be careful not to exaggerate the facts or make false statements. Rather, she must present the facts in such a way that the reader could reasonably infer that Peretto was negligent and that his negligence caused Baranski's injuries and losses.

What if her research into the case had given Lopez reason to believe that a fact was probably true even though she could not verify it? She could still include the statement in the complaint by prefacing it with the phrase, "On information and belief." This language would indicate to the court that plaintiff Baranski has good reason to believe the truth of the statement, but that the evidence for it either had not yet been obtained or might not hold up under close scrutiny.

BE CLEAR AND CONCISE. The most effective complaints are clear and concise. Brevity and simplicity are required under FRCP 8(a). When drafting the complaint, Lopez should use clear language and favor simple and direct statements over more complex wording. Lopez should only include facts that are absolutely necessary for the complaint. By reducing the body of the complaint to the simplest possible terms, Lopez achieves greater clarity and minimizes the possibility of divulging attorney Gilmore's trial strategies or hinting at a possible defense that the opponent might use.

OUTLINE HARMS SUFFERED AND REMEDY SOUGHT. After telling Baranski's story, Lopez adds one or more paragraphs outlining the harms suffered by the plaintiff and the remedy sought. In general, it is preferable that all allegations of damages—such as hospital costs, lost wages, and auto-repair expenses—be included in a single paragraph, as in Exhibit 10.2, Paragraph 10, at the top of page 281. Lopez should check the relevant court rules to see whether the court requires that certain damages (Baranski's lost wages, for example) be alleged in a separate paragraph.

Prayer for Relief

Paralegal Lopez includes a paragraph at the end of the complaint, similar to the one shown in Exhibit 10.2, asking that judgment be entered for the plaintiff and appropriate relief be granted. This **prayer for relief** will indicate that plaintiff Baranski is seeking money damages to compensate her for the harms that she suffered.

prayer for relief
A statement at the end of the complaint requesting that the court grant relief to the plaintiff.

EXHIBIT 10.2
The Complaint

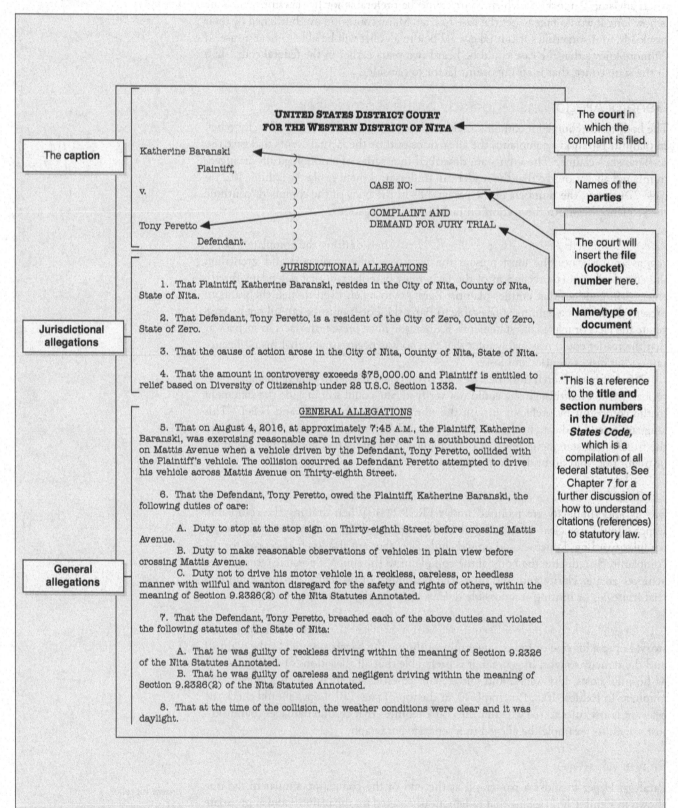

The caption

UNITED STATES DISTRICT COURT
FOR THE WESTERN DISTRICT OF NITA

Katherine Baranski

       Plaintiff,

v.

Tony Peretto

       Defendant.

)
)
)
)
)
)
)
)
)

CASE NO: _____

COMPLAINT AND
DEMAND FOR JURY TRIAL

The **court** in which the complaint is filed.

Names of the **parties**

The court will insert the **file (docket) number** here.

Name/type of document

Jurisdictional allegations

JURISDICTIONAL ALLEGATIONS

1. That Plaintiff, Katherine Baranski, resides in the City of Nita, County of Nita, State of Nita.

2. That Defendant, Tony Peretto, is a resident of the City of Zero, County of Zero, State of Zero.

3. That the cause of action arose in the City of Nita, County of Nita, State of Nita.

4. That the amount in controversy exceeds $75,000.00 and Plaintiff is entitled to relief based on Diversity of Citizenship under 28 U.S.C. Section 1332.

*This is a reference to the **title and section numbers** in the *United States Code,* which is a compilation of all federal statutes. See Chapter 7 for a further discussion of how to understand citations (references) to statutory law.

GENERAL ALLEGATIONS

5. That on August 4, 2016, at approximately 7:45 A.M., the Plaintiff, Katherine Baranski, was exercising reasonable care in driving her car in a southbound direction on Mattis Avenue when a vehicle driven by the Defendant, Tony Peretto, collided with the Plaintiff's vehicle. The collision occurred as Defendant Peretto attempted to drive his vehicle across Mattis Avenue on Thirty-eighth Street.

6. That the Defendant, Tony Peretto, owed the Plaintiff, Katherine Baranski, the following duties of care:

    A. Duty to stop at the stop sign on Thirty-eighth Street before crossing Mattis Avenue.
    B. Duty to make reasonable observations of vehicles in plain view before crossing Mattis Avenue.
    C. Duty not to drive his motor vehicle in a reckless, careless, or heedless manner with willful and wanton disregard for the safety and rights of others, within the meaning of Section 9.2326(2) of the Nita Statutes Annotated.

General allegations

7. That the Defendant, Tony Peretto, breached each of the above duties and violated the following statutes of the State of Nita:

    A. That he was guilty of reckless driving within the meaning of Section 9.2326 of the Nita Statutes Annotated.
    B. That he was guilty of careless and negligent driving within the meaning of Section 9.2326(2) of the Nita Statutes Annotated.

8. That at the time of the collision, the weather conditions were clear and it was daylight.

Continued

EXHIBIT 10.2

The Complaint—Continued

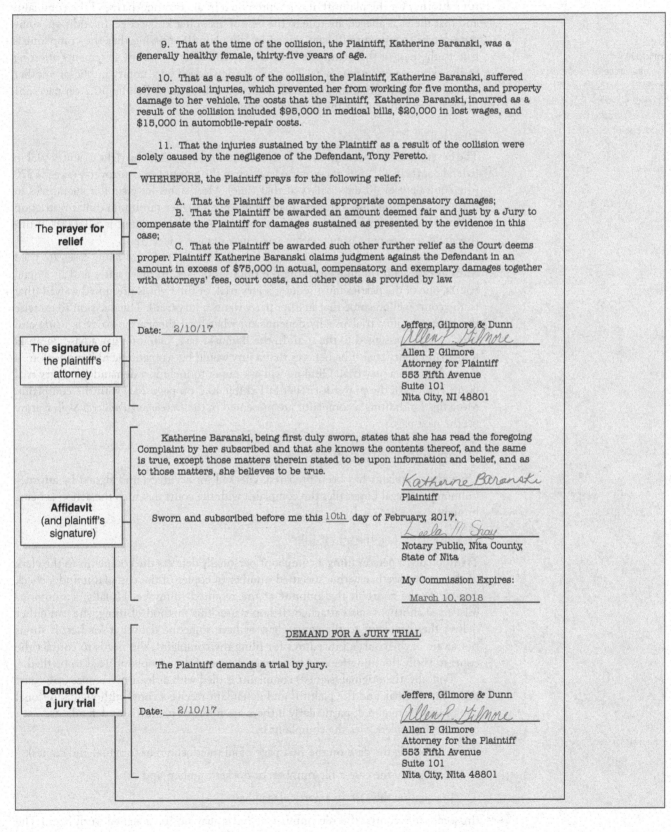

9. That at the time of the collision, the Plaintiff, Katherine Baranski, was a generally healthy female, thirty-five years of age.

10. That as a result of the collision, the Plaintiff, Katherine Baranski, suffered severe physical injuries, which prevented her from working for five months, and property damage to her vehicle. The costs that the Plaintiff, Katherine Baranski, incurred as a result of the collision included $95,000 in medical bills, $20,000 in lost wages, and $15,000 in automobile-repair costs.

11. That the injuries sustained by the Plaintiff as a result of the collision were solely caused by the negligence of the Defendant, Tony Peretto.

WHEREFORE, the Plaintiff prays for the following relief:

A. That the Plaintiff be awarded appropriate compensatory damages;

B. That the Plaintiff be awarded an amount deemed fair and just by a Jury to compensate the Plaintiff for damages sustained as presented by the evidence in this case;

C. That the Plaintiff be awarded such other further relief as the Court deems proper. Plaintiff Katherine Baranski claims judgment against the Defendant in an amount in excess of $75,000 in actual, compensatory, and exemplary damages together with attorneys' fees, court costs, and other costs as provided by law.

The prayer for relief

Date: 2/10/17

Jeffers, Gilmore & Dunn

Allen P. Gilmore

Allen P Gilmore
Attorney for Plaintiff
553 Fifth Avenue
Suite 101
Nita City, NI 48801

The signature of the plaintiff's attorney

Katherine Baranski, being first duly sworn, states that she has read the foregoing Complaint by her subscribed and that she knows the contents thereof, and the same is true, except those matters therein stated to be upon information and belief, and as to those matters, she believes to be true.

Katherine Baranski

Plaintiff

Sworn and subscribed before me this 10th day of February, 2017.

Leela M Shay

Notary Public, Nita County,
State of Nita

My Commission Expires:

March 10, 2018

Affidavit (and plaintiff's signature)

DEMAND FOR A JURY TRIAL

The Plaintiff demands a trial by jury.

Jeffers, Gilmore & Dunn

Allen P. Gilmore

Allen P Gilmore
Attorney for the Plaintiff
553 Fifth Avenue
Suite 101
Nita City, Nita 48801

Demand for a jury trial

Date: 2/10/17

Signature

In federal practice, the signature following the prayer for relief certifies that the plaintiff's attorney (or the plaintiff, if not represented by an attorney) has read the complaint and that the facts alleged are true to the best of his or her knowledge. In addition, some state courts require an affidavit signed by the plaintiff verifying that the complaint is true to the best of the plaintiff's knowledge. Affidavits are sworn statements attesting to the existence of certain facts. They are acknowledged by a notary public or another official authorized to administer such oaths or affirmations. Exhibit 10.2 on page 281 illustrates an affidavit for the Baranski complaint.

Demand for a Jury Trial

The Seventh Amendment to the U.S. Constitution guarantees the right to a jury trial in federal courts in all "suits at common law" when the amount in controversy exceeds $20 (the equivalent of 40 days' salary at that time). Most states have similar guarantees in their own constitutions, although many states put a higher minimum dollar restriction on the guarantee (for example, in Maryland the minimum amount is $10,000). If this threshold requirement is met, either party may request a jury trial.

The right to a trial by jury does not have to be exercised, and many cases are tried without one, with the judge making the findings of fact. In most states and in federal courts, one of the parties must request a jury trial, or the right is presumed waived (that is, the court will presume that neither party wants a jury trial). The decision to exercise the right to a jury trial usually depends on what legal theory the party is using and which judge is assigned to the trial. In the Baranski case, Gilmore may advise Baranski to demand a jury trial if he believes that a jury would be sympathetic to her position. If Baranski wants a jury trial, Gilmore will ask Lopez to include a demand for a jury trial (as in Point B of the prayer for relief in Exhibit 10.2 on page 281) with the complaint. More tips for drafting a complaint are presented in the *Developing Paralegal Skills* feature on the next page.

Filing the Complaint

Once the complaint has been prepared, checked for accuracy, and signed by attorney Gilmore, paralegal Lopez files the complaint with the court in which the action is being brought.

Traditional Method of Filing

Traditionally, a person filing a complaint personally delivers the complaint to the clerk of the court, together with a specified number of copies of the complaint and a check payable to the court in the amount of the required filing fee. Usually, a summons (discussed shortly) is also attached. If Lopez uses this method of filing, she can either deliver the complaint to the court clerk or have someone deliver it for her. If she is not aware of the court's procedures for filing the complaint, she needs to contact the court to verify the filing fee and how many copies of the complaint need to be filed.

Typically, the original (signed) complaint is filed with at least two copies (the court keeps the original, and the plaintiff and defendant receive a copy), although additional copies may be required, particularly if there are multiple plaintiffs or defendants.

The court clerk files the complaint by:

- stamping the date on the first page of all the documents (original and copies);
- assigning the case a file number, or docket number; and
- assigning the case to a particular judge.

(In some state courts, the file number or judge may not be assigned until later.) The clerk then returns the date-stamped copies to the person who delivered the documents for service on the defendant (to be discussed shortly).

affidavit
A written statement of facts, confirmed by the oath or affirmation of the party making it and sworn before a person having the authority to administer the oath or affirmation.

DEVELOPING PARALEGAL SKILLS

A CHECKLIST FOR DRAFTING A COMPLAINT IN A FEDERAL CIVIL CASE

Civil cases begin when a complaint is filed in court. To draft a complaint, you need to know the facts your client alleges and the law that supports your client's claim for relief. You need to review notes from client interviews and meetings with the attorneys, factual materials (e.g., police or hospital reports), and preliminary research. It is a good idea to review complaints from similar cases handled by your firm in the past. They can give you a feel for the appropriate writing style. Form books also provide guidance on how to draft particular claims. It is also critical to check the appropriate court's rules for local requirements.

For civil suits in federal court, FRCP 8 sets out the required elements. State rules have equivalent provisions. Generally, local rules will cover the typeface, type and size of paper, and other such matters.

A well-drafted complaint contains the information needed to answer the following questions:

- Who is the plaintiff? Use the plaintiff's legal name and include a statement of the jurisdiction where the plaintiff is a legal resident. If the plaintiff is suing as the representative of someone else, identify the relationship.

- Who is the defendant? It is critical to use the defendant's correct legal name so that you sue the proper person or firm. You also need to provide the defendant's legal residence.

- Why is the suit being filed in this court? How does the court have jurisdiction over the case? List the specific statutes involved. For example, list 28 U.S.C. 1331 for federal question jurisdiction, 28 U.S.C. 1332 for diversity-of-citizenship jurisdiction, or 42 U.S.C. 1983 for civil

rights violations. Remember, the court must have jurisdiction over both the cause of action and defendants.

- Did any administrative prerequisites have to be satisfied prior to filing suit? If so, how?

- Is the claim timely filed (within the relevant statute of limitations)?

- What are the facts that make up the plaintiff's case? State these accurately, clearly, and briefly. Give names and dates where known.

- What are the legal claims made by the plaintiff? Draft each claim in a separate "count" in the complaint.

- Are there special pleading requirements for particular claims (e.g., fraud)? How has the plaintiff satisfied them?

- What is the plaintiff asking for? Clearly describe the relief the plaintiff wants—is it monetary damages? An injunction? Declaratory relief? Attorneys' fees and costs? Prejudgment interest? Postjudgment interest? Are special damages requested (such as statutory damages or punitive damages)?

- Who is the attorney filing the suit? Include an appropriate signature block for the lawyer to sign, certifying that she has conducted a reasonable inquiry into the facts that support the claim.

- Is a jury requested? Check to see if the claim is one for which a jury is available. Find out whether the attorney overseeing the case wants to request a jury. If so, you need to include the appropriate language demanding a jury trial.

All parts of the complaint should be written in clear, direct English. Professionalism is appreciated by a court.

E-Filing

Instead of delivering a paper document to the court, Lopez may be able to file the complaint electronically. Electronic filing is becoming more common. Because of the reduced time and paperwork involved, electronic filing can result in savings for attorneys, clients, and the courts. With e-filing, registered attorneys can file case documents over the Internet at any time right up to the filing deadline. (Go to **pacer.gov** to see the service for the federal court system.)

electronic filing (e-filing) system
An online system that enables attorneys to file case documents with courts twenty-four hours a day, seven days a week.

The security of the e-filing process is important. Only registered parties may access a court's e-filing system. As with most secure electronic communications, the registered party has a user ID and a password. An attorney may give a paralegal authority to use the system on his or her behalf. Consent of the parties to use e-filing may be required. Once parties agree to e-filing, the court assigns a docket number to the case. From that point forward, all documents filed by consenting parties must use the system. Often, documents must be formatted as secure PDF files so that they cannot be altered. The parties must provide e-mail addresses for notification of service of documents.

A party to an action being handled by e-filing may have the right to request hard copies of documents. When hard copies are used, they are to include a clear notice that they have been filed electronically. Special steps are taken to protect private information, such as Social Security numbers, credit-card information, a minor child's name, or trade secrets. Fees for documents filed are paid electronically. Therefore, in many cases, all paperwork and communications between the parties and the court may be electronic.

Service of Process

service of process
The delivery of the summons and the complaint to a defendant.

Before the court can exercise jurisdiction over the defendant, the court must have proof that the defendant was notified of the lawsuit. Serving the summons and complaint—that is, officially delivering these documents to the defendant in a lawsuit—is referred to as service of process.

The Summons

summons
A document served on a defendant in a lawsuit informing the defendant that a legal action has been commenced against him or her and that the defendant must appear in court or respond to the plaintiff's complaint within a specified period of time.

The summons identifies the parties to the lawsuit, as well as the court in which the case will be heard, and directs the defendant to respond to the complaint within a specified period of time. In the Baranski case, paralegal Lopez will prepare a summons by filling out a form similar to that shown in Exhibit 10.3 below. Lopez also prepares a cover sheet for the case (a preprinted form), as is required in federal courts and in most state courts.

EXHIBIT 10.3
A Summons in a Civil Action

UNITED STATES DISTRICT COURT
FOR THE WESTERN DISTRICT OF NITA

Katherine Baranski)
           Plaintiff,)
v.)
Tony Peretto)
           Defendant.)

Civil Action, File Number 14-14335-NI

Summons

To the above-named Defendant:

You are hereby summoned and required to serve upon A. P. Gilmore, Jeffers, Gilmore & Dunn, plaintiff's attorney, whose address is 553 Fifth Avenue, Suite 101, Nita City, NI 48801, an answer to the complaint which is herewith served upon you, within 20 days after service of this summons upon you, exclusive of the day of service. If you fail to do so, judgment by default will be taken against you for the relief demanded in the complaint.

C. H. Hynek   February 10, 2017
CLERK   DATE

John Dolan
BY DEPUTY CLERK

If the case were being brought in a state court, Lopez would deliver the summons to the court clerk at the same time she delivers the complaint. In federal court cases, as will be discussed, the complaint may already have been filed under the FRCP provisions relating to waiver of notice.

After the clerk files the complaint and signs, seals, and issues the summons, attorney Gilmore is responsible for making sure that the summons and complaint are served on defendant Peretto. The service of the complaint and summons must happen within a specific time—120 days under FRCP 4(m)—after the complaint has been filed.

Serving the Complaint and Summons

How service of process occurs depends on the rules of the court or jurisdiction in which the lawsuit is brought. Under FRCP 4(c)(2), service of process in federal court cases may be effected "by any person who is not a party and who is at least 18 years of age." Paralegal Lopez, for example, could serve the summons and complaint by personally delivering it to defendant Peretto. Alternatively, she could make arrangements for someone else to do so, subject to approval of attorney Gilmore.

Most law firms contract with independent companies that provide process service in the local area. In some cases, the attorney might request that the court have a U.S. marshal or other federal official serve the summons. See the U.S. Marshals Service website for a discussion of their services and the service requirements in each state. A good discussion can be found at **usmarshals.gov/process/summons-complaint.htm**. For a list of process methods in the states, see **usmarshals.gov/process/state.htm**.

Under FRCP 4(e)(1), service of process in federal court cases may be performed "pursuant to the law of the state in which the district court is located." Some state courts require that a public officer, such as a sheriff, serve the complaint and summons.

ALTERNATIVE SERVICE METHODS.   Although the most common way to serve process on a defendant is through personal service as described above, other methods are permissible at times, depending on the jurisdiction. *Substituted service* is a method of service allowed by law in place of personal service, such as service by certified mail or e-mail. In general, substituted service is not favored. The paralegal and attorney need to know the types of service authorized by the laws in the relevant state.

PROOF OF SERVICE.   Regardless of how the summons is served, attorney Gilmore will need proof that defendant Peretto actually received the summons. In federal court cases, unless service is made by a U.S. marshal or other official, the process server fills out and signs a form similar to the return-of-service form shown in Exhibit 10.4 on the following page. This form is then submitted to the court as proof of service.

return-of-service form
A document signed by a process server and submitted to the court to prove that a defendant received a summons.

JURISDICTIONS VARY.   Paralegal Lopez must be careful to comply with the service requirements of the court in which plaintiff Baranski's suit has been filed. If service is not properly made, defendant Peretto has legal grounds (basis) for asking the court to dismiss the case against him. The court cannot exercise jurisdiction over Peretto until he has been properly notified of the lawsuit being brought against him.

Serving Corporate Defendants

In cases involving corporate defendants, the summons and complaint may be served on an officer or a *registered agent* (representative) of the corporation. The name of a corporation's registered agent and its business address can usually be obtained from the secretary of state's office in the state in which the company is incorporated or in any state in which it does business.

Finding the Defendant

Because some defendants may be difficult to locate, paralegals sometimes have to search for a defendant so that process can be served. Information sources include telephone

EXHIBIT 10.4
A Return-of-Service Form

RETURN OF SERVICE

Service of the Summons and Complaint was made by me	DATE 2/11/17
NAME OF SERVER Elena Lopez	TITLE Paralegal

Check one box below to indicate appropriate method of service

☒ Served personally upon the defendant. Place where served: ___Defendant Peretto's Home: 1708 Johnston Drive, Zero City, Zero 59806___

☐ Left copies thereof at the defendant's dwelling house or usual place of abode with a person of suitable age and discretion then residing therein. Name of person with whom the summons and complaint were left: _____

☐ Returned unexecuted: _____

☐ Other (specify): _____

DECLARATION OF SERVER

I declare under penalty of perjury under the laws of the United States of America that the foregoing information contained in the Return of Service and Statement of Service Fees is true and correct.

Executed on ___2/11/17___   *Elena Lopez*
                Date   Signature of Server

308 University Avenue, Nita City, Nita 48804
Address of Server

directories, banks, former business partners or fellow workers, credit bureaus, Social Security offices, insurance companies, landlords, state and county tax rolls, utility companies, automobile-registration bureaus, bureaus of vital statistics, and the post office. (Chapter 11 discusses these and other sources that the paralegal might consult when trying to locate parties or witnesses in lawsuits.)

The Defendant Can Waive Service

Often the defendant is aware that a lawsuit is being filed (often the plaintiff's attorney has been in contact with the defendant and indicated that a complaint would be filed). A plaintiff can request the defendant to *waive* (give up) the right to be formally served with a summons. FRCP 4(d) sets forth the procedure by which a plaintiff's attorney can request the defendant to accept service of the documents through the mail or "other reliable means." Most states have similar rules.

The aim of FRCP 4(d) is to reduce the costs associated with service of process. As an incentive, defendants who agree to waive formal service of process under the federal rules receive additional time to respond to the complaint (sixty days, compared with the twenty days that a defendant normally has to respond to the complaint under FRCP 12). Some state rules of civil procedure provide other incentives, such as making a party who will not agree to waive service pay for reasonable expenses thereafter incurred in serving or attempting to serve the party.

The Defendant's Response

Once a defendant receives the plaintiff's complaint, the defendant must respond to the complaint within a specified time (typically twenty days). If the defendant fails to respond within that time, the plaintiff can ask the court to enter a default judgment against the defendant. The defendant will then be liable for all damages the plaintiff is claiming and loses the opportunity to defend against the claim in court.

In the Baranski case, assume that defendant Peretto consults with an attorney, Elizabeth Cameron, to decide on a course of action. Before Cameron advises Peretto on the matter, she will investigate plaintiff Baranski's claim and obtain evidence of what happened at the time of the accident. She may ask her paralegal, Gordon McVay, to call anyone who may have witnessed the accident and any police officers who were at the scene. Cameron will also ask McVay to gather relevant documents, including the traffic ticket Peretto received at the time of the accident and any reports filed by the police. If all goes well, Cameron and McVay will complete their investigation in a few days and then assess the results.

Most cases are dropped by the plaintiff or settled out of court before they go to trial. But even if Peretto's attorney suspects that an out-of-court settlement might be preferable to a trial, she will draft a response to Baranski's claim. She knows that if Peretto does not respond to the complaint within the proper time period, the court could enter a default judgment against him.

The Answer

A defendant's answer must respond to each allegation in the plaintiff's complaint. FRCP 8(b) permits the defendant to admit or deny the truth of each allegation. Peretto's attorney may advise him to admit to some of the allegations in Baranski's complaint, because doing so narrows the number of issues in dispute. Allegations not denied by the defendant are deemed to have been admitted.

If Peretto does not know whether a particular allegation is true or false, Cameron may indicate that in the answer. This puts the burden of proving the allegation on Baranski. It is not necessary for Peretto's attorney to include in the answer any of the reasons for the denial of particular allegations in Baranski's complaint. These reasons may be revealed during the discovery phase of the litigation process (discussed later in this chapter).

Exhibit 10.5 on the following two pages illustrates the responses that Peretto might make in his answer. Like the complaint, the answer begins with a caption and ends with the attorney's signature. It may also include an affidavit signed by the defendant and/or a demand for a jury trial, as in Exhibit 10.5.

ANSWER AND AFFIRMATIVE DEFENSES.   A defendant may assert in the answer a reason why he or she should not be held liable for the plaintiff's injuries even if the facts, as alleged by the plaintiff, are true. This is called raising an affirmative defense.

For example, Peretto's attorney might also raise the defense of *contributory negligence.* That is, she could argue that even though Peretto's car collided with Baranski's, Baranski was also negligent because she was exceeding the speed limit when the accident occurred. The plaintiff's role in contributing to the accident could result in reduced or no damages for her. Although affirmative defenses are directed toward the plaintiff, the plaintiff is not required to file additional pleadings in response to these defenses.

ANSWER AND COUNTERCLAIM.   Peretto's attorney may assert one or more counterclaims. A counterclaim is like a reverse lawsuit. The defendant asserts a claim against the plaintiff for injuries the defendant suffered from the same incident. For example, Peretto might contend that Baranski lost control of her car and skidded into Peretto's car, causing him to be injured. This allegation would be a counterclaim. The plaintiff is then required to reply to any counterclaims made by the defendant.

default judgment
A judgment entered by a clerk or court against a party who has failed to appear in court to answer or defend against a claim that has been brought against him or her by another party.

answer
A defendant's response to a plaintiff's complaint.

affirmative defense
A response to a plaintiff's claim that does not deny the plaintiff's facts but attacks the plaintiff's legal right to bring an action.

counterclaim
A claim made by a defendant in a civil lawsuit against the plaintiff; in effect, a counterclaiming defendant is suing the plaintiff.

EXHIBIT 10.5

The Answer

UNITED STATES DISTRICT COURT
FOR THE WESTERN DISTRICT OF NITA

Katherine Baranski	)	
Plaintiff,	)	CASE NO. 14-14335-NI
	)	Honorable Harley M. Larue
v.	)	
	)	
	)	ANSWER AND
Tony Peretto	)	DEMAND FOR JURY TRIAL
Defendant.	)	

JURISDICTIONAL ALLEGATIONS

1. Defendant lacks sufficient information to form a belief as to the truth of the allegations contained in paragraph 1 of Plaintiff's Complaint.

2. Defendant admits the allegations contained in paragraph 2 of Plaintiff's Complaint.

3. Defendant admits the allegations contained in paragraph 3 of Plaintiff's Complaint.

4. Defendant lacks sufficient information to form a belief as to the truth of the allegations contained in paragraph 4 of Plaintiff's Complaint.

GENERAL ALLEGATIONS

5. Defendant admits the allegations contained in paragraph 5 of Plaintiff's Complaint.

6. Defendant admits the allegations contained in paragraph 6 of Plaintiff's Complaint.

7. Defendant contends that he was operating his vehicle properly and denies the allegations contained in paragraph 7 of Plaintiff's Complaint for the reason that the allegations are untrue.

8. Defendant admits the allegation contained in paragraph 8 of Plaintiff's Complaint.

9. Defendant lacks sufficient information to form a belief as to the truth of the allegation contained in paragraph 9 of Plaintiff's Complaint.

10. Defendant lacks sufficient information on the proximate cause of Plaintiff's injuries to form a belief as to the truth of the averments contained in paragraph 10 of Plaintiff's Complaint.

11. Defendant denies the allegation of negligence contained in paragraph 11 of Plaintiff's Complaint.

---

cross-claim

A claim asserted by a defendant in a civil lawsuit against another defendant or by a plaintiff against another plaintiff.

CROSS-CLAIM.   If a complaint names multiple defendants, the answer filed by one defendant might be followed by a cross-claim, in which the defendant asserts a claim against another defendant. (Note that cross-claims may also be filed by one plaintiff against another plaintiff in the same case.) For example, suppose that plaintiff Baranski had been struck by two vehicles, one belonging to defendant Peretto and one belonging to Leon Balfour. If Peretto and Balfour had been named as co-defendants in Baranski's complaint, Peretto's attorney might have filed an answer to Baranski's complaint that included a cross-claim against Balfour. The party against whom the cross-claim is brought is required to reply to (answer) the claim.

EXHIBIT 10.5

The Answer—Continued

<u>NEW MATTER AND AFFIRMATIVE DEFENSES</u>

Although denying that the Plaintiff is entitled to the relief prayed for in the Plaintiff's Complaint, Defendant further states that the Plaintiff is barred from recovery hereunder by reason of the following:

1. That the Plaintiff's injuries were proximately caused by her own contributory negligence and want of due care under the circumstances prevailing at the time of the accident.

2. That the Plaintiff was exceeding the posted speed limit at the time and place of the accident and therefore was guilty of careless and negligent driving within the meaning of Section 9.2325(1) of the Nita Statutes Annotated.

3. That the Plaintiff failed to exercise that standard of care that a reasonably prudent person would have exercised under the same or similar conditions for her own safety and that her own negligence, contributory negligence, and/or comparative negligence caused or was a contributing factor to the incident out of which the Plaintiff's cause of action arises.

4. The Defendant reserves the right, by an appropriate Motion, to move the Court to amend the Defendant's Answer to the Plaintiff's Complaint, to allege other New Matters and Affirmative Defenses as may be revealed by discovery yet to be had and completed in this case.

WHEREFORE, the Defendant prays for a judgment of no cause of action with costs and attorneys' fees to be paid by the Plaintiff.

Cameron & Strauss, P.C.

Elizabeth A. Cameron

Date: 2/25/17

Elizabeth A. Cameron
Attorney for the Defendant
310 Lake Drive
Zero City, ZE 59802

Tony Peretto, being first duly sworn, states that he has read the foregoing Answer by him subscribed and that he knows the contents thereof, and the same is true, except those matters therein stated to be upon information and belief, and as to those matters, he believes to be true.

Tony Peretto

Defendant

Laura Curtis

Sworn and subscribed before me this 25th day of February, 2017.

Notary Public, Zero County,
State of Zero

My Commission Expires:
December 8, 2018

<u>DEMAND FOR A JURY TRIAL</u>

The Defendant demands a trial by jury.

Cameron & Strauss, P.C.

Elizabeth A. Cameron

Date: 2/25/17

Elizabeth A. Cameron
Attorney for the Defendant
310 Lake Drive
Zero City, Zero 59802

Under the federal rules, a defendant who has a claim against the plaintiff related to the same incident is normally required to file a counterclaim within the defendant's pleading. A party who fails to do so may lose the possibility of asserting the claim at a later date. This requirement is intended to prevent multiple lawsuits between the same parties.

Filing a Motion

A **motion** is a request submitted to the court by an attorney on behalf of his or her client. When one party files a motion with the court, that party must also send to, or serve on, the opposing party a *notice of motion*. The notice informs the opposing party that the motion has been filed and indicates when the court will hear the motion. The notice gives the opposing party an opportunity to prepare for the hearing.

The **motion to dismiss**, as the phrase implies, requests the court to dismiss the case for reasons provided in the motion. Defendant Peretto's attorney, for example, could file a motion to dismiss if she believed that Peretto had not been properly served, that the complaint had been filed in the wrong court, that the statute of limitations for that type of lawsuit had expired, or that the complaint did not state a claim for which relief (a remedy) could be granted. See Exhibit 10.6 on the facing page for an example of a motion to dismiss.

If Peretto's attorney decides to file a motion to dismiss Baranski's claim, she may want to attach **supporting affidavits**—sworn statements as to certain facts that may contradict allegations made in the complaint. Peretto's attorney may also have her paralegal draft a **memorandum of law** (which is called a *brief* in some states) to be submitted along with the motion to dismiss and the accompanying affidavits. The memorandum of law presents the legal basis for the motion, citing any statutes and cases that support it. A supporting affidavit gives factual support to the motion to dismiss, while the memorandum of law provides the legal grounds for the dismissal of the claim.

The Scheduling Conference

After the complaint and answer have been filed, the court typically schedules a conference to consult with the attorneys for both sides. (A party not represented by an attorney attends the conference himself or herself.) Following this meeting, the judge enters a *scheduling order* that sets out the time limits within which pretrial events (such as the pleadings, the discovery, and the final pretrial conference) must be completed, as well as the date of the trial. Under FRCP 16(b), the scheduling order should be entered "as soon as practicable but in any event within 90 days after the appearance of a defendant and within 120 days after the complaint has been served on a defendant." The purpose of this meeting is to enable the court to manage the case and establish time restrictions given the nature of the case.

Traditional Discovery Tools

Before a trial begins, the parties can use a number of procedural devices to obtain information and gather evidence about the case. Baranski's attorney, for example, will want to know how fast Peretto was driving, whether he had been drinking, and whether he saw the stop sign. The process of obtaining information from the opposing party or from other witnesses is known as **discovery**.

Purpose of Discovery

Discovery serves several purposes. It preserves evidence from witnesses who might not be available at the time of the trial or whose memories will fade as time passes. It can lead to an out-of-court settlement if one party decides that the opponent's case is too strong to challenge. If the case does go to trial, discovery prevents surprises by giving parties access to evidence that might otherwise be hidden. This allows both parties to learn as much as they can about what to expect at a trial before they reach the courtroom. It also serves to narrow the issues so the trial focuses on the main questions in the case.

The FRCP and similar rules in the states set forth the guidelines for discovery activity. Discovery is intended to give the parties access to witnesses, documents, records, and other evidence that the opposing side has. The rules governing discovery are also designed to make sure that a witness or a party is not unduly harassed, that **privileged information**

---

motion
A procedural request or application presented by an attorney to the court on behalf of a client.

motion to dismiss
A motion filed by the defendant in which the defendant asks the court to dismiss the case for a specified reason, such as improper service, lack of personal jurisdiction, or the plaintiff's failure to state a claim for which relief can be granted.

supporting affidavit
An affidavit accompanying a motion that is filed by an attorney on behalf of his or her client. The sworn statements in the affidavit provide a factual basis for the motion.

memorandum of law
A document (known as a *brief* in some states) that delineates the legal theories, statutes, and cases on which a motion is based.

discovery
Formal investigation prior to trial. Opposing parties use various methods, such as interrogatories and depositions, to obtain information from each other and from witnesses to prepare for trial.

privileged information
Confidential communications between certain individuals, such as an attorney and his or her client, that are protected from disclosure except under court order.

EXHIBIT 10.6
A Motion to Dismiss

**UNITED STATES DISTRICT COURT
FOR THE WESTERN DISTRICT OF NITA**

Katherine Baranski)
　　　　　Plaintiff,)
　　　　　　　　　　　)　　CASE NO. 14-14335-NI
v.)　　Honorable Harley M. Larue
　　　　　　　　　　　)
　　　　　　　　　　　)　　MOTION TO DISMISS
Tony Peretto)
　　　　　Defendant.)

The Defendant, Tony Peretto, by his attorney, moves the court to dismiss the above-named action because the statute of limitations governing the Plaintiff's claim has expired, as demonstrated in the memorandum of law that is being submitted with this motion. The Plaintiff therefore has no cause of action against the Defendant.

Cameron & Strauss, P.C.

Date: 2/20/17

Elizabeth A. Cameron
Elizabeth A. Cameron
Attorney for the Defendant
310 Lake Drive
Zero City, ZE 59802

(communications that ordinarily may not be disclosed in court) is safeguarded, and that only matters relevant to the case at hand are discoverable. Courts generally allow broad discovery so that there are fewer surprises at trial.

Discovery methods include interrogatories, depositions, requests for production and physical examination, and requests for admission. Remember, as with most legal matters, you have an obligation to keep all such information confidential, as discussed in the *Ethics Watch* feature on the following page.

Interrogatories

Interrogatories are written questions that must be answered, in writing, by the parties to the lawsuit and then signed by the parties under oath. In the Baranski case, attorney Gilmore may ask paralegal Lopez to draft interrogatories to be sent to defendant Peretto.

Drafting Interrogatories

All discovery documents, including interrogatories, normally begin with a caption similar to the complaint caption illustrated earlier in this chapter. Following the caption, Lopez adds the name of the party who must answer the interrogatories, instructions to be followed by the party, and definitions of certain terms used in the interrogatories. The body of the document is the interrogatories themselves—that is, the questions that the opposing party must answer. Interrogatories end with a signature line for the attorney, followed by the attorney's name and address.

REVIEW THE FILE. Before drafting the questions, Lopez carefully reviews the case file (including the pleadings and the evidence and other information she obtained during her preliminary investigation into Baranski's claim). She will consult with Gilmore on the litigation strategy he believes should be pursued as the case moves forward. For further guidance, she might consult form books containing sample interrogatories, as well as interrogatories used in similar cases handled by the firm.

interrogatories
A series of written questions for which written answers are prepared and then signed under oath by a party to a lawsuit (the plaintiff or the defendant).

ETHICS WATCH

KEEPING CLIENT INFORMATION CONFIDENTIAL

As it happens, attorney Gilmore's legal assistant, Lopez, is a friend of plaintiff Baranski's sister. Lopez learns from the results of Baranski's medical examination that Baranski has a serious illness. Lopez is sure that the sister, who quarreled with Baranski two months ago and hasn't spoken to her since, is unaware of the illness and would probably be hurt if she learned that Lopez knew of it and didn't tell her so she could make amends with Baranski.

Should Lopez tell her friend about the illness? No. This is confidential information at this point, which Lopez only became aware of by virtue of her job. Should the information be revealed publicly during the course of the trial, Lopez would be free to disclose it to her friend if the friend still remained unaware of it. In the meantime, Lopez is ethically (and legally) obligated to protect the information from anyone who is not working on the case, including her friend.

This behavior is consistent with the NFPA *Model Disciplinary Rules and Ethical Considerations*, Section EC-1.5(f): "A paralegal shall not engage in any indiscreet communications concerning clients."

COURTS MAY LIMIT THE NUMBER OF INTERROGATORIES.   Depending on the complexity of the case, interrogatories may be few or in the hundreds. Exhibit 10.7 on the following two pages illustrates the types of interrogatories that have traditionally been used in cases similar to the Baranski-Peretto case.

Many state courts limit the number of interrogatories that can be used. FRCP 33 limits the number in federal court cases to twenty-five (unless a greater number are allowed by stipulation of the parties or by court order). Before drafting interrogatories, the paralegal should check the rules of the court in which an action is filed to find out if there are limits.

Answering Interrogatories

After receiving the interrogatories, Peretto must answer them within a specified time (thirty days under FRCP 33) in writing and under oath. Depending on the rules of the court, answers to interrogatories can often be handled electronically. Peretto will likely have substantial guidance from his attorney and his attorney's paralegal in forming his answers. He must answer each question truthfully because he is under oath. His attorney will counsel him, though, on how to phrase his answers so that they are truthful and strategically sound. For example, she will advise him on how to limit his answers to prevent disclosing more information than necessary.

Depositions

Like interrogatories, depositions are given under oath. However, depositions are usually conducted orally (except in rare circumstances when the party cannot be deposed in person or by telephone or videoconference). Furthermore, unlike interrogatories, they may be taken from witnesses as well as parties.

In a deposition, the attorney is able to question the person being deposed (the deponent) *in person* and follows up with new questions that come to mind. The attorney

deposition
A pretrial question-and-answer proceeding, usually conducted orally, in which a party or witness answers an attorney's questions. The answers are given under oath, and the session is recorded.

deponent
A party or witness who testifies under oath during a deposition.

EXHIBIT 10.7

Sample Interrogatories

UNITED STATES DISTRICT COURT
FOR THE WESTERN DISTRICT OF NITA

Katherine Baranski)
        Plaintiff,)
)   CASE NO. 14-14335-NI
v   )   Honorable Harley M. Larue
)
)   PLAINTIFF'S FIRST
Tony Peretto   )   INTERROGATORIES
        Defendant.)   TO DEFENDANT

PLEASE TAKE NOTICE that the following Interrogatories are directed to you under the provisions of Rule 26(a)(5) and Rule 33 of the Federal Rules of Civil Procedure. You are requested to answer these Interrogatories and to furnish such information in answer to the Interrogatories as is available to you.

You are required to serve integrated Interrogatories and Answers to these Interrogatories under oath, within thirty (30) days after service of them upon you. The original answers are to be retained in your attorney's possession, and a copy of the answers is to be served upon Plaintiff's counsel.

The answers should be signed and sworn to by the person making answer to the Interrogatories.

When used in these Interrogatories the term "Defendant," or any synonym thereof, is intended to and shall embrace and include, in addition to said Defendant, all agents, servants and employees, representatives, attorneys, private investigators, or others who are in possession of or who may have obtained information for or on behalf of the Defendant.

These Interrogatories shall be deemed continuing, and supplemental answers shall be required immediately upon receipt thereof if Defendant, directly or indirectly, obtains further or different information from the time answers are served until the time of trial.

1. Were you the driver of an automobile involved in an accident with Plaintiff on August 4, 2016, at about 7:45 A.M. at the intersection of Mattis Avenue and Thirty-eighth Street, in Nita City, Nita? If so, please state:

    (a) Your name;
    (b) Every name you have used in the past;
    (c) The dates you used each name;
    (d) The date and place of your birth.

2. Please list your current residence and all residences you occupied in the five years preceding your move to your current residence, including complete addresses, dates of residence, and names of owners or managers.

3. Please indicate where you are presently employed and where you were employed during the five years preceding the beginning of your current employment. In so doing, please indicate the following:

    (a) The names, addresses, and telephone numbers of each employer or place of business, including the dates during which you worked there;
    (b) How many hours you worked, on average, per week;
    (c) The names, addresses, and telephone numbers of your supervisors (or owners of the business);
    (d) The nature of the work that you performed.

4. At the time of the incident, were you acting as an agent or employee for any person? If so, state:

    (a) The name, address, and telephone number of that person;
    (b) A description of your duties.

5. At the time of the incident, did you have a driver's license? If so, state:

    (a) The state or other issuing entity;
    (b) The license number and type;
    (c) The date of issuance and expiration;
    (d) Any violations, offenses, or restrictions against your license.

Continued

EXHIBIT 10.7

Sample Interrogatories—Continued

6. Indicate whether you have ever had your driver's license suspended, revoked, or canceled and whether you have ever been denied the issuance of a driver's license for mental or physical reasons. If you have, please indicate the date and state of such occurrence as well as the reasons for it.

7. At the time of the incident, did you or any other person have any physical, emotional, or mental disability or condition that may have contributed to the occurrence of the incident? If so, for each person state:

    (a) The name, address, and telephone number;
    (b) The nature of the disability or condition;
    (c) The name, address, and telephone number of any qualified person who treated or diagnosed the condition and the dates of such treatment;
    (d) The manner in which the disability or condition contributed to the occurrence of the incident.

8. Within twenty-four hours before the incident, did you or any person involved in the incident use or take any of the following substances: alcoholic beverage, marijuana, or other drug or medication of any kind (prescription or not)? If so, for each person state:

    (a) The name, address, and telephone number;
    (b) The nature or description of each substance;
    (c) The quantity of each substance used or taken;
    (d) The date and time of day when each substance was used or taken;
    (e) The address where each substance was used or taken;
    (f) The name, address, and telephone number of each person who was present when each substance was used or taken;
    (g) The name, address, and telephone number of any health-care provider that prescribed or furnished the substance and the condition for which it was prescribed or furnished.

9. For each time you have had your vision checked within the last five years, please indicate the following:

    (a) The date and reason for the vision examination;
    (b) The name, address, and telephone number of the examiner;
    (c) The results and/or actions taken.

10. For each time you have had your hearing checked within the last five years, please indicate the following:

    (a) The date and reason for the hearing examination;
    (b) The name, address, and telephone number of the examiner;
    (c) The results and/or actions taken.

[Additional questions would be asked relating to the accident, including questions concerning road conditions and surface, posted speed limits, shoulders and curbs on the road, general character of the neighborhood, when the defendant noticed the plaintiff's vehicle, where it was located and the speed at which the plaintiff was traveling, whether there were other vehicles between the plaintiff's and the defendant's vehicles, and so forth.]

Dated: : 2/15/17 _____

_____
Allen P. Gilmore
Attorney for Plaintiff

is not limited in the number of questions asked in a deposition, whereas most courts limit the number of interrogatory questions. Moreover, because the questioning is often done in person, the deponent must answer without asking an attorney how to respond.

When both the defendant and the plaintiff are located in the same jurisdiction, the site of the deposition is usually the offices of the attorney requesting the deposition. When the parties are in different jurisdictions, other arrangements may be made. In the Baranski case, attorney Gilmore may go to Peretto's city and depose Peretto in the office of Peretto's attorney, Cameron. Or the parties may agree to do a videoconference or phone call for the deposition.

Procedure for Taking Depositions

The attorney wishing to depose a party or witness must give reasonable notice in writing to all other parties in the case and to the deposed. This is done by serving the opposing

EXHIBIT 10.8

Notice of Taking Deposition

UNITED STATES DISTRICT COURT
FOR THE WESTERN DISTRICT OF NITA

Katherine Baranski)
      Plaintiff,)
)
v)
)
)
Tony Peretto)
      Defendant.)
	CASE NO. 14-14335-NI
	Honorable Harley M. Larue
	
	NOTICE OF TAKING
	DEPOSITION

TO: Elizabeth A. Cameron
      Cameron & Strauss, P.C.
      310 Lake Drive
      Zero City, ZE 59802

PLEASE TAKE NOTICE that Katherine Baranski, by and through her attorneys, Jeffers, Gilmore & Dunn, will take the deposition of Tony Peretto on Wednesday, April 16, 2017, at 1:30 P.M., at the law offices of Cameron & Strauss, P.C., 310 Lake Drive, Zero City, ZE 59802, pursuant to the Federal Rules of Civil Procedure, before a duly authorized and qualified notary and stenographer.

Dated: March 20, 2017

Jeffers, Gilmore & Dunn

Allen P. Gilmore

Allen P. Gilmore
Attorney for Katherine Baranski
553 Fifth Avenue, Suite 101
Nita City, NI 48801

---

attorney (or attorneys) with a notice of the time and place of the deposition and the name of the person being examined (see Exhibit 10.8 above).

If the person scheduled to be deposed will not attend voluntarily, a paralegal may need to prepare a subpoena for deposition and submit it to the clerk of the court for signature. Generally, a subpoena is an order issued by the court clerk directing a party to appear and to testify at trial, as will be discussed in Chapter 12. A *subpoena for deposition* orders the person to appear at a deposition rather than in a court proceeding. A subpoena should also be prepared if the attorney wants the deponent to bring certain documents or tangible things to the deposition (this is called a *subpoena duces tecum*). Court rules differ on how subpoenas may be issued. Attorneys are often allowed to issue them in the name of the court.

Under FRCP 30 and 31, court permission is required for depositions to be taken before the parties have made the initial disclosures required by Rule 26 (discussed later in this chapter). Also, court approval may be required if either party wants to take more than one deposition from the same person or more than a total of ten depositions in the case. Always check the relevant court rules when planning discovery strategy.

subpoena
A document commanding a person to appear at a certain time and place to give testimony concerning a certain matter.

Drafting Deposition Questions

Depositions are conducted by attorneys. Paralegals may attend depositions but do not ask questions. Deposition questions are often drafted by paralegals, however. In the Baranski case, for example, Gilmore might ask Lopez to draft questions for a deposition of defendant Peretto or someone else, such as an eyewitness to the accident. For Peretto's deposition, Lopez might draft questions similar to those presented in Exhibit 10.9 on page 297. Gilmore can then use Lopez's questions as a checklist during the deposition.

Note, though, that Gilmore's questions are not limited to the questions in the list. Unforeseen questions may arise as Gilmore learns new information during the deposition.

Also, the deponent's answer to one question may reveal the answer to another, so not all the questions on the checklist will need to be asked.

Preparing the Client for a Deposition

No attorney can predict a deponent's answers beforehand. Spontaneous and sometimes contradictory statements can seriously damage the deponent's case. For this reason, the deposed parties and their lawyers prepare for depositions by formulating answers to likely questions. For example, if defendant Peretto's attorney plans to depose plaintiff Baranski, attorney Gilmore might have Baranski come to the office for a run-through of possible questions that Peretto's attorney might ask her.

This preparation does not mean that the lawyer tells the deponent what to say. Instead, the lawyer offers suggestions as to how the answers to certain questions should be phrased. The answers must be truthful, but the truth can be presented in many ways.

A practice deposition can also help laypeople become accustomed to the unfamiliar format and can reduce stress. This lessens the chances that the witness will make an error during the deposition due to nervousness. For example, Gilmore would caution Baranski to limit her responses to the questions and not engage in speculative answers. If Baranski was asked whether she had ever been involved in an automobile accident before, for example, Gilmore would probably caution her to give a simple (but truthful) "yes" or "no" answer. Gilmore normally would permit Baranski to provide additional information only in response to precisely phrased questions.

The Role of the Deponent's Attorney

The deponent's attorney attends the deposition, but the attorney's role is limited. Under FRCP 30, the attorney may instruct a deponent to not answer a question only when necessary to preserve a privilege, to enforce a limitation directed by the court, or to present a motion to terminate the deposition. In other words, if Baranski was deposed by Peretto's attorney, Cameron, she would have to answer Cameron's questions even if the questions were not clearly relevant to the issues of the case—unless the court had previously limited this line of questioning. The deponent's attorney, Gilmore, could object only to questions that called for privileged information to be disclosed. Under Rule 30, that attorney is required to state objections concisely, in a nonargumentative and nonsuggestive manner.

The deponent's attorney or the other party's attorney may also ask questions during the deposition to clarify a point or to establish facts needed for a motion. These questions are asked after the attorney conducting the deposition has finished. After the deponent's attorney has asked questions, the attorney conducting the deposition has another chance to ask questions. This continues until everyone is done.

As will be discussed shortly, deposition proceedings are recorded. If both attorneys agree, they can go "off the record" to clarify a point or discuss a disputed issue. Depositions are stressful and tempers often flare. In the event that the deposition can not be conducted in an orderly fashion, the attorney conducting the deposition may have to terminate it.

The Deposition Transcript

deposition transcript
The official transcription of the recording taken during a deposition.

Every utterance made during a deposition is recorded. A court reporter usually records the deposition proceedings and creates an official deposition transcript. Methods of recording a deposition include stenographic recording (a traditional method that involves the use of a shorthand machine or written shorthand), digital audio recording, digital video recording, or some combination of these methods. Rule 30(b)(2) of the FRCP states that unless the court orders otherwise, a deposition "may be recorded by sound, sound-and-visual, or stenographic means."

impeach
To call into question the credibility of a witness by challenging the truth or accuracy of his or her trial statement.

Either party may use the deposition transcript during the trial to prove a particular point or to impeach (call into question) the credibility of a witness who says something during the trial different from what was stated during the deposition. For example, a

EXHIBIT 10.9

Sample Deposition Questions

<u>DEPOSITION QUESTIONS</u>

1. Please state your full name and address for the record.
2. Please state your age, birth date, and Social Security number.
3. What is your educational level, and what employment position do you hold?
4. Do you have a criminal record, and if so, for what?
5. Have you been involved in previous automobile accidents? What driving violations have you had? Has your driver's license ever been suspended?
6. What is your medical history? Have you ever had health problems? Are you in perfect health? Were you in perfect health at the time of the accident?
7. Do you wear glasses or contact lenses? If so, for what condition? Were you wearing your glasses or contacts at the time the accident occurred?
8. Do you take medication of any kind?
9. Do you have any similar lawsuits or any claims pending against you?
10. Who is your automobile insurer? What are your policy limits?
11. Were there any passengers in your vehicle at the time of the accident?
12. Describe your vehicle. What was the mechanical condition of your vehicle at the time of the accident? Do you do your own mechanical work? If so, what training do you have in maintaining and repairing automobiles? Had you taken your vehicle to a professional mechanic's shop prior to the accident?
13. Please state the date on which the accident occurred.
14. Where were you prior to the accident, for at least the six hours preceding the accident?
15. Where were you going when the accident occurred, and for what purpose?
16. What were you doing during the last few moments before the accident? Were you smoking, eating, drinking, or chewing gum?
17. What were you thinking about just before the accident occurred?
18. What route did you take to reach your destination, and why did you take this particular route?
19. Describe the weather conditions at the time of the accident.
20. Please recite the facts of how the accident occurred.
21. Please describe the area in which the accident occurred. Were there many cars and pedestrians on the streets? Were there traffic controls, obstructions, or the like?
22. What was your location, and in what direction were you going?
23. When did you see the plaintiff's automobile approaching?
24. How far away were you when you first saw the auto? What was your rate of speed?
25. Did your vehicle move forward or was it pushed backward by the impact?
26. When did you first apply your brakes? Were your brakes functioning properly?
27. Did you attempt to avoid the accident? If so, how?
28. Did you receive a traffic ticket as a result of the accident?
29. Do you own the vehicle that you were driving at the time of the accident?
30. Were you acting within the scope of your employment when the accident occurred?
31. What were the conditions of the parties affected by the accident just after the accident occurred?
32. Did you attempt to provide first aid to any party?
33. How did the plaintiff leave the scene, and what was the plaintiff's physical condition?
34. What was the damage to your vehicle, and has it been repaired?

witness in the Baranski case might state during the deposition that Peretto *did not* stop at the stop sign before crossing Mattis Avenue. If, at trial, the witness states that Peretto *did* stop at the stop sign before crossing Mattis Avenue, Baranski's attorney could challenge the witness's credibility on the basis of the deposition transcript. Exhibit 10.10 on the next page shows a page from a transcript of a deposition conducted by Gilmore in the case. The deponent was Julia Williams, an eyewitness to the accident. On the transcript, the letter "Q" precedes each question asked by Gilmore, and "A" precedes each of Williams's answers.

Summarizing and Indexing the Deposition Transcript

Typically, the paralegal summarizes the deposition transcript. The summary, which along with the transcript will become part of the litigation file, allows members of the litigation team to review the information obtained from deponents during depositions.

EXHIBIT 10.10

A Deposition Transcript (Excerpt)

67	Q: Where were you at the time of the accident?
68	A: I was on the southwest corner of the intersection.
69	Q: Are you referring to the intersection where Thirty-eighth Street crosses Mattis Avenue?
70	A: Yes.
71	Q: Why were you there at the time of the accident?
72	A: Well, I was on my way to work. I usually walk down Mattis Avenue to the hospital.
73	Q: So you were walking to work down Mattis Avenue and you saw the accident?
74	A: Yes.
75	Q: What did you see?
76	A: Well, as I was about to cross the street, a dark green van passed within three feet of me and ran the
77	stop sign and crashed into another car.
78	Q: Can you remember if the driver of the van was a male or a female?
79	A: Yes. It was a man.
80	Q: I am showing you a picture. Can you identify the man in the picture?
81	A: Yes. That is the man who was driving the van.
82	Q: Do you wear glasses?
83	A: I need glasses only for reading. I have excellent distance vision.
84	Q: How long has it been since your last eye exam with a doctor?
85	A: Oh, just a month ago, with Dr. Sullivan.

page 4

If Lopez summarizes the deposition transcript of Julia Williams, the transcript is likely summarized sequentially—that is, in the order in which it was given during the deposition—as shown in Exhibit 10.11 on the facing page. Notice that the summary includes the page and line numbers in the deposition transcript where the full text of the information can be found.

Often, in addition to summarizing the transcript, the paralegal provides an index. It is a list of topics (such as education, employment status, injuries, and medical costs) followed by the relevant page and line numbers of the deposition transcript. Together, the summary and the index allow anyone involved in the case to locate information quickly. More tips for summarizing a deposition are provided in the *Developing Paralegal Skills* feature on page 300.

Requests for Production and Physical Examination

Another form of discovery is a request for the production of documents or tangible things or for permission to enter property for inspection and other purposes. FRCP 34 authorizes each party to request evidence from any other party. If the item requested is large or cannot be "produced" for some reason (Peretto's van for example), then the party can request permission to enter on the other party's land to inspect, test, sample, and photograph the item. In federal courts, the duty of disclosure under FRCP 26 has greatly decreased the need to file such production requests.

| Case: | Baranski v. Peretto | Attorney: Allen P. Gilmore |
| | Plaintiff 15773 | Legal Assistant: Elena Lopez |

Deponent: Julia Williams   Date: March 17, 2017
3801 Mattis Avenue
Nita City, Nita 48800

Page	Line(s)	
		* * * *
4	72–77	Williams stated that she was on the way to work at the time of the accident. She was about to cross the street when Peretto's car ("a dark green van") passed within three feet of her, ran the stop sign, and crashed into Baranski's car.
4	80–81	When shown a picture of Peretto, she identified him as the driver of the green van.
4	82–83	Williams has excellent distance vision and does not require corrective lenses. She does need reading glasses for close work.
		* * * *

EXHIBIT 10.11
A Deposition Summary (Excerpt)

When the mental or physical condition of a party is in controversy, the opposing party may request the court to order the party to submit to a physical or mental examination by a licensed examiner. For example, if Peretto claims that Baranski's injuries were the result of a preexisting medical condition rather than the collision, defense attorney Cameron may file a request to have Baranski examined by a physician. Because the existence, nature, and extent of Baranski's injuries are important in calculating the damages that she might be able to recover from Peretto, the court may grant the request.

Requests for Admission

During discovery, a party can also request that the opposing party admit the truth of matters relating to the case. For example, Baranski's attorney can request that Peretto admit that he owned the car involved in the accident. Such admissions save time at trial because the parties do not spend time proving admitted facts. Any matter admitted under such a request is established as true for the trial. FRCP 36 permits requests for admission but requires that a request cannot be made, without the court's permission, before the pre-discovery meeting of the attorneys.

The Duty to Disclose under FRCP 26

Each party has a duty to disclose to the other party specified types of information prior to the discovery stage of litigation. Under FRCP Rule 26(f), once a lawsuit is brought, the parties (the plaintiff and defendant and/or their attorneys) must schedule a pre-discovery meeting to discuss the nature of the lawsuit, any defenses that may be raised against the claims being brought, and possibilities for promptly settling or otherwise resolving the dispute. The meeting should take place as soon as practicable but at least fourteen days before a scheduling conference is held or a scheduling order issued.

Either at this meeting or within ten days after it, the parties must also make the initial disclosures described below and submit to the court a plan for discovery. As the trial date approaches, the attorneys must make subsequent disclosures relating to witnesses, documents, and other relevant information.

DEVELOPING PARALEGAL SKILLS

DEPOSITION SUMMARIES

After a deposition is taken, each attorney orders a copy of the deposition transcript. Copies may be obtained in printed form or in an electronic file. When the transcript is received, the paralegal's job is to prepare a summary of the testimony that was given. The summary is typically only a few pages in length.

The legal assistant must be very familiar with the lawsuit and the legal theories that are being pursued so that he or she can point out possible inconsistencies in the testimony or between the testimony and the pleadings. The paralegal might also give special emphasis to any testimony that will help to prove the client's case in court.

After the deposition summary has been created, the paralegal places the summary in the litigation file, usually in a special discovery folder or binder within the larger

file. The deposition summary will be used to prepare for future depositions, to prepare pretrial motions, and to impeach witnesses at the trial, should they give contradictory testimony.

TIPS FOR SUMMARIZING A DEPOSITION

- Find out how the deposition is to be summarized—by chronology, by legal issue, by factual issues, or otherwise.
- Read through the deposition transcript and mark important pages.
- Be sure to include a reference to the page and line that is being summarized.
- Take advantage of software that can assist in summarizing the deposition transcript.

These rules do not replace the methods of discovery discussed in the preceding section. Rather, they impose a duty on attorneys to disclose specified information to opposing counsel early in the litigation process so that discovery time and costs can be reduced. Attorneys use discovery tools (such as depositions and interrogatories) to obtain information, but they cannot do so until the pre-discovery meeting has been held and initial disclosures have been made.

Initial Disclosures

FRCP 26(a)(1) requires each party to disclose the following information to the other party at an initial meeting of the parties or within ten days of the meeting:

- The name, address, and telephone number of any person likely to have "discoverable information" and the nature of that information.

- A copy or "description by category and location" of all documents, data, and other "things in the possession, custody, or control of the party" relevant to the dispute.

- A computation of the damages claimed by the disclosing party. The party must make available to the other party for inspection and copying the documents on which the computation is based.

- Copies of any insurance policies that cover the injuries or harms alleged in the lawsuit and that may pay part or all of a judgment resulting from the dispute.

In the Baranski case, Gilmore and Lopez must quickly assemble all relevant information, documents, and other evidence gathered during client interviews and preliminary investigation. Lopez prepares copies of the documents—or a description of them—for Gilmore's review and signature. These will be filed with the court and sent to Peretto's attorney. In the information disclosed, Gilmore and Lopez must include even information that might damage Baranski's position. They need not disclose *privileged information*, however, such as confidential discussions between Baranski and Gilmore.

Failure to Disclose

A party is not excused from disclosing relevant information simply because the party has not yet completed an investigation into the case or because the other party has not yet made disclosures. FRCP 37(c) makes clear that the failure to make initial disclosures can result in serious sanctions.

If a party fails to make required disclosures, that party will not be able to use the information as evidence at trial. In addition, the court may impose other sanctions, such as ordering the party to pay reasonable expenses, including attorneys' fees, created by the failure to disclose. In sum, Gilmore and Lopez need to make sure that all relevant information (that is not privileged) is disclosed, or Gilmore will not be able to use it in court (and may face other sanctions).

Discovery Plan

As mentioned above, at the initial meeting of the parties, the attorneys must work out a discovery plan and submit a report describing the plan to the court within ten days of the meeting. The type of information to be included in the discovery plan is illustrated in Exhibit 10.12 on the following page, which shows Form 35, a form created for this purpose. As indicated by the form, Rule 26(f) allows the attorneys room to negotiate details of discovery, including time schedules to be followed.

In the Baranski case, paralegal Lopez will make sure that attorney Gilmore takes a copy of Form 35 with him to the initial pre-discovery meeting of the parties to use as a checklist, along with tentative dates by which they believe they can have completed discovery. After the attorneys decide on the details of the plan to be proposed to the court, Gilmore may have Lopez draft a final version of the plan for his review and signature.

discovery plan
A plan formed by the attorneys litigating a lawsuit, on behalf of their clients, that indicates the types of information that will be disclosed by each party to the other prior to trial, the testimony and evidence that each party will or may introduce at trial, and the general schedule for pretrial disclosures and events.

Subsequent Disclosures

In addition to the initial disclosures just discussed, each party must make other disclosures prior to trial. All subsequent disclosures must also be in writing, signed by the attorneys, and filed with the court. These include information relating to expert witnesses, other witnesses, and exhibits that may be used at trial.

Expert Witnesses

Under FRCP 26(a)(2), parties must disclose to other parties the names of expert witnesses who may be called to testify during the trial. Additionally, the following information about each expert must be disclosed in a report signed by the expert witness:

- A statement by the expert indicating the opinions that will be expressed, the basis for the opinions, and the data or information considered by the witness when forming the opinions.

- Exhibits that will be used to summarize or support the opinions.

- The qualifications of the expert witness, including a list of all publications authored by the witness in the last ten years.

- The compensation to be paid to the expert witness.

- A list of other cases in which the witness has testified as an expert at trial or by deposition in the preceding four years.

These disclosures must be made at times set by the court. If the court does not indicate any times, then they must be made at least ninety days before the trial date.

EXHIBIT 10.12

Form 35—Report of Parties' Planning Meeting (Discovery Plan)

[Caption and Names of Parties]

1. Pursuant to Fed. R. Civ. P. 26(f), a meeting was held on _____(date)_____ at _____(place)_____ and was attended by:

_____(name)_____ for plaintiff(s) _____(party name)_____
_____(name)_____ for defendant(s) _____(party name)_____
_____(name)_____ for defendant(s) _____(party name)_____

2. Pre-Discovery Disclosures. The parties [have exchanged] [will exchange by _____(date)_____] the information required by [Fed. R. Civ. P. 26(a)(1)] [(local rule _____)].

3. Discovery Plan. The parties jointly propose to the court the following discovery plan: [Use separate paragraphs or subparagraphs as necessary if parties disagree.]

Discovery will be needed on the following subjects:
_____(brief description of subjects on which discovery will be needed)_____
All discovery commenced in time to be completed by _(date)_. [Discovery on_(issue for early discovery)_
to be completed by _____(date)_____.]
Maximum of ____ interrogatories by each party to any other party. [Responses due ____ days after service.]
Maximum of ____ requests for admission by each party to any other party. [Responses due ____ days after service.]
Maximum of ____ depositions by plaintiff(s) and ____ by defendant(s).
Each deposition [other than of _____] limited to maximum of ____ hours unless extended by agreement of parties.
Reports from retained experts under Rule 26(a)(2) due:
    from plaintiff(s) by _____(date)_____.
    from defendant(s) by _____(date)_____.
Supplementations under Rule 26(e) due _(time(s) or intervals(s))_.

4. Other Items. [Use separate paragraphs or subparagraphs as necessary if parties disagree.]

The parties [request] [do not request] a conference with the court before entry of the scheduling order.
The parties request a pretrial conference in_____(month and year)_____.
Plaintiff(s) should be allowed until _(date)_ to join additional parties and until _(date)_ to amend the pleadings.
Defendant(s) should be allowed until _(date)_ to join additional parties and until _(date)_ to amend the pleadings.
All potentially dispositive motions should be filed by_(date)_.
Settlement [is likely] [is unlikely] [cannot be evaluated prior to _(date)_] [may be enhanced by use of the following alternative
    dispute resolution procedure: _____].
Final lists of witnesses and exhibits under Rule 26(a)(3) should be due
    from plaintiff(s) by _(date)_.
    from defendant(s) by _(date)_.
Parties should have _____ days after service of final lists of witnesses and exhibits to list objections under Rule 26(a)(3).
The case should be ready for trial by _(date)_ [and at the time is expected to take approximately _(length of time)_].
[Other matters.]

Date: _____

Other Pretrial Disclosures

Under FRCP 26(a)(3), each party must also disclose to the other party the following information about witnesses who will testify at trial or any exhibits that may be used:

- A list of the names, addresses, and telephone numbers of other witnesses who may be called during the trial to give testimony. The list must indicate whether the witness "will" or "may" be called.

- A list of witnesses whose deposition testimony may be offered during the trial and a transcript of the relevant sections of the deposition testimony, if the testimony was not taken stenographically.

- A list of exhibits that indicates which exhibits will and may be offered.

These disclosures must be made at least thirty days before trial, unless the court orders otherwise. Once disclosures have been made, the opposing party has fourteen days to file with the court any objections to the use of any deposition or exhibit. If objections are not made, they are presumed to be waived (unless a party can show good cause why he or she failed to object to the disclosures previously).

An attorney's duty to disclose relevant information is ongoing throughout the pretrial stage. Any time an attorney learns new relevant supplemental information concerning statements or responses made earlier, that information must be disclosed to the other party. An important task for many paralegals is keeping track of the opposing parties' discovery requests so the attorney can be alerted if a supplemental filing is necessary.

Discovery of Electronic Evidence

Electronic evidence, or e-evidence, includes computer-generated or electronically recorded information, such as e-mail, voice mail, Facebook, Google+, Instagram, or Twitter postings on social media sites, blog posts, documents, and other data that may be posted on a cloud server. E-evidence has become increasingly important because it can reveal facts found only in electronic format. The FRCP and state rules specifically allow discovery of electronic "data compilations." As in other areas of the practice of law, electronic tools are playing a growing part of discovery.

The Advantages of Electronic Evidence

Most information stored on computers is never printed on paper. When a person works on a computer, information is recorded on a hard drive even if not "saved" by the user. This information, called metadata, is the hidden data kept by the computer about a file, including location, path, creator, date created, date last accessed, earlier versions, passwords, and formatting. It reveals information about how, when, and by whom a file was created, accessed, modified, and transmitted. This information can only be obtained from the file in its electronic format.

E-Mail Communications

Billions of e-mails are sent annually. E-mail has become fertile ground for evidence in litigation and has been the "smoking gun" in some cases. Many people converse casually in e-mail communications, as if talking to a friend. This makes e-mail believable and compelling evidence—which can be damaging if discovered by outsiders.

In addition, in its electronic form, e-mail contains information that provides links to other e-mails, e-mail attachments, erased files, and metadata. Metadata reveal the identity of any person who received copies of an e-mail message (even "blind" copies). Thus, e-evidence can be used to trace a message to its true originator, reconstruct an e-mail conversation, and establish a timeline of the events in dispute (who knew what, when). Attorneys also use it to verify clients' claims or discredit the claims of the opposition.

Deleted Files Can Be Retrieved

A major advantage of e-evidence is that even deleted files can often be retrieved from within a computer. Deleting a file does not destroy the data, but simply makes the space occupied by the file available to be overwritten by new information. Until that space is actually used for new data (which may never occur), experts can retrieve the deleted record.

The use of backup drives and cloud storage makes it even less likely that simply erasing a file actually deletes it. Online storage servers are often themselves backed up so it is possible to locate copies of files deleted from individual computers. Postings on blogs or other websites may be accessed using backups of a Web-hosting service. Never assume that a file from a computer connected to a network is gone just because it was erased from that computer.

The same is true of e-mails and other messages. Many people think that when they delete an e-mail and empty the "trash," the message is gone. As just described, however, deleted data remain on the computer until overwritten by new data (or wiped out by

metadata
Embedded electronic data recorded by a computer in association with a particular file, including location, path, creator, date created, date last accessed, hidden notes, earlier versions, passwords, and formatting. Metadata reveal information about how, when, and by whom a document was created, accessed, modified, and transmitted.

utility software) and usually remain in a central server. Similarly, tweets may have been "re-tweeted," blog posts may have been distributed through networks of servers, and so forth.

Experts have even been able to retrieve data, in whole or in part, from computers that have been damaged by water, fire, or severe impact. Therefore, do not assume that e-evidence is not available just because a file was deleted, a computer was damaged, or a utility program was run. Technical issues in discovery are growing ever more complex, as discussed in *Technology and Today's Paralegal* on the facing page.

The Sources of Electronic Evidence

The key to conducting electronic discovery is developing an understanding of the kinds of information it can provide so you know where to look for particular information. Generally, data can be located in active files, in backup files, or as residual data. Active files are currently accessible on the computer (documents and e-mail, for example). Backup files have been copied to other locations such as flash drives or to remote servers. Residual data appear to be gone but are still recoverable from somewhere on the computer system by special software.

Backup Data

Backup files can be a hidden treasure for the legal team. Reviewing backup copies of documents and e-mail provides useful information about how a particular matter progressed over several weeks or months. Because the location of the data depends on the backup practice in use, you need to find out what the policy is as soon as you can during discovery. See the *Developing Paralegal Skills* feature on page 306 for more tips on e-discovery.

Backup files contain not only e-mail messages and word-processing documents, but also other embedded information that can be useful. When computers are networked, audit trails that keep track of network usage may be available. An audit trail will tell you who accessed the system, when it was accessed, and whether those who accessed the system copied, downloaded, modified, or deleted any files. Some word-processing software allows users to insert hidden comments or track changes while drafting and revising documents. These comments and revisions can also be accessed from the electronic version of the backup file.

Other Sources of E-Evidence

Electronic evidence is not limited to the data on computer systems. It includes *all* electronically recorded information, such as voice mail, video, electronic calendars, and phone logs on smartphones, iPads, tablets, laptops, and other devices that digitally store data. Use traditional discovery tactics (such as interrogatories and depositions) to find out about other sources of potential e-evidence. Consider all possible sources that might prove fruitful, but such requests must be reasonable and in good faith.

The Special Requirements of Electronic Evidence

While courts allow discovery of electronic evidence, judges know that electronic evidence can be manipulated. To ensure that the evidence obtained during discovery will be admissible, you must do two things. First, make sure that you obtain an exact image copy of the electronic evidence. Second, make sure you can prove that nothing has been changed from the time the image copy was made. Keeping a backup copy of the material as received from the other party is one way to do this. Your law firm will likely have policies on how to handle e-evidence.

Acquiring an Image Copy

To use any evidence, you must convince the court that it is authentic. In the case of electronic evidence, you must show that the electronic version is the same as the version that was present on the target system. The way to do this is to have an image copy made.

TECHNOLOGY AND TODAY'S PARALEGAL

WHO BEARS THE COSTS OF ELECTRONIC DISCOVERY?

Traditionally, the party responding to a discovery request pays the expenses involved in obtaining the requested materials. If compliance would be too burdensome or costly, however, the judge could either limit the scope of the request or shift some or all of the costs to the requesting party. How do these traditional rules governing discovery apply to requests for electronic evidence?

WHY COURTS MIGHT SHIFT THE COSTS OF ELECTRONIC DISCOVERY

Electronic discovery has dramatically increased the costs associated with complying with discovery requests. It is no longer simply a matter of photocopying paper documents. Now the responding party may need to hire computer forensics (qualified scientific) experts to make "image" copies of desktop, laptop, and server hard drives, as well as removable storage media (such as flash drives), backup drives, and server-based systems, voice mail, smartphones, and any other form of digitally stored data.

In cases involving multiple parties or large corporations with many offices and employees, the electronic discovery process can easily run into hundreds of thousands of dollars—or more.

COSTLY DISCOVERY

For example, Viacom, which owns Comedy Central and other television channels, sued YouTube, owned by Google, for more than $1 billion. Viacom claimed that YouTube committed copyright violations by allowing clips from Viacom's television shows to be posted on YouTube without Viacom's permission.[a] Viacom hired a company, BayTSP, to search for possible violations on YouTube. BayTSP identified more than 150,000 clips posted on YouTube. Viacom claimed losses from each such posting.

YouTube demanded to see evidence of the violations. BayTSP estimated that it had gathered more than 1 million documents, all electronic, related to the clip postings. It protested to the court that the document request was unreasonable. BayTSP spent 2,000 hours over six months searching and reviewing the documents. Using electronic filters, it narrowed the list to 650,000 potentially relevant documents. The court allowed YouTube's request for these documents to go forward. Given the amount at stake in the litigation, YouTube was within its rights, and BayTSP had to provide the records. The cost of document production would be borne by BayTSP or, the court noted, probably by Viacom because BayTSP worked for it. The court held, however, that when costs are burdensome, a court may order the costs to be split between defendant and plaintiff.

WHAT FACTORS DO COURTS CONSIDER IN DECIDING TO SHIFT COSTS?

When is it appropriate for a court to shift cost from one party to another in discovery? The FRCP advisory committee lists seven factors:

1. the specificity of the discovery request;
2. the quantity of information available from other and more easily accessed sources;
3. the failure to produce relevant information that seems likely to have existed but is no longer available on more easily accessed sources;
4. the likelihood of finding relevant responsive information that cannot be obtained from other, more easily accessed sources;
5. predictions as to the importance and usefulness of the further information;
6. the importance of the issues at stake in the litigation;
7. and the parties' resources.[b]

TECHNOLOGY TIP

Paralegals should keep in mind not only the high costs of some electronic discovery requests but the possibility that the court may shift some of these costs. Suppose, for example, you are assisting a corporate defendant in a product liability lawsuit brought by a plaintiff who was seriously harmed by one of the defendant's products. If the plaintiff requests extensive electronic evidence during discovery, the defendant corporation may be required to pay a significant portion of the costs of the requested discovery.

---

a. *Viacom International v. YouTube, Inc.*, 2009 WL 102808 (N.D.Cal. 2009).

b. Fed.R.Civ.P. 26(b)(2).

DEVELOPING PARALEGAL SKILLS

ELECTRONIC DISCOVERY

Paralegals must be prepared to deal with electronic discovery. This means not only formulating electronic discovery plans, but making sure to preserve the integrity of any electronic evidence acquired. It is important, too, to remember that e-evidence is fragile. Although—as discussed in the chapter—it may be difficult to permanently delete files from a computer system, it is not impossible. Every time a user enters new data, loads new software, or performs routine maintenance procedures, the data on the computer are permanently altered.

Firms with careful data retention policies regularly perform procedures to eliminate such files. Just booting up a computer can change dates and times on numerous files. The following are general guidelines to follow in conducting e-discovery.

TIPS FOR CONDUCTING E-DISCOVERY

- Immediately write a preservation-of-evidence letter to all parties involved, including your client, at the outset

of the case. This letter informs the parties that they have a duty to take immediate action to preserve any potential electronic evidence.

- Use interrogatories to gather information about the opposing party's computer system so that you can learn about the various technologies used by that party.

- Follow up with depositions. Once you know the names of the parties who oversee the system or have special knowledge of it, take depositions from them.

- After you have found out the details of where electronic evidence is located, draft a request for production of the evidence.

- When the e-evidence is acquired, determine how best to manage, review, and interpret the data, which may involve using the services of an outside company that specializes in this field. Special software can help manage files of millions of e-mails or large amounts of other e-evidence.

Suppose the target system is a computer hard drive. Making an image copy involves creating an electronic image of the drive being copied. The copy would capture all data, including residual data. This is different from the usual file-by-file copying method.

Making an image copy of a computer drive is best left to an expert in computer forensics. These experts collect, preserve, and analyze electronic evidence and testify in court if needed.

Preserving the Chain of Custody

Once you have acquired an exact copy of the electronic evidence, you must establish and maintain a chain of custody to avoid any claims that the evidence has been tampered with. The phrase chain of custody refers to the movement and location of evidence from the time it is obtained to the time it is presented in court.

It is crucial when dealing with electronic evidence to track the evidence from its original source to its submission to the court. Tracking provides the court assurance that nothing has been added, changed, or deleted. The original image copy should be protected so it is tamperproof, labeled as the original, and kept in a secure location. Typically, a forensic specialist copies the original data that are write-protected and scanned for viruses. You may need to review the evidence only on a secure computer not connected to the Internet to protect data integrity.

Federal Rule of Evidence 502

The use of electronic evidence can result in a huge number of documents being made available to an opposing party. This availability has increased the number of documents accidentally released. In many cases, for example, a party had the right to access e-mails

chain of custody
A series describing the movement and location of evidence from the time it is obtained to the time it is presented in court. The court requires that evidence be preserved in the condition in which it was obtained if it is to be admitted into evidence at trial.

of the opposing party relating to a particular matter. While attempts are made to filter out non-relevant e-mails, some e-mails that should have been protected by attorney-client confidentiality rules have been accidentally included among the thousands of e-mails seen by the opposing party.

To deal with this problem, Congress changed Federal Rule of Evidence 502. Under it, if there is an accidental release of material that should have been protected, the court may rule that protection was not waived by accidental disclosure. Courts consider the following factors in deciding if a privileged document has been lost to the opposing party or is still protected:

1. the reasonableness of precautions taken to prevent inadvertent disclosure in view of the extent of document production,

2. the number of inadvertent disclosures,

3. the extent of the disclosures,

4. the promptness of steps taken to remedy the disclosure, and

5. whether interests of justice would be served by relieving the party of its error of disclosing a protected document.

Paralegals often play a key role in organizing documents, so they must be alert to such issues. In complex cases involving a huge number of electronic documents, firms that are experts in such matters can be hired to help filter and sort documents.

Maintenance of Electronic Records

To this point we have considered the collection of electronic matter. A related issue for all firms is the need to put in place a records management system before litigation arises to minimize the burden of responding to discovery requests. Because litigation is a virtual certainty for many businesses, the up-front investment is often worthwhile.

Do Not Keep What Is Not Needed

The key to an e-discovery-ready records-management system is to ensure that records are properly categorized and stored. Records not required by business needs or legal requirements are destroyed and "scrubbed" from computers by programs that ensure actual deletion of the material. In a recent survey, more than two-thirds of corporate legal departments sought a records-management system that covered everything from data preservation to production of documents.

Cost and Risk Controls

Important issues for clients are controlling costs and reducing risks. Among the most costly aspects of document production is review for relevance and privilege, a process that may consume more than half of a litigation budget. Automated processes can help reduce costs by excluding documents based on criteria such as file type, dates, storage location, or the presence or absence of key words.

Risk control refers to the measures used to identify, preserve, and organize documents. Errors can lead to fines or other penalties. Among the most difficult issues to address is how to handle e-mail and calendar archives. Not only must the e-mails themselves be saved, but also the metadata about the e-mails, such as storage location, creation dates and times, path information, and so on.

Paralegals working in the corporate setting find proper record maintenance a key part of document control. Records—both paper and electronic—that are no longer legally required to be maintained are destroyed. This helps prevent a party in litigation from going on a "fishing" expedition into documents that may date back in time beyond what is required. When records are not well monitored, open access to electronic media is more likely to be allowed by a court. Similarly, law firms should be proactive in careful record organization and maintenance to protect the firm and its clients.

Pretrial Motions

As we discussed earlier in the chapter, and as shown in Exhibit 10.13 below, there are a number of motions that may be made before trial. In Chapter 6 we noted that many conflicts are settled by some form of alternative dispute resolution before trial. When that happens, and the parties reach a settlement agreement, the court is informed and, after reviewing the agreement, usually approves it and dismisses the case.

Summary Judgment

If there is no settlement, one of the last substantive motions likely to be filed before trial is a motion for summary judgment. The party filing the motion is asking the court to grant a judgment in his or her favor without a trial because there is no real disagreement about the relevant facts. Once discovery is complete, the parties can argue that

motion for summary judgment
A motion that may be filed by either party in which the party asks the court to enter judgment in his or her favor without a trial. A motion for summary judgment can be supported by evidence outside the pleadings, such as witnesses' affidavits, answers to interrogatories, and other evidence obtained prior to or during discovery.

EXHIBIT 10.13
Pretrial Motions

MOTION TO DISMISS

A motion filed by the defendant in which the defendant asks the court to dismiss the case for a specified reason, such as improper service, lack of personal jurisdiction, or the plaintiff's failure to state a claim for which relief can be granted. A plaintiff would file a motion to dismiss against a counterclaim or cross-claim.

MOTION TO STRIKE

A motion filed by a party in which the party asks the court to strike (delete) material from another party's filing. Motions to strike help to clarify the underlying issues by removing paragraphs that are redundant or irrelevant to the action.

MOTION TO MAKE MORE DEFINITE AND CERTAIN

A motion filed by the defendant to compel the plaintiff to clarify the basis of the plaintiff's cause of action. The motion is filed when the defendant believes that the complaint is too vague or ambiguous for the defendant to respond to it in a meaningful way. Similarly, a plaintiff might file such a motion about a counterclaim or cross-claim.

MOTION TO COMPEL DISCOVERY

A motion that may be filed by either party in which the party asks the court to compel the other party to comply with a discovery request. If a party refuses to allow the opponent to inspect and copy certain documents, for example, the party requesting the documents may make a motion to compel production of the documents.

MOTION FOR JUDGMENT ON THE PLEADINGS

After all pleadings have been filed, either party may file this motion. It may be used when there are no facts in dispute, only a question of how the law will apply to the undisputed facts.

MOTION FOR SUMMARY JUDGMENT

A motion that may be filed by either party in which the party asks the court to enter judgment in his or her favor without a trial. Unlike a motion for judgment on the pleadings, a motion for summary judgment can be supported by evidence outside the pleadings, such as witnesses' affidavits, answers to interrogatories, and other evidence obtained prior to or during discovery.

no material (relevant) facts are in dispute and the only question is how the law applies to undisputed facts.

Considerations by the Court

When the court considers a motion for summary judgment, it considers the evidence the parties have gathered for trial. To support the motion, a party submits evidence obtained, such as depositions and interrogatories, and argues that, given the facts, the other party cannot prevail at trial. The court reviews the evidence in the light most favorable to the nonmoving party. That is, the court must be satisfied that it has drawn all permissible inferences in that party's favor in interpreting the evidence. This motion is more likely to be successfully used by the defendant, but in about a quarter of cases in which the motion is used, it is successful for the plaintiff.

Motion by Defendant

In the Baranski case, for example, suppose it is established that Peretto was in another state at the time of the accident. Peretto's attorney could make a motion for summary judgment in Peretto's favor and attach to the motion a witness's sworn statement that Peretto was in the other state at the time of the accident. Unless Baranski's attorney could bring in other evidence to show that Peretto was at the scene of the accident, Peretto's motion for summary judgment would be granted.

A motion for summary judgment would also be appropriate if Baranski had previously signed a release waiving her right to sue Peretto on the claim. In that situation, attorney Cameron would attach a copy of the release to the motion before filing the motion with the court. Cameron would also prepare a memorandum of law in support of the motion. When the court heard the motion, Cameron would argue that execution of the waiver barred Baranski from pursuing her claim against Peretto.

Burden of Proof

The burden would then shift to Gilmore to show that the release was invalid or otherwise not binding on Baranski. If the judge believed that Baranski involuntarily signed the release, then the judge would grant the motion. If Gilmore convinced the judge that there was an issue concerning the validity of the release, such as evidence that the release signed by Baranski had been procured by fraud, then the judge would deny the motion for summary judgment and permit the case to go to trial. The validity of the release would then be determined at trial by the fact finder.

KEY TERMS AND CONCEPTS

Chapter Summary / Civil Litigation: Before the Trial

CIVIL LITIGATION—A BIRD'S-EYE VIEW

1. *Pretrial settlements*—Throughout the pretrial stage of litigation, the attorney and paralegal attempt to help the parties reach a settlement at the same time as they are preparing the case for trial.

2. *Procedural requirements*—Although civil lawsuits vary from case to case in terms of complexity, cost, and detail, all civil litigation involves similar procedural steps, as described in Exhibit 10.1 on page 272.

The Federal Rules of Civil Procedure (FRCP) govern civil cases in federal courts and what must be done during various stages of litigation. Each state has adopted its own rules of civil procedure, which are often similar to the FRCP. Many courts also have (local) rules of procedure that supplement the federal or state rules.

THE PRELIMINARIES

1. *The initial client interview*—The first step occurs when an attorney meets with a client who wishes to bring a lawsuit against another party. Before the meeting, the paralegal checks to ensure that representing the client would not create a conflict of interest. The attorney normally conducts the initial client interview, although the paralegal often attends and may make arrangements for subsequent meetings.

2. *Preliminary investigation*—Once the attorney agrees to represent the client in the lawsuit and the client has signed the retainer agreement, the attorney and paralegal undertake a preliminary investigation to determine the facts alleged by the client and gain other information relating to the case.

3. *Creating the litigation file*—A litigation file is created to hold all documents and records pertaining to the lawsuit. Each law firm or legal department has procedures for organizing and maintaining litigation files. Generally, the file expands as the case progresses to include subfiles for the pleadings, discovery, and other documents relating to the litigation.

THE PLEADINGS

The pleadings inform each party of the claims of the other and detail the facts, charges, and defenses involved in the litigation. Pleadings typically consist of the plaintiff's complaint, the defendant's answer, and any counterclaim or cross-claim.

1. *Drafting the complaint*—A complaint states the claim(s) that plaintiff is making against the defendant. A lawsuit is initiated by filing a complaint with the clerk of the appropriate court.

   a. The complaint includes a caption, jurisdictional allegations, general allegations (body of the complaint) detailing the cause of action, a prayer for relief, a signature, and, if appropriate, a demand for a jury trial.

   b. A complaint can be filed either by personal delivery of the papers to the court clerk or, if the court permits, by electronic filing. The procedural requirements of courts that allow electronic filing vary and must be followed carefully.

2. *Filing the complaint*—The document is filed in paper or electronically. E-filing is becoming more common;

some states have statewide systems, and some courts require e-filing.

3. *Service of process*—Typically, the defendant is notified of a lawsuit by delivery of the complaint and a summons (called service of process). The summons identifies the parties to the suit, identifies the court in which the case has been filed, and directs the defendant to respond to the complaint within a specified time period.

   a. Although often the complaint and summons are personally delivered to the defendant, other methods of service are allowed in some situations.

   b. In federal cases and in many states, the defendant can waive, or give up, the right to be personally served with the summons and complaint (and accept service by mail, for example).

   c. Under FRCP 4, if the defendant waives service of process, the defendant receives additional time to respond to the complaint.

4. *The defendant's response*—On receiving the complaint, the defendant has several options.

a. The defendant may submit an answer that denies wrongdoing or asserts an affirmative defense against the plaintiff's claim, such as the plaintiff's contributory negligence. The answer may be followed by a counterclaim, in which the defendant asserts a claim against the plaintiff arising out of the same incident; or it may be followed by a cross-claim, in which the defendant makes claims against another defendant named in the complaint.

b. The defendant may make a motion to dismiss the case. It asserts that, even assuming the facts of the complaint are true, the plaintiff has failed to state a cause of action or there are other grounds for dismissal of the suit.

5. *The scheduling conference*—The court may hold a conference to consult attorneys on both sides for case management purposes.

TRADITIONAL DISCOVERY TOOLS

Before trial, the attorney for each party undertakes a formal investigative process called discovery to obtain evidence helpful to the client's case.

1. *Interrogatories*—Interrogatories are written questions that the parties to the lawsuit must answer, in writing and under oath. The FRCP and some states' rules limit the number of questions that may be asked and the number of interrogatories that may be filed.

2. *Depositions*—Depositions are given under oath, but unlike interrogatories, may be taken from witnesses as well as from the parties to the lawsuit. Also, the attorney is able to question the deponent (the person being deposed) in person. There is no limit on the number of questions that may be asked. Usually, a court reporter records the official transcript of the deposition.

3. *Requests for production and physical examination*—During discovery, the attorney for either side may request that another party produce documents or other tangible things, or allow the attorney access to them for inspection. When the mental or physical condition of a party is in controversy, the opposing party may request the court to order the party to submit to an examination.

4. *Requests for admission*—A party can request that the opposing party admit the truth of matters relating to the case. Such admissions save time at trial because the parties do not have to spend time proving facts on which they agree.

THE DUTY TO DISCLOSE UNDER FRCP 26

In federal court, FRCP 26 requires that attorneys cooperate in forming a discovery plan early in litigation. It also requires attorneys to disclose relevant information *automatically*. Only after initial disclosures have been made can attorneys resort to the use of traditional discovery tools. An attorney's duty to disclose relevant information continues throughout the pretrial stage.

1. *Initial disclosures*—Each party must disclose information about persons likely to have discoverable information, a copy of relevant information or descriptions of it, information about the damages requested, and information about insurance that may apply.

2. *Failure to disclose*—Should a party fail to disclose relevant information, court sanctions may be imposed.

3. *Discovery plan*—Must be reported within ten days of the initial meeting of the attorneys.

4. *Subsequent disclosures*—After the initial disclosure, parties in civil litigation must tell each other before trial about expert witnesses to be used, the names of witnesses, and the evidence to be presented at trial.

DISCOVERY OF ELECTRONIC EVIDENCE

Electronic evidence includes computer-generated or electronically recorded information, such as e-mail, voice mail, spreadsheets, and other documents. Federal rules and state rules allow discovery of evidence in electronic form.

1. *Advantages of e-evidence*—Electronic evidence often provides more information than paper discovery, because it can reveal facts found only in electronic format. In addition, the computer contains hidden data (metadata) about documents and e-mail that can be useful. Even files deleted by the user can be retrieved from residual data in the computer.

2. *Sources of e-evidence*—E-evidence may be located in computers, in the backup data copied to removable media or remote servers, or in deleted files. Other sources for e-evidence include voice mail, social media, phone logs, and so forth.

3. *Special requirements of e-evidence*—To ensure that e-evidence is admissible at trial, obtain an exact image copy of the original data. Preserving the integrity of e-evidence is essential for it to be admissible. Key steps include making an exact image of the original data and preserving the chain of custody until trial.

MAINTENANCE OF ELECTRONIC RECORDS

Firms should have proactive policies to organize all documents. When discovery occurs, documents from previous cases are more likely to be protected if clearly organized and shown to not be relevant to the current litigation. Many firms also destroy all copies of records no longer required by law to be maintained so as to prevent their resurrection in future litigation.

PRETRIAL MOTIONS

Various motions may be filed by either party during or after the discovery stage of litigation. A motion for summary judgment is common. It asks the court to enter judgment without a trial and can be supported by evidence outside the pleadings (including affidavits, depositions, and interrogatories). The motion is not granted if key facts are in dispute.

QUESTIONS FOR REVIEW

1. Describe what takes place during the initial client interview. Who conducts this interview, the attorney or the paralegal? Why?

2. Describe the pleadings in a civil lawsuit. How does each type of pleading affect the litigation? If a defendant fails to respond to the plaintiff's complaint within a specified time period, what can happen?

3. What is service of process? What are the methods of serving a complaint on a defendant in a federal court lawsuit? What happens if the defendant is not properly served?

4. When does discovery take place, and what does it involve? List three traditional discovery devices that can be used to obtain information prior to trial. Is electronic evidence discoverable?

5. What is the duty to disclose under FRCP 26? What happens if there is a failure to disclose?

6. What pretrial motions are discussed in this chapter? What is the purpose of each motion?

ETHICS QUESTION

A client who is suing her employer for employment discrimination calls paralegal DeShawn from her employer-issued smartphone to discuss her case against her employer. Later, the client e-mails documents to DeShawn from her office computer that may be used as evidence in her upcoming trial. What ethical issues do the client's actions raise? What are DeShawn's ethical obligations in this situation? The law firm's obligations?

PRACTICE QUESTIONS AND ASSIGNMENTS

1. Assume that you work for attorney Tara Jolans of Adams & Tate, 1000 Town Center, Suite 500, White Tower, Michigan. Jolans has decided to represent Sandra Nelson in her lawsuit against David Namisch. Based on the following information and the material in the chapter, draft a complaint to be filed in the U.S. District Court for the Eastern District of Michigan.

Sandra Nelson is the plaintiff in a lawsuit resulting from an automobile accident. Sandra was turning left at a traffic light at the intersection of Jefferson and

Mack Streets while the left-turn arrow was green. In the intersection, she was hit from the side by a 2014 Toyota Camry driven by David Namisch, who failed to stop at the light. The accident occurred on June 3, 2016, at 11:30 P.M. David lives in New York, was visiting his family in Michigan, and just prior to the accident had been out drinking with his brothers. Several witnesses saw the accident. One of the witnesses called the police.

Sandra was not wearing her seat belt at the time of the accident, and she was thrown against the windshield, sustaining massive head injuries. When the police and ambulance arrived, they did not think that she would make it to the hospital alive, but she survived. She wants to claim damages of $500,000 for medical expenses, $65,000 for lost wages, and $75,000 for property damage to her Mercedes. The accident was reported in the local newspaper, complete with photographs.

2. Using Exhibit 10.3, A Summons in a Civil Action, on page 284, draft a summons to accompany the complaint against David Namisch. David's address is 1000 Main Street, Apartment 63, New York, NY 10009. The court clerk's name is David T. Brown.

3. Review Exhibit 10.7, Sample Interrogatories. Draft the first ten questions for a set of interrogatories to be directed to the plaintiff, Sandra Nelson, based on the facts given in Question 1 above. How do the interrogatories for Sandra Nelson differ from those in the sample?

4. In an employment discrimination lawsuit, the plaintiff printed over 400 e-mails related to her discrimination claim. Her former employer produced only 120 e-mail messages in response to a discovery request for e-mails between management and human resources. The employer claimed that additional e-mails were stored on backup tapes and would be extremely costly to produce. What would the judge consider in determining whether to order the employer to produce additional e-mails?

5. Open a saved Word document. Find the properties tab and open it. The document properties contain the document's metadata. Find and write down the document's author, creation date, date last revised, and the name of the person who revised it What is one way in which metadata could be used in a trial?

GROUP PROJECT

This project addresses the issue of the discoverability of social networking information.

Student one will do an Internet search on whether information on social networking sites such as Facebook is discoverable.

Student two will assume it is discoverable, and will research who has to provide it—the user of a social networking account, or the social networking site itself.

Student three will research whether penalties apply if the postings on a social networking site are removed (known as spoliation of evidence) after a lawsuit begins. If the information is removed, is the removal permanent?

Student four will present the group's findings in a one-page paper.

INTERNET PROJECTS

1. Locate the complaint in the *Viacom International v. YouTube* case discussed in the *Technology and Today's Paralegal* feature on page 305 by going to **dmlp.org/sites/citmedialaw.org/files/2008-04-28-Viacom%20First%20Amended%20Complaint.pdf**. Read the complaint and answer these questions:

   a. In which court was the complaint filed?

   b. Who are the plaintiffs?

   c. Who are the defendants?

   d. What is the basis of the court's jurisdiction?

   e. What was the nature of the cause of action—that is, what legal claim was asserted?

   f. What remedies did the plaintiffs request?

2. Do an Internet search to locate the following for your state:

   a. *State court rules.* Provide the URL of the Web page where the court rules are located.

   b. *Summons and return-of-service forms.* Take a screenshot of both of these forms and print them.

   c. *Filing fees for civil lawsuits.* Print the Web page showing the filing fees.

   d. Do your state courts have an electronic filing system? Attach a screenshot of the Web page indicating whether and what type of electronic system your state courts use.

e. Is there a website for your local trial court? If so, find the court rules and determine whether electronic filing is available. Provide the URL to this court's website.

3. Go to the federal courts website at **uscourts.gov/ about-federal-courts/court-role-and-structure**.

a. What is the function of the district courts?

b. Click on the court locator. How many federal districts are located in your state? Which one are you located in?

c. Use the court locator to access your district court's website. Provide the court's Web address.

d. Does your district court's website provide access to its local court rules? If so, print a screen shot of the first page of the rules.

e. Does the website provide information on filing fees? If so, what is the cost of filing a civil lawsuit?

f. Does the website offer access to forms? If so, print a screenshot showing a list of the forms provided.

g. Does the website provide information on electronic filing? If so, review it and answer these questions:

1. What is PACER?

2. What is CM/ECF?

h. Does the website provide information on tours of the court? Consider taking a tour!

▰ END NOTES

1. Nita and Zero are fictitious states invented for this hypothetical example.

2. The body of the complaint described in this section is a *fact pleading*, in which sufficient factual circumstances must be alleged to convince the court that the plaintiff has a cause of action. State courts often require fact pleadings, whereas federal courts only require *notice pleading*. FRCP 8(a) requires only that the complaint have "a short and plain statement of the claim showing that the pleader is entitled to relief." Fact pleading and notice pleading are not totally different—that is, the same allegation of facts could be in the body of a complaint submitted to either a federal or a state court. Federal courts simply have fewer requirements in this respect, and therefore they are often more attractive to litigants.

Trial Procedures

CHAPTER OUTLINE

CHAPTER OBJECTIVES

After completing this chapter, you will know:

- How attorneys prepare for trial and how paralegals assist in this task.

- How jurors are selected and the roles of attorneys and their legal assistants in the selection process.

- The various phases of a trial and trial-related tasks that paralegals often perform.

- The options available to the losing party after the verdict is in.

- How a case is appealed to a higher court for review.

Introduction

Trials cost time and money, so parties to lawsuits often try to avoid going to trial. Pretrial negotiations between the parties and their attorneys often lead to an out-of-court settlement. Using the pretrial motions discussed in Chapter 10, the parties may try to end the litigation after the pleadings are filed or while discovery takes place. In many cases, parties opt for alternative dispute resolution (ADR), such as mediation or arbitration. Recall from Chapter 6 that ADR is not always optional. Some state and federal courts *mandate* that a dispute be mediated before the parties are permitted to bring the dispute before a court. If the parties fail to settle their dispute, the case will go to trial.

To illustrate how attorneys and paralegals prepare for trial, we continue using the hypothetical scenario developed in Chapter 10, in which Katherine Baranski (the plaintiff) is suing Tony Peretto (the defendant) for negligence. In the Baranski-Peretto case, Allen Gilmore is the attorney for plaintiff Baranski, and Gilmore's paralegal is Elena Lopez. Defendant Peretto's attorney is Elizabeth Cameron, and Cameron's legal assistant is Gordon McVay. In preparing for trial, paralegals use a wide range of evolving skills as discussed in the *Developing Paralegal Skills* feature below.

Preparing for Trial

As the trial date approaches, the attorneys for the plaintiff and the defendant and their paralegals complete trial preparations. The paralegals collect and organize the documents and other evidence relating to the dispute. They may create a trial-preparation

DEVELOPING PARALEGAL SKILLS

NEW TOOLS IN TRIAL PREPARATION

Attorneys' trial tactics are evolving to include more sophisticated presentations, creating a greater need for paralegals with design and technology skills. Exhibits are no longer simply copies of documents blown up to larger sizes, but also include elaborate video presentations.

In addition, technology is changing how litigation is being conducted outside the courtroom. Web research on opposing witnesses may uncover valuable information to use in discrediting them. However, you must also do thorough Internet-based research about *your* witnesses before you present them. Otherwise, opposing counsel may reveal some facts about your witnesses that you do not know, because they did not tell you embarrassing information.

Some of the less sophisticated work formerly done by paralegals is now automated, creating a demand for paralegals with higher skill levels. For example, electronic indexing makes document retrieval faster and more accurate, enhancing cross-examination. Some courtrooms even allow for real-time transmission of transcribed testimony outside the courtroom, allowing paralegals back in the office to be scouring a witness's testimony for inconsistencies as they occur.

One of the impacts of these changes is a need for paralegals reviewing electronic evidence to be familiar with the programs used to create records. This knowledge enables them to explore issues such as documents' metadata (electronic data on document creation and revision) within records, which might provide additional evidence beyond the text of the document itself. For instance, documents created with document creators such as Microsoft Word include a record showing the person who created it, when it was created, and when it was altered. Such information can be crucial in cases where the parties disagree about the sequence of events.

checklist similar to the one in Exhibit 12.1 below. Settlement negotiations often continue before and throughout the trial; however, both sides must assume that the trial court will decide the issue. Hence, they must be prepared for trial.

At this point in the litigation, plaintiff Baranski's attorney, Gilmore, focuses on legal strategy and how he can best use the information learned during the pleadings and discovery stages when presenting Baranski's case to the court. He will meet with his client and with his key witnesses to make last-minute preparations for trial. He might also meet with defendant Peretto's attorney to try to settle the dispute. Gilmore's paralegal, Elena Lopez, notifies witnesses of the trial date and helps Gilmore prepare for trial. For example, she makes sure that all exhibits to be used during the trial are ready and verifies that the trial notebook (discussed shortly) is in order.

Contacting and Preparing Witnesses

Typically, the paralegal is responsible for ensuring that witnesses are available and in court on the day of the trial. As mentioned before, a witness is any person asked to testify at trial. The person may be an eyewitness, an official witness (such as a police officer), an expert witness, or anyone with knowledge relevant to the lawsuit.

Several types of negligence lawsuits require expert witnesses. As discussed in the preceding chapter, an expert witness has specialized knowledge in a particular field.

EXHIBIT 12.1
Trial-Preparation Checklist

TWO MONTHS BEFORE THE TRIAL

____ Review the status of the case and inform the attorney of any depositions, interrogatories, or other discovery procedures that need to be completed before trial.
____ Interview witnesses and prepare witness statements.
____ Review deposition transcripts/summaries, answers to interrogatories, witness statements, and other information obtained about the case. Inform the attorney of any further discovery that should be undertaken prior to trial.
____ Begin preparing the trial notebook.

ONE MONTH BEFORE THE TRIAL

____ Make a list of the witnesses who will testify at the trial for the trial notebook.
____ Prepare a subpoena for each witness, and arrange to have the subpoenas served.
____ Prepare any exhibits that will be used at trial and reserve any special equipment (such as for a PowerPoint presentation) that will be needed at the trial.
____ Draft *voir dire* (jury selection) questions and perhaps prepare a jury profile.
____ Prepare motions and memoranda.
____ Continue assembling the trial notebook.

ONE WEEK BEFORE THE TRIAL

____ Check the calendar and call the court clerk to confirm the trial date.
____ Complete the trial notebook. Keep electronic copies of everything.
____ Make sure that all subpoenas have been served.
____ Prepare the client and witnesses for trial.
____ Make the final arrangements (housing, transportation, and the like) for the client or witnesses, as necessary.
____ Check with the attorney to verify how witnesses should be paid (for lost wages, travel expenses, and the like).
____ Make final arrangements to have all equipment, documents, and other items in the courtroom on the trial date.

ONE DAY BEFORE THE TRIAL

____ Meet with others on the trial team to coordinate last-minute efforts.
____ Have a final pretrial meeting with the client.

Such witnesses are often called to testify in negligence cases, because one element to be proved in a negligence case is the reasonableness of the defendant's actions. In medical-malpractice cases, for example, it takes someone with specialized knowledge in the defendant physician's area of practice to establish the reasonableness of the defendant's actions.

Contacting Witnesses and Issuing Subpoenas

In the Baranski case, attorney Gilmore and paralegal Lopez have lined up witnesses to testify on behalf of their client. Lopez informs the witnesses that the trial date is set and that they will be expected to appear at the trial to testify. A *subpoena* (an order issued by the court clerk directing a person to appear in court—see Chapter 10) is served on each of the witnesses to ensure the witness's presence in court. A subpoena to appear in a federal court is shown in Exhibit 12.2 on the next page. Although not shown here, a return-of-service form, similar to the one illustrated in Chapter 10 on page 286, will be attached to the subpoena to verify that the witness received it.

Unless already familiar with the court's requirements, Lopez checks with the court clerk to learn what fees and documents she needs to take to court to obtain the subpoena. In some court systems, attorneys, as officers of the court, may issue subpoenas. The subpoena is then served on the witness. Paralegals may serve subpoenas, but they are commonly served by a process server.

When contacting *friendly* witnesses (those favorable to Baranski's position), Lopez should take care to explain that all witnesses are served with subpoenas, as a precaution, and to tell all witnesses when they can expect the subpoena. Otherwise, a friendly witness might believe that Gilmore and Lopez did not trust him to keep a promise to appear in court and be offended.

Preparing Witnesses for Trial

No prudent attorney puts a non-hostile witness on the stand unless the attorney has discussed the testimony beforehand with that person. Advance preparation makes a big difference to the testimony that a witness provides. The time devoted to preparing a witness varies depending on the size of the case, the importance of the witness's testimony, and whether the attorney believes the witness will communicate clearly and effectively in court. Additional time is needed to prepare witnesses who are relatively inexperienced, are not very articulate, or are especially nervous about testifying.

TELL WITNESSES WHAT TO EXPECT.   Prior to trial, Gilmore and Lopez meet with each witness to prepare her or him for trial. Gilmore will discuss the types of questions that he intends to ask the witness in court and the questions that he expects the opposing attorney to ask. He also tells the witness that during cross-examination opposing counsel will ask leading questions and may try to confuse the witness or attack his or her statements. Gilmore may recommend that the witness answer the opponent's questions in as few words as possible while not appearing to be overly defensive. The attorney may not, of course, tell the witness what to say in response to questions.

Gilmore also reviews with the witness any statements the witness made about the case, particularly if the statements were given under oath (such as during a deposition). It is important that a witness understand that during the trial, he may be asked about inconsistencies between statements previously given or between trial testimony and prior statements. Additionally, Gilmore may review the substantive legal issues involved in the case and discuss how the witness's testimony will affect the outcome of those issues. As the *In the Office* feature on page 353 notes, remember that you are often dealing with confidential information that must be protected.

ROLE-PLAYING.   If a witness needs additional preparation, Gilmore or Lopez may engage in role-playing with the witness. Such rehearsal is often valuable in helping the witness to understand more fully how questioning will proceed and what tactics may be involved in the opposing attorney's questions. It also may alleviate some of the witness's

EXHIBIT 12.2

A Supoena

AO 88 (Rev. 2/06) Subpoena in a Civil Case

Issued by the

UNITED STATES DISTRICT COURT

——————————— WESTERN DISTRICT OF NITA ———————————

Katherine Baranski	**SUBPOENA IN A CIVIL CASE**
V.	
Tony Peretto	CASE NUMBER 17-14335-NI

TO: Julia Williams
      3765 Mattis Avenue
      Nita City, NI 48800

[X] YOU ARE COMMANDED to appear in the United States District Court at the place, date, and time specified below to testify in the above case.

PLACE OF TESTIMONY	COURT ROOM
4th and Main Nita City, NI	B
	DATE AND TIME 8/4/17 10:00 A.M.

[ ] YOU ARE COMMANDED to appear at the place, date, and time specified below to testify at the taking of a deposition in the above case.

PLACE OF DEPOSITION	DATE AND TIME

[ ] YOU ARE COMMANDED to produce and permit inspection and copying of the following documents or objects at the place, date, and time specified below (list documents or objects):

PLACE	DATE AND TIME

[ ] YOU ARE COMMANDED to permit inspection of the following premises at the date and time specified below.

PREMISES	DATE AND TIME

Any organization not a party to this suit that is subpoenaed for the taking of a deposition shall designate one or more officers, directors, or managing agents, or other persons who consent to testify on its behalf, and may set forth, for each person designated, the matters on which the person will testify. Federal Rules of Civil Procedure, 30(b)(6).

ISSUING OFFICER SIGNATURE AND TITLE (INDICATE IF ATTORNEY FOR PLAINTIFF OR DEFENDANT)	DATE
Allen P. Gilmore, Attorney for the Plaintiff	July 13, 2017

ISSUING OFFICER'S NAME, ADDRESS AND PHONE NUMBER
Allen P. Gilmore, Jeffers, Gilmore & Dunn,
553 Fifth Avenue, Suite 101, Nita City, NI 48801   (616) 555-9690

(See Rule 45, Federal Rules of Civil Procedure, Parts C & D on Reverse)

If action is pending in district other than district of issuance, state district under case number.

IN THE OFFICE

PROTECTING CONFIDENTIAL INFORMATION

Many of the materials related to cases are confidential. To protect the interests of clients, help make sure that information is not exposed to visitors to the office or to other employees who do not have a need to know information related to a particular case. Keep materials put away when you are not working on them. Because most work is done on computers, close files on your computer when you leave your desk so other people cannot read what is there. Computers can be easily locked. Entering your password returns you to the same point, so you do not have to close all files.

Be particularly careful with laptops, iPads, and flash drives outside of the office. Losing a computer or drive with confidential documents can be disastrous. Make sure all devices with files are password protected. Also, notice that many people talk on the phone as if no one around them is listening. Be cautious when talking about legal matters, especially on a cell phone out of the office.

fears. In addition, Lopez might take the witness to the courtroom in which the trial will take place to familiarize her with the trial setting. As testifying is often stressful, anything that the paralegal can do to reduce a witness's discomfort will help the witness to better control her responses when testifying and thus will benefit the client.

NUMEROUS DETAILS. Paralegals are often responsible for handling the details in preparing witnesses for court. For example, Lopez might recommend appropriate clothing and grooming or tell the witness where to look and how to remain calm and composed when speaking to the court. If the witness will be asked about any exhibits or evidence (such as photographs or documents), Lopez will show these items to the witness. Lopez will update the witness as to when she will probably be called to testify.

Exhibits and Displays

Paralegals frequently prepare exhibits or displays to present at trial. Gilmore may wish to show the court a photograph of plaintiff Baranski's car taken after the accident occurred, a diagram of the intersection, an enlarged document (such as a police report), or other relevant evidence. Lopez will be responsible for making sure that exhibits are properly prepared and ready for trial. If any exhibits require special equipment, such as an easel, projector, or laptop, Lopez must also make sure that these will be available in the courtroom and properly set up when needed.

The Trial Notebook

To present Baranski's case effectively, Gilmore needs to have all relevant documents in the courtroom. He also needs to be able to locate them quickly. To accomplish these goals, Lopez prepares a trial notebook and sets up computer files. Traditionally, the trial notebook has been a binder containing trial-related materials separated by tabbed divider sheets. Most lawyers today rely primarily on documents kept in computers, but paper copies are still common. The discussion here applies to both.

trial notebook
Traditionally, a binder that contains copies of all the documents and information that an attorney will need to have at hand during the trial.

Key Materials

Lopez meets with Gilmore to discuss what he wants to include in the trial notebook for Baranski's case and how the notebook should be organized. Gilmore tells Lopez that the organization of the notebook should make it possible to find quickly whatever documents they may need during the trial. Lopez should include the following materials in the notebook:

- Copies of the pleadings.
- Interrogatories.
- Deposition transcripts and summaries.
- Pretrial motions and any recent rulings on them.
- A list of exhibits and a case outline indicating when they will be used.
- A witness list, the order in which witnesses will testify, and the questions to be asked of each witness.
- Relevant cases or statutes that Gilmore plans to cite.
- Additional documents important to have close at hand during the trial.

Note that many of the above materials will be scanned and saved in files on a laptop or elsewhere.

Lopez will create a general index to the notebook or computer file's contents and place this index at the front of the notebook. She may also create an index for each section of the binder or computer file and place those indexes at the beginnings of the sections. Paralegals sometimes use a notebook computer and a software retrieval system to help them quickly locate documents, especially in complicated cases involving thousands of documents. Careful, consistent organization of computer files is critical.

Protect Original Documents

When preparing a traditional trial notebook, remember that the notebook should not contain the original documents but copies of them from when they were scanned. The original documents (unless needed as evidence at trial) should remain in the firm's files, for security (should the trial notebook be misplaced) and for access by staff in the office during trial.

Lopez will not wait until the last minute to prepare the trial notebook and electronic files. At the outset of the lawsuit, she makes copies of the pleadings and other documents as they are generated to include in the notebook. That way, just before the trial, she is free to attend to other pressing needs. As discussed in this chapter, high-tech presentations are changing trial-preparation tasks (see the *Technology and Today's Paralegal* feature on the facing page).

Pretrial Conference

pretrial conference
A conference prior to trial in which the judge and the attorneys litigating the suit discuss settlement possibilities, clarify the issues in dispute, and schedule forthcoming trial-related events.

motion *in limine*
A motion requesting that certain evidence not be brought out at the trial, such as prejudicial, irrelevant, or legally inadmissible evidence.

Before the trial begins, the attorneys usually meet with the trial judge in a pretrial conference to explore the possibility of resolving the case and, if a settlement is not possible, to determine how the trial will be conducted. In particular, the court or the parties may attempt to clarify the issues in dispute and establish ground rules to restrict such matters as the admissibility of certain types of evidence. For example, Gilmore might have Lopez draft a motion *in limine*[1] (a motion to limit evidence) to submit to the judge at this time. The motion requests the judge to order that certain evidence not be brought out at trial.

To illustrate: Suppose Baranski had been arrested in the past for illegal drug possession. Gilmore knows that the arrest, if introduced by the defense at trial, might prejudice the jury against Baranski. Because the arrest is not relevant to the case and potentially prejudicial, Gilmore might submit a motion *in limine* to keep the defense from presenting evidence of the arrest. Exhibit 12.3 on page 356 presents a sample motion *in limine*. With the motion, Gilmore would include affidavits and/or a memorandum of law (a brief)—documents discussed in Chapter 10—to convince the judge why the motion should be granted.

TECHNOLOGY AND TODAY'S PARALEGAL

TAKE ADVANTAGE OF THE LATEST TOOLS

As you have seen, cases can involve huge document files and preparation of motions and other court documents. A growing number of programs exist to help keep documents organized, provide details related to trials, remind you of schedules, and assist in making sure research is comprehensive. A few are discussed here.

TRIAL-RELATED PROGRAMS AND APPS

Westlaw Legal Calendaring uses Microsoft Outlook to keep track of litigation-related dates based on court rules governing a case. (**legalsolutions.thomsonreuters.com/law-products/solutions/legal-calendaring**)

A number of apps can help you in various ways. An easy-to-use iPad app, *Trialpad*, is designed to assist in trial preparation. Users are able to organize and create sharp-looking displays of trial exhibits. (**itunes.apple.com/us/app/trialpad-organize-present/id828542236?mt=8**)

IJuror is a jury-selection app that provides a seating chart and allows entry of information on each prospective juror. (**itunes.apple.com/us/app/ijuror/id372486285?mt=8**)

Just like Westlaw's *Legal Calendaring*, the *Court Days Pro* app lets the user calculate dates and deadlines based on a customizable database of court rules and statutes. (**itunes.apple.com/us/app/court-days-pro-rules-based/id419708480?mt=8**)

BROWSER TOOLS

Bestlaw is a browser extension, available to download for free, that enhances usability of WestlawNext. This product allows the user to copy *Bluebook* citations, open documents in free sources before opening them on Westlaw, and instantly look up case information on platforms such as Google Scholar, Wikipedia, and Cornell LII. (**bestlaw.io**)

For frequent users of PACER (discussed in Chapter 8), *Recapthelaw* (**recapthelaw.org**) is a browser extension that allows users to add to a free, open repository of public court records. Whenever a document is purchased from PACER, this feature automatically places the document in a public repository hosted by the Internet Archive. The benefit of sharing is realized when the RECAP extension alerts users that a document they are searching for was already uploaded to the public repository and is now accessible for free.

Powered by Cornell Legal Information Institute, *Jureeka!* (**jureeka.blogspot.com**) turns legal citations found in Web pages into hyperlinks.

TECHNOLOGY TIP

Technologies can make a litigation paralegal's job easier, especially in cases that involve extensive documentation. All programs have their limitations, so you want to be sure you fully understand how a program works—what it does and what it does not do—so you do not miss critical information.

Once the pretrial conference has concluded, both parties turn their attention to the trial itself. Assuming that a jury will hear the trial, one more step is necessary before the trial begins: selecting the jurors who will hear the trial and render a verdict on the dispute.

Jury Selection

Before the trial gets under way, a panel of potential jurors must be assembled. The clerk of the court usually notifies local residents by mail that they have been selected for jury duty. Selecting prospective jurors varies, depending on the court, but often they are randomly selected from lists of registered voters or licensed drivers. The persons

EXHIBIT 12.3

Motion *in Limine*

A. P. Gilmore
Jeffers, Gilmore & Dunn
553 Fifth Avenue
Suite 101
Nita City, NI 48801
(616) 555-9690

Attorney for Plaintiff

**UNITED STATES DISTRICT COURT
FOR THE WESTERN DISTRICT OF NITA**

Katherine Baranski)
        Plaintiff,)
)   CASE NO. 17-14335-NI
v.   )   Honorable Harley M. Larue
)
)   MOTION IN LIMINE
Tony Peretto)
        Defendant.)

The Plaintiff respectfully moves the Court to prohibit counsel for the Defendant from directly or indirectly introducing or making any reference during the trial to the Plaintiff's arrest in 2008 for the possession of illegal drugs.

The grounds on which this motion is based are stated in the accompanying affidavits and memorandum.

Date: 6/18/17   *Allen P. Gilmore*

                                    Allen P. Gilmore
                                      Attorney for the Plaintiff

---

selected report to the courthouse on the date specified (unless they are granted exceptions or waivers). At the court, they are gathered into a pool of jurors, and the process of selecting jurors who will actually hear the case begins. Although some trials require twelve-person juries, civil matters can be heard by a jury of as few as six persons in many states. Federal court juries are usually chosen from a wider geographic area than are state court juries. The different demographics are a reason an attorney might prefer one court rather than the other.

Voir Dire

Both the plaintiff's attorney and the defendant's attorney have some input into the ultimate makeup of the jury. Each attorney usually questions prospective jurors in a proceeding known as *voir dire*.[2] Litigators know the importance of the *voir dire* process. It helps to pick the right jury, but also is a time for attorneys to introduce themselves and their clients to the jury before the trial even begins.

Legal assistants may work with their attorneys to write up questions to ask jurors during *voir dire*. Because the jurors will have filled out forms giving basic information about themselves, the questions can be tailored accordingly. The idea is to uncover biases on the part of prospective jurors and to find persons who might identify with the plights of their respective clients.

Typically, the legal team for each side has already developed an idea of what kind of person would be most sympathetic toward or most likely to vote in favor of its client. In complex cases, experts may be hired to help create a juror profile.

voir dire

A proceeding in which attorneys for the plaintiff and the defendant ask prospective jurors questions to determine whether any potential juror is biased or has any connection with a party to the action or with a prospective witness.

Jury selection may last an hour or days, depending on the complexity of the case and the rules and preferences of the particular court or judge. In some courts, the judge questions prospective jurors using queries prepared and submitted by the attorneys. In other courts, the judge has each juror answer a list of standard questions and gives each attorney a small amount of time to ask follow-up questions. When large numbers of prospective jurors are involved, the attorneys (or the judge) may direct their questions to groups of jurors as opposed to individual jurors to reduce the time spent choosing a jury.

Jury Selection Experts and Tools

Picking a jury is a critical step in a trial. The famous litigator Clarence Darrow claimed "almost every case is won or lost when the jury is sworn." Picking a jury is often done by instinct. Experienced trial lawyers gauge whether a juror is likely to be sympathetic to their clients based on gut reactions, on stereotypes about marital status, race, religion, occupation, or on other factors. Today, jury selection is becoming a big business when the stakes are high. Now, significant sums are spent on jury consultants who promise to use science to help lawyers pick a jury. Consultants helped pick juries in the $253 million Vioxx products liability case, for example.

By using online search tools, paralegals and assisting attorneys can discover valuable information about prospective jurors from their online "digital shadow." A prospective juror may appear in court dressed professionally, but his Facebook profile may feature wild partying. Spotting such information may help a lawyer defending a DWI case decide to keep the party animal on the jury, reasoning that he is more likely to sympathize with the defendant. As the amount of information available online about people increases, having the skills to quickly find revealing information is ever more valuable for the paralegal.

Challenges during *Voir Dire*

During *voir dire*, the attorney for each side decides if there are any individuals he or she would like to prevent from serving as jurors in the case. The attorney may exercise a challenge to exclude a particular person from the jury. There are two types of challenges available to both sides in a lawsuit: challenges for cause and peremptory challenges.

challenge
An attorney's objection, during *voir dire*, to the inclusion of a particular person on the jury.

Challenges for Cause

The attorney can exercise a challenge for cause if the prospective juror is biased against the client or case for some reason. For example, if a juror states during *voir dire* that she dislikes immigrants and the client is foreign born, the attorney can exercise a challenge for cause. Each side can exercise an *unlimited* number of challenges for cause. Because most people are not forthcoming about their biases, the attorney must be able to prove sufficiently to the court that the person cannot be an objective juror in the case. Often, the judge will ask the challenged juror follow-up questions and then determine if the juror can likely be objective.

challenge for cause
A *voir dire* challenge to exclude a potential juror from serving on the jury for a reason specified by an attorney in the case.

Peremptory Challenges

Both attorneys may exercise a *limited* number of peremptory challenges without giving any reason to the court as to why they object to a particular juror. In most cases, peremptory challenges are the only challenges exercised (because there is often no proof that any juror is biased). A juror may be excused from serving on the jury for any reason, including her facial expressions or nonverbal behavior during the questioning. Peremptory challenges based on race or sex, however, are illegal.

Because the number of peremptory challenges is limited (a court may allow only three, for example), attorneys must exercise peremptory challenges carefully. Litigators conserve their peremptory challenges to eliminate the prospective jurors who appear the most hostile.

peremptory challenge
A *voir dire* challenge to exclude a potential juror from serving on the jury without any supporting reason or cause. Peremptory challenges based on racial or gender criteria are illegal.

Procedure for Challenges

Typically, *voir dire* takes place in the courtroom, and the attorneys question the six to twelve prospective jurors who are seated in the jury box. Other prospective jurors may be seated in the courtroom, so that as one person is excused, another person can take his place in the jury box. The procedure varies depending on the jurisdiction.

Often, rather than making challenges orally in front of the jury, the attorneys write down on a piece of paper which juror they wish to challenge, and the paper is given to the judge. The judge thanks and dismisses the prospective juror, and the process starts over with the next individual. Then the remaining prospective jurors do not know which side dismissed a person and so are less likely to guess why.

The Paralegal's Role during *Voir Dire*

As mentioned, paralegals help develop a jury profile and draft questions asked during *voir dire*. In addition, a paralegal can assist an attorney by providing another pair of eyes and ears during the jury selection process. Attorneys frequently rely on the observations of other members of the legal team who are present during the questioning.

If paralegal Lopez attends *voir dire* with attorney Gilmore in the Baranski case, she will watch all jurors as the attorneys question them. Because Lopez is not participating in the questioning, she is free to observe the prospective jurors. She can report any verbal or nonverbal actions she observed that Gilmore might not have noticed. Suppose that as Gilmore is questioning one juror, another juror is frowning with disapproval at Baranski. Gilmore might not notice this and Lopez can bring it to his attention. As the *Ethics Watch* feature on the following page notes, you must limit contact with jurors.

Alternate Jurors

Because unforeseeable circumstances or illness may necessitate that one or more of the sitting jurors be dismissed, the court often seats several *alternate jurors*. Depending on the rules of the particular jurisdiction, a court might have two or three alternate jurors present throughout the trial. If a juror has to be excused during the trial, then an alternate can take his place without disrupting the proceedings. Unless they replace jurors, alternates do not participate in jury deliberations at the end of the trial.

The Trial

Once the jury members are seated, the judge swears in the jury, and the trial begins. During the trial, the attorneys present their cases to the jury. While the attorneys concentrate on the trial, their paralegals can coordinate the logistical aspects of the trial and observe the trial proceedings. Because Lopez is thoroughly familiar with the case and Gilmore's legal strategy, she will be a valuable ally during the trial. She will anticipate Gilmore's needs and provide appropriate reminders or documents.

The Paralegal's Duties

Prior to each trial day, Lopez assembles the documents and materials needed and makes sure that Gilmore has within reach any documents or exhibits he needs for questioning parties or witnesses. At the end of the day, Lopez organizes the materials, decides what will be needed for the next day, and files the documents that can remain in the office.

Lopez also monitors each witness's testimony to ensure that it is consistent with previous statements made by the witness. She has the relevant deposition transcript (and summary) at hand when a witness takes the stand. She follows the deposition transcript (or summary) of each witness during testimony. This way, she can pass a note to Gilmore if he misses any inconsistencies in the testimony.

Lopez also observes how the jury responds to witnesses and their testimony or to the attorneys. She will take notes during the trial on these observations as well as on

ETHICS WATCH

COMMUNICATING WITH JURORS

Suppose that you are the paralegal working on the Baranski case with attorney Gilmore, and you run into one of the jurors in the grocery store. The juror approaches you and says, "You know, I didn't really understand what that witness, Williams, was saying. Did she really see the accident? Also, is it true that Mrs. Baranski will never be able to walk normally again?" You know the answers to these questions, and you would like the juror to know the truth. You also know that it would enhance Baranski's chances of winning the case if this juror were as familiar with the factual background as you are.

What should you do?

1. Explain to the juror that neither you nor a juror is permitted to discuss a case they are hearing with anyone.
2. Inform the juror that as a paralegal, you have an ethical duty to abide by the professional rules of conduct governing the legal profession. One of these rules prohibits *ex parte* (private) communications with jurors about a case being tried.
3. Report the conversation to attorney Gilmore, who may decide to tell the judge about it.

These actions are consistent with NFPA's *Model Code of Ethics and Professional Responsibility*, Section EC-1.2(a), "A paralegal shall not engage in any *ex parte* communications involving the courts or any other adjudicatory body [a person or panel that makes a legal decision] in an attempt to exert undue influence or to obtain advantage or the benefit of only one party," and Section EC-1.5(f), "A paralegal shall not engage in any indiscreet communications concerning clients." They are also consistent with the NALA *Code of Ethics*, Canon 9, "A paralegal must do all other things incidental, necessary, or expedient for the attainment of the ethics and responsibilities as defined by statute or rule of court."

Reprinted by permission of the National Federation of Paralegal Associations, Inc. (NFPA®); www.paralegals.org.; Copyright 1975; Adopted 1975; Revised 1979, 1988, 1995, 2007. Reprinted with permission of NALA, the Association for Paralegals–Legal Assistants. Inquiries should be directed to NALA, 1516 S. Boston, #200, Tulsa, OK 74119, www.nala.org.

the points being stressed and the evidence introduced by opposing counsel. At the end of the day, Lopez and Gilmore may review the day's events, and Lopez's "trial journal" provides a ready reference to what happened in the courtroom.

Opening Statements

The trial both opens and closes with attorneys' statements to the jury. In their opening statements, the attorneys give a brief version of the facts and the supporting evidence they will use during the trial. Because some trials can take weeks or even months, it is helpful for jurors to hear a summary of the story that will unfold during the trial.

The opening statement is a kind of "road map" that describes the destination that each attorney hopes to reach and outlines how he or she plans to reach it. Plaintiff Baranski's attorney, Gilmore, focuses on such things as his client's lack of fault and the injuries that she sustained when she was hit by defendant Peretto's car. Peretto's attorney, Cameron, highlight the points that weaken Baranski's claim (Cameron might

opening statement
An attorney's statement to the jury at the beginning of the trial. The attorney briefly outlines the evidence that will be offered during the trial and the legal theory that will be pursued.

point out that Baranski was speeding) or otherwise suggest that Peretto did not commit a wrongful act. Note that the defendant's attorney has the right to reserve her opening statement until after the plaintiff's case has been presented.

The Plaintiff's Case

Once the opening statements have been made, Gilmore will present the plaintiff's case first. Because he is the plaintiff's attorney, he has the burden of proving that defendant Peretto was negligent.

Direct Examination

Gilmore will call eyewitnesses to the stand and ask them to tell the court about the events that led to the accident. This questioning is known as direct examination. For example, Gilmore will call Julia Williams, an eyewitness who saw the accident, and ask her questions such as those presented in Exhibit 12.4 below. He will also call other witnesses, including the police officer and ambulance driver who were summoned to the accident. Gilmore will try to elicit responses from these witnesses that strengthen Baranski's case—or at least that do not weaken it.

During direct examination, attorney Gilmore usually will not be permitted to ask *leading questions*, which are questions that lead the witness to a particular desired response (see Chapter 11). A leading question might be something like the following: "So, Mrs. Williams, you noticed that the defendant ran the stop sign, right?" If Mrs. Williams answers "yes," she has, in effect, been "led" to this answer by Gilmore's leading question. Leading questions discourage witnesses from telling their stories in their own words.

When Gilmore is dealing with *hostile witnesses* (uncooperative witnesses or those testifying on behalf of the other party), however, he is normally permitted to ask leading questions. This is because hostile witnesses may be uncommunicative and unwilling to

direct examination
The examination of a witness by the attorney who calls the witness to the stand to testify on behalf of the attorney's client.

EXHIBIT 12.4
Direct Examination—
Sample Questions

ATTORNEY:	Mrs. Williams, please explain how you came to be at the scene of the accident.	
WITNESS:	Well, I was walking north on Mattis Avenue toward Nita City Hospital, where I work as a nurse.	
ATTORNEY:	Please describe for the court, in your own words, exactly what you observed when you reached the intersection of Mattis Avenue and Thirty-eighth Street.	
WITNESS:	I was approaching the intersection when I saw the defendant run the stop sign on Thirty-eighth Street and crash into the plaintiff's car.	
ATTORNEY:	Did you notice any change in the speed at which the defendant was driving as he approached the stop sign?	
WITNESS:	No. He didn't slow down at all.	
ATTORNEY:	Mrs. Williams, are you generally in good health?	
WITNESS:	Yes.	
ATTORNEY:	Have you ever had any problems with your vision?	
WITNESS:	No. I wear reading glasses for close work, but I see well in the distance.	
ATTORNEY:	And how long has it been since your last eye examination?	
WITNESS:	About a month or so ago, I went to Dr. Sullivan for an examination. He told me that I needed reading glasses but that my distance vision was excellent.	

describe the events they witnessed. If Gilmore asked a hostile witness what she observed on the morning of August 4 at 7:45 A.M., for example, the witness might respond, "I saw two trucks driving down Mattis Avenue." That answer might be true, but it has nothing to do with the Baranski-Peretto accident. Therefore, to elicit relevant information from this witness, Gilmore would be permitted to use leading questions to force the witness to respond to the question at issue.

Cross-Examination

After Gilmore has finished questioning a witness on direct examination, Peretto's attorney, Cameron, begins her cross-examination of that witness. During her cross-examination, Cameron is primarily concerned with reducing the witness's credibility in the eyes of the jury and the judge. Attorneys typically use leading questions during cross-examination (because the witness is hostile). Generally, experienced trial attorneys ask only questions to which they know the answers—otherwise a question might elicit testimony from the witness that further supports the opponent's case.

cross-examination
The questioning of an opposing witness during the trial.

MAKE THE QUESTIONS RELEVANT. Cameron formulates questions for Gilmore's witnesses based on the witnesses' answers in depositions and interrogatories. Discovery usually provides attorneys with a good idea as to what areas of questioning may prove fruitful. If a witness's testimony on the witness stand differs materially from the answers previously given, or contradicts some other item of evidence (physical evidence or testimony of another witness), the attorney can use this discrepancy to attack the witness's credibility.

FOCUS ON CREDIBILITY. The defendant's attorney must generally confine her cross-examination to matters that were brought up during direct examination or that relate to a witness's credibility. This restriction is not followed in all states, however, and ultimately both the nature and extent of the cross-examination are subject to the discretion of the trial judge. In any event, Cameron's interrogation may not extend to matters unrelated to the case. She normally may not introduce evidence that a witness for the plaintiff is a smoker or dislikes children, for example, unless she can demonstrate that such facts are relevant to the case.

In general, Cameron may try to uncover relevant physical infirmities of the plaintiff's witnesses (poor eyesight or hearing), as well as any evidence of bias (such as a witness's habit of playing golf with Baranski every Saturday). Some questions that Cameron might ask Julia Williams, Gilmore's eyewitness, are presented in Exhibit 12.5 on the following page.

Redirect and Recross

After defendant Peretto's attorney has finished cross-examining each witness, plaintiff Baranski's attorney will try to repair any damage done to the credibility of the witness's testimony—or to the case itself. Gilmore does this by again questioning the witness and allowing the witness to explain her answer. This is known as redirect examination.

redirect examination
The questioning of a witness following the adverse party's cross-examination.

If Cameron's cross-examination revealed that one of Gilmore's eyewitnesses to the accident had vision problems, for example, Gilmore could ask the witness whether she was wearing glasses or contact lenses at the time of the accident. Gilmore might have the witness demonstrate to the court that she has adequate vision by having her identify an object at the far end of the courtroom. Because redirect examination is primarily used to improve the credibility of cross-examined witnesses, it is limited to matters raised during cross-examination. (If Cameron chooses not to cross-examine a particular witness, then there can be no redirect examination by Gilmore.)

Following Gilmore's redirect examination, Cameron is given an opportunity for recross-examination. Gilmore would then have another opportunity for more direct examination and so on until both sides are done. When both attorneys have finished with the first witness, Gilmore calls succeeding witnesses in Baranski's case. Each will be subject to cross-examination (and redirect and recross, if necessary).

recross-examination
The questioning of an opposing witness following the adverse party's redirect examination.

EXHIBIT 12.5

Cross-Examination—
Sample Questions

ATTORNEY:	You have just testified that you were approaching the intersection when the accident occurred. Isn't it true that you stated earlier, under oath, that you were at the intersection at the time of the accident?
WITNESS:	Well, I might have, but I think I said that I was close to the intersection.
ATTORNEY:	In fact, you said that you were at the intersection. Now, you say that you were approaching it. Which is it?
WITNESS:	I was approaching it, I suppose.
ATTORNEY:	Okay. Exactly where were you when the accident occurred?
WITNESS:	I think that I was just in front of the Dairy Queen when the accident happened.
ATTORNEY:	Mrs. Williams, the Dairy Queen on Mattis Avenue is at least seventy-five yards from the intersection of Mattis Avenue and Thirty-eighth Street. Is it your testimony today that you noticed the defendant's car from seventy-five yards away as it was approaching the intersection on Mattis Avenue?
WITNESS:	Well, no, I guess not.
ATTORNEY:	Isn't it true that there were a lot of other cars driving on the road that morning?
WITNESS:	Yes.
ATTORNEY:	And you had no reason to be paying particular attention to the defendant's car, did you?
WITNESS:	Not really.
ATTORNEY:	In fact, you did not see the defendant's car until after the collision occurred, did you, Mrs. Williams?

Motion for a Directed Verdict

After attorney Gilmore has presented his case for Baranski, then Cameron, as counsel for defendant Peretto, may make a motion for a directed verdict (also known as a *motion for judgment as a matter of law* in federal courts). Cameron will be arguing to the court that the plaintiff's attorney has not offered enough evidence to support a claim against Peretto. If the judge agrees and grants the motion, then judgment is entered for Peretto, the case is dismissed, and the trial is over. A sample motion for judgment as a matter of law is shown in Exhibit 12.6 on page 364.

The motion for a directed verdict (judgment as a matter of law) is not common because only cases that involve genuine factual disputes are permitted to proceed to trial in the first place. If the judge had believed that Baranski's case was flawed before the trial started, then the judge would probably have granted a pretrial motion to dismiss the case, thereby avoiding the expense of a trial. Occasionally, however, the witnesses' testimony unexpectedly leaves a crucial element unproven. In that event, the court may grant the defendant's motion for a directed verdict.

motion for a directed verdict
A motion (also known as a *motion for judgment as a matter of law* in the federal courts) requesting that the court grant a judgment in favor of the party making the motion on the ground that the other party has not produced sufficient evidence to support his or her claim.

The Defendant's Case

Assuming the court denies the motion for a directed verdict, the two attorneys now reverse their roles. Cameron presents evidence demonstrating the weaknesses of plaintiff Baranski's claims against defendant Peretto. She essentially follows the same procedure used by Gilmore when he presented Baranski's side of the story. Cameron calls witnesses to the stand and questions them. After her direct examination of each witness, the witnesses are subject to possible cross-examination by Gilmore, redirect examination by Cameron, recross-examination by Gilmore, and so on.

In her presentation of the defendant's case, Cameron attempts to counter the points made by Gilmore. Cameron and her paralegal, McVay, may have to prepare new

At trial, attorneys and paralegals must have close at hand all of the documents and information that they may need to refer to during the proceedings. Typically, these materials are contained in the trial notebook, which may consist of several binders. Increasingly, for complex litigation, attorneys and paralegals retrieve necessary documents from offline or online databases using laptop computers. When might it be preferable to have physical documents rather than scanned documents in a digital file?

© Edler von Rabenstein/www.Shutterstock.com.

exhibits and memoranda of law in addition to those originally prepared. The need to prepare additional exhibits and memoranda may arise when the plaintiff's attorney pursues a strategy different from the one anticipated by the defense team. Depending on Cameron's strategy, she may choose to begin by exposing weaknesses in the plaintiff's case (by asserting that Baranski was speeding, for example) or by presenting Peretto's version of the accident. In either case, McVay, like Lopez, keeps track of the materials brought to court each day.

Once Cameron has finished presenting her case, Gilmore will offer evidence to *rebut* (refute) evidence introduced by Cameron in Peretto's behalf. After Gilmore's rebuttal, if any, both attorneys make their closing arguments to the jury.

Closing Arguments

In their **closing arguments**, the attorneys summarize their presentations and argue in their clients' favor. A closing argument should include all major points that support the client's case. It should emphasize the shortcomings of the opposing party's case. Jurors view a closing argument with some skepticism if it merely recites the central points of a party's claim or defense without also responding to the unfavorable facts or issues raised by the other side. Of course, neither attorney wants to focus too much on the other side's position, but the elements of the opposing position need to be acknowledged and their flaws highlighted.

Both attorneys will want to organize their presentations so they can explain their arguments and show the jury how their arguments are supported by the evidence. Once both attorneys have completed their remarks, the case will be submitted to the jury, and the attorneys' role in the trial will be finished.

Jury Instructions

Before the jurors begin deliberations, the judge gives the jury a **charge**. The judge sums up the case and instructs the jurors on the rules of law that apply. (In some courts, jury

closing argument
The argument made by each side's attorney after the cases for the plaintiff and defendant have been presented. Closing arguments are made prior to the jury charge.

charge
The judge's instruction to the jury setting forth the rules of law that the jury must apply in reaching its decision, or verdict.

EXHIBIT 12.6

Motion for Judgment
as a Matter of Law

Elizabeth A. Cameron
Cameron & Strauss, P.C.
310 Lake Drive
Zero City, ZE 59802
(616) 955-6234

Attorney for Defendant

UNITED STATES DISTRICT COURT
FOR THE WESTERN DISTRICT OF NITA

Katherine Baranski	)	
Plaintiff,	)	CASE NO. 17-14335-NI
	)	Honorable Harley M. Larue
v.	)	
	)	
	)	MOTION FOR JUDGMENT
Tony Peretto	)	AS A MATTER OF LAW
Defendant.	)	

The Defendant, Tony Peretto, at the close of the Plaintiff's case, moves the court to withdraw the evidence from the consideration of the jury and to find the Defendant not liable.

As grounds for this motion, Defendant Peretto states that:

(1) No evidence has been offered or received during the trial of the above-entitled cause of action to sustain the allegations of negligence contained in Plaintiff Baranski's complaint.

(2) No evidence has been offered or received during the trial proving or tending to prove that Defendant Peretto was guilty of any negligence.

(3) The proximate cause of Plaintiff Baranski's injuries was not due to any negligence on the part of Defendant Peretto.

(4) By the uncontroverted evidence, Plaintiff Baranski was guilty of contributory negligence, which was the sole cause of the Plaintiff's injuries.

Date: _7/21/17_

Elizabeth A. Cameron
Elizabeth A. Cameron
Attorney for the Defendant

---

instructions are given prior to closing arguments and may even be given at some other point during trial proceedings.) These often include definitions of legal terms relevant to the case and standard instructions on deliberations. In addition, the charge usually contains a request for findings of fact, typically phrased in an "if, then" format.

For example, in the portion of the charge presented in Exhibit 12.7 on the facing page, the jury is first asked to decide if the defendant was negligent. *If* the jury decides that the defendant was negligent, *then* the jury must decide whether the defendant's negligence caused the plaintiff's injuries. This format helps to channel the jurors' deliberations.

Each side typically submits a proposed charge to the court before the trial begins, and an attorney's trial strategy will likely be linked to the charges. The paralegal may draft proposed instructions for the attorney's review. There are standard form charges in most jurisdictions. Court opinions and your firm's case files may have helpful examples of language from similar cases. Because errors in the charge can lead an appellate court

EXHIBIT 12.7

Jury Charge—Request
for Findings of Fact

The jury is requested to answer the following questions:

(1) Do you find by a preponderance of the evidence that the defendant was negligent?

Answer: (yes or no) _____

If your answer to question (1) is "yes," go on to question (2).
If your answer to question (1) is "no," stop here.

(2) Do you find by a preponderance of the evidence that the defendant's negligence was a proximate (direct) cause of the plaintiff's injuries?

Answer: (yes or no) _____

If your answer to question (2) is "yes," go on to question (3).
If your answer to question (2) is "no," stop here.

(3) Do you find that the plaintiff was negligent?

Answer: (yes or no) _____

If your answer to question (3) is "yes," go on to question (4).
If your answer to question (3) is "no," then skip down to question (6).

(4) Do you find that the plaintiff's negligence was a proximate (direct) cause of the accident and injuries that she suffered?

Answer: (yes or no) _____

If your answer is "yes," go on to question (5).
If your answer is "no," skip to question (6).

(5) Taking 100% as the total fault causing the accident and injuries, what percentage of the total fault causing the accident and injuries do you attribute to:

the defendant _____

the plaintiff _____

(If you find that a party has no fault in causing the accident, then attribute 0% of the fault to that party.)

(6) Disregarding any negligence or fault on the part of the plaintiff, what sum of money would reasonably compensate the plaintiff for her claimed injury and damage?

Answer: $ _____

to reverse a judgment, it is critical to get the charge right. The judge, however, has the final decision as to what instructions are submitted to the jury.

The Verdict

Following its receipt of the charge, the jury begins deliberations. Once it has reached a decision, the jury issues a verdict in favor of one of the parties. If the jury finds a party owes damages on a claim or counterclaim, the jury specifies the amount to be paid to the other party. Following the announcement of the verdict, the jurors are discharged.

verdict
A formal decision made by a jury.

Usually, immediately after the verdict has been announced and the jurors discharged, the party in whose favor the verdict was issued makes a motion asking the judge to issue a *judgment*—the court's final word on the matter—consistent with the jury's verdict. If the jury in the Baranski case finds that Peretto was negligent and awards Baranski damages of $85,000, the judge will order Peretto to pay the plaintiff that amount.

Posttrial Motions and Procedures

Every trial must have a winner and a loser. Although civil litigation is an expensive and cumbersome process, the losing party may wish to pursue the matter further after the verdict.

Assume that Baranski wins at trial and is awarded $85,000 in damages. Cameron, as defendant Peretto's attorney, may file a posttrial motion or appeal the decision to a higher court. Note that even though Baranski won the case, she could also appeal the judgment. For example, she might appeal the case on the ground that she should have received $170,000 in damages instead of $85,000, arguing that the latter amount inadequately compensates her for the harms that she suffered as a result of Peretto's negligence.

Motions after the Trial

motion for judgment notwithstanding the verdict
A motion (also referred to as a *motion for judgment as a matter of law* in federal courts) requesting that the court grant judgment in favor of the party making the motion on the ground that the jury verdict against him or her was unreasonable or erroneous.

Assume that Cameron believes that the verdict for Baranski is not supported by the evidence. She may file a motion for judgment notwithstanding the verdict (also known as a *motion for judgment as a matter of law* in federal courts). By filing this motion, Cameron asks the judge to enter a judgment in favor of Peretto on the ground (basis) that the jury verdict in favor of Baranski was unreasonable and erroneous. Cameron may file this motion only if she previously filed a motion for a directed verdict (or judgment as a matter of law) during the trial. She must file the motion within ten days following the entry of judgment against Peretto.

Supporting Affidavit

Similar to most motions in federal court, this motion must be accompanied by a supporting affidavit or a memorandum of law, or brief (discussed in Chapter 10). The judge then determines whether the jury's verdict was reasonable in view of the evidence presented at trial. Such motions are rarely granted.

Motion for a New Trial

motion for a new trial
A motion asserting that the trial was so fundamentally flawed (because of error, newly discovered evidence, prejudice, or other reason) that a new trial is needed to prevent a miscarriage of justice.

Rule 50 of the Federal Rules of Civil Procedure permits either party to file a motion for a new trial. Such a motion may be submitted along with a motion for judgment notwithstanding the verdict. A motion for a new trial is a far more drastic tactic because it asserts that the trial was so pervaded by error or so fundamentally flawed that a new trial should be held. For a motion for a new trial to have a reasonable chance of being granted, the motion must allege serious problems such as jury misconduct, prejudicial jury instructions, excessive or inadequate damages, or the existence of newly discovered evidence (but not if the evidence could have been discovered earlier through the use of reasonable care).

Similar to other posttrial motions in federal courts, the motion for a new trial must be filed within ten days following the entry of the judgment. Exhibit 12.8 on the facing page illustrates a motion for judgment as a matter of law or, in the alternative, for a new trial.

Appealing the Verdict

appeal
The process of seeking a higher court's review of a lower court's decision for the purpose of correcting or changing the lower court's judgment or decision.

If Cameron's posttrial motions are unsuccessful or if she decides not to file them, she may still file an appeal. The purpose of an appeal is to have the trial court's decision reversed or modified by an appellate court. As discussed in Chapter 6, appellate courts, or courts of appeals, are *reviewing* courts, not trial courts. No new evidence is presented to the appellate court and there is no jury.

The appellate court reviews the trial court's proceedings to decide whether the trial court erred in applying the law to the facts of the case, in instructing the jury, or in administering the trial generally. Appellate courts rarely tamper with a trial court's findings of fact because the judge and jury were in a better position than the appellate court to evaluate the credibility of witnesses, the nature of the evidence, and the like.

As grounds for the appeal, Cameron, might argue that the trial court erred in one of the ways mentioned in the preceding paragraph. Unless she believes that a reversal of the

EXHIBIT 12.8
Motion for Judgment as a
Matter of Law or for a New Trial

Elizabeth A. Cameron
Cameron & Strauss, P.C.
310 Lake Drive
Zero City, ZE 59802
(616) 955-6234

Attorney for Defendant

**UNITED STATES DISTRICT COURT
FOR THE WESTERN DISTRICT OF NITA**

Katherine Baranski	)	CASE NO. 17-14335-NI
Plaintiff,	)	Honorable Harley M. Larue
	)	
v.	)	MOTION FOR JUDGMENT AS
	)	A MATTER OF LAW OR, IN
	)	THE ALTERNATIVE,
Tony Peretto	)	MOTION FOR A NEW TRIAL
Defendant.	)	

The Defendant, Tony Peretto, moves this Court, pursuant to Rule 50(b) of the Federal Rules of Civil Procedure, to set aside the verdict and judgment entered on August 15, 2017, and to enter instead a judgment for the Defendant as a matter of law. In the alternative, and in the event the Defendant's motion for judgment as a matter of law is denied, the Defendant moves the Court to order a new trial.

The grounds for this motion are set forth in the attached memorandum.

Date: 8/18/17

Elizabeth A. Cameron
Elizabeth A. Cameron
Attorney for the Defendant

judgment is likely, however, she will probably advise Peretto not to appeal the case, as an appeal adds to the costs already incurred by Peretto in defending against Baranski's claim.

Notice of Appeal

When the appeal involves a federal district court decision, the **appellant** (the party appealing the decision) must file a notice of appeal with the district court that rendered the judgment. The clerk of the court then notifies the **appellee** (the party against whom the appeal is taken) as well as the court of appeals. The clerk forwards to the appellate court a transcript of the trial court proceedings, along with related pleadings and exhibits. These materials constitute the **record on appeal**.

The Appellate Brief and Oral Arguments

When a case is appealed, the attorneys for both parties submit written *briefs* that present their positions on the issues to be reviewed by the appellate court. The briefs outline each party's view of the proper application of the law to the facts. In preparing the briefs, the attorneys cite relevant pages of the court records. Paralegals often index and summarize the record to assist in the brief writing. These tasks are similar to the organization and summarizing of discovery materials before trial.

After the appellate court has reviewed the briefs, the court usually sets a time for both attorneys to argue their positions before the panel of judges. The attorneys then present their arguments and answer any questions the judges might have. Generally, the attorneys' arguments before an appellate court are limited in both the time allowed for

appellant
The party who takes an appeal from one court to another; sometimes referred to as the *petitioner.*

appellee
The party against whom an appeal is taken—that is, the party who opposes setting aside or reversing the judgment; sometimes referred to as the *respondent.*

record on appeal
The items submitted during the trial (pleadings, motions, briefs, and exhibits) and the transcript of the trial proceedings that are forwarded to the appellate court for review when a case is appealed.

argument and the scope of the argument. Following oral arguments, the judges decide the matter and issue a formal written opinion, which normally is published in the relevant reporter (see Chapter 7).

The Appellate Court's Options

Once they have reviewed the record and heard oral arguments, if any, the judges have several options. In the Baranski case, if the appellate court decided to uphold the trial court's decision, then the judgment for Baranski would be affirmed. If the judges decided to reverse the trial court's decision, then Peretto would no longer be obligated to pay the damages awarded to Baranski by the trial court. The court might also affirm or reverse a decision *in part*. For example, the judges might affirm the jury's finding that Peretto was negligent but remand the case—that is, send it back to the trial court—for further proceedings on another issue (such as the extent of Baranski's damages). An appellate court can also *modify* a lower court's decision. If, for example, the appellate court decided that the jury awarded an excessive amount in damages, the appellate court might reduce the award.

The decision of the appellate court may sometimes be appealed further. A state intermediate appellate court's decision may be appealed to the state supreme court. A federal appellate court's decision may be appealed to the United States Supreme Court. The higher courts decide whether or not they will review the case. These courts normally are not *required* to review cases. Recall from Chapter 6 that although thousands of cases are submitted to the United States Supreme Court each year, it hears fewer than ninety. (An action decided in a state court has a somewhat greater chance of being reviewed by the state supreme court.)

Enforcing the Judgment

The uncertainties of the litigation process are compounded by the lack of guarantees that a judgment will be enforceable. *Developing Paralegal Skills* on the facing page discusses this practical problem. It is one thing to have a court enter a judgment in your favor; it is another to collect the funds to which you are entitled from the opposing party. Even if the jury awarded Baranski the full amount of damages requested ($170,000), for example, she might not, in fact, "win" anything. Peretto's auto insurance coverage might have expired before the accident, in which event it would not cover damages. Alternatively, Peretto's insurance coverage might be limited to $30,000, meaning that Peretto would have to pay the remaining $140,000 personally.

If Peretto did not have that amount or he simply refused to pay, then Baranski would need to go back to court and request that it issue a writ of execution—an order, usually issued by the clerk of the court, directing the sheriff to seize (take temporary ownership of) Peretto's assets. Assets may have to be sold. The proceeds would be used to pay the damages owed to Baranski. Any excess proceeds of the sale would go back to Peretto.

Judgment Creditor

Even as a judgment creditor (one who has obtained a court judgment against a debtor), Baranski may not be able to obtain the full amount of the judgment from Peretto. Laws protecting debtors provide that certain property (such as a debtor's home up to a specific value and tools used by the debtor in his trade) is *exempt* from seizure. Exempt property cannot be seized and sold to pay debts owed to judgment creditors.

Similar exemptions would apply if Peretto declared bankruptcy. Thus, even though Baranski won at trial, she, like many others who are awarded damages, might not be able to collect what she is owed. However, judgments constitute liens (legal claims) for significant time periods. If the financial circumstances of the debtor—such as Peretto—improve in the future, recovery may be possible. There are many roles for paralegals in

affirm
To uphold the judgment of a lower court.

reverse
To overturn the judgment of a lower court.

remand
To send a case back to a lower court for further proceedings.

writ of execution
A writ that puts in force a court's decree or judgment.

judgment creditor
A creditor who is legally entitled, by a court's judgment, to collect the amount of the judgment from a debtor.

DEVELOPING PARALEGAL SKILLS

LOCATING ASSETS

Paralegal Myra Cullen works for a firm that represented Jennifer Roth in a lawsuit brought against Best Eatery, a restaurant. Roth won $500,000 in a lawsuit for damages she suffered when she fell and broke her leg in the restaurant's lobby on a rainy morning. Best Eatery's liability insurance will pay only a portion of Roth's award.

Myra has been assigned to investigate Best Eatery's assets to determine how the judgment might be collected. She knows from pretrial discovery that John Dobman owns Best Eatery as a sole proprietor, which means that he is personally liable for the debts of the business. Myra contacts the county register of deeds to research the value of the property on which Best Eatery is located and any other property owned by John Dobman. The county clerk's deed records can be searched via the Internet. Myra knows, however, that after conducting an online search she will need to verify the information obtained. She writes down the document numbers provided online so that she can quickly access the information at the clerk's office.

Myra determines that Dobman's equity (market value minus mortgage outstanding) in the property on which Best Eatery is located is at least $700,000, which could cover any shortfall in the damages. Because the equity in the restaurant is sufficient to cover the award, Myra simply notes the record number of Dobman's other real property (his house) in the client's file.

TIPS FOR LOCATING ASSETS

- Ask what property the defendant owns during discovery, such as in interrogatories.
- Locate the address of the property (you can do this on the Internet).
- Go to the register of deeds (usually online) to learn about any liens filed against the property and the amount of any mortgage loan.
- Check with a real estate agent or an appraiser as to the market value of the property. Tax appraisal values can be accessed online.
- Deduct the liens and the mortgage debt from the market value to determine the defendant's equity.

collecting judgments, including researching defendants' assets, filing liens, and so on. Many of the skills used in pretrial investigations are useful here.

Social Media Tools at Work

The difficulty of enforcing court judgments, coupled with the high costs accompanying litigation (including attorneys' fees, court costs, and the litigants' time costs), are reasons why most disputes are settled out of court, before or during the trial.

Enforcing judgments is another area where a paralegal's social media skills can pay dividends. Search engines and other tools can be used to look for social media postings that give evidence of valuable assets. Does a judgment debtor have pictures on his Facebook page showing a new boat or vacation home? People often reveal important clues about their lifestyles in social settings that can help locate assets that could be used to satisfy a judgment.

Judgment debtors' digital shadows may be a useful source of information for developing questions that can be used in a post-verdict deposition taken in the search for assets. Be sure to check out their spouses, children, and other relatives as well. If a husband or wife tweets about the generous gift he or she received just before trial, the asset may be able to be recaptured through collection proceedings against the defendant.

Finally, the *Featured Contributor* reminds us, on pages 370 and 371, of the roles the paralegal plays in the litigation process.

FEATURED CONTRIBUTOR

THE COMPLEX ROLES IN LITIGATION

Regina C. Graziani, Esq.

BIOGRAPHICAL NOTE

Regina C. Graziani serves the Paralegal Studies Program at the University of Hartford in Connecticut as both director and instructor. She received her law degree from Villanova University. She is an immediate past co-chair of the Paralegals Section of the Connecticut Bar Association and a past member of the Connecticut Bar Association's House of Delegates. Graziani is a member of the Committee on Insurance Programs for the Bar of the Connecticut Bar Association. She also is co-chair of the Hartford County Bar Association's Paralegal Committee. Attorney Graziani has been a member of the greater Hartford legal community for over 20 years, beginning her career as a litigation paralegal in a major Hartford law firm, where she specialized in large-case management. As an attorney, she focuses on the representation of regulated industrial, financial, and commercial establishments, as well as a small number of citizen plaintiffs in state and federal court, especially in environmental law.

CIVIL LITIGATION

While litigators are often viewed poorly, litigation plays an important role in our society. It is the method by which disputes are settled in a civilized manner.

When parties cannot resolve a dispute on their own, they take it to the courthouse. A trier of fact (jury) and a trier of law (judge) apply precedent to the facts of the matter and reach a decision that is consistent with prior decisions that are similar

unless there is a substantive reason for not applying precedent. As citizens and practitioners, we know (or are able to determine) what the law is—what the consequence for a specified behavior is or what the compensation is for an injury.

PRACTICE

Civil litigation requires patience, an appreciation of strategy, and attention to detail. The litigation process is about strategy: which

KEY TERMS AND CONCEPTS

parties will be sued, in which court, and under which causes of action. Each of those decisions is strategic. The plaintiff must determine whether to file the complaint in state court or federal court, and must analyze the benefits and detriments of filing in each court, and ultimately select the one that is most beneficial to the matter.

Once discovery is entered, consideration is given as to which discovery tools will be used. Tools are selected on the basis of which will yield the most valuable results. Cost may also be a criterion. Depositions are expensive and a client may not be able to afford them; we must determine how else to best obtain the information needed. When faced with a request to produce documents, the scale of the request must be determined, as it possibly could range from millions of pages to a single document.

There is an art to drafting interrogatories, requests for production, and requests for admission. The key is what information is needed to prove the plaintiff's cause of action, or to break down the plaintiff's case (as a defendant). All reports, statements, tests, and documents must be reviewed to ascertain what facts are known and what evidence is needed to meet the burden of proof. Once that determination is made, the interrogatories, requests for production, or requests for admission are crafted narrowly and precisely to elicit the necessary information. Discovery is like a large puzzle. Each party has some pieces, but needs more to determine what the picture is. As the picture is developed, a party may realize that its case is not as strong as it first appeared, and settlement may be desirable.

Preparing for trial can be daunting. A good paralegal has the ability to organize the documents and create a trial notebook for the attorney's use during trial. The notebook contains the important documents and pleadings that have been filed during the course of the litigation, among other documents.

The value of a paralegal in litigation does not end with the preparation for trial. A paralegal plays a significant role during the trial as well and may operate electronic media that are used to present exhibits to the jury. Most likely, the paralegal created the product that is viewed by the jury. The days of bringing a trifold display or an enlarged copy of a document are gone; we use electronic methods. A paralegal may also be charged with note taking during the testimony of witnesses, in preparation for cross-examination or rebuttal. The paralegal may also watch jurors during testimony to try to read their expressions.

PARALEGAL'S ROLE

A successful litigation paralegal is highly motivated, pays attention to detail, possesses strong written and oral skills, is curious, and is competent with technology.

The litigation paralegal is invaluable to the attorney. One may undertake many tasks under the supervision of an attorney. Aside from providing legal advice to the client, signing documents that require an attorney's signature, appearing in court, and asking questions at a deposition, the paralegal can do most any other litigation task. From conducting research on the causes of action to drafting the complaint to assembling the trial notebook, the paralegal is an important and invaluable member of the litigation team.

Discovery is like a large puzzle."

Chapter Summary / Trial Procedures

PREPARING FOR TRIAL

Before trial, attorneys for both sides and their paralegals gather and organize evidence, documents, and other materials relating to the case. A comprehensive checklist ensures that nothing is overlooked during this stage.

1. *Contacting and preparing witnesses*—Paralegals often assist in contacting and issuing subpoenas to witnesses, as well as in preparing witnesses for trial.

2. *Exhibits and displays*—Paralegals assume responsibility for making sure that all exhibits and displays are ready by trial; technology in this area is changing rapidly.

3. *Trial notebook*—A comprehensive trial notebook is critical when preparing for trial and at trial, and often afterward. Paralegals may be responsible for obtaining and organizing copies of all relevant documents.

PRETRIAL CONFERENCE

Before trial, the attorneys for both sides meet with the trial judge in a pretrial conference to decide whether a settlement is possible or, if not, to decide how the trial will be conducted and what types of evidence will be admissible.

It is not uncommon for one or both of the attorneys to make a motion in *limine*, which asks the court to keep certain evidence from being offered at the trial.

JURY SELECTION

1. *Voir dire*—During the *voir dire* process, attorneys for both sides question potential jurors to determine whether any potential jurors should be excluded from the jury.

2. Online searches for information about prospective jurors may provide helpful information in the selection process. Consultants may be employed in complex cases.

3. *Challenges during* voir dire—Attorneys for both sides can exercise an unlimited number of challenges for cause on the basis of prospective jurors' bias against the client or case. Attorneys can exercise a limited number of peremptory challenges without giving any reason to the court for excluding a potential juror.

4. *Paralegals' role during* voir dire—Paralegals may help prepare jury profiles and observe prospective jurors to gain insights into the potential jurors' views of the case.

5. *Alternate jurors*—In case of illness or other problem during a trial, an alternate juror may be called to step in so the trial may proceed.

THE TRIAL

Once the jury has been selected and seated, the trial begins.

1. If the paralegal attends the trial, she may coordinate witnesses' appearances, track the testimony of witnesses and compare it with sworn statements that the witnesses made before the trial, and provide the attorney with reminders or documents when necessary.

2. *Opening statements*—The trial begins with opening statements in which the attorneys briefly outline their versions of the facts of the case and the evidence they will offer to support their views.

3. *Plaintiff's case*—Following the opening statements, the plaintiff's attorney presents evidence supporting the claims, including the testimony of witnesses.

   a. In direct examination, the attorney questions witnesses who are called to testify.

   b. Following direct examination by the plaintiff's attorney, the defendant's attorney may cross-examine the witness.

   c. If the witness was cross-examined, the plaintiff's attorney may question the witness on redirect examination, after which the defendant's attorney may question the witness on recross-examination.

4. *Motion for a directed verdict*—After the plaintiff's attorney has presented his client's case, the defendant's attorney may make a motion for a directed verdict (a motion for judgment as a matter of law). It asserts that the plaintiff has not offered enough evidence to support the claim against the defendant. If the judge grants the motion, the case is dismissed.

5. *Defendant's case*—The attorneys reverse roles, and the defendant's attorney presents evidence and testimony to refute the plaintiff's claims. Witnesses called to the stand by the defendant's attorney are subject to direct examination by that attorney, cross-examination by the plaintiff's attorney, and possible redirect examination and recross-examination.

6. *Closing arguments*—After the defendant's attorney has finished her presentation, both attorneys give closing arguments. The arguments summarize the major points that support the client's case and emphasize shortcomings in the opposing party's case.

7. *Jury instructions*—Following the attorneys' closing arguments (or, in some courts, at some other point), the judge instructs the jury in a charge—a document that includes statements of the applicable law and a review of the facts as presented during the trial. The jury must not disregard the judge's instructions as to what the applicable law is and how it should be applied to the facts of the case as interpreted by the jury.

8. *Verdict*—Once the jury reaches a decision, it issues a verdict in favor of one of the parties and is discharged. The court then enters a judgment.

POSTTRIAL MOTIONS AND PROCEDURES

After the verdict has been pronounced and the trial concluded, the losing party's attorney may file a posttrial motion or an appeal.

1. *Posttrial motions*—A motion for judgment notwithstanding the verdict (a motion for judgment as a matter of law) asks the judge to enter a judgment in favor of the losing party in spite of the verdict because the verdict was not supported by the evidence or was otherwise in error. A motion for a new trial asserts that the trial was so flawed—by juror misconduct or other pervasive errors—that a new trial should be held.

2. *Appealing the verdict*—The attorney may, depending on the client's wishes, appeal the decision to an appellate court for review. Appeals are usually filed only when the attorney believes there is a good chance of reversal.

   a. In an appeal, the appellant must file a notice of appeal with the court that rendered the judgment. The clerk forwards the trial record to the reviewing court.

   b. The parties then file appellate briefs arguing their positions. Later, they are given the opportunity to present oral arguments before the appellate panel.

   c. The appellate court decides whether to affirm, reverse, remand, or modify the trial court's judgment.

   d. The appellate court's decision may sometimes be appealed further (to the state supreme court, for example).

ENFORCING THE JUDGMENT

Even though a plaintiff wins a lawsuit for damages, it may be difficult to enforce the judgment against the defendant, particularly if the defendant has few assets. The paralegal is often involved in locating assets so the attorney can request a writ of execution (court order to seize property) to try to collect the amount the client is owed.

■ QUESTIONS FOR REVIEW

1. What role does the paralegal play in pretrial preparation of witnesses, exhibits, and displays for trial? How are the trial notebooks prepared?

2. Describe the juror selection process. What is the difference between a peremptory challenge and a challenge for cause?

3. What are the different phases of a trial? List the process steps in attorneys' questioning of witnesses. What is the difference between direct examination and cross-examination?

4. Describe the procedure for filing an appeal. What factors does an attorney consider when deciding whether a case should be appealed? Can the jury decide matters of law?

5. What is a writ of execution? What is a judgment creditor?

■ ETHICS QUESTION

During the course of a products liability trial, a juror consulted the website **howstuffworks.com** to better understand components in the piece of equipment involved in the case. Aaron, a paralegal for the defense attorney, overheard two jurors discussing the information as they left the jury box. The information that the juror had learned would be beneficial to the defendant, whom Aaron's boss is defending in the case. What should Aaron do in this situation?

■ PRACTICE QUESTIONS AND ASSIGNMENTS

1. Using the material from this chapter, identify the different phases of a trial (opening statement, direct examination, cross-examination, motion for directed verdict, closing statement, verdict, posttrial motions) in the hypothetical situations below:

   a. The plaintiff's attorney asks the witness, "Mrs. Wong, could you explain what you observed at the scene of the accident on January 17, 2016?"

   b. The defense attorney makes a motion saying that the plaintiff's attorney has not offered enough evidence to support a claim against the defendant.

   c. The defense attorney asks the plaintiff's witness, "Mr. Bashara, isn't it true that you were drinking alcohol immediately before you were involved in the car accident?"

   d. The plaintiff's attorney gives her version of the facts and supporting evidence that she will use to prove her case during the trial.

2. Using the material presented in the chapter, identify the motion that would be filed in each of the following situations:

   a. A plaintiff's attorney loses a case, and she believes that her loss is due to prejudicial jury instructions given by the judge.

   b. The defendant's key witness died during trial and there was no way to obtain the testimony he would have provided. As a result, key evidence was not presented, and the defendant was unable to prove his case.

   c. In the same case (see Question 2b above), the plaintiff's attorney made an appropriate motion, which was not granted, and ultimately lost the lawsuit. Thus, according to the plaintiff's attorney, the judgment was not supported by the evidence.

   d. The defense attorney saw the grisly photographs of an accident that the plaintiff's attorney has in her file. The defense attorney is concerned that these photographs would unfairly prejudice a jury against the defendant during the trial.

3. During jury selection for a medical malpractice trial, three employees of the insurance company that carried the malpractice insurance for the doctor and hospital being sued were members of the jury pool. Should employees of an insurance company be allowed to serve on the jury? If not, discuss the challenges that the plaintiff's attorney could raise to have them removed.

4. Attorney Johnson calls witness Roberta Looper to the stand to testify. When the judge asks Roberta to raise her hand to be sworn in, Roberta refuses, saying that she is an atheist and cannot swear an oath to God on the Bible. Given the material covered in previous chapters on the First Amendment, can the judge make Roberta take the oath? Can the judge refuse to let her testify? What alternative might there be for Roberta to swear to tell the truth?

5. A contractor filed a whistleblower lawsuit against a city in federal court for nonrenewal of her contract as the city's food drive coordinator. The plaintiff's co-worker offered opinion testimony (as a lay witness) about the contractor's contribution to the food drive's success and growth. Should the co-worker's opinion testimony be allowed? Explain.

6. Indicate what action the appellate court has taken in each hypothetical below (affirmed, modified, or reversed the trial court's decision or remanded the case for further proceedings):

   a. A trial court finds for the plaintiff in the amount of $150,000 in a case in which the plaintiff slipped and fell in a grocery store. The court of appeals finds that while the plaintiff is entitled to damages, the damages awarded by the jury are excessive. The appellate court sends the case back to the trial court for reevaluation of the amount of damages awarded.

   b. A trial court finds that the plaintiff was slandered by the defendant. On appeal, the court of appeals finds that the trial court admitted evidence that it should not have allowed and holds that without this evidence, there was no slander.

   c. A trial court finds that the defendant breached a contract and owes the plaintiff $1,000,000 in damages. The defendant appeals, claiming that the damages are not supported by the evidence. The court of appeals agrees with the trial court's decision.

7. Using Exhibit 12.2 on page 352, draft a subpoena for a friendly witness using the following facts:

   Simon Kolstad, whose address is 100 Schoolcraft Road, Del Mar, California, is a witness to be subpoenaed in *Sumner v. Hayes*, a civil lawsuit filed in the U.S. District Court for the Eastern District of Michigan, case number 15-123492. He is being subpoenaed by the plaintiff's attorney, Marvin W. Green, whose office is located at 300 Penobscot Building, 705 Premier Ave., Detroit, Michigan. Kolstad is to appear in Room 6 of the courthouse, which is located at 231 Lafayette Boulevard, Detroit, Michigan, at 2:30 P.M. on January 10, 2017.

GROUP PROJECT

The group should research how a paralegal might use social media sites to find information about jurors.

Student one will use online sources (and library sources, if necessary) to find out what kinds of information are available online about potential jurors. Student one should summarize how this information could be used during *voir dire*.

Students two and three will research whether investigation of this nature is ethical, and if so, under what circumstances it might become unethical.

Student four will create a presentation to share the group's results with the rest of the class.

INTERNET PROJECTS

1. Browse the Jury Research Institute website at **juryresearchinstitute.com**.

   a. Write a one-page summary of the services that the company provides.

   b. Go to "Browse our Experience," click on "Notable Cases," and review the verdicts. After doing so, do you think that it is worthwhile to hire a jury consultant? From the information found in "Notable Cases," who tends to hire jury consultants?

2. Review **bloglawonline.blogspot.com/2010/02/juror-use-of-social-media-state-by.html** for your state's court rules and model jury instructions prohibiting jurors' use of social media and Internet research. (If no information is listed for your state, select another state for which jury instructions are provided.) Print a copy of the jury instructions and then give your opinion on whether

they offer sufficient warning to jurors. Explain the reasons for your opinion.

3. Do an Internet search for your state's court rules for civil cases. Look up how many challenges for cause are allowed during *voir dire*. How many peremptory challenges are permitted?

4. Do an Internet search for a local civil trial court clerk's Web page. See if the trial schedule is available online; if not, call the court clerk's office to obtain a schedule. Go and observe a trial or other evidentiary hearing for two to three hours. Write a two-page summary of what you observed and learned, recording the phase of the trial, the types of witnesses testifying, the evidence being presented, and any motions made. Be sure to include the name of the court you visited, the date, and the judge's name.

END NOTES

1. Pronounced in *lim*-uh-nay.

2. Pronounced vwahr *deer*. These old French words mean "to speak the truth." In legal language, the phrase refers to the process of questioning jurors to learn about their backgrounds, attitudes, and similar attributes.

CHAPTER 13

Criminal Law and Procedures

CHAPTER OUTLINE

CHAPTER OBJECTIVES

After completing this chapter, you will know:

- The difference between crimes and other wrongful acts.

- The two elements required for criminal liability and some of the most common defenses that are raised in defending against criminal charges.

- Major categories of crimes and some common types of crimes.

- The constitutional rights of persons accused of crimes.

- The basic steps involved in criminal procedure, from the time a crime is reported to the resolution of the case.

- How and why criminal litigation procedures differ from civil litigation procedures.

Introduction

Each year, more than 10 million people are arrested on criminal charges and enter the criminal justice system. Therefore, it is no wonder that many attorneys and paralegals work on criminal law cases. In fact, about one in every five paralegals spends most of her or his work time on criminal law.

Public prosecutors, who are employed by the government, prosecute criminal cases. The chief public prosecutor in federal criminal cases is called a U.S. attorney. Assistant U.S. attorneys conduct most trials for those cases. In cases tried in state or local courts, the public prosecutor may be referred to as a *prosecuting attorney, state prosecutor, district attorney, county attorney,* or *city attorney.* Defendants in criminal cases may hire private attorneys to defend them. If a defendant cannot afford to hire an attorney, the court will appoint one. Everyone accused of a crime that may result in a jail sentence has a right to counsel, and court-appointed attorneys ensure this right. Some court-appointed defense lawyers work for organizations funded by the states. These are usually called public defenders. Others are private attorneys appointed to represent a particular defendant.

In this chapter, we provide an overview of criminal law and procedure. We begin by explaining the nature of crime and the key differences between criminal law and civil law. We then discuss the elements of criminal liability and some of the many types of crime. We emphasize the constitutional protections that come into play when a person is accused of a crime, and focus on how and why criminal procedures differ from civil procedures. As the *Featured Contributor* notes on the following two pages, paralegals need certain talents to be effective in the criminal justice arena.

public prosecutor
An individual, acting as a trial lawyer, who initiates and conducts criminal cases in the government's name and on behalf of the people.

public defender
Court-appointed defense counsel. A lawyer appointed by the court to represent a criminal defendant who is unable to pay to hire private counsel.

Defining Crime

What is a crime? To answer, we begin by distinguishing crimes from other wrongs, such as torts—and, hence, criminal law from tort, or civil, law. Major differences between civil law and criminal law are summarized in Exhibit 13.1 on page 380. After discussing the differences, we explain how one act can qualify as both a crime and a tort. We then describe classifications of crimes and jurisdiction over criminal acts.

Key Differences between Civil Law and Criminal Law

A crime can be distinguished from other wrongful acts, such as torts, in that a crime is an *offense against society as a whole.* Criminal defendants are prosecuted by public officials on behalf of the state, as mentioned above, not by their victims or other private parties. In practice, however, the cooperation of the victim is usually important. The prosecutor can file criminal charges even if the victim does not wish to cooperate, but that makes a successful prosecution less likely. In addition, those who have committed crimes are subject to penalties, including fines, imprisonment, and, in some cases, death.

crime
A broad term for violations of law that are punishable by the state and are codified by legislatures. The objective of criminal law is to protect the public.

As will be discussed in Chapter 14, tort remedies—remedies for civil wrongs—are generally intended to compensate the injured party (by awarding money damages, for example). Criminal law, however, is concerned with punishing the wrongdoer in an attempt to deter others from similar actions.

Statutory Basis

Another factor distinguishing criminal law from tort law is that criminal law is primarily statutory law. Essentially, a crime is whatever a legislature has declared to be a crime. Although the U.S. Congress defines federal crimes, most crimes are defined by state legislatures.

FEATURED CONTRIBUTOR

PARALEGALS AND CRIMINAL LITIGATION

Steven C. Kempisty, Esq.

BIOGRAPHICAL NOTE

Steven Kempisty is a graduate of the State University of New York at Fredonia and the Massachusetts School of Law at Andover. A licensed attorney, he joined Bryant & Stratton College in 1999 and has served as program director for the two-year paralegal program at the Liverpool, New York, campus since 2009. Mr. Kempisty also is a member of the Financial Industry Regulatory Authority (FINRA), where he is an arbitration panelist. His main fields of interest are contract and corporations work.

One of the most important things I tell new students is: "*Law & Order* is a nice program; please understand that it is fiction. The practice of law, especially criminal law and procedure, is not how Hollywood portrays it."

Our legal system can be very complex and cumbersome. The criminal court system often has "logjammed" dockets. Criminal law professionals are often overworked and may have more cases than can be handled by even the most skilled individual. Three important rules for those who wish to become part of the legal profession are: be available, be organized, and be prepared.

BE AVAILABLE

Criminal law provides vital protections to the accused. Government officials take their jobs seriously, and skilled defense attorneys are just as committed as they represent their clients. Being available could mean doing anything from:

1. Reviewing files.

2. Reading over old affidavits and looking at all information.

3. Reading and organizing deposition statements.

4. Looking over police reports.

5. Looking over many different records that may be germane to a case, ranging from old tax records to old indictments.

6. Answering the phone.

7. Rereading the initial interview of a client.

8. Reviewing numerous pages of statutes, cases, and footnotes.

Standards of Proof

The burden of proof required in criminal and civil cases is another difference. Because the state has extensive resources at its disposal when prosecuting criminal cases, there are procedural safeguards to protect the rights of defendants. One of these safeguards is the higher burden of proof in a criminal case. In a civil case, the plaintiff usually must prove a case by a *preponderance of the evidence*. Under this standard, the plaintiff must convince the court that, based on the evidence presented by both parties, it is more likely than not that the plaintiff's allegation is true.

In a criminal case, in contrast, the state must prove its case beyond a reasonable doubt—that is, normally every juror in a criminal case must be convinced, beyond a reasonable doubt, of the defendant's guilt. The higher standard of proof in criminal cases reflects a fundamental social value—a belief that it is worse to convict an innocent individual than to let a guilty person go free. We will look at other safeguards later in the chapter, in the context of criminal procedure.

beyond a reasonable doubt
The standard used to determine the guilt or innocence of a person charged with a crime. To be guilty of a crime, a suspect must be proved guilty "beyond and to the exclusion of every reasonable doubt."

9. Researching on Westlaw or Lexis.

10. Being skilled and capable in storing, managing, and organizing many forms of electronically stored information (ESI)

Some of these tasks may seem mundane, but finding information that is helpful to a case, whether for a prosecutor or defense counsel, is important.

Being available to weed through and organize endless paperwork is hugely valuable to a legal team. It needs to be done. Being available to complete this task, although it appears thankless, will be valued and appreciated.

BE ORGANIZED

Organization is never overrated. Every legal textbook will mention the importance of discovery, document production, and organizing information. Becoming organized is especially important for deposition testimony, for material evidence that may be challenged under hearsay rules, and for keeping the order of your case flowing logically so as to best represent your side in an issue.

Colleagues have told me more than once that they missed an opportunity at some point in a case simply because they were not organized on a particular issue of evidence or procedure. Work together on the organization of a file and case so as to avoid confusion among the team members. The fundamental importance of organization on a legal team is everyone understanding the system and the legal team's goals.

BE PREPARED

Being prepared would appear to be common sense. What I mean is, be prepared for the unexpected since we must "expect the unexpected." With evidentiary disclosure there should never be any surprises or cliff-hanging elements of a case that magically appear the day of trial. However, witnesses get cold feet, unorganized people lose important documents, people leave, and subpoenas are defied.

During the many hours that a legal team puts into a case, there can be shifts. When a curveball is thrown, one must seek assistance, seek a continuance or adjournment, but remain calm and carry on. There is no such thing as the perfect plan in law, but being prepared for all problems means they can be handled properly. Panicking will not get the job done.

CONCLUSION

In my very first case I had a client who did not speak English. I had to hire an interpreter for myself and for court appearances with the client. One time the interpreter was late. I was in a panic. A veteran colleague of mine was in court and talked me through the problem. I had forgotten that the client could read and write some in English, so we could progress. My interpreter eventually showed up and we proceeded. My colleague taught me a valuable lesson: Remain focused and calm. To do so, we must be organized and prepared with all relevant information to assist our clients properly.

> The practice of law, especially criminal law and procedure, is not how Hollywood portrays it."

Victimless Crimes

Yet another factor that distinguishes criminal law from tort law is the fact that a criminal act does not necessarily involve a victim, in the sense that the act directly and physically harms another. If Marissa grows marijuana in her backyard for her personal use, she may not be physically or directly harming another's interests, but she is nonetheless committing a crime (in most states and under federal law). Why? Because she is violating a rule of society that has been enacted into law by elected representatives of the people.

Civil Liability for Criminal Acts

Note that a person who commits a crime may be subject to both civil and criminal liability. Suppose Joe is walking down the street, minding his own business, when suddenly an attacker stabs Joe, seriously injuring him. A police officer arrests the wrongdoer. In

EXHIBIT 13.1

Civil Law and
Criminal Law Compared

Issue	Under Civil Law	Under Criminal Law
Area of concern	Rights and duties between individuals and between persons and government	Offenses against society as a whole
Wrongful act	Harm to a person or to a person's property	Violation of a statute that prohibits a certain activity
Party who brings suit	Person who suffered harm	The state
Standard of proof	Preponderance of the evidence	Beyond a reasonable doubt
Remedy	Damages to compensate for the harm or a decree to achieve an equitable result	Punishment (fine, removal from public office, imprisonment, or death)

separate legal actions, the attacker may be subject both to criminal prosecution by the state and to a tort (civil) lawsuit brought by Joe. Exhibit 13.2 on the facing page illustrates how the same act can result in both a tort action and a criminal action against the wrongdoer.

Classifications of Crimes

Crimes are generally divided into two broad classifications: felonies and misdemeanors.

Felonies

felony
A crime—such as arson, murder, assault, or robbery—that carries the most severe sanctions. Sanctions range from one year in a state or federal prison to life imprisonment or (in some states) the death penalty.

A **felony** is a serious crime that may be punished by imprisonment for more than one year. In some states, certain felonies are punishable by death. Examples of felonies include murder, rape, robbery, arson, and grand larceny. (You will read more about these and other crimes later in the chapter.)

Felonies are commonly classified by degree. The Model Penal Code,[1] for example, provides for four degrees of felony:

1. *capital offenses*, for which the maximum penalty is death,
2. *first degree felonies*, punishable by a maximum penalty of life imprisonment,
3. *second degree felonies*, punishable by a maximum of ten years' imprisonment, and
4. *third degree felonies*, punishable by up to five years' imprisonment.

Misdemeanors

misdemeanor
A crime less serious than a felony, punishable by a fine or incarceration for up to one year in jail (not a state or federal penitentiary).

A **misdemeanor** is a crime that may be punished by incarceration of not more than one year. If incarcerated, the guilty party goes to a local jail instead of prison. A misdemeanor, by definition, is not a serious crime. Under federal law and in most states, a misdemeanor is any crime that is not defined by statute as a felony. State legislatures specify what crimes are classified as felonies or misdemeanors and what the potential punishment for each type of criminal act may be. Examples of misdemeanors include prostitution, disturbing the peace, and public intoxication.

Petty Offenses

petty offense
In criminal law, the least serious kind of wrong, such as a traffic or building-code violation.

Certain criminal or quasi-criminal actions, such as violations of building codes, are termed petty offenses, or *infractions*. In most jurisdictions, such actions are considered a subset of misdemeanors. Some states, however, classify them separately.

Jurisdiction over Crimes

Most crimes are defined in state statutes, and the states have jurisdiction in cases involving these crimes. Federal jurisdiction extends to thousands of crimes. If a federal law

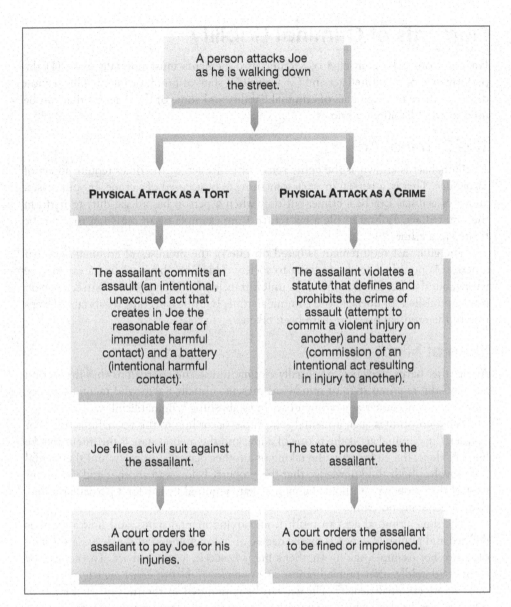

EXHIBIT 13.2

Tort (Civil) Lawsuit and Criminal Prosecution for the Same Act

A person attacks Joe as he is walking down the street.

PHYSICAL ATTACK AS A TORT

The assailant commits an assault (an intentional, unexcused act that creates in Joe the reasonable fear of immediate harmful contact) and a battery (intentional harmful contact).

Joe files a civil suit against the assailant.

A court orders the assailant to pay Joe for his injuries.

PHYSICAL ATTACK AS A CRIME

The assailant violates a statute that defines and prohibits the crime of assault (attempt to commit a violent injury on another) and battery (commission of an intentional act resulting in injury to another).

The state prosecutes the assailant.

A court orders the assailant to be fined or imprisoned.

defines a certain action as a crime, federal jurisdiction exists. Generally, federal criminal jurisdiction applies to crimes that:

1. occur outside the jurisdiction of a state,

2. involve interstate commerce or communications,

3. interfere with the operation of the federal government or its agents, or

4. are directed at citizens or property located outside the United States.

Consider just one example: Burning down a person's home in Dallas is arson under Texas law. Burning down a Dallas post office, which is federal property, would be a federal crime. Burning down a warehouse used by Amazon.com—a building used in interstate commerce—would be a federal crime, but may be prosecuted under state law.

A challenging legal issue today concerns how a state or the federal government can exercise jurisdiction over criminal acts that are committed via the Internet, which knows no geographical borders. Often either the state or the federal government may prosecute such a matter.

Elements of Criminal Liability

For a person to be convicted of a crime, two elements must normally exist: (1) the performance of a criminal act and (2) a specified state of mind, or intent. This section describes these two elements of criminal liability and some of the defenses that can be used to avoid liability for crimes.

The Criminal Act

A criminal act is known as the *actus reus*,[2] or guilty act. Most crimes require an act of *commission*. That is, a person must *do* something to be accused of a crime. In some cases, an act of *omission* can be a crime, but only when a person has a legal duty to perform the omitted act. Failure to file a tax return is an example of an omission that can be treated as a crime.

The guilty-act requirement is based on one of the premises of criminal law—that a person is punished for harm done to society. Thinking about stealing a car may be wrong, but the thought does no harm unless translated into action. Of course, a person can be punished for *attempting* to commit a crime, but normally only if substantial steps toward the criminal objective have been taken.

State of Mind

An act that harms society is not legally a crime unless the court finds that the second element—the required state of mind—was present. Usually a wrongful mental state, or *mens rea*,[3] is necessary as a wrongful act in establishing criminal liability.

What constitutes such a mental state varies according to the wrongful action. For murder, the criminal act is the taking of a life, and the mental state is the intent to take life. For theft, the guilty act is the taking of another person's property, and the mental state involves both the knowledge that the property belongs to another and the intent to steal that property. Without the mental state required by law for a particular crime, there is generally no crime.

The same criminal act can result from varying mental states, and how a crime is defined and punished depends on the degree of "wrongfulness" of the defendant's state of mind. For example, taking another's life is *homicide*, a criminal act. The act can be committed coldly, after premeditation, as in *murder in the first degree*, which carries the most severe criminal penalty. The act can be committed in the heat of passion, as in *voluntary manslaughter*, which carries a less severe penalty than murder. Or the act can be committed as a result of criminal negligence (reckless driving, for example), as in *involuntary manslaughter*. In each of these situations, the law recognizes a different degree of wrongfulness, and the harshness of the punishment depends on the degree to which the act of killing another was an *intentional* act.

Corporate Criminal Liability

A corporation may be held liable for crimes committed by its agents and employees within the course and scope of their employment. Obviously, corporations cannot be imprisoned, but they can be fined or denied certain legal privileges.

Corporate directors and officers are personally liable for the crimes they commit, regardless of whether the crimes were committed for their personal benefit or on the corporation's behalf. Additionally, corporate directors and officers may be held liable for the actions of employees under their supervision. Under what has become known as the responsible corporate officer doctrine, a court may impose criminal liability on a corporate officer regardless of whether she or he participated in, directed, or even knew about a given criminal violation.

For example, in one case the chief executive officer of a supermarket chain was held personally liable for sanitation violations in corporate warehouses where rodents contaminated food. The case was eventually heard by the United States Supreme

Court, which held that the corporate officer was personally liable not because he intended the crime or even knew about it but because he was in a "responsible relationship" to the corporation and had the power to prevent the violation.[4] Courts have used similar reasoning to impose criminal liability on corporate managers who allowed harm to the environment in violation of federal law, such as the Clean Water Act (discussed in Chapter 19).

Defenses to Criminal Liability

A person accused of a crime will typically offer a defense—a reason why he or she should not be found guilty. Asserting that a defendant lacks the required criminal intent for a specific crime is one way of defending against criminal liability. This defense and others are discussed below. No one charged with a crime is obligated to offer a defense. The government must prove guilt beyond a reasonable doubt even if the defendant does not offer any particular defense but simply tries, at trial, to point out defects in government claims and evidence.

defense
The evidence and arguments presented in the defendant's support in a criminal action or lawsuit.

The Required Mental State Is Lacking

Proving that a defendant did or did not possess the required mental state for a given crime is difficult because a person's state of mind cannot be known. For example, assume that Jackson shot and killed Avery. Jackson is arrested and charged with the crime of murder. Jackson contends that he did not commit murder because he was too high on drugs to know what he was doing and thus lacked the required mental state for murder—intent to kill. Jackson claims that, at most, he committed the crime of involuntary manslaughter. There will have to be some facts in evidence tending to show that Jackson was indeed so under the influence of drugs that he could not have intended to kill Avery.

Criminal defendants may assert that they lacked the required degree of criminal intent for other reasons, including:

- *insanity* (the inability to distinguish between right and wrong due to diminished mental capacity),

- *duress* (which exists when one is forced to commit a specific act), or

- *mistake* (for example, taking someone else's property, such as a briefcase, thinking that it is one's own).

Protection of Persons or Property

We all have the right to protect ourselves from physical attacks by others. This is the right of self-defense. In most states, the force we use to protect ourselves must be reasonable under the circumstances. The force used must be justified by the degree of threat posed in a given situation. If someone is about to take your life, the use of *deadly force* (shooting that person with a gun, for example) might be deemed reasonable. If, however, someone in a shopping mall tries to steal a bag you are carrying, you normally do not have a right to shoot the thief, because there was no physical threat to your person.

self-defense
The legally recognized privilege to protect oneself or one's property against injury by another. The privilege of self-defense protects only acts that are reasonably necessary to protect oneself or one's property.

DEFENSE OF OTHERS. Similarly, we have the right to use force in defense of others if they are threatened with imminent harm. If you and a friend are walking down a city street one night and someone attacks and threatens to kill your friend, you are justified in responding with reasonable force to protect your friend. As with self-defense, the reasonableness of the force used is judged in view of the nature of the threat.

defense of others
The use of reasonable force to protect others from harm.

DEFENSE OF PROPERTY. We also have the right to use reasonable force in the defense of property. In particular, if someone is trespassing on our property or is stealing our property, we have the right to use force to stop the trespassing or prevent the theft. Again, the amount of force used must be reasonable. Because human life has a

defense of property
The use of reasonable force to protect one's property from harm threatened by another. The use of deadly force in defending one's property is seldom justified.

higher value than property, deadly force is normally not allowed in the protection of property unless the thief or trespasser poses a threat to human life.

Depending on the situation, the *castle* (or *stand your ground*) *doctrine* may come into play. This doctrine is based on the common law concept that you have a right to defend your home (your castle), yourself, your property, or an innocent person from the illegal acts of another. In general, if an intruder is in a home, the legal residents of the home do not have a *duty to retreat*. Rather, they have an express right to *stand their ground*. About half the states have expressed this principle in legislation, but the details of how the principle is applied vary across the states.

Statutes of Limitations

With some exceptions, such as for the crime of murder, statutes of limitations apply to crimes. In other words, criminal cases must be prosecuted within a certain number of years. If a criminal action is brought after the statutory time period has expired, the accused can raise the statute of limitations as a defense.

Other Defenses

Further defenses include *mistaken identity*, and a defendant may offer an *alibi* (proof that the defendant was somewhere else at the time of the crime, for example).

Because criminal law brings the force of the state to bear against the individual, law enforcement authorities must abide by the letter of procedural law when arresting and prosecuting a person accused of a crime. If they do not, the defendant may be able to use the prosecution's violations of procedural laws as a defense, depending on the nature of the right that was violated and the degree of violation.

Types of Crimes

The number of acts categorized as criminal is nearly endless. Federal, state, and local laws provide for the classification and punishment of thousands of different criminal acts. Traditionally, though, crimes have been grouped into five broad categories, or types: violent crime (crimes against persons), property crime, public order crime, white-collar crime, and organized crime.

Violent Crime

Crimes against persons, because they cause others to suffer harm or death, are referred to as *violent crimes*. Murder is a violent crime. So are sexual assault, rape, and assault and battery (discussed further in Chapter 14). Robbery—the taking of money, personal property, or any other article of value from a person by means of force or fear—is another violent crime. Typically, states have more severe penalties for *aggravated robbery*—robbery with the use of a deadly weapon—than for simple robbery. Many crimes carry greater penalties if a deadly weapon is involved.

Each violent crime is further classified by degree, depending on the circumstances surrounding the criminal act. These include the intent of the person committing the crime, whether a weapon was used, and the level of pain and suffering experienced by the victim. For example, traditionally, killing another human being could result in one of three different offenses, depending on the defendant's intent: murder (if the killing was intentional), voluntary manslaughter (if intentional but provoked), or involuntary manslaughter (if the killing was unintentional but resulted from criminal negligence or an unlawful act, such as drunk driving).

Most states follow these basic classifications of homicide but add degrees of murder to provide penalties of different severity. For example, deliberate and premeditated killing is usually first degree murder (a *capital offense*—a crime possibly punishable by death). First degree murder may also include killings committed during certain types of

robbery
The taking of money, personal property, or any other article of value from a person by means of force or fear.

felonies, such as arson, burglary, rape, or robbery. When a person is killed during other types of felonies, the charge is likely to be second degree murder, which is typically not punishable by death.

Property Crime

The most common type of criminal activity is property crime—a crime in which the goal of the offender is some form of economic gain or damage to property. Robbery is a form of property crime, as well as a violent crime, because the offender seeks to gain the property of another by use of force or the threat of force (which creates fear). Other property crimes are discussed next.

Burglary

Burglary usually involves breaking and entering onto the property of another with the intent to commit a felony. A burglary does not necessarily involve theft. The defendant may have intended to commit some other felony and still be guilty of burglary.

burglary
Breaking and entering onto the property of another with the intent to commit a felony.

Larceny

Any person who wrongfully or fraudulently takes and carries away another person's personal property is guilty of larceny. In other words, larceny is "stealing." To be guilty of larceny, the accused must have intended to deprive the owner permanently of the property. Larceny does not involve force or fear (as in robbery) or breaking into a building (as in burglary). Taking company products and supplies home for personal use, if one is not authorized to do so, is larceny. Many states have expanded the definition of larceny to include thefts of computer files, computer time, and electricity.

larceny
The wrongful or fraudulent taking and carrying away of another person's personal property with the intent to deprive the person permanently of the property.

Obtaining Goods by False Pretenses

It is a criminal act to obtain goods by means of false pretenses—for example, buying groceries with a check knowing that there are insufficient funds to cover it. Statutes dealing with such illegal activities vary from state to state.

Receiving Stolen Goods

It is a crime to receive stolen goods. The recipient of such goods need not know the true identity of the owner or the thief. All that is necessary is that the recipient knew or *should have known* that the goods were stolen (which implies the intent to deprive the owner of those goods). In other words, if someone sells you a new laptop for fifty dollars from the back of a truck full of laptops, you may be guilty of receiving stolen property.

Arson

The willful and malicious burning of a building (and, in some states, personal property) owned by another is the crime of arson. Every state also has a special statute that covers burning a building for the purpose of collecting insurance.

arson
The willful and malicious burning of a building (and, in some states, personal property) owned by another; arson statutes have been extended to cover the intentional destruction of any building, regardless of ownership, by fire or explosion.

Forgery

The fraudulent making or altering of any writing in a way that changes the legal rights and liabilities of another is forgery. If, without authorization, Tyler signs Ben's name to the back of a check made out to Ben, Tyler is committing forgery. Forgery also includes changing trademarks, falsifying public records, counterfeiting, and altering a legal document.

forgery
The fraudulent making or altering of any writing in a way that changes the legal rights and liabilities of another.

Public Order Crime

Societies outlaw activities considered to be contrary to public values and morals. Today, the most common public order crimes include public drunkenness, gambling, and illegal drug use. These are sometimes referred to as victimless crimes because they potentially harm only the offender. Nevertheless, legislatures have deemed these acts as detrimental to society because they create an environment that gives rise to property crimes, violent crimes, or those that damage the "fabric" of society.

Some of these crimes can result in property forfeitures. For example, someone who transports illegal drugs in his car may lose the car to the government as well as suffer a prison term.

White-Collar Crime

Crimes that typically occur in the business context are commonly referred to as white-collar crimes. A famous white-collar criminal is Bernard Madoff, who pleaded guilty to defrauding clients of his failed investment firm that lost billions of dollars. Although there is no official definition of white-collar crime, the term is popularly used to mean an illegal act or series of acts committed by a person or business entity using some nonviolent means. Usually, this kind of crime is committed in relationship to a legitimate occupation. Many, but not all, corporate crimes fall into this category.

Embezzlement

When a person entrusted with another person's property fraudulently takes it, embezzlement occurs. Typically, embezzlement involves an employee who steals funds. Banks face this problem, and so do businesses in which officers or accountants "cook" the books to cover up the taking of funds for their own benefit. Embezzlement is not larceny, because the wrongdoer does not physically take the property from the possession of another, and it is not robbery, because force or fear is not used.

Mail and Wire Fraud

One of the most potent weapons against white-collar criminals is the Mail Fraud Act. Under this act, it is a federal crime (mail fraud) to use the mails, which includes e-mail, to defraud the public. Illegal use of the mails must involve (1) mailing or causing someone else to mail (or e-mail) something written, printed, or photocopied for the purpose of executing a scheme to defraud and (2) a contemplated or an organized scheme to defraud by false pretenses. If, for example, Johnson advertises by mail the sale of a cure for cancer that he knows has no medical validity, he can be prosecuted for fraudulent use of the mails.

Federal law also makes it a crime (called *wire fraud*) to use the telephone to defraud. Under the same statute, it is a crime to use almost any means of public communication, such as radio, television, or the Internet, to defraud.

Bribery

Basically, three types of bribery are considered crimes: bribery of public officials, commercial bribery, and bribery of foreign officials. The attempt to influence a public official to act in a way to serve a private interest is a crime. As an element of this crime, intent must be proved. The bribe can be anything the recipient considers to be valuable. Realize that *the crime of bribery occurs when the bribe is offered*. It does not matter whether the bribe is accepted. *Accepting a bribe* is a separate crime.

Typically, people make commercial bribes to obtain information, cover up an inferior product, or secure new business. For example, a person in one business may offer an employee in a competing business some type of payoff in exchange for trade secrets or pricing schedules. A so-called *kickback*, or payoff for special favors, is commercial bribery in some situations, such as secretly paying a company's purchasing agent to order goods from a particular supplier. Bribing foreign officials to obtain favorable business contracts is also a crime under U.S. law even though the payment takes place in another country.

Bankruptcy Fraud

Federal bankruptcy law allows many individuals and businesses to be relieved of oppressive debt through bankruptcy proceedings, as explained in Chapter 19. Criminal violations may occur during various stages of bankruptcy. A creditor, for example, may file a false claim against a debtor, which is a crime. Also, a debtor may fraudulently transfer assets to favored parties before or after the petition for bankruptcy is filed. For example, a company-owned automobile may be "sold" at a bargain price to a trusted friend or relative. It is also a crime for the debtor to fraudulently conceal property during bankruptcy, such as by hiding gold coins.

Theft of Trade Secrets

As will be discussed in Chapter 15, trade secrets are a form of intellectual property that is extremely valuable for many businesses. The Economic Espionage Act made the theft of trade secrets a federal crime. The act also made it a federal crime to buy or possess trade secrets, knowing that the trade secrets were stolen or otherwise acquired without the owner's authorization. Conviction can result in a prison sentence and a large fine.

Additionally, the law provides that any property acquired as a result of the violation, and any property used in the commission of the violation, are subject to criminal *forfeiture*—meaning that the government can take the property. A theft of trade secrets conducted via the Internet, for example, could result in the forfeiture of every computer or other device used to facilitate the violation.

Insider Trading

A person who obtains "inside information" about the plans or financial status of a corporation with publicly traded stock can make profits by using the information to guide decisions about the purchase or sale of the stock. Insider trading is a violation of securities law that subjects the violator to criminal penalties. One who possesses inside information and who has a duty not to disclose it to outsiders may not profit from the purchase or sale of securities based on that information until the information is public. Thus, a paralegal who knows that a client of the law firm is about to announce a merger—which will increase the price of the company's stock—cannot buy the stock before the announcement.

insider trading
Trading in the stock of a publicly listed corporation based on inside information. One who possesses inside information and has a duty not to disclose it to outsiders may not profit from the purchase or sale of securities based on that information until the information is available to the public.

Organized Crime

As mentioned, white-collar crime takes place within the confines of the legitimate business world. *Organized crime*, in contrast, operates *illegitimately* by, among other things, providing illegal goods and services. For organized crime, the traditional preferred markets are gambling, prostitution, illegal narcotics, and loan sharking (lending funds at very high interest rates), along with more recent ventures into counterfeiting, credit-card scams, and hacking computers for financial data.

Money Laundering

The profits from illegal activities, particularly illegal drug transactions, are tens of billions of dollars a year. Under federal law, banks and other financial institutions are required to report currency transactions involving more than $10,000 or that are otherwise suspicious. Consequently, those who engage in illegal activities face difficulties in depositing their cash profits from illegal transactions.

As an alternative to simply storing cash from illegal transactions in a safe-deposit box, wrongdoers and racketeers have invented ways to launder "dirty" money to make it "clean." This money laundering is done through legitimate businesses. Suppose Matt, a successful drug dealer, becomes a partner with a restaurant owner. Little by little, the restaurant shows increasing revenue because Matt falsely reports income obtained

money laundering
Falsely reporting income that has been obtained through criminal activity, such as illegal drug transactions, as income obtained through a legitimate business enterprise to make the "dirty" money "clean."

through drug dealing as restaurant income. As a partner in the restaurant, Matt is able to report the "profit" as legitimate income on which he pays federal and state taxes. He can then spend that after-tax income without worrying that his lifestyle may exceed the level possible with his reported income.

The Racketeer Influenced and Corrupt Organizations Act (RICO)

To curb the entry of organized crime into the legitimate business world, Congress passed the Racketeer Influenced and Corrupt Organizations Act (RICO). The act makes it a federal crime to (1) use income obtained from racketeering activity to purchase any interest in an enterprise, (2) acquire or maintain an interest in an enterprise through racketeering activity, (3) conduct or participate in the affairs of an enterprise through racketeering activity, or (4) conspire to do any of the preceding activities. RICO is used more often to attack white-collar crime than organized crime.

Racketeering activity is not a new type of crime created by RICO. Rather, RICO incorporates by reference many federal crimes and state felonies and declares that if a person commits *two* of these offenses, he is guilty of "racketeering activity." Any person found guilty of a violation is subject to a fine of up to $25,000 per violation, imprisonment for up to twenty years, or both. Additionally, the statute provides that those who violate RICO may be required to forfeit any assets, in the form of property or cash, that were acquired as a result of the alleged illegal activity or that were "involved in" or an "instrumentality of" the activity.

Cyber Crimes

cyber crime
A crime that occurs online, in the virtual community of the Internet, as opposed to the physical world.

Many crimes are committed with computers and occur in cyberspace. These crimes fall under the broad label of cyber crime. Most cyber crimes are not "new" crimes. Rather, they are existing crimes in which the Internet is the instrument of wrongdoing. The challenge for law enforcement is to apply traditional laws—which were designed to protect persons from physical harm or to safeguard their physical property—to new methods of committing crime.

Cyber Theft

In cyberspace, thieves are not subject to the physical limitations of the "real" world. A thief with Internet access could, in theory, steal data stored in a networked computer anywhere on earth.

Financial Crimes

Computer networks provide opportunities for employees to commit crimes that involve serious economic losses. For example, employees of a company's accounting department can transfer funds among accounts with little effort and often with less risk than is involved in paper transactions. Business dependence on computer operations has left many companies vulnerable to sabotage, fraud, embezzlement, and the theft of proprietary data.

Identity Theft

identity theft
The theft of a form of identification, such as a name, date of birth, and Social Security number, which is then used to access the victim's financial resources.

A form of cyber theft that has become particularly troublesome is identity theft. It occurs when the wrongdoer steals identification information—such as name, date of birth, and Social Security number—and uses that to access the victim's financial resources or get credit in his name. The Internet provides not only another way to steal personal information but a way for those who steal information to use items such as stolen credit-card numbers while protected by anonymity.

Cyberstalking

California passed the first antistalking law in 1990, in response to the murders of six women by stalkers. The law made it a crime to harass or follow a person while making a "credible threat" that puts the person in reasonable fear for her safety or the safety of her immediate family. Most states and the federal government followed with similar antistalking legislation.

Later, it became clear that these laws, which required a "physical act" such as following the victim, were insufficient. They could not protect persons against cyberstalking, in which the perpetrator harasses the victim using the Internet, e-mail, Facebook, Twitter, or some other electronic communication. Federal and state laws now include threats made through electronic communication devices.

Hacking

Hackers who break into computers without authorization often commit cyber theft. Sometimes, however, the principal aim of hackers is to cause random data errors on others' computers or otherwise disrupt the target's business.

It is difficult to know how frequently hackers succeed in breaking into databases across the United States. The FBI reports that only a minority of security breaches are reported to a law enforcement agency. Admitting to a breach would be admitting to a certain degree of incompetence, which could damage reputations.

Prosecuting Cyber Crimes

The Internet has raised new issues in the investigation of crimes and the prosecution of offenders. As discussed in Chapter 6, the issue of jurisdiction presents difficulties in cyberspace. Identifying the wrongdoers can be very difficult. Cyber criminals do not leave physical traces, such as fingerprints, as evidence of their crimes. Electronic "footprints" can be hard to find and follow, and many are in foreign countries.

A significant federal statute specifically addressing cyber crime is the Counterfeit Access Device and Computer Fraud and Abuse Act. It provides, among other things, that a person who accesses or attempts to access a computer online, without authority, to obtain classified, restricted, or protected data is subject to criminal prosecution. Such data could include financial and credit records, medical records, legal files, national security files, and other confidential information in government or private computers.

The crime has two elements: accessing a computer without authority and taking the data. This theft is a felony if it is committed for a commercial purpose or for private financial gain or if the value of the stolen data (or computer time) exceeds $5,000. Penalties include fines and imprisonment for up to twenty years. In addition, a victim of computer theft can bring a civil suit against the violator to obtain damages, an injunction, and other relief.

Social Media and Criminal Justice

Both law enforcement officers and criminals use social media tools, and paralegals working regularly in criminal law need to keep up with the latest developments. Some law enforcement social media is open only to police department employees, such as Law Officer Connect. Other sites are open to anyone interested in the issues. Sites such as **ConnectedCOPS.net** keep up with developments in social media and criminal law.

Use of Social Media

Criminals use social media to seek out victims and to organize group criminal activity. Flash mobs have been organized via Twitter to create opportunities to "grab and snatch"

cyberstalking
The crime of stalking in cyberspace. The cyberstalker usually finds the victim through Internet chat rooms, newsgroups, bulletin boards, or e-mail and proceeds to harass that person or put the person in reasonable fear for his or her safety or the safety of his or her immediate family.

hacker
A person who uses one computer to break into another.

items from stores. As a result, law enforcement officials are taking more interest in obtaining records from smartphones or social media sites as part of their investigations.

Law enforcement agencies are expanding their use of social media in solving crimes. For example, the FBI has created a popular YouTube channel featuring videos describing wanted criminals. The FBI's YouTube video on former mob boss and fugitive James "Whitey" Bulger was part of a social media campaign that ultimately led to the tip that Bulger was living in an apartment in California. Bulger's capture came after a 20-year manhunt, showing the power of social media campaigns.

Similarly, police in Tacoma, Washington, used social media evidence to confirm that victims and suspects in a triple homicide knew each other. Utah police discovered photos on a convicted sex offender's social media account that showed forbidden contact with two youths. A Colorado detective created a photo lineup from social networking profile photos, helping victims to identify the suspects.

Proper Evidence

Paralegals assisting in criminal defenses should determine whether their clients have a presence on such sites and, if so, whether or not the information about them can be protected from police investigators. The law in this area is not settled. The courts consider the following factors, in addition to the usual requirements of relevance and reliability, in determining if evidence from social media sites deserves privacy protection:

1. Did a password or other form of privacy protection exist to protect the information?

2. Did the affected party have a reasonable expectation of privacy even if no password protection was used (e.g., was the material accessible to outsiders)?

3. Did the police have a reasonable suspicion or probable cause to investigate the social networking site, or were they simply engaged in a "fishing expedition"?

4. Is there a reason to believe the evidence is a reliable representation of what the person posted, or might it have been hacked?

Social media also impact the courtroom. A juror in a Pennsylvania criminal case posted updates on the case on Twitter and Facebook. In a Florida criminal case, several jurors used Google to look up definitions of terms and to learn about evidence excluded by the judge. That led to a mistrial. An alert paralegal watches the jury for signs of use of smartphones or tablets during trial and checks open jury-member sites on Facebook and such, because such activities can be highly prejudicial to either side.

Paralegals working in both criminal defense and criminal prosecution need to keep up to date on the latest developments in social media technology to do their jobs. Not only do they need this knowledge to do their own jobs, it helps to anticipate what the other side in the case is going to do next.

Constitutional Safeguards

From the time a crime is reported until the trial concludes, law enforcement officers and prosecutors must follow specific procedures that protect an accused person's constitutional rights. Before allowing a case to go to trial, the prosecutor and paralegals assigned to the case review pretrial events closely to make sure that requirements have been properly observed. Defense attorneys and their legal assistants investigate and review the actions of arresting and investigating police officers in an attempt to obtain grounds for a dismissal of the charges against their clients.

Safeguards in the Bill of Rights

The U.S. Constitution provides specific procedural safeguards to protect persons accused of crimes against potentially arbitrary or unjust use of government power.

Safeguards are spelled out in Amendments to the U.S. Constitution and are summarized below. (The full text of the Constitution is presented in Appendix I.)

1. The Fourth Amendment prohibits unreasonable searches and seizures and requires a showing of probable cause (discussed shortly) before a search or an arrest warrant may be issued.

2. The Fifth Amendment requires that no one shall be deprived of "life, liberty, or property without due process of law." Due process of law means that the government must follow a set of reasonable, fair, and standard procedures (that is, criminal procedural law) in any action against a citizen.

3. The Fifth Amendment prohibits double jeopardy (trying someone twice for the same criminal offense).

4. The Fifth Amendment guarantees that no person shall be "compelled in any criminal case to be a witness against himself." This is known as the privilege against compulsory self-incrimination.

5. The Sixth Amendment guarantees a speedy and public trial, a trial by jury, the right to confront witnesses, and the right to a lawyer at various stages in some proceedings.

6. The Eighth Amendment prohibits excessive bail and fines, as well as cruel and unusual punishment.

due process of law
Fair, reasonable, and standard procedures that must be used by the government in any legal action against a citizen. The Fifth Amendment to the U.S. Constitution prohibits the deprivation of "life, liberty, or property without due process of law."

double jeopardy
To place at risk (jeopardize) a person's life or liberty twice. The Fifth Amendment to the Constitution prohibits a second prosecution for the same criminal offense.

self-incrimination
The act of giving testimony that implicates oneself in criminal wrongdoing. The Fifth Amendment to the Constitution states that no person "shall be compelled in any criminal case to be a witness against himself."

DEVELOPING PARALEGAL SKILLS

KEEP UP WITH EVOLVING DISCOVERY TECHNOLOGY

Technology is revolutionizing criminal law practice by enhancing what police can discover when investigating crimes. Criminal prosecutions involve not just witness testimony, but evidence collected with the latest scientific techniques. Paralegals working in criminal law need to educate themselves on how these technologies work so they can prepare arguments for and against admissibility of high-tech evidence.

Technologies moving from science fiction to reality include the following:

• Facial recognition software facilitates identification of suspects outside of traditional police lineups. It works off underlying bone structure, so cosmetic changes to hairstyles or beards will not fool it.

• Handheld spectrometers allow investigators in the field to detect drug residues and other substances at levels invisible to the naked eye.

• Fluorescent dyes react to blood and can reveal even tiny droplets of blood that are otherwise invisible.

Once blood-spatter data are collected, simulations can suggest the type of weapon used, how a wound was inflicted, and whether the assailant was left- or right-handed.

• Portable lasers allow crime scene investigators to locate tiny bits of evidence, such as a fragment from a strand of hair.

• 3-D scanning allows instant re-creation of crime scenes on laptops at the scene, giving police faster access to important information.

• Firearms databases allow police to distinguish bullets fired from different guns as accurately as fingerprints distinguish individual people.

All this technology can help solve crimes, but police or prosecutors can also misuse each piece. Paralegals on both sides of a case need to understand these technologies to effectively argue their relevance and admissibility in individual cases.

The Exclusionary Rule

exclusionary rule
In criminal procedure, a rule under which any evidence obtained in violation of the accused's constitutional rights, as well as any evidence derived from illegally obtained evidence, will not be admissible in court.

Under what is known as the exclusionary rule, evidence obtained in violation of the rights spelled out in the Fourth, Fifth, and Sixth Amendments normally is excluded from trial, along with evidence derived from the improperly obtained evidence. Evidence derived from illegally obtained evidence is known as the "fruit of the poisonous tree." For example, if drugs are discovered during an illegal search, the search is "the poisonous tree," and the drugs are the "fruit," which normally will be excluded from evidence if the case is brought to trial. As the *Developing Paralegal Skills* feature on the preceding page notes, rapid advances in the ability to detect evidence means paralegals must keep on top of new technology to understand possible pitfalls.

The purpose of the exclusionary rule is to deter police from conducting warrantless searches and engaging in other misconduct. The rule is sometimes criticized because it can lead to injustice. Some defendants have "gotten off on a technicality" because law enforcement personnel failed to observe procedural requirements. Even though a defendant may be obviously guilty, if the evidence of that guilt was obtained improperly, it normally cannot be used against the defendant in court.

The *Miranda* Rule

In *Miranda v. Arizona,*[5] a case decided in 1966, the United States Supreme Court established the rule that individuals who are arrested must be informed of certain constitutional rights, including their Fifth Amendment right to remain silent and their Sixth Amendment right to counsel.

Miranda rights
Certain constitutional rights of accused persons taken into custody by law enforcement officials, such as the right to remain silent and the right to counsel, as established by the United States Supreme Court's decision in *Miranda v. Arizona*.

These rights, called *Miranda* rights, are listed in Exhibit 13.3 below. If the arresting officers fail to inform a criminal suspect of these constitutional rights, any statements the suspect makes normally are not admissible in court. It is important to note that the police are not required to give *Miranda* warnings until the individual is placed in custody. Thus, if a person who is not in custody makes voluntary admissions to an officer, these statements are admissible.

The exact meaning of the *Miranda* rule is subject to frequent tests in the courts. The Supreme Court has held that a confession need not be excluded even though the police failed to inform a suspect in custody that his attorney had tried to reach him by telephone. Furthermore, the Court has stated that a suspect's conviction will not be overturned solely on the ground that law enforcement personnel coerced the suspect into making a confession if other, legally obtained evidence admitted at trial is enough to justify the conviction without the confession.

EXHIBIT 13.3
The *Miranda* Rights

On taking a criminal suspect into custody and before any interrogation takes place, law enforcement officers are required to communicate the following rights and facts to the suspect:

1. **The right to remain silent.**
2. **That any statements made may be used against the person in a court of law.**
3. **The right to talk to a lawyer and to have a lawyer present while being questioned.**
4. **If the person cannot afford to hire a lawyer, the right to have a lawyer provided at no cost.**

In addition to being advised of these rights, the suspect must be asked if he or she understands the rights and whether he or she wishes to exercise the rights or waive (not exercise) the rights.

Criminal Procedures Prior to Prosecution

Although the Constitution guarantees due process of law to persons accused of committing crimes, the steps in bringing a criminal action vary across jurisdictions and type of crime. In this section, we provide an overview of the basic procedures that take place before an individual is prosecuted for a crime. Exhibit 13.4 on the following page illustrates a general outline of criminal procedure in both federal and state cases. Because of the procedural variations, however, a paralegal involved in a criminal case needs to learn the specific requirements that apply to the case.

Arrest and Booking

An arrest occurs when the police take a person into custody and charge that person with a crime. (Often the interaction with the police is captured on video.) After the arrest and a search, the police typically take the suspect to a *holding facility* (usually at the police station or a jail), where booking occurs. Booking is the process of entering a suspect's name, the offense for which the suspect is being held, and the time of arrival into the police log (computer). The suspect is fingerprinted and photographed, told the reason for the arrest, and allowed to make a phone call.

If the crime is not serious, the officer may then release the suspect on personal recognizance—that is, on the suspect's promise to appear before a court at a later date. Otherwise, the suspect may be held in custody pending an initial appearance in court (usually within a few days).

Law enforcement personnel are in control of the arrest and booking of suspects. Paralegals and attorneys usually are not involved until after an arrest has been made. The defense will, however, look closely to see that the proper procedure was followed in the arrest of the client. An officer can legally arrest a person with or without a warrant if the officer has probable cause to believe that the person committed a crime (discussed shortly). Before an officer questions a suspect who has been arrested, the officer must give the *Miranda* warning.

Detention Is Not an Arrest

An arrest differs from a *stop* or *detention*, such as a traffic stop. Police officers have a right to stop and detain a person if they have a *reasonable suspicion* that the person committed, or is about to commit, a crime. Reasonable suspicion is a lower standard than probable cause—because a stop is much less invasive than an arrest. It means, for example, that based on reasonable suspicion an officer can stop a person who seems to match the description of an assailant in the neighborhood. The officer can even "frisk" the person being detained (pat down the person's clothes) to make sure the person is not carrying a weapon. There can be no arrest, however, without probable cause.

Probable Cause

The requirement of probable cause is a key factor that is assessed repeatedly throughout the stages of criminal proceedings. The first stage, arrest, requires probable cause. In an arrest, probable cause exists if there is a substantial likelihood that a crime was committed and that the suspect committed the crime. Probable cause involves a *likelihood*—not just a possibility—that the suspect committed the crime. The probable cause requirement comes from the Fourth Amendment, which prohibits unreasonable searches and seizures.

If a police officer sees a crime being committed, the officer can arrest the suspect on the spot without a warrant, because the probable cause requirement is met. If a crime is reported to the police, the police must decide whether there is enough information about the alleged wrongdoer's likely guilt to establish probable cause to arrest. What is

arrest
To take into custody a person suspected of criminal activity.

booking
The process of entering a suspect's name, offense, and arrival time into the police log (blotter) following his or her arrest.

probable cause
Reasonable grounds to believe the existence of facts warranting certain actions, such as the search or arrest of a person.

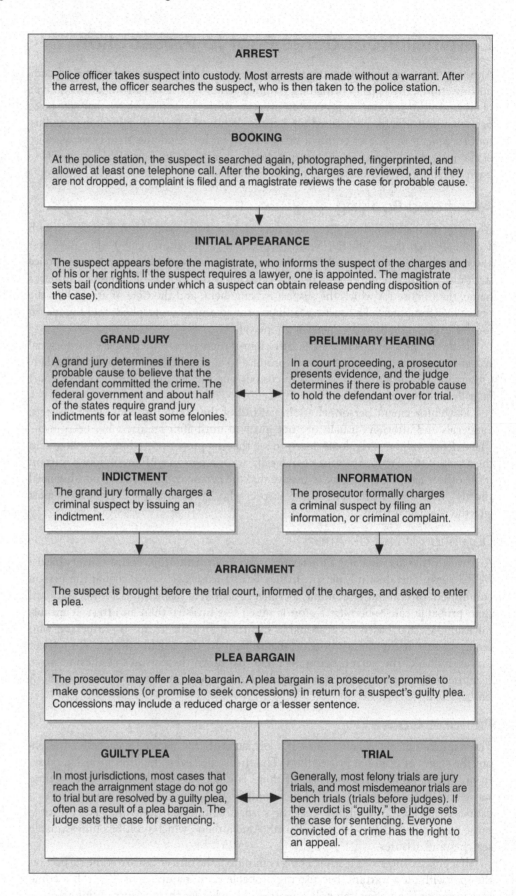

ARREST

Police officer takes suspect into custody. Most arrests are made without a warrant. After the arrest, the officer searches the suspect, who is then taken to the police station.

BOOKING

At the police station, the suspect is searched again, photographed, fingerprinted, and allowed at least one telephone call. After the booking, charges are reviewed, and if they are not dropped, a complaint is filed and a magistrate reviews the case for probable cause.

INITIAL APPEARANCE

The suspect appears before the magistrate, who informs the suspect of the charges and of his or her rights. If the suspect requires a lawyer, one is appointed. The magistrate sets bail (conditions under which a suspect can obtain release pending disposition of the case).

GRAND JURY

A grand jury determines if there is probable cause to believe that the defendant committed the crime. The federal government and about half of the states require grand jury indictments for at least some felonies.

PRELIMINARY HEARING

In a court proceeding, a prosecutor presents evidence, and the judge determines if there is probable cause to hold the defendant over for trial.

INDICTMENT

The grand jury formally charges a criminal suspect by issuing an indictment.

INFORMATION

The prosecutor formally charges a criminal suspect by filing an information, or criminal complaint.

ARRAIGNMENT

The suspect is brought before the trial court, informed of the charges, and asked to enter a plea.

PLEA BARGAIN

The prosecutor may offer a plea bargain. A plea bargain is a prosecutor's promise to make concessions (or promise to seek concessions) in return for a suspect's guilty plea. Concessions may include a reduced charge or a lesser sentence.

GUILTY PLEA

In most jurisdictions, most cases that reach the arraignment stage do not go to trial but are resolved by a guilty plea, often as a result of a plea bargain. The judge sets the case for sentencing.

TRIAL

Generally, most felony trials are jury trials, and most misdemeanor trials are bench trials (trials before judges). If the verdict is "guilty," the judge sets the case for sentencing. Everyone convicted of a crime has the right to an appeal.

considered probable cause varies across jurisdictions. Usually, if the suspect is at home at the time of the arrest, the police need to obtain an arrest warrant (unless the police chased the suspect to the home or some other emergency circumstance exists).

DEVELOPING PARALEGAL SKILLS

THE PROSECUTOR'S OFFICE—WARRANT DIVISION

Kathy Perello works as a paralegal in the warrant division of the county prosecutor's office. Officer McCarthy gives her the paperwork from the prosecutor that authorizes the arrest of a burglary suspect and requests that Kathy prepare an arrest warrant. Officer McCarthy will take the warrant to the court, swear to the truth of its contents, and ask the judge to sign the warrant so that he can make the arrest.

CHECKLIST FOR PREPARING A WARRANT

- Obtain written authorization from a prosecutor before initiating the warrant procedure.
- Obtain a copy of the suspect's criminal history.
- Use the above to prepare the warrant.
- Verify that the police record matches that of the suspect.
- Make sure that the crime and the suspect are both specifically described.
- Review the typed warrant to ensure that it includes any other required terms.
- Call the officer to pick up the warrant and take it to a judge for a determination of probable cause.

Warrants

Often, the police try to gather information to help them determine whether a suspect should be arrested. If, after investigating the matter, the police decide to arrest the suspect, they must obtain an **arrest warrant**, which is typically issued by a judge. To obtain the warrant, the police must convince the official, usually through supporting affidavits, that probable cause exists. The warrant process is discussed further in the *Developing Paralegal Skills* feature above.

SEARCH WARRANTS.   Probable cause is also required to obtain a **search warrant**. A warrant authorizes police officers or other investigators to search specifically named persons or property for evidence and to seize evidence if they find it. Probable cause requires law enforcement officials to have trustworthy evidence that would convince a reasonable person that the proposed search or seizure is more likely justified than not. The Fourth Amendment prohibits general warrants. It requires a description of what will be searched or seized. The search cannot extend beyond what is described in the warrant.

WHEN WARRANT NOT NEEDED.   There are exceptions to the requirement for a search warrant. For example, if an officer is arresting a person (with either an arrest warrant or sufficient probable cause) and sees drug paraphernalia "in plain view," no warrant is required to seize that evidence. Exceptions also exist when it is likely that the items sought will be removed or destroyed before a warrant can be obtained or when an officer is in hot pursuit of a suspect.

Investigation after the Arrest

The police often must find and interview witnesses and conduct searches (of the suspect's home or car, for example) to collect evidence. Witnesses may view the suspect in a *lineup*, in which the suspect appears with a group of several others. In more serious cases, detectives may take charge of the investigation.

arrest warrant
A written order, based on probable cause and typically issued by a judge, commanding that the person named on the warrant be arrested by the police.

search warrant
A written order, based on probable cause and issued by a judge or public official (magistrate), commanding that police officers or criminal investigators search a specific person, place, or property to obtain evidence.

As the police review the evidence, they may conclude that there is not enough evidence to justify recommending the case for prosecution. If so, the suspect is released, and no charges are filed. The police can still recommend prosecution later if more evidence is obtained. Or the police may decide to change the offense with which the suspect is being charged. The police may also decide to release the suspect with a warning or a referral to a social-service agency. Unless the suspect is released at this point in the criminal process, control over the case moves from the police to the public prosecutor.

The Prosecution Begins

Prosecution of a criminal case begins when the police inform the public prosecutor of the alleged crime, provide the reports written by the arresting and investigating officers, and turn over their evidence. The prosecutor may investigate the case further by interviewing the suspect, the officers, and witnesses, and by gathering other evidence. The prosecutor's legal assistants often participate in these tasks. Based on a review of the police file or an investigation, the prosecutor decides whether to take the case to trial or drop the case and allow the suspect to be released.

Major reasons for releasing the suspect include insufficient evidence and unreliable witnesses. If you are working for a client, by now you are keeping close track of all details such as witnesses as *In the Office* discusses on page 398.

Prosecutorial Discretion

Prosecutors have broad discretion. If they decide to pursue a case, they decide what charges to file. Because prosecutions are expensive and resources are limited, most prosecutors do not go forward with a case unless they are confident that they can prove the case in court. Typically, a prosecutor who decides to file a case alleges as many criminal offenses as could be proved based on the facts. If the defendant is facing numerous charges, the likelihood is greater that the prosecutor will get a conviction on at least one. The chances are also greater that the defendant will plead guilty to one or more of the offenses in exchange for having other charges dropped.

If the decision is made to prosecute, the prosecutor must take the necessary procedures to formally charge the person before the court. Procedures vary depending on the jurisdiction and the type of case. Often, misdemeanor charges are handled differently than felony charges. Some prosecutors may file complaints involving misdemeanor charges. A grand jury indictment (discussed shortly) is used for felony charges in some jurisdictions, but in most cases a grand jury in not used. The prosecutor files an information, as discussed below. The way a criminal case is initiated is one area of criminal procedure that varies substantially among the states. Keep this in mind as you read the following subsections.

Complaint and Initial Appearance

The criminal litigation process may begin with filing a *complaint* (see Exhibit 13.5 on the facing page). The complaint includes a statement of the charges that are being brought against the suspect, who now becomes a criminal defendant. Because the defendant is in the court system, prosecutors must show that they have legal grounds to proceed. They must show probable cause that the defendant committed a crime.

Initial Appearance

In most jurisdictions, defendants are taken before a judge or magistrate soon after arrest. During this *initial appearance*, the judge makes sure that the person appearing is the person named in the complaint, informs the defendant of the charges made in the complaint, and advises the defendant of the right to counsel and the right to remain silent. If a defendant cannot afford to hire an attorney, a public defender or member

EXHIBIT 13.5

A Complaint

AO 91 (Rev. 11/11) Criminal Complaint

UNITED STATES DISTRICT COURT
for the

United States of America	)	
v.	)	Case No.
	)	
	)	
	)	
Defendant(s)	)	

CRIMINAL COMPLAINT

I, the complainant in this case, state that the following is true to the best of my knowledge and belief.

On or about the date(s) of _____ in the county of _____ in the

_____ District of _____ , the defendant(s) violated:

Code Section   Offense Description

This criminal complaint is based on these facts:

☐ Continued on the attached sheet.

_____
Complainant's signature

_____
Printed name and title

Sworn to before me and signed in my presence.

Date: _____

_____
Judge's signature

City and state: _____

_____
Printed name and title

Source: http://www.uscourts.gov/uscourts/FormsAndFees/Forms/AO091.pdf

of the private bar may be appointed to represent the defendant (the defendant may be asked to fill out an application for appointed counsel).

Bail

The judge must make a decision whether to set bail or release the defendant until the next court date. Bail is an amount paid by the defendant to the court as insurance that the defendant will show up for future court appearances. If the defendant shows up as promised, the court returns the funds. Courts often use standard bail schedules, which set the bail for specific kinds of cases, and may deny bail for more serious crimes. The Eighth Amendment prohibits "excessive bail," and a defendant can request a hearing to seek a reduction in bail.

If the court sets bail in an amount that the defendant is unable to pay, the defendant (or the defendant's attorney or paralegal) can arrange with a *bail bondsperson* to post a bail bond on the defendant's behalf. The bail bondsperson promises to pay the bail amount to the court if the defendant fails to return for further proceedings. In return, the bail bondsperson receives a payment from the defendant, usually 10 percent of the bail amount.

bail
The amount of money or conditions set by the court to ensure that an individual accused of a crime will appear for further criminal proceedings. If the accused person provides bail, whether in cash or by means of a bail bond, then the person is released from jail.

IN THE OFFICE

MULTIPLE BENEFITS OF GOOD RECORDS

One job as a paralegal may be to make sure that witnesses are in court at the proper time. This relates to the attorney's duty of competence. Suppose that despite all your efforts a witness fails to appear in court. Your supervising attorney is upset and asks you how it could have happened.

You show the attorney:

- the memorandum of your interview with the client, in which you noted that the witness was willing to testify,

- the receipt from the certified letter that you sent to the witness, which contained the subpoena, indicating that the witness had received it, and

- telephone memos of calls you made to the witness prior to the trial in which the witness agreed to be in court on the date of the trial, as well as follow-up calls you made immediately before and then during the trial to confirm appearance.

Although your documentation is not a cure for the problem presented by the missing witness, it provides evidence—should it be necessary—that neither you nor the attorney was negligent.

Preliminary Hearing

preliminary hearing
An initial hearing in which a judge or magistrate decides whether there is probable cause to believe that the defendant committed the crime with which he or she is charged.

The defendant again appears before a magistrate or judge at a preliminary hearing. During this hearing, the judge determines whether the evidence presented is sufficient to establish probable cause to believe the defendant committed the crime as charged. This may be the first adversarial proceeding in which both sides are represented by counsel. Paralegals may become involved in the process at this point by assisting in preparation for the hearing.

The prosecutor may present witnesses, who may be cross-examined by defense counsel (the defense rarely presents its witnesses prior to trial). A defendant who intends to plead guilty usually waives the right to a preliminary hearing to help move things along more quickly. In many jurisdictions, however, the preliminary hearing is required in certain felony cases.

If the judge or magistrate finds the evidence insufficient to establish probable cause, either the charge is reduced to a lesser one or charges are dropped altogether and the defendant is released. If the magistrate believes there is sufficient evidence to establish probable cause, the prosecutor issues an information. The information (which may also be called an accusation or complaint) is the formal charge against the defendant and binds over the defendant for further proceedings. Usually the defendant is arraigned and the case proceeds to trial.

information
A formal criminal charge made by a prosecutor without a grand jury indictment.

Grand Jury Review

grand jury
A group of citizens called to decide whether probable cause exists to believe that a suspect committed the crime with which he or she has been charged and thus should stand trial.

The federal government and about half of the states use a grand jury—not a prosecutor—to make the decision as to whether a case should go to trial in many felony cases. In other words, a grand jury's indictment is an alternative to a prosecutor's information to initiate the criminal litigation process.

A grand jury is a group of citizens called to decide whether there is probable cause to believe that the defendant committed the crime charged and therefore should go to trial. Even in cases in which grand jury review is not used and an information is submitted, the prosecutor may call a grand jury to evaluate the evidence against a suspect, which will indicate to the prosecutor the relative strength or weakness of the case.

At a preliminary hearing, a judge or a magistrate evaluates the evidence against the defendant. If the evidence is sufficient to establish probable cause (reasonable grounds to believe that the defendant committed the crime with which he or she is charged), the prosecutor issues an information, and the defendant is bound over for further proceedings. Paralegals often assist either the defendant or the prosecutor in preparing for preliminary hearings. What might some of the duties of a paralegal be?

The grand jury sits in closed session and hears only evidence presented by the prosecutor—the defendant cannot present evidence at this hearing. Normally, the defendant and the defendant's attorney are not allowed to attend grand jury proceedings—although in some cases the prosecutor calls the defendant as a witness. The prosecutor presents to the grand jury the evidence the state has against the defendant, including photographs, documents, tangible items, test results, and the testimony of witnesses.

If the grand jury finds that probable cause exists, it issues an indictment[6] against the defendant called a *true bill.* An overwhelming majority of the cases that prosecutors bring to grand juries result in an indictment. The indictment (or information, if that is used instead) is filed with the trial court and becomes the formal charge against the defendant. An example of an indictment is shown in Exhibit 13.6 on the following page.

Arraignment

At the arraignment, the defendant is informed of the charges and must respond to the charges by entering a plea: guilty, not guilty, or *nolo contendere,* which is Latin for "I will not contest it" and is often called a no-contest plea. A plea of no contest is neither an admission of guilt nor a denial of guilt—but it operates like a guilty plea in that the defendant is convicted.

The primary reason for pleading no contest is so that the plea cannot later be used against the defendant in a civil trial. For example, if a defendant pleads guilty to assault, the admission of guilt can be used to impose civil liability, whereas with a no-contest plea, the plaintiff in the civil suit must prove the defendant committed the assault. No-contest pleas are thus useful for the defendant who could be sued in a civil action for damages caused to a person or property.

At the arraignment, the defendant can move to have the charges dismissed, which happens in a fair number of cases. The defendant may claim, for example, that the case should be dismissed because the statute of limitations for the crime in question has lapsed. Most frequently, the defendant pleads guilty to the charge or to a lesser charge that has been agreed on through plea bargaining between the prosecutor and the defendant. If the defendant pleads guilty, no trial is necessary, and the defendant is sentenced based on the plea. If the defendant pleads not guilty, the case is set for trial.

indictment
A charge or written accusation, issued by a grand jury, that probable cause exists to believe that a person has committed a crime for which he or she should stand trial.

arraignment
A court proceeding in which the suspect is formally charged with the criminal offense stated in the indictment. The suspect then enters a plea (guilty, not guilty, or *nolo contendere*) in response.

nolo contendere
Latin for "I will not contest it." A criminal defendant's plea in which he or she chooses not to challenge, or contest, the charges brought by the government. Although the defendant will still be convicted and sentenced, the plea neither admits nor denies guilt.

plea bargaining
The process by which the accused and the prosecutor in a criminal case work out a mutually satisfactory disposition of the case, subject to court approval. Usually, plea bargaining involves the defendant's pleading guilty to a lesser offense in return for a lighter sentence.

[Title of Court and Cause]

The Grand Jury charges that:

On or about _____ , 20__ , at _____ , _____ , in the _____ District of _____ , _____ , having been convicted of knowingly acquiring and possessing a SNAP/Food Stamp EBT card in a manner not authorized by the provisions of Chapter 51, Title 7, United States Code, and the regulations issued pursuant to said chapter, a felony conviction, in the federal district court for the _____ District of _____ , and sentenced on _____ , 20__ , did knowingly possess a firearm that had been transported in and affecting commerce, to wit: an OMC Pistol, Back Up 380 Caliber, serial number _____ ; all in violation of Section 1202(a)(1) of Title 18, United States Code, Appendix.

A True Bill

_____ ,
Foreperson.

_____ ,
United States Attorney.

Pretrial Motions

Defense attorneys and their paralegals search for and are alert to any violation of the defendant's rights. Many pretrial motions are based on possible violations of the defendant's rights as provided by the Constitution and criminal procedural law. We discuss here a few of the most common motions filed in a criminal case.

The specific requirements for pretrial motions vary by jurisdiction. Not every jurisdiction allows every type of pretrial motion, and the standards used by judges to evaluate motions may differ as well. A motion is generally accompanied by a pleading that sets forth the legal argument in support of the motion. A memorandum of law, a brief, affidavits, or supporting points and authorities may be filed to support a pleading.

Motions to Suppress

motion to suppress evidence
A motion requesting that certain evidence be excluded from consideration during the trial.

One of the most common motions made by defense attorneys is the motion to suppress evidence. A motion to suppress asserts that the evidence against the defendant was illegally obtained and should be excluded (inadmissible). Typically, this is filed when an officer performs a search without probable cause, seizes evidence, and then arrests the defendant based on that evidence.

Suppose an officer stops the defendant's vehicle because his taillight is out and then searches the defendant's trunk, finding illegal narcotics. The defendant is charged with possession. A motion to suppress would be appropriate here (and probably successful) because the officer did not have probable cause to search the trunk when carrying out the traffic stop.

The defense attorney normally prepares the motion and submits a brief in support of the motion. (These motions and memoranda may be drafted by paralegals.) Exhibit 13.7 on pages 401 and 402 shows a sample memorandum. Often, the attorney requests the court to allow oral argument on the motion, although in some jurisdictions it is automatic. If the court conducts a hearing on the motion, the attorneys for both sides may call witnesses (police officers and others who were present) to testify, and the judge makes a ruling. If the judge grants the motion to exclude evidence, the prosecution may not be able to prove its case against the defendant and drops the charges.

EXHIBIT 13.7
Memorandum in Support of a Motion to Suppress

[Attorney for Defendant]

SUPERIOR COURT OF THE STATE OF NITA
FOR THE COUNTY OF NITA

THE PEOPLE OF THE STATE OF NITA,	)	Case No.: C45778
Plaintiff,	)	D.A. No.: A39996
	)	
	)	**MEMORANDUM OF LAW IN SUPPORT**
v.	)	**OF MOTION TO SUPPRESS**
	)	
	)	DATE: 10-27-17
	)	TIME: 1:15
Eduardo Jose Mendez,	)	Estimated Time: 45 min.
Defendant.	)	No. of Witnesses: 1

Defendant, Eduardo Jose Mendez, by and through his attorney the Public Defender of the County of Nita, respectfully submits the following memorandum of law in support of his motion to Suppress.

STATEMENT OF FACTS

On or about September 23, 2017, at approximately 02:15, Officer Ramirez observed Mr. Mendez riding his bicycle in the area of 1300 Elm St. and 500 C St. It was drizzling, and few people walked the streets. Officer Ramirez indicated that the area is known for narcotic activity and that he believed Mr. Mendez had been participating or was about to participate in narcotic activity.

Mr. Mendez was on his bicycle at the corner of Elm and C St. when Officer Ramirez approached him. He indicated that Mr. Mendez appeared to be nervous and was sweating profusely. He asked Mr. Mendez what he was doing, and Mr. Mendez responded that he was waiting for his girlfriend. Officer Ramirez conducted a pat-down search for weapons. He felt several hard objects inside Mr. Mendez's pants pockets and asked Mr. Mendez if he had a knife in his pocket. Mr. Mendez consented to a search of his pockets, and Officer Ramirez found only a wooden pencil.

Without asking for permission, and without notice, Officer Ramirez reached for and grabbed Mr. Mendez's baseball cap. The officer took the cap off of Mr. Mendez's head. He felt the outside of the cap and with his fingers manipulated a small soft lump in Mr. Mendez's cap. He went through the cap and moved the side material of the cap. He found a small plastic package burnt on one end. He opened the package. Officer Ramirez found a small amount of an off-white powder substance inside the package.

ARGUMENT

I. MR. MENDEZ'S FOURTH AMENDMENT RIGHT TO PRIVACY WAS VIOLATED BECAUSE THE OFFICER'S DETENTION OF MR. MENDEZ WAS NOT JUSTIFIED BY REASONABLE SUSPICION

A person has been seized within the meaning of the Fourth Amendment if, in view of all the circumstances surrounding the incident, a reasonable person would have believed that he was not free to leave. *United States v. Mendenhall,* 446 U.S. 544, 554 (1980). Here, Officer Ramirez seized Mr. Mendez when he stopped to question him. Mr. Mendez submitted to Officer Ramirez's show of authority when he responded to the questioning. Mr. Mendez's belief that he was not free to leave is evidenced by his actions during the seizure. He appeared nervous and kept looking around in all directions as if looking for someone to help him. A reasonable person such as Mr. Mendez, in view of all of the circumstances, would have believed and in fact did believe he was not free to leave. Therefore, the officer's initial stop was a seizure.

* * * *

Continued

Motions to Dismiss

A motion can be filed to dismiss charges pending against the defendant. Motions to dismiss in criminal cases often assert that the defendant's constitutional rights—or required criminal procedures—have been violated. The defense might argue that the prosecution waited too long to prosecute the case in violation of the Sixth Amendment

EXHIBIT 13.7
Memorandum in Support of a Motion to Suppress—Continued

Officer Ramirez did not have reasonable suspicion to stop Mr. Mendez. He fails to point to specific facts causing him to suspect criminal activity was afoot. Officer Ramirez notes in his police report that he "felt" that defendant "had been participating or was about to participate in narcotic activity." The officer also indicated that he believed the area was known for narcotic activity. However, "Persons may not be subjected to invasions of privacy merely because they are in or are passing through a high-crime area." *McCally-Bey v. Kirner,* 24 F.Supp.3d 389 (N.D. Nita 2002).

These observations taken as a whole and Officer Ramirez's explanation do not rise to the requisite level of reasonable suspicion necessary to invade the privacy of a citizen.

II. OFFICER RAMIREZ'S PAT-DOWN SEARCH EXCEEDED ITS SCOPE WHEN HE SEARCHED THE BASEBALL CAP AND MANIPULATED ITS CONTENTS

Under the *Terry* doctrine, a search is referred to as a "frisk." *Terry v. Ohio,* 392 U.S. 1 (1968). A *frisk* is justified only if the officer reasonably believes that the person is armed and dangerous. A frisk is a pat-down of a person's outer clothing. It is limited in scope to its purpose, which is to search for weapons. Even slightly lingering over a package because it feels like it contains drugs exceeds the scope of the search. *Minnesota v. Dickerson,* 508 U.S. 366 (1993). An officer cannot manipulate a package or a substance that is clearly not a weapon through an individual's clothing during a *Terry* pat-down search.

* * * *

III. OFFICER RAMIREZ DID NOT HAVE PROBABLE CAUSE TO CONDUCT A WARRANTLESS SEARCH OF MR. MENDEZ

* * * *

IV. ALL EVIDENCE OBTAINED AS A RESULT OF AN UNLAWFUL DETENTION MUST BE SUPPRESSED AS TAINTED EVIDENCE; FRUIT OF THE POISONOUS TREE

* * * *

* * * *

As discussed above, the detention of Mr. Mendez did not meet constitutionally established standards of reasonableness. Hence, all evidence obtained as a result of such unlawful detention is inadmissible. In addition, all evidence seized as a result of the arrest that followed from his unlawful detention is inadmissible as fruit of the poisonous tree.

* * * *

For the above-mentioned reasons, all evidence obtained as a result of Mr. Mendez's detention, illegal search, and subsequent arrest in this case must be suppressed.

Dated:

Respectfully submitted,

_____
Attorney for Defendant

---

right to a speedy and public trial (sometimes called a *speedy trial motion*). The defense files the motion with a supporting memorandum, which may argue that the defendant has been prejudiced by the delay, that witnesses are no longer available, and that a fair trial cannot be had. If the judge agrees, the case is dismissed.

Because it may eliminate charges against a client without subjecting the client to the risks of a jury trial, the motion to dismiss is one of the most useful motions for the defense to file. A paralegal who becomes skilled at writing persuasive motions to dismiss will be a valuable asset to the defense team.

Other Common Motions

Just as in civil cases, attorneys in criminal cases may file motions *in limine* (discussed in Chapter 12 on page 354) to keep certain evidence out of the trial. A defense attorney whose client has prior criminal convictions may file a motion *in limine* requesting the court to prevent any evidence of these convictions from being offered by the prosecution. The prosecutor may also file such motions to keep possibly prejudicial evidence from being admitted (such as concerning a victim's reputation).

In some cases the defense files motions appropriate to the matter:

- When there is a good deal of pretrial publicity, the defense may make a motion for a change of venue asking the court to relocate the trial.

- When the judge has publicly displayed bias or personally knows a party or witnesses in a case, the defense may file a motion to recuse asking the trial judge to remove himself from the case. If the motion is granted, a different judge will hear the case.

- When a case involves more than one defendant, the defense counsel may file a motion to sever (separate) the cases for purposes of trial.

Various other motions—including motions to reduce the charges against the defendant, to obtain evidence during discovery, or to extend the trial date—may also be made prior to the trial. As with motions made during the civil litigation process, each motion must be accompanied by supporting affidavits and/or legal memoranda.

motion for a change of venue
A motion requesting that a trial be moved to a different location to ensure a fair and impartial proceeding, for the convenience of the parties, or for some other acceptable reason.

motion to recuse
A motion to remove a particular judge from a case.

motion to sever
A motion to try multiple defendants separately.

Discovery

In preparing for trial, public prosecutors, defense attorneys, and paralegals engage in discovery (including depositions and interrogatories), interview and subpoena witnesses, prepare exhibits and a trial notebook, examine documents and evidence, and do other tasks necessary to effectively prosecute or defend the defendant. Although similar to civil litigation in these respects, criminal discovery is generally more limited, and the time constraints are different. The *Developing Paralegal Skills* feature on the following page gives some useful tips for discovery in criminal cases.

During discovery, defendants are generally entitled to obtain any evidence in the possession of the prosecutor relating to the case, including statements previously made by the defendant, objects, documents, and reports of tests and examinations. The prosecutor must hand over evidence that tends to show the defendant's innocence as well as evidence of the defendant's guilt. Defendants are given this right to offset the fact that the prosecution (the state) has more resources at its disposal than the defendant (an individual citizen).

Some state statutes allow the prosecutor access to materials that the defense intends to introduce as evidence in the trial. In some jurisdictions, when the defense attorney requests discovery of case materials from the prosecutor, the defense is required to disclose similar materials to the prosecutor in return. In the absence of such statutes, courts have generally refused discovery to the prosecution. This judicial restraint is intended to protect the defendant from self-incrimination, as guaranteed by the Fifth Amendment to the U.S. Constitution (see Appendix I).

The Trial

Only a small fraction of the criminal cases brought by the state go to trial. Some defendants are released without charges, or the charges against them are dropped. Most defendants plead guilty to the offense or to a lesser offense prior to trial. Plea bargaining often occurs in criminal proceedings, from the arraignment to the date of trial or even during a trial. Because a trial is expensive and the outcome uncertain, both sides have an incentive to negotiate a plea.

Although some criminal trials go on for weeks and are highly publicized, most criminal trials last less than one week (often only a few days). The trial is conducted in much the same way as a civil trial. The prosecutor and the defense attorney make opening

DEVELOPING PARALEGAL SKILLS

DISCOVERY IN THE CRIMINAL CASE

A law firm is defending Taylor Rogers in an attempted murder case. He allegedly shot a person in a drive-by shooting on the expressway. Lee Soloman, a paralegal, is working on the case. Today, as the result of a successful discovery motion that his supervising attorney received from the court, Lee has obtained copies of all evidence that the prosecuting attorney has in his file. Lee's job is to create the discovery file and then work with the material in the file to prepare the case.

TIPS FOR CRIMINAL DISCOVERY

- Create a discovery file containing sections for the defendant's statements, witnesses' statements, police reports, tests, and other evidence.

- Review the evidence and prepare a memo summarizing it.

- Review the memo and/or evidence with your supervising attorney.

- If the supervising attorney agrees, contact witnesses and obtain statements.

- Interview police officers involved in the arrest or who were at the crime scene.

statements, examine and cross-examine witnesses, and summarize positions in closing arguments. Graphics may be used for illustration. These are discussed in the *Developing Paralegal Skills* feature on the facing page and in *Ethics Watch* on page 406. Following closing arguments, the jury is instructed and sent to deliberate. When the jury renders a verdict, the trial comes to an end. There are, however, some major procedural differences between criminal trials and civil trials, as discussed next.

The Presumption of Innocence

In criminal trials, the defendant is innocent until proved guilty. The prosecutor bears the burden of proving the defendant guilty as charged. Defendants do not have to prove their innocence. In fact, they are not required to present any evidence to counter the state's accusations (although it is usually in their best interests to provide some defense). Even a defendant who actually committed the crime is innocent at law unless the prosecutor presents sufficient evidence to convince the jury or judge of guilt.

Not only does the state bear the burden of proving the defendant guilty, but it also is held to a high standard of proof. The prosecution must prove its case *beyond a reasonable doubt*. It is not enough for the jury (or judge) to think that the defendant is probably guilty. The members of the jury must be firmly convinced of guilt. The jurors receive instructions such as, "If you think there is a real possibility that he is not guilty, you *must* give him the benefit of the doubt and find him not guilty."

The Privilege against Self-Incrimination

The Fifth Amendment to the Constitution states that no person can be forced to give testimony that might be self-incriminating. Therefore, a defendant does not have to testify at trial. Witnesses may also refuse to testify on this ground. For example, if a witness, while testifying, is asked a question which, if answered, would reveal her own criminal wrongdoing, the witness may "take the Fifth" and refuse to testify on the ground that the testimony may incriminate her. It does not prevent defendants from being required

DEVELOPING PARALEGAL SKILLS

PREPARING GRAPHIC PRESENTATIONS

Melanie Hofstadter, a paralegal who is about to retire from her job, is training her replacement. Melanie works for a law firm that specializes in criminal law and has assisted the attorneys countless times with trial preparations. Now she is instructing the new paralegal, Keera Mason, on how to prepare graphic presentations for the attorneys' courtroom use.

Melanie explains that trial graphics are classified into three main types: fact graphics, concept graphics, and case graphics.

1. Fact graphics show only the facts on which both parties agree—for example, a time line indicating the order in which events occurred.

2. Concept graphics are used to educate the judge and jury about ideas with which they may not be familiar, such as the general procedures involved in DNA fingerprinting.

3. Case graphics, or analytical graphics, illustrate the basis of the defense or allegation; for example, a flowchart could be used to show how certain facts are related and how they lead to a specific conclusion.

Melanie gives Keera a document that contains a list of tips and suggestions that Keera should keep in mind when preparing trial graphics.

TIPS FOR PREPARING A GRAPHIC PRESENTATION

- Remember that less can be more. A good graphic presentation should be simple and straightforward. Trim excess words and punctuation from charts, lists, and diagrams; using incomplete sentences and simple phrases is acceptable in graphic presentations.

- Use boldfaced text and easy-to-read fonts.

- Keep plenty of "white space" in the graphic displays.

- Know what you want the reader to focus on, and eliminate all distractions.

- Remember that it is your job to make it easy for the jury to see, read, and understand your points. Don't overburden the graphic displays with too much information or detail.

- Keep in mind that the main purpose of trial graphics is to focus attention on the points that you want to emphasize or highlight, not to focus attention on the actual presentation or display.

to provide physical samples (such as blood); submit to fingerprinting, photography, or measurements; write or speak for identification purposes; appear in court; or make a gesture or assume a particular position.

The Right to a Speedy Trial

The Sixth Amendment requires a speedy and public trial for criminal prosecutions but does not specify what is meant by "speedy." The federal Speedy Trial Act (18 USC §3161-3174) also sets time limits. Federal Rule of Criminal Procedure 48 also gives courts discretion to dismiss cases not brought to trial promptly. Most states have similar statutes and rules.

Generally, criminal cases are brought to trial much more quickly than civil cases. A defendant who remains in custody prior to trial, for example, may be tried within thirty to forty-five days from the date of arraignment. If the defendant (or the defendant's attorney) needs more time to prepare a defense, the defendant may give up the right to be tried as quickly but will still go to trial within a few months, typically. As noted in Chapter 5, the Sixth Amendment also guarantees accused persons the right to confront and cross-examine witnesses against them.

Reprinted by permission of the National Federation of Paralegal Associations, Inc. (NFPA®), www.paralegals.org.; Copyright 1975. Adopted 1975, Revised 1979, 1988, 1995, 2007. Reprinted with permission of NALA, the Association for Paralegals–Legal Assistants. Inquiries should be directed to NALA, 1516 S. Boston, #200, Tulsa, OK 74119, www.nala.org.

ETHICS WATCH

THE IMPORTANCE OF ACCURACY

In preparing exhibits for trial, especially when creating an exhibit from raw data, it is important that the paralegal ensure that the exhibit is accurate and not misleading. If erroneous evidence is introduced in court and challenged by opposing counsel, your supervising attorney may face serious consequences. By preparing an inaccurate exhibit (for example, by miscalculating a column of figures), the paralegal may jeopardize the attorney's professional reputation by causing the attorney to breach a professional duty.

This paralegal responsibility comes from the following codes:

• NALA *Code of Ethics*, Canon 10: "A paralegal's conduct is guided by bar associations' codes of professional responsibility and rules of professional conduct."

• NFPA *Model Code of Ethics and Professional Responsibility*, Section EC-1.3: "A paralegal shall maintain a high standard of professional conduct."

The Requirement for a Unanimous Verdict

acquittal
A certification or declaration following a trial that the individual accused of a crime is innocent, or free from guilt, in the eyes of the law and is thus absolved of the charges.

Of the criminal cases that go to trial, most are tried by a jury. In most jurisdictions, jury verdicts in criminal cases must be *unanimous* for acquittal or conviction. In other words, all twelve jurors (some states allow smaller juries) must agree that the defendant is either guilty or not guilty.

If the jury cannot reach unanimous agreement on whether to acquit or convict the defendant, the result is a hung jury. When the jury is hung, the defendant may be tried again, but often the case is not retried. The requirement for unanimity is important because if even one juror is not convinced of the defendant's guilt, the defendant is not convicted. Thus, the prosecuting attorney must make as strong a case as possible, while the defense attorney can aim at persuading some jurors to have doubts. As in all litigation, throughout a trial, a law firm must take steps to maintain the security of its information, as discussed in the *Technology and Today's Paralegal* feature on the facing page.

hung jury
A jury whose members are so irreconcilably divided in their opinions that they cannot reach a verdict. The judge in this situation may order a new trial.

Sentencing

sentence
The punishment, or penalty, ordered by the court to be inflicted on a person convicted of a crime.

When a defendant is found guilty by a trial court (or pleads guilty to an offense without a trial), the judge will pronounce a sentence, which is the penalty imposed on anyone convicted of a crime. Often, the sentence is pronounced in a separate proceeding.

Limited Role of Jury

Unless the prosecutor is seeking the death penalty, the jury normally is not involved in sentencing the defendant. Jurors are dismissed after they return a verdict, and the judge either sentences the defendant on the spot or schedules a future appearance for sentencing. At the sentencing hearing, the judge usually listens to arguments from both attorneys concerning the factors in "aggravation and mitigation" (that is, why the defendant's punishment should be harsh or lenient).

TECHNOLOGY AND TODAY'S PARALEGAL

EVOLVING SECURITY AND FORENSIC TOOLS

Technologies used in law offices change frequently. Be aware of developments that affect the functioning of a law office and can destroy the security of information sent to other parties. Technology can pose threats to the security of information as well as offer new opportunities in the collection and evaluation of evidence.

PROTECTING SECURITY

New technology can mean that documents believed to be secure are not. For example, members of the media were able to read parts of a confidential settlement that had been redacted (blacked out) in the settlement of a lawsuit involving Facebook and ConnectU. The computer codes that supposedly hid some information from public view were bypassed in electronic copies of documents released to the press, allowing reporters to see the private information. The lawyers for ConnectU claimed to have received $65 million from Facebook in the settlement, but the press could see the amount was actually $31 million. ConnectU fired the law firm that made the mistake.

KNOWING WHERE PEOPLE ARE OR WERE

Global positioning system (GPS) devices are now built into many vehicles. Information collected by these devices may allow investigators to determine the location of a vehicle (and therefore a suspect) at a given point in time, which can help in criminal investigations.

Federal rules now require cell phones to support GPS information so that 911 emergency calls can be pinpointed by location. This can be important in criminal investigations, because it enables an investigator to find out the location of persons and their cell phones, even if they did not call 911.

USING DIGITAL FORENSIC EXPERTS

The use of digital forensic experts in litigation is increasing. Professionals can assist in the evaluation of digital material and identify when it has been compromised and is no longer trustworthy. Just as the use of DNA evidence has helped to convict some people accused of crimes and free others falsely accused, digital evidence is playing an increasing role in helping to establish guilt or innocence.

TECHNOLOGY TIP

The rapid evolution of technology means that law firms must watch for possibilities not envisioned before. Web sites such as **eLawExchange.com** provide information about innovations affecting law and about how to find experts when needed. Paralegals should use such resources to keep up to date with evolving technologies.

Range of Penalties

Most criminal statutes set forth a maximum and minimum penalty that should be imposed for a violation. Thus, judges often have some discretion in sentencing defendants. The judge typically sentences the offender to one or more of the following:

- Incarceration in a jail or a prison.
- Probation (formal or informal).
- Fines or other financial penalties.
- Public work service (for less serious offenses).
- Class attendance (for offenses such as domestic violence and alcohol- or drug-related crimes).
- Death (in some states).

In federal and many state cases, the defense and prosecutor prepare sentencing memoranda, arguing for particular sentences. For more serious crimes, the federal courts use the

Federal Sentencing Guidelines (which can be found online) to help determine sentences. Paralegals are often involved in helping to draft sentencing memoranda and organize supporting documents, such as letters of support for the defendant or statements from the victim for a prosecutor. In some states, victims have the right to address the court and may have an attorney or paralegal assist them in preparing their statements.

Incarceration

Defendants sentenced to incarceration will go to a county jail for less serious offenses (involving sentences of less than one year) or a state or federal prison for serious crimes (involving sentences of more than one year).

The judge may consider alternatives to jail time. Defendants may be placed on house arrest and wear an electronic device that notifies authorities if they leave a designated area. Defendants who have alcohol or drug problems may sometimes be allowed to satisfy the incarceration portion of a sentence in an inpatient rehabilitation program. In some states, defendants may be allowed to satisfy short periods of custody time (ten to thirty days) by checking into the jail on weekends only or by participating in a supervised release program, which enables them to stay employed.

Probation

probation
When a convicted defendant is released from confinement but is still under court supervision for a period of time.

A part of many sentences is probation. Typically, defendants are sentenced to less than the maximum penalty and placed on probation with certain conditions for a set time. In such cases, the sentence imposed is said to be *suspended*. If the person fails to meet the conditions of probation, probation may be revoked, and the person may be sentenced to custody time up to the maximum for the offense.

COMBINATION OF PENALTIES.　If convicted of driving while under the influence, for example, a defendant might be sentenced to two days in jail, three years of informal probation, a fine of $3,000, and ten days of public work service (picking up roadside trash, for example). The court could also require the defendant to attend a first-offenders program (meeting twice a week for six to eight weeks and costing several thousand dollars). If the defendant does not do all of these things, the court can revoke probation and sentence the person to spend up to a year in jail.

TYPES OF PROBATION.　Probation can be either formal or informal. In formal probation, which is typical in felony cases, the defendant is required to meet regularly with a probation officer. The defendant may be required to submit to drug and alcohol testing, to possess no firearms, and to avoid socializing with those who might be engaging in criminal activity, for example.

Defendants on informal probation do not have a probation officer, but they may be required to comply with certain conditions. This could include paying a fine, performing public work service, participating in specified programs (such as attending Alcoholics Anonymous meetings or anger management classes), and not violating the law.

Diversion

diversion program
In some jurisdictions, an alternative to prosecution that is offered to certain felony suspects to deter them from future unlawful acts.

In many states, diversion programs are available to defendants charged with certain offenses. Diversion is an alternative to prosecution. Generally, these programs suspend criminal prosecution for a certain period of time and require that the defendant complete specified conditions—such as attending special classes and not getting in trouble with the police—during that time. If the person fulfills the diversion requirements, the case will be dismissed. If the defendant fails to complete the diversion satisfactorily, the criminal prosecution springs back to life, and the defendant is prosecuted for the crime.

The objective is to deter the defendant from further wrongdoing by offering an incentive—namely, a way to avoid any record of conviction. Diversion is a good option for defendants who want to avoid having convictions on their records. Most defendants who are eligible for diversion choose that option and thus do not proceed to trial.

Appeal

Persons convicted of crimes have a right of appeal. Most felony convictions are appealed to an intermediate court of appeal. In some states, there is no intermediate court of appeal, so the appeal goes directly to the state's highest appellate court, usually called the supreme court of the state. Most convictions that result in supervised release or fines are not appealed, but a high percentage of the convictions that result in prison sentences are appealed. About 10 percent of such convictions are reversed on appeal. The most common reason for reversal is that the trial court admitted improper evidence, such as evidence obtained by a search that did not meet constitutional requirements.

If a conviction is overturned on appeal, the defendant may or may not be tried again, depending on the reason for the reversal and on whether the case was reversed with or without prejudice. A decision reversed "with prejudice" means that no further action can be taken on the claim or cause. A decision reversed "without prejudice" may be tried again.

KEY TERMS AND CONCEPTS

acquittal 406
actus reus 382
arraignment 399
arrest 393
arrest warrant 395
arson 385
bail 397
beyond a reasonable doubt 378
booking 393
burglary 385
crime 377
cyber crime 388
cyberstalking 389
defense 383
defense of others 383
defense of property 383
diversion program 408
double jeopardy 391
due process of law 391

embezzlement 386
exclusionary rule 392
felony 380
forgery 385
grand jury 398
hacker 389
hung jury 406
identity theft 388
indictment 399
information 398
insider trading 387
larceny 385
mens rea 382
Miranda rights 392
misdemeanor 380
money laundering 387
motion for a change of venue 403
motion to recuse 403

motion to sever 403
motion to suppress evidence 400
nolo contendere 399
petty offense 380
plea bargaining 399
preliminary hearing 398
probable cause 393
probation 408
public defender 377
public prosecutor 377
responsible corporate officer doctrine 382
robbery 384
search warrant 395
self-defense 383
self-incrimination 391
sentence 406
white-collar crime 386

Chapter Summary / Criminal Law and Procedures

DEFINING CRIME

1. *Key differences between civil and criminal law*—Crimes are distinguished from civil wrongs, such as torts, in several ways:

    a. Crimes are deemed to be offenses against society as a whole.

    b. Tort (civil) litigation involves lawsuits between private parties; criminal litigation involves the state's prosecution of a wrongdoer.

    c. Crimes are defined as such by state legislatures or the federal government.

d. In criminal cases the state must prove the defendant's guilt beyond a reasonable doubt. In civil cases, the plaintiff proves a case by a preponderance of the evidence.

e. A criminal act need not involve a victim.

2. *Civil liability for criminal acts*—Those who commit crimes may be subject to both criminal and civil liability, such as when a person commits an assault, but the legal actions are separate matters.

3. *Classification of crimes*—Crimes fall into two basic classifications: felonies and misdemeanors.

   a. Felonies are more serious crimes (such as murder, rape, and robbery) for which penalties may range from imprisonment for a year or longer to (in some states) death.

   b. Misdemeanors are less serious crimes (such as prostitution, disturbing the peace, and public intoxication) for which penalties may include imprisonment for up to a year. Petty offenses, or infractions, such as violations of building codes, are usually a subset of misdemeanors.

4. *Jurisdiction over crimes*—Most crimes fall under state statutes and state prosecution, but there is a long list of federal criminal acts, too.

ELEMENTS OF CRIMINAL LIABILITY

For criminal liability to exist, the state must meet certain standards of proof:

1. *The criminal act*—Most crimes require that the defendant be shown to have committed or attempted to commit an act, *actus reus*, the guilty act.

2. *State of mind*—The defendant must also have had the required state of mind, *mens rea*, or intent to do a criminal act.

3. *Corporate criminal liability*—Corporations may be held liable for crimes. Corporate officers and directors may be held personally liable for the crimes of the corporation.

4. *Defenses to criminal liability*—Criminal liability may be avoided if the state of mind required for the crime was lacking or another defense against liability can be raised. Defenses include self-defense, defense of others, defense of property, and the running of a statute of limitations.

TYPES OF CRIMES

Many acts are defined as criminal by federal and state laws. The five traditional major categories of crimes are as follows:

1. *Violent crime*—Crimes that cause another person to suffer harm or death are violent crimes, such as murder, rape, robbery, and assault and battery.

2. *Property crime*—When the offender takes or damages the property of another. Property crimes include burglary, larceny (stealing), obtaining goods by false pretenses, receiving stolen goods, arson, and forgery.

3. *Public order crime*—Crimes involving behavior society has deemed inappropriate, such as public drunkenness and illegal drug use, are public order crimes.

4. *White-collar crime*—Illegal acts committed by individuals or business entities in the course of legitimate business—for example, embezzlement, mail or wire fraud, bribery, theft of trade secrets, and insider trading—are white-collar crimes.

5. *Organized crime*—The criminal enterprises that provide illegal goods and services such as gambling, prostitution, and illegal narcotics. Money from such activities will be made to appear legitimate by money laundering. The Racketeer Influenced and Corrupt Organizations Act (RICO) is applied to a wide range of activities.

CYBER CRIMES

Cyber crimes are committed with computers, typically by using the Internet to achieve illegal ends. Cyber crimes include theft of money or data, identity theft, cyberstalking, and hacking. Prosecuting cyber crimes presents new challenges to law enforcement and the courts.

SOCIAL MEDIA AND CRIMINAL JUSTICE

Social media tools are used by law enforcement authorities, so legal providers must know the boundaries of such use when defending clients.

1. *Use of social media*—Criminals are making greater use of social media to exploit victims, so law enforcement is responding by monitoring transmissions and gathering records of transmissions.

2. *Proper evidence*—Lawyers, when defending those accused of crimes, look to see if client rights have been violated in the collection of evidence by investigators' improper access to social media.

CONSTITUTIONAL SAFEGUARDS

Specific procedures must be followed in arresting and prosecuting a criminal suspect to safeguard constitutional rights.

1. *Safeguards in the Bill of Rights*—Persons accused of crimes have rights, including protection against unreasonable searches and seizures, the right to due process of law, protection against double jeopardy, protection against self-incrimination (the right to remain silent), the right to a speedy and public trial, the right to confront witnesses and be represented by an attorney, and protection against excessive bail and cruel and unusual punishment.

2. *Exclusionary rule*—Evidence obtained in violation of a defendant's constitutional rights normally must be excluded from trial, along with evidence derived from illegally obtained evidence.

3. Miranda *rule*—At the time a criminal suspect is taken into custody, the arresting officers must inform the suspect of his or her rights by reading the *Miranda* warnings. Evidence or confession obtained in violation of the suspect's rights will normally not be admissible in court. The Supreme Court has made exceptions to the *Miranda* rule.

CRIMINAL PROCEDURES PRIOR TO PROSECUTION

The initial procedure undertaken by the police after a crime is reported or observed includes steps that must be followed properly for a case to proceed.

1. *Arrest and booking*—Officers take a person into custody and charge the person with a crime. The suspect is usually taken to a holding facility (jail) where the person is detained while being booked (entered into the police log). Police must show probable cause for the accusation and, in many cases, need an arrest warrant issued by a judge.

2. *Investigation after the arrest*—Police may need to interview witnesses, collect evidence, execute search warrants, and take other steps in making the case that a suspect should be prosecuted.

THE PROSECUTION BEGINS

Police make a report of the alleged crime to a public prosecutor.

1. *Prosecutorial discretion*—The prosecutor decides, based on a review of the evidence, if the case should proceed or the accusations dropped.

2. *Complaint and initial appearance*—A complaint against an accused person includes a statement of charges; upon being served with a complaint, the person formally becomes a defendant. There will be an initial appearance before a judge or magistrate, and the defendant is usually released on personal recognizance or must post bail.

3. *Preliminary hearing*—Appearance before a judge will determine if there is sufficient evidence to show probable cause so as to allow the matter to proceed.

4. *Grand jury review*—The federal government and many states use a grand jury to obtain an indictment in certain felony cases; only with such an indictment will the case go to trial. In other cases the prosecutor provides an information for prosecution to proceed.

5. *Arraignment*—The defendant is formally charged in court and enters a plea. Often the parties have agreed to a plea bargain that will terminate proceedings at this point.

6. *Pretrial motions*—If the case proceeds, various motions may be entered, often by the defense, such as a motion to suppress evidence or a motion to dismiss the case.

7. *Discovery*—In criminal cases, the defendant is entitled to obtain any evidence relating to the case possessed by the prosecution, including documents, statements previously made by the defendant, objects, reports of tests or examinations, and other evidence.

THE TRIAL

Most criminal cases are settled before they get to trial through plea bargaining. Most criminal trials last less than one week and differ from civil trials in a few major ways.

1. *The presumption of innocence*—The defendant is innocent until the prosecutor proves the defendant's guilt to the jury (or judge) beyond a reasonable doubt. The defendant is not required to present any evidence at the trial.

2. *The privilege against self-incrimination*—The defendant and witnesses cannot be forced to testify if such testimony would be incriminating.

3. *The right to a speedy trial*—Defendants have a right to a speedy and public trial. Even if they waive that right, criminal cases usually go to trial more quickly than civil cases.

4. *The requirement for a unanimous verdict*—Most criminal cases are tried by juries. Generally, all jurors must reach agreement to acquit or convict the defendant.

5. *Sentencing*—The judge sentences a defendant who has been found guilty (or who pleads guilty or no contest), often at a separate proceeding. Most criminal statutes set forth a range of penalties that can be imposed, and judges are free to select the appropriate penalty within that range. Typically, sentences involve fines, imprisonment, and probation (including conditions of probation).

6. *Diversion*—A defendant may be sentenced to a diversion program, which results in dismissal of the case provided the defendant complies with the requirements of diversion (which vary by state).

7. *Appeal*—If the defendant loses at trial, he or she may appeal the case to a higher court. A small percentage of criminal cases are reversed on appeal.

■ QUESTIONS FOR REVIEW

1. What are the key differences between civil and criminal law?

2. What two elements are required for criminal liability?

3. What are the five traditional types of crime? What defenses can be raised against criminal liability?

4. What are cyber crimes? What role has social media played in these crimes? What factors determine whether social media evidence deserves privacy protection?

5. Which constitutional amendments provide rights to a person accused of a crime, and what rights are provided? What are *Miranda* rights, and which amendments provide the basis for *Miranda* rights?

6. List and explain the basic steps involved in criminal procedure from the time a crime is reported to the resolution of the case.

7. Explain what happens during sentencing. Describe the different types of penalties and alternatives that exist. What happens during an appeal?

■ ETHICS QUESTION

A man who was not a lawyer opened a law office and filled out a court registration form using the Social Security number, birth date, faked law school credential, and last name of a real lawyer. He filed a lawsuit in federal court unbeknownst to the supposed plaintiffs in the case. When visited by undercover FBI agents, the man told the agents that he would represent them for a $5,000 retainer and would charge $400 an hour. What crime did he commit? What state regulatory statute related to the practice of law was violated?

■ PRACTICE QUESTIONS AND ASSIGNMENTS

1. Identify each of the following crimes by its classification (infraction, misdemeanor, felony):

   a. Jerry refuses to put his trash out at the curb for the weekly trash pickup. Instead, he lets it collect on the side of his garage, where it is an eyesore and attracts rats to the neighborhood. The police department receives complaints from his neighbors and gives Jerry a citation for violating the trash ordinance.

   b. Neehan is arrested for being under the influence of drugs in public. She faces a possible jail sentence of six months.

c. Susanna is arrested for forging Martha's name on the back of a check made out to Martha and then depositing the check into her own bank account. The penalty includes confinement for over one year in prison on conviction.

2. Using the material presented in the chapter on state of mind, identify the type of homicide (involuntary manslaughter, voluntary manslaughter, first or second degree murder) committed in each of the following situations:

   a. David, while driving in an intoxicated state, crashes into another car and kills its occupants.

   b. David, after pulling up next to his wife at a stoplight and observing her passionately kissing another man, smashes into her car and kills her.

   c. David, who is angry with his boss for firing him, plans to kill his boss by smashing his car into his boss's car, killing his boss and making it look like a car accident. David carries out his plan, kills his boss, and survives the accident.

3. Identify the following criminal procedures:

   a. Ani is charged with the crime of arson. She pleads not guilty and is bound over for trial in the district court.

   b. Reyna is taken to the police station, searched, photographed, fingerprinted, and allowed to make one telephone call.

   c. A jury of Barbara's peers reviews the evidence against her and determines whether probable cause exists and whether the prosecutor should proceed to trial for manslaughter.

   d. Police officers stop Miguel on the street because his description matches that of a reported gas-station robber. He is three blocks from the gas station when they stop him. They question him, search him, and find that he has a pocketful of $20 and $50 bills—the same denominations that were reported by the gas-station attendant as having been stolen. The police read Miguel his rights and take him to the police station.

   e. Andrew is taken before a magistrate, where the charges against him are read and counsel is appointed. His request to be set free on bail is denied.

   f. In exchange for a guilty plea to manslaughter, the prosecutor agrees to drop the more serious murder charges against Maria.

4. Mona was laid off from her manufacturing job three years ago. Her unemployment compensation has run out, as has her severance package, and she has few prospects for finding work. Mona learns that a former co-worker has died. She thinks that if she can file a tax return using the co-worker's name and Social Security number, she can collect a tax refund. Mona takes the woman's name and looks up her Social Security number on the Social Security Death Master File website. In January 2016, Mona files the tax return in the deceased's name. She receives a refund check. Mona decides that this is a quick and easy way to make money, so she continues to take names from obituaries reported in the media and file more false tax returns until she has collected over $100,000. What crimes has Mona committed?

5. The police pick up Larry and take him to the station for questioning in a local murder case. They detain him for three days. After two days of questioning, Larry says, "I want an attorney. You haven't let me call my attorney." It is late, and Larry's attorney does not answer the phone, but she receives the message first thing in the morning on the third day that Larry is in custody and heads directly to the police station, where she secures Larry's release. She confirms that the police failed to tell Larry that he had the right to have an attorney present and did not give him any of his other *Miranda* rights. What will be the result if the information Larry gave to the police is used against him in court?

6. After answering a few background questions regarding his name and title, a government official took the Fifth Amendment eighty-two times during the course of a hearing on corruption charges. What does taking the Fifth Amendment eighty-two times say about guilt or innocence? Does taking the Fifth Amendment protect the official from self-incrimination?

7. A women's clothing boutique posted information on Facebook about a leopard-print dress with hot-pink and lime-green accents that was stolen from the store. The theft was captured on security video. Shortly after the store's posting, a Facebook selfie of a woman wearing the dress, captioned "Love my new dress," was forwarded to the store owner. The owner contacted the police, who arrested the woman pictured in the selfie. What crime was committed?

8. During a criminal trial involving child pornography charges, the defendant's lawyer returned late from the lunch recess. The trial resumed, and the defendant had no lawyer present for seven minutes. During that time, prosecutors introduced incriminating evidence. When the lawyer returned from lunch, he did not object to the testimony that had been presented while he was absent. The defendant was convicted and sentenced to life in prison. Which of the defendant's rights were violated? Can an argument be made that his conviction should be overturned?

■ GROUP PROJECT

This project involves researching CryptoWall ransomeware.

Student one will locate the *New York Times* article, "How My Mom Got Hacked" and provide a summary of the facts and legal issues.

Student two will locate and summarize an article discussing the CryptoWall cyber attack on the Dickson County, Tennessee, Sheriff's Office. Student three will locate the online Internet Crime Complaint Center and provide information on how to file a complaint with the agency. Student four will locate and summarize an article on **abajournal.com** about a lawyer who clicked on an e-mail link and lost $289,000. The group will make a recommendation on how law offices can avoid becoming victims of cyber crimes and how do respond if they do.

■ INTERNET PROJECTS

1. Go to the FBI's YouTube channel at **youtube.com/user/fbi**. Watch a video clip on a wanted person and provide the following information:

   a. Who is the suspect, and what crime or crimes has he or she allegedly committed?

   b. Is a reward being offered?

   c. What information is the FBI seeking?

   d. How do persons with information provide it to the FBI?

2. Locate the First Circuit Court of Appeal's decision in *In re Tsarnaev*, 775 F.3d 457 (1st Cir. 2015), available at **media.ca1.uscourts.gov/pdf.opinions/14-2362P-01A.pdf**. Answer the following questions about the case:

   a. What is a writ of *mandamus*? You can look up the definition at **law.cornell.edu**.

   b. What did the court decide? Why?

   c. Give a one-sentence explanation of why this defendant was prosecuted.

   d. Why did one of the judges dissent? What were his reasons?

   e. Discuss the issue of jury impartiality with respect to the media attention the *Tsarnaev* case received.

3. Review the American Bar Association (ABA) Standing Committee on Ethics and Professional Responsibility Formal Opinion 466 at **abajournal.com/files/Formal_Opinion_466_FINAL_04_23_14.pdf**.

   a. What does the ABA conclude that an attorney may ethically do to research jurors' or potential jurors' Internet presence (including social media sites) prior to and during a trial?

   b. Do an online search for the ethics opinion of your state's bar association on this issue. How does it compare to the ABA's opinion? Which opinion has precedence in your state?

   c. What is an attorney's obligation if she finds evidence of juror or potential juror misconduct that is criminal or fraudulent? What should a paralegal do if she is performing research for the attorney and discovers a juror's or potential juror's criminal or fraudulent misconduct?

■ END NOTES

1. The American Law Institute (mentioned in Chapter 5) issued the Official Draft of the Model Penal Code in 1962. The Model Penal Code was designed to assist state legislatures in reexamining and recodifying state criminal laws. Uniformity among the states is not as important in criminal law as in other areas of the law. Crime varies with local circumstances, and it is appropriate that punishments vary accordingly.

2. Pronounced *ak*-tus *ray*-us.

3. Pronounced menz *ray*-uh.

4. *United States v. Park*, 421 U.S. 658, 95 S.Ct. 1903, 44 L.Ed.2d 489 (1975).

5. 384 U.S. 436, 86 S.Ct. 1602, 16 L.Ed.2d 694 (1966).

6. Pronounced in-*dite*-ment.

Key Elements of the Law

CONTRACT

CHAPTER 14

Tort Law, Product Liability, and Consumer Law

CHAPTER OUTLINE

Introduction

The Basis of Tort Law

Intentional Torts

Negligence

Cyber Torts: Defamation Online

Strict Liability

Product Liability

Consumer Law

CHAPTER OBJECTIVES

After completing this chapter, you will know:

- What a tort is, the purpose of tort law, and the basic categories of torts.

- The four elements of negligence.

- What is meant by strict liability and the underlying policy for imposing strict product liability.

- What defenses can be raised in product liability actions.

- Some of the ways in which the government protects consumers against unfair business practices and harmful products.

Introduction

Torts are wrongful actions. In fact, the word *tort* is French for "wrong." Through tort law, society seeks to compensate those who have suffered injuries as a result of the wrongful conduct of others. Although some torts, such as trespass, originated in the English common law, the field of tort law continues to expand. As new ways to commit wrongs—such as the use of the Internet to commit wrongful acts—are recognized, the courts extend the principles of tort law to cover these wrongs.

Here, we discuss some of the primary concepts of tort law and how they are being applied today. We also consider *product liability*, which is a major area of tort law under which sellers can be held liable for defective products. In the final pages of the chapter, we look at a growing body of law designed to protect the health and safety and the credit of consumers.

tort
A civil wrong not arising from a breach of contract; a breach of a legal duty that causes harm or injury to another.

The Basis of Tort Law

Two notions serve as the basis of all torts: wrongs and compensation. Tort law recognizes that some acts are wrong because they cause injuries to others. In a tort action, one person or group brings suit against another person or group to obtain compensation (money damages) or other relief for the harm suffered.

Because tort suits involve *private* wrongs, they are distinguishable from criminal actions, which involve *public* wrongs. A government prosecutor brings criminal actions against individuals who are accused of committing acts that are wrongs against society (crimes are usually defined by statutes, as discussed in Chapter 13). Some acts may result in both a tort lawsuit and a criminal prosecution.

The purpose of tort law is to provide remedies for the invasion of protected interests or rights—such as people's interests in physical safety, privacy, freedom of movement, and reputation—that society seeks to protect. We first discuss two broad categories of torts: *intentional torts* and *negligence*. The classification of a particular tort depends largely on how it occurs (intentionally or unintentionally) and the circumstances. We then examine the concept of *strict liability*, a doctrine under which a defendant may be held liable for harm or injury to another regardless of intention or fault.

When thinking about torts, it is important to focus on the elements of the tort. A plaintiff must prove the elements to succeed in a tort claim. These are important to know, as they will affect your work. In analyzing a client's tort claim you will check to make sure there is evidence to prove each element of the tort.

elements
The issues and facts that the plaintiff must prove to succeed in a tort claim.

Intentional Torts

An intentional tort, as the term implies, requires *intent*. Hence, intent is an element of intentional torts. In tort law, intent does not necessarily mean that the person accused (who is sometimes called the tortfeasor) intended to harm someone. Rather, it means that the actor intended the consequences of an act or knew or should have known that certain consequences would result from an act. Thus, pushing another person—even if done in fun and without any bad intent—is an intentional tort if an injury results. We should know that if we shove someone, it is possible he will fall.

There are two categories of intentional torts. There are intentional torts against persons and intentional torts against property. We look at both categories.

intentional tort
A wrongful act knowingly committed.

tortfeasor
One who commits a tort.

Intentional Torts against Persons

Intentional torts against persons include assault and battery, false imprisonment, intentional infliction of emotional distress, defamation, invasion of the right to privacy, appropriation, misrepresentation, and wrongful interference.

Assault

An assault is any communication or action intended to make another person fearful of immediate physical harm. In other words, an assault is a threat that a reasonable person would believe. The tort law of assault protects our interest in freedom from fear of harmful or offensive contact. The occurrence of apprehension is enough to justify compensation. The elements of assault are:

1. an act intended to cause an apprehension of harmful or offensive contact, and
2. an act that causes fear of imminent bodily harm.

Battery

The *completion* of the threat, if it results in harm to the plaintiff, is a battery, which is defined as harmful or offensive physical contact *intentionally* performed.

> **EXAMPLE 14.1** Suppose Ivan threatens Jean with a gun, then shoots her. Pointing the gun at Jean is an assault. Firing of the gun (if the bullet hits Jean) is a battery.

Tort law for battery protects our right to personal security and safety. The contact can be physically harmful, or it can be merely offensive (such as an unwelcome kiss). The contact can involve any part of the body or anything attached to it—for example, an item of clothing or a purse. Whether the contact is offensive or not is determined by the *reasonable person standard* (discussed later). The contact can be made by the defendant or by some force the defendant sets in motion—for example a rock thrown or food poisoned. The elements of battery are:

1. an intent to cause an unwanted contact, and
2. the unwanted, offensive, and harmful contact.

COMPENSATION. If the plaintiff shows that there was offensive contact, or fear of such contact, and the jury agrees, the plaintiff has a right to compensation. There is no need to show that the defendant acted out of malice. The underlying motive does not matter, only the intent to bring about the harmful or offensive contact to the plaintiff. Proving a motive is not necessary but is often relevant and makes a case stronger.

DEFENSES TO ASSAULT AND BATTERY. A number of legally recognized defenses, or reasons why plaintiffs should not obtain compensation they are seeking, can be raised by defendants in tort actions. Later, we review defenses that can be raised in many tort cases. The following defenses may be used by a defendant who is sued for assault, battery, or both:

- *Consent.* When a person gives permission to the act that damages her, there is generally no liability (legal responsibility) for the damage done. For instance, if Suzi consents to being kissed, Bryan can raise this as a defense if she sues for battery.

- *Self-defense.* A person defending her life or physical well-being can claim self-defense. In situations of both *real* and *apparent* danger, a person may use whatever force is *reasonably* necessary to prevent harmful contact. Thus, if Simon assaults Linda with a knife, she can claim this defense if Simon sues her for hitting him with a baseball bat.

- *Defense of others.* A person can act in a reasonable manner to protect others who are in real or apparent danger. If Fred offensively grabs Rafic's wife and Rafic hits Fred, Rafic can raise this as a defense if Fred tries to sue him for battery.

- *Defense of property.* People can use reasonable force in attempting to remove intruders from their homes (see the discussion of the castle doctrine in Chapter 13 on page 384). Generally, force that is likely to cause death or great bodily injury should not be used just to protect property. For instance, if you catch someone in the act of breaking into your garage, you can use non-deadly force to stop that person without being liable for battery.

The defendant bears the burden of proving the facts necessary to be able to rely on these defenses. The plaintiff must, of course, respond to such defenses when they are raised.

False Imprisonment

False imprisonment is the intentional confinement or restraint of another person's activities without justification. The elements of false imprisonment are:

false imprisonment
The intentional confinement or restraint of a person against his or her will.

1. intent to confine or restrain a person, and
2. actual confinement in boundaries not of the plaintiff's choosing.

False imprisonment interferes with the freedom to move without restraint. The confinement can be accomplished through the use of physical barriers, restraint, or threats of physical force. It is essential that the person being restrained not comply with the restraint willingly, but one does not have to resist physically to be subject to restraint.

Stores are often sued for false imprisonment after they have attempted to confine a suspected shoplifter for questioning. (An example is provided in the *Developing Paralegal Skills* feature below.) Under the "privilege to detain" granted to merchants in some states, a merchant can use the defense of *probable cause* to justify delaying a suspected shoplifter. Probable cause exists when the evidence to support the belief that a person is guilty outweighs the evidence against that belief. Although laws governing false imprisonment vary from state to state, generally they require that any detention be conducted in a *reasonable* manner and for only a *reasonable* length of time.

DEVELOPING PARALEGAL SKILLS

A CLAIM OF FALSE IMPRISONMENT

Julie Waterman works for a small law firm. She is interviewing a new client who detained a customer in his store for suspected shoplifting. Now he is facing a lawsuit brought by the customer for false imprisonment. Julie will gather as much information as she can about the incident and summarize what she learns in a memorandum for the attorney to review later. Before the interview, Julie checks the relevant state law governing false imprisonment. During the interview, Julie makes sure that she covers the topics on her checklist for determining false imprisonment.

CHECKLIST FOR DETERMINING FALSE IMPRISONMENT

- Did the client have cause to believe that the customer was shoplifting? What made the client suspect that the customer took merchandise without paying for it?

- Did the customer resist the detention?

- How long did the client detain the customer? Fifteen minutes? An hour? Was the duration of the detention reasonable?

- Was the customer in a reasonably comfortable environment during the detention? Was he prevented from leaving the store?

- Was the customer subjected to abusive or accusatory words or to any indignity while being confined?

- Were all procedures used to detain the customer reasonable?

Focusing on legal standards for such incidents helps the attorney determine the likely outcome of litigation in this contentious area.

Intentional Infliction of Emotional Distress

intentional infliction
of emotional distress
Intentional, extreme, and outrageous
conduct resulting in severe emotional distress to another.

The tort of intentional infliction of emotional distress (or mental distress) involves these elements:

1. outrageous conduct by the defendant
2. intent to commit the act or conduct involved
3. causation
4. severe emotional distress in the plaintiff.

EXAMPLE 14.2 Suppose a prankster calls Erica and says that her husband has just been killed in a horrible accident. As a result, Erica suffers intense mental pain. The caller's behavior is extreme and outrageous conduct that exceeds the bounds of decency accepted by society and is therefore actionable (serving as the basis for a lawsuit).

actionable
Capable of serving as the basis of a
lawsuit. An actionable claim can be
pursued in a lawsuit or other court
action.

Courts in some jurisdictions require that the emotional distress be evidenced by some physical symptom, illness, or emotional disturbance that can be documented by a psychiatric consultant or other medical professional.

Defamation

defamation
Anything published or publicly spoken that causes injury to another's
good name, reputation, or character.

slander
Defamation in oral form.

libel
Defamation in writing or other published form (such as videotape).

Wrongfully harming a person's good reputation is the tort of defamation. The law imposes a general duty on all persons to refrain from making false, damaging statements about others. Breaching this duty orally involves the tort of slander. Breaching it in writing involves the tort of libel. The tort of defamation also arises when a false statement is made about a person's product, business, or title to property.

The common law defines four types of false statements that are considered defamation *per se* (meaning that no proof of injury or harm is required for these false statements to be actionable):

- That a person has a loathsome communicable disease.
- That a person committed improprieties while engaging in a profession.
- That a person has committed or has been imprisoned for a serious crime.
- That an unmarried woman is unchaste.

THE PUBLICATION REQUIREMENT.   The tort of defamation requires the publication of a statement or statements that hold an individual up to contempt, ridicule, or hatred. Publication here means that the defamatory statements are communicated to third parties.

EXAMPLE 14.3 If Crystal writes Andrew a private letter accusing him of embezzling funds, the action does not constitute libel. If Juan calls Rita dishonest and incompetent when no one else is around, the action does not constitute slander. In neither case was the message communicated to a third party.

If a third party overhears defamatory statements by chance, the courts usually hold that this constitutes publication. Defamatory statements made on the Internet are actionable as well. Anyone who republishes or repeats defamatory statements, knowing them to be false, is liable even if that person reveals the source of the statements.

DEFENSES AGAINST DEFAMATION.   Truth is normally an absolute defense against a defamation charge. In other words, if the defendant in a defamation suit can prove that his allegedly defamatory statements were true, the defendant will not be liable.

privilege
In tort law, the ability to act contrary
to another person's right without
that person's having legal redress for
such acts. Privilege may be raised as
a defense to defamation.

Another defense that is sometimes raised is that the statements were privileged communications and thus the defendant is immune from liability. Privileged communications are of two types: absolute and qualified. Only in judicial proceedings and certain legislative proceedings is an *absolute* privilege granted. For example, statements made in the courtroom by attorneys and judges during a trial are absolutely privileged, as are statements made by legislators during debate in a legislature. A *qualified*, or *conditional*, privilege applies when a statement is related to a matter of public interest or when the statement is necessary to protect a person's private interest and is made to another person with an interest in the same subject matter.

In general, false and defamatory statements that are made about *public figures* (public officials and persons who get a lot of publicity) and that are published in the media are privileged if they are made without actual malice. To be made with actual malice, a statement must be made *with either knowledge of falsity or a reckless disregard of the truth*. Statements made about public figures, especially when they are made through the media, are usually related to matters of general public interest. Furthermore, public figures usually have access to the media to respond to defamatory statements. Hence, public figures have a greater burden of proof in defamation cases (they must prove actual malice) than do private individuals.

actual malice
Real and demonstrated evil intent. In a defamation suit, a statement made about a public figure normally must be made with actual malice (with either knowledge of its falsity or a reckless disregard of the truth) for liability to be incurred.

Invasion of the Right to Privacy

A person has a right to solitude and freedom from prying public eyes—in other words, to privacy. The Supreme Court has held that a fundamental right to privacy is implied by various amendments to the U.S. Constitution. Some state constitutions explicitly provide for privacy rights. In addition, a number of federal and state statutes protect individual rights in specific areas. Tort law also safeguards these rights through the tort of *invasion of privacy*. Four acts qualify as an invasion of privacy:

- *The use of a person's name, picture, or other likeness for commercial purposes without permission.* This tort, which is usually referred to as the tort of appropriation, will be examined shortly.

- *Intrusion into a person's affairs or seclusion.* For example, invading someone's home or snooping in someone's briefcase is an invasion of privacy. The tort has been held to extend to eavesdropping by wiretap, hacking into a computer, the unauthorized viewing of a bank account, and window peeping.

- *Publication of information that places a person in a false light.* This could be a story attributing to the person ideas not held or actions not taken. (Publishing such a story could involve the tort of defamation as well.)

- *Public disclosure of private facts about an individual that an ordinary person would find objectionable.* A newspaper account of a private citizen's sex life or financial affairs could be an actionable invasion of privacy.

The Electronic Privacy Information Center (EPIC) is a good resource on privacy issues. Go to **epic.org** for more information. How privacy issues are relevant at work is discussed in the *In the Office* feature on the following page.

Appropriation

The use by one person of another person's name or likeness without permission and for the benefit of the user is the tort of appropriation. A person's right to privacy normally includes the right to the exclusive use of his identity.

appropriation
In tort law, the use by one person of another person's name, likeness, or other identifying characteristic without permission and for the benefit of the user.

EXAMPLE 14.4 An example of appropriation can be found in the case brought by Vanna White, the hostess of the popular television game show *Wheel of Fortune*, against Samsung Electronics. Without White's permission, Samsung included in an advertisement for its video recorders a depiction of a robot dressed in a wig, gown, and jewelry, posed in a scene that resembled the *Wheel of Fortune* set, in a stance for which White was famous. The court held in White's favor, holding that the tort of appropriation does not require the use of a celebrity's name or exact likeness. The court stated that Samsung's robot ad left "little doubt" as to the identity of the celebrity whom the ad was meant to depict.

IN THE OFFICE

ONLINE PRIVACY

A pressing issue in the online world is the privacy rights of employees who use company-provided Internet access. Law firms routinely provide paralegals and other employees with computers and smartphones with which to access e-mail and the Internet. What if a paralegal uses his work computer and e-mail to make sexually explicit or unprofessional comments about other employees? Can a paralegal claim a right to privacy in the personal e-mail sent from his office computer? Does it matter if the paralegal used a personal e-mail address from a work-provided device?

Most courts that have considered the question have concluded that employees have no reasonable expecta-tion of privacy in e-mails sent from office computers. This is true even when employees were not informed that the employer could read their e-mails. The employer has a legal and ethical obligation to prevent harassment and discrimination in the workplace. Although employers who provide Internet access to employees can usually monitor or access their employees' e-mail messages without liability for invasion of privacy, they would not be allowed by most courts to publicly disclose the contents of an employee's personal e-mails. Always assume your employer can see e-mail sent from work and a history of your Web activity. Avoid using employer-provided electronic devices for personal purposes.

Misrepresentation (Fraud)

Misrepresentation leads another to believe in a condition that is different from the condition that actually exists. This is often accomplished through a false or an incorrect statement. The tort of fraudulent misrepresentation, or fraud, involves intentional deceit for personal gain—not misrepresentations innocently made by someone who is unaware of the facts.

fraudulent misrepresentation
Any misrepresentation, either by mis-statement or omission of a material fact, knowingly made with the intention of deceiving another and on which a reasonable person would and does rely to his or her detriment.

ELEMENTS OF FRAUD.   The tort of fraudulent misrepresentation includes several elements:

- Misrepresentation of facts or conditions with knowledge that they are false or with reckless disregard for the truth.
- Intent to induce another to rely on the misrepresentation.
- Justifiable reliance by the deceived party.
- Causal connection between the misrepresentation and the harm suffered.
- Damages suffered as a result of the reliance.

Fraud exists when a person represents as a fact something he knows is untrue. It is fraud to claim that a roof does not leak if you know it does. Facts can be objectively determined, unlike *seller's talk* or hype.

EXAMPLE 14.5 If Harry says, "I am the best accountant in town," that is seller's talk, not fraud. The speaker is not trying to represent something as fact, because the term *best* is subjective (open to interpretation) and because a "reasonable person" would not rely on Harry's statement.

FACT VERSUS OPINION.   Normally, the tort of misrepresentation or fraud occurs only when there is reliance on a *statement of fact*. Sometimes, however, reliance on a *statement of opinion* may involve the tort of misrepresentation if the person making the statement of opinion has a superior knowledge of the subject matter.

EXAMPLE 14.6 When a lawyer makes a statement of opinion about the law in a state in which the lawyer is licensed to practice, a court would hold reliance on such a statement to be equivalent to reliance on a statement of fact.

Wrongful Interference

Some lawsuits involve situations in which a person or business is accused of wrongfully interfering with the business of another. These business torts are generally divided into two categories: wrongful interference with a contractual relationship and wrongful interference with a business relationship.

business tort
Wrongful interference with another's business rights.

WRONGFUL INTERFERENCE WITH A CONTRACTUAL RELATIONSHIP.   The area of tort law relating to intentional interference with a contractual relationship has expanded in recent years. Three elements are necessary to establish the tort of wrongful interference with a contractual relationship:

1. a valid, enforceable contract exists between two parties,

2. a third party knows that this contract exists, and

3. the third party *intentionally* causes either of the two parties to breach the contract.

The contract may be between a firm and its employees or a firm and its customers. Sometimes a competitor of a firm draws away one of the firm's key employees. If the original employer can show (1) that the competitor induced the employee to leave in breach of a contract and (2) that the employee would not otherwise have broken the contract, then the employer may be entitled to compensation from the competitor.

WRONGFUL INTERFERENCE WITH A BUSINESS RELATIONSHIP.   Wrongful interference with a business relationship occurs when a party unreasonably interferes with another's business in an attempt to gain a larger share of the market. The elements of a wrongful interference with a business relationship are:

1. defendant knew or had reason to know that a third party and the plaintiff are in a business relationship or are considering doing business together, and

2. defendant intentionally interfered in the relationship.

There is a difference between competitive methods that do not give rise to tort liability and predatory behavior—actions undertaken with the intention of unlawfully driving competitors completely out of the market. The distinction usually depends on whether a business is attempting to attract customers in general or to target customers who have shown an interest in a similar product or service of a specific competitor.

predatory behavior
Business behavior that is undertaken with the intention of unlawfully driving competitors out of the market.

EXAMPLE 14.7 If a shopping center contains two shoe stores, an employee of Store A cannot be sent to the entrance of Store B to divert customers to Store A. This type of activity is the tort of wrongful interference with a business relationship, commonly considered to be an unfair trade practice.

DEFENSES TO WRONGFUL INTERFERENCE.   A person will not be liable for the tort of wrongful interference with a contractual or business relationship if it can be shown that the interference was justified, or permissible. Good faith competitive behavior is a permissible interference even if it results in the breaking of a contract.

EXAMPLE 14.8 If Antonio's Meats advertises so effectively that Beverly's Supermarket breaks its contract with Otis Meat Company, Otis Meat will be unable to recover against Antonio's Meats on a wrongful interference theory. Public policy favors free competition through honest advertising.

Intentional Torts against Property

Intentional torts against property include trespass to land, trespass to personal property, and conversion. These torts are wrongful actions that interfere with legally recognized rights to land or personal property. The law distinguishes real property from personal property (see Chapter 16). *Real property* is land and things "permanently" attached to the land. *Personal property* consists of movable items. Thus, a house is real property, whereas the furniture inside the house is personal property. Money and stocks and bonds are also personal property. (See this chapter's *Technology and Today's Paralegal* feature on the facing page for a discussion of how spam can constitute the tort of interference with personal property.)

Trespass to Land

trespass to land
The entry onto, above, or below the surface of land owned by another without the owner's permission.

A **trespass to land** occurs whenever a person, without permission, enters onto land that is owned by another, causes anything to enter onto the land, remains on the land, or permits anything to remain on it. The elements are:

1. plaintiff has lawful possession of the property at the time of the trespass,
2. there is an unauthorized entry by defendant, and
3. there is damage suffered by the plaintiff.

Actual harm to the land is not an essential element of this tort because the tort is designed to protect the right of owners to exclusively possess their property. Common trespasses include walking or driving on the land, shooting a gun over the land, throwing rocks at a building that belongs to someone else, causing water to back up on someone else's land, and placing part of one's building or fence on an adjoining landowner's property.

TRESPASS CRITERIA, RIGHTS, AND DUTIES.   The owner of the real property must show that a person is a trespasser. For example, a person who ignores "private property" signs and enters, uninvited, onto the property is clearly a trespasser. A guest in your home is an invitee, not a trespasser—unless she has been asked to leave but refuses. Any person who enters onto your property to commit an illegal act (such as a thief) is a trespasser, with or without posted signs. Normally, a trespasser must pay for any damage caused to the property and can be removed from the premises through the use of reasonable force without the owner being liable for assault and battery.

Further, a property owner owes no duty of care to a trespasser. If a trespasser sneaks across your backyard and breaks a leg when he steps in a hole in your lawn, he cannot sue you for having a hole in the lawn.

DEFENSES AGAINST TRESPASS TO LAND.   The most common defense to trespass is that the trespass was justified. For example, when a trespasser enters to assist someone in danger, a defense exists. Another defense exists when the trespasser can show that he had permission to come onto the land for a specified purpose, such as to deliver a package. Note that the property owner can revoke such permission. If the property owner asks the person delivering the package to leave and the person refuses, the package delivery person becomes a trespasser.

Trespass to Personal Property

trespass to personal property
The unlawful taking or harming of another's personal property; interference with another's right to the exclusive possession of his or her personal property.

Whenever any individual unlawfully harms the personal property of another or otherwise interferes with the owner's right to exclusively possess that personal property, **trespass to personal property** occurs. The elements of trespass to personal property are:

1. lawful possession of the property by the plaintiff and
2. unauthorized entry on or use of the property by the defendant.

TECHNOLOGY AND TODAY'S PARALEGAL

IDENTITY THEFT, SPAM, AND RELATED LEGAL ISSUES

The Internet offers a huge range of valuable services, from shopping to filing legal documents. Its popularity means that deceptive and destructive practices constantly evolve and cause problems. These problems can have legal dimensions. As a paralegal, you should be aware of problems, efforts to control them, and resources that can provide assistance.

IDENTITY THEFT

Identity theft causes much grief and tens of billions of dollars in financial losses annually. We hear horror stories about individuals having their accounts drained and their credit ruined. Most of the losses, however, fall on businesses victimized by the use of stolen financial information and other valuable data.

One type of identity theft involves *phishing*. A perpetrator "fishes" for financial data and passwords by posing as a legitimate bank, PayPal, the IRS, a credit-card company, or other reputable source. The *phisher* sends an official looking e-mail asking the recipient to "update" or "confirm" vital information. Once those data are received, the phisher quickly drains accounts.

Various government agencies provide information about identify theft and advice about preventing it or dealing with its effects:

- The Federal Trade Commission offers information at **ftc.gov**. Enter "Identity Theft" in the search box.

- At the Department of Justice website, **justice.gov**, enter "Identify Theft" in the search box.

- The Social Security Administration offers advice about stolen Social Security numbers at **ssa.gov**.

Private sources include the Identity Theft Resources Center at **idtheftcenter.org** and the Privacy Rights Clearinghouse at **privacyrights.org**.

Only give out personal information such as credit-card or bank account numbers when you verify the identity of the person you are speaking with, or when you confirm that the website you are using is secure.

THE FEDERAL CAN-SPAM ACT

Bulk, unsolicited e-mail, or *spam*, imposes a burden on an ISP's equipment as well as on e-mail recipients. Spam accounts for a high percentage of all e-mail. When dealing with clients who market goods or services through commercial e-mails, paralegals need to understand laws regulating spam. An important federal law in this area is the Controlling the Assault of Non-Solicited Pornography and Marketing (CAN-SPAM) Act. You can find information about it at the Federal Trade Commission's website. Go to **ftc.gov** and enter "CAN-SPAM" in the search box.

SPAMMING AS A TORT

Spamming may be a tort if it interferes with a computer system's functioning. A number of plaintiffs have successfully sued, under tort law, when spam overloaded a business's computer system or impaired a business's computer equipment. In these cases, spamming was held to constitute unauthorized interference with the use of the personal property of another, which is a trespass to personal property. Because a great deal of spam comes from other countries, however, tort actions are limited in their effectiveness.

TECHNOLOGY TIP

Paralegals in consumer law need to keep up to date on issues such as identity theft to protect the firm's clients and assets. Paralegals should also be familiar with the resources available to those who have complaints and with laws regulating spam and hacking.

EXAMPLE 14.9 Suppose a student takes another student's paralegal book as a practical joke and hides it so that the owner is unable to find it for a week before the final exam. In this situation, the student has engaged in a trespass to personal property.

If it can be shown that trespass to personal property was warranted, then a defense exists. Most states, for example, allow automobile repair shops to hold a customer's car (under what is called an *artisan's lien*) when the customer refuses to pay for repairs already completed. Not all service providers can do this, however. Veterinarians are generally not permitted to keep a pet until the bill owed for pet treatment has been paid.

Conversion

conversion
The act of wrongfully taking or retaining a person's personal property and placing it in the service of another.

Whenever personal property is wrongfully taken from its owner, the act of conversion occurs. The elements of conversion are:

1. the plaintiff has rightful possession of personal property,
2. the defendant intentionally interferes with that right, and
3. the interference deprives the plaintiff of the possession or use of the property.

Conversion is any act depriving an owner of personal property without that owner's permission and without just cause. When conversion occurs, the lesser offense of trespass to personal property usually occurs as well. If the initial taking of the property is unlawful, there is trespass. Keeping the property is conversion. Even if the owner permitted the initial taking of the property, failure to return it may still be conversion. Conversion is the civil side of crimes related to theft. A store clerk who steals merchandise from the store commits a crime and engages in the tort of conversion at the same time.

Even if a person mistakenly believed that she was entitled to the goods, a tort of conversion may occur.

EXAMPLE 14.10 Someone who buys stolen goods may be guilty of conversion even if she did not know that the goods were stolen. If the true owner brings a tort action against the buyer, the buyer must return the property to the owner or pay the owner the value of the property (despite having paid the thief).

Negligence

negligence
The failure to exercise the standard of care that a reasonable person would exercise in similar circumstances.

The tort of negligence occurs when someone suffers injury because of another's failure to meet a required *duty of care*. The elements of the tort of negligence are:

1. the defendant owed a duty of care to the plaintiff,
2. the defendant breached that duty,
3. the plaintiff suffered a legally recognizable injury, and
4. the defendant's breach caused the injury suffered.

In contrast to intentional torts, in torts involving negligence, the one committing the tort did not intend to commit the initial act or to bring about the consequences of the act. Rather, the actor's legally careless conduct creates a *risk* of such consequences. If no risk is created, there is no negligence. The risk must be foreseeable—that is, it must be such that a reasonable person engaging in the same activity would anticipate the risk and guard against it.

Many of the actions discussed in the section on intentional torts constitute negligence if the element of intent is missing.

EXAMPLE 14.11 If Juan intentionally shoves Naomi, who falls and breaks an arm as a result, Juan will have committed the intentional tort of battery. If Juan carelessly bumps into Naomi on the stairway because he is running down the stairs, and she falls and breaks an arm as a result, Juan's action will constitute negligence. In either situation, Juan has committed a tort.

Next, we elaborate on each of the four elements of negligence.

The Duty of Care and Its Breach

duty of care
The duty of all persons, as established by tort law, to exercise reasonable care in dealings with others. Failure to exercise due care, which is normally determined by the reasonable person standard, is the tort of negligence.

Central to the tort of negligence is the concept of a duty of care. This arises from the belief that for people to live together in society, some actions can be tolerated and some cannot. Some actions are right and some are wrong. Some actions are reasonable and some are not. The basic principle underlying the duty of care is that people are free to act as they please so long as their actions do not infringe on the interests of others.

Reasonable Person Standard

The law of torts defines and measures the duty of care by the reasonable person standard. In determining whether a duty of care has been breached, the courts ask how a reasonable person would act in the same circumstances. This standard is not necessarily how a particular person would act. That is, it is how a judge or jury thinks a person of ordinary sense should have acted under circumstances similar to those in the matter in question. That we must exercise a reasonable standard of care in our activities is a pervasive concept in the law. Many of the issues dealt with in later chapters have to do with this duty.

In negligence cases, the degree of care to be exercised depends on the defendant's occupation or profession, relationship with the plaintiff, and other factors. Generally, a breach of the duty of care is determined on a case-by-case basis. The outcome depends on how the trial court judge (or jury) decides a reasonable person in the defendant's position would have acted in the circumstances of the case. Next we examine the degree of care typically expected of property owners and professionals.

reasonable person standard
The standard of behavior expected of a hypothetical "reasonable person"; the standard against which negligence is measured and that must be observed to avoid liability for negligence.

The Duty of Property Owners

Property owners are expected to exercise reasonable care to protect invited persons coming onto their property from harm. Owners who rent or lease property to tenants are expected to exercise reasonable care to ensure that the tenants and their guests are not harmed in common areas, such as stairways and laundry rooms, by keeping them in safe condition.

DUTY TO BUSINESS INVITEES.
Retailers and other businesses that invite persons to come onto their premises have a duty to exercise reasonable care to protect those persons, who are considered business invitees.

business invitee
A person, such as a customer or a client, who is invited onto business premises by the owner of those premises for business purposes.

> **EXAMPLE 14.12** If you entered a supermarket, slipped on a wet floor from a spilled product, and suffered injuries, the owner of the supermarket could well be liable for damages. Liability could be imposed if, when you slipped, there was no sign warning that the floor was wet and no other steps had been taken to remove the slip danger. A court would likely hold that the business owner failed to exercise a reasonable degree of care in protecting the store's customers against foreseeable risks about which the owner knew or *should have known*. That a patron might slip on the wet floor and be injured as a result was a foreseeable risk, and the owner should have taken care to avoid this risk or to warn the customer of it.

The owner also has a duty to discover and remove any hidden dangers that might injure a customer or other invitee.

OPEN AND OBVIOUS RISKS.
Some risks, of course, are so obvious that the owner need not warn of them. For instance, a business owner does not need to warn customers to open a door before attempting to walk through it. Other risks, however, even though they may seem obvious to a business owner, may not be so in the eyes of another, such as a child.

> **EXAMPLE 14.13** A hardware store owner may not think it is necessary to warn customers that a stepladder leaning against the back wall of the store could fall down and harm them. It is possible, though, that a child could tip the ladder over or climb on it and be hurt as a result. In that case, the store could be held liable for leaving the ladder in an accessible area.

The Duty of Professionals

If a person has special knowledge or skill, the person's conduct must be consistent with that status. Professionals—including physicians, architects, engineers, accountants, contractors, lawyers, and others—are required to have the standard knowledge and ability expected of members of the profession. In determining what is reasonable care for professionals, their training, standards of the profession, and expertise are taken into account. In other words, an accountant cannot defend against a lawsuit for negligence by stating, "But I was not familiar with the technical rules of accounting." Furthermore, a business is held to the standard of care expected of knowledgeable people in that line of work. Thus, an auto repair shop cannot deny knowledge of the proper procedures for an oil change.

If a professional violates the duty of care toward a client, the professional may be sued for malpractice. For example, a patient might sue a physician for *medical malpractice*. Thus, a surgeon who did not follow standard procedures and thereby injured a patient would have negligently committed medical malpractice. Similarly, a client might sue an attorney for *legal malpractice* (discussed in Chapter 4) for failure to demonstrate the knowledge expected of a competent member of the bar.

The Injury Requirement and Damages

To recover damages (receive compensation), the plaintiff in a tort lawsuit must prove that she or he suffered a *legally recognizable* injury—some loss, harm, wrong, or invasion of a legally protected interest. This is generally true in lawsuits for intentional torts as well as lawsuits for negligence.

Essentially, the purpose of tort law is to compensate for legally recognized injuries resulting from wrongful acts. If no harm or injury results from a given negligent action, there is nothing to compensate.

EXAMPLE 14.14 If you carelessly bump into a passerby, who stumbles and falls as a result, you may be liable in tort if the passerby is injured in the fall. If the person is unharmed, however, there normally could be no suit for damages, because no injury was suffered.

Compensatory Damages

compensatory damages
A money award equivalent to the actual value of injuries or damages sustained by the aggrieved party.

The purpose of tort law is to compensate injured parties for damages suffered, not to punish people for the wrongs that they commit. Compensatory damages are intended to compensate, or reimburse, a plaintiff for actual losses—to make the plaintiff "whole." Occasionally, however, punitive damages are also awarded in tort lawsuits.

Punitive Damages

punitive damages
Money damages awarded to a plaintiff to punish the defendant and deter future similar conduct.

Punitive damages are intended to punish the wrongdoer and deter others from similar wrongdoing. Punitive damages are rarely awarded in lawsuits for ordinary negligence. They are more likely to be awarded in cases involving intentional torts. However, if the defendant's negligent conduct was particularly reckless or willful, a plaintiff has a greater chance of prevailing. For example, in the *Exxon Valdez* oil spill in Alaska, a jury awarded $5 billion in punitive damages against Exxon in addition to $287 million in actual damages. (This award was later reduced to $507.5 million on appeal.)

Causation

causation in fact
Causation brought about by an act or omission without which an event would not have occurred.

Another element necessary to a tort is *causation*. If a person fails in a duty of care and someone suffers injury, the wrongful activity must have caused the harm for a tort to be committed. In deciding whether there is causation, the court must address two questions:

- *Is there causation in fact?* Did the injury occur because of the defendant's act, or would it have occurred anyway? If an injury would not have occurred without the defendant's act, then there is causation in fact. Causation in fact can usually be

Paralegals who work in the area of tort law often assist in litigation involving automobile accidents. Investigating the facts of the accident and preparing sketches are usually an important aspect of the paralegal's job. What is the relationship between fact investigation and preparation of sketches for trial?

determined by the use of the *but for* test: "but for" the wrongful act, the injury would not have occurred.

EXAMPLE 14.15 Annie runs a red light and runs into Joe's car. The accident would not have occurred but for Annie's running the red light, so she is liable.

- *Was the act the proximate cause of the injury?* Proximate cause, or legal cause, exists when the connection between an act and an injury is strong enough to justify imposing liability.

EXAMPLE 14.16 Arnie runs a red light and hits Nicki's car. Her car has explosives in the trunk, and they explode when the car is hit. The explosion hurts bystanders. The injured bystanders cannot sue Arnie. His negligence was the cause in fact of the accident, but it was not the proximate cause of the bystanders' injuries. The likelihood of that incident was so remote, Arnie could not have foreseen that possibility. The bystanders may be able to sue Nicki, however, because it is not reasonable to transport explosives in the trunk of a car.

Both questions must be answered in the affirmative for liability in tort to arise. If a defendant's action constitutes causation in fact but a court decides that the action is not the proximate cause of the plaintiff's injury, the causation requirement has not been met—and the defendant normally will not be liable to the plaintiff. Notice in the discussion of these matters the detailed information that is required. The *Featured Contributor* on the following pages discusses the kind of research that may be required in a liability case.

proximate cause
Legal cause; exists when the connection between an act and an injury is strong enough to justify imposing liability.

Defenses to Negligence

Defendants often defend against negligence claims by asserting that the plaintiffs have failed to prove the existence of one or more of the required elements for negligence. Additionally, there are three basic *affirmative* defenses to negligence claims that defendants can raise to avoid or reduce their liability even if the facts are as the plaintiff claims: (1) assumption of risk, (2) superseding cause, and (3) contributory or comparative negligence.

FEATURED CONTRIBUTOR

IN-DEPTH RESEARCH AND ATTENTION TO DETAIL

Kenneth O'Neil Salyer

BIOGRAPHICAL NOTE

Kenneth O'Neil Salyer earned his undergraduate, J.D., and Master of Arts in Teaching degrees at the University of Louisville. He is licensed to practice law in the state of Kentucky and has litigated tort, products liability, and real estate matters. He has served as chair of the legal studies department at a college in Louisville. Mr. Salyer consults with colleges across the country about online education and remains active in the legal community. He is the head coach for the University of Louisville undergraduate moot court teams.

"Neil," said the managing partner, "I need you to go with Laura to research the history of asbestos-insulation installation in Kentucky buildings prior to 1965." I received this directive during my third year of law school while clerking at a personal-injury defense firm that specialized in mass torts and products liability cases. Without any construction or engineering experience, I was severely overwhelmed and woefully underprepared to

execute this task successfully. I knew the firm was defending certain businesses in mesothelioma litigation, but had no idea why the history of asbestos insulation was so important, and worse, no idea how to find the answer.

The aforementioned "Laura" was the managing partner's lead paralegal; she had worked on asbestos and mesothelioma cases for longer than I had been with the firm. Without hesita-

Assumption of Risk

A plaintiff who voluntarily enters into a risky situation, knowing the risk involved, will not be allowed to recover. This is the defense of assumption of risk. The requirements of this defense are (1) knowledge of the risk and (2) voluntary assumption of the risk. Remember, the defendant has the burden of proof of establishing these.

The risk can be assumed by express agreement, or the assumption of risk can be implied by the plaintiff's knowledge of the risk and subsequent conduct.

> **EXAMPLE 14.17** Bob, a race car driver, enters a NASCAR race. Because he knows there is a risk of being killed or injured in a crash, a liability suit in case of an accident is unlikely to be successful.

Of course, the plaintiff does not assume a risk different from or greater than the risk normally carried by the activity. In the scenario just mentioned, the race driver does not assume the risk that the operators of the raceway will do nothing about an oil slick on the track.

In emergency situations, risks are not considered assumed. Neither are they assumed when a statute protects a class of people from harm and a member of the class is injured by the harm.

> **EXAMPLE 14.18** Employees are protected by statute from harmful working conditions and therefore do not assume the risks associated with the workplace. An employee who is injured will generally be compensated regardless of fault under state workers' compensation statutes (to be discussed in Chapter 18).

assumption of risk
Voluntarily taking on a known risk; a defense against negligence that can be used when the plaintiff has knowledge of and appreciates a danger and voluntarily exposes himself or herself to the danger.

tion, she took me under her wing and quickly taught me what it takes to be a topflight legal professional in the competitive world of tort and products liability litigation.

We logged countless hours traveling across the state to every library with an engineering or construction section housing historical records. We found engineering specs from the 1950s, scoured old building codes, and located regional "best practices," all in an effort to better equip our attorneys in their upcoming mass tort litigation.

Once all the information had been gathered, Laura explained how to piece it together like a jigsaw puzzle. We had to determine the questions and then formulate the answers to provide the managing partner the necessary knowledge to become an expert in this non-legal field. I quickly learned that exceptionally good attorneys are not just experts at the law; they also become experts in the fields in which they litigate. This expertise comes not only from personal research and knowledge, but also the research performed by their trusted paralegals.

For this case, the attorney needed to know and understand the common practices at the time the buildings in question were built, as well as asbestos research that was readily available at the time. Both of these would help determine liability of the business and the builder.

> **Good attorneys become experts in the fields in which they litigate"**

Laura taught me many things about success in the legal field: extreme attention to detail, thinking outside the box when presented with complex questions, and most importantly, going above and beyond what was necessary to ensure success for a client. Our days of traversing the state and sitting in dark, damp libraries flipping through moldy records helped the clients prove to the jury that they acted in good faith by following standard procedures of the time.

After law school, and throughout my years as a litigator, I always made sure a competent, trustworthy paralegal was by my side. I never walked into trial without feeling I knew more about the subject at hand than opposing counsel. Simply stated, this would have been impossible without the help of knowledgeable, driven, and exceptional paralegals.

When I began teaching students how to be effective paralegals, Laura's early lessons never left my mind. An intimate understanding of the law is important, but it is not the only skill one needs to be an effective, high-performing paralegal. Your attention to detail and ability to think outside the box when addressing in-class questions, homework, and more will be key to success when you enter the highly professional and stressful world of a legal professional.

Superseding Cause

An unforeseeable intervening event may break the connection between a wrongful act and an injury to another. If so, it acts as a *superseding cause*—that is, it relieves a defendant of liability for injuries caused by the intervening event.

EXAMPLE 14.19 Suppose that Derrick keeps a container of gasoline in the trunk of his car. Carrying the gasoline creates a foreseeable risk and is negligent. If Derrick's car crashes into a tree, causing the gasoline can to explode, Derrick will be liable for injuries sustained by passing pedestrians because of his negligence. If lightning striking the car causes the explosion, however, the lightning supersedes Derrick's original negligence as a cause of the damage, because the lightning strike was so unlikely as to not be foreseeable.

Contributory and Comparative Negligence

All people are expected to exercise a reasonable degree of care in looking out for themselves. In a few jurisdictions, recovery for injury resulting from negligence is prevented if the plaintiff was also negligent. This is the defense of contributory negligence. Under the common law doctrine of contributory negligence, any negligence by the plaintiff means the plaintiff will not recover damages.

Most states apply the doctrine of comparative negligence. Here, the plaintiff's negligence and the defendant's negligence are compared and the liability for damages distributed accordingly. Some jurisdictions have adopted a "pure" form of comparative negligence that allows the plaintiff to recover, even if his fault is greater than that of

contributory negligence
A theory in tort law under which a complaining party's own negligence contributed to his or her injuries. Contributory negligence is an absolute bar to recovery in some jurisdictions.

comparative negligence
A theory in tort law under which the liability for injuries resulting from negligent acts is shared by all persons who were guilty of negligence (including the injured party) on the basis of each person's proportionate carelessness.

the defendant. For example, if the plaintiff was 80 percent at fault and the defendant 20 percent at fault, the plaintiff may recover 20 percent of her damages. Many states' comparative negligence statutes, however, contain a "50 percent" rule by which the plaintiff recovers nothing if he was more than 50 percent at fault.

Special Negligence Doctrines and Statutes

There are a number of special doctrines and statutes relating to negligence. We examine only a few of them here.

Negligence *Per Se*

negligence *per se*
An action or failure to act in violation of a statutory requirement.

Certain conduct, whether it consists of an action or a failure to act, may be treated as negligence *per se* (*per se* means "in or of itself"). Negligence *per se* may occur if an individual violates a statute or an ordinance providing for a criminal penalty and that violation causes another to be injured. The injured person must prove:

1. that the statute sets out what standard of conduct is expected, when and where it is expected, and of whom it is expected,

2. that she is in the class intended to be protected by the statute, and

3. that the statute was designed to prevent the type of injury that was suffered.

The standard of conduct required by the statute is the duty that the defendant owes to the plaintiff, and a violation of the statute is the breach of that duty.

EXAMPLE 14.20 A statute requires property owners to keep buildings in safe condition and may subject owners to a criminal penalty, such as a fine, if the building is not kept safe. The statute is meant to protect those who are rightfully in the building. Thus, if an owner, without sufficient excuse, violates the statute and a tenant is injured as a result, then most courts will hold that the owner's unexcused violation of the statute establishes a breach of a duty of care—the owner's violation is negligence *per se*.

Special Negligence Statutes

Good Samaritan statute
A state statute stipulating that persons who provide emergency services to others in peril—unless they do so recklessly, thus causing further harm—cannot be sued for negligence.

dram shop act
A state statute that imposes liability on the owners of bars, as well as those who serve alcoholic drinks to the public, for injuries resulting from accidents caused by intoxicated persons when the sellers or servers of alcoholic drinks contributed to the intoxication.

cyber tort
A tort committed by use of the Internet.

Many states have enacted statutes prescribing responsibilities in certain circumstances. Most states have what are called Good Samaritan statutes. Under these, persons who receive voluntary aid from others cannot turn around and sue the "Good Samaritans" for negligence. These laws were passed largely to protect medical personnel who volunteer their services in emergency situations to those in need, such as people hurt in car accidents.

Many states have passed dram shop acts. A bar owner or bartender may be held liable for injuries caused by a person who became intoxicated while drinking at the bar or who was already intoxicated when served by the bartender. In some states, statutes impose liability on *social hosts* (persons hosting parties) for injuries caused by guests who became intoxicated at the hosts' homes. For liability to be imposed, it is unnecessary to prove that the bar owner, bartender, or social host was negligent.

Cyber Torts: Defamation Online

Who should be held liable for cyber torts, or torts committed in cyberspace? For example, who should be held liable when someone posts a defamatory message online? Should an Internet service provider (ISP) that provides access to the Internet be liable for the remark?

Cyber torts (like cyber crimes, discussed in Chapter 13) are not new torts as much as they are new ways of committing torts that present special issues of proof. How, for example, can it be proved that an online defamatory remark was "published," which requires that a third party see or hear it? How can the identity of the person who made the remark be discovered?

Liability of Internet Service Providers

Online forums allow anyone—customers, employees, or crackpots—to complain about a business firm's personnel, policies, practices, or products. Regardless of whether the complaint is justified, it might have an impact on the business. One question that created problems for the courts was whether providers of such forums could be held liable for defamatory statements. Congress responded with the Communications Decency Act, which states that Internet service providers, or "interactive computer service providers," are not liable for such material.[1]

Piercing the Veil of Anonymity

A problem for anyone who seeks to sue for online defamation is discovering the identity of the person who posted the defamatory message. ISPs can disclose personal information about their customers only when ordered to do so by a court. Because of this, businesses and individuals have resorted to lawsuits against unidentified "John Does." Then, using the authority of the courts, they might obtain from the ISPs the identities of the persons responsible for the messages.

EXAMPLE 14.21 Eric Hvide, former chief executive of a company called Hvide Marine, sued a number of "John Does" who had posted allegedly defamatory statements about him and his company on online message boards. Hvide sued the John Does for libel in a Florida court. The court ruled that Yahoo and AOL had to reveal the identities of the defendant Does. Hvide was then able to amend his complaint to substitute the names of the actual individuals for the "John Does" listed in his original complaint.

In some cases, the rights of plaintiffs in such situations have been balanced against the defendants' rights to free speech. Some courts have concluded that more than a bare allegation of defamation is required to outweigh an individual's right to anonymity in the exercise of free speech.

Strict Liability

Intentional torts and torts of negligence involve acts that depart from a reasonable standard of care and cause injuries. Under the doctrine of strict liability, liability for injury is imposed for reasons other than fault. Traditionally, strict liability was imposed for damages proximately caused by an abnormally dangerous or exceptional activity.

Abnormally dangerous activities have three characteristics. The activities:

1. involve potential harm, of a serious nature, to persons or property,

2. involve a high degree of risk that cannot be completely guarded against by the exercise of reasonable care, and

3. are not commonly performed in the community or area.

The primary basis of liability is the creation of an extraordinary risk. Even if blasting with dynamite in construction is performed with all reasonable care, for instance, there is still a risk of injury. Balancing that risk against the potential for harm, the person engaged in the activity will pay for any injury it causes. Knowing that they will be liable for any injuries, those engaged in such activities have strong incentives to use extreme caution.

The most significant application of strict liability is in the area of *product liability*—liability of manufacturers and sellers for harmful or defective products. This is a newer application of the doctrine of strict liability.

strict liability
Liability regardless of fault. In tort law, strict liability may be imposed on a merchant who introduces into commerce a good that is so defective as to be unreasonably dangerous.

Product Liability

Those who manufacture or sell goods can be held liable for injuries and damages caused by defects under the law of **product liability**. Liability is based on the notion that manufacturers are better able to bear the cost of injury than innocent victims. In addition, requiring producers to pay for injuries caused by their products encourages them to make safer products. The kinds of issues that arise for paralegals who work in this area of law are discussed in the *Developing Paralegal Skills* feature below.

Theories of Product Liability

A party who is injured by a defective product can bring a suit against the product's seller or manufacturer under several theories. These theories include negligence, misrepresentation, and strict product liability.

Product Liability Based on Negligence

If a manufacturer fails to exercise due care to make a product safe, *any person* who is injured by the product can sue the manufacturer for negligence. The plaintiff does not have to be the person who bought the product. The manufacturer must use due care in designing the product, selecting the materials, producing and assembling the product, testing and inspecting the product for safety, and placing adequate warnings on the label to inform users of dangers.

Product Liability Based on Misrepresentation

When a manufacturer or seller misrepresents the quality, nature, or appropriate use of a product, and the user is injured as a result, the basis of liability may be the tort of fraud.

DEVELOPING PARALEGAL SKILLS

HANDLING PRODUCT-RELATED CLAIMS

Product liability cases make up almost 7% of personal injury cases in the United States. These affect products used in every American home, from cars to toys. For example, there are over 200,000 toy-related injuries annually. Product-related injuries can be caused by anything from choking on a small part in a toy to an electric vehicle's battery catching fire.

If a client brings a product liability case to your firm, there are important steps to take in the course of the investigation of the claim. You must attempt to locate and preserve the product that allegedly caused the injury. This may require quick action. If an individual is injured in a car accident in which you suspect there may be a product defect as a cause, you will need to contact the owner (if different from your client), garage, towing company, or police impound lot that has possession of the vehicle

and ask them to refrain from any work on or disposal of the vehicle. You will also want to inspect it as soon as possible. You will need photographs, a secure chain of custody for the product, and an expert inspection of it.

If an injury led to an ambulance or police call, you will want to secure authenticated copies of any tapes of the calls or records created. If anyone saw a doctor as a result of the product's malfunction, you will need his or her medical records. If someone died, you will want his or her death certificate and autopsy report (if any). Getting these records and any witness statements quickly is important to your supervising attorney's evaluation of the case.

Product liability cases often involve considerable technical evidence. Knowing the scientific and engineering terms and being able to interact with experts in these areas will make you a more effective paralegal.

Generally, the misrepresentation must have been made knowingly or with reckless disregard for the facts, and the party must have intended the user to rely on the statement.

Strict Product Liability

Under the doctrine of strict liability, a manufacturer that has exercised reasonable care can still be held liable if a product is defective and injures someone. Strict product liability reflects the general principle that the law should protect consumers from unsafe and dangerous products. The rule of strict liability is also applicable to the suppliers of component parts that are used in the final product.

Strict liability will be imposed if the plaintiff can establish the following six requirements:

1. The product must be in a defective condition when the defendant sells it.

2. The defendant must normally be engaged in the business of selling the product.

3. The product must be unreasonably dangerous to the user or consumer because of its defective condition (in most states).

4. The plaintiff must incur physical harm to self or property by use or consumption of the product.

5. The defective condition must be the proximate cause of the injury or damage.

6. The goods must not have been substantially changed from the time the product was sold to the time the injury was sustained.[2]

Note that the plaintiff is not required to show why or how the product became defective. The plaintiff must only prove that the unreasonably dangerous product caused the injury and that the condition of the product was essentially the same as when it was sold. A product may be unreasonably dangerous due to a flaw in the manufacturing process, a design defect, or an inadequate warning.

> **unreasonably dangerous product**
> A product that is defective to the point of threatening a consumer's health and safety. A product will be considered unreasonably dangerous if it is dangerous beyond the expectation of the ordinary consumer or if a less dangerous alternative was economically feasible for the manufacturer, but the manufacturer failed to produce it.

MANUFACTURING DEFECTS.   A product that departs from its intended design, even though all possible care was exercised in the preparation and marketing of the product, has a manufacturing defect. Liability is imposed on the manufacturer (and possibly on the wholesaler and retailer) regardless of whether the manufacturer acted "reasonably."

DESIGN DEFECTS.   A product has a design defect if the foreseeable risks of harm posed by the product could have been reduced or avoided by adopting an economically feasible, reasonable alternative design. The *Ethics Watch* feature on the next page discusses how work and personal life can conflict even in this area of law.

WARNING DEFECTS.   A product may also be deemed to be defective because of inadequate instructions or warnings in situations in which the risk of harm was foreseeable and could have been avoided if a proper warning had been given.

In evaluating the adequacy of warnings, courts consider the risks of the product and whether the content of the warning was understandable to the expected user.[3] For example, children would likely respond better to bright, bold, simple warning labels, whereas adults may benefit from more detailed information.

Sellers must warn those who purchase their products of harms that can result from the *foreseeable misuse* of the product. The key is the foreseeability of the misuse. Sellers are not required to take precautions against every possible unusual use of their products.

Defenses to Product Liability

There is no duty to warn about risks that are obvious or commonly known. Gas stations do not have to warn consumers to avoid drinking gasoline. Knives are supposed to be sharp. Warnings about *obvious risks* do not add to the safety of a product and could even detract from it by making other warnings seem less significant.

ETHICS WATCH

CONFIDENTIALITY AND PRODUCT LIABILITY

Paralegals who work in the area of product liability may find themselves in a sticky situation. For example, suppose your firm represents a particular toy manufacturer. The toy firm sells a toy that is popular for young children. The toy, however, is apparently defective and has injured a few children. It has not been recalled. Everything you know about this toy you have learned from the work you have done on the case.

Should you talk to your attorney about the possibility of discussing with the client the possibility of a voluntary recall? Suppose some of your friends have children around that age. Can you warn your friends about the defective toy? If you tell one person, you may violate the ethical rule of confidentiality. What if you don't warn someone and that person's child is injured?

This is just one example of ethical dilemmas that may arise for paralegals who work in the area of product liability. In circumstances such as these, it is advisable to consult your supervising attorney for direction.

The issue discussed here is related to the NALA *Code of Ethics and Professional Responsibility*, Canon 4: "A paralegal must use discretion and professional judgment commensurate with knowledge and experience but must not render independent legal judgment in place of an attorney." It is also related to the NFPA *Model Code of Ethics*, Section EC 1.5: "A paralegal shall preserve all confidential information provided by the client or acquired from other sources before, during, and after the course of the professional relationship."

Reprinted by permission of the National Federation of Paralegal Associations, Inc.(NFPA®). www.paralegals.org.; Copyright 1975; Adopted 1975; Revised 1979, 1988, 1995, 2007. Reprinted with permission of NALA, the Association for Paralegals–Legal Assistants. Inquiries should be directed to NALA, 1516 S. Boston, #200, Tulsa, OK 74119, www.nala.org.

To avoid liability under product liability, the defendant can show that there is no basis for the plaintiff's claim or that the plaintiff has not met the requirements for liability. For example, if the suit alleges a product caused an injury and the defendant proves that the product did not cause the plaintiff's injury, the defendant will not be liable. Defendants may also assert the affirmative defenses discussed next.

Assumption of Risk

The obviousness of a risk and a user's decision to proceed in the face of that risk may be a defense in a product liability suit. For example, if a buyer ignored a product recall by the seller, a court might conclude that the buyer had assumed the risk. To establish this defense, the defendant must show that:

1. the plaintiff knew and appreciated the risk created by the product defect, and

2. the plaintiff voluntarily assumed the risk, even though it was unreasonable to do so.

Product Misuse

Defendants can also claim that the plaintiff misused the product. This defense is similar to claiming that the plaintiff assumed the risk. Here, however, the use was not the one for which the product was designed. If the misuse is reasonably foreseeable, the seller must take measures to guard against it, such as by warning consumers, but if a consumer does something dangerous, such as use a chain saw to trim toenails, the chainsaw maker is not liable.

Comparative Negligence

Developments in the area of comparative negligence (discussed earlier in this chapter) have affected the doctrine of strict liability. Most jurisdictions consider the negligent or intentional actions of both the plaintiff and the defendant when apportioning liability and damages.

Consumer Law

Since the 1960s, many laws have been passed to protect the health and safety of consumers. A consumer is a person who purchases, for private use, goods or services from business firms. Sources of consumer protection exist at all levels of government. Exhibit 14.1 below indicates some of the areas of consumer law regulated by statutes that are expanded by regulations. Many federal agencies have an office of consumer affairs, and most states have one or more such offices, including the offices of state attorneys general, to assist consumers.

All statutes, agency rules, and common law judicial decisions that serve to protect the interests of consumers are classified as consumer law. Because of the wide variation among state consumer protection laws, our primary focus here is on federal legislation—specifically, on legislation governing deceptive advertising, labeling and packaging, sales, health protection, product safety, and credit protection. However, as Exhibit 14.1 shows, states also provide protection for business practices that can injure consumers.

consumer
A person who buys products and services for personal or household use.

consumer law
Statutes, agency rules, and judicial decisions protecting consumers of goods and services.

Deceptive Sales Practices

Under the common law, if a seller misrepresented the quality, price, or availability of a certain product, the consumer's recourse was to sue the seller for fraud or for breach of contract. Fraud requires proof of *intent* to misrepresent the product's usefulness to the buyer. Frequently, the burden of having to prove intent was too great, and consumers were left with little or no legal recourse against deceptive practices. Whether the claim

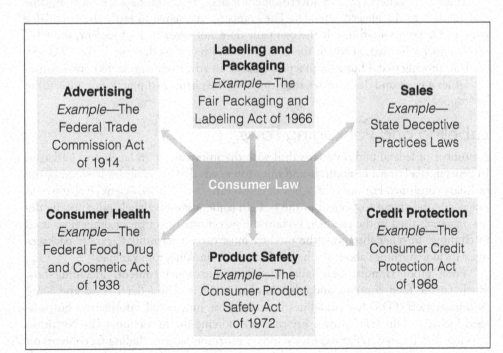

EXHIBIT 14.1

Selected Areas of Consumer Law Regulated by Statutes

is fraud or breach of contract, litigation is costly, so consumers rarely pursue actions involving relatively small losses, even if they would be likely to win the cases.

Today, various agencies, both federal and state, are empowered to protect consumers from deceptive business practices. At the federal level, the most important agency is the Federal Trade Commission (FTC). The Federal Trade Commission Act authorizes the FTC to determine what constitutes a deceptive practice. The FTC policy on deception holds that a practice is deceptive and subject to agency action if:

1. there is misrepresentation or omission of information in a communication to consumers,

2. the deception is likely to mislead a reasonable consumer, and

3. the deception is material—it is likely to be misleading to the detriment of consumers.

This broad definition allows the FTC to attack a wide variety of business practices, as do statutes such as the California Civil Code, Chapter 3, which concerns deceptive practices. Besides such general regulations, there are more specific areas of regulation, as we see next.

Deceptive Advertising

Over the past several decades, consumers have received increased protection against deceptive advertising. Deceptive advertising comes in many forms. Deception may arise from a false statement or claim about a company's own products or a competitor's products. Some advertisements contain "half-truths," meaning that the information presented is true but incomplete, leading consumers to a false conclusion.

EXAMPLE 14.22 The makers of Campbell's soups advertised that most Campbell's soups were low in fat and cholesterol and thus were helpful in fighting heart disease. What the ads did not say was that Campbell's soups are high in sodium and that high-sodium diets may increase the risk of heart disease. The FTC ruled that Campbell's claims were thus deceptive.

Generally the test for whether an ad is deceptive is *whether a reasonable consumer would be deceived by the ad.*

If the FTC believes that an advertisement is deceptive, it drafts a formal complaint and sends it to the alleged offender. The company may agree to settle the complaint without further proceedings. If the company does not agree to a settlement, the FTC can conduct a hearing, at which the company can present its defense. If the FTC succeeds in proving that a business practice, such as an advertisement, is deceptive, it usually issues a cease-and-desist order requiring that the challenged practice or advertising be stopped.

Labeling and Packaging Laws

A number of federal and state laws deal with the information on labels and packages. In general, labels must be accurate and must use words that are easily understood by the ordinary consumer. For instance, a box of cereal cannot be labeled "giant" if that would exaggerate the amount of cereal in the box. In some instances, labels must specify the raw materials used in the product, such as the percentage of cotton or other fiber used in clothing. In other instances, the product must carry a warning. Cigarette packages must include warnings about the health hazards of smoking, for example.

Food products must bear labels detailing nutritional content, including how much fat the food contains and what kind of fat it is. The federal Food and Drug Administration (FDA) has guidelines to standardize nutritional information on packaged foods, and the FTC plays a key role in enforcing the restrictions. The Nutrition Labeling and Education Act requires standard nutrition facts (including fat content) on

deception
In consumer law, a material misrepresentation or omission in information that is likely to mislead a reasonable consumer to his or her detriment.

deceptive advertising
Advertising that misleads consumers, either by unjustified claims concerning a product's performance or by failure to disclose relevant information concerning the product's composition or performance.

cease-and-desist order
An administrative or judicial order prohibiting a person or business firm from conducting activities that an agency or court has deemed illegal.

food labels, regulates the use of such terms as *fresh*, *low fat*, and *organic*, and, subject to FDA approval, authorizes certain health claims.

Sales Transactions

Many laws that protect consumers require the disclosure of terms in sales transactions and provide rules governing certain sales, such as door-to-door sales, mail-order sales, and the receipt of unsolicited merchandise. One FTC regulation, for example, requires sellers to give consumers three days to cancel any door-to-door sale. In addition, the FTC requires that consumers be notified in Spanish of this right if the oral negotiations for the sale were in Spanish. The FTC also has rules requiring sellers of some goods and services (such as used cars and funeral services) to disclose particular information to consumers. Most states have enacted laws specifically governing consumer sales transactions or broad consumer deception that apply to a wide range of practices.

Consumer Health and Safety

Regulating the labeling and packaging of products helps to promote consumer health and safety. But there is a difference between regulating information about a product and regulating the content of the product.

> **EXAMPLE 14.23** Tobacco products have not been altered by regulation or banned despite their known hazards. Rather, regulations require producers to warn consumers about the hazards of tobacco. If people choose to use tobacco products with knowledge of the risks to their health, that is their choice.

We now look at several laws that regulate the actual products made available to consumers.

In 1906, Congress passed the Pure Food and Drug Act, which was the first legislation aimed at protecting consumers against impure and misbranded food and drug products. In 1938, the Federal Food, Drug and Cosmetic Act was passed to strengthen the 1906 law. These acts and later amendments established standards for foods, specified safe levels of food additives, and regulated some aspects of food advertising. They also required that drugs must be proved effective as well as safe before they could receive permission to be sold. The Food and Drug Administration enforces most of the statutes involving food and drugs, but the Department of Agriculture has jurisdiction over some food products.

Still other statutes, categorized as product-safety acts, regulate the distribution of hazardous or defective products. One example is the Consumer Product Safety Act, enacted to protect consumers from dangerous products. The Consumer Product Safety Commission, which was created by the act, conducts research on the safety of products and maintains a clearinghouse on the risks associated with various products. The Commission sets standards for consumer products and bans the sale of products it deems hazardous to consumers. Products banned include unsafe fireworks, cribs, and toys, as well as many products containing asbestos, lead, or vinyl chloride.

Consumer Credit Protection

Because of the extensive use of credit by American consumers, credit protection has become an important area of consumer protection legislation. One of the most significant statutes regulating the credit and credit-card industry is the Truth-in-Lending Act (TILA), the name commonly given to Title 1 of the Consumer Credit Protection Act, passed by Congress in 1968 and greatly expanded since then.

The Truth-in-Lending Act

The TILA is basically a *disclosure law*. It is administered by the Consumer Financial Protection Bureau (CFPB) and requires sellers and lenders to disclose credit terms or loan terms so that borrowers can shop around for the best financing arrangements.

TILA requirements apply only to entities that, in the ordinary course of business, lend money, sell on credit, or arrange for the extension of credit. Sales or loans made between two consumers do not come under the act. Additionally, the act only protects persons (not businesses). Under TILA, terms of a credit instrument must be clearly and conspicuously (obviously) disclosed and must follow regulations. This law provides that a consumer can cancel a contract if a creditor fails to follow exactly the required procedures.

EQUAL OPPORTUNITY.   The Equal Credit Opportunity Act (ECOA) amended TILA in 1974. It prohibits the denial of credit solely on the basis of race, religion, national origin, color, gender, marital status, age, or whether or not a credit applicant receives public-assistance benefits. Creditors may not collect information about any of these characteristics from an applicant and may not require the signature of an applicant's spouse, other than as a joint applicant.

CREDIT CARDS.   The TILA also contains provisions regarding credit cards. One provision limits the liability of a cardholder to $50 per card for unauthorized charges made before the creditor is notified that the card has been lost. Another provision prohibits a credit-card company from billing a consumer for any unauthorized charges on a credit card that was improperly issued by the company. Further provisions of the act concern billing disputes related to credit-card purchases. The act outlines specific procedures and time deadlines for both the consumer and the credit-card company to follow in settling a dispute.

The Credit Card Accountability Responsibility and Disclosure (CARD) Act of 2009 also provides protection for credit card holders. It limits the fees credit-card companies can charge for various services, thereby reducing the average cost of possessing a credit card. The main impact is not on interest rate but on fees for such things as late payments, fees for charging more than the approved credit limit, and unexpected rate increases over time. The CARD Act focuses on transparent information provided in plain language by card issuers. The Consumer Financial Protection Bureau is responsible for implementing the statute.

Fair Credit Reporting

Lenders use *credit reports* to decide whether and how much to lend to prospective borrowers. To protect consumers against inaccurate credit reporting, Congress enacted the Fair Credit Reporting Act. It provides that consumer credit reporting agencies—such as Equifax, TransUnion, and Experian—may issue credit reports only for specified purposes. This includes the extension of credit, the issuance of insurance policies, and compliance with a court order. A report may also be issued in response to a consumer's request for a copy of her own credit report. When a consumer is denied credit or insurance on the basis of a credit report, the consumer must be notified of that fact and of the name and address of the credit-reporting agency that issued the credit report.

Under the act, consumers may request the source of any information being given out by a credit agency, as well as the identity of any party that received an agency's report. Consumers also have access to the information contained about them in a credit reporting agency's files. If a consumer discovers that these files contain inaccurate information, the agency, on the consumer's written request, must investigate. If the investigation reveals that the information is unverifiable or inaccurate, the agency must delete it within a reasonable period of time.

Fair and Accurate Credit Transactions Act

To help combat identity theft, Congress passed the Fair and Accurate Credit Transactions (FACT) Act. It established a fraud alert system so that consumers who suspect that they have been victimized by identity theft can place an alert on their credit files. The act also requires the major credit reporting agencies to provide consumers with free copies of their own credit reports every twelve months. Since 2008, the act has required that financial institutions work with the FTC to identify "red flag" indicators of identity theft and to develop rules on how to dispose of sensitive credit information.

The FACT Act gives consumers who have been victimized by identity theft some assistance in rebuilding their credit reputations. For example, credit reporting agencies must stop reporting allegedly fraudulent account information once the consumer establishes that identify theft has occurred. Business owners and creditors are required to provide consumers with copies of any records that can help the consumer prove that a particular account or transaction is fraudulent (a forged signature, for example).

Fair Debt-Collection Practices

Congress passed the Fair Debt Collection Practices Act (FDCPA) to curb abuses by collection agencies. The act applies to debt-collection agencies that regularly attempt to collect debts on behalf of someone else.

The act prohibits contacting consumers at their place of employment if the employers object, contacting consumers at inconvenient times, and contacting consumers if attorneys represent them. The act also prohibits debt-collection agencies from contacting most third parties about a debt unless authorized to do so by a court, using harassment and intimidation (such as abusive language), using false or misleading information, and communicating with the consumer after receipt of a notice that the consumer is refusing to pay the debt except to advise the consumer of legal action being taken by the agency.

EXAMPLE 14.24 West Asset Management, a debt collector, was sued for harassment under the FDCPA for repeatedly calling a widow and trying to convince her to pay a debt owed by her deceased husband to Bank of America. The widow had no obligation to repay the debt, as Bank of America and the debt collector knew. A Florida court held that both Bank of America and the debt collector could be liable for improper debt-collection tactics.

Garnishment Proceedings

Creditors have numerous remedies available to them when consumers fail to pay their debts. Among these remedies is garnishment. Garnishment occurs when a creditor, after complying with procedures mandated by state law, legally seizes a portion of a debtor's property (usually wages) in the possession of a third party (such as an employer). The creditor must obtain an *order of garnishment* from the court. It allows the creditor to have access to the debtor's wages while they are in the control of the employer. Laws governing garnishment vary considerably from state to state.

Both federal and state laws limit the amount that can be taken from a debtor's take-home pay. The federal Consumer Credit Protection Act provides that a debtor can keep either 75 percent of the net earnings per week or a sum equivalent to the pay for thirty hours of work at federal minimum wage rates, whichever is greater. State laws also provide dollar exemptions, and these amounts are often larger than those provided by federal law.

Employers dislike garnishment proceedings. Such proceedings impose time costs on employers (possible appearance at court hearings, record-keeping costs, and the like). To protect the job security of employees whose wages are subject to garnishment, federal law provides that garnishment of an employee's wages usually cannot be grounds for that employee's dismissal. The *Developing Paralegal Skills* feature on the following page discusses this issue further with respect to the role that may involve a paralegal.

garnishment
A proceeding in which a creditor legally seizes a portion of a debtor's property (such as wages) that is in the possession of a third party (such as an employer).

DEVELOPING PARALEGAL SKILLS

DISCHARGED FOR GARNISHMENT

Eva White works as a paralegal for a firm that specializes in employment law. A business client has called Eva's supervising attorney to ask for advice concerning garnishment. Basically, the client wants to know if he can fire an employee so that he can avoid having to comply with garnishment proceedings that have been initiated against the employee. The attorney has asked Eva to research recent case law and current statutes and regulations on the question of whether an employer may fire an employee for this reason.

Eva goes online to research garnishment and locates a case in which an employee was fired two days after his employer received notice of garnishment. The case turned on whether the employer had notice that the garnishment proceedings had already been initiated against the employee. She reads the case and finds a citation to the statute. Eva's next step is to check the statute itself to ensure that she has up-to-date knowledge of how the statute is being applied.

CHECKLIST FOR LEGAL RESEARCH

- Locate statutes and regulations issued under the statutes.
- Locate case law to see how the statute and regulations have been interpreted and applied and whether the statute has been found to be unconstitutional.
- Update your case law findings by checking a citator (see Chapter 8) to make sure that the holding in the case is still good law.
- Update the statute by checking the pocket part or using a citator to see if the statute has been amended or repealed.

KEY TERMS AND CONCEPTS

actionable   420
actual malice   421
appropriation   421
assault   418
assumption of risk   430
battery   418
business invitee   427
business tort   423
causation in fact   428
cease-and-desist order   438
comparative negligence   431
compensatory damages   428
consumer   437
consumer law   437
contributory negligence   431
conversion   426

cyber tort   432
deception   438
deceptive advertising   438
defamation   420
dram shop act   432
duty of care   426
elements   417
false imprisonment   419
fraudulent misrepresentation   422
garnishment   441
Good Samaritan statute   432
intentional infliction of
   emotional distress   420
intentional tort   417
libel   420
negligence   426

negligence *per se*   432
predatory behavior   423
privilege   420
product liability   434
proximate cause   429
punitive damages   428
reasonable person standard   427
slander   420
strict liability   433
tort   417
tortfeasor   417
trespass to land   424
trespass to personal property   424
unreasonably dangerous
   product   435

Chapter Summary / Tort Law, Product Liability, and Consumer Law

THE BASIS OF TORT LAW

Two notions serve as the basis of all torts: wrongs and compensation. Tort law recognizes that some acts are wrong because they cause injuries to others. A *tort* is a civil wrong. In a tort action, one person or group brings a personal-injury suit against another person or group to obtain compensation (money damages) or other relief for the harm suffered. Tort law provides remedies for the invasion of protected interests, such as physical security, privacy, freedom of movement, and reputation. Torts fall into two broad classifications: *intentional torts* and *negligence*.

INTENTIONAL TORTS

Intentional torts are when the actor intended to perform an act that resulted in an injury to a protected right of another party.

1. *Intentional torts against persons*—Intentional acts that violate protected interests under the common law.

    a. An assault is an intentional act that causes another person to be apprehensive or fearful of immediate harm. A battery is an assault that results in physical contact. Defenses to such actions include consent, self-defense, and the defense of others and of property.

    b. False imprisonment is the intentional confinement or restraint of another person's movement without justification.

    c. An intentional act that amounts to extreme and outrageous conduct that results in severe emotional distress to another can be the basis of a suit for intentional infliction of emotional (mental) distress.

    d. A false statement, not made under privilege, that is communicated to a third person and that causes damage to a person's reputation may be defamation. If spoken it is slander; if in print, it is libel. Defenses include the privilege to relay the information, such as in the news, or to protect another interest.

    e. Invasion of the right to privacy is the use of a person's name or likeness for commercial purposes without permission, wrongful intrusion into a person's private activities, publication of information that places a person in a false light, or disclosure of private facts that an ordinary person would find objectionable.

    f. The use of another person's name, likeness, or other identifying characteristic without permission and for the benefit of the user is the intentional tort of appropriation.

    g. Misrepresentation or fraud is a false representation made by one party, by misstatement of facts or conduct, with the intent of deceiving another, and on which the other reasonably relies to his detriment, thereby suffering a loss.

    h. Knowing, intentional interference by a third party with an enforceable contractual relationship or an established business relationship between other parties for the purpose of advancing the economic interests of the third party is the tort of wrongful interference.

2. *Intentional torts against property*—Intentional acts by a party that violate interests of others protected at common law.

    a. Trespass to land is the invasion of another's real property without consent or privilege.

    b. Unlawfully damaging or interfering with the owner's right to use, possess, or enjoy personal property is the tort of trespass to personal property.

    c. Conversion is a tort in which personal property is taken from its rightful owner.

NEGLIGENCE

Negligence is the careless performance of a legally required duty or the failure to perform a legally required act. Elements that must be proved are that a legal duty of care existed to another party, that the defendant breached that duty, and that the breach caused damage or injury to another.

1. *The duty of care and its breach*—Negligence involves the failure to exercise the duty of care expected of all parties. We are held to the standard of a reasonable person under the circumstances. For businesses, this means an obligation to provide safe premises for clients. Professionals must meet the standards

expected of knowledgeable members of their area of expertise.

2. *The injury requirement and damages*—A plaintiff in a negligence suit must have sustained an injury that produced legally recognized damages. Most commonly, plaintiffs receive compensatory damages, but when the actions of a defendant are particularly offensive, punitive damages may be added.

3. *Causation*—The injury must be logically attributable to the violation of a protected interest by the defendant because there is a cause in fact or proximate cause.

4. *Defenses to negligence*—A defendant may plead an affirmative defense in negligence cases: assumption

of risk, superseding cause, and contributory negligence by the plaintiff.

5. *Special negligence doctrines and statutes*—Negligence *per se* is a type of negligence that may occur if a person violates a statute or an ordinance providing for a criminal penalty and the violation causes another to be injured. There are special negligence statutes such as dram shop acts and Good Samaritan laws that prescribe duties and responsibilities in certain circumstances. The violation of such statutes will impose civil liability or help protect a party accused of negligence.

CYBER TORTS: DEFAMATION ONLINE

General tort principles are extended to cover cyber torts, or torts that occur in cyberspace, such as online defamation. Federal and state statutes may also apply to certain forms of cyber torts.

1. *Liability of Internet service providers*—ISPs are generally protected from suit when they have been the

method of transmission of damaging information, as long as they have taken reasonable steps to protect against abuse of their services.

2. *Piercing the veil of anonymity*—ISPs may be required to provide the names of their clients who have been accused of torts. The law is still evolving on this point.

STRICT LIABILITY

The doctrine of strict liability is old but has been expanded over time to apply to more areas of tort law. Under it, a person or company may be held liable, regardless of the degree of care exercised, for damages or injuries caused by a product or activity.

1. *Abnormally dangerous activities*—Strict liability applies to those engaged in particularly dangerous activities, such as with toxic chemicals and explo-

sives. All burden is placed on those who engage in such activities or use such materials, so they have strong incentives to protect others against injury and will be held liable for any injuries related to such activities.

2. *Other applications of strict liability*—The most important application of the doctrine of strict liability is in the area of defective products.

PRODUCT LIABILITY

The makers of products can be liable in tort to injuries and damages caused by defective products. This is an old doctrine that has evolved over time.

1. *Theories of product liability*—Suits for product liability may be based on negligence, in which it is alleged that due care was not used by the manufacturer in designing, producing, or testing the product before selling it, or there was a failure to place adequate warnings on the product. It may be based on misrepresentation, when the seller misrepresents the quality, nature, or appropriate use of the product, and the user is injured as a result. Strict product liability occurs when a manufacturer exercised a reasonable care, but the product was defective and injury resulted. Most suits claim there was a defect in the production process, or there was a design defect that caused the product to

be more dangerous than it should have been, or there was a failure to warn of dangers in the product.

2. *Defenses to product liability*—If sued, a producer can offer several defenses: assumption of risk—the user or consumer knew of the risk of harm and voluntarily assumed it; product misuse—the user or consumer misused the product in a way unforeseeable by the manufacturer; comparative negligence—the plaintiff and the defendant should share liability under the doctrine of comparative negligence if the plaintiff's misuse of the product contributed to the risk of injury; and commonly known dangers. If a defendant succeeds in convincing the court that a plaintiff's injury resulted from a commonly known danger, such as the danger associated with using a sharp knife, the defendant will not be liable.

CONSUMER LAW

Statutes, agency rules, and common law judicial decisions that serve to protect the interests of consumers are classified as consumer law. There are many federal consumer protection statutes, in addition to a wide variety of state consumer protection statutes. Some state statutes provide more protection than that afforded by the federal laws discussed below.

1. *Deceptive sales practices*—The Federal Trade Commission (FTC) has authority to investigate and sue firms engaged in deceptive business practices that could injure a reasonable consumer. The agency also issues regulations to define certain deceptive practices. State attorneys general have broad powers to attack deceptive practices.

2. *Deceptive advertising*—Advertising that misleads consumers or that is based on false claims is prohibited by the FTC. Generally, the test for whether an ad is deceptive is whether a reasonable consumer would be deceived by the ad. The FTC can require the advertiser to stop the challenged advertising, often by getting a court to issue a cease-and-desist order.

3. *Labeling and packaging*—Manufacturers must comply with labeling or packaging requirements for their specific products. In general, labels must be accurate and not misleading. Food products must bear labels detailing their nutritional content, and standards must be met before a product can use terms like *fresh* and *organic* on the label.

4. *Sales transactions*—Many federal laws regulate the disclosure of terms to consumers in sales transactions, particularly in door-to-door and mail-order sales. The FTC conducts most of the federal regulation of sales. States have broad statutes that allow them to sue firms for harmful sales practices that cover a wide range of activities.

5. *Consumer health and safety*—Laws protecting the health and safety of consumers regulate the content of a food, drug, or other item. The Federal Food, Drug and Cosmetic Act protects consumers against impure and misbranded foods and drugs. The act establishes food standards, specifies safe levels of food additives, and regulates some aspects of food advertising. The Consumer Product Safety Act seeks to protect consumers from risk of injury from hazardous products. The Consumer Product Safety Commission may ban the sale of hazardous products.

6. *Consumer credit protection*—Credit protection has become an important area regulated by federal consumer protection legislation. Among the most important is the Truth-in-Lending Act (TILA). It is a disclosure law requiring sellers and lenders to disclose credit terms or loan terms so that individuals can shop around to compare terms. This law also provides for the following:

a. *Equal credit opportunity*—Prohibits creditors from discriminating on the basis of race, religion, national origin, color, gender, marital status, or age.

b. *Credit-card protection*—Limits the liability of card-holders for unauthorized charges made on unsolicited credit cards. The CARD Act limits fees for various actions by credit-card holders and requires clear information about card pricing.

c. *Credit-card rules*—TILA provides detailed rules that apply in case of a dispute between a credit-card holder and the bank that issued the card.

The Fair Credit Reporting Act protects consumers against inaccurate credit reporting and provides that credit reports can only be issued for certain purposes. Consumers are entitled to receive a copy of their credit report on request and to be notified any time they are denied credit or insurance based on the report. The reporting agency must conduct an investigation if the consumer contests any information on the credit report.

The Fair and Accurate Credit Transactions Act helps protect against identity theft by establishing a national fraud-alert system for credit users; by requiring major credit-reporting agencies to provide consumers with free copies of their credit reports every twelve months; by requiring that account numbers on credit-card receipts be shortened; and by assisting victims of identity theft in reestablishing their credit reputations.

The Fair Debt Collection Practices Act prohibits debt collectors from using unfair debt-collection practices, such as contacting debtors at their place of employment if their employers object, contacting debtors at unreasonable times, contacting third parties about the debt unless authorized to do so by a court, and harassing debtors.

Garnishment is when a creditor has the right to seize a portion of the debtor's property (such as wages) in the possession of a third party (such as an employer) to satisfy a debt. The creditor must comply with specific procedures mandated by state law.

■ QUESTIONS FOR REVIEW

1. Define tort. What is the purpose of tort law? What are the main categories of torts, and how do they differ?

2. Define intentional tort. List the elements of assault, battery, intentional infliction of emotional distress, and defamation. How do intentional torts against persons differ from cyber torts?

3. List and define the four elements of negligence. Why is the duty of care for professionals different from the duty of an ordinary person? What are the affirmative defenses to a negligence action?

4. What is product liability? What are the three legal theories for product liability suits? List and define the affirmative defenses to a product liability suit.

5. List and describe the six areas of federal consumer law discussed in the chapter. Do states have consumer protection laws? If so, what level of consumer protection do state laws provide?

■ ETHICS QUESTION

Chloee is a new legal assistant interviewing a client who wants to sue the manufacturer of an allegedly defective elliptical-training machine. The client claims that while using the machine, it stopped suddenly, causing him to fall off and seriously injure his hip. Near the end of the interview, the client asks Chloee whether she thinks he has a good case. Chloee responds, "Well, as you know, I'm a paralegal, and I cannot give legal advice. Personally, though, I think that you do have a good case." Has Chloee violated her ethical duties? How would you have handled the situation?

■ PRACTICE QUESTIONS AND ASSIGNMENTS

1. Bob is driving to work for his morning shift at the plant when he encounters strikers who are picketing and blocking the entrance to the factory. Bob cannot afford to lose his job, so he decides to cross the picket line. When he attempts to drive through, the picketers surround his car and begin to rock and push it. Bob's car is spun around and ends up in oncoming traffic. Bob suffers a panic attack and his anxiety disorder is aggravated so that he cannot work. Does Bob have a tort claim against the picketers? If so, which torts were committed?

2. During the Ebola crisis, hospitals throughout the United States set up protocols for handling Ebola patients, including providing an Ebola checklist for use by emergency room staff. When the first Ebola patient was initially seen at a Texas hospital's emergency room, he reported a fever and flu-like symptoms (classic symptoms of the Ebola virus) and told the emergency room staff that he had just come from Liberia, a country with a severe Ebola outbreak. The patient was treated for the flu, given antibiotics, and sent home. Despite the presence of Ebola symptoms and his recent arrival from Liberia, his illness was not reported to any authorities. The man returned three days later by ambulance, deathly ill. He was admitted to the hospital, was diagnosed with Ebola, and died within a few days. On which tort law theory discussed in the chapter might the hospital be liable?

3. Two middle-school girls labeled a male gym teacher a "perv" and "creeper." They spread false rumors that he inappropriately touched students and peeked into the girls' locker room. The girls' parents shared these falsehoods about the teacher with their friends. The teacher was cleared of allegations of criminal behavior and filed a lawsuit against the parents for spreading false rumors about his behavior. Under which tort theory would the teacher file a suit?

4. A law school has an open admissions policy, and because of an antiquated state law, it accepts students with the equivalent of an associate's degree. Once admitted, students must earn a grade of "C" or better in all courses to stay enrolled. Many students flunk out. Several disgruntled students start a blog where they complain about the law school's policies. Over time, more students post on the blog, and some of the statements are untrue. The law school sues for online defamation, naming the defendants as John Does. Will the Internet Service Provider (ISP) have to reveal the identities of the defendant Does? How do the rights of the plaintiff balance against the defendants' First Amendment rights to free speech? Can the ISP be held liable for the defamation?

5. Carmen buys a television set manufactured by AKI Electronics. She is going on vacation, so she takes the set to her mother's house for her mother to use. Because the set is defective, it explodes, causing considerable damage to her mother's house. Carmen's mother sues AKI for the damage to her house. Discuss the product liability theories under which Carmen's mother can recover from AKI.

■ GROUP PROJECT

This project asks you to research the ignition-switch recall by General Motors (GM) in 2014.

Student one will locate and summarize articles describing the problem with ignition switches on GM vehicles, when and how the problem was discovered, and what injuries or deaths resulted from the defective ignition switches.

Student two will locate and summarize articles on why product-liability lawsuits against GM were not a viable alternative in 2014.

Student three will locate and summarize articles on the Congressional testimony of GM's executives on the ignition-switch issue and describe what remedies resulted for persons who were injured or for the families of those who died.

Student four will compile the summaries and present them to the class.

■ INTERNET PROJECTS

Go to FindLaw's Consumer Protection website at **consumer.findlaw.com/**.

a. Select a topic of interest to you and browse through the listings. Write a one-page synopsis of what you found about the topic. Include the URL for the topic in your answer.

b. For the same topic, write a one-page summary of applicable laws referenced on the website. Note any government agencies that oversee consumer protection on this topic, Print and attach a copy of a pertinent page of the website.

■ END NOTES

1. 47 U.S.C. Section 230.
2. *Restatement (Second) of Torts*, Section 402A.
3. *Restatement (Third) of Torts: Products Liability*, Section 2, Comment h.

CHAPTER 15

Contracts and Intellectual Property Law

CHAPTER OUTLINE

Introduction

Requirements to
Form a Valid Contract

Defenses to
Contract Enforceability

Sales Contracts and Warranties

Contract Performance
and Remedies

Online Contracting and
Electronic Signatures

Intellectual Property Law

CHAPTER OBJECTIVES

After completing this chapter, you will know:

- The requirements for forming a valid contract and the circumstances under which contracts are not enforceable.

- The remedies available when a contract is breached, or broken.

- The nature and legal validity of an electronic signature.

- The nature and forms of intellectual property.

- What conduct gives rise to a violation of intellectual property rights.

448

Introduction

The law governs most activities. Simple, everyday transactions—such as buying a gallon of milk at a convenience store or installing a new app on your smartphone—are subject to laws that define the rights and duties of the parties involved. This chapter covers two of the most important areas of law—contracts and sales. Paralegals routinely help attorneys deal with disputes involving contract and sales law. Because such disputes often deal with complicated issues, paralegals need to understand the principles of these areas.

Another field of law that has become increasingly important involves intellectual property, such as patents, trademarks, and copyrights. As you will learn later in the chapter, the value of intellectual property has increased because of the massive flow of ideas and innovations. Attorneys and their paralegals are frequently called on to help clients register and protect various forms of intellectual property.

Requirements to Form a Valid Contract

Contract law deals with, among other things, the keeping of promises. A promise is an assurance that one will or will not do something in the future. As mentioned in Chapter 2, a *contract* is any agreement (based on a promise or an exchange of promises) that can be enforced in court.

promise
An assurance that one will or will not do something in the future.

Bilateral and Unilateral Contracts

Two types of contracts are *bilateral* and *unilateral*. Most contracts are bilateral. The exchange of a promise for a promise creates a bilateral contract. Yvonne offers to sell Sean her car for $10,000, and he accepts, saying he will have the money tomorrow. When people make a unilateral contract, they exchange a promise for an act:

EXAMPLE 15.1 Yvonne tells Devon she will pay him $100 if he will detail her car. He says nothing but then details the car. Because he completed the requested act, Yvonne owes him $100.

Both types of contracts are valid, although they may be referred to by different names. Some states do not use the term *unilateral contract*.

Contract Validity

If a client alleges that a party has breached (failed to perform) a contract, the first issue that your supervising attorney and you need to examine is whether a *valid contract* (a contract that will be enforced by a court) was ever formed. To form a valid contract, four basic requirements must be met:

- **Agreement.** An agreement includes an offer and an acceptance. One party must offer to enter into a legal agreement, and another party must accept the terms of the offer.

- **Consideration.** Promises made by parties must be supported by legally sufficient and bargained-for consideration (something of value that is received or promised to convince a person to make a deal, as discussed shortly).

- **Contractual capacity.** Both parties entering into the contract must have the contractual capacity to do so. The law must recognize them as qualified competent parties.

- **Legality.** The contract's purpose must be to accomplish some goal that is legal and not against public policy.

If any of these elements is lacking, no contract was formed. We look more closely at these requirements in the following subsections.

Agreement

agreement
A meeting of the minds, and a requirement for a valid contract. Agreement involves two distinct events: an offer to form a contract and the acceptance of that offer by the offeree.

A contract is, in essence, an agreement between two or more parties. If the parties fail to reach an agreement on the terms of the contract, no contract exists. Ordinarily, agreement is evidenced by two events: an *offer* and an *acceptance*. One party offers a certain bargain to another party, who then accepts that bargain. When contracts are drafted with the assistance of an attorney, it is possible that both parties to the agreement will want to use the same attorney. That raises special issues, as noted in the *Ethics Watch* feature below.

Offer

offer
A promise or commitment to do or refrain from doing some specified thing in the future.

offeror
The party making the offer.

An offer is a promise or commitment to do or not do some specified thing in the future. Three elements are necessary for an offer to be effective:

- The offeror (the party making the offer) must have the *intent to be bound* by the offer.

- The terms of the offer must be *reasonably certain*, or *definite*, so that the parties and the court can determine the terms of the contract. (In contracts for the sale

ETHICS WATCH

POTENTIAL CONFLICTS OF INTEREST

It is not uncommon for two parties to come together and want an attorney to write a contract that represents an agreement, such as to build an apartment building together. This raises an obvious conflict-of-interest issue. Can the attorney represent both parties in a contract? Conflict rules prevent an attorney from simultaneously representing adverse parties in a legal proceeding. On the one hand, the parties could write up a legally binding contract without an attorney. On the other hand, should a dispute arise over the contract, assisting one party will necessarily be adverse to the other. In this situation, there should be careful research on the rules on waiving conflicts in their state.

If the state has adopted the 2002 Revision of the Model Rules (discussed in Chapter 4), the attorney must obtain the informed consent of each party in writing. This means the attorney must explain the risks of having one attorney draw up a contract for two people and also must discuss the alternatives. Then the two parties must sign a consent form.

Paralegals often have a role to play in these situations, such as conducting an initial interview with the parties. The position of a paralegal in such circumstances is covered by the NALA *Code of Ethics and Professional Responsibility*, Canon 2: "A paralegal may perform any task which is properly designated and supervised by an attorney, as long as the attorney is ultimately responsible to the client, maintains a direct relationship with the client, and assumes professional responsibility for the work product."

of goods, discussed later, the requirement of definiteness is relaxed somewhat so that a contract can exist even if certain terms are left "open," or unspecified.)

• The offer must be communicated to the offeree (the party to whom the offer is made).

offeree
The party to whom the offer is made.

Offers made in jest, in undue excitement, or in obvious anger do not meet the intent requirement.

EXAMPLE 15.2 Al and Sue ride to work together each day in Sue's car, which she bought for $18,000 six months ago. One cold morning, Al and Sue get into the car, but Sue cannot get it started. Angry, she yells, "I'll sell you this stupid car for $100!" Al writes Sue a check for $100. Has a contract to sell the car been formed? If Al consulted with your supervising attorney, claiming that Sue had breached a contract because she had refused to give him the car, what would the attorney say? The attorney would tell Al that a reasonable person would have recognized under the circumstances that Sue's offer was not serious—she did not intend to be bound but was simply frustrated. Therefore, no valid contract was formed.

Similarly, an offer will not be effective if it is too ambiguous in its terms.

EXAMPLE 15.3 Kim wants to sell her set of legal encyclopedias but has not mentioned a price. Jamal says to Kim, "I'll buy your encyclopedias and pay for them next week." In this situation, no contract results, because no price was set.

Note that when considering a dispute, the courts evaluate it from the standpoint of a reasonable person.

EXAMPLE 15.4 Jeff has been attempting to buy some land from Raul for months. One night, while drinking together at a bar, Jeff offers Raul $20,000 for the land. Raul agrees and the two sign a simple agreement while in the bar. Raul later claims he did not mean it and refuses to sell. Because a reasonable person would think this was an agreement to sell, Raul has agreed to sell despite his mental reservation.

Advertisements

Advertisements are generally not offers but are invitations to make an offer. When an ad is "clear, definite, and explicit" and leaves nothing open for negotiation, however, it may be an offer.

EXAMPLE 15.5 A Pepsi ad encouraged consumers to accumulate "Pepsi Points" by buying Pepsi products. The ad showed many items, from sunglasses to hats, that the consumer could acquire. The final item was a military fighter jet, listed for 7,000,000 points. When someone got the points and demanded the jet, Pepsi refused to deliver it, and the consumer sued. The court ruled that the advertisement was not an offer because an objective, reasonable person would not have considered the commercial to be an offer. (You can find the commercial on YouTube by searching for "Harrier Jet Pepsi." There are two versions—one from before the lawsuit and one from after it.)

Termination of the Offer

Once an offer has been communicated, the party to whom the offer was made can accept the offer, reject the offer, or make a counteroffer. If a party accepts the offer, a contract is formed (provided the other requirements to form a contract are met). If the party rejects the offer, the offer is terminated. That is, the offer no longer stands (and the offeree cannot take the offeror up on the offer later). The offeree also has the option of rejecting the offer and can also make an offer—called a counteroffer.

COUNTEROFFER. In a counteroffer, the offeree becomes the offeror—offering to form a contract with different terms.

A real estate paralegal reviews the terms of a purchase offer with a potential home buyer to ensure that all of the contract's terms are clear. What is the role of the paralegal during real estate transactions?

© Goodluz/www.Shutterstock.com.

EXAMPLE 15.6 Dilan offers to work for Wayne for $50,000 a year. Wayne responds, "Your price is too high. I'll hire you for $40,000." Wayne's response is a counteroffer, because it terminates Dilan's offer and creates a new offer by Wayne.

Both a rejection of the offer and the making of a counteroffer terminate the original offer. The original offer can also be terminated if the party making the offer withdraws the offer before it has been accepted (called *revoking* the offer). If the offer has already been accepted, however, then both parties are bound in contract.

OTHER BASES FOR TERMINATION. An offer also terminates automatically in some circumstances, such as when the subject matter of the offer is destroyed, one of the parties dies or becomes incompetent, or a new law is passed that makes the contract illegal. Additionally, an offer ends if a period of time is specified in the offer and the offer is not accepted within that period. If no time for acceptance is specified in the offer, the offer expires when a *reasonable* period of time has passed. What constitutes a reasonable period in the eyes of the court varies, depending on the circumstances.

Acceptance

acceptance
In contract law, the offeree's indication to the offeror that the offeree agrees to be bound by the terms of the offeror's offer, or proposal to form a contract.

mirror image rule
A common law rule that requires that the terms of the offeree's acceptance adhere exactly to the terms of the offeror's offer for a valid contract to be formed.

A party's acceptance of the offer results in a legally binding contract if the other elements of a valid contract are present. The acceptance must be *unequivocal*—that is, the terms of the offer must be accepted exactly as stated by the offeror. This principle of contract law is known as the mirror image rule—the terms of the acceptance must be the same as ("mirror") the terms of the offer. If the acceptance is subject to new conditions or if the terms of the acceptance materially change the original offer, the acceptance may be deemed a counteroffer that implicitly rejects the original offer.

EXAMPLE 15.7 Sara agrees to sell her house to Jamil for $221,000. When he signs the contract, Jamil adds a note that he wants Sara to leave her furniture in the living room. That is not a valid acceptance; it is a counteroffer because Jamil added a new condition. Unless Sara wants to accept, the deal is dead if she wishes to sell to someone else.

PROPER COMMUNICATION. Another requirement, for most types of contracts, is that the acceptance be communicated to the offeror. An issue in contract formation has to do with the timeliness of acceptances. The general rule is that acceptance of an offer is timely if it is made before the offer is terminated.

Problems arise, however, when the parties involved are not dealing face-to-face. In such cases, acceptance takes effect at the time the acceptance is communicated via the mode expressly or impliedly authorized by the offeror. This is the mailbox rule. Under this rule, if the offer states that it must be accepted by mail, the acceptance becomes valid the moment it is deposited in the mail or sent by e-mail.

REASONABLENESS STANDARD. Often, the party making an offer does not indicate how acceptance must be made. In those cases, acceptance may be made in any manner that is *reasonable under the circumstances*. Several factors determine whether the acceptance is reasonable: the nature of the circumstances at the time the offer was made, the means used to transmit the offer, and the reliability of the offer's delivery.

EXAMPLE 15.8 An offer is sent by FedEx overnight because an acceptance is urgently required. In this situation, the offeree's acceptance by fax or e-mail will be deemed reasonable.

In contracts formed on the Internet, the issues of timeliness and method of acceptance usually do not arise. This is because persons often accept online offers simply by clicking on the box "I agree" or "I accept." Such click-on agreements are widely used in the formation of contracts online (as discussed later).

Consideration

Another requirement for a valid contract is consideration. Consideration is usually defined as something of value—such as money or the performance of an action not otherwise required—that is given in exchange for a promise. Promises are generally not enforceable without consideration.

EXAMPLE 15.9 You give your friend $1,000 in exchange for her promise to take care of your house and garden for six months. This promise normally will be enforceable, because consideration has been given. Your consideration is $1,000. Your friend's consideration is the assumption of an obligation (taking care of the house and garden) that she otherwise would not assume.

Both parties to the contract must give consideration for the contract to be enforceable. Many disputes arise when one party argues there is a lack of consideration. Consideration is required by the common law. In contrast, most civil law countries, such as Germany and France, do not require consideration for a contract to be valid.

Elements of Consideration

Often, consideration is divided into two parts: (1) something of *legal value* must be given in exchange for the promise, and (2) there must be a *bargained-for* exchange. The "something of legal value" may consist of a return promise that is bargained for. It may also consist of performance, which may be an act, a forbearance, or the creation, modification, or destruction of a legal relationship. Forbearance involves not doing something one has a legal right to do.

EXAMPLE 15.10 When you are twenty-one, your grandfather promises to pay you $10,000 if you agree not to smoke any cigarettes before the age of twenty-five. Your consideration in this situation is refraining from smoking cigarettes.

mailbox rule
A rule providing that an acceptance of an offer takes effect at the time it is communicated via the mode expressly or impliedly authorized by the offeror, rather than at the time it is actually received by the offeror. If acceptance is to be by mail, for example, it becomes effective the moment it is placed in the mailbox.

click-on agreement
An agreement that arises when a buyer, engaging in a transaction on a computer, indicates his or her assent to be bound by the terms of an offer by clicking on a button that says, for example, "I agree"; sometimes referred to as a click-on license or a click-wrap agreement.

consideration
Something of value, such as money or the performance of an action not otherwise required, that motivates the formation of a contract. Each party must give consideration for the contract to be binding.

Contract Change Requires New Consideration

Once a contract has been formed, the general common law rule is that the terms of a contract cannot be modified without further consideration. For instance, after making the deal in the example just given, your grandfather cannot modify the terms by requiring you not to drink alcohol before age 25 for the same $10,000—you would have to receive additional consideration for this new agreement.

Legal Sufficiency of Consideration

For a binding contract to be created, consideration must be *legally sufficient*. To be legally sufficient, consideration for a promise must be either *legally detrimental to the promisee or legally beneficial to the promisor*. A party can incur legal detriment either by promising to give legal value (such as the payment of money) or by a forbearance or a promise of forbearance.

The requirement of consideration is what distinguishes contracts from gifts.

EXAMPLE 15.11 You promise to give your friend $1,000 as a gift, and she says she will be very happy to receive your gift. In this situation, no contract results, because your friend has given no legally sufficient consideration.

Adequacy of Consideration

Adequacy of consideration refers to the fairness of the bargain. In general, a court will not question the adequacy of consideration if the consideration is legally sufficient. Parties are normally free to bargain as they wish. If people could sue merely because they had entered into a bad bargain, the courts would be overloaded with frivolous suits.

EXAMPLE 15.12 Alonzo sells his 2014 Mercedes Benz, which is in excellent condition, to Herb for $3,000, even though the car is worth much more. Later Alonzo says he wants the car back because he must have been out of his mind to sell it for so little. The court normally will not invalidate a contract as long as it was made freely by a sane person. Courts are generally not in the business of ensuring that deals are based on fair market value.

A court may consider the adequacy of consideration in terms of its value because inadequate consideration may indicate fraud, duress, undue influence, or a lack of bargained-for exchange. It may also reflect a party's incompetence (for example, an individual might have been too intoxicated or senile to make a contract).

Promissory Estoppel

In some circumstances, contracts will be enforced even though consideration is lacking. Under the doctrine of **promissory estoppel**, a person who has reasonably and substantially relied on the promise of another may obtain some measure of recovery. The following elements are required:

promissory estoppel
A doctrine under which a promise is binding if the promise is clear and definite, the promisee justifiably relies on the promise, the reliance is reasonable and substantial, and justice will be better served by enforcement of the promise.

- There must be a clear and definite promise.
- The promisee must justifiably rely on the promise.
- The reliance normally must be of a substantial and definite character.
- Justice will be better served by enforcement of the promise.

If these requirements are met, a promise may be enforced even though it is not supported by consideration. In essence, the promisor will be *estopped* (prevented) from asserting the lack of consideration as a defense.

EXAMPLE 15.13 Your uncle tells you, "I'll pay you $500 a week so you won't have to work while you are in college." In reliance on your uncle's promise, you quit your job. Your uncle then refuses to pay you, putting you in financial trouble. Under the doctrine of promissory estoppel, you may be able to enforce such a promise.

Contractual Capacity

For a contract to be deemed valid, the parties to the contract must have contractual capacity—the legal ability or competence to enter into a contractual relationship. Courts generally presume the existence of contractual capacity, but there are some situations in which capacity is lacking or questionable. In many instances, a party may have the capacity to enter into a valid contract but also have the right to avoid liability under it.

contractual capacity
The threshold mental capacity required by law for a party who enters into a contract to be bound by that contract.

Minors

Minors usually are not legally bound by contracts. Subject to certain exceptions, the contracts entered into by a minor are *voidable* (they can be canceled, or avoided) at the option of that minor. The minor has the option of *disaffirming* (renouncing) the contract and setting aside the contract and all legal obligations arising from it. An adult who enters into a contract with a minor, however, cannot avoid his contractual duties on the ground that the minor can do so. Unless the minor exercises the option to set aside the contract, the adult party is bound by it.

Intoxication and Mental Capacity

Intoxication is a condition in which a person's normal capacity to act or think is inhibited by alcohol or some other drug. Under the common law rule, if the person was sufficiently intoxicated to lack mental capacity, the transaction is voidable at the option of the intoxicated person even if the intoxication was purely voluntary. In spite of the common law rule, most courts rarely permit contracts to be avoided on this basis.

If a person has been adjudged mentally incompetent by a court of law and a guardian has been appointed, any contract made by the mentally incompetent person is *void*—no contract exists. Only the guardian can enter into binding legal duties on the incompetent person's behalf. Even if the court has not previously ruled that the person is mentally incompetent, the contract may be avoided if incompetence is proved.

EXAMPLE 15.14 Rita, who suffers from Alzheimer's disease, signs a contract to buy ten new vacuum cleaners. If the contract is challenged and it can be proved that Rita did not understand what she was doing at the time she signed the contract, the contract will not be valid.

The issue of contractual capacity is discussed further in the *Developing Paralegal Skills* feature on the following page.

Legality

A contract to do something that is prohibited by federal or state statutory law is illegal and, as such, void from the outset and unenforceable. For example, a contract to buy a liver from another person is void because it is illegal. No court would enforce the contract if a lawsuit were brought for breach of contract. Any contract to commit an illegal act is unenforceable.

In some instances, the subject matter of the contract is not illegal, but one of the parties is not legally authorized to perform the contract. For example, all states require that members of certain occupations—including physicians, lawyers, real estate brokers, architects, electricians, contractors, and stockbrokers—obtain licenses allowing them to practice. When a person enters into a contract with an unlicensed individual for services that should be performed by a licensed professional, the contract may still be enforceable, depending on the nature of the licensing statute.

Some states expressly provide that the lack of a license in certain occupations bars the enforcement of work-related contracts. If there is no express provision, one must look to the underlying purpose of the licensing requirements for a particular occupation. If the purpose is to protect the public from unauthorized practitioners, a contract involving an unlicensed individual normally is unenforceable. If the underlying purpose of the statute is to raise government revenues, however, a contract entered into with an

DEVELOPING PARALEGAL SKILLS

ASSESSING CONTRACTUAL CAPACITY

You are a legal assistant for Jeff Barlow. He asks you to draft a contract for Margaret Klaus, a seventy-nine-year-old widow. In the contract, Margaret will transfer all of her shares in NAPO Corporation to her nephew Jeremy. In return, Jeremy promises to take care of Margaret for the rest of her life. Barlow is leaving on vacation and asks you to have the document completed and to arrange for a meeting with the client and her nephew to sign the contract when he returns.

You learn that the stock being conveyed is worth a huge sum. More importantly, you begin to have doubts about Margaret's mental status. You have talked to her several times a week for three weeks. She often calls you by different names, repeats herself, and does not remember what you just told her. Although Jeremy has been living with Margaret for the past six months, whenever Margaret calls, she is alone and seems to be frightened. Now that you have finished the contract, you wonder if Margaret is capable of genuine consent and whether Jeremy has too much influence over her. What should you do?

TIPS FOR DEALING WITH SUSPICIONS OF INCOMPETENCE

- Document everything. Keep a record of all the conversations you had with the client that led you to suspect a lack of contractual capacity, as well as any other facts that contributed to your suspicions (if you discovered the person was taking medication for mental illness, for example).

- Do not discuss your suspicions with *anyone* except your supervising attorney. Making such statements about a person can damage her reputation, and you may even be held liable for defamation.

- Remember, it is the attorney's job to take into consideration the client's contractual capacity, not yours. You just want to make Barlow aware of the situation in an effort to protect the client's best interests.

unlicensed practitioner generally is enforceable—although the unlicensed person may be fined.

Additionally, some contracts are not enforced because the court deems them to be contrary to public policy. For example, contracts that restrain trade (anticompetitive contracts) and contracts that are so oppressive to innocent parties that they are deemed *unconscionable* (unconscionable contracts will be discussed shortly) are not enforceable owing to the negative impact they would have on society.

Defenses to Contract Enforceability

Two competent parties enter into a contract for a legal purpose. The agreement is supported by consideration. The contract thus meets the four requirements for a valid contract. Nonetheless, the contract may be unenforceable if the parties have not genuinely assented (agreed) to its terms, if the contract is so oppressive to one of the parties that a court will refuse to enforce it, or if the contract is not in the proper form—such as in writing, if the law requires it to be in writing.

Concern about enforceability means that at least part of a contract is likely to come from an existing contract known to contain the necessary elements. As the *Technology and Today's Paralegal* feature on the facing page notes, there are many sources for form contracts that paralegals can consult.

TECHNOLOGY AND TODAY'S PARALEGAL

CONTRACT FORMS

Before the printing press was invented, every contract form had to be handwritten. Since the advent of printing, many standard contract forms have been readily available at low cost. With the Internet, preprinted forms are unnecessary, as attorneys and paralegals can customize contract forms for each situation.

ONLINE CONTRACT FORMS

A large variety of contract forms, as well as other legal and business forms, is available online. For example, at **forms.lp.findlaw.com**, you can access thousands of legal forms for lawyers, businesses, and the public. The contracts range from basic sales contracts to sample software licensing agreements. Many are available free of charge. PublicLegal also offers a number of free contract forms and links to other online resources at **ilrg.com**.

Another source for contract forms is 'Lectric Law Library's collection of forms at **lectlaw.com**. Select "Free Online Legal Forms" and you will see a list of forms by area. This site includes forms for the assignment of a contract, a contract for the sale of a business, and many others.

Yet another source is **uslegalforms.com,** which has numerous forms available in many areas of practice. Not only can you search for contracts by content area (such as real estate or employment), but you can look up state-specific forms (separation agreements, for example). Most forms are available for a nominal fee. Similar types of services are available at many other sites, including **legal-forms-now.com**, **findforms.com**, and **allaboutforms.com**.

TECHNOLOGY TIP

Online contract forms are a great resource for paralegals. Thousands of forms can be easily accessed and customized for use in particular transactions. Keep in mind, though, that the contracts you find online will not necessarily be valid for your state or situation. You must always research the contract requirements in your state to verify that you are using the appropriate form. At a minimum, the forms can save significant time in piecing together needed parts of a document. You can then focus on the parts relevant to a particular matter your firm is handling.

Genuineness of Assent

Lack of genuineness of assent can be used as a defense to the contract's enforceability. Genuineness of assent may be lacking because of a mistake, fraudulent misrepresentation, undue influence, or duress.

genuineness of assent
Knowing and voluntary assent to the contract terms. If a contract is formed as a result of mistake, misrepresentation, undue influence, or duress, genuineness of assent is lacking, and the contract will be voidable.

Mistake

It is important to distinguish between *mistakes of fact* and *mistakes of value or quality*. If a mistake concerns the future market value or quality of the object of the contract, the mistake is one of *value*, and either party normally can enforce the contract. Each party is considered to have assumed the risk that the value would change or prove to be different from what he or she thought. Without this rule, almost any party who did not receive what he or she considered a fair bargain could argue mistake.

MISTAKE OF FACT.   Only a mistake of fact allows a contract to be avoided. Mistakes of fact occur in two forms—*unilateral* and *mutual (bilateral)*. A unilateral mistake occurs when one party to the contract makes a mistake as to some material fact—that is, a fact important to the subject matter of the contract. The general rule is that a unilateral mistake does not give the mistaken party any right to relief from the contract. There are some exceptions to this rule, however.

unilateral mistake
Mistake as to a material fact on the part of only one party to a contract. In this situation, the contract is normally enforceable against the mistaken party, with some exceptions.

material fact
A fact that is important to the subject matter of the contract.

rescission
A remedy in which the contract is canceled and the parties are returned to the positions they occupied before the contract was made.

mutual mistake
Mistake as to the same material fact on the part of both parties to a contract. In this situation, either party can cancel the contract.

EXAMPLE 15.15 A contractor's written bid to remodel a house was $10,000 because he made a mistake in addition and left off the last zero. In this situation, the contract resulting from the bid can be rescinded. (Rescission is the act of canceling, or nullifying, a contract.)

MUTUAL MISTAKE.   When *both* of the parties are mistaken about the same material fact, a mutual mistake has occurred, and either party can cancel the contract.

EXAMPLE 15.16 At Perez's art gallery, Diana buys a painting of a landscape. Both Diana and Perez believe that the painting is by the famous artist Vincent van Gogh. Later, Diana discovers that the painting is a fake. Because neither Perez nor Diana was aware of this material fact when they made their deal, Diana can rescind (cancel) the contract and recover the purchase price of the painting.

Fraudulent Misrepresentation

When an innocent party is fraudulently induced to enter into a contract, the contract usually can be avoided because that party has not *voluntarily* consented to its terms. Normally, the innocent party can either rescind (cancel) the contract and be restored to her original position or enforce the contract and seek damages for any injuries resulting from the fraud.

You read about the tort of fraud in Chapter 14. In the context of contract law, fraudulent misrepresentation occurs when one party to a contract misrepresents a material fact to the other party, with the intention of deceiving the other party, and the other party justifiably relies on the misrepresentation. To collect damages, a party must also have been injured. A party may still be able to avoid the contract in some states without proving that she was injured by the fraud, however.

Note that the misrepresentation may be based on conduct as well as oral or written statements.

EXAMPLE 15.17 Gene is contracting to buy Rachelle's horse. While showing Gene the horse, Rachelle skillfully keeps the horse's head turned one way so that Gene does not see that the horse is blind in one eye. Rachelle's conduct constitutes fraud.

Undue Influence

Undue influence arises from special kinds of relationships in which one party can greatly influence another party, thus overcoming that party's free will. As was illustrated in *Developing Paralegal Skills* on page 456, caretakers may unduly influence elderly people. In addition, attorneys may unduly influence clients, and parents may unduly influence children. The essential feature of undue influence is that the party being taken advantage of does not exercise free will in entering into a contract. A contract entered into under excessive or undue influence lacks genuine assent and is voidable.

Duress

Assent to the terms of a contract is not genuine if one of the parties is *forced* into the agreement. Forcing a party to do something, including entering into a contract, through fear created by threats is legally defined as *duress*. In addition, blackmail or extortion to induce consent to a contract constitutes duress. Duress is both a defense to the enforcement of a contract and a ground for the rescission of a contract.

Unconscionable Contracts

Ordinarily, a court does not look at the fairness or equity of a contract. For example, a court normally will not inquire into the adequacy of consideration. Persons are assumed to be reasonably intelligent, and the court does not come to their aid just because they have made unwise or foolish bargains.

In certain circumstances, a bargain is so oppressive to one of the parties that the court will refuse to enforce the contract. This is called an unconscionable contract. Contracts entered into because of one party's vastly superior bargaining power may be deemed unconscionable. These situations usually involve an adhesion contract, which is a contract drafted by the dominant party and then presented to the other—the adhering party—on a "take-it-or-leave-it" basis.

The Statute of Frauds

An otherwise valid contract may be unenforceable if it is not in the proper form. To ensure that there is reliable proof of the agreement, certain contracts are required to be in writing. If a contract is required by law to be in writing and there is no written evidence of the contract, it may not be enforceable.

Every state has a statute that specifies what types of contracts must be in writing or be evidenced by a written document. This is commonly referred to as the Statute of Frauds. Although the statutes vary slightly, the following contracts are normally required to be in writing:

- Contracts involving interests in land or anything attached to land, such as buildings, minerals, or timber.

- Contracts that cannot be performed within one year after formation.

- Collateral, or secondary, contracts, such as promises to be responsible for the debts of another.

- Promises made in consideration of marriage, such as prenuptial agreements (discussed in Chapter 17).

- Contracts for the sale of goods for $500 or more. (This is under the Uniform Commercial Code, not the common law.)

Note that the test for determining whether an oral contract is enforceable under the "one-year rule" is not whether an agreement is *likely* to be performed within one year but whether performance is *possible* within one year. Exhibit 15.1 below illustrates the one-year rule.

unconscionable contract
A contract that is so oppressive to one of the parties that the court will refuse to enforce the contract.

adhesion contract
A contract drafted by the dominant party and then presented to the other—the adhering party—on a "take-it-or-leave-it" basis.

Statute of Frauds
A state statute that requires certain types of contracts to be in writing to be enforceable.

EXHIBIT 15.1

The One-Year Rule

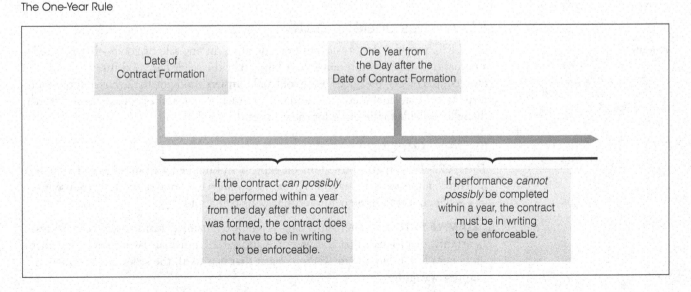

Sales Contracts and Warranties

Uniform Commercial Code (UCC)
Statutes adopted by all states, in part or in whole, that contain uniform laws governing business transactions as defined in the code.

sales contract
A contract for the sale of goods, as opposed to a contract for the sale of services, real property, or intangible property. Sales contracts are governed by Article 2 of the Uniform Commercial Code.

The principles we have been discussing come from the common law of contracts. Recall from Chapter 5 that legislatures can pass laws that replace common law principles. That is what happened in the case of the Uniform Commercial Code (UCC). Sales contracts—or, more specifically, contracts for the sale of goods—are governed by state statutes based on Article 2 of the UCC. The UCC is one of the many uniform laws created by the American Law Institute and the National Conference of Commissioners on Uniform State Laws. The UCC was first issued in 1952 and has since been revised to reflect the changing customs and needs of business. The UCC has been adopted, in whole or in part, by all states. State codes are not necessarily called the Uniform Commercial Code. In Ohio, for example, UCC provisions are part of the Ohio Commercial Code.

Researching matters involving the sale of goods usually requires using specialized legal resources because UCC provisions are generally the same (uniform) across states. Decisions from other states are more of a persuasive authority than is the case in other areas of law. Commentary by the Uniform Law Commission on the UCC provisions is also important.

The Scope of UCC Article 2

Two things should be kept in mind about Article 2 of the UCC. First, it deals with the sale of *goods*, not real property (real estate), services, or intangible property. Second, the rules may vary depending on whether the buyer or seller is a merchant. You should always note the subject matter of a contract dispute. If the subject is goods, then the UCC likely governs. If it is real estate or services, then the common law principles apply.

As under the common law, the parties to sales contracts are free to fashion the terms as they wish. The UCC normally comes into play only when a dispute arises over ambiguous or missing terms. Note that the UCC does not replace the common law of contracts. A contract for the sale of goods is also subject to the common law requirements of agreement, consideration, contractual capacity, and legality. Similarly, the common law defenses against contract formation or enforceability also apply to sales contracts. If the UCC has not modified a common law principle, then the common law governs. In other words, the general rule is that when the UCC addresses a particular matter, the UCC governs. When the UCC is silent, then the common law of contracts applies.

Warranties under the UCC

warranty
An express or implied promise by a seller that specific goods to be sold meet certain criteria, or standards of performance, on which the buyer may rely.

The UCC provides that a warranty of title arises in any sale of goods—that is, a seller automatically warrants (promises) to a buyer that the seller has good title to (legitimate ownership rights in) the goods being sold and transfers good title to the buyer. If the goods turn out to be stolen, for example, and the buyer has to return the goods to the real owner, the seller is liable to the buyer for the value of the goods.

Express Warranty

The UCC also contains provisions on express and implied warranties as to the quality or nature of the goods being sold. An *express warranty* is an oral or written promise made by a seller concerning the nature of the goods being sold.

EXAMPLE 15.18 The statement, "This is a new Craftsman lawn mower" is an express warranty, or promise, that the mower is indeed a Craftsman lawn mower and that it is new. If you buy the mower and learn that it is used, the seller has breached an express warranty.

Implied Warranties

Under the UCC, every merchant makes an *implied warranty of merchantability* when goods are sold. The goods must be merchantable—that is, they must be "reasonably fit for the ordinary purposes for which such goods are used." Examples of unmerchantable goods are a light bulb that explodes when switched on, hamburger meat that contains bits of glass, and a new boat that leaks. Goods sold by merchants must also be fit for the particular purpose for which they are sold. For *implied warranty of fitness for a particular purpose* to arise, the buyer must rely on the seller's skill or judgment in selecting suitable goods.

EXAMPLE 15.19 Suppose Kathleen indicated to the sellers of a horse, who were knowledgeable horse dealers, that she planned to use the horse for breeding. In this case, the horse was to be used for a particular, nonordinary purpose. When Kathleen later discovered the horse was incapable of reproducing, she could rely on the implied warranty of fitness to recover the purchase price.

Disclaimers

The UCC permits express and implied warranties to be disclaimed, provided the buyer is made aware of the disclaimers at the time the contract is formed. To disclaim an implied warranty of fitness for a particular purpose, the disclaimer must be in writing and be conspicuous (printed in larger or contrasting type or in a different color, for example).

Generally speaking, unless circumstances indicate otherwise, the implied warranties are disclaimed by the expression "as is," "with all faults," or similar language that is commonly understood by both parties as meaning that there are no implied or express warranties. An example of the application of these issues in the practice of contract law is presented in the *Developing Paralegal Skills* below.

DEVELOPING PARALEGAL SKILLS

CONTRACT REVIEW

Sam Thompson works as a paralegal for a corporation. One of his jobs is to review contracts between the corporation and outside vendors. He is reviewing a contract for the corporation's purchase of fifty new tablet devices from an outside vendor.

The contract, which is a preprinted form contract, was submitted by the vendor and consists of thirty paragraphs of "fine print." The vendor has filled in the blanks in the form for terms such as price and quantity. As Sam reads the contract, he comes across a warranty disclaimer provision. Sam realizes that this contract provision means that there will be no warranty of merchantability or fitness for a particular purpose for the new tablet devices. They are taken "as is." He makes a note to tell his supervising attorney about this provision. The attorney will want to inform management of this limitation on warranties.

TIPS FOR REVIEWING A CONTRACT

- Find out which contract provisions are acceptable to the client.
- Obtain the original copy of the contract.
- Read each provision carefully.
- Be certain you understand the meaning of each provision. If you are uncertain, find out what a provision means. Do not rely on the formulaic language in standard contract forms.
- Prepare a memo explaining the client's rights and liabilities under the contract.
- In the memo, mention any contract terms and provisions that the client might find objectionable.

Contract Performance and Remedies

A party's contractual duties, under a common law contract or a contract formed under the UCC, can be terminated in several ways. The most common way to terminate contractual duties, however, is by the performance of those duties. Failure to perform contractual duties as promised results in a breach of contract. When one party breaches a contract, the other party (the nonbreaching party) can seek remedies.

Contract Performance

Conditions expressly stated in a contract must be fully satisfied for complete performance to take place. A party who in good faith performs substantially all terms of a contract can usually enforce the contract against the other party under the doctrine of *substantial performance*. Generally, performance that provides a party with the important and essential benefits of a contract, in spite of any omission or deviation from the terms, is substantial performance. Because substantial performance is not perfect, the other party is entitled to damages to compensate for the part of the contract not completed.

Impossibility of Performance

After a contract has been made, performance may become impossible in an objective sense ("it can't be done," rather than "I can't do it").

> **EXAMPLE 15.20** Colter promises to sell his car to Janine the next day for $4,500. Colter is in an accident later that day. Because the car has been damaged or destroyed, Colter cannot deliver the car that was promised, and Janine does not have to accept the damaged vehicle even if Colter has it repaired.

Similarly, a party to a contract may die prior to performance, or performance may become illegal because of a change in the law. In these situations, the law excuses parties from their contractual performance duties under the doctrine of *impossibility of performance*.

Commercial Impracticability

Under the doctrine of *commercial impracticability*, courts may excuse parties from their obligations when the performance becomes much more difficult or expensive than contemplated at the time the contract was formed. For someone to invoke this doctrine, however, anticipated performance must become *extremely* difficult or costly.

> **EXAMPLE 15.21** Delbert's Trucking agreed to carry a load of freight each day for a year from Molly's Factory to a train station four miles away. Delbert's and Molly's agreed that the price would be $40 per day. Two months later, the road Delbert's used was torn out by highway crews for reconstruction work expected to take six months. As a result, Delbert's must travel 30 miles to get to the train station. Molly's cannot expect Delbert's to fulfill the contract at the original price. Unexpected cost conditions have greatly changed, making fulfillment of the contract impracticable.

Contract Remedies

A *remedy* is the relief provided for an innocent party when the other party has breached the contract. It is the means employed to enforce a right or to redress an injury. The most common remedies available to a nonbreaching party include damages, rescission, restitution, reformation, and specific performance.

Damages

A breach of contract entitles the nonbreaching party to sue for money damages (see Chapter 4). Damages are designed to compensate a party for the loss of the bargain. Generally, innocent parties are to be placed in the position they would have occupied had the contract been fully performed.

---

performance
In contract law, the fulfillment of duties arising under a contract; the normal way of discharging contractual obligations.

breach of contract
The failure, without legal excuse, of a contractual party to perform the obligations assumed in a contract.

COMPENSATORY DAMAGES.   Damages compensating the nonbreaching party for the loss of the bargain are known as *compensatory damages*. These damages compensate the injured party only for damages actually sustained and proved to have arisen directly from the loss of the bargain caused by the breach of contract. They simply replace what was lost because of the breach.

Compensatory damages are the difference between the value of the breaching party's promised performance and the value of actual performance. This amount is reduced by any loss that the injured party has avoided. In addition, the injured party may be able to recover *incidental damages*—expenses resulting directly from the breach of contract, such as those incurred to obtain performance from another source.

EXAMPLE 15.22 You are hired to perform certain services during August for $3,000, but the employer breaches the contract and you find another job that pays only $500. You can recover $2,500 as compensatory damages. In addition, as incidental damages, you can recover any expenses you incurred in finding the other job.

Damages in contracts cases must be reasonably certain, not based on speculation. This often comes up in cases where the plaintiff alleges that the defendant's breach caused lost profits for the plaintiff. Lost future profits may be established based on past profits, which raises difficulties for new businesses that have no track record.

CONSEQUENTIAL DAMAGES.   *Consequential damages*, or *special damages*, are a type of compensatory damages. Consequential damages are caused by circumstances beyond the contract itself. They flow from the results of a breach. For consequential damages to be awarded, the breaching party must have known (or have had reason to know) that circumstances would cause the nonbreaching party to suffer additional losses.

EXAMPLE 15.23 Glenda contracts with Eric to ship an item she needs to repair her printing press. The contract clearly states that Glenda must receive the item by Monday or she will not be able to print advertising posters for a customer and will lose $10,000. If Eric is late in shipping, Glenda normally can recover the consequential damages caused by the delay (that is, the $10,000 in losses).

LIQUIDATED DAMAGES.   Parties may specify an amount to be paid in the event of a future breach of the contract. This amount, called *liquidated damages*, must be reasonably related to the damages that may be suffered if the contract is not fulfilled. Liquidated damages are a form of compensatory damages. They may not be designed to serve as a *penalty* to deter a party from breaching a contract.

IN THE OFFICE

LISTEN UP

Hearing is not the same as listening. Many people are not good listeners. We often hear what we want to hear as we filter information through our own experiences and interests. When clients talk, focus carefully on what they say, as they may reveal information you had not anticipated. Observing their body language is also important.

Showing empathy and interest encourages clients to share more information, which may prove useful in handling legal issues. Taking an active interest in what others say, whether clients or co-workers, can increase your productivity and earn you recognition as a person who helps solve problems.

EXAMPLE 15.24 Shondra is planning to open a new store in a shopping center on June 1. The owner of the center assures her the store space will be ready. But what if it is not? Shondra will be stuck with inventory she will have to put in storage, employees who cannot work, and so forth. The parties may agree that if the store space is not ready when promised, the shopping center will pay Shondra $500 a day in liquidated damages to compensate her for her expenses. That would be reasonable, but if the contract had stated the damages were to be $50,000 a day, it would be a penalty that could not be enforced, as the amount is not reasonably related to the loss suffered.

PUNITIVE DAMAGES.   *Punitive damages* are not available in an action for breach of contract. They are intended to punish guilty parties, and contract law is not concerned with punishing guilt. Its purpose is to compensate a party for the loss of a bargain, no more and no less. However, if a tort such as fraud or negligence is involved, punitive damages may be appropriate. In such situations, a tort claim may be added.

Rescission, Restitution, and Reformation

As already discussed, *rescission* is essentially an action to undo, or terminate, a contract—to return the contracting parties to the positions they occupied prior to the transaction. When fraud, a mistake, duress, undue influence, misrepresentation, or lack of contractual capacity is present, rescission is available. The failure of one party to perform entitles the other party to rescind the contract.

Generally, to rescind a contract, the parties must make **restitution** to each other by returning goods, property, or funds previously conveyed. If physical property or goods can be returned, they must be. If the property or goods have been consumed, the restitution must be made in an equivalent dollar amount.

When the parties have imperfectly expressed their agreement in writing, the equitable remedy of **reformation** may also be available. In breach of contract cases, this remedy occurs when the court revises a contract to reflect the true intention of the parties—if a mutual mistake occurred, for example.

Specific Performance

The equitable remedy of **specific performance** calls for the performance of the act promised in the contract. Normally, specific performance is not granted unless the party's legal remedy (money damages) is inadequate. For this reason, contracts for the sale of goods rarely qualify for specific performance—substantially identical goods can be bought or sold in the market. If the contract involves unique goods, however, such as a painting or a rare book, a court will grant specific performance.

Generally, courts refuse to grant specific performance of contracts for personal services—contracts that require one party to work personally for another party. Public policy discourages involuntary servitude, and ordering one party to perform personal services against her will amounts to a type of servitude. Moreover, the courts do not want to monitor personal-service contracts.

EXAMPLE 15.25 If you contract with a famous artist to paint your portrait and the artist later refuses to perform, the court will not compel the artist to perform. The court cannot assure meaningful performance in such situations.

Remedies for Breach of Sales Contracts

Remedies for breach of a contract for the sale of goods are designed to put the aggrieved party in as good a position as if the other party had fully performed. The seller's remedies for breach include the right to stop or withhold delivery of the goods and the right to recover damages or the purchase price of the goods from the buyer.

The buyer's remedies include:

---

restitution
An equitable remedy under which a person is restored to his or her original position prior to loss or injury, or placed in the position that he or she would have been in had the breach not occurred.

reformation
An equitable remedy granted by a court to correct, or "reform," a written contract so that it reflects the true intentions of the parties.

specific performance
An equitable remedy requiring exactly the performance that was specified in a contract; usually granted only when money damages would be an inadequate remedy and the subject matter of the contract is unique (for example, real property).

1. the right to reject *nonconforming goods* (goods that do not conform to those specifically agreed on in the contract) or improperly delivered goods,

2. the right to *cover* (buy goods elsewhere and recover from the seller the extra cost of obtaining the substitute goods),

3. the right to recover damages, and

4. in certain circumstances, the right to obtain specific performance of the sales contract.

Online Contracting and Electronic Signatures

Today, many contracts are formed over the Internet. In general, the courts apply the traditional principles of contract law in cyberspace. Many disputes concerning contracts formed online tend to center on the specific terms of the contract and whether the parties voluntarily agreed to those terms.

Online Offers and Acceptances

Generally, the terms of an online offer should be as comprehensive as the terms in an offer made in a written (paper) document. Possible contingencies should be anticipated and provided for in the offer. Because jurisdictional issues often arise with online transactions, dispute-settlement provisions, such as arbitration clauses, are frequently used. The offer should be displayed on the screen so as to be easily readable and clear. An online offer should also include some mechanism, such as providing an "I agree" or "I accept" box, by which a customer accepts the offer.

Click-On Agreements

As described earlier, a click-on agreement (also sometimes called a *click-on license, click-through agreement,* or *click-wrap agreement*) arises when a buyer, completing a transaction on a computer, indicates assent to be bound by the terms of an offer by clicking on a button that says "I agree" or "I accept." The terms may be contained on a website through which the buyer is obtaining goods or services, or they may appear when software is loaded. The courts normally enforce click-on agreements.

EXAMPLE 15.26 Aaron is downloading a new program. A message pops up on the screen with a window through which Aaron can read the licensing agreement. (Note that a contract involving software usually grants a license by which a party is given the right to use the software but does not own the software.) Even if Aaron clicks on the "I agree" box below the window without reading the terms, he will nonetheless be bound by the terms of that agreement.

Shrink-Wrap Agreements

A **shrink-wrap agreement** is an agreement whose terms are expressed inside the box in which the goods are packaged. *Shrink-wrap* refers to the plastic that may cover the box. Usually, the party who opens the box is told that he agrees to the terms by keeping whatever is in the box.

shrink-wrap agreement
An agreement whose terms are expressed in a document located inside the box in which the goods (usually software) are packaged.

EXAMPLE 15.27 Abdul orders a new computer that is sent by FedEx. When he receives the computer, he finds that the box also contains an agreement setting forth the terms of the sale, including what remedies are available. The document states that Abdul's use of the computer for more than thirty days is construed as an acceptance of the terms.

In many cases, a shrink-wrap agreement is between the manufacturer of the hardware or software and the ultimate buyer-user of the product, although it may be between a retailer and a buyer. Thus, the terms typically concern warranties, remedies, and other issues associated with the use of the product.

Generally, the courts have enforced the terms of shrink-wrap agreements with one exception: If a court finds that the buyer learned of the shrink-wrap terms *after* the parties entered into a contract, the court may conclude that those terms were proposals for additional terms and were not part of the contract unless the buyer expressly agreed to them.

EXAMPLE 15.28 When Abdul entered into the contract to purchase the computer, he was not informed in the online materials that any dispute regarding his purchase had to be arbitrated. He used the computer and a month later it failed and lost all the data he had entered. He then discovered that the shrink-wrap agreement included an arbitration clause. In that situation, a court may conclude that the arbitration clause—which Abdul did not know about—was a proposal rather than part of the agreement.

E-Signatures

In some instances, a contract cannot be enforced unless it is signed by the party against whom enforcement is sought. An issue in Internet transactions has to do with how electronic signatures, or e-signatures, can be created and verified on e-contracts.

In the days when many people could not write, documents were often signed with an "X." Then handwritten signatures became common, followed by typed signatures, printed signatures, and, most recently, digital signatures, which are transmitted electronically. In the evolution of signature technology, the question of what constitutes a valid signature is a major issue—without consensus on what constitutes a valid signature, little business could be accomplished.

Today, several technologies allow electronic documents to be signed. The use of a trusted program such as Adobe EchoSign helps ensure that signatures are valid. Because paralegals are frequently responsible for obtaining the necessary signatures on legal documents, some knowledge of digital signatures and alternative technologies is useful.

e-signature
An electronic sound, symbol, or process attached to or logically associated with a record and executed or adopted by a person with the intent to sign the record, according to the Uniform Electronic Transactions Act.

State Laws Governing E-Signatures

Most states have laws governing e-signatures. In an attempt to create uniformity among these laws, the National Conference of Commissioners on Uniform State Laws and the American Law Institute issued the Uniform Electronic Transactions Act (UETA). It has been adopted, at least in part, by forty-seven states (the other three states have other laws to recognize such signatures). The UETA states that a signature or a contract may not be denied legal effect or enforceability solely because it is in electronic form.

Under the UETA, an *e-signature* is broadly defined as "an electronic sound, symbol, or process attached to or logically associated with a record and executed or adopted by a person with the intent to sign the record." In other words, the signature does not have to be created by any specific technology and can be simply a person's name typed at the end of an e-mail message. The parties do have to agree to conduct business electronically for the UETA provisions to apply. Also, the UETA states that it does not apply to (or change) the provisions of the UCC and does not apply to wills and trusts.

Federal Law on E-Signatures and E-Documents

Congress enacted the Electronic Signatures in Global and National Commerce Act (E-SIGN Act) to provide that no contract, record, or signature may be "denied legal effect" solely because it is in an electronic form. In other words, an electronic signature is as valid as a signature on paper, and an electronic document can be as enforceable as a paper one. For an e-signature to be enforceable, the contracting parties must have agreed to use e-signatures. For an e-document to be valid, it must be in a form that can be retained and accurately reproduced.

The E-SIGN Act does not apply to every document. Contracts and documents that are exempt include court papers, divorce decrees, evictions, foreclosures, health-insurance terminations, prenuptial agreements, and wills.

Electronic contracting has expanded to include many possibilities. From a remote location, a person can open an account with a financial institution, obtain a mortgage or other loan, buy insurance, retain an attorney, and purchase real estate over the Internet. Payments and transfers of funds can be done entirely online. By using e-contracts, a person can avoid the time and costs associated with producing, delivering, signing, and returning paper documents.

Intellectual Property Law

The contract law had its origins hundreds of years ago. Now we move to an area of law that, although it has existed for some time, has rapidly grown in importance in recent years. Most people think of wealth in terms of houses, land, cars, stocks, and bonds. Wealth, however, also includes intellectual property, the products that result from intellectual, creative processes. As the *Developing Paralegal Skills* feature below notes, complex strategic issues involving intellectual property (IP) are becoming more important in law practice.

intellectual property
Property resulting from intellectual, creative processes.

Although it is an abstract term, intellectual property is nonetheless wholly familiar to virtually everyone. *Trademarks, copyrights, trade secrets,* and *patents* are all forms of intellectual property. This book is copyrighted. If you drink a Coke™ you consume a product with a trademarked name, made by a formula that is a trade secret, advertised

DEVELOPING PARALEGAL SKILLS

NEW STRATEGIES IN INTELLECTUAL PROPERTY

A growing area of practice in intellectual property (IP) law involves licensing agreements between owners of patents, copyrights, and trademarks. Not only do IP owners often license rights to other businesses, but strategies to reduce taxes often lead firms to put their collection of IP rights in a subsidiary. For example, the band U2 moved the IP rights to their music to the Netherlands to reduce taxes on their royalties. Similarly, Google used what is called the "double Irish" strategy. It licensed the European rights to its search and advertising business to Google Ireland Holdings, based in Bermuda, where taxes are low. It operates the business through Google Ireland Limited, which passes the revenue to the Bermuda-based company.

A key part of any licensing or IP-based tax strategy is proper valuation of the intellectual property rights involved. Paralegals are often involved in documenting the value of the IP rights, which must be done with great care. For patents, you might be asked to research the following:

• Is the patent in force in the relevant jurisdiction, and have all fees been paid?

• Are there related patents listed in the foreign or domestic patent applications? If so, who owns them?

• What is the scope of the patent claim? Were there any amendments that narrow or broaden the scope made during the application process?

• Is there any past or pending litigation involving the patent?

• Are there any "blocking" patents, i.e., patents on which this patent infringes?

• Is the patent protected in relevant foreign jurisdictions?

By researching these types of questions and documenting the answers, a paralegal can assist in establishing a fair valuation for IP rights that will enable firms to negotiate the sale of rights or to claim appropriate tax benefits.

using copyrighted material, and manufactured with patented equipment. The apps you use, the movies you see, and the music you listen to are all forms of intellectual property.

The need to protect creative works was voiced by the framers of the U.S. Constitution more than two hundred years ago: Article I, Section 8, of the Constitution authorized Congress "[t]o promote the Progress of Science and useful Arts, by securing for limited Times to Authors and Inventors the exclusive Right to their respective Writings and Discoveries." Laws protecting patents, trademarks, and copyrights are designed to protect and reward inventive and artistic creativity. Exhibit 15.2 below summarizes the forms of intellectual property, how they are acquired, and what remedies are available for *infringement*, or unauthorized use.

Growing Value of Intellectual Property

The study of intellectual property law is important because intellectual property has taken on increasing significance. In the digital age, the value of the world's intellectual property exceeds the value of physical property, such as machines and houses.

EXHIBIT 15.2

Forms of Intellectual Property

	Definition	How Acquired	Duration	Remedy for Infringement
Patent	A grant from the government that gives an inventor exclusive rights to an invention.	By filing a patent application with the U.S. Patent and Trademark Office and receiving its approval.	For inventions, 20 years from the date of application; for design patents, 14 years from the date of application.	Money damages, including royalties and lost profits, *plus* attorneys' fees. Damages may be tripled for intentional infringements.
Copyright	The right of an author or a creator of a literary or artistic work or other production (such as a computer program) to have the exclusive use of that work for a given period of time.	Automatic (once the work or creation is put in tangible form). Only the *expression* of an idea (and not the idea itself) can be protected by copyright.	For authors: the life of the author plus 70 years. For publishers: 95 years after the date of publication or 120 years after creation.	Actual damages plus profits received by the party who infringed or statutory damages under the Copyright Act, *plus* costs and attorneys' fees in either situation.
Trademark	A distinctive word, name, symbol, or device that an entity uses to distinguish its goods or services from those of others. The owner has the exclusive right to use that mark.	1. At common law, created by use of the mark. 2. Registration with the U.S. Patent and Trademark Office; mark must already be in use or be placed in use within the following six months.	Unlimited, as long as the mark is in use. To continue notice by registration, holder must renew between the fifth and sixth years and, thereafter, every ten years.	1. Injunction prohibiting future use of mark. 2. Actual damages plus profits received by the party who infringed. 3. Destruction of articles that infringed. 4. *Plus* costs and attorneys' fees.
Trade Secret	A business secret that makes a company or product unique and that would be of value to a competitor. Trade secrets include customer lists, plans, and research and development.	Through the development of the information and processes that constitute the business secret.	Unlimited, so long as not revealed to others (once a trade secret is revealed to others, it is no longer secret).	Money damages for misappropriation (the Uniform Trade Secrets Act also permits punitive damages if willful), *plus* costs and attorneys' fees.

Ownership rights in intangible intellectual property are more important to the prosperity of U.S. companies than are their tangible assets. Because of the importance of obtaining and protecting intellectual property rights, attorneys and paralegals with specialized knowledge in this area are in great demand in law firms and in corporations.

Patents

A patent is a grant from the government that gives an inventor the exclusive right to make, use, and sell an invention for a period of twenty years from the date of filing the application for a patent. Patents for designs, as opposed to inventions, are given for a fourteen-year period. To secure a patent, the applicant must demonstrate to the satisfaction of examiners at the U.S. Patent and Trademark Office that the invention, discovery, process, or design is genuine, novel, useful, and not obvious in light of current technology. In case of a race to invent and protect, the law protects the first to file for a patent, not the first to invent. A patent holder gives notice to all that an article or design is patented by placing on it the word *Patent* or *Pat.* and the patent number.

Filing patents is complicated and is a specialized area of law. One may become a *patent agent* by passing the patent bar examination; a law degree is not required, but advanced technical knowledge is. A lawyer who passes the patent bar is a patent attorney. Often, patents must be filed in multiple nations, so the expense of dealing with the different requirements in Europe and Japan can be considerable.

If a firm makes, uses, or sells another's patented design, product, or process without permission, it commits the tort of patent infringement. Patent infringement may exist even though the patent owner has not put the patented product in commerce. Patent infringement may also occur even though not all features or parts of an invention are copied. With respect to a patented process, however, all steps or their equivalent must be copied for infringement to exist.

patent
A government grant that gives an inventor the exclusive right or privilege to make, use, or sell an invention for a limited time period.

Copyrights

Literary or artistic productions (including computer software) are protected under copyright law. A copyright gives the creator of a work the right to the exclusive use of that work for a given period of time. The Copyright Act of 1976, as amended, governs copyrights. Works are automatically given statutory copyright protection for the life of the author plus 70 years. For works by more than one author, the copyright expires 70 years after the death of the last surviving author. For copyrights owned by publishing houses, the copyright expires 95 years from the date of publication or 120 years from the date of creation, whichever is first.

Copyrights can be registered with the U.S. Copyright Office in Washington, D.C. (but registration is not required). It is a simple and inexpensive process. A copyright owner also no longer needs to place a © or *Copyright* on the work to have the work protected against infringement. Chances are that if somebody created it, somebody owns it.

copyright
The exclusive right of an author (or other creator) to publish, print, or sell an intellectual production for a statutory period of time.

What Can Be Copyrighted?

It is not possible to copyright an *idea*. Others may freely use the ideas embodied in a work. What is copyrightable is how an idea is *expressed*. When an idea and an expression are inseparable, the expression cannot be copyrighted. Generally, anything that is not an original expression of an idea does not qualify for copyright protection. Facts widely known to the public are not copyrightable. Page numbers normally are not copyrightable because they follow a sequence known to everyone. Mathematical calculations are not copyrightable. The key requirement to obtain copyright protection is originality, but the work need not have market value.

Copyright Infringement

When the form or expression of an idea is copied, an infringement of copyright occurs. The reproduction does not have to be exactly the same as the original, nor does it have to reproduce the original in its entirety.

Penalties or remedies can be imposed on those who infringe copyrights. These range from actual damages (damages based on the actual harm caused to the copyright holder by the infringement) or statutory damages. Damages provided for under the Copyright Act for willful infringement is up to $150,000 per work. In most instances damages are $750 to $30,000 per work at the discretion of the court. When many copyrighted songs have been downloaded and improperly distributed, the total damages can be huge.

An exception to liability for copyright infringement is made under the "fair use" doctrine. Under the Copyright Act, a person or organization can in certain situations reproduce copyrighted material without paying royalties (fees paid to the copyright holder for the privilege of reproducing the copyrighted material). Generally, the courts determine whether a particular use is fair on a case-by-case basis.

Trademarks and Related Property

trademark
A distinctive mark, motto, device, or emblem that a manufacturer stamps, prints, or otherwise affixes to the goods it produces so that they can be identified on the market and their origins made known. Once a trademark is established (under the common law or through registration), the owner is entitled to its exclusive use.

A **trademark** is a distinctive mark, motto, or emblem that a manufacturer stamps, prints, or otherwise affixes to the goods it produces so they can be distinguished from the goods of other manufacturers and merchants. Examples of trademarks are brand-name labels on jeans, luggage, shoes, and other products. Generally, to be protected under trademark law, a mark must be distinctive. A distinctive mark might consist of an uncommon or invented word (such as *Xerox, Exxon,* or *Google*) or words used in an uncommon or fanciful way (such as *English Leather* for an aftershave lotion instead of for leather processed in England).

At common law, the person who used a symbol or mark to identify a business or product was protected in the use of that trademark. Today, trademarks are usually registered with the federal government. The registration process is easy and the Trademark Office website allows you to search all existing marks. A mark can be registered with the Trademark Office (1) if it is already in commerce or (2) if the applicant intends to put the mark into commerce within six months.

A person need not have registered a trademark in order to sue for trademark infringement, but registration furnishes proof of the date the owner began using the trademark. Only those trademarks that are deemed sufficiently distinctive from competing trademarks will be protected.

Trade dress is an extension of trademark. It applies to the look and feel of a product or service. For example, Home Depot stores have orange signage. Because the company has invested in developing that distinctive look, and it is well recognized by consumers, other home supply stores cannot imitate the orange motif claimed by Home Depot. Similarly, Owens Corning insulation is colored pink. The company has spent large sums in advertisements featuring the pink product. The color is not functional; it is distinctive to the product, so other insulation makers cannot use the color.

Trade Names

trade name
A term that is used to indicate part or all of a business's name and that is directly related to the business's reputation and goodwill. Trade names are protected under the common law (and under trademark law, if the business's name is the same as its trademark).

Trademarks apply to *products*. The term **trade name** is used to indicate part or all of a business's name, such as McDonald's. Unless the trade name is also used as a trademark (as with Coca-Cola, for example), the name is not protected under federal trademark law. Trade names are protected under the common law, however. Holiday Inns, Inc., which does business as (d/b/a) Holiday Inn, for example, could sue a motel owner who used that name or a portion of it (such as "Holiday Motels") without permission. As with trademarks, trade names must be actually used to receive protection.

Trademark Infringement

Registration of a trademark gives notice that the trademark belongs to the registrant. The registrant is allowed to use the symbol ® to indicate that the mark has been registered. Whenever that trademark is copied partly or in whole by another party (intentionally or unintentionally), the trademark has been infringed and the owner can sue. The extent of protection depends on real use and recognition of the mark in the market. The fact that a mark owner thinks her business will be global does not matter if in fact it is small and not known. Marks are limited to specific goods or services in the areas in which a firm actually operates. If a mark is truly famous, such as Nike, then it receives protection in all markets.

Trademark Dilution

Historically, federal trademark law prohibited the unauthorized use of the same mark on competing or "related" goods or services only when such use would be likely to confuse consumers. The federal Trademark Dilution Act extends that protection.

Trademark *dilution* occurs when a trademark is used, without authorization, in a way that diminishes the distinctive quality of the mark. Unlike trademark infringement, a dilution cause of action does not require proof that consumers are likely to be confused by a connection between the unauthorized use and the mark. For this reason, the products (or services) involved do not have to be similar. In addition, a famous mark may be diluted not only by the use of an *identical* mark but also by the use of a *similar* mark.

Trade Secrets

Business processes and information that are not (or cannot be) patented, copyrighted, or trademarked may be protected against appropriation by a competitor as trade secrets. Trade secrets consist of customer lists, plans, research and development, pricing information, marketing techniques, production techniques, and generally anything that is in fact not known outside the company and that would have value to a competitor.

trade secret
Information or processes that give a business an advantage over competitors who do not know the information or processes.

What Is Protected?

Unlike copyright and trademark protection, protection of trade secrets extends both to ideas and to their expression. Of course, the secret formula, method, or other information must be disclosed to some persons, particularly to key employees. Businesses must actively protect their trade secrets. The owner of the secret must restrict access to the knowledge and, commonly, all employees who use the process or information agree, by a signed confidentiality agreement, never to divulge or use the information outside of the company.

To protect intellectual property a firm must know what assets it possesses. See this chapter's *Featured Contributor* article on pages 472 and 473 on auditing intellectual property.

Misappropriation of Trade Secrets

One who discloses or uses another's trade secret, without a privilege to do so, is liable to the other if (1) he or she discovered the secret by improper means or (2) the disclosure or use constitutes a breach of confidence. The theft of confidential business data through industrial espionage, such as when a business taps into a competitor's computer, is a theft of trade secrets and is actionable.

At one time, virtually all law with respect to trade secrets was common law. In an effort to reduce the unpredictability of the law in this area, the Uniform Trade Secrets Act (UTSA) was proposed. Today, it has been adopted in forty-seven states. New York and Massachusetts have not adopted it; North Carolina has a statute similar to the UTSA. Under the UTSA, a plaintiff can also recover punitive damages for willful misappropriation of business secrets.

A federal statute, the Economic Espionage Act, also addresses trade secret theft. While its focus is on the theft of trade secrets that are sold to foreign entities, it also applies to domestic theft. Violations of the statute can result in a prison term and significant fines.

FEATURED CONTRIBUTOR

STRATEGIES FOR PROTECTING INTELLECTUAL PROPERTY: THE INTELLECTUAL PROPERTY AUDIT

Deborah E. Bouchoux

BIOGRAPHICAL NOTE

Deborah E. Bouchoux is an attorney licensed to practice in the District of Columbia. She has been involved in paralegal education for more than twenty years. Bouchoux teaches in the Paralegal Studies Program at Georgetown University in Washington, D.C., and serves as a member of the advisory board for the program.

Ms. Bouchoux is a frequent lecturer for the National Capital Area Paralegal Association and is the author of *Intellectual Property: The Law of Trademarks, Copyrights, Patents, and Trade Secrets*, as well as *Protecting Your Company's Intellectual Property: A Practical Guide to Trademarks, Copyrights, Patents, and Trade Secrets*.

Because clients are often unaware of the value of their intangible assets or intellectual property, many law firms conduct intellectual property audits for their clients. The audit will identify the intellectual property owned by the client, and the legal team and the client will then develop strategies to protect and exploit that property. Audits are also conducted when a company sells its assets or merges with another entity. The buyer will want to know what type of intellectual property assets the selling company possesses so that it will know what assets it is acquiring and can ensure that it will not be inheriting infringement lawsuits. For example, after Apple bought Beats Electronics in May 2014, Bose Corporation sued Beats for infringement of its noise-canceling headphone patents (with the case settling later in 2014). This type of audit is often referred to as a due-diligence review.

THE NEED FOR INTELLECTUAL PROPERTY AUDITS

Clients may not understand the value of their intellectual property portfolios and the need to protect their rights. They may be using unique marketing materials that should be copyrighted, slogans that should be trademarked, inventions that may be patentable, and confidential information that should be protected as trade secrets. Without protection, valuable rights may be lost. For example, the disclosure of confidential information may lead to a loss of trade-secret rights and result in declining profits.

Once companies realize what intellectual property they own, they can use that intellectual property to create revenue. Trademarks, copyrights, patents, and trade secrets can all be licensed to others for fees to generate a continuing revenue stream for the company. IBM reportedly earns more than $1 billion annually from licensing and sales of its intellectual property,

and Hewlett-Packard's website identifies its intellectual property assets that are available to be licensed.

Routinely conducted audits also save the client time. In the event the client wishes to borrow money from a bank, it will have an accurate and up-to-date list of its intellectual property assets that can then be pledged as collateral to ensure repayment of the loan to the bank. Similarly, if the company is the subject of an acquisition, it will have a current list of the intellectual property assets the buyer will be acquiring and will only need to update the information since the last audit, ensuring that the acquisition can be completed promptly. If there are agreements in place that would restrict a buyer from using the seller's intellectual property, the transaction price can be restructured to account for such a loss, or an insurance policy can be included as part of the terms.

STRATEGIES FOR CONDUCTING AN INTELLECTUAL PROPERTY AUDIT

There are several steps in conducting a successful intellectual property audit. These steps are explored in the following subsections.

Designating the Team. The law firm should designate an attorney and paralegal to serve as representatives of the firm, and the company should select an individual who will serve as the company's team leader. Together, these individuals will be primarily responsible for conducting the audit and can answer any questions that may arise in the course of the audit. The team should have a preliminary meeting to discuss the scope and nature of the audit. For example, the client will need to determine whether only U.S. materials will be reviewed or whether consideration will be given to seeking protection in foreign countries for certain trademarks and patents. The involvement of legal counsel ensures that any matters discussed are subject to the attorney-client privilege and remain confidential.

Preparing the Audit Questionnaire. The legal team should prepare a worksheet or questionnaire for the client that is designed to elicit information from the client about its intellectual property assets. Paralegals play a significant role in drafting the audit questionnaire. The audit questionnaire will typically ask the following:

- Does the client use any specific names, logos, or slogans in advertising its products and services?

- Are any written materials used in marketing (such as brochures, newspaper or Web-based advertisements, and materials used for presentations)?

- Has the client developed any inventions, products, software, or processes?

- Does the client use any software or products owned by another entity?

- Does the client use any confidential methods or processes in developing and marketing its products and services, including financial forecasts, marketing plans, and customer lists?

- Has the company ever been sued for or accused of infringing another party's intellectual property rights?

- How does the company control access to its valuable and proprietary materials to protect against inadvertent disclosure or misappropriation of these materials?

- Do employment, confidentiality, nondisclosure, and noncompete contracts exist to protect proprietary materials?

The questionnaire should be tailored to the needs of the client. For example, companies engaged in telecommunications services or software development will need detailed sections designed to obtain information on software products and proprietary information. In contrast, companies engaged in consulting will likely have no "products" that need protection but will have a wealth of written materials that should be protected as trade secrets or registered as copyrights.

Conducting the Audit. On receiving the questionnaire, the client should begin gathering the materials that are responsive to the questionnaire. The legal team will then review the materials that the client has assembled to determine which materials can be protected under intellectual property law. If the client has a website, it should be carefully reviewed to ensure not only that the site is protected under copyright law but also that it does not infringe on the rights of another party by, for example, using another's copyrighted music or artwork. Paralegals often coordinate the time and manner of the audit by scheduling the audit date, arranging for a conference room, and ensuring that a photocopy machine is available to copy documents that are responsive to the questionnaire. Generally, the audit is conducted at the client's office because this is where the pertinent materials and documents are located.

Writing the Audit Report. After conducting the audit, the legal team prepares a written report for the client summarizing the results of the audit. The report identifies all of the intellectual property owned by the client and makes recommendations for its continued protection and maintenance. For example, the audit may disclose that the client uses a distinctive slogan in its advertising materials or that title to some of the intellectual property assets is unclear or out of date. The legal team will then recommend that the slogan be registered as a trademark and that the chain of title be corrected to reflect current ownership of the intellectual property.

POSTAUDIT ACTIVITY

After the audit is complete, the legal team, and particularly the paralegal, will begin preparing applications to register trademarks, copyrights, and patents and will develop written policies to protect the client's trade secrets. The team will need to ensure that the U.S. Patent and Trademark Office and Copyright Office records accurately reflect ownership of the company's trademarks, patents, and copyrights. Contracts will need to be drafted for the client to use when it hires independent contractors to develop certain products, such as software. Such contracts will clarify that the company will own all rights to any work products produced by those independent contractors. License agreements may need to be drafted so that the company can license its intellectual property to others to use. Internet and social use policies may be needed so that all employees are aware of the confidential nature of the company's electronic communications. The company will be advised to review materials used by its competitors to ensure that the competitors do not infringe on the company's valuable intellectual property rights—by using a trademark that is confusingly similar to one owned by the company, for example. Finally, the paralegal will implement a docketing system to ensure that the client's intellectual property rights are maintained. For example, the paralegal should calendar the dates for maintenance and renewal of company trademarks and maintenance of patents. The paralegal should also schedule the date of the next intellectual property audit.

Paralegals play a significant role in drafting the audit questionnaire."

KEY TERMS AND CONCEPTS

Chapter Summary / Contracts and Intellectual Property Law

REQUIREMENTS TO FORM A VALID CONTRACT

A contract is any agreement (based on a promise or an exchange of promises) that can be enforced in court. To form a valid contract, four basic requirements must be met.

1. *Agreement*—An agreement includes an offer and an acceptance. One party must offer to enter into a legal agreement, and another party must accept the terms of the offer.

   a. An offer is a promise to do or to refrain from doing some specified thing in the future.

   b. The offeror must have the intent to be bound, the terms must be reasonably certain or definite, and the offer must be communicated to the offeree.

   c. Both a rejection of the offer and the making of a counteroffer terminate the original offer. The offer is also terminated if the party making the offer withdraws the offer before it has been accepted. Otherwise, the offer expires after a reasonable period of time has passed.

   d. An offer may automatically terminate by law if the subject matter is destroyed, one party dies or becomes incompetent, or the contract becomes illegal.

   e. The terms of the acceptance must be the same as ("mirror") the terms of the offer.

   f. Acceptance of an offer is timely if it is made before the offer is terminated. Acceptance takes effect at the time the acceptance is communicated via the mode expressly or impliedly authorized by the offeror. This is called the *mailbox rule.*

   g. If the contract does not specify the method of acceptance, an offer may be accepted by any means that is reasonable under the circumstances.

2. *Consideration*—Consideration is usually defined as "something of value"—such as money or the performance of an action—given in exchange for a promise.

   a. To be legally sufficient, consideration must involve a legal detriment to the promisee, a legal benefit to the promisor, or both.

   b. In general, a court will not question the adequacy of consideration (fairness of the bargain). Courts will inquire into the adequacy of consideration only when fraud, undue influence, duress, or incompetence is involved.

   c. Some contracts may be enforced (or partially enforced) under the doctrine of promissory estoppel even though consideration is lacking.

3. *Contractual capacity*—The parties to the contract must have the legal ability to enter into a contractual relationship. Courts generally presume contractual capacity unless one party is a minor, intoxicated, or mentally incompetent.

4. *Legality*—A contract to do something that is prohibited by federal or state statutory law is illegal and, as such, void from the outset and thus unenforceable.

a. Contracts entered into by persons who do not have a license, when one is required by statute, may not be enforceable.

b. Some contracts are not enforced because the court deems them to be contrary to public policy.

DEFENSES TO CONTRACT ENFORCEABILITY

A contract that meets all the above requirements may not be enforceable if (1) the parties have not genuinely assented (agreed) to its terms, (2) the contract is so oppressive to one of the parties that a court will refuse to enforce it, or (3) the contract is not in the proper form.

1. *Genuineness of assent*—A contract can be avoided if there was a lack of real consent. This may be due to mistake of material fact (not value) when both parties are mistaken (mutual mistake). Lack of consent could also be based on fraudulent misrepresentation in making the contract, or be a result of undue influence (when free will is overcome by another party) or duress (making a contract under fear or a threat).

2. *Unconscionable contracts*—When a contract is so oppressive to one of the parties that a court will refuse to enforce it, the oppressed party will be excused from performance. These situations usually involve an adhesion contract, which is a contract drafted by the dominant party and presented on a "take-it-or-leave-it" basis.

3. *Statute of Frauds*—Every state has a Statute of Frauds, which is a statute that specifies what types of contracts must be in writing (or be evidenced by a written document). The following types of contracts are normally required to be in writing:

   a. Contracts involving interests in land.

   b. Contracts that cannot by their terms be performed within one year from the day after the date of formation.

   c. Collateral, or secondary, contracts, such as promises to answer for the debt or duty of another.

   d. Promises made in consideration of marriage.

   e. Contracts for the sale of goods priced at $500 or more.

SALES CONTRACTS AND WARRANTIES

States have statutes to replace common law contracts in certain areas of commerce.

1. *The scope of UCC Article 2*—The Uniform Commercial Code (UCC) governs contracts for the sale of goods (as opposed to real property or services). The UCC primarily comes into play when disputes arise over ambiguous or missing terms and when the buyer or seller is a merchant.

2. *Warranties under the UCC*—The UCC contains provisions on express and implied warranties that arise when goods are sold. For example, under the UCC, every merchant warrants that the goods are reasonably fit for the ordinary purpose for which such goods are used.

CONTRACT PERFORMANCE AND REMEDIES

The most common way to terminate contractual duties under a common law contract or UCC-based contract is by the performance of those duties. Failure to perform contractual duties as promised results in a breach of the contract.

1. *Contract performance*—Performance that provides a party with the important and essential benefits of a contract, in spite of deviations from the terms, is substantial performance. Because substantial performance is not in full compliance with the contract, the other party is entitled to damages to compensate for the failure to comply with the contract. However, if, after a contract has been made, performance becomes objectively impossible (the subject matter is destroyed, for example), then performance is excused because of impossibility or commercial impracticability.

2. *Contract remedies*—When there is a breach, remedies can include the following:

   a. Money damages are a legal remedy designed to compensate a party for the loss of the bargain.

      1. Compensatory damages compensate the injured party for damages actually sustained. Incidental damages are for expenses caused directly by a breach of contract, such as the cost of obtaining performance from another source.

      2. Consequential damages flow from the party's breach and were foreseeable at the time the contract was formed.

      3. Liquidated damages are an amount specified in the contract in case of a failure to perform.

b. The following equitable remedies are available only in limited circumstances:

   1. Rescission is an action to undo or cancel the contract. When a contract is rescinded, restitution must be made.

   2. Reformation is an action in which the court rewrites the contract to reflect the parties' true agreement.

   3. Specific performance, which requires a party to perform the contract, is available when money damages are an inadequate remedy.

3. *Remedies for breach of sales contracts*—The UCC may provide additional remedies to buyers and sellers (such as the buyer's right to reject nonconforming goods).

ONLINE CONTRACTING AND ELECTRONIC SIGNATURES

Many contracts are formed over the Internet. How the courts apply the traditional rules of contract law is an increasingly important issue. Generally, the terms of the offer should be just as comprehensive as in written documents. The method of acceptance should also be specified.

1. *Online offers and acceptances*—As with regular contracts, it is best to have clear terms to reduce grounds for later disputes. The courts enforce click-on agreements where the buyer accepts the offer by clicking "I agree" or something similar. Similarly, shrink-wrap agreements, when the terms are expressed inside or on the box in which the goods are packaged, are agreed to by keeping the goods. Courts enforce such agreements unless the buyer learned of the terms after entering the contract.

2. *E-signatures*—Digital signatures verify the identity of parties to a contract. A party's signature can be electronically encoded onto a key or card that is verified by a third party or can be digitally captured and attached to the electronic document.

3. *State laws governing e-signatures*—The Uniform Electronic Transactions Act (UETA), which governs e-signatures, has been adopted, at least in part, by forty-seven states.

4. *Federal law on e-signatures and e-documents*—The Electronic Signatures in Global and National Commerce Act (E-SIGN Act) gave validity to e-signatures by providing that no contract, record, or signature may be "denied legal effect" solely because it is in electronic form.

INTELLECTUAL PROPERTY LAW

Intellectual property—the products that result from intellectual, creative processes—is becoming increasingly valuable. The following are the four basic types of intellectual property rights. If a party infringes on these rights, the owner of the property can file suit and possibly obtain damages.

1. *Patent*—A grant from the government that gives an inventor the exclusive right to make, use, and sell an invention.

2. *Copyright*—The right of an author or a creator of a literary or artistic work or other production (such as a computer program) to have the exclusive use of that work for a given period of time.

3. *Trademarks and related property*—A distinctive mark or motto that a manufacturer stamps, prints, or affixes to goods so that its products are distinguishable from those of others. Trademarks apply to products, whereas trade names apply to business names. Infringements and dilution of marks are bases for suits for unauthorized use of the property.

4. *Trade secret*—A business secret that makes a particular company or product unique and that would be of value to a competitor (such as customer lists, plans, and research and development).

■ QUESTIONS FOR REVIEW

1. What are the four basic requirements for forming a valid contract? Are there any circumstances in which the court will enforce the parties' agreement even though it lacks consideration? What defenses can be used against a claim of breach of contract?

2. Consideration, a requirement for a valid contract, is defined as *something of value*. What items, other than money, meet this definition? Explain how consideration distinguishes a contract from a gift.

3. What is the Uniform Commercial Code (UCC), and to what types of contracts does it apply? How does the UCC affect the common law of contracts? What warranties exist under the UCC?

4. Describe the remedies that are available when a contract is breached. What is specific performance, and in what circumstances is it available?

5. What kinds of electronic contracts do the courts enforce? What constitutes an electronic signature, and what makes it valid? What state and federal laws govern electronic signatures and contracts?

6. List the four major forms of intellectual property and describe what intellectual property is. Why is it significant in the law today?

ETHICS QUESTION

Shayna is a paralegal at a bank. She reviews a package of loan documents for a complex commercial transaction that has been submitted by the lawyers for the borrower. She does not fully understand one provision in the documents that eliminates the need for a guarantor. A guarantor promises that the loan will be repaid in the event that the borrower fails to do so, an important protection for the bank.

Shayna does not include this provision in her summary to her supervising attorney, and the loan goes through without the guarantee. Later the borrower defaults on the loan and the bank is out several million dollars. What ethics rules have been violated? What might be the outcome for Shayna? For her supervising attorney?

PRACTICE QUESTIONS AND ASSIGNMENTS

1. Using the material on contract law in this chapter, identify which contract below is a bilateral contract and which is a unilateral contract:

   a. Juanita offers to sell Mier her laptop for $200. Mier agrees and tells her he will meet her in the cafeteria at noon the next day with cash.

   b. Jonah e-mails Michael and offers Michael $5,000 to paint his house green during the first week of June. Michael does not respond to Jonah's e-mail, but arrives at Jonah's house on June 1st and begins painting it green.

2. Bernie, the sole owner of a small business, has a large piece of used farm equipment for sale. He offers to sell the equipment to Hank for $10,000. Discuss what happens to the offer in the following situations:

   a. Bernie dies prior to Hank's acceptance; at the time he accepts, Hank is unaware of Bernie's death.

   b. The night before Hank accepts, a fire destroys the equipment.

3. Using the material on acceptances presented in this chapter, identify which situation below will result in a contract:

   a. Kelly offers to sell her used algebra textbook to Patrick for $50. He responds, "Maybe—if I have enough money once I get my book refund later this week."

   b. Kirk offers Kristina $50 for her textbook. Kristina says, "Sure. I'll drop it off in the morning."

4. Using the material on contract law presented in this chapter, identify which defenses the defendants in the following hypothetical cases might use in an action for breach of contract:

   a. Mrs. Martinez, a Spanish-speaking immigrant, buys a washing machine and signs a financing agreement that allows her to pay for it in monthly installments. The agreement contains a clause that allows the store to repossess the appliance if she misses a payment. Mrs. Martinez misses the next-to-the-last payment. The store notifies Mrs. Martinez that she has breached her contract and that it intends to repossess the washing machine. How might Mrs. Martinez defend against the store's action?

   b. Sally orally agrees to purchase a farm from her lifelong friend, Fred. She promises to pay Fred $120,000 for the farm. She trusts Fred, so she does not put the deal in writing. A few days later, Fred sells the same property to Nell for $140,000. Fred and Nell put their agreement in writing. When Sally learns of Fred's contract with Nell, she sues Fred for breach of contract. What is Fred's defense?

   c. Rob enters into a contract with Tom to sell Tom fifty sweaters in Christmas colors and featuring Christmas designs. The first shipment of sweaters is due on October 1, 2017. When the sweaters are not delivered, Tom calls Rob and learns that the factory where the sweaters were to be produced has burned down. Tom, who is upset because he needed the sweaters for his Christmas catalog sales, sues Rob for breach of contract. What is Rob's defense?

5. Joel goes to an expensive restaurant in New York for lunch. He orders the special, pasta with white truffles.

The price is not given, and he does not ask the waiter how much it costs. When the bill arrives at the end of the meal, Joel is flabbergasted—he was charged $175 for his entrée. Does a dinner meet the definition of a sale of goods under the UCC? If so, does the UCC rule apply that where the buyer and seller have agreed to a contract but have not agreed on the price, the price must be a reasonable price for the goods, and not the price that the seller demands?

6. Using the requirements for an offer that were stated in the chapter, draft a simple offer to purchase a used iPad from a classmate. Make sure that the offer is definite and certain. Next, write an explanation (in one or two paragraphs) of how you would communicate the offer to the person, how long the offer would remain open, and what method of acceptance you would prefer.

7. Based on the material on intellectual property law presented in the chapter, in which of the following situations would a court likely hold Maruta liable for copyright or trademark infringement?

   a. At the library, Maruta photocopies ten pages from a scholarly journal relating to a topic on which she is writing a term paper.

   b. Maruta makes leather handbags and sells them in her small leather shop. She advertises her handbags as "Vutton handbags," hoping that customers might mistakenly assume that they were made by Vuitton, the well-known maker of high-quality luggage and handbags.

   c. Maruta owns a video game store. She buys a copy of the latest games from various developers. She makes copies to rent or sell to her customers.

8. Rosalia, a very experienced paralegal, works in a firm specializing in appellate law practice. She prepares many legal briefs along with her supervising attorney, and sometimes her supervising attorney just reviews, signs, and files the briefs. Recently, it has come to the firm's attention that several fee-based online legal research databases have been reproducing the firm's legal briefs in their databases and selling access to them. Rosalia's supervising attorney has obtained copyright registration over many of their briefs and is considering suing for copyright infringement. Explain whether Rosalia and her supervising attorney have a case, or whether the reproduction of the briefs represents fair use.

◢ GROUP PROJECT

In this project, each group will analyze advertisements to determine if they can be offers.

Students one and two will review the Pepsi Harrier Jet commercials (numbers one and two) on **YouTube.com** to determine the differences between the two ads. (These ads are discussed on page 451.)

Student three should locate the U.S. Second Circuit Court of Appeals opinion in this case on Google Scholar

and create a list of the reasons the court gave for finding that the first ad was held not to be enforceable.

Student four will play the two commercials for the class, explaining how they differ and offering support for the court's opinion that no legal offer was made.

◢ INTERNET PROJECTS

1. Go to the list of contract provisions found on the Ask the Lawyer website at **vlany.org/askthelawyer.info/ what-are-some-key-contract-provisions/**.

   a. How many different types of clauses are discussed? Write out a list with a one-sentence explanation of each provision.

   b. Go to FindLaw's site on business contracts at **contracts.corporate.findlaw.com**. There, you can access contracts listed by industry, by type, or by company name. Select a contract to view. Note the name of the contract and its general purpose. Does the contract use all of the clauses (reflecting typi-

   cal contract provisions) that you noted in question 1a above? List the clauses used and provide a one-sentence summary of each provision.

2. Do an Internet search to locate your state or local paralegal association. Contact it to find an intellectual property law paralegal to interview. Learn about her educational background and work history, how she got her job, and what her day-to-day work entails. Prepare a three- to five- paragraph summary of your interview, including the paralegal's name and place of employment.

NALA's *Code of Ethics and Professional Responsibility*

A paralegal must adhere strictly to the accepted standards of legal ethics and to the general principles of proper conduct. The performance of the duties of the paralegal shall be governed by specific canons as defined herein so that justice will be served and goals of the profession attained. (See *Model Standards and Guidelines for Utilization of Legal Assistants*, Section II.)

The canons of ethics set forth hereafter are adopted by the National Association of Legal Assistants, Inc., as a general guide intended to aid paralegals and attorneys. The enumeration of these rules does not mean there are not others of equal importance although not specifically mentioned. Court rules, agency rules, and statutes must be taken into consideration when interpreting the canons.

Canons of Ethics

Definition

Legal assistants, also known as paralegals, are a distinguishable group of persons who assist attorneys in the delivery of legal services. Through formal education, training and experience, legal assistants have knowledge and expertise regarding the legal system and substantive and procedural law which qualify them to do work of a legal nature under the supervision of an attorney.

NALA members also adopted the ABA definition of a legal assistant/paralegal, as follows:

> A legal assistant or paralegal is a person qualified by education, training or work experience who is employed or retained by a lawyer, law office, corporation, governmental agency or other entity who performs specifically delegated substantive legal work for which a lawyer is responsible. (Adopted by the ABA in 1997)

Canon 1

A paralegal must not perform any of the duties that attorneys only may perform nor take any actions that attorneys may not take.

Canon 2

A paralegal may perform any task which is properly delegated and supervised by an attorney, as long as the attorney is ultimately responsible to the client, maintains a direct relationship with the client, and assumes professional responsibility for the work product.

Canon 3

A paralegal must not: (a) engage in, encourage, or contribute to any act which could constitute the unauthorized practice of law; and (b) establish attorney-client relationships, set fees, give legal opinions or advice, or represent a client before a court or agency unless so authorized by that court or agency; and (c) engage in conduct or take any action which would assist or involve the attorney in a violation of professional ethics or give the appearance of professional impropriety.

Canon 4

A paralegal must use discretion and professional judgment commensurate with knowledge and experience but must not render independent legal judgment in place of an attorney. The services of an attorney are essential in the public interest whenever such legal judgment is required.

Canon 5

A paralegal must disclose his or her status as a paralegal at the outset of any professional relationship with a client, attorney, a court or administrative agency or personnel thereof, or a member of the general public. A paralegal must act prudently in determining the extent to which a client may be assisted without the presence of an attorney.

Canon 6

A paralegal must strive to maintain integrity and a high degree of competency through education and training with respect to professional responsibility, local rules and practice, and through continuing education in substantive areas of law to better assist the legal profession in fulfilling its duty to provide legal service.

Canon 7

A paralegal must protect the confidences of a client and must not violate any rule or statute now in effect or hereafter enacted controlling the doctrine of privileged communications between a client and an attorney.

Canon 8

A paralegal must disclose to his or her employer or prospective employer any pre-existing client or personal relationship that may conflict with the interests of the employer or prospective employer and/or their clients.

Canon 9

A paralegal must do all other things incidental, necessary, or expedient for the attainment of the ethics and responsibilities as defined by statute or rule of court.

Canon 10

A paralegal's conduct is guided by bar associations' codes of professional responsibility and rules of professional conduct.

NALA's *Model Standards and Guidelines for Utilization of Paralegals*

NALA's study of the professional responsibility and ethical considerations of paralegals is ongoing. This research led to the development of the NALA *Model Standards and Guidelines for Utilization of Paralegals*. This guide summarizes case law, guidelines, and ethical opinions of the various states affecting paralegals. It provides an outline of minimum qualifications and standards necessary for paralegal professionals to assure the public and the legal profession that they are, indeed, qualified. The following is a listing of the standards and guidelines.

The annotated version of the *Model Standards and Guidelines* was last revised in 2007. It is online at **www.nala.org** (select "Model Standards and Guidelines for Utilization of Paralegals" from the "About Paralegals" menu), where detailed comments are provided about each guideline.

Preamble

Proper utilization of the services of legal assistants contributes to the delivery of cost-effective, high-quality legal services. Legal assistants and the legal profession should be assured that measures exist for identifying legal assistants and their role in assisting attorneys in the delivery of legal services. Therefore, the National Association of Legal Assistants, Inc., hereby adopts these Standards and Guidelines as an educational document for the benefit of legal assistants and the legal profession.

History

The National Association of Legal Assistants adopted this Model in 1984. At the same time the following definition of a legal assistant was adopted:

> Legal assistants, also known as paralegals, are a distinguishable group of persons who assist attorneys in the delivery of legal services. Through formal education, training, and experience, legal assistants have knowledge and expertise regarding the legal system and substantive and procedural law which qualify them to do work of a legal nature under the supervision of an attorney.

Historically, there have been similar definitions adopted by various legal professional organizations. Recognizing the need for one clear definition the NALA membership approved a resolution in July 2001 to adopt the legal assistant definition of the American Bar Association (ABA). This definition continues to be utilized today.

Definition

A legal assistant or paralegal is a person qualified by education, training, or work experience who is employed or retained by a lawyer, law office, corporation, governmental agency, or other entity who performs specifically delegated substantive legal work for which a lawyer is responsible. (Adopted by the ABA in 1997 and by NALA in 2001.)

Standards

A legal assistant should meet certain minimum qualifications. The following standards may be used to determine an individual's qualifications as legal assistant:

Successful completion of the Certified Legal Assistant (CLA)/Certified Paralegal (CP) certifying examination of the National Association of Legal Assistants, Inc.;

1. Graduation from an ABA-approved program of study for legal assistants;
2. Graduation from a course of study for legal assistants which is institutionally accredited but not ABA approved, and which requires not less than the equivalent of 60 semester hours of classroom study;
3. Graduation from a course of study for legal assistants, other than those set forth in (1) and (2) above, plus not less than six months of in-house training as a legal assistant;
4. A baccalaureate degree in any field, plus not less than six months of in-house training as a legal assistant;
5. A minimum of three years of law-related experience under the supervision of an attorney, including at least six months of in-house training as a legal assistant; or
6. Two years of in-house training as a legal assistant.

For purposes of these Standards, "in-house training as a legal assistant" means attorney education of the employee concerning legal assistant duties and these Guidelines. In addition to review and analysis of assignments, the legal assistant should receive a reasonable amount of instruction directly related to the duties and obligations of the legal assistant.

Guidelines

These Guidelines relating to standards of performance and professional responsibility are intended to aid legal assistants and attorneys. The ultimate responsibility rests with an attorney who employs legal assistants to educate them with respect to the duties they are assigned and to supervise the manner in which such duties are accomplished.

Guideline 1

Legal assistants should:

- Disclose their status as legal assistants at the outset of any professional relationship with a client, other attorneys, a court or administrative agency or personnel thereof, or members of the general public;

- Preserve the confidences and secrets of all clients; and
- Understand the attorney's Rules of Professional Responsibility and these Guidelines in order to avoid any action which would involve the attorney in a violation of the Rules, or give the appearance of professional impropriety.

Guideline 2

Legal assistants should not:

- Establish attorney-client relationships;
- Set legal fees, give legal opinions or advice;
- Represent a client before a court, unless authorized to do so by said court;
- Engage in, encourage, or contribute to any act which could constitute the unauthorized practice of law.

Guideline 3

Legal assistants may perform services for an attorney in the representation of a client, provided:

- The services performed by the legal assistant do not require the exercise of independent professional legal judgment;
- The attorney maintains a direct relationship with the client and maintains control of all client matters;
- The attorney supervises the legal assistant;
- The attorney remains professionally responsible for all work on behalf of the client, including any actions taken or not taken by the legal assistant in connection therewith; and
- The services performed supplement, merge with, and become the attorney's work product.

Guideline 4

In the supervision of a legal assistant, consideration should be given to:

- Designating work assignments that correspond to the legal assistant's abilities, knowledge, training, and experience;
- Educating and training the legal assistant with respect to professional responsibility, local rules and practices, and firm policies;
- Monitoring the work and professional conduct of the legal assistant to ensure that the work is substantively correct and timely performed;
- Providing continuing education for the legal assistant in substantive matters through courses, institutes, workshops, seminars, and in-house training; and
- Encouraging and supporting membership and active participation in professional organizations.

Guideline 5

Except as otherwise provided by statute, court rule or decision, administrative rule or regulation, or the attorney's rules of professional responsibility, and within the preceding parameters and proscriptions, a legal assistant may perform any function delegated by an attorney, including but not limited to the following:

- Conduct client interviews and maintain general contact with the client after the establishment of the attorney-client relationship, so long as the client is aware of the status and function of the legal assistant, and the client contact is under the supervision of the attorney.
- Locate and interview witnesses, so long as the witnesses are aware of the status and function of the legal assistant.

- Conduct investigations and statistical and documentary research for review by the attorney.
- Conduct legal research for review by the attorney.
- Draft legal documents for review by the attorney.
- Draft correspondence and pleadings for review by and signature of the attorney.
- Summarize depositions, interrogatories, and testimony for review by the attorney.
- Attend executions of wills, real estate closings, depositions, court or administrative hearings, and trials with the attorney.
- Author and sign letters providing the legal assistant's status is clearly indicated and the correspondence does not contain independent legal opinions or legal advice.

Conclusion

These Standards and Guidelines were developed from generally accepted practices. Each supervising attorney must be aware of the specific rules, decisions, and statutes applicable to legal assistants within his/her jurisdiction.

NFPA's *Model Code of Ethics and Professional Responsibility and Guidelines for Enforcement*

Preamble

The National Federation of Paralegal Associations, Inc. ("NFPA®"), is a professional organization comprised of paralegal associations and individual paralegals throughout the United States and Canada. Members of NFPA® have varying backgrounds, experiences, education, and job responsibilities that reflect the diversity of the paralegal profession. NFPA® promotes the growth, development, and recognition of the paralegal profession as an integral partner in the delivery of legal services.

In May 1993 NFPA® adopted its Model Code of Ethics and Professional Responsibility ("Model Code") to delineate the principles for ethics and conduct to which every paralegal should aspire.

Many paralegal associations throughout the United States have endorsed the concept and content of NFPA®'s Model Code through the adoption of their own ethical codes. In doing so, paralegals have confirmed the profession's commitment to increase the quality and efficiency of legal services, as well as recognized its responsibilities to the public, the legal community, and colleagues.

Paralegals have recognized, and will continue to recognize, that the profession must continue to evolve to enhance their roles in the delivery of legal services. With increased levels of responsibility comes the need to define and enforce mandatory rules of professional conduct. Enforcement of codes of paralegal conduct is a logical and necessary step to enhance and ensure the confidence of the legal community and the public in the integrity and professional responsibility of paralegals.

In April 1997 NFPA® adopted the Model Disciplinary Rules ("Model Rules") to make possible the enforcement of the Canons and Ethical Considerations contained in the NFPA® Model Code. A concurrent determination was made that the Model Code of Ethics and Professional Responsibility, formerly aspirational in nature, should be recognized as setting forth the enforceable obligations of all paralegals.

The Model Code and Model Rules offer a framework for professional discipline, either voluntarily or through formal regulatory programs.

§1. NFPA® Model Disciplinary Rules and Ethical Considerations

1.1 A Paralegal Shall Achieve and Maintain a High Level of Competence.

Ethical Considerations

EC-1.1(a) A paralegal shall achieve competency through education, training, and work experience.

EC-1.1(b) A paralegal shall aspire to participate in a minimum of twelve (12) hours of continuing legal education, to include at least one (1) hour of ethics education, every two (2) years in order to remain current on developments in the law.

EC-1.1(c) A paralegal shall perform all assignments promptly and efficiently.

1.2 A Paralegal Shall Maintain a High Level of Personal and Professional Integrity.

Ethical Considerations

EC-1.2(a) A paralegal shall not engage in any *ex parte* communications involving the courts or any other adjudicatory body in an attempt to exert undue influence or to obtain advantage or the benefit of only one party.

EC-1.2(b) A paralegal shall not communicate, or cause another to communicate, with a party the paralegal knows to be represented by a lawyer in a pending matter without the prior consent of the lawyer representing such other party.

EC-1.2(c) A paralegal shall ensure that all timekeeping and billing records prepared by the paralegal are thorough, accurate, honest, and complete.

EC-1.2(d) A paralegal shall not knowingly engage in fraudulent billing practices. Such practices may include, but are not limited to: inflation of hours billed to a client or employer; misrepresentation of the nature of tasks performed; and/or submission of fraudulent expense and disbursement documentation.

EC-1.2(e) A paralegal shall be scrupulous, thorough, and honest in the identification and maintenance of all funds, securities, and other assets of a client and shall provide accurate accounting as appropriate.

EC-1.2(f) A paralegal shall advise the proper authority of nonconfidential knowledge of any dishonest or fraudulent acts by any person pertaining to the handling of the funds, securities, or other assets of a client. The authority to whom the report is made shall depend on the nature and circumstances of the possible misconduct (for example, ethics committees of law firms, corporations and/or paralegal associations, local or state bar associations, local prosecutors, administrative agencies, etc.). Failure to report such knowledge is in itself misconduct and shall be treated as such under these rules.

1.3 A Paralegal Shall Maintain a High Standard of Professional Conduct.

Ethical Considerations

EC-1.3(a) A paralegal shall refrain from engaging in any conduct that offends the dignity and decorum of proceedings before a court or other adjudicatory body and shall be respectful of all rules and procedures.

EC–1.3(b) A paralegal shall avoid impropriety and the appearance of impropriety and shall not engage in any conduct that would adversely affect his/her fitness to practice. Such conduct may include, but is not limited to: violence, dishonesty, interference with the administration of justice, and/or abuse of a professional position or public office.

EC–1.3(c) Should a paralegal's fitness to practice be compromised by physical or mental illness, causing that paralegal to commit an act that is in direct violation of the Model Code/Model Rules and/or the rules and/or laws governing the jurisdiction in which the paralegal practices, that paralegal may be protected from sanction upon review of the nature and circumstances of that illness.

EC–1.3(d) A paralegal shall advise the proper authority of nonconfidential knowledge of any action of another legal professional that clearly demonstrates fraud, deceit, dishonesty, or misrepresentation. The authority to whom the report is made shall depend on the nature and circumstances of the possible misconduct (for example, ethics committees of law firms, corporations and/or paralegal associations, local or state bar associations, local prosecutors, administrative agencies, etc.). Failure to report such knowledge is in itself misconduct and shall be treated as such under these rules.

EC–1.3(e) A paralegal shall not knowingly assist any individual with the commission of an act that is in direct violation of the Model Code/Model Rules and/or the rules and/or laws governing the jurisdiction in which the paralegal practices.

EC–1.3(f) If a paralegal possesses knowledge of future criminal activity, that knowledge must be reported to the appropriate authority immediately.

1.4 A Paralegal Shall Serve the Public Interest by Contributing to the Improvement of the Legal System and Delivery of Quality Legal Services, Including *Pro Bono Publico* Services.

Ethical Considerations

EC–1.4(a) A paralegal shall be sensitive to the legal needs of the public and shall promote the development and implementation of programs that address those needs.

EC–1.4(b) A paralegal shall support efforts to improve the legal system and access thereto and shall assist in making changes.

EC–1.4(c) A paralegal shall support and participate in the delivery of *Pro Bono Publico* services directed toward implementing and improving access to justice, the law, the legal system, or the paralegal and legal professions.

EC–1.4(d) A paralegal should aspire annually to contribute twenty-four (24) hours of *Pro Bono Publico* services under the supervision of an attorney or as authorized by administrative, statutory, or court authority to:

1. persons of limited means; or
2. charitable, religious, civic, community, governmental, and educational organizations in matters that are designed primarily to address the legal needs of persons with limited means; or
3. individuals, groups, or organizations seeking to secure or protect civil rights, civil liberties, or public rights.

The twenty-four (24) hours of *Pro Bono Publico* services contributed annually by a paralegal may consist of such services as detailed in this EC-1.4(d), and/or administrative matters designed to develop and implement the attainment of this aspiration as detailed above in EC-1.4(a) & (c), or any combination of the two.

1.5 A Paralegal Shall Preserve All Confidential Information Provided by the Client or Acquired from Other Sources before, during, and after the Course of the Professional Relationship.

Ethical Considerations

EC–1.5(a) A paralegal shall be aware of and abide by all legal authority governing confidential information in the jurisdiction in which the paralegal practices.

EC–1.5(b) A paralegal shall not use confidential information to the disadvantage of the client.

EC–1.5(c) A paralegal shall not use confidential information to the advantage of the paralegal or of a third person.

EC–1.5(d) A paralegal may reveal confidential information only after full disclosure and with the client's written consent; or, when required by law or court order; or, when necessary to prevent the client from committing an act that could result in death or serious bodily harm.

EC–1.5(e) A paralegal shall keep those individuals responsible for the legal representation of a client fully informed of any confidential information the paralegal may have pertaining to that client.

EC–1.5(f) A paralegal shall not engage in any indiscreet communications concerning clients.

1.6 A Paralegal Shall Avoid Conflicts of Interest and Shall Disclose Any Possible Conflict to the Employer or Client, as Well as to the Prospective Employers or Clients.

Ethical Considerations

EC–1.6(a) A paralegal shall act within the bounds of the law, solely for the benefit of the client, and shall be free of compromising influences and loyalties. Neither the paralegal's personal or business interest, nor those of other clients or third persons, should compromise the paralegal's professional judgment and loyalty to the client.

EC–1.6(b) A paralegal shall avoid conflicts of interest that may arise from previous assignments, whether for a present or past employer or client.

EC–1.6(c) A paralegal shall avoid conflicts of interest that may arise from family relationships and from personal and business interests.

EC–1.6(d) In order to be able to determine whether an actual or potential conflict of interest exists a paralegal shall create and maintain an effective record-keeping system that identifies clients, matters, and parties with which the paralegal has worked.

EC–1.6(e) A paralegal shall reveal sufficient nonconfidential information about a client or former client to reasonably ascertain if an actual or potential conflict of interest exists.

EC–1.6(f) A paralegal shall not participate in or conduct work on any matter where a conflict of interest has been identified.

EC–1.6(g) In matters where a conflict of interest has been identified and the client consents to continued representation, a paralegal shall comply fully with the implementation and maintenance of an Ethical Wall.

1.7 A Paralegal's Title Shall Be Fully Disclosed.

Ethical Considerations

EC-1.7(a) A paralegal's title shall clearly indicate the individual's status and shall be disclosed in all business and professional communications to avoid misunderstandings and misconceptions about the paralegal's role and responsibilities.

EC-1.7(b) A paralegal's title shall be included if the paralegal's name appears on business cards, letterhead, brochures, directories, and advertisements.

EC-1.7(c) A paralegal shall not use letterhead, business cards, or other promotional materials to create a fraudulent impression of his/her status or ability to practice in the jurisdiction in which the paralegal practices.

EC-1.7(d) A paralegal shall not practice under color of any record, diploma, or certificate that has been illegally or fraudulently obtained or issued or which is misrepresentative in any way.

EC-1.7(e) A paralegal shall not participate in the creation, issuance, or dissemination of fraudulent records, diplomas, or certificates.

1.8 A Paralegal Shall Not Engage in the Unauthorized Practice of Law.

Ethical Considerations

EC-1.8(a) A paralegal shall comply with the applicable legal authority governing the unauthorized practice of law in the jurisdiction in which the paralegal practices.

§2. NFPA Guidelines for the Enforcement of the Model Code of Ethics and Professional Responsibility

2.1 Basis for Discipline

2.1(a) Disciplinary investigations and proceedings brought under authority of the Rules shall be conducted in accord with obligations imposed on the paralegal professional by the Model Code of Ethics and Professional Responsibility.

2.2 Structure of Disciplinary Committee

2.2(a) The Disciplinary Committee ("Committee") shall be made up of nine (9) members including the Chair.

2.2(b) Each member of the Committee, including any temporary replacement members, shall have demonstrated working knowledge of ethics/professional responsibility-related issues and activities.

2.2(c) The Committee shall represent a cross section of practice areas and work experience. The following recommendations are made regarding the members of the Committee.

1. At least one paralegal with one to three years of law-related work experience.
2. At least one paralegal with five to seven years of law-related work experience.
3. At least one paralegal with over ten years of law-related work experience.
4. One paralegal educator with five to seven years of work experience, preferably in the area of ethics/professional responsibility.
5. One paralegal manager.

6. One lawyer with five to seven years of law-related work experience.

7. One lay member.

2.2(d) The Chair of the Committee shall be appointed within thirty (30) days of its members' induction. The Chair shall have no fewer than ten (10) years of law-related work experience.

2.2(e) The terms of all members of the Committee shall be staggered. Of those members initially appointed, a simple majority plus one shall be appointed to a term of one year, and the remaining members shall be appointed to a term of two years. Thereafter, all members of the Committee shall be appointed to terms of two years.

2.2(f) If for any reason the terms of a majority of the Committee will expire at the same time, members may be appointed to terms of one year to maintain continuity of the Committee.

2.2(g) The Committee shall organize from its members a three-tiered structure to investigate, prosecute, and/or adjudicate charges of misconduct. The members shall be rotated among the tiers.

2.3 Operation of Committee

2.3(a) The Committee shall meet on an as-needed basis to discuss, investigate, and/or adjudicate alleged violations of the Model Code/Model Rules.

2.3(b) A majority of the members of the Committee present at a meeting shall constitute a quorum.

2.3(c) A Recording Secretary shall be designated to maintain complete and accurate minutes of all Committee meetings. All such minutes shall be kept confidential until a decision has been made that the matter will be set for hearing as set forth in Section 6.1 below.

2.3(d) If any member of the Committee has a conflict of interest with the Charging Party, the Responding Party, or the allegations of misconduct, that member shall not take part in any hearing or deliberations concerning those allegations. If the absence of that member creates a lack of a quorum for the Committee, then a temporary replacement for the member shall be appointed.

2.3(e) Either the Charging Party or the Responding Party may request that, for good cause shown, any member of the Committee not participate in a hearing or deliberation. All such requests shall be honored. If the absence of a Committee member under those circumstances creates a lack of a quorum for the Committee, then a temporary replacement for that member shall be appointed.

2.3(f) All discussions and correspondence of the Committee shall be kept confidential until a decision has been made that the matter will be set for hearing as set forth in Section 6.1 below.

2.3(g) All correspondence from the Committee to the Responding Party regarding any charge of misconduct and any decisions made regarding the charge shall be mailed certified mail, return receipt requested, to the Responding Party's last known address and shall be clearly marked with a "Confidential" designation.

2.4 Procedure for the Reporting of Alleged
Violations of the Model Code/Disciplinary Rules

2.4(a) An individual or entity in possession of nonconfidential knowledge or information concerning possible instances of misconduct shall make a confidential written report to the Committee within thirty (30) days of obtaining same. This report shall include all details of the alleged misconduct.

2.4(b) The Committee so notified shall inform the Responding Party of the allegation(s) of misconduct no later than ten (10) business days after receiving the confidential written report from the Charging Party.

2.4(c) Notification to the Responding Party shall include the identity of the Charging Party, unless, for good cause shown, the Charging Party requests anonymity.

2.4(d) The Responding Party shall reply to the allegations within ten (10) business days of notification.

2.5 Procedure for the Investigation of a Charge of Misconduct

2.5(a) Upon receipt of a Charge of Misconduct ("Charge"), or on its own initiative, the Committee shall initiate an investigation.

2.5(b) If, upon initial or preliminary review, the Committee makes a determination that the charges are either without basis in fact or, if proven, would not constitute professional misconduct, the Committee shall dismiss the allegations of misconduct. If such determination of dismissal cannot be made, a formal investigation shall be initiated.

2.5(c) Upon the decision to conduct a formal investigation, the Committee shall:

1. mail to the Charging and Responding Parties within three (3) business days of that decision notice of the commencement of a formal investigation. That notification shall be in writing and shall contain a complete explanation of all Charge(s), as well as the reasons for a formal investigation, and shall cite the applicable codes and rules;
2. allow the Responding Party thirty (30) days to prepare and submit a confidential response to the Committee, which response shall address each charge specifically and shall be in writing; and
3. upon receipt of the response to the notification, have thirty (30) days to investigate the Charge(s). If an extension of time is deemed necessary, that extension shall not exceed ninety (90) days.

2.5(d) Upon conclusion of the investigation, the Committee may:

1. dismiss the Charge upon the finding that it has no basis in fact;
2. dismiss the Charge upon the finding that, if proven, the Charge would not constitute Misconduct;
3. refer the matter for hearing by the Tribunal; or
4. in the case of criminal activity, refer the Charge(s) and all investigation results to the appropriate authority.

2.6 Procedure for a Misconduct Hearing before a Tribunal

2.6(a) Upon the decision by the Committee that a matter should be heard, all parties shall be notified and a hearing date shall be set. The hearing shall take place no more than thirty (30) days from the conclusion of the formal investigation.

2.6(b) The Responding Party shall have the right to counsel. The parties and the Tribunal shall have the right to call any witnesses and introduce any documentation that they believe will lead to the fair and reasonable resolution of the matter.

2.6(c) Upon completion of the hearing, the Tribunal shall deliberate and present a written decision to the parties in accordance with procedures as set forth by the Tribunal.

2.6(d) Notice of the decision of the Tribunal shall be appropriately published.

2.7 Sanctions

2.7(a) Upon a finding of the Tribunal that misconduct has occurred, any of the following sanctions, or others as may be deemed appropriate, may be imposed upon the Responding Party, either singularly or in combination:

1. Letter of reprimand to the Responding Party; counseling;
2. Attendance at an ethics course approved by the Tribunal; probation;

3. Suspension of license/authority to practice; revocation of license/authority to practice;

4. Imposition of a fine; assessment of costs; or

5. In the instance of criminal activity, referral to the appropriate authority.

2.7(b) Upon the expiration of any period of probation, suspension, or revocation, the Responding Party may make application for reinstatement. With the application for reinstatement, the Responding Party must show proof of having complied with all aspects of the sanctions imposed by the Tribunal.

2.8 Appellate Procedures

2.8(a) The parties shall have the right to appeal the decision of the Tribunal in accordance with the procedure as set forth by the Tribunal.

Definitions

APPELLATE BODY means a body established to adjudicate an appeal to any decision made by a Tribunal or other decision-making body with respect to formally heard Charges of Misconduct.

CHARGE OF MISCONDUCT means a written submission by any individual or entity to an ethics committee, paralegal association, bar association, law enforcement agency, judicial body, government agency, or other appropriate body or entity, that sets forth non-confidential information regarding any instance of alleged misconduct by an individual paralegal or paralegal entity.

CHARGING PARTY means any individual or entity who submits a Charge of Misconduct against an individual paralegal or paralegal entity.

COMPETENCY means the demonstration of: diligence, education, skill, and mental, emotional, and physical fitness reasonably necessary for the performance of paralegal services.

CONFIDENTIAL INFORMATION means information relating to a client, whatever its source, that is not public knowledge nor available to the public. ("Non-Confidential Information" would generally include the name of the client and the identity of the matter for which the paralegal provided services.)

DISCIPLINARY COMMITTEE means any committee that has been established by an entity such as a paralegal association, bar association, judicial body, or government agency to: (a) identify, define, and investigate general ethical considerations and concerns with respect to paralegal practice; (b) administer and enforce the Model Code and Model Rules and; (c) discipline any individual paralegal or paralegal entity found to be in violation of same.

DISCIPLINARY HEARING means the confidential proceeding conducted by a committee or other designated body or entity concerning any instance of alleged misconduct by an individual paralegal or paralegal entity.

DISCLOSE means communication of information reasonably sufficient to permit identification of the significance of the matter in question.

ETHICAL WALL means the screening method implemented in order to protect a client from a conflict of interest. An Ethical Wall generally includes, but is not limited to, the following elements: (1) prohibit the paralegal from having any connection with the matter; (2) ban discussions with or the transfer of documents to or from the paralegal; (3) restrict access to files; and (4) educate all members of the firm, corporation, or entity as to the separation of the paralegal (both organizationally and physically) from the pending matter. For more information regarding the Ethical Wall, see the NFPA publication entitled "The Ethical Wall—Its Application to Paralegals."

EX PARTE means actions or communications conducted at the instance and for the benefit of one party only, and without notice to, or contestation by, any person adversely interested.

INVESTIGATION means the investigation of any charge(s) of misconduct filed against an individual paralegal or paralegal entity by a Committee.

LETTER OF REPRIMAND means a written notice of formal censure or severe reproof administered to an individual paralegal or paralegal entity for unethical or improper conduct.

MISCONDUCT means the knowing or unknowing commission of an act that is in direct violation of those Canons and Ethical Considerations of any and all applicable codes and/or rules of conduct.

PARALEGAL is synonymous with "Legal Assistant" and is defined as a person qualified through education, training, or work experience to perform substantive legal work that requires knowledge of legal concepts and is customarily but not exclusively performed by a lawyer. This person may be retained or employed by a lawyer, law office, governmental agency, or other entity or may be authorized by administrative, statutory, or court authority to perform this work.

PRO BONO PUBLICO means providing or assisting to provide quality legal services in order to enhance access to justice for persons of limited means; charitable, religious, civic, community, governmental, and educational organizations in matters that are designed primarily to address the legal needs of persons with limited means; or individuals, groups, or organizations seeking to secure or protect civil rights, civil liberties, or public rights.

PROPER AUTHORITY means the local paralegal association, the local or state bar association, committee(s) of the local paralegal or bar association(s), local prosecutor, administrative agency, or other tribunal empowered to investigate or act upon an instance of alleged misconduct.

RESPONDING PARTY means an individual paralegal or paralegal entity against whom a Charge of Misconduct has been submitted.

REVOCATION means the rescission of the license, certificate, or other authority to practice of an individual paralegal or paralegal entity found in violation of those Canons and Ethical Considerations of any and all applicable codes and/or rules of conduct.

SUSPENSION means the suspension of the license, certificate, or other authority to practice of an individual paralegal or paralegal entity found in violation of those Canons and Ethical Considerations of any and all applicable codes and/or rules of conduct.

TRIBUNAL means the body designated to adjudicate allegations of misconduct.

NALS *Code of Ethics and Professional Responsibility*

Members of NALS are bound by the objectives of this association and the standards of conduct required of the legal profession.

Every member shall:

- Encourage respect for the law and the administration of justice;
- Observe rules governing privileged communications and confidential information;
- Promote and exemplify high standards of loyalty, cooperation, and courtesy;
- Perform all duties of the profession with integrity and competence; and
- Pursue a high order of professional attainment.

Integrity and high standards of conduct are fundamental to the success of our professional association. This Code is promulgated by the NALS and accepted by its members to accomplish these ends.

Canon 1

Members of this association shall maintain a high degree of competency and integrity through continuing education to better assist the legal profession in fulfilling its duty to provide quality legal services to the public.

Canon 2

Members of this association shall maintain a high standard of ethical conduct and shall contribute to the integrity of the association and the legal profession.

Canon 3

Members of this association shall avoid a conflict of interest pertaining to a client matter.

Canon 4

Members of this association shall preserve and protect the confidences and privileged communications of a client.

Canon 5

Members of this association shall exercise care in using independent professional judgment and in determining the extent to which a client may be assisted without the presence of a lawyer and shall not act in matters involving professional legal judgment.

Canon 6

Members of this association shall not solicit legal business on behalf of a lawyer.

Canon 7

Members of this association, unless permitted by law, shall not perform paralegal functions except under the direct supervision of a lawyer and shall not advertise or contract with members of the general public for the performance of paralegal functions.

Canon 8

Members of this association, unless permitted by law, shall not perform any of the duties restricted to lawyers or do things which lawyers themselves may not do and shall assist in preventing the unauthorized practice of law.

Canon 9

Members of this association not licensed to practice law shall not engage in the practice of law as defined by statutes or court decisions.

Canon 10

Members of this association shall do all other things incidental, necessary, or expedient to enhance professional responsibility and participation in the administration of justice and public service in cooperation with the legal profession.

Paralegal Associations

NFPA Associations

National Federation of Paralegal
Associations (NFPA); please see
paralegals.org for updates.

Region I

Alaska Association of Paralegals
alaskaparalegals.org

Hawaii Paralegal Association
hawaiiparalegal.org

Oregon Paralegal Association
oregonparalegals.org

Sacramento Valley Paralegal Association
svpa.org

Washington State Paralegal Association
wspaonline.org

Region II

Arkansas Paralegal Association
arkansasparalegal.org

Baton Rouge Paralegal Association
brparalegals.com

Dallas Area Paralegal Association
dallasparalegals.org

Illinois Paralegal Association
ipaonline.org

Kansas Paralegal Association
ksparalegals.org

Minnesota Paralegal Association
mnparalegals.org

Missouri Paralegal Association
missouriparalegalassoc.org

New Orleans Paralegal Association
nopa.onefireplace.com

Paralegal Association of Wisconsin
wisconsinparalegal.org

Rocky Mountain Paralegal Association
(CO, NE, SD, UT, WY)
rockymtnparalegal.org

Region III

Cleveland Association of Paralegals
capohio.org

Georgia Association of Paralegals
gaparalegal.org

Greater Lexington Paralegal Association
lexingtonparalegals.org

Indiana Paralegal Association
indianaparalegals.org

Memphis Paralegal Association
memphisparalegalassoc.org

Michiana Paralegal Association (IN, MI)
michianaparalegalassociation.org

Middle Tennessee Paralegal Association
mtpa.memberlodge.org

Northeast Indiana Paralegal Association
niparalegal.org

Paralegal Association of Central Ohio
pacoparalegals.org

South Florida Paralegal Association
sfpa.info

Tampa Bay Paralegal Association
tbpa.org

Region IV

Bucks County Paralegal Association
buckscoparalegals.com

Central Pennsylvania Paralegal Association
centralpaparalegals.com

Chester County Paralegal Association
chescoparalegal.org

Lycoming County Paralegal Association (PA)
lycolaw.org/lcpa/main.htm

Maryland Association of Paralegals
mdparalegals.org

Montgomery County Paralegal
Association (PA)
montcoparalegals.org

National Capital Area Paralegal Association
ncapa.com

Paralegal Association of Northern Virginia
panv.org

Philadelphia Association of Paralegals
philaparalegals.com

Pittsburgh Paralegal Association
pghparalegals.org

South Jersey Paralegal Association
sjpaparalegals.org

Region V

Capital District Paralegal Association (NY)
cdpa.info

Central Connecticut Paralegal Association
ctparalegals.org

Central Massachusetts Paralegal Association
cmpa.net

Connecticut Association of Paralegals
ct-cap.com

Massachusetts Paralegal Association
massparalegal.org

New Haven County Association of Paralegals
nhcap.org

New York City Paralegal Association
nyc-pa.org

Paralegal Association of New Hampshire
panh.org

Paralegal Association of Rochester
rochesterparalegal.org

Rhode Island Paralegal Association
riparalegals.org

Vermont Paralegal Organization
vtparalegal.org

Western Massachusetts Paralegal
Association
wmassparalegal.org

Western New York Paralegal Association
wnyparalegals.org

NALA State and Local Affiliates

This list is current as of the publication date. For updates, please check the NALA web site (nala.org).

Alabama

Alabama Association of Paralegals
alabamaparalegals.net

Alaska

Fairbanks Association of Legal Assistants
fairbanksparalegal.com

Arizona

Arizona Paralegal Association
azparalegal.org

Maricopa County Association of Paralegals
mcaparalegals.org

Tucson Paralegal Association
tucsonparalegals.org

Arkansas

Arkansas Paralegal Alliance
arkansasparalegalalliance.org

California

Fresno Paralegal Association
fresnoparalegal.org

Inland Counties Association of Paralegals
icaponline.wildapricot.org

Los Angeles Paralegal Association
lapa.org

Orange County Paralegal Association
ocparalegal.org

Paralegal Association of Santa Clara
County
pascco.org

San Diego Paralegal Association
sdparalegals.org

Ventura County Paralegal Association
vcparalegal.org

Colorado

Legal Assistants of the Western Slope
ws-laws.com

Florida

Central Florida Paralegal Association
cfpainc.com

Gulf Coast Paralegal Association
gcpa.info

Northeast Florida Paralegal Association
nefpa.org

Northwest Florida Paralegal Association
nwfpa.com

Paralegal Association of Florida
pafinc.org

South Florida Paralegal Association
sfpa.info

Southwest Florida Paralegal Association
swfloridaparalegals.com

Tampa Bay Paralegal Association
tbpa.org

Georgia

Atlanta Paralegal Association
atlantaparalegal.org

Illinois

Central Illinois Paralegal Association
ciparalegal.org

Iowa

Iowa Association of Legal
Assistants.Paralegals
ialanet.org

Kansas

Heartland Paralegal Association
(Kansas City)
heartlandparalegalassociation.weebly.com

Kansas Association of Legal
Assistants.Paralegals
kansas.gov/kala

Kentucky

Kentucky Paralegal Association
kypa.org

Louisiana

Louisiana State Paralegal Association
la-paralegals.org

Michigan

Great Lakes Paralegal Association
glpa-michigan.org

Mississippi

Mississippi Paralegal Association
msparalegals.org

Missouri

St. Louis Paralegal Association
stlpa.org

Montana

Montana Association of Legal
Assistants*Paralegals
malanet.org

Nebraska

Nebraska Paralegal Association
nebraskaparalegal.org

Nevada

Las Vegas Valley Paralegal Association
lvvpa.org

Sierra Nevada Association of Paralegals
snapreno.com

New Jersey

Paralegal Association of New Jersey
laanj.org

North Carolina

Guilford Paralegal Association
guilfordparalegalassociation.org

Metrolina Paralegal Association (Charlotte)
charlotteareaparalegals.com

North Carolina Paralegal Association
ncparalegal.org

North Dakota

Red River Valley Paralegal Association
rrvpa.org

Western Dakota Association of Legal Assistants
wdala.org

Ohio

Paralegal Association of Northwest Ohio
panonet.org

Oklahoma

Central Oklahoma Association of Legal Assistants
coala.cc

Oklahoma Paralegal Association
okparalegal.org

Tulsa Area Paralegal Association
tulsaparalegals.org

Oregon

Pacific Northwest Paralegal Association
pnpa.org

Pennsylvania

Lancaster Area Paralegal Association
lapaparalegals.com

South Carolina

Charleston Association of Legal Assistants
calasc.org

South Carolina Upstate Paralegal Association
scupa.org

South Dakota

South Dakota Paralegal Association
sdparalegals.com

Tennessee

Greater Memphis Paralegal Alliance
memphisparalegals.org

Smoky Mountain Paralegal Association
smparalegal.org

Tennessee Paralegal Association
tnparalegal.org

Texas

Capital Area Paralegal Association
capatx.org

El Paso Paralegal Association
elppa.org

Houston Association of Bankruptcy Paralegals
houstonbankruptcyparalegals.org

Houston Corporate Paralegal Association
hcpa.cc

Houston Paralegal Association
hpa.wildapricot.org

J.L. Turner Legal Association
jltla.org

North Texas Paralegal Association
ntparalegals.org

Northeast Texas Association of Paralegals
ntaparalegals.org

South Texas Organization of Paralegals
stopweb.org

Southeast Texas Association of Paralegals
setap.org

Texas Panhandle Paralegal Association
txtppa.webs.com

West Texas Paralegal Association
westtexasparalegalassociation.org

Utah

Utah Paralegal Association
utparalegalassn.org

Virginia

Richmond Paralegal Association
richmondparalegals.org

Roanoke Valley Paralegal Association
rvpa.org

Tidewater Paralegal Association
tidewaterparalegalassociation.org

Virginia Peninsula Paralegal Association
vappa.org

West Virginia

Legal Assistants/Paralegals of Southern West Virginia
lapswv.org

Wisconsin

Madison Area Paralegal Association
madisonparalegal.org

Wyoming

Legal Assistants of Wyoming
lawyo.com

NALS State and Chapter Associations

NALS, the Association for Legal Professionals, has state and chapter affiliates as listed below. For additional details, consult the NALS Resource Center at **nals.org**.

Alabama

Alabama-AALS
alabama-als.org

BLSA (Birmingham)
blsa-al.com

Mobile Legal Professionals Association MALS
malsmontgomery.blogspot.com

Alaska

NALS of Anchorage
nalsofanchorage.org

Arizona

NALS of Arizona
nalsofarizona.org

NALS of Phoenix
nalsofphoenix.org

NALS of Tucson and Southern Arizona
nalsoftucson.org

Arkansas

AALS–The Association for Arkansas Legal Support Professionals
aalsonline.org

Greater Little Rock Legal Support Professionals
greaterlittlerocklsp.com

Northeast Arkansas Legal Support Professionals
nealsp.org

California

NALS of Orange County
nalsoc.com

Georgia

Cobb County Legal Professional Association
facebook.com/CobbCountyLegal ProfessionalsAssociation

NALS of Atlanta
nalsofatlanta.org

Idaho

IDALS
idals.org

Maine

NALS of Maine
nalsofmaine.org

Michigan

Grand Traverse Area Legal Professionals
facebook.com/pages/Grand-Traverse-Area-
Legal-Professionals/195505783799263

Jackson County Legal Support
   Professionals
nalsofjacksoncounty.com

NALS of Detroit
nalsofdetroit.org

NALS of Greater Kalamazoo
nalsofgreaterkalamazoo.org/Home_Page.php

NALS of Lansing
nalsoflansing.org

NALS of Michigan
nalsofmichigan.org

NALS of West Michigan
nalsofwmi.org

Mississippi

Gulf Coast Association for Legal Support
   Professionals
gulfcoastalsp.org

Mississippi Legal Professionals Association
mississippilpa.org

Missouri

Heart of America Legal Professionals
   Association (Kansas City)
halpa.org

Kansas City Legal Secretaries Association
kclsa.net

NALS of Greater St. Louis
nalsofgreaterstlouis.org

NALS of Missouri
nalsofmissouri.org

Springfield Area Legal Support
   Professionals
salsp.org

Nevada

NALS of Las Vegas,
nalsoflasvegas.org

New Jersey

NJALS
njals.org

New York

NALS of Nassau County
nalsofnewyorkinc.org/
NALS-of-Nassau-County

NALS of New York
nalsofnewyorkinc.org

NALS of New York City
nalsofnewyorkinc.org/
NALS-of-New-York-City

NALS of Suffolk County
nalsofnewyorkinc.org/
NALS-of-Suffolk-County

Ohio

NALS of Northeast Ohio
nalsofneo.org

Oregon

Central Oregon Legal Professionals
nalsor.org/COLP/index.htm

Legal Professionals of Douglas County
nalsor.org/douglas/index.htm

Mt. Hood Legal Professionals
nalsor.org/Mt_Hood/index.htm

NALS of Lane County
nalsor.org/Lane/index.htm

NALS of Mid-Willamette Valley
nalsor.org/MWValley/index.htm

NALS of Oregon
nalsor.org

NALS of Portland
nalsor.org/Portland/index.htm

NALS of Southern Oregon Coast
nalsor.org/SouthernOregonCoast/
index.htm

Pennsylvania

NALS of Pennsylvania
palegal.org

NALS of Philadelphia
nalsofphiladelphia.org

South Carolina

Legal Staff Professionals of Greenville
lspg.org

Legal Staff Professionals of South Carolina
lspsc.org

Tennessee

MLSA—Legal Professionals of Memphis
memphislsa.org

NALS of Nashville
nalsnashville.wordpress.com

Texas

Austin Legal Professionals Association
austinlpa.org

El Paso County Legal Support Professionals
epalp.org

Houston Association of Legal Professionals
houstonalp.org

San Antonio Legal Secretaries Association
sanantoniolsa.org

Texas Association of Legal Professionals
texasalp.org

Waco Legal Professionals Association
wacolpa.com

Virginia

VALS—The Association for Legal
   Professionals
v-a-l-s.org

Virginia Beach Legal Staff Association
vblsa.org

Washington

NALS of Greater Seattle
nalsofgs.org

NALS of Kitsap County
nalsofkitsap.org

NALS of Washington
nalsofwashington.org

Wisconsin

Bay Area Association for Legal
   Professionals
facebook.com/pages/Bay-Area-Association-for-
Legal-Professionals-BAALP/104811499581040

Legal Personnel of South Central
   Wisconsin
lpscw.org

Wisconsin Association for Legal
   Professionals
wisconsinalp.org

F

Information on NALA's CP Program

Certification

In the working environment, professional certification is a time honored process respected by both employers and those within the career field. The following is a definition used by many to describe professional certification:

> *Professional certification is a voluntary process by which a nongovernmental entity grants a time-limited recognition to an individual after verifying that the individual has met predetermined, standardized criteria. (Source: Rops, Mickie S., CAE, Understanding the Language of Credentialing, American Society of Association Executives, May 2002.)*

The definition hits the high points. Certification is voluntary, not imposed by government. It is time limited, which means that those with the certification must fulfill ongoing educational requirements to keep the certification current, and the criteria for certification [are] recognized in the community. Keep these aspects in mind as you read more about the CP program.

Administration

The NALA Certifying Board for Paralegals is responsible for content, standards and administration of the Certified Paralegal Program. It is composed of paralegals who have received an Advanced Paralegal Certification designation, attorneys and paralegal educators.

In the technical areas of statistical analyses, examination construction, reliability and validity tests, the Board contracts with a professional consulting firm offering expertise in these areas as well as in occupational research. Technical analyses of the Certified Paralegal examination are conducted on an ongoing basis to ensure the integrity of the examination. Content analyses of the test design, accuracy of questions, and topic/subject mix for each exam section are ongoing processes of the Certifying Board. The Board also utilizes the occupational data available through surveys of legal assistants and other means, including review of textbooks and research within the field of paralegal education. Through these analyses and procedures, the Board is assured that the examination reflects and responds to work-place realities and demands.

Background and Numbers

Established in 1976, the Certified Paralegal (then known as the CLA—Certified Legal Assistant) program has enabled the profession to develop a strong and responsive self-regulatory program offering a nationwide credential for legal assistants. The Certified Paralegal program establishes and serves as a:

- National professional standard for legal assistants.
- Means of identifying those who have reached this standard.
- Credentialing program responsive to the needs of paralegals and responsive to the fact that this form of self-regulation is necessary to strengthen and expand development of this career field.
- Positive, ongoing, voluntary program to encourage the growth of the paralegal profession, attesting to and encouraging a high level of achievement.

As of March 2015, there are 18,289 Certified Paralegals and over 3,400 Advanced Certified Paralegals in the United States. Over 28,000 paralegals have participated in this program. [Go to **www.nala.org**, select "Certification," and find the appropriate links under "Background and Numbers"] to see the distribution of Certified Paralegals across the United States [and] the distribution of Advanced Certified Paralegals. The growth of these programs is impressive.

The Certified Paralegal Credential

Use of the CP credential signifies that a paralegal is capable of providing superior services to firms and corporations. National surveys consistently show Certified Paralegals are better utilized in a field where attorneys are looking for a credible, dependable way to measure ability. The credential has been recognized by the American Bar Association as a designation which marks a high level of professional achievement. The CLA or CP credential has also been recognized by over 47 legal assistant organizations and numerous bar associations.

For information concerning standards of professional credentialing programs, you may want to see the article: "The Certified Legal Assistant Program and the United States Supreme Court Decision in *Peel v. Attorney Registration and Disciplinary Committee of Illinois.*" [It is available at **www.nala.org** under the "Certification" tab.] In this case, the United States Supreme Court addressed the issue concerning the utilization of professional credentials awarded by private organizations. In *Peel v. Attorney Registration and Disciplinary Committee of Illinois*, 110 S.Ct. 2281 (1990), the Court suggested that a claim of certification is truthful and not misleading if it meets certain standards. This article details those standards in terms of the standards of the NALA Certified Paralegal Program.

Is It CLA or CP?

The terms "legal assistant" and "paralegal" are synonymous terms. The terms are defined as such throughout the United States in state supreme court rules, statutes, ethical opinions, bar association guidelines and other similar documents. These are the same documents which provide recognition of the paralegal profession and encourage the use of paralegals in the delivery of legal services.

NALA has become increasingly aware that while the terms are defined as identifying the same professional, a preference in terms is emerging. Different geographic areas use one term more than another. For this reason, we filed for a certification mark "CP" with the U.S. Patent and Trademark Office. The certification mark was successfully registered on July 20, 2004.

Those who are admitted to the Certified Paralegal program today and successfully complete the examination are awarded a "Certified Paralegal" certificate and may use the credential "CP." Those who renew their certification are also awarded the "Certified Paralegal" certificate and encouraged to use the credential "CP." However, some with this certification continue to use the credential, "CLA".

CLA is a certification mark duly registered with the U.S. Patent and Trademark Office (No. 113199). CP® is a certification duly registered with the U.S. Patent and Trademark Office (No. 78213275). Any unauthorized use of these credentials is strictly forbidden.

Am I a Certified Paralegal?

Occasionally, paralegals call themselves "certified" by virtue of completing a paralegal training course, or another type of preparatory education. Although a school may award a certificate of completion, this is not the same as earning professional certification by an entity such as NALA. In this instance the school's certificate is designation of completion of a training program.

How the Certified Paralegal Exam Is Developed

The Certifying Board provides oversight for the development and ongoing maintenance of the examination. The Certifying Board, NALA certification program staff, and trained subject matter experts work in partnership with a qualified psychometric consultant to ensure the examination is developed and maintained in a manner consistent with generally accepted psychometric, educational testing practices, and national accreditation standards for certification programs.

The Certifying Board selects diverse groups of qualified subject matter experts (SMEs) to participate in exam development activities throughout the exam development and maintenance process. Activities that involve subject matter expert participation include creating job analysis surveys, creating test content outlines, writing and reviewing exam items, and establishing the passing point for exams. Ad-hoc committees and/or working groups of subject matter experts composed of Certifying Board members, paralegals, attorneys, educators, and other outside experts may be assembled for these tasks.

Job analysis studies are conducted approximately every six years to identify and validate the knowledge and skills which will be measured by the examination sections. The results of the job analysis studies serve as the basis for the exam specifications. These exam specifications, with weights for each content area, are approved by the Certifying Board.

Qualified subject matter experts write and review items for the exam. Subject matter expert item writers and reviewers complete mandatory training provided by the certification program on item writing/review for certification examinations. Items are subject to multiple levels of review and analysis before being used as graded items on the exam.

The Certifying Board oversees a continual process of item writing, review and evaluation to ensure that exam content remains up-to-date, accurate, and consistent with the content outline.

Updates to Exam Specifications

The previous model for the Certified Paralegal Examination consisted of a five-part examination on the subjects of Communications, Ethics, Judgment & Analytical Ability, Legal Research, and Substantive Law. The Substantive Law section consisted of a test on the American Legal System plus four additional tests based on specialty practice areas. Examinees could select the four areas from a list of nine practice areas.

In April of 2013, NALA Certifying Board announced new specifications for the Certified Paralegal examination beginning with the September 2013 testing window. These modifications are based on a careful and detailed analysis of the findings of the 2012 Job Analysis study conducted by the Board in consultation with PSI Psychometric Consulting Services.

The new examination specifications call for adjustments to the number of points per subjects within all sections of the examination. No new subjects were introduced in any examination area.

The most significant modification to the examination is the elimination of several practice area tests under the Substantive Law section. It was demonstrated by the job analysis study that, on a nationwide basis, few paralegals utilize the knowledge and skills tested by these practice area examination sections on a regular and routine basis in the workplace.

In addition, the option to select questions from certain specialty practice areas will no longer be available to examinees. All examinees will take the same Substantive Law section of the examination, as is the case with all other sections of the Certified Paralegal examination.

Effective with the September 2013 testing and subsequent testing sessions, the Substantive Law section consists of questions on the following subjects:

- American Legal System
- Civil Litigation
- Business Organizations
- Contracts

With these modifications, the Certifying Board has listened to member and nonmember paralegals and has applied findings of the job analysis study to the exam specifications. The Certifying Board strives to link the Certified Paralegal examination directly to the day to day duties and responsibilities of paralegals in the workplace. The modifications demonstrate a continued effort to ensure the Certified Paralegal examination remains an accurate and relevant reflection of today's paralegals.

Examination Descriptions

The Certified Paralegal examination is divided into five sections. Examinees are asked to demonstrate knowledge by responding to true/false, multiple choice and matching questions requiring knowledge of the subject and reading comprehension skills. Analytical skills are further tested by an essay question on the Judgment & Analytical Ability section. Any form of test question (true/false, multiple choice, essay) may be used at any time on the Certified Paralegal examination. Sections of the examination are:

- Communications
- Ethics
- Legal Research
- Judgment & Analytical Ability
- Substantive Law
  - American Legal System
  - Civil Litigation
  - Contracts
  - Business Organizations

For a detailed list of current exam specifications, see **www.nala.org** and look under "Certification" for details of passing requirements on the five-part examination.

Advanced Paralegal Certification

Commitment to continued growth and life-long learning is the hallmark of a professional. Once a Certified Paralegal's career is launched, there will be a need for advanced CLE programs as one changes areas of practice, or is met with more challenging assignments. The Advanced Paralegal Certification program is designed to recognize this effort.

Advanced Paralegal Certification is available to those with a current Certified Paralegal certification. The advanced certification programs are written with the understanding that a person seeking advanced certification has already mastered the Certified Paralegal examination and has demonstrated knowledge and skills in areas of written communications, legal research, ethics, judgment and legal analysis, the American legal system, as well as general knowledge of four specialty areas of practice.

[You can go directly to the APC site at **www.nala.org/apc.aspx**.] Below is a summary of the APC program.

Background

The Certified Paralegal certification program offers professional certification for paralegals immediately upon completion of their training. In 1982, NALA instituted the CLA Specialty program, to recognize a Certified Paralegal's specialized knowledge in a specialty area of practice. In 2002, a special task force was appointed to look at the CLA Specialty Certification program and see if changes were needed. The Task Force determined it was time to redesign and restructure the program. The result is the Advanced Paralegal Certification program, a web-based, curriculum-based certification program.

APC Program—Curriculum-Based Certification

The curriculum-based certification is an accepted model of certification and professional development programs throughout the United States and across numerous occupations. This is certification based on specific course material.

An assessment component is part of the curriculum-based program. Participants are required to demonstrate mastery of the course material throughout the process. Both the educational and assessment components are on-line.

A curriculum-based model assumes that participants will discuss course material and consult outside sources, including colleagues, reference books, and specialty practice area experts. The focus is on education and learning specific subject matter rather than testing, which has already been done by the Certified Paralegal Examination to ensure that candidates have the requisite analytical, research, and writing skills.

Many years in development, this program increases access to advanced certification for paralegals working in specific practice areas.

Courses

APC courses are developed by the APC board and experienced technical writers. The courses are about 20 hours in length. The length of time spent on the courses will vary based on one's understanding of the material. Also, the courses include additional reading material and cases.

Advanced Paralegal Certification programs are now offered in the following areas: [Go to **www.nala.org/apc.aspx** and click on the appropriate links for details on these APC courses.]

- Contracts Management/Contracts Administration
- Discovery
- Social Security Disability
- Trial Practice (January 2007)
- Alternative Dispute Resolution (March 2008)
- Business Organizations: Incorporated Entities (June 2008)
- Trademarks (March 2009)
- Personal Injury—Core Course (February 2010)
- Personal Injury—8 Practice Area Courses (March 2010)
- Land Use (October 2010)
- Criminal Litigation (March 2011)
- Commercial Bankruptcy (October 2011)

- Family Law–Child Custody, Child Support, Visitation (November 2012)
- Real Estate Principles (March 2013)
- Family Law–Division of Property and Spousal Support (June 2013)
- Business Organizations: Noncorporate Entities (October 2013)
- Family Law–Dissolution Case Management (March 2014)
- E-Discovery (June 2014)
- Family Law–Adoption and Assisted Reproduction (December 2014)

APC Board

The Advanced Paralegal Certification program of NALA is administered by a board composed of experienced paralegals, attorneys, paralegal educators, and paralegal managers. The Chair of the APC board is also a member of the NALA Board of Directors. All paralegals on the APC board have received the advanced certification credential. The board relies heavily on the expertise of technical writers and professional testing consultants.

For Certified Paralegals

Paralegals who have a valid Certified Paralegal certification credential from NALA and successfully complete an APC Course are awarded use of the ACP credential to signify this outstanding achievement. In addition, Certified Paralegals may also receive 20 hours of continuing legal education credit for completion of an advanced program. For the Personal Injury program, 20 hours of credit is awarded for completion of the Personal Injury Core Course; 10 hours is awarded for completion of a Personal Injury practice area course.

Paralegals who do not have the Certified Paralegal certification are welcome to participate in these advanced programs. The credential will not be awarded, however.

Information on NFPA's PCCE™ and PACE® Examinations

The National Federation of Paralegal Associations (NFPA) sponsors the Paralegal CORE Competency Exam™ (PCCE™) and Paralegal Advanced Competency Exam (PACE) so practicing paralegals can display their abilities. See the NFPA website at **paralegals.org** for more detail about these exams. (Information about these exams from the NFPA website is reprinted here with permission.)

Paralegal CORE Competency Exam™

The Paralegal CORE Competency Exam™ (PCCE™) was developed to assess the knowledge, skills and ability of early-career and entry-level paralegals. It became available in November of 2011. The handbook is available as a PDF download. The exam is administered by computer at Prometric Test Centers throughout the United States and Canada. For full details, please refer to the brochure.

The PCCE Study Guide 1st Edition is now available! It can be ordered from our online form for addresses in the United States and Canada. Call NFPA headquarters for other destinations.

The application fee is $215, payable by credit card (only) through the application website. You have 90 days to take the test from the date your application is accepted. To comply with the Americans with Disabilities Act (ADA) and Title VII of the Civil Rights Act, special testing accommodations will be considered for individuals with disabilities recognized by the ADA. Appendix D of the handbook contains a form for these requests.

Scoring runs for the exam are processed quarterly, with individuals receiving their certificates and score reports approximately six to eight weeks after the scoring run is processed.

On June 11, 2011, 188 paralegals took the PCCE pilot test at 12 test sites across the country. Of the paralegals who completed the test, 146 achieved a passing score of 550 or better. Those paralegals were the very first CORE Registered Paralegals™ and have earned the right to use the CRP™ credential. Since then, many more paralegals have joined their ranks.

PCCE Review Course by API

The on-line PCCE Review Course is jointly offered by NFPA and the Advanced Paralegal Institute (API) and is provided through Computer Mediated Distance Learning. The seven week on-line course prepares candidates to sit for the PCCE.

Paralegal Advanced Competence Exam® (PACE®)

At the 1994 mid-year meeting the NFPA membership voted overwhelmingly to develop an exam which could become a standard used by state legislative bodies to gauge the competency level of experienced paralegals. The PACE program launched in 1996.

The exam was developed by a professional testing firm in conjunction with an independent task force including paralegals, lawyers, paralegal educators and content specialists from the general public who are legal advocates. It is administered by computer in a proctored testing facility, consists of 200 multiple-choice questions and must be completed in four hours, although many candidates complete it in two.

The questions are not practice-area specific, but are hypothetical issues testing advanced application of general knowledge, paralegal experience, and critical analysis ability to identify the correct answer. The exam covers tasks that experienced paralegals routinely perform, regardless of the practice area or geographic region in which they live. These tasks were organized into 5 domains: Administration of Client Legal Matters (23%); Development of Client Legal Matters (30%); Factual and Legal Research (22%); Factual and Legal Writing (20.5%), and Office Administration (4.5%). Ethics are included in all of the above domains, as are technology and terminology.

As the utilization of paralegals increases and the roles they play become more varied, the legal profession has come to recognize the Registered Paralegal (RP®) credential as a signal of excellence.

Requirements to Sit for PACE

Requirements for a paralegal to take PACE include work experience and education. The paralegal cannot have been convicted of a felony nor be under suspension, termination, or revocation of a certificate, registration, or license by any entity. Additionally, the candidate's experience must meet one of the following four options:

- An associate's degree in paralegal studies obtained from an institutionally accredited school, and/or ABA approved paralegal education program; and six (6) years' substantive paralegal experience; OR
- A bachelor's degree in any course of study obtained from an institutionally accredited school school and three (3) years of substantive paralegal experience; OR
- A bachelor's degree and completion of a paralegal program with an institutionally accredited school, said paralegal program may be embodied in a bachelor's degree; and two (2) years' substantive paralegal experience; OR
- Four (4) years' substantive paralegal experience on or before December 31, 2000.

Reprinted by permission of the National Federation of Paralegal Associations, Inc. (NFPA®), www.paralegals.org.

Information on NALS Certification

NALS, The Association for Legal Professionals, offers certification for Professional Paralegals (PP), Professional Legal Secretaries (PLS), and Accredited Legal Professionals (ALP). For details on the certifications check the website at **nals.org**. (Information about certification from the NALS website is reprinted here with permission.)

Advance Your Career

NALS offers members and nonmembers the opportunity to sit for three unique certifications dedicated to the legal services profession. The exams are of varying levels and are developed by professionals in the industry. Each of the three certifications is developed by NALS and takes advantage of the more than 84 years of experience and dedication to the legal services industry only NALS has to offer. NALS has the certification for you, whether you are beginning a career in the legal industry or are a veteran paralegal ready to display your skills.

- **Accredited Legal Professional (ALP)**
  Current Number Certified: 3,251 (as of 02/15)

  One way to demonstrate your preparedness for the demanding field of law is by becoming an ALP®. This is NALS' entry-level examination for those entering the legal support profession. This designation is awarded after passing a four-hour, three-part exam. Attaining this goal demonstrates your commitment and aptitude for succeeding in the ever-changing legal environment.

- **Professional Legal Secretary (PLS)**
  Current Number Certified: 5,751 (as of 02/15)

  How do your skills compare with the hallmark of a professional? PLS® is the designation for lawyer's assistants who want to be identified as exceptional. Certification is received after passing a one-day, four-part exam which demonstrates not only dedication to professionalism, but acceptance of the challenge to be exceptional.

- **Professional Paralegal (PP)**
  Current Number Certified: 586 (as of 02/15)
  Are you looking for a way to establish your credentials nationwide as a Professional Paralegal? Established in 2004 at our members' request, the PP® designation is an attainable goal for paralegals who wish to be identified as exceptional in all areas of law. The certificate is received after passing a one-day, four-part exam.

Preparing for Exams

- **Required Textbooks**
- **NALS Online Store**—Information on mock exams and other materials to help you prepare.
- **NALS Online Study Group**—To assist those preparing for their exams, NALS will hold a series of WebEd sessions with coverage over all parts of the exam, as well as exam specific reviews for the ALP, PLS, and the Professional Paralegal (PP). The series will wrap up with a general session on test-taking tips.
- **NALS Basic or Advanced Legal Training Course**—Many states and local chapters sponsor the NALS Legal Training Course. This course emulates a classroom study style in preparing for the exam. Check the NALS Calendar for an upcoming course in your area.
- **Stetson University**—NALS Online Basic Legal Training Program—An excellent option for individuals at locations without a local NALS chapter. This course is highly interactive and is taught by practicing lawyers.

The Constitution
of the United States

Preamble

We the People of the United States, in Order to form a more perfect Union, establish Justice, insure domestic Tranquility, provide for the common defence, promote the general Welfare, and secure the Blessings of Liberty to ourselves and our Posterity, do ordain and establish this Constitution for the United States of America.

Article I

Section 1.   All legislative Powers herein granted shall be vested in a Congress of the United States, which shall consist of a Senate and House of Representatives.

Section 2.   The House of Representatives shall be composed of Members chosen every second Year by the People of the several States, and the Electors in each State shall have the Qualifications requisite for Electors of the most numerous Branch of the State Legislature.

No Person shall be a Representative who shall not have attained to the Age of twenty five Years, and been seven Years a Citizen of the United States, and who shall not, when elected, be an Inhabitant of that State in which he shall be chosen.

Representatives and direct Taxes shall be apportioned among the several States which may be included within this Union, according to their respective Numbers, which shall be determined by adding to the whole Number of free Persons, including those bound to Service for a Term of Years, and excluding Indians not taxed, three fifths of all other Persons. The actual Enumeration shall be made within three Years after the first Meeting of the Congress of the United States, and within every subsequent Term of ten Years, in such Manner as they shall by Law direct. The Number of Representatives shall not exceed one for every thirty Thousand, but each State shall have at Least one Representative; and until such enumeration shall be made, the State of New Hampshire shall be entitled to chuse three, Massachusetts eight, Rhode Island and Providence Plantations one, Connecticut five, New York six, New Jersey four, Pennsylvania eight, Delaware one, Maryland six, Virginia ten, North Carolina five, South Carolina five, and Georgia three.

When vacancies happen in the Representation from any State, the Executive Authority thereof shall issue Writs of Election to fill such Vacancies.

The House of Representatives shall chuse their Speaker and other Officers; and shall have the sole Power of Impeachment.

Section 3.   The Senate of the United States shall be composed of two Senators from each State, chosen by the Legislature thereof, for six Years; and each Senator shall have one Vote.

Immediately after they shall be assembled in Consequence of the first Election, they shall be divided as equally as may be into three Classes. The Seats of the Senators of the first Class shall be vacated at the Expiration of the second Year, of the second Class at the Expiration of the fourth Year, and of the third Class at the Expiration of the sixth Year, so that one third may be chosen every second Year; and if Vacancies happen by Resignation, or otherwise, during the Recess of the Legislature of any State, the Executive thereof may make temporary Appointments until the next Meeting of the Legislature, which shall then fill such Vacancies.

No Person shall be a Senator who shall not have attained to the Age of thirty Years, and been nine Years a Citizen of the United States, and who shall not, when elected, be an Inhabitant of that State for which he shall be chosen.

The Vice President of the United States shall be President of the Senate, but shall have no Vote, unless they be equally divided.

The Senate shall chuse their other Officers, and also a President pro tempore, in the Absence of the Vice President, or when he shall exercise the Office of President of the United States.

The Senate shall have the sole Power to try all Impeachments. When sitting for that Purpose, they shall be on Oath or Affirmation. When the President of the United States is tried, the Chief Justice shall preside: And no Person shall be convicted without the Concurrence of two thirds of the Members present.

Judgment in Cases of Impeachment shall not extend further than to removal from Office, and disqualification to hold and enjoy any Office of honor, Trust, or Profit under the United States: but the Party convicted shall nevertheless be liable and subject to Indictment, Trial, Judgment, and Punishment, according to Law.

Section 4.   The Times, Places and Manner of holding Elections for Senators and Representatives, shall be prescribed in each State by the Legislature thereof; but the Congress may at any time by Law make or alter such Regulations, except as to the Places of chusing Senators.

The Congress shall assemble at least once in every Year, and such Meeting shall be on the first Monday in December, unless they shall by Law appoint a different Day.

Section 5.   Each House shall be the Judge of the Elections, Returns, and Qualifications of its own Members, and a Majority of each shall constitute a Quorum to do Business; but a smaller Number may adjourn from day to day, and may be authorized to compel the Attendance of absent Members, in such Manner, and under such Penalties as each House may provide.

Each House may determine the Rules of its Proceedings, punish its Members for disorderly Behavior, and, with the Concurrence of two thirds, expel a Member.

Each House shall keep a Journal of its Proceedings, and from time to time publish the same, excepting such Parts as may in their Judgment require Secrecy; and the Yeas and Nays of the Members of either House on any question shall, at the Desire of one fifth of those Present, be entered on the Journal.

Neither House, during the Session of Congress, shall, without the Consent of the other, adjourn for more than three days, nor to any other Place than that in which the two Houses shall be sitting.

Section 6.   The Senators and Representatives shall receive a Compensation for their Services, to be ascertained by Law, and paid out of the Treasury of the United States. They shall in all Cases, except Treason, Felony and Breach of the Peace, be privileged from Arrest during their Attendance at the Session of their respective Houses, and in going to and returning from the same; and for any Speech or Debate in either House, they shall not be questioned in any other Place.

No Senator or Representative shall, during the Time for which he was elected, be appointed to any civil Office under the Authority of the United States, which shall have been created, or the Emoluments whereof shall have been increased during such time; and no Person holding any Office under the United States, shall be a Member of either House during his Continuance in Office.

Section 7. All Bills for raising Revenue shall originate in the House of Representatives; but the Senate may propose or concur with Amendments as on other Bills.

Every Bill which shall have passed the House of Representatives and the Senate, shall, before it become a Law, be presented to the President of the United States; If he approve he shall sign it, but if not he shall return it, with his Objections to the House in which it shall have originated, who shall enter the Objections at large on their Journal, and proceed to reconsider it. If after such Reconsideration two thirds of that House shall agree to pass the Bill, it shall be sent together with the Objections, to the other House, by which it shall likewise be reconsidered, and if approved by two thirds of that House, it shall become a Law. But in all such Cases the Votes of both Houses shall be determined by Yeas and Nays, and the Names of the Persons voting for and against the Bill shall be entered on the Journal of each House respectively. If any Bill shall not be returned by the President within ten Days (Sundays excepted) after it shall have been presented to him, the Same shall be a Law, in like Manner as if he had signed it, unless the Congress by their Adjournment prevent its Return in which Case it shall not be a Law.

Every Order, Resolution, or Vote, to which the Concurrence of the Senate and House of Representatives may be necessary (except on a question of Adjournment) shall be presented to the President of the United States; and before the Same shall take Effect, shall be approved by him, or being disapproved by him, shall be repassed by two thirds of the Senate and House of Representatives, according to the Rules and Limitations prescribed in the Case of a Bill.

Section 8. The Congress shall have Power To lay and collect Taxes, Duties, Imposts and Excises, to pay the Debts and provide for the common Defence and general Welfare of the United States; but all Duties, Imposts and Excises shall be uniform throughout the United States;

To borrow Money on the credit of the United States;

To regulate Commerce with foreign Nations, and among the several States, and with the Indian Tribes;

To establish an uniform Rule of Naturalization, and uniform Laws on the subject of Bankruptcies throughout the United States;

To coin Money, regulate the Value thereof, and of foreign Coin, and fix the Standard of Weights and Measures;

To provide for the Punishment of counterfeiting the Securities and current Coin of the United States;

To establish Post Offices and post Roads;

To promote the Progress of Science and useful Arts, by securing for limited Times to Authors and Inventors the exclusive Right to their respective Writings and Discoveries;

To constitute Tribunals inferior to the supreme Court;

To define and punish Piracies and Felonies committed on the high Seas, and Offenses against the Law of Nations;

To declare War, grant Letters of Marque and Reprisal, and make Rules concerning Captures on Land and Water;

To raise and support Armies, but no Appropriation of Money to that Use shall be for a longer Term than two Years;

To provide and maintain a Navy;

To make Rules for the Government and Regulation of the land and naval Forces;

To provide for calling forth the Militia to execute the Laws of the Union, suppress Insurrections and repel Invasions;

To provide for organizing, arming, and disciplining, the Militia, and for governing such Part of them as may be employed in the Service of the United States, reserving to the States respectively, the Appointment of the Officers, and the Authority of training the Militia according to the discipline prescribed by Congress;

To exercise exclusive Legislation in all Cases whatsoever, over such District (not exceeding ten Miles square) as may, by Cession of particular States, and the Acceptance of Congress, become the Seat of the Government of the United States, and to exercise like Authority over all Places purchased by the Consent of the Legislature of the State in which the Same shall be, for the Erection of Forts, Magazines, Arsenals, dock-Yards, and other needful Buildings;—And

To make all Laws which shall be necessary and proper for carrying into Execution the foregoing Powers, and all other Powers vested by this Constitution in the Government of the United States, or in any Department or Officer thereof.

Section 9. The Migration or Importation of such Persons as any of the States now existing shall think proper to admit, shall not be prohibited by the Congress prior to the Year one thousand eight hundred and eight, but a Tax or duty may be imposed on such Importation, not exceeding ten dollars for each Person.

The privilege of the Writ of Habeas Corpus shall not be suspended, unless when in Cases of Rebellion or Invasion the public Safety may require it.

No Bill of Attainder or ex post facto Law shall be passed.

No Capitation, or other direct, Tax shall be laid, unless in Proportion to the Census or Enumeration herein before directed to be taken.

No Tax or Duty shall be laid on Articles exported from any State.

No Preference shall be given by any Regulation of Commerce or Revenue to the Ports of one State over those of another: nor shall Vessels bound to, or from, one State be obliged to enter, clear, or pay Duties in another.

No Money shall be drawn from the Treasury, but in Consequence of Appropriations made by Law; and a regular Statement and Account of the Receipts and Expenditures of all public Money shall be published from time to time.

No Title of Nobility shall be granted by the United States: And no Person holding any Office of Profit or Trust under them, shall, without the Consent of the Congress, accept of any present, Emolument, Office, or Title, of any kind whatever, from any King, Prince, or foreign State.

Section 10. No State shall enter into any Treaty, Alliance, or Confederation; grant Letters of Marque and Reprisal; coin Money; emit Bills of Credit; make any Thing but gold and silver Coin a Tender in Payment of Debts; pass any Bill of Attainder, ex post facto Law, or Law impairing the Obligation of Contracts, or grant any Title of Nobility.

No State shall, without the Consent of the Congress, lay any Imposts or Duties on Imports or Exports, except what may be absolutely necessary for executing its inspection Laws: and the net Produce of all Duties and Imposts, laid by any State on Imports or Exports, shall be for the Use of the Treasury of the United States; and all such Laws shall be subject to the Revision and Controul of the Congress.

No State shall, without the Consent of Congress, lay any Duty of Tonnage, keep Troops, or Ships of War in time of Peace, enter into any Agreement or Compact with another State, or with a foreign Power, or engage in War, unless actually invaded, or in such imminent Danger as will not admit of delay.

Article II

Section 1. The executive Power shall be vested in a President of the United States of America. He shall hold his Office during the Term of four Years, and, together with the Vice President, chosen for the same Term, be elected, as follows:

Each State shall appoint, in such Manner as the Legislature thereof may direct, a Number of Electors, equal to the whole Number of Senators and Representatives to which the State may be entitled in the Congress; but no Senator or Representative, or Person holding an Office of Trust or Profit under the United States, shall be appointed an Elector.

The Electors shall meet in their respective States, and vote by Ballot for two Persons, of whom one at least shall not be an Inhabitant of the same State with themselves. And they shall make a List of all the Persons voted for, and of the Number of Votes for each; which List they shall sign and certify, and transmit sealed to the Seat of the Government of the United States, directed to the President of the Senate. The President of the Senate shall, in the Presence of the Senate and House of Representatives, open all the Certificates, and the Votes shall then be counted. The Person having the greatest Number of Votes shall be the President, if such Number be a Majority of the whole Number of Electors appointed; and if there be more than one who have such Majority, and have an equal Number of Votes, then the House of Representatives shall immediately chuse by Ballot one of them for President; and if no Person have a Majority, then from the five highest on the List the said House shall in like Manner chuse the President. But in chusing the President, the Votes shall be taken by States, the Representation from each State having one Vote; A quorum for this Purpose shall consist of a Member or Members from two thirds of the States, and a Majority of all the States shall be necessary to a Choice. In every Case, after the Choice of the President, the Person having the greater Number of Votes of the Electors shall be the Vice President. But if there should remain two or more who have equal Votes, the Senate shall chuse from them by Ballot the Vice President.

The Congress may determine the Time of chusing the Electors, and the Day on which they shall give their Votes; which Day shall be the same throughout the United States.

No person except a natural born Citizen, or a Citizen of the United States, at the time of the Adoption of this Constitution, shall be eligible to the Office of President; neither shall any Person be eligible to that Office who shall not have attained to the Age of thirty five Years, and been fourteen Years a Resident within the United States.

In Case of the Removal of the President from Office, or of his Death, Resignation or Inability to discharge the Powers and Duties of the said Office, the same shall devolve on the Vice President, and the Congress may by Law provide for the Case of Removal, Death, Resignation or Inability, both of the President and Vice President, declaring what Officer shall then act as President, and such Officer shall act accordingly, until the Disability be removed, or a President shall be elected.

The President shall, at stated Times, receive for his Services, a Compensation, which shall neither be increased nor diminished during the Period for which he shall have been elected, and he shall not receive within that Period any other Emolument from the United States, or any of them.

Before he enter on the Execution of his Office, he shall take the following Oath or Affirmation: "I do solemnly swear (or affirm) that I will faithfully execute the Office of President of the United States, and will to the best of my Ability, preserve, protect and defend the Constitution of the United States."

Section 2.   The President shall be Commander in Chief of the Army and Navy of the United States, and of the Militia of the several States, when called into the actual Service of the United States; he may require the Opinion, in writing, of the principal Officer in each of the executive Departments, upon any Subject relating to the Duties of their respective Offices, and he shall have Power to grant Reprieves and Pardons for Offenses against the United States, except in Cases of Impeachment.

He shall have Power, by and with the Advice and Consent of the Senate to make Treaties, provided two thirds of the Senators present concur; and he shall nominate, and by and with the Advice and Consent of the Senate, shall appoint Ambassadors, other public Ministers and Consuls, Judges of the supreme Court, and all other Officers of the United States, whose Appointments are not herein otherwise provided for, and which shall be established by Law; but the Congress may by Law vest the Appointment of such inferior Officers, as they think proper, in the President alone, in the Courts of Law, or in the Heads of Departments.

The President shall have Power to fill up all Vacancies that may happen during the Recess of the Senate, by granting Commissions which shall expire at the End of their next Session.

Section 3.   He shall from time to time give to the Congress Information of the State of the Union, and recommend to their Consideration such Measures as he shall judge necessary and expedient; he may, on extraordinary Occasions, convene both Houses, or either of them, and in Case of Disagreement between them, with Respect to the Time of Adjournment, he may adjourn them to such Time as he shall think proper; he shall receive Ambassadors and other public Ministers; he shall take Care that the Laws be faithfully executed, and shall Commission all the Officers of the United States.

Section 4.   The President, Vice President and all civil Officers of the United States, shall be removed from Office on Impeachment for, and Conviction of, Treason, Bribery, or other high Crimes and Misdemeanors.

Article III

Section 1.   The judicial Power of the United States, shall be vested in one supreme Court, and in such inferior Courts as the Congress may from time to time ordain and establish. The Judges, both of the supreme and inferior Courts, shall hold their Offices during good Behaviour, and shall, at stated Times, receive for their Services a Compensation, which shall not be diminished during their Continuance in Office.

Section 2.   The judicial Power shall extend to all Cases, in Law and Equity, arising under this Constitution, the Laws of the United States, and Treaties made, or which shall be made, under their Authority;—to all Cases affecting Ambassadors, other public Ministers and Consuls;—to all Cases of admiralty and maritime Jurisdiction;—to Controversies to which the United States shall be a Party;—to Controversies between two or more States;—between a State and Citizens of another State;—between Citizens of different States;—between Citizens of the same State claiming Lands under Grants of different States, and between a State, or the Citizens thereof, and foreign States, Citizens or Subjects.

In all Cases affecting Ambassadors, other public Ministers and Consuls, and those in which a State shall be a Party, the supreme Court shall have original Jurisdiction. In all the other Cases before mentioned, the supreme Court shall have appellate Jurisdiction, both as to Law and Fact, with such Exceptions, and under such Regulations as the Congress shall make.

The Trial of all Crimes, except in Cases of Impeachment, shall be by Jury; and such Trial shall be held in the State where the said Crimes shall have been committed; but when not committed within any State, the Trial shall be at such Place or Places as the Congress may by Law have directed.

Section 3.   Treason against the United States, shall consist only in levying War against them, or, in adhering to their Enemies, giving them Aid and Comfort. No Person shall be convicted of Treason unless on the Testimony of two Witnesses to the same overt Act, or on Confession in open Court.

The Congress shall have Power to declare the Punishment of Treason, but no Attainder of Treason shall work Corruption of Blood, or Forfeiture except during the Life of the Person attainted.

Article IV

Section 1. Full Faith and Credit shall be given in each State to the public Acts, Records, and judicial Proceedings of every other State. And the Congress may by general Laws prescribe the Manner in which such Acts, Records and Proceedings shall be proved, and the Effect thereof.

Section 2. The Citizens of each State shall be entitled to all Privileges and Immunities of Citizens in the several States.

A Person charged in any State with Treason, Felony, or other Crime, who shall flee from Justice, and be found in another State, shall on Demand of the executive Authority of the State from which he fled, be delivered up, to be removed to the State having Jurisdiction of the Crime.

No Person held to Service or Labour in one State, under the Laws thereof, escaping into another, shall, in Consequence of any Law or Regulation therein, be discharged from such Service or Labour, but shall be delivered up on Claim of the Party to whom such Service or Labour may be due.

Section 3. New States may be admitted by the Congress into this Union; but no new State shall be formed or erected within the Jurisdiction of any other State; nor any State be formed by the Junction of two or more States, or Parts of States, without the Consent of the Legislatures of the States concerned as well as of the Congress.

The Congress shall have Power to dispose of and make all needful Rules and Regulations respecting the Territory or other Property belonging to the United States; and nothing in this Constitution shall be so construed as to Prejudice any Claims of the United States, or of any particular State.

Section 4. The United States shall guarantee to every State in this Union a Republican Form of Government, and shall protect each of them against Invasion; and on Application of the Legislature, or of the Executive (when the Legislature cannot be convened) against domestic Violence.

Article V

The Congress, whenever two thirds of both Houses shall deem it necessary, shall propose Amendments to this Constitution, or, on the Application of the Legislatures of two thirds of the several States, shall call a Convention for proposing Amendments, which, in either Case, shall be valid to all Intents and Purposes, as part of this Constitution, when ratified by the Legislatures of three fourths of the several States, or by Conventions in three fourths thereof, as the one or the other Mode of Ratification may be proposed by the Congress; Provided that no Amendment which may be made prior to the Year One thousand eight hundred and eight shall in any Manner affect the first and fourth Clauses in the Ninth Section of the first Article; and that no State, without its Consent, shall be deprived of its equal Suffrage in the Senate.

Article VI

All Debts contracted and Engagements entered into, before the Adoption of this Constitution shall be as valid against the United States under this Constitution, as under the Confederation.

This Constitution, and the Laws of the United States which shall be made in Pursuance thereof; and all Treaties made, or which shall be made, under the Authority of the United States, shall be the supreme Law of the Land; and the Judges in every State shall be bound thereby, any Thing in the Constitution or Laws of any State to the Contrary notwithstanding.

The Senators and Representatives before mentioned, and the Members of the several State Legislatures, and all executive and judicial Officers, both of the United States and of the several States, shall be bound by Oath or Affirmation, to support this Constitution; but no religious Test shall ever be required as a Qualification to any Office or public Trust under the United States.

Article VII

The Ratification of the Conventions of nine States shall be sufficient for the Establishment of this Constitution between the States so ratifying the Same.

Amendment I [1791]

Congress shall make no law respecting an establishment of religion, or prohibiting the free exercise thereof; or abridging the freedom of speech, or of the press; or the right of the people peaceably to assemble, and to petition the Government for a redress of grievances.

Amendment II [1791]

A well regulated Militia, being necessary to the security of a free State, the right of the people to keep and bear Arms, shall not be infringed.

Amendment III [1791]

No Soldier shall, in time of peace be quartered in any house, without the consent of the Owner, nor in time of war, but in a manner to be prescribed by law.

Amendment IV [1791]

The right of the people to be secure in their persons, houses, papers, and effects, against unreasonable searches and seizures, shall not be violated, and no Warrants shall issue, but upon probable cause, supported by Oath or affirmation, and particularly describing the place to be searched, and the persons or things to be seized.

Amendment V [1791]

No person shall be held to answer for a capital, or otherwise infamous crime, unless on a presentment or indictment of a Grand Jury, except in cases arising in the land or naval forces, or in the Militia, when in actual service in time of War or public danger; nor shall any person be subject for the same offence to be twice put in jeopardy of life or limb; nor shall be compelled in any criminal case to be a witness against himself, nor be deprived of life, liberty, or property, without due process of law; nor shall private property be taken for public use, without just compensation.

Amendment VI [1791]

In all criminal prosecutions, the accused shall enjoy the right to a speedy and public trial, by an impartial jury of the State and district wherein the crime shall have been committed, which district shall have been previously ascertained by law, and to be informed of the nature and cause of the accusation; to be confronted with the witnesses against him; to have compulsory process for obtaining witnesses in his favor, and to have the Assistance of Counsel for his defence.

Amendment VII [1791]

In Suits at common law, where the value in controversy shall exceed twenty dollars, the right of trial by jury shall be preserved, and no fact tried by jury, shall be otherwise reexamined in any Court of the United States, than according to the rules of the common law.

Amendment VIII [1791]

Excessive bail shall not be required, nor excessive fines imposed, nor cruel and unusual punishments inflicted.

Amendment IX [1791]

The enumeration in the Constitution, of certain rights, shall not be construed to deny or disparage others retained by the people.

Amendment X [1791]

The powers not delegated to the United States by the Constitution, nor prohibited by it to the States, are reserved to the States respectively, or to the people.

Amendment XI [1798]

The Judicial power of the United States shall not be construed to extend to any suit in law or equity, commenced or prosecuted against one of the United States by Citizens of another State, or by Citizens or Subjects of any Foreign State.

Amendment XII [1804]

The Electors shall meet in their respective states, and vote by ballot for President and Vice-President, one of whom, at least, shall not be an inhabitant of the same state with themselves; they shall name in their ballots the person voted for as President, and in distinct ballots the person voted for as Vice-President, and they shall make distinct lists of all persons voted for as President, and of all persons voted for as Vice-President, and of the number of votes for each, which lists they shall sign and certify, and transmit sealed to the seat of the government of the United States, directed to the President of the Senate;—The President of the Senate shall, in the presence of the Senate and House of Representatives, open all the certificates and the votes shall then be counted;—The person having the greatest number of votes for President, shall be the President, if such number be a majority of the whole number of Electors appointed; and if no person have such majority, then from the persons having the highest numbers not exceeding three on the list of those voted for as President, the House of Representatives shall choose immediately, by ballot, the President. But in choosing the President, the votes shall be taken by states, the representation from each state having one vote; a quorum for this purpose shall consist of a member or members from two-thirds of the states, and a majority of all states shall be necessary to a choice. And if the House of Representatives shall not choose a President whenever the right of choice shall devolve upon them, before the fourth day of March next following, then the Vice-President shall act as President, as in the case of the death or other constitutional disability of the President.—The person having the greatest number of votes as Vice-President, shall be the Vice-President, if such number be a majority of the whole number of Electors appointed, and if no person have a majority, then from the two highest numbers on the list, the Senate shall choose the Vice-President; a quorum for the purpose shall consist of two-thirds of the whole number of Senators, and a majority of the whole number shall be necessary to a choice. But no person constitutionally ineligible to the office of President shall be eligible to that of Vice-President of the United States.

Amendment XIII [1865]

Section 1. Neither slavery nor involuntary servitude, except as a punishment for crime whereof the party shall have been duly convicted, shall exist within the United States, or any place subject to their jurisdiction.

Section 2. Congress shall have power to enforce this article by appropriate legislation.

Amendment XIV [1868]

Section 1. All persons born or naturalized in the United States, and subject to the jurisdiction thereof, are citizens of the United States and of the State wherein they reside. No State shall make or enforce any law which shall abridge the privileges or immunities of citizens of the United States; nor shall any State deprive any person of life, liberty, or property, without due process of law; nor deny to any person within its jurisdiction the equal protection of the laws.

Section 2.   Representatives shall be apportioned among the several States according to their respective numbers, counting the whole number of persons in each State, excluding Indians not taxed. But when the right to vote at any election for the choice of electors for President and Vice President of the United States, Representatives in Congress, the Executive and Judicial officers of a State, or the members of the Legislature thereof, is denied to any of the male inhabitants of such State, being twenty-one years of age, and citizens of the United States, or in any way abridged, except for participation in rebellion, or other crime, the basis of representation therein shall be reduced in the proportion which the number of such male citizens shall bear to the whole number of male citizens twenty-one years of age in such State.

Section 3.   No person shall be a Senator or Representative in Congress, or elector of President and Vice President, or hold any office, civil or military, under the United States, or under any State, who having previously taken an oath, as a member of Congress, or as an officer of the United States, or as a member of any State legislature, or as an executive or judicial officer of any State, to support the Constitution of the United States, shall have engaged in insurrection or rebellion against the same, or given aid or comfort to the enemies thereof. But Congress may by a vote of two-thirds of each House, remove such disability.

Section 4.   The validity of the public debt of the United States, authorized by law, including debts incurred for payment of pensions and bounties for services in suppressing insurrection or rebellion, shall not be questioned. But neither the United States nor any State shall assume or pay any debt or obligation incurred in aid of insurrection or rebellion against the United States, or any claim for the loss or emancipation of any slave; but all such debts, obligations and claims shall be held illegal and void.

Section 5.   The Congress shall have power to enforce, by appropriate legislation, the provisions of this article.

Amendment XV [1870]

Section 1.   The right of citizens of the United States to vote shall not be denied or abridged by the United States or by any State on account of race, color, or previous condition of servitude.

Section 2.   The Congress shall have power to enforce this article by appropriate legislation.

Amendment XVI [1913]

The Congress shall have power to lay and collect taxes on incomes, from whatever source derived, without apportionment among the several States, and without regard to any census or enumeration.

Amendment XVII [1913]

Section 1.   The Senate of the United States shall be composed of two Senators from each State, elected by the people thereof, for six years; and each Senator shall have one vote. The electors in each State shall have the qualifications requisite for electors of the most numerous branch of the State legislatures.

Section 2.   When vacancies happen in the representation of any State in the Senate, the executive authority of such State shall issue writs of election to fill such vacancies: Provided, That the legislature of any State may empower the executive thereof to make temporary appointments until the people fill the vacancies by election as the legislature may direct.

Section 3. This amendment shall not be so construed as to affect the election or term of any Senator chosen before it becomes valid as part of the Constitution.

Amendment XVIII [1919]

Section 1. After one year from the ratification of this article the manufacture, sale, or transportation of intoxicating liquors within, the importation thereof into, or the exportation thereof from the United States and all territory subject to the jurisdiction thereof for beverage purposes is hereby prohibited.

Section 2. The Congress and the several States shall have concurrent power to enforce this article by appropriate legislation.

Section 3. This article shall be inoperative unless it shall have been ratified as an amendment to the Constitution by the legislatures of the several States, as provided in the Constitution, within seven years from the date of the submission hereof to the States by the Congress.

Amendment XIX [1920]

Section 1. The right of citizens of the United States to vote shall not be denied or abridged by the United States or by any State on account of sex.

Section 2. Congress shall have power to enforce this article by appropriate legislation.

Amendment XX [1933]

Section 1. The terms of the President and Vice President shall end at noon on the 20th day of January, and the terms of Senators and Representatives at noon on the 3d day of January, of the years in which such terms would have ended if this article had not been ratified; and the terms of their successors shall then begin.

Section 2. The Congress shall assemble at least once in every year, and such meeting shall begin at noon on the 3d day of January, unless they shall by law appoint a different day.

Section 3. If, at the time fixed for the beginning of the term of the President, the President elect shall have died, the Vice President elect shall become President. If the President shall not have been chosen before the time fixed for the beginning of his term, or if the President elect shall have failed to qualify, then the Vice President elect shall act as President until a President shall have qualified; and the Congress may by law provide for the case wherein neither a President elect nor a Vice President elect shall have qualified, declaring who shall then act as President, or the manner in which one who is to act shall be selected, and such person shall act accordingly until a President or Vice President shall have qualified.

Section 4. The Congress may by law provide for the case of the death of any of the persons from whom the House of Representatives may choose a President whenever the right of choice shall have devolved upon them, and for the case of the death of any of the persons from whom the Senate may choose a Vice President whenever the right of choice shall have devolved upon them.

Section 5. Sections 1 and 2 shall take effect on the 15th day of October following the ratification of this article.

Section 6. This article shall be inoperative unless it shall have been ratified as an amendment to the Constitution by the legislatures of three-fourths of the several States within seven years from the date of its submission.

Amendment XXI [1933]

Section 1. The eighteenth article of amendment to the Constitution of the United States is hereby repealed.

Section 2. The transportation or importation into any State, Territory, or possession of the United States for delivery or use therein of intoxicating liquors, in violation of the laws thereof, is hereby prohibited.

Section 3. This article shall be inoperative unless it shall have been ratified as an amendment to the Constitution by conventions in the several States, as provided in the Constitution, within seven years from the date of the submission hereof to the States by the Congress.

Amendment XXII [1951]

Section 1. No person shall be elected to the office of the President more than twice, and no person who has held the office of President, or acted as President, for more than two years of a term to which some other person was elected President shall be elected to the office of President more than once. But this Article shall not apply to any person holding the office of President when this Article was proposed by the Congress, and shall not prevent any person who may be holding the office of President, or acting as President, during the term within which this Article becomes operative from holding the office of President or acting as President during the remainder of such term.

Section 2. This article shall be inoperative unless it shall have been ratified as an amendment to the Constitution by the legislatures of three-fourths of the several States within seven years from the date of its submission to the States by the Congress.

Amendment XXIII [1961]

Section 1. The District constituting the seat of Government of the United States shall appoint in such manner as the Congress may direct:

A number of electors of President and Vice President equal to the whole number of Senators and Representatives in Congress to which the District would be entitled if it were a State, but in no event more than the least populous state; they shall be in addition to those appointed by the states, but they shall be considered, for the purposes of the election of President and Vice President, to be electors appointed by a state; and they shall meet in the District and perform such duties as provided by the twelfth article of amendment.

Section 2. The Congress shall have power to enforce this article by appropriate legislation.

Amendment XXIV [1964]

Section 1. The right of citizens of the United States to vote in any primary or other election for President or Vice President, for electors for President or Vice President, or for Senator or Representative in Congress, shall not be denied or abridged by the United States, or any State by reason of failure to pay any poll tax or other tax.

Section 2. The Congress shall have power to enforce this article by appropriate legislation.

Amendment XXV [1967]

Section 1. In case of the removal of the President from office or of his death or resignation, the Vice President shall become President.

Section 2.   Whenever there is a vacancy in the office of the Vice President, the President shall nominate a Vice President who shall take office upon confirmation by a majority vote of both Houses of Congress.

Section 3.   Whenever the President transmits to the President pro tempore of the Senate and the Speaker of the House of Representatives his written declaration that he is unable to discharge the powers and duties of his office, and until he transmits to them a written declaration to the contrary, such powers and duties shall be discharged by the Vice President as Acting President.

Section 4.   Whenever the Vice President and a majority of either the principal officers of the executive departments or of such other body as Congress may by law provide, transmit to the President pro tempore of the Senate and the Speaker of the House of Representatives their written declaration that the President is unable to discharge the powers and duties of his office, the Vice President shall immediately assume the powers and duties of the office as Acting President.

Thereafter, when the President transmits to the President pro tempore of the Senate and the Speaker of the House of Representatives his written declaration that no inability exists, he shall resume the powers and duties of his office unless the Vice President and a majority of either the principal officers of the executive department or of such other body as Congress may by law provide, transmit within four days to the President pro tempore of the Senate and the Speaker of the House of Representatives their written declaration that the President is unable to discharge the powers and duties of his office. Thereupon Congress shall decide the issue, assembling within forty-eight hours for that purpose if not in session. If the Congress, within twenty-one days after receipt of the latter written declaration, or, if Congress is not in session, within twenty-one days after Congress is required to assemble, determines by two-thirds vote of both Houses that the President is unable to discharge the powers and duties of his office, the Vice President shall continue to discharge the same as Acting President; otherwise, the President shall resume the powers and duties of his office.

Amendment XXVI [1971]

Section 1.   The right of citizens of the United States, who are eighteen years of age or older, to vote shall not be denied or abridged by the United States or by any State on account of age.

Section 2.   The Congress shall have power to enforce this article by appropriate legislation.

Amendment XXVII [1992]

No law, varying the compensation for the services of the Senators and Representatives, shall take effect, until an election of Representatives shall have intervened.

Spanish Equivalents for Important Legal Terms in English

Abandoned property: bienes abandonados

Acceptance: aceptación; consentimiento; acuerdo

Acceptor: aceptante

Accession: toma de posesión; aumento; accesión

Accommodation indorser: avalista de favor

Accommodation party: firmante de favor

Accord: acuerdo; convenio; arregio

Accord and satisfaction: transacción ejecutada

Act of state doctrine: doctrina de acto de gobierno

Administrative law: derecho administrativo

Administrative process: procedimiento o metódo administrativo

Administrator: administrador (-a)

Adverse possession: posesión de hecho susceptible de proscripción adquisitiva

Affirmative action: acción afirmativa

Affirmative defense: defensa afirmativa

After-acquired property: bienes adquiridos con posterioridad a un hecho dado

Agency: mandato; agencia

Agent: mandatorio; agente; representante

Agreement: convenio; acuerdo; contrato

Alien corporation: empresa extranjera

Allonge: hojas adicionales de endosos

Answer: contestación de la demande; alegato

Anticipatory repudiation: anuncio previo de las partes de su imposibilidad de cumplir con el contrato

Appeal: apelación; recurso de apelación

Appellate jurisdiction: jurisdicción de apelaciones

Appraisal right: derecho de valuación

Arbitration: arbitraje

Arson: incendio intencional

Articles of partnership: contrato social

Artisan's lien: derecho de retención que ejerce al artesano

Assault: asalto; ataque; agresión

Assignment of rights: transmisión; transferencia; cesión

Assumption of risk: no resarcimiento por exposición voluntaria al peligro

Attachment: auto judicial que autoriza el embargo; embargo

Bailee: depositario

Bailment: depósito; constitución en depósito

Bailor: depositante

Bankruptcy trustee: síndico de la quiebra

Battery: agresión; física

Bearer: portador; tenedor

Bearer instrument: documento al portador

Bequest or legacy: legado (de bienes muebles)

Bilateral contract: contrato bilateral

Bill of lading: conocimiento de embarque; carta de porte

Bill of Rights: declaración de derechos

Binder: póliza de seguro provisoria; recibo de pago a cuenta del precio

Blank indorsement: endoso en blanco

Blue sky laws: leyes reguladoras del comercio bursátil

Bond: título de crédito; garantía; caución

Bond indenture: contrato de emisión de bonos; contrato del ampréstito

Breach of contract: incumplimiento de contrato

Brief: escrito; resumen; informe

Burglary: violación de domicilio

Business judgment rule: regla de juicio comercial

Business tort: agravio comercial

Case law: ley de casos; derecho casuístico

Cashier's check: cheque de caja

Causation in fact: causalidad en realidad

Cease-and-desist order: orden para cesar y desistir

Certificate of deposit: certificado de depósito

Certified check: cheque certificado

Charitable trust: fideicomiso para fines benéficos

Chattel: bien mueble

Check: cheque

Chose in action: derecho inmaterial; derecho de acción

Civil law: derecho civil

Close corporation: sociedad de un solo accionista o de un grupo restringido de accionistas

Closed shop: taller agremiado (emplea solamente a miembros de un gremio)

Closing argument: argumento al final

Codicil: codicilo

Collateral: garantía; bien objeto de la garantía real

Comity: cortesía; cortesía entre naciones

Commercial paper: instrumentos negociables; documentos a valores commerciales

Common law: derecho consuetudinario; derecho común; ley común

Common stock: acción ordinaria

Comparative negligence: negligencia comparada

Compensatory damages: daños y perjuicios reales o compensatorios

Concurrent conditions: condiciones concurrentes

Concurrent jurisdiction: competencia concurrente de varios tribunales para entender en una misma causa

Concurring opinion: opinión concurrente

Condition: condición

Condition precedent: condición suspensiva

Condition subsequent: condición resolutoria

Confiscation: confiscación

Confusion: confusión; fusión

Conglomerate merger: fusión de firmas que operan en distintos mercados

Consent decree: acuerdo entre las partes aprobado por un tribunal

Consequential damages: daños y perjuicios indirectos

Consideration: consideración; motivo; contraprestación

Consolidation: consolidación

Constructive delivery: entrega simbólica

Constructive trust: fideicomiso creado por aplicación de la ley

Consumer protection law: ley para proteger el consumidor

Contract: contrato

Contract under seal: contrato formal o sellado

Contributory negligence: negligencia de la parte actora

Conversion: usurpación; conversión de valores

Copyright: derecho de autor

Corporation: sociedad anómina; corporación; persona juridica

Co-sureties: cogarantes

Counterclaim: reconvención; contrademanda

Counteroffer: contraoferta

Course of dealing: curso de transacciones

Course of performance: curso de cumplimiento

Covenant: pacto; garantía; contrato

Covenant not to sue: pacto or contrato a no demandar

Covenant of quiet enjoyment: garantía del uso y goce pacífico del inmueble

Creditors' composition agreement: concordato preventivo

Crime: crimen; delito; contravención

Criminal law: derecho penal

Cross-examination: contrainterrogatorio

Cure: cura; cuidado; derecho de remediar un vicio contractual

Customs receipts: recibos de derechos aduaneros

Damages: daños; indemnización por daños y perjuicios

Debit card: tarjeta de dé bito

Debtor: deudor

Debt securities: seguridades de deuda

Deceptive advertising: publicidad engañosa

Deed: escritura; título; acta translativa de domino

Defamation: difamación

Delegation of duties: delegación de obligaciones

Demand deposit: depósito a la vista

Depositions: declaración de un testigo fuera del tribunal

Devise: legado; deposición testamentaria (bienes inmuebles)

Direct examination: interrogatorio directo; primer interrogatorio

Directed verdict: veredicto según orden del juez y sin participación activa del jurado

Disaffirmance: repudiación; renuncia; anulación

Discharge: descargo; liberación; cumplimiento

Disclosed principal: mandante revelado

Discovery: descubrimiento; producción de la prueba

Dissenting opinion: opinión disidente

Dissolution: disolución; terminación

Diversity of citizenship: competencia de los tribunales federales para entender en causas cuyas partes intervinientes son cuidadanos de distintos estados

Divestiture: extinción premature de derechos reales

Dividend: dividendo

Docket: orden del día; lista de causas pendientes

Domestic corporation: sociedad local

Draft: orden de pago; letrade cambio

Drawee: girado; beneficiario

Drawer: librador

Duress: coacción; violencia

Easement: servidumbre

Embezzlement: desfalco; malversación

Eminent domain: poder de expropiación

Employment discrimination: discriminación en el empleo

Entrepreneur: empresario

Environmental law: ley ambiental

Equal dignity rule: regla de dignidad egual

Equity security: tipo de participación en una sociedad

Estate: propiedad; patrimonio; derecho

Estop: impedir; prevenir

Ethical issue: cuestión ética

Exclusive jurisdiction: competencia exclusiva

Exculpatory clause: cláusula eximente

Executed contract: contrato ejecutado

Execution: ejecución; cumplimiento

Executor: albacea

Executory contract: contrato aún no completamente consumado

Executory interest: derecho futuro

Express contract: contrato expreso

Expropriation: expropriación

Federal question: caso federal

Fee simple: pleno dominio; dominio absoluto

Fee simple absolute: dominio absoluto

Fee simple defeasible: dominio sujeta a una condición resolutoria

Felony: crimen; delito grave

Fictitious payee: beneficiario ficticio

Fiduciary: fiduciaro

Firm offer: oferta en firme

Fixture: inmueble por destino, incorporación a anexación

Floating lien: gravamen continuado

Foreign corporation: sociedad extranjera; U.S. sociedad constituída en otro estado

Forgery: falso; falsificación

Formal contract: contrato formal

Franchise: privilegio; franquicia; concesión

Franchisee: persona que recibe una concesión

Franchisor: persona que vende una concesión

Fraud: fraude; dolo; engaño

Future interest: bien futuro

Garnishment: embargo de derechos

General partner: socio comanditario

General warranty deed: escritura translativa de domino con garantía de título

Gift: donación

Gift *causa mortis*: donación por causa de muerte

Gift *inter vivos*: donación entre vivos

Good faith: buena fe

Good faith purchaser: comprador de buena fe

Holder: tenedor por contraprestación

Holder in due course: tenedor legítimo

Holographic will: testamento ológrafico

Homestead exemption laws: leyes que exceptúan las casas de familia de ejecución por duedas generales

Horizontal merger: fusión horizontal

Identification: identificación

Implied-in-fact contract: contrato implícito en realidad

Implied warranty: guarantía implícita

Implied warranty of merchantability: garantía implícita de vendibilidad

Impossibility of performance: imposibilidad de cumplir un contrato

Imposter: imposter

Incidental beneficiary: beneficiario incidental; beneficiario secundario

Incidental damages: daños incidentales

Indictment: auto de acusación; acusación

Indorsee: endorsatario

Indorsement: endoso

Indorser: endosante

Informal contract: contrato no formal; contrato verbal

Information: acusación hecha por el ministerio público

Injunction: mandamiento; orden de no innovar

Innkeeper's lien: derecho de retención que ejerce el posadero

Installment contract: contrato de pago en cuotas

Insurable interest: interés asegurable

Intended beneficiary: beneficiario destinado

Intentional tort: agravio; cuasidelito intenciónal

International law: derecho internaciónal

Interrogatories: preguntas escritas sometidas por una parte a la otra o a un testigo

Inter vivos trust: fideicomiso entre vivos

Intestacy laws: leyes de la condición de morir intestado

Intestate: intestado

Investment company: compañia de inversiones

Issue: emisión

Joint tenancy: derechos conjuntos en un bien inmueble en favor del beneficiario sobreviviente

Judgment *n.o.v.*: juicio no obstante veredicto

Judgment rate of interest: interés de juicio

Judicial process: acto de procedimiento; proceso jurídico

Judicial review: revisión judicial

Jurisdiction: jurisdicción

Larceny: robo; hurto

Law: derecho; ley; jurisprudencia

Lease: contrato de locación; contrato de alquiler

Leasehold estate: bienes forales

Legal rate of interest: interés legal

Legatee: legatario

Letter of credit: carta de crédito

Levy: embargo; comiso

Libel: libelo; difamación escrita

Life estate: usufructo

Limited partner: comanditario

Limited partnership: sociedad en comandita

Liquidation: liquidación; realización

Lost property: objetos perdidos

Majority opinion: opinión de la mayoría

Maker: persona que realiza u ordena; librador

Mechanic's lien: gravamen de constructor

Mediation: mediación; intervención

Merger: fusión

Mirror image rule: fallo de reflejo

Misdemeanor: infracción; contravención

Mislaid property: bienes extraviados

Mitigation of damages: reducción de daños

Mortgage: hypoteca

Motion to dismiss: excepción parentoria

Mutual fund: fondo mutual

Negotiable instrument: instrumento negociable

Negotiation: negociación

Nominal damages: daños y perjuicios nominales

Novation: novación

Nuncupative will: testamento nuncupativo

Objective theory of contracts: teoria objetiva de contratos

Offer: oferta

Offeree: persona que recibe una oferta

Offeror: oferente

Order instrument: instrumento o documento a la orden

Original jurisdiction: jurisdicción de primera instancia

Output contract: contrato de producción

Parol evidence rule: regla relativa a la prueba oral

Partially disclosed principal: mandante revelado en parte

Partnership: sociedad colectiva; asociación; asociación de participación

Past consideration: causa o contraprestación anterior

Patent: patente; privilegio

Pattern or practice: muestra o práctica

Payee: beneficiario de un pago

Penalty: pena; penalidad

Per capita: por cabeza

Per stirpes: por estirpe

Perfection: perfeción

Performance: cumplimiento; ejecución

Personal defenses: excepciones personales

Personal property: bienes muebles

Plea bargaining: regateo por un alegato

Pleadings: alegatos

Pledge: prenda

Police powers: poders de policia y de prevención del crimen

Policy: póliza

Positive law: derecho positivo; ley positiva

Possibility of reverter: posibilidad de reversión

Precedent: precedente

Preemptive right: derecho de prelación

Preferred stock: acciones preferidas

Premium: recompensa; prima

Presentment warranty: garantía de presentación

Price discrimination: discriminación en los precios

Principal: mandante; principal

Privity: nexo jurídico

Privity of contract: relación contractual

Probable cause: causa probable

Probate: verificación; verificación del testamento

Probate court: tribunal de sucesiones y tutelas

Proceeds: resultados; ingresos

Profit: beneficio; utilidad; lucro

Promise: promesa

Promisee: beneficiario de una promesa

Promisor: promtente

Promissory estoppel: impedimento promisorio

Promissory note: pagaré; nota de pago

Promoter: promotor; fundador

Proximate cause: causa inmediata o próxima

Proxy: apoderado; poder

Punitive, or exemplary, damages: daños y perjuicios punitivos o ejemplares

Qualified indorsement: endoso con reservas

Quasi contract: contrato tácito o implícito

Quitclaim deed: acto de transferencia de una propiedad por finiquito, pero sin ninguna garantía sobre la validez del título transferido

Ratification: ratificación

Real property: bienes inmuebles

Reasonable doubt: duda razonable

Rebuttal: refutación

Recognizance: promesa; compromiso; reconocimiento

Recording statutes: leyes estatales sobre registros oficiales

Redress: reporacíon

Reformation: rectificación; reforma; corrección

Rejoinder: dúplica; contrarréplica

Release: liberación; renuncia a un derecho

Remainder: substitución; reversión

Remedy: recurso; remedio; reparación

Replevin: acción reivindicatoria; reivindicación

Reply: réplica

Requirements contract: contrato de suministro

Res judicata: cosa juzgada; res judicata

Rescission: rescisión

Respondeat superior: responsabilidad del mandante o del maestro

Restitution: restitución

Restrictive indorsement: endoso restrictivo

Resulting trust: fideicomiso implícito

Reversion: reversión; sustitución

Revocation: revocación; derogación

Right of contribution: derecho de contribución

Right of reimbursement: derecho de reembolso

Right of subrogation: derecho de subrogación

Right-to-work law: ley de libertad de trabajo

Robbery: robo

Rule 10b-5: Regla 10b-5

Sale: venta; contrato de compreventa

Sale on approval: venta a ensayo; venta sujeta a la aprobación del comprador

Sale or return: venta con derecho de devolución

Sales contract: contrato de compraventa; boleto de compraventa

Satisfaction: satisfacción; pago

Scienter: a sabiendas

S corporation: S corporación

Secured party: acreedor garantizado

Secured transaction: transacción garantizada

Securities: volares; titulos; seguridades

Security agreement: convenio de seguridad

Security interest: interés en un bien dado en garantía que permite a quien lo detenta venderlo en caso de incumplimiento

Service mark: marca de identificación de servicios

Shareholder's derivative suit: acción judicial entablada por un accionista en nombre de la sociedad

Signature: firma; rúbrica

Slander: difamación oral; calumnia

Sovereign immunity: immunidad soberana

Special indorsement: endoso especial; endoso a la orden de una person en particular

Specific performance: ejecución precisa, según los términos del contrato

Spendthrift trust: fideicomiso para pródigos

Stale check: cheque vencido

Stare decisis: acatar las decisiones, observar los precedentes

Statutory law: derecho estatutario; derecho legislado; derecho escrito

Stock: acciones

Stock warrant: certificado para la compra de acciones

Stop-payment order: orden de suspensión del pago de un cheque dada por el librador del mismo

Strict liability: responsabilidad uncondicional

Summary judgment: fallo sumario

Tangible property: bienes corpóreos

Tenancy at will: inguilino por tiempo indeterminado (según la voluntad del propietario)

Tenancy by sufferance: posesión por tolerancia

Tenancy by the entirety: locación conyugal conjunta

Tenancy for years: inguilino por un término fijo

Tenancy in common: specie de copropiedad indivisa

Tender: oferta de pago; oferta de ejecución

Testamentary trust: fideicomiso testamentario

Testator: testador (-a)

Third party beneficiary contract: contrato para el beneficio del tercero-beneficiario

Tort: agravio; cuasidelito

Totten trust: fideicomiso creado por un depósito bancario

Trade acceptance: letra de cambio aceptada

Trade name: nombre comercial; razón social

Trademark: marca registrada

Traveler's check: cheque del viajero

Trespass to land: ingreso no autorizado a las tierras de otro

Trespass to personal property: violación de los derechos posesorios de un tercero con respecto a bienes muebles

Trust: fideicomiso; trust

Ultra vires: ultra vires; fuera de la facultad (de una sociedad anónima)

Unanimous opinion: opinión unámine

Unconscionable contract or clause: contrato leonino; cláusula leonino

Underwriter: subscriptor; asegurador

Unenforceable contract: contrato que no se puede hacer cumplir

Unilateral contract: contrato unilateral

Union shop: taller agremiado; empresa en la que todos los empleados son miembros del gremio o sindicato

Universal defenses: defensas legitimas o legales

Usage of trade: uso comercial

Usury: usura

Valid contract: contrato válido

Venue: lugar; sede del proceso

Vertical merger: fusión vertical de empresas

Void contract: contrato nulo; contrato inválido, sin fuerza legal

Voidable contract: contrato anulable

Voir dire: examen preliminar de un testigo a jurado por el tribunal para determinar su competencia

Voting trust: fideicomiso para ejercer el derecho de voto

Waiver: renuncia; abandono

Warranty of habitability: garantía de habitabilidad

Watered stock: acciones diluídos; capital inflado

White-collar crime: crimen administrativo

Writ of attachment: mandamiento de ejecución; mandamiento de embargo

Writ of *certiorari*: auto de avocación; auto de certiorari

Writ of execution: auto ejecutivo; mandamiento de ejecución

Writ of *mandamus*: auto de mandamus; mandamiento; orden judicial

Glossary

A

ABA-approved program A legal or paralegal educational program that satisfies the standards for paralegal training set forth by the American Bar Association.

acceptance In contract law, the offeree's indication to the offeror that the offeree agrees to be bound by the terms of the offeror's offer, or proposal to form a contract.

acquittal A certification or declaration following a trial that the individual accused of a crime is innocent, or free from guilt, in the eyes of the law and is thus absolved of the charges.

actionable Capable of serving as the basis of a lawsuit. An actionable claim can be pursued in a lawsuit or other court action.

active listening The act of listening attentively to the speaker's message and responding by giving appropriate feedback to show that you understand what the speaker is saying; restating the speaker's message in your own words to confirm that you accurately interpreted what was said.

actual malice Real and demonstrated evil intent. In a defamation suit, a statement made about a public figure normally must be made with actual malice (with either knowledge of its falsity or a reckless disregard of the truth) for liability to be incurred.

actus reus A guilty (prohibited) act. The commission of a prohibited act is one of the two essential elements required for criminal liability; the other element is the intent to commit a crime.

address block The part of a letter that indicates to whom the letter is addressed. The address block is placed in the upper left-hand portion of the letter, above the salutation (and reference line, if one is included).

adhesion contract A contract drafted by the dominant party and then presented to the other—the adhering party—on a "take-it-or-leave-it" basis.

adjudicate To resolve a dispute using a neutral decision maker.

administrative agency A federal or state government agency established to perform a specific function. Administrative agencies are authorized by legislative acts to make and enforce rules relating to the purpose for which they were established.

administrative law A body of law created by administrative agencies in the form of rules, regulations, orders, and decisions in order to carry out their duties and responsibilities.

administrative law judge (ALJ) One who presides over an administrative agency hearing and who has the power to administer oaths, take testimony, rule on questions of evidence, and make determinations of fact.

administrator A person appointed by a court to serve as a personal representative for a person who died intestate, who made a will but failed to name an executor, or whose executor cannot serve.

adoption A procedure in which persons become the legal parents of a child who is not their biological child.

Advanced Paralegal Certification (APC) A credential awarded by the National Association of Legal Assistants to a Certified Paralegal (CP) or Certified Legal Assistant (CLA) whose competency in a legal specialty has been certified based on an examination of the paralegal's knowledge and skills in the specialty area.

adversarial system of justice A legal system in which the parties to a lawsuit are opponents, or adversaries, and present their cases in the light most favorable to themselves. The impartial decision maker (the judge or jury) determines who wins based on an application of the law to the evidence presented.

affidavit A written statement of facts, confirmed by the oath or affirmation of the party making it and sworn before a person having the authority to administer the oath or affirmation.

affirm To uphold the judgment of a lower court.

affirmative defense A response to a plaintiff's claim that does not deny the plaintiff's facts but attacks the plaintiff's legal right to bring an action.

agency A relationship between two persons in which one person (the agent) represents or acts in the place of the other (the principal).

agent A person who is authorized to act for or in the place of another person (the principal).

agreement A meeting of the minds, and a requirement for a valid contract. Agreement involves two distinct events: an offer to form a contract and the acceptance of that offer by the offeree.

alimony Financial support paid to a former spouse after a marriage has been terminated. The alimony may be permanent or temporary (rehabilitative).

allegation A party's statement, claim, or assertion made in a pleading to the court. The allegation sets forth the issue that the party expects to prove.

alternative dispute resolution (ADR) The resolution of disputes in ways other than those involved in the traditional judicial process. Negotiation, mediation, and arbitration are forms of ADR.

American Arbitration Association (AAA) The major organization offering arbitration services in the United States.

American Association for Paralegal Education (AAfPE) A national organization of paralegal educators; the AAfPE was established in 1981 to promote high standards for paralegal education.

American Bar Association (ABA) A voluntary national association of attorneys. The ABA plays an active role in developing educational and ethical standards for attorneys and in pursuing improvements in the administration of justice.

annotation A brief comment, an explanation of a legal point, or a case summary found in a case digest or other legal source.

annulment A court decree that invalidates (nullifies) a marriage. Although the marriage itself is deemed nonexistent, children of a marriage that is annulled are deemed legitimate.

answer A defendant's response to a plaintiff's complaint.

appeal The process of seeking a higher court's review of a lower court's decision for the purpose of correcting or changing the lower court's judgment or decision.

appellant The party who takes an appeal from one court to another; sometimes referred to as the *petitioner*.

appellate court A court that reviews decisions made by lower courts, such as trial courts; a court of appeals.

appellate jurisdiction The power of a court to hear and decide an appeal; the authority of a court to review cases that have already been tried in a lower court and to make decisions about them without holding a trial.

appellee The party against whom an appeal is taken—that is, the party who opposes setting aside or reversing the judgment; sometimes referred to as the *respondent*.

appropriation In tort law, the use by one person of another person's name, likeness, or other identifying characteristic without permission and for the benefit of the user.

arbitration A method of settling disputes in which a dispute is submitted to a disinterested third party (other than a court), who issues a decision that may or may not be legally binding.

arbitration clause A clause in a contract providing that, in case of a dispute, the parties will determine their rights through arbitration rather than the judicial system.

arraignment A court proceeding in which the suspect is formally charged with the criminal offense stated in the indictment. The suspect then enters a plea (guilty, not guilty, or *nolo contendere*) in response.

arrest To take into custody a person suspected of criminal activity.

arrest warrant A written order, based on probable cause and typically issued by a judge, commanding that the person named on the warrant be arrested by the police.

arson The willful and malicious burning of a building (and, in some states, personal property) owned by another; arson statutes have been extended to cover the destruction of any building, regardless of ownership, by fire or explosion.

articles of incorporation The document filed with the appropriate state official, usually the secretary of state, when a business is incorporated. State statutes usually prescribe what kind of information must be contained in the articles of incorporation.

assault Any word or action intended to make another person apprehensive or fearful of immediate physical harm; a reasonably believable threat.

associate attorney An attorney working for a law firm who is not a partner and does not have an ownership interest in the firm. Associates are usually less experienced attorneys and may be invited to become partners after working for the firm for several years.

assumption of risk Voluntarily taking on a known risk; a defense against negligence that can be used when the plaintiff has knowledge of and appreciates a danger and voluntarily exposes himself or herself to the danger.

attorney-client privilege A rule of evidence requiring that confidential communications between a client and his or her attorney (relating to their professional relationship) be kept confidential, unless the client consents to disclosure.

authentication The process of establishing the genuineness of an item that is to be introduced as evidence in a trial.

automatic stay A suspension of all judicial proceedings upon the occurrence of an independent event. Under the Bankruptcy Code, the moment a petition to initiate bankruptcy proceedings is filed, all litigation or other legal action by creditors against a debtor and the debtor's property is suspended.

award In the context of ADR, the decision rendered by an arbitrator.

B

bail The amount of money or conditions set by the court to ensure that an individual accused of a crime will appear for further criminal proceedings. If the accused person provides bail, whether in cash or by means of a bail bond, then the person is released from jail.

bankruptcy court A federal court of limited jurisdiction that hears only bankruptcy proceedings.

bankruptcy estate In bankruptcy proceedings, all of the debtor's interests in property currently held and wherever located, as well as interests in certain property to which the debtor becomes entitled within 180 days after filing for bankruptcy.

bankruptcy law The body of federal law that governs bankruptcy proceedings. The twin goals of bankruptcy law are (1) to protect a debtor by giving him or her a fresh start and (2) to ensure that creditors competing for a debtor's assets are treated fairly.

bankruptcy trustee A person appointed by the bankruptcy court to administer the debtor's estate in the interests of both the debtor and the creditors. The basic duty of the bankruptcy trustee is to collect and reduce to cash the estate in property and to close up the estate as speedily as is compatible with the best interests of the parties.

battery The intentional and offensive touching of another without lawful justification.

beyond a reasonable doubt The standard used to determine the guilt or innocence of a person charged with a crime. To be guilty of a crime, a suspect must be proved guilty "beyond and to the exclusion of every reasonable doubt."

bigamy The act of entering into marriage with one person while still legally married to another.

Bill of Rights The first ten amendments to the U.S. Constitution.

billable hours Hours or fractions of hours that attorneys and paralegals spend in work that requires legal expertise and that can be billed directly to clients.

binder A written, temporary insurance policy.

binding authority Any source of law that a court must follow when deciding a case. Binding authorities include constitutions, statutes, and regulations that govern the issue being decided, as well as court decisions that are controlling precedents within the jurisdiction.

binding mediation A form of ADR in which a mediator attempts to facilitate agreement between the parties but then issues a legally binding decision if no agreement is reached.

bonus An end-of-the-year payment to a salaried employee in appreciation for that employee's overtime work, diligence, or dedication to the firm.

booking The process of entering a suspect's name, offense, and arrival time into the police log (blotter) following his or her arrest.

breach To violate a legal duty by an act or a failure to act.

breach of contract The failure, without legal excuse, of a contractual party to perform the obligations assumed in a contract.

briefing a case Summarizing a case. A case brief gives the full citation, the factual background and procedural history, the issue or issues raised, the court's decision, the court's holding, and the legal reasoning on which the court based its decision. It may also include conclusions or notes concerning the case made by the one briefing it.

burglary Breaking and entering onto the property of another with the intent to commit a felony.

business invitee A person, such as a customer or a client, who is invited onto business premises by the owner of those premises for business purposes.

business tort Wrongful interference with another's business rights.

bylaws A set of governing rules adopted by a corporation or other association.

C

case law Rules of law announced in court decisions.

case of first impression A case presenting a legal issue that has not yet been addressed by a court in a particular jurisdiction.

case on "all fours" A case in which all four elements (the parties, the circumstances, the legal issues involved, and the remedies sought) are very similar to those in the case being researched.

case on point A case involving factual circumstances and issues that are similar to those in the case being researched.

causation in fact Causation brought about by an act or omission without which an event would not have occurred.

cease-and-desist order An administrative or judicial order prohibiting a person or business firm from conducting activities that an agency or court has deemed illegal.

certificate of incorporation or corporate charter The document issued by a state official, usually the secretary of state, granting a corporation legal existence and the right to function.

certification Formal recognition by a private group or a state agency that a person has satisfied the group's standards of ability, knowledge, and competence; ordinarily accomplished through the taking of an examination.

Certified Legal Assistant (CLA) or Certified Paralegal (CP) A legal assistant whose legal competency has been certified by the National Association of Legal Assistants following an examination that tests the legal assistant's knowledge and skills.

chain of custody A series describing the movement and location of evidence from the time it is obtained to the time it is presented in court. The court requires that evidence be preserved in the condition in which it was obtained if it is to be admitted into evidence at trial.

challenge An attorney's objection, during *voir dire*, to the inclusion of a particular person on the jury.

challenge for cause A *voir dire* challenge to exclude a potential juror from serving on the jury for a reason specified by an attorney in the case.

charge The judge's instruction to the jury setting forth the rules of law that the jury must apply in reaching its decision, or verdict.

checks and balances A system in which each of the three branches of the national government—executive, legislative, and judicial—exercises a check on the actions of the other two branches.

child support The financial support necessary to provide for a child's needs. Commonly, when a marriage is terminated, the noncustodial spouse agrees or is required by the court to make child-support payments to the custodial spouse.

chronologically In a time sequence; naming or listing events in the time order in which they occurred.

circumstantial evidence Indirect evidence offered to establish, by inference, the likelihood of a fact that is in question.

citation In case law, a reference to a case by the name of the case, the volume number and name of the reporter in which the case can be found, the page number on which the case begins, and the year. In statutory and administrative law, a reference to the title number, name, and section of the code in which a statute or regulation can be found.

citator A book or online service that provides the history and interpretation of a statute, regulation, or court decision and a list of the cases, statutes, and regulations that have interpreted, applied, or modified a statute or regulation.

citing case A case listed in a citator that cites the case being researched.

civil law Law dealing with the definition and enforcement of private rights, as opposed to criminal matters.

civil law system A system of law based on a code rather than case law, often originally from the Roman Empire; the predominant system of law in the nations of continental Europe and the nations that were once their colonies.

click-on agreement An agreement that arises when a buyer, engaging in a transaction on a computer, indicates his or her assent to be bound by the terms of an offer by clicking on a button that says, for example, "I agree"; sometimes referred to as a click-on license or a click-wrap agreement.

close corporation A corporation owned by a small group of shareholders, often family members; also called a closely held corporation. Shares in close corporations cannot be publicly traded on the stock market, and often other restrictions on stock transfer apply. Some close corporations qualify for special tax status as S corporations.

closed-ended question A question phrased in such a way that it elicits a simple "yes" or "no" answer.

closing In a letter, an ending word or phrase placed above the signature, such as "Sincerely" or "Very truly yours."

closing argument The argument made by each side's attorney after the cases for the plaintiff and defendant have been presented. Closing arguments are made prior to the jury charge.

code A systematic and topically organized presentation of laws, rules, or regulations.

common law A body of law developed from custom or judicial decisions in English and U.S. courts and not by a legislature.

common law marriage A marriage that is formed by mutual consent and without a marriage license or ceremony. The couple must be eligible to marry, have a present and continuing agreement to be a couple, live together as a couple, and hold themselves out to the public as a couple. Many states do not recognize common law marriages.

community property In certain states, all property acquired during a marriage, except for inheritances or gifts received during the marriage by either marital partner. Each spouse has a one-half ownership interest in community property.

comparative negligence A theory in tort law under which the liability for injuries resulting from negligent acts is shared by all persons who were guilty of negligence (including the injured party) on the basis of each person's proportionate carelessness.

compensatory damages A money award equivalent to the actual value of injuries or damages sustained by the aggrieved party.

complaint The pleading made by a plaintiff or a charge made by the state alleging wrongdoing on the part of the defendant.

concurrent jurisdiction Jurisdiction that exists when two different courts have the power to hear a case. For example, some cases can be heard in either a federal or a state court.

confirmation letter A letter that summarizes an oral conversation to provide a permanent record of the discussion.

conflict of interest A situation in which two or more duties or interests come into conflict, as when an attorney attempts to represent opposing parties in a legal dispute.

conflicts check A procedure for determining whether an agreement to represent a potential client will result in a conflict of interest.

consideration Something of value, such as money or the performance of an action not otherwise required, that motivates the formation of a contract. Each party must give consideration for the contract to be binding.

constitutional law Law based on the U.S. Constitution and the constitutions of the states.

constructive discharge A termination of employment that occurs when the employer causes the employee's working conditions to be so intolerable that a reasonable person in the employee's position would feel compelled to quit.

consumer A person who buys products and services for personal or household use.

consumer-debtor A debtor whose debts are primarily consumer debts—that is, debts for purchases that are primarily for household or personal use.

consumer law Statutes, agency rules, and judicial decisions protecting consumers of goods and services.

contingency fee A legal fee that consists of a specified percentage (such as 30 percent) of the amount the plaintiff recovers in a civil lawsuit. The fee is paid only if the plaintiff wins the lawsuit (recovers damages).

continuing legal education (CLE) programs Courses through which attorneys and other legal professionals extend their education beyond school.

contract An agreement (based on a promise or an exchange of promises) that can be enforced in court.

contractual capacity The threshold mental capacity required by law for a party who enters into a contract to be bound by that contract.

contributory negligence A theory in tort law under which a complaining party's own negligence contributed to his or her injuries. Contributory negligence is an absolute bar to recovery in some jurisdictions.

conversion The act of wrongfully taking or retaining a person's personal property and placing it in the service of another.

copyright The exclusive right of an author (or other creator) to publish, print, or sell an intellectual production for a statutory period of time.

corporate law Law that governs the formation, financing, merger and acquisition, and termination of corporations, as well as the rights and duties of those who own and run the corporation.

counterclaim A claim made by a defendant in a civil lawsuit against the plaintiff; in effect, a counterclaiming defendant is suing the plaintiff.

court of equity A court that decides controversies and administers justice according to the rules, principles, and precedents of equity.

court of law A court in which the only remedies were things of value, such as money. Historically, in England, courts of law were different from courts of equity.

cram-down provision A provision of the Bankruptcy Code that allows a court to confirm a debtor's Chapter 11 reorganization plan even though only one class of creditors has accepted it. To exercise the court's right under this provision, the court must demonstrate that the plan does not discriminate unfairly against any creditors and is fair and equitable.

crime A broad term for violations of law that are punishable by the state and are codified by legislatures. The objective of criminal law is to protect the public.

criminal law Law that governs and defines those actions that are crimes and that subjects persons convicted of crimes to punishment imposed by the government (a fine or jail time).

cross-claim A claim asserted by a defendant in a civil lawsuit against another defendant or by a plaintiff against another plaintiff.

cross-examination The questioning of an opposing witness during the trial.

cyber crime A crime that occurs online, in the virtual community of the Internet, as opposed to the physical world.

cyber tort A tort committed by use of the Internet.

cyberstalking The crime of stalking in cyberspace. The cyberstalker usually finds the victim through Internet chat rooms, newsgroups, bulletin boards, or e-mail and proceeds to harass that person or put the person in reasonable fear for his or her safety or the safety of his or her immediate family.

D

damages Money awarded as a remedy for a civil wrong, such as a breach of contract or a tort (wrongful act).

debtor in possession (DIP) In Chapter 11 bankruptcy proceedings, a debtor who is allowed, for the benefit of all concerned, to maintain possession of the estate in bankruptcy (the business) and to continue business operations.

deception In consumer law, a material misrepresentation or omission in information that is likely to mislead a reasonable consumer to his or her detriment.

deceptive advertising Advertising that misleads consumers, either by unjustified claims concerning a product's performance or by failure to disclose relevant information concerning the product's composition or performance.

deed A document by which title to property is transferred from one party to another.

defamation Anything published or publicly spoken that causes injury to another's good name, reputation, or character.

default judgment A judgment entered by a clerk or court against a party who has failed to appear in court to answer or defend against a claim that has been brought against him or her by another party.

defendant A party against whom a lawsuit is brought.

defense The evidence and arguments presented in the defendant's support in a criminal action or lawsuit.

defense of others The use of reasonable force to protect others from harm.

defense of property The use of reasonable force to protect one's property from harm threatened by another. The use of deadly force in defending one's property is seldom justified.

demand letter A letter in which one party explains its legal position in a dispute and requests that the recipient take some action, such as paying money owed.

deponent A party or witness who testifies under oath during a deposition.

deposition A pretrial question-and-answer proceeding, usually conducted orally, in which a party or witness answers an attorney's questions. The answers are given under oath, and the session is recorded.

deposition transcript The official transcription of the recording taken during a deposition.

dicta A Latin term referring to nonbinding (nonprecedential) judicial statements that are not directly related to the facts or issues presented in the case and thus are not essential to the holding.

digest A compilation in which brief summaries of court cases are arranged by subject and subdivided by jurisdiction and court.

direct evidence Evidence directly establishing the existence of a fact.

direct examination The examination of a witness by the attorney who calls the witness to the stand to testify on behalf of the attorney's client.

director A person elected by the shareholders to direct corporate affairs.

disbarment A severe disciplinary sanction in which an attorney's license to practice law in the state is revoked because of unethical or illegal conduct.

discharge The termination of an obligation. A discharge in bankruptcy terminates the debtor's obligation to pay the debts discharged by the court.

discovery Formal investigation prior to trial. Opposing parties use various methods, such as interrogatories and depositions, to obtain information from each other and from witnesses to prepare for trial.

discovery plan A plan formed by the attorneys litigating a lawsuit, on behalf of their clients, that indicates the types of information that will be disclosed by each party to the other prior to trial, the testimony and evidence that each party will or may introduce at trial, and the general schedule for pretrial disclosures and events.

dissolution The formal disbanding of a partnership or a corporation.

diversion program In some jurisdictions, an alternative to prosecution that is offered to certain felony suspects to deter them from future unlawful acts.

diversity of citizenship Under the Constitution, a basis for federal district court jurisdiction over a lawsuit between (1) citizens of different states, (2) a foreign country and citizens of a state or states, or (3) citizens of a state and citizens of a foreign country. The amount in controversy must be more than $75,000 before a federal court can exercise jurisdiction in such cases.

dividend A distribution of profits to corporate shareholders, disbursed in proportion to the number of shares held.

divorce A formal court proceeding that legally dissolves a marriage.

docket The list of cases entered on the court's calendar and scheduled to be heard by the court.

double billing Billing more than one client for the same billable time period.

double jeopardy To place at risk (jeopardize) a person's life or liberty twice. The Fifth Amendment to the Constitution prohibits a second prosecution for the same criminal offense.

dram shop act A state statute that imposes liability on the owners of bars, as well as those who serve alcoholic drinks to the public, for injuries resulting from accidents caused by intoxicated persons when the sellers or servers of alcoholic drinks contributed to the intoxication.

due process of law Fair, reasonable, and standard procedures that must be used by the government in any legal action against a citizen. The Fifth Amendment to the U.S. Constitution prohibits the deprivation of "life, liberty, or property without due process of law."

duty of care The duty of all persons, as established by tort law, to exercise reasonable care in dealings with others. Failure to exercise due care, which is normally determined by the reasonable person standard, is the tort of negligence.

E

e-signature An electronic sound, symbol, or process attached to or logically associated with a record and executed or adopted by a person with the intent to sign the record, according to the Uniform Electronic Transactions Act.

early neutral case evaluation A form of ADR in which a neutral third party evaluates the strengths and weaknesses of the disputing parties' positions; the evaluator's opinion forms the basis for negotiating a settlement.

easement The right of a person to make limited use of another person's real property without taking anything from the property.

elder law A relatively new legal specialty that involves serving the needs of older clients, such as estate planning and making arrangements for long-term care.

electronic filing (e-filing) system An online system that enables attorneys to file case documents with courts twenty-four hours a day, seven days a week.

elements The issues and facts that the plaintiff must prove to succeed in a tort claim.

emancipation The legal relinquishment by a child's parents or guardian of the legal right to exercise control over the child. Usually, a child who moves out of the parents' home and supports himself or herself is considered emancipated.

embezzlement The fraudulent appropriation of the property or money of another by a person entrusted with that property or money.

eminent domain The power of a government to take land for public use from private citizens for just compensation.

employment at will A common law doctrine under which employment is considered to be "at will"—that is, either party may terminate the employment relationship at any time and for any reason, unless a contract or statute specifies otherwise.

employment manual A firm's handbook or written statement that specifies the policies and procedures that govern the firm's employees and employer-employee relationships.

enabling legislation A statute enacted by a legislature that authorizes the creation of an administrative agency and specifies the name, purpose, composition, and powers of the agency being created.

environmental impact statement (EIS) A statement required by the National Environmental Policy Act for any major federal action that will significantly affect the quality of the environment. The statement must analyze the action's impact on the environment and explore alternative actions that might be taken.

environmental law All state and federal laws or regulations enacted or issued to protect the environment and preserve environmental resources.

equitable principles and maxims Propositions or general statements of rules of law that are frequently involved in equity jurisdiction.

estate administration The process in which a decedent's personal representative settles the affairs of the decedent's estate (collects assets, pays debts and taxes, and distributes the remaining assets to heirs); the process is usually overseen by a probate court.

estate planning Making arrangements, during a person's lifetime, for the transfer of that person's property to others on the person's death. Estate planning often involves executing a will or establishing a trust fund to provide for others, such as a spouse or children, on a person's death.

ethical wall A term that refers to the procedures used to create a screen around an attorney, a paralegal, or another member of a law firm to shield him or her from information about a case in which there is a conflict of interest.

evidence Anything that is used to prove the existence or nonexistence of a fact.

exclusionary rule In criminal procedure, a rule under which any evidence obtained in violation of the accused's constitutional rights, as well as any evidence derived from illegally obtained evidence, will not be admissible in court.

exclusive jurisdiction Jurisdiction that exists when a case can be heard only in a particular court, such as a federal court.

executor A person appointed by a testator to serve as a personal representative on the testator's death.

expense slip A slip of paper on which any expense, or cost, that is incurred on behalf of a client (such as the payment of court fees or long-distance telephone charges) is recorded.

expert witness A witness with professional training or substantial experience qualifying him or her to testify as to his or her opinion on a particular subject.

eyewitness A witness who testifies about an event that he or she observed or experienced firsthand.

F

false imprisonment The intentional confinement or restraint of a person against his or her will.

family law Law relating to family matters, such as marriage, divorce, child support, and child custody.

federal question A question that pertains to the U.S. Constitution, acts of Congress, or treaties. It provides a basis for jurisdiction by the federal courts as authorized by Article III, Section 2, of the Constitution.

Federal Rules of Civil Procedure (FRCP) The rules controlling all procedural matters in civil trials brought before the federal district courts.

federal system The system of government established by the Constitution, in which the national government and the state governments share sovereign power.

fee simple absolute Ownership rights entitling the holder to use, possess, or dispose of the property however he or she chooses during his or her lifetime.

felony A crime—such as arson, murder, assault, or robbery—that carries the most severe sanctions. Sanctions range from one year in a state or federal prison to life imprisonment or (in some states) the death penalty.

fiduciary relationship A relationship involving a high degree of trust and confidence.

fixed fee A fee paid to the attorney by his or her client for having provided a specified legal service, such as the creation of a simple will.

forgery The fraudulent making or altering of any writing in a way that changes the legal rights and liabilities of another.

forms file A reference file containing copies of the firm's commonly used legal documents and informational forms. The documents in the forms file serve as models for drafting new documents.

foster care A temporary arrangement in which a family is paid by the state to care for a child for a limited period of time, often pending adoption.

fraudulent misrepresentation Any misrepresentation, either by misstatement or omission of a material fact, knowingly made with the intention of deceiving another and on which a reasonable person would and does rely to his or her detriment.

freelance paralegal A paralegal who operates his or her own business and provides services to attorneys on a contract basis. A freelance paralegal works under the supervision of an attorney, who assumes responsibility for the paralegal's work product.

friendly witness A witness who is biased against your client's adversary or sympathetic toward your client in a lawsuit or other legal proceeding.

G

garnishment A proceeding in which a creditor legally seizes a portion of a debtor's property (such as wages) that is in the possession of a third party (such as an employer).

general licensing Licensing in which all individuals within a specific profession or group (such as paralegals) must meet licensing requirements imposed by the state in order to legally practice their profession.

general partner A partner who participates in managing the business of a partnership and has all the rights and liabilities that arise under traditional partnership law.

genuineness of assent Knowing and voluntary assent to the contract terms. If a contract is formed as a result of mistake, misrepresentation, undue influence, or duress, genuineness of assent is lacking, and the contract will be voidable.

Good Samaritan statute A state statute stipulating that persons who provide emergency services to others in peril—unless they do so recklessly, thus causing further harm—cannot be sued for negligence.

grand jury A group of citizens called to decide whether probable cause exists to believe that a suspect committed the crime with which he or she has been charged and thus should stand trial.

guardian *ad litem* A person appointed by the court to represent the interests of a child or a mentally incompetent person before the court.

H

hacker A person who uses one computer to break into another.

headnote A note, usually a paragraph long, near the beginning of a reported case summarizing the court's ruling on an issue.

hearsay Testimony that is given in court by a witness who relates not what he or she knows personally but what another person said. Hearsay is generally not admissible as evidence.

holding The binding legal principle, or precedent, that is drawn from the court's decision in a case.

homestead exemption A law permitting the debtor to retain the family home, either in its entirety or up to a specified dollar amount, free from the claims of unsecured creditors or trustees in bankruptcy.

hornbook A single-volume scholarly discussion, or treatise, on a particular legal subject.

hostile witness A witness who is biased against your client or friendly toward your client's adversary in a lawsuit or other legal proceeding; an adverse witness.

hung jury A jury whose members are so irreconcilably divided in their opinions that they cannot reach a verdict. The judge in this situation may order a new trial.

hypothetical question A question based on hypothesis, conjecture, or fiction.

I

identity theft The theft of a form of identification, such as a name, date of birth, or Social Security number, which is then used to access the victim's financial resources.

impeach To call into question the credibility of a witness by challenging the truth or accuracy of his or her trial statement.

independent adoption A privately arranged adoption, as when a doctor, lawyer, or other person puts a couple seeking to adopt a child in contact with a pregnant woman who has decided to give up her child for adoption.

independent contractor A person who is hired to perform a specific undertaking but who is free to choose how and when to perform the work. An independent contractor may or may not be an agent.

indictment A charge or written accusation, issued by a grand jury, that probable cause exists to believe that a person has committed a crime for which he or she should stand trial.

information A formal criminal charge made by a prosecutor without a grand jury indictment.

informative letter A letter that conveys information to a client, a witness, an adversary's counsel, or some other person regarding a legal matter (such as the date, time, place, and purpose of a meeting) or a cover letter that accompanies other documents being sent to a person or court.

injunction A court decree ordering a person to do or to refrain from doing a certain act.

insider trading Trading in the stock of a publicly listed corporation based on inside information. One who possesses inside information and has a duty not to disclose it to outsiders may not profit from the purchase or sale of securities based on that information until the information is available to the public.

insurable interest An interest either in a person's life or well-being or in property that is sufficiently substantial to justify insuring against injury to or death of the person or damage to the property.

insurance A contract by which an insurance company (the insurer) promises to pay a sum of money or give something of value to another (either the insured or the beneficiary) to compensate for a specified loss.

intellectual property Property that results from intellectual, creative processes. Copyrights, patents, and trademarks are examples of intellectual property.

intentional infliction of emotional distress Intentional, extreme, and outrageous conduct resulting in severe emotional distress to another.

intentional tort A wrongful act knowingly committed.

inter vivos **trust** A trust created by the grantor (settlor) and effective during the grantor's lifetime—that is, a trust not established by a will.

international law The law that governs relations among nations. International customs and treaties are generally considered to be two of the most important sources of international law.

interrogatories A series of written questions for which written answers are prepared and then signed under oath by a party to a lawsuit (the plaintiff or the defendant).

interviewee The person who is being interviewed.

intestacy laws State statutes that specify how property will be distributed when a person dies intestate.

intestate The state of having died without a valid will.

investigation plan A plan that lists each step involved in obtaining and verifying facts and information relevant to the legal problem being investigated.

J

joint and several liability Shared and individual liability. In partnership law, joint and several liability means that a third party may sue all of the partners (jointly) or one or more of the partners separately (severally). This is true even if one of the partners sued did not participate in, ratify, or know about whatever gave rise to the cause of action.

joint custody Custody of a child that is shared by the parents following the termination of a marriage.

joint liability Shared liability. In partnership law, partners incur joint liability for partnership obligations and debts.

joint tenancy The joint ownership of property by two or more co-owners in which each co-owner owns an undivided portion of the property. On the death of one of the joint tenants, his or her interest automatically passes to the surviving joint tenant or tenants.

judgment The court's final decision regarding the rights and claims of the parties to a lawsuit.

judgment creditor A creditor who is legally entitled, by a court's judgment, to collect the amount of the judgment from a debtor.

jurisdiction The authority of a court to hear and decide a specific case.

justiciable controversy A controversy that is real and substantial, as opposed to hypothetical or academic.

K

key number A number (accompanied by the symbol of a key) corresponding to a specific topic within West's key-number system to facilitate legal research of case law.

KeyCite An online citator on Westlaw that can trace case history, retrieve secondary sources, categorize legal citations by legal issue, and perform other functions.

L

laches An equitable doctrine that bars a party's right to legal action if the party has neglected for an unreasonable length of time to act on his or her rights.

larceny The wrongful or fraudulent taking and carrying away of another person's personal property with the intent to deprive the person permanently of the property.

law A body of rules of conduct established and enforced by the controlling authority (the government) of a society.

law clerk A law student working as an apprentice with a law firm to gain practical experience.

lay witness A witness who can truthfully and accurately testify on a fact in question without having specialized training or knowledge; an ordinary witness.

leading question A question that suggests, or "leads to," a desired answer. Interviewers may use leading questions to elicit responses from witnesses who otherwise would not be forthcoming.

lease In real property law, a contract by which the owner of real property (the landlord) grants to a person (the tenant) an exclusive right to use and possess the property, usually for a specified period of time, in return for rent or some other form of payment.

legal administrator An administrative employee of a law firm who manages day-to-day operations. In smaller law firms, legal administrators are usually called office managers.

legal custody Custody of a child that confers on the parent the right to make major decisions about the child's life without consulting the other parent.

legal nurse consultant (LNC) A nurse who consults with legal professionals and others about medical aspects of legal claims or issues. Legal nurse consultants normally must have at least a bachelor's degree in nursing and significant nursing experience.

legal technician or **independent paralegal** A paralegal who offers services directly to the public without attorney supervision. Independent paralegals assist consumers by supplying them with forms and procedural knowledge relating to simple or routine legal procedures.

legalese Legal language that is hard for the general public to understand.

libel Defamation in writing or other published form (such as videotape).

licensing A government's official act of granting permission to an individual, such as an attorney, to do something that would be illegal in the absence of such permission.

limited liability company (LLC) A hybrid form of business organization authorized by a state in which the owners of the business have limited liability and taxes on profits are passed through the business entity to the owners.

limited liability partnership (LLP) A hybrid form of business organization authorized by a state that allows professionals to enjoy the tax benefits of a partnership while limiting in some way the normal joint and several liability of partners.

limited partner One who invests in a limited partnership but does not play an active role in managing the operation of the business. Unlike general partners, limited partners are only liable for partnership debts up to the amounts that they have invested.

limited partnership A partnership consisting of one or more general partners and one or more limited partners.

liquidation In regard to corporations, the process by which corporate assets are converted into cash and distributed among creditors and shareholders according to specific rules of preference. In regard to bankruptcy, a proceeding under Chapter 7 of the Bankruptcy Code (often referred to as *ordinary*, or *straight*, bankruptcy) in which a debtor states his or her debts and turns all assets over to a trustee, who sells the nonexempt assets and distributes the proceeds to creditors. With certain exceptions, the remaining debts are then discharged, and the debtor is relieved of the obligation to pay the debts.

litigation The process of working a lawsuit through the court system.

litigation paralegal A paralegal who specializes in assisting attorneys in the litigation process.

long arm statute A state statute that permits a state to obtain jurisdiction over nonresidents. The nonresidents must have certain "minimum contacts" with that state for the statute to apply.

M

mailbox rule A rule providing that an acceptance of an offer takes effect at the time it is communicated via the mode expressly or impliedly authorized by the offeror, rather than at the time it is actually received by the offeror. If acceptance is to be by mail, for example, it becomes effective the moment it is placed in the mailbox.

malpractice Professional misconduct or negligence—the failure to exercise due care—on the part of a professional, such as an attorney or a physician.

managing partner The partner in a law firm who makes decisions relating to the firm's policies and procedures and who generally oversees the business operations of the firm.

marital property All property acquired during the course of a marriage, apart from inheritances and gifts made to one or the other of the spouses.

material fact A fact that is important to the subject matter of the contract.

mediation A method of settling disputes outside of court by using the services of a neutral third party, who acts as a communicating agent between the parties; a method of dispute settlement that is less formal than arbitration.

memorandum of law A document (known as a *brief* in some states) that delineates the legal theories, statutes, and cases on which a motion is based.

mens rea A wrongful mental state, or intent. A wrongful mental state is a requirement for criminal liability. What constitutes a wrongful mental state varies according to the nature of the crime.

metadata Embedded electronic data recorded by a computer in association with a particular file, including location, path, creator, date created, date last accessed, hidden notes, earlier versions, passwords, and formatting. Metadata reveal information about how, when, and by whom a document was created, accessed, modified, and transmitted.

mini-trial A private proceeding that assists disputing parties in determining whether to take their case to court. Each party's attorney briefly argues the party's case before the other party and (usually) a neutral third party, who acts as an adviser. If the parties fail to reach an agreement, the adviser issues an opinion as to how a court would likely decide the issue.

***Miranda* rights** Certain constitutional rights of accused persons taken into custody by law enforcement officials, such as the right to remain silent and the right to counsel, as established by the United States Supreme Court's decision in *Miranda v. Arizona*.

mirror image rule A common law rule that requires that the terms of the offeree's acceptance adhere exactly to the terms of the offeror's offer for a valid contract to be formed.

misdemeanor A crime less serious than a felony, punishable by a fine or incarceration for up to one year in jail (not a state or federal penitentiary).

money laundering Falsely reporting income that has been obtained through criminal activity, such as illegal drug transactions, as income obtained through a legitimate business enterprise to make the "dirty" money "clean."

mortgage A written instrument giving a creditor an interest in the debtor's property as security for a debt.

motion A procedural request or application presented by an attorney to the court on behalf of a client.

motion for a change of venue A motion requesting that a trial be moved to a different location to ensure a fair and impartial proceeding, for the convenience of the parties, or for some other acceptable reason.

motion for a directed verdict A motion (also known as a *motion for judgment as a matter of law* in the federal courts) requesting that the court grant a judgment in favor of the party making the motion on the ground that the other party has not produced sufficient evidence to support his or her claim.

motion for a new trial A motion asserting that the trial was so fundamentally flawed (because of error, newly discovered evidence, prejudice, or other reason) that a new trial is needed to prevent a miscarriage of justice.

motion for judgment notwithstanding the verdict A motion (also referred to as a *motion for judgment as a matter of law* in federal courts) requesting that the court grant judgment in favor of the party making the motion on the ground that the jury verdict against him or her was unreasonable or erroneous.

motion for summary judgment A motion that may be filed by either party in which the party asks the court to enter judgment in his or her favor without a trial. A motion for summary judgment can be supported by evidence outside the pleadings, such as witnesses' affidavits, answers to interrogatories, and other evidence obtained prior to or during discovery.

motion *in limine* A motion requesting that certain evidence not be brought out at the trial, such as prejudicial, irrelevant, or legally inadmissible evidence.

motion to dismiss A motion filed by the defendant in which the defendant asks the court to dismiss the case for a specified reason, such as improper service, lack of personal jurisdiction, or the plaintiff's failure to state a claim for which relief can be granted.

motion to recuse A motion to remove a particular judge from a case.

motion to sever A motion to try multiple defendants separately.

motion to suppress evidence A motion requesting that certain evidence be excluded from consideration during the trial.

mutual mistake Mistake as to the same material fact on the part of both parties to a contract. In this situation, either party can cancel the contract.

N

National Association of Legal Assistants (NALA) One of the two largest national paralegal associations in the United States; formed in 1975. NALA is actively involved in paralegal professional development.

National Federation of Paralegal Associations (NFPA) One of the two largest national paralegal associations in the United States; formed in 1974. NFPA is actively involved in paralegal professional development.

national law Law that relates to a particular nation (as opposed to international law).

negligence The failure to exercise the standard of care that a reasonable person would exercise in similar circumstances.

negligence *per se* An action or failure to act in violation of a statutory requirement.

negotiation A process in which parties attempt to settle their dispute voluntarily, with or without attorneys to represent them.

networking Making personal connections and cultivating relationships with people in a certain field, profession, or area of interest.

no-fault divorce A divorce in which neither party is deemed to be at fault for the breakdown of the marriage.

nolo contendere Latin for "I will not contest it." A criminal defendant's plea in which he or she chooses not to challenge, or contest, the charges brought by the government. Although the defendant will still be convicted and sentenced, the plea neither admits nor denies guilt.

O

offer A promise or commitment to do or refrain from doing some specified thing in the future.

offeree The party to whom the offer is made.

offeror The party making the offer.

office manager An administrative employee who manages the day-to-day operations of a firm. In larger law firms, office managers are usually called legal administrators.

officer A person hired by corporate directors to assist in the management of the day-to-day operations of the corporation.

online dispute resolution (ODR) The resolution of disputes with the assistance of an organization that offers dispute resolution services via the Internet.

open-ended question A question phrased in such a way that it elicits a relatively unguided and lengthy narrative response.

opening statement An attorney's statement to the jury at the beginning of the trial. The attorney briefly outlines the evidence that will be offered during the trial and the legal theory that will be pursued.

opinion A statement by the court setting forth the applicable law and the reasons for its decision in a case.

opinion (advisory) letter A letter from an attorney to a client containing a legal opinion on an issue raised by the client's question or legal claim. The opinion is based on a detailed analysis of the law.

order for relief A court's grant of assistance to a complainant.

ordinance An order, rule, or law enacted by a municipal or county government to govern a local matter as allowed by state or federal legislation.

original jurisdiction The power of a court to take a case, try it, and decide it.

P

paralegal or legal assistant A person qualified by education, training, or work experience who is employed or retained by a lawyer, law office, corporation, governmental agency, or other entity and who performs specifically delegated substantive legal work, for which a lawyer is responsible.

paralegal manager An employee in a law firm who is responsible for overseeing the paralegal staff and paralegal professional development.

parallel citation A second (or third) citation for a given case. When a case is published in more than one reporter, each citation is a parallel citation to the other(s).

partner A person who operates a business jointly with one or more other persons. Each partner is a co-owner of the business firm.

partnership An association of two or more persons to carry on, as co-owners, a business for profit.

party With respect to lawsuits, the plaintiff or the defendant. Some cases involve multiple parties (more than one plaintiff or defendant).

passive listening The act of listening attentively to the speaker's message and responding to the speaker by providing verbal or nonverbal cues that encourage the speaker to continue; in effect, saying, "I'm listening, please go on."

patent A government grant that gives an inventor the exclusive right or privilege to make, use, or sell an invention for a limited time period.

paternity suit A lawsuit brought by an unmarried mother to establish that a certain person is the biological father of her child. DNA testing or a comparable procedure is often used to determine paternity.

peremptory challenge A *voir dire* challenge to exclude a potential juror from serving on the jury without any supporting reason or cause. Peremptory challenges based on racial or gender criteria are illegal.

performance In contract law, the fulfillment of duties arising under a contract; the normal way of discharging contractual obligations.

personal liability An individual's personal responsibility for debts or obligations. The owners of sole proprietorships and partnerships are personally liable for the debts and obligations incurred by their businesses. If their firms go bankrupt or cannot meet debts, the owners will be personally responsible for the debts.

personal property Any property that is not real property. Generally, any property that is movable or intangible is classified as personal property.

persuasive authority Any legal authority, or source of law, that a court may look to for guidance but on which it need not rely in making its decision. Persuasive authorities include cases from other jurisdictions, discussions in legal periodicals, and so forth.

persuasive precedent A precedent decided in another jurisdiction that a court may either follow or reject but that is entitled to careful consideration.

petition for divorce The document filed with the court to initiate divorce proceedings. The requirements governing the form and content of a divorce petition vary from state to state.

petition in bankruptcy An application to a bankruptcy court for relief in bankruptcy; a filing for bankruptcy. The official forms required for a petition in bankruptcy must be completed accurately, sworn to under oath, and signed by the debtor.

petty offense In criminal law, the least serious kind of wrong, such as a traffic or building-code violation.

plaintiff A party who initiates a lawsuit.

plea bargaining The process by which the accused and the prosecutor in a criminal case work out a mutually satisfactory disposition of the case, subject to court approval. Usually, plea bargaining involves the defendant's pleading guilty to a lesser offense in return for a lighter sentence.

pleadings Statements by the plaintiff and the defendant that detail the facts, charges, and defenses involved in the litigation.

pocket part A pamphlet containing recent cases or changes in the law that is used to update legal encyclopedias and other legal authorities. It is called a "pocket part" because it slips into a pocket, or sleeve, in the front or back binder of the volume.

policy In insurance law, a contract for insurance coverage. The policy spells out the precise terms and conditions as to what will and will not be covered under the contract.

potentially responsible party (PRP) A party who may be liable under the Comprehensive Environmental Response, Compensation, and Liability Act, or Superfund. Any person who generated hazardous waste, transported hazardous waste, owned or operated a waste site at the time of disposal, or currently owns or operates a site may be responsible for some or all of the cleanup costs involved in removing the hazardous substances.

prayer for relief A statement at the end of the complaint requesting that the court grant relief to the plaintiff.

precedent A court decision that furnishes authority for deciding later cases in which similar facts are presented.

predatory behavior Business behavior that is undertaken with the intention of unlawfully driving competitors out of the market.

preemption A doctrine under which a federal law preempts, or takes precedence over, conflicting state and local laws.

preference In bankruptcy proceedings, the debtor's favoring of one creditor over others by making payments or transferring property to that creditor at the expense of the rights of other creditors. The bankruptcy trustee is allowed to recover payments made to one creditor in preference over another.

preliminary hearing An initial hearing in which a judge or magistrate decides if there is probable cause to believe that the defendant committed the crime with which he or she is charged.

premium In insurance law, the price paid by the insured for insurance protection for a specified period of time.

prenuptial agreement A contract formed between two persons who are contemplating marriage to provide for the disposition of property in the event of a divorce or the death of one of the spouses after they have married.

pretrial conference A conference prior to trial in which the judge and the attorneys litigating the suit discuss settlement possibilities, clarify the issues in dispute, and schedule forthcoming trial-related events.

primary source of law In legal research, a document that establishes the law on a particular issue, such as a case decision, legislative act, administrative rule, or presidential order.

principal In agency law, a person who, by agreement or otherwise, authorizes another person (the agent) to act on the principal's behalf in such a way that the acts of the agent become binding on the principal.

privilege In tort law, the ability to act contrary to another person's right without that person's having legal redress for such acts. Privilege may be raised as a defense to defamation.

privileged information Confidential communications between certain individuals, such as an attorney and his or her client, that are protected from disclosure except under court order.

probable cause Reasonable grounds to believe the existence of facts warranting certain actions, such as the search or arrest of a person.

probate The process of "proving" the validity of a will and ensuring that the instructions in a valid will are carried out.

probate court A court having jurisdiction over proceedings concerning the settlement of a person's estate.

probation When a convicted defendant is released from confinement but is still under court supervision for a period of time.

procedural law Rules that define the manner in which the rights and duties of individuals are enforced.

product liability The legal liability of manufacturers, sellers, and lessors of goods to consumers, users, and bystanders for injuries or damages that are caused by the goods.

professional corporation (PC) A corporation formed by professionals, such as attorneys or accountants. Each member of the firm is liable for his or her own malpractice, but is generally protected by limited liability as in the corporate form.

professional limited liability company (PLLC) An organizational form law firms may use in most states to help limit personal liability by separating individuals and the legal entity, the firm.

promise An assurance that one will or will not do something in the future.

promissory estoppel A doctrine under which a promise is binding if the promise is clear and definite, the promisee justifiably relies on the promise, the reliance is reasonable and substantial, and justice will be better served by enforcement of the promise.

proof of claim A document filed with a bankruptcy court by a creditor to inform the court of a claim against a debtor's property. The proof of claim lists the creditor's name and address, as well as the amount that the creditor asserts is owed to the creditor by the debtor.

property settlement The division of property between spouses on the termination of a marriage.

proximate cause Legal cause; exists when the connection between an act and an injury is strong enough to justify imposing liability.

public defender Court-appointed defense counsel. A lawyer appointed by the court to represent a criminal defendant who is unable to pay to hire private counsel.

public law number An identification number assigned to a statute.

public policy A governmental policy based on widely held societal values.

public prosecutor An individual, acting as a trial lawyer, who initiates and conducts criminal cases in the government's name and on behalf of the people.

publicly held corporation A corporation whose shares are eligible to be publicly traded in securities markets, such as the New York Stock Exchange.

punitive damages Money damages awarded to a plaintiff to punish the defendant and deter future similar conduct.

R

real estate Land and things permanently attached to the land, such as houses, buildings, and trees.

real property Immovable property consisting of land and the buildings and plant life thereon.

reasonable person standard The standard of behavior expected of a hypothetical "reasonable person"; the standard against which negligence is measured and that must be observed to avoid liability for negligence.

record on appeal The items submitted during the trial (pleadings, motions, briefs, and exhibits) and the transcript of the trial proceedings that are forwarded to the appellate court for review when a case is appealed.

recross-examination The questioning of an opposing witness following the adverse party's redirect examination.

redirect examination The questioning of a witness following the adverse party's cross-examination.

reference line The portion of the letter that indicates the matter to be discussed, such as "RE: Summary of Cases Applying the Family and Medical Leave Act of 1993." The reference line is placed just below the address block and above the salutation.

reformation An equitable remedy granted by a court to correct, or "reform," a written contract so that it reflects the true intentions of the parties.

Registered Paralegal (RP) A paralegal whose competency has been certified by the National Federation of Paralegal Associations after successful completion of the Paralegal Advanced Competency Exam (PACE).

relevant evidence Evidence tending to prove or disprove the fact in question. Only relevant evidence is admissible in court.

remand To send a case back to a lower court for further proceedings.

remedy The means by which a right is enforced or the violation of a right is prevented or compensated for.

remedy at law A remedy available in a court of law. Money damages and items of value are awarded as a remedy at law.

remedy in equity A remedy allowed by courts in situations where remedies at law are not appropriate. Remedies in equity are based on rules of fairness, justice, and honesty.

reporter A book in which court cases are published, or reported.

reprimand A disciplinary sanction in which an attorney is rebuked for misbehavior. Although a reprimand is the mildest sanction for attorney misconduct, it is serious and may significantly damage the attorney's reputation in the legal community.

rescission A remedy in which the contract is canceled and the parties are returned to the positions they occupied before the contract was made.

respondeat superior A doctrine in agency law under which a principal-employer may be held liable for the wrongful acts committed by agents or employees acting within the scope of their agency or employment.

responsible corporate officer doctrine A common law doctrine under which the court may impose criminal liability on a corporate officer for actions of employees under her or his supervision regardless of whether she or he participated in, directed, or even knew about those actions.

restitution An equitable remedy under which a person is restored to his or her original position prior to loss or injury, or placed in the position that he or she would have been in had the breach not occurred.

restraining order A court order that requires one person (such as an abusing spouse) to stay away from another (such as an abused spouse).

restrictive covenants Agreements between an employer and employee that the employee will not attempt to compete with the employer for a specified period after employment ends.

retainer An advance payment made by a client to a law firm to cover part of the legal fees and/or costs that will be incurred on that client's behalf.

retainer agreement A signed document stating that the attorney or the law firm has been hired by the client to provide certain legal services and that the client agrees to pay for those services.

return-of-service form A document signed by a process server and submitted to the court to prove that a defendant received a summons.

reverse To overturn the judgment of a lower court.

reversible error A legal error at the trial court level that is significant enough to have affected the outcome of the case. It is grounds for reversal of the judgment on appeal.

risk A prediction concerning potential loss based on known and unknown factors.

risk management Planning that is undertaken to reduce the risk of loss from known and unknown events. In the context of insurance, risk management involves transferring certain risks from the insured to the insurance company.

robbery The taking of money, personal property, or any other article of value from a person by means of force or fear.

rulemaking The actions undertaken by administrative agencies when formally adopting new regulations or amending old ones.

rules of evidence Rules governing the admissibility of evidence in trial courts.

S

sales contract A contract for the sale of goods, as opposed to a contract for the sale of services, real property, or intangible property. Sales contracts are governed by Article 2 of the Uniform Commercial Code.

salutation In a letter, the formal greeting to the addressee. The salutation is placed just below the reference line.

search warrant A written order, based on probable cause and issued by a judge or public official (magistrate), commanding that police officers or criminal investigators search a specific person, place, or property to obtain evidence.

secondary source of law In legal research, any publication that indexes, summarizes, or interprets the law, such as a legal encyclopedia, a treatise, or an article in a law review.

secured creditor A lender, seller, or any other person in whose favor there is a security interest.

self-defense The legally recognized privilege to protect oneself or one's property against injury by another. The privilege of self-defense protects only acts that are reasonably necessary to protect oneself or one's property.

self-incrimination The act of giving testimony that implicates oneself in criminal wrongdoing. The Fifth Amendment to the Constitution states that no person "shall be compelled in any criminal case to be a witness against himself."

self-regulation The regulation of the conduct of a professional group by members of the group. Self-regulation involves establishing ethical or professional standards of behavior with which members of the group must comply.

sentence The punishment, or penalty, ordered by the court to be inflicted on a person convicted of a crime.

separate property Property that a spouse owned before the marriage, plus inheritances and gifts acquired by the spouse during the marriage.

service of process The delivery of the summons and the complaint to a defendant.

settlement agreement An out-of-court resolution to a legal dispute, which is agreed to by the parties in writing. A settlement agreement may be reached at any time prior to or during a trial.

sexual harassment In the employment context, (1) the hiring or granting of job promotions or other benefits in return for sexual favors (*quid pro quo* harassment) or (2) language or conduct that is so sexually offensive that it creates a hostile working environment (hostile-environment harassment).

share A unit of stock; a measure of ownership interest in a corporation.

shareholder One who has an ownership interest in a corporation through the purchase of corporate shares, or stock.

Shepard's An online citator on LexisNexis that provides a list of all the authorities citing a particular case, statute, or other legal authority.

shrink-wrap agreement An agreement whose terms are expressed in a document located inside the box in which the goods (usually software) are packaged.

slander Defamation in oral form.

slip opinion A judicial opinion published shortly after the decision is made and not yet included in a case reporter or advance sheets.

sole proprietorship The simplest form of business organization, in which the owner is the business. Anyone who does business without creating a formal business entity has a sole proprietorship.

specific performance An equitable remedy requiring exactly the performance that was specified in a contract; usually granted only when money damages would be an inadequate remedy and the subject matter of the contract is unique (for example, real property).

staff attorney An attorney hired by a law firm as an employee. A staff attorney has no ownership rights in the firm and will not be invited to become a partner in the firm.

standing to sue A sufficient stake in a controversy to justify bringing a lawsuit. To have standing to sue, the plaintiff must demonstrate an injury or a threat of injury.

stare decisis The doctrine of precedent, under which a court is obligated to follow earlier decisions of that court or higher courts within the same jurisdiction. This is a major characteristic of the common law system.

state bar association An association of attorneys within a state. In most states, an attorney must be a member of the state bar association to practice law in the state.

statute A written law enacted by a legislature under its constitutional lawmaking authority.

Statute of Frauds A state statute that requires certain types of contracts to be in writing to be enforceable.

statute of limitations A statute setting the maximum time period within which certain actions can be brought to court or rights enforced. After the period of time has run, no legal action can be brought.

statutory law The body of written laws enacted by the legislature.

strict liability Liability regardless of fault. In tort law, strict liability may be imposed on a merchant who introduces into commerce a good that is so defective as to be unreasonably dangerous.

submission agreement A written agreement to submit a legal dispute to an arbitrator or arbitrating panel for resolution.

subpoena A document commanding a person to appear at a certain time and place to give testimony concerning a certain matter.

substantive law Law that defines the rights and duties of individuals with respect to each other's conduct and property.

summary jury trial (SJT) A settlement method in which a trial is held but the jury's verdict is not binding. The verdict acts as a guide to both sides in reaching an agreement during mandatory negotiations that follow the trial. If a settlement is not reached, both sides have the right to a full trial later.

summons A document served on a defendant in a lawsuit informing the defendant that a legal action has been commenced against him or her and that the defendant must appear in court or respond to the plaintiff's complaint within a specified period of time.

support personnel Employees who provide clerical, secretarial, or other support to the legal, paralegal, and administrative staff of a law firm.

supporting affidavit An affidavit accompanying a motion that is filed by an attorney on behalf of his or her client. The sworn statements in the affidavit provide a factual basis for the motion.

supremacy clause The provision in Article VI of the U.S. Constitution that declares the Constitution, laws, and treaties of the United States "the supreme Law of the Land."

suspension A serious disciplinary sanction in which an attorney who has violated an ethical rule or a law is prohibited from practicing law in the state for a specified or an indefinite period of time.

syllabus A brief summary of the holding and legal principles involved in a reported case, which is followed by the court's official opinion.

T

tenancy in common A form of co-ownership of property in which each party owns an undivided interest that passes to his or her heirs at death.

testamentary trust A trust that is created by will and that does not take effect until the death of the testator.

testate The condition of having died with a valid will.

testator One who makes a valid will.

third party A person or entity not directly involved in an agreement (such as a contract), legal proceeding (such as a lawsuit), or relationship (such as an attorney-client relationship).

time slip A record documenting, for billing purposes, the hours (or fractions of hours) that an attorney or a paralegal worked for each client, the date on which the work was done, and the type of work done.

tort A civil wrong not arising from a breach of contract; a breach of a legal duty that causes harm or injury to another.

tortfeasor One who commits a tort.

trade journal A newsletter, magazine, or other periodical that provides a certain trade or profession with information (products, trends, or developments) relating to that trade or profession.

trade name A term that is used to indicate part or all of a business's name and that is directly related to the business's reputation and goodwill. Trade names are protected under the common law (and under trademark law, if the business's name is the same as its trademark).

trade secret Information or processes that give a business an advantage over competitors who do not know the information or processes.

trademark A distinctive mark, motto, device, or emblem that a manufacturer stamps, prints, or otherwise affixes to the goods it produces so that they can be identified on the market and their origins made known. Once a trademark is established (under the common law or through registration), the owner is entitled to its exclusive use.

treatise In legal research, a work that provides a systematic, detailed, and scholarly review of a particular legal subject.

treaty An agreement, or compact, formed between two independent nations.

trespass to land The entry onto, above, or below the surface of land owned by another without the owner's permission.

trespass to personal property The unlawful taking or harming of another's personal property; interference with another's right to the exclusive possession of his or her personal property.

trial court A court in which cases begin and in which questions of fact are examined.

trial notebook Traditionally, a binder that contains copies of all the documents and information that an attorney will need to have at hand during the trial.

trust An arrangement in which property is transferred by one person (the grantor, or settlor) to another (the trustee) for the benefit of a third party (the beneficiary).

trust account A bank account in which one party (the trustee, such as an attorney) holds funds belonging to another person (such as a client); a bank account into which funds advanced to a law firm by a client are deposited. Also called an *escrow account*.

U

unauthorized practice of law (UPL) The performance of actions defined by a legal authority, such as a state legislature, as constituting the "practice of law" without authorization to do so.

unconscionable contract A contract that is so oppressive to one of the parties that the court will refuse to enforce the contract.

underwriter In insurance law, the insurer, or the one assuming a risk in return for the payment of a premium.

Uniform Commercial Code (UCC) Statutes adopted by all states, in part or in whole, that contain uniform laws governing business transactions as defined in the code.

unilateral mistake Mistake as to a material fact on the part of only one party to a contract. In this situation, the contract is normally enforceable against the mistaken party, with some exceptions.

unreasonably dangerous product A product that is defective to the point of threatening a consumer's health and safety. A product will be considered unreasonably dangerous if it is dangerous beyond the expectation of the ordinary consumer or if a less dangerous alternative was economically feasible for the manufacturer, but the manufacturer failed to produce it.

U.S. trustee A government official who performs administrative tasks that a bankruptcy judge would otherwise have to perform.

V

venue The geographic district in which an action is tried and from which the jury is selected.

verdict A formal decision made by a jury.

vicarious liability Legal responsibility placed on one person for the acts of another.

visitation rights The right of a noncustodial parent to have contact with his or her child. Grandparents and stepparents may also be given visitation rights.

voir dire A proceeding in which attorneys for the plaintiff and the defendant ask prospective jurors questions to determine whether any potential juror is biased or has any connection with a party to the action or with a prospective witness.

W

warranty An express or implied promise by a seller that specific goods to be sold meet certain criteria, or standards of performance, on which the buyer may rely.

white-collar crime A crime that typically occurs in a business context; popularly used to refer to an illegal act or series of acts committed by a person or business entity using nonviolent means.

wiki A Web page that can be added to and modified by anyone or by authorized users who share the site. The most famous example is Wikipedia.

will A document directing how and to whom the maker's property and obligations are to be transferred on his or her death.

winding up The process of winding up all business affairs (collecting and distributing the firm's assets) after a partnership or corporation has been dissolved.

witness A person who is asked to testify under oath at a trial.

witness statement The written record of the statements made by a witness during an interview, signed by the witness.

work product An attorney's mental impressions, conclusions, and legal theories regarding a case being prepared on behalf of a client. Work product normally is regarded as privileged information.

workers' compensation laws State statutes that establish an administrative procedure for compensating workers for injuries that arise out of or in the course of their employment, regardless of fault.

workout An out-of-court negotiation in which a debtor enters into an agreement with a creditor or creditors for a payment or plan to discharge the debtor's debt.

writ of *certiorari* A writ from a higher court asking a lower court to send it the record of a case for review. The United States Supreme Court uses *certiorari* to review most of the cases it decides to hear.

writ of execution A writ that puts in force a court's decree or judgment.

wrongful discharge An employer's termination of an employee's employment in violation of the law.

Index